The Rough Start Guide to Capitalization Tables

Understanding Ownership, Equity, Dilution, and Control in Startups

PRSC Whitley with Akasha Rehn
Rhubarb Bridge Publishing ▪ Silicon Fen ▪ British Isles

* * *

Contents

* * *

The Rough Start Guide to Capitalization Tables

First Edition

Published by Rhubarb Bridge Publishing

12345678910

Also in the series:

The Rough Start Guide to Term Sheets and Negotiation
The Rough Start Guide to Raising from Angels and Family
The Rough Start Guide to Starting a Security Firm
The Rough Start Guide to Starting a Private Detective Agency
The Rough Start Guide to Launching an Enforcement Agency

Disclaimer

This book is not legal advice. It is not investment advice. It is not tax advice. It is not accounting advice.

Capitalization tables sit at the intersection of company law, securities regulation, tax planning, governance, employment incentives, and fundraising strategy. These areas vary by jurisdiction and can change over time. A structure that is sensible in one country, at one stage, or for one type of company may be wholly unsuitable elsewhere.

The purpose of this book is to help the reader understand the ideas, mechanics, risks, and strategic consequences that sit behind startup ownership structures. It is written to improve awareness and judgment, not to replace qualified professional advisers.

If you are forming a company, issuing shares, building an employee option plan, preparing for outside investment, or negotiating with angels or venture capital firms, you should obtain advice from appropriately qualified legal, financial, and tax professionals in the relevant jurisdiction.

Neither the author nor the publisher accepts responsibility for loss, liability, or damage arising from reliance on the contents of this book.

Preface

Most people do not go looking for a book on capitalization tables because they are curious about spreadsheets.

They go looking because something has happened.

A founder has started a company and suddenly been asked how many shares exist. A cofounder wants to know what percentage is fair. An investor asks for a revised cap table before a meeting. A lawyer mentions dilution, pre money valuation, or preferred stock. An employee is promised options and wants to know whether those options mean anything at all. Somewhere in the middle of all this, somebody realises that ownership is not a side issue. It is the structure underneath everything.

That is what this book is about.

A capitalization table looks harmless. At first glance it is just a record. A list of names, a number of shares, a percentage next to each one. But that apparent simplicity is misleading. The cap table determines who owns the company, who gets diluted, who gets rewarded, who gets control, who gets paid first at exit, and who discovers too late that the numbers they thought they understood never meant what they thought they meant.

It is one of the most important documents in the life of a startup, and one of the least understood.

This book is written for readers arriving from different directions. Some will know nothing about venture finance and simply want to raise money without making a catastrophic mistake. Others will come from law, finance, economics, accounting, or academic study and will want a deeper explanation of how ownership, control, and capital interact. Both readers are welcome here. The aim is not to talk down to the beginner or slow down the more advanced reader. The aim is to build understanding in layers, beginning with the foundations and moving steadily into the deeper mechanics of startup equity.

The subject is bigger than a spreadsheet.

A cap table is a practical tool, yes, but it is also a record of bargaining power. It reflects how founders divide a business at birth, how risk is priced, how future workers are incentivised, how investors protect themselves, and how control can move away from the people who created the company in the first place. It is where law meets ambition, where mathematics meets personality, and where optimism meets negotiation.

In that sense, the capitalization table is one of the clearest windows into the reality of startup life.

People often speak about funding as though it were a simple event. An investor arrives, writes a cheque, and the company grows. Reality is more complex. Every funding round changes the ownership structure. Every change in ownership affects incentives. Every attempt to protect one stakeholder creates pressure somewhere else. The cap table is where those changes become visible.

This book exists to make that visibility useful.

It will explain what a capitalization table is, how it begins, how it evolves, why dilution is not always disaster, why percentages can be deceptive, why preferred shares matter, why option pools alter the future before it arrives, and why a founder with a large stake can still lose control. It will also show why a well kept cap table is not merely tidy administration but strategic self defence.

If you are building a company, considering investment, advising founders, studying venture finance, or trying to understand how ownership actually works once real money enters the room, this book is for you.

What follows is not just a guide to a document.

It is a guide to one of the hidden operating systems of modern business.

Introduction

Before there is revenue, there is ownership.

Before there is a board, there is ownership.

Before there is investment, dilution, control, or exit, there is ownership.

Most startups begin in a strange emotional state. The founders are usually thinking about products, prototypes, customers, code, design, hiring, survival, and belief. They are trying to make something real before the world has fully agreed that it exists. In that early rush, ownership can feel abstract. Founders may split the business casually, promise equity informally, or create shares without understanding what those shares will later be asked to carry. For a while, this seems manageable. Then the outside world arrives.

The outside world asks harder questions.

How many shares are authorised. How many are issued. Who owns what. Are founder shares vested. Is there an option pool. What happens if a new investor arrives. What rights sit behind the percentages. What class of shares are outstanding. What does the company look like after a seed round, after a SAFE, after a note conversion, after Series A. The founders who thought they owned a business suddenly realise they are standing inside a structure that can be measured, negotiated, and altered.

That structure is the capitalization table.

A capitalization table, often shortened to cap table, is the ownership ledger of a company. At its most basic, it records who holds shares and in what quantity. Yet that plain description hides its significance. The cap table is not only an administrative record. It is the map of economic claims inside the company. It shows who stands to gain from success, who will be diluted when capital is raised, who may influence decisions, and who may walk away with more than everyone else when the company is sold.

This is why serious investors inspect the cap table early. It tells them whether the company has been structured sensibly or carelessly. It tells them whether the founders understand ownership or merely assume they do. It tells them whether future rounds are likely to be clean or painful. It tells them whether there is enough room left in the company for employee incentives, strategic hires, and new capital. It can even hint at future conflict.

A bad cap table can poison a good company.

A messy founder split can breed resentment. An oversized early grant can suffocate later flexibility. An option pool created too late can surprise and anger founders. Convertible instruments can quietly build up pressure in the background. Investor protections can make percentages look more flattering than the economic reality. A cap table that looks fine on the surface can conceal a structure that becomes chaotic the moment serious financing begins.

And yet, none of this means the cap table should be feared.

It should be understood.

Once understood, it becomes one of the clearest tools available to the founder, investor, advisor, or serious student of startup finance. It turns vague discussion into measurable structure. It allows

* * *

ONE

The First Shock of Ownership

What a Founder Thinks They Own

At the beginning, ownership feels almost fictional. A founder has an idea, perhaps a prototype, perhaps only notes, sketches, code fragments, customer conversations, or a conviction strong enough to survive ridicule, exhaustion, and the indifference of other people. In that phase the company does not yet feel like a legal structure with defined economic rights. It feels personal. It feels like an extension of will. The founder believes, often sincerely and not entirely irrationally, that the company is theirs because they imagined it first, named it first, worried about it first, and gave it those first invisible sacrifices which no later investor, employee, or adviser will ever fully see. They think of ownership in the moral sense before they ever think of it in the legal or financial one.

That is the first misunderstanding, and it is so common that it barely looks like an error at all. The founder is not wrong to feel that the company is theirs. In the human sense, it often is. They are the original source of motion. Without them there would have been no first step, no initial risk, no period in which the business existed only because one person kept insisting it should. Yet startups do not remain in the human sense for very long. The moment the business enters the world of incorporation, shares, agreements, advisors, employees, and investors, that instinctive feeling of possession collides with a harder and much less sentimental reality. What the founder believes they own and what they are actually recorded as owning may differ sharply, and that gap can become one of the defining tensions in the life of a company.

Most founders begin by thinking in wholes. They say my company, my business, my app, my technology, my invention. The language itself encourages confusion. It suggests absolute possession, as though a company were a bicycle in a garage or a camera bought with cash. But a company is not owned in that way. It is not a physical object whose possession is settled by custody. It is a legal entity, and legal entities are owned through structured claims.

Those claims are represented by shares or equivalent rights, and those shares are subject to rules, classes, restrictions, and future alteration. The founder may feel they own one hundred percent of the business simply because no one else has yet appeared with a formal claim. That feeling may last until the first cofounder discussion, the first casual promise to an early helper, the first accountant's question, the first solicitor's correction, or the first investor meeting in which someone asks to see the cap table. Suddenly the thing that felt whole must be divided, described, and defended.

This is where the romance of founding gives way to arithmetic, and many founders resent that transition because arithmetic feels like reduction. It appears to shrink the imaginative act into a spreadsheet. Yet the spreadsheet is not what reduces the company. It reveals the structure that was always going to matter once other people became involved. Every founder who hopes to hire, raise capital, reward staff, bring in expertise, or eventually sell or list the business is, knowingly or not, entering a system where ownership must be formalised. The cap table does not desecrate the dream. It is the mechanism by which the dream becomes legible to other people.

The problem is that founders usually meet this mechanism too late. They often encounter it not as a natural part of company formation but as an interruption. They are trying to build momentum. They want money, introductions, technical help, product progress, customer traction. Then some investor or lawyer insists on precision. Who owns what. How many shares exist. Were founder shares vested. Has anyone been promised equity informally. Is there an option pool. Are there convertible instruments already in circulation. What rights attach to the outstanding stock. The founder who thought ownership was obvious now discovers that obviousness carries no weight. The market does not recognise emotional authorship. It recognises enforceable claims.

That discovery can feel unfair, especially to first time founders. They have often done the hardest part already, which is to create something from almost nothing. They may have worked without salary, absorbed the initial risk, and kept the project alive while everyone else waited to see whether it would fail. Then, just as the outside world begins to care, that same outside world starts dissecting the company into percentages and rights.

The founder may interpret this as a kind of theft, or at least as a coldness that fails to honour the origin story. There is some truth in that reaction. Finance is cold. Law is cold.

Capital is cold. None of them naturally bends toward the founder's sense of personal creation. They ask instead what has been issued, what has been agreed, and what can be enforced.

But the founder's emotional model of ownership is not merely incomplete because it ignores law. It is incomplete because it ignores time. Founders often imagine ownership as a static condition. They think they own the company now, therefore they will continue to own it in some meaningful way later. Yet startup ownership is dynamic from the moment the company begins interacting with other people. If there are two founders, ownership must be split. If there is an early employee, some claim may be reserved. If there is outside money, new shares may be issued. If there is an option pool, future dilution has already begun in principle even before the options are exercised. If there are preferred shares, the founder may still appear to own a substantial percentage while the economic reality underneath has changed decisively. The founder starts with a feeling of entirety and is then forced to learn that ownership is a moving ratio within a structure designed to evolve.

This is one reason so many young companies suffer avoidable conflict. Founders negotiate early ownership as if they are dividing a treasure chest when in reality they are defining a future system of adjustment. A founder who says, with confidence, that they own half the company may not understand what that half actually means after two rounds of dilution, an option pool expansion, a note conversion, and a preference stack that pays investors first at exit. Another founder may proudly say that they retained eighty percent after their first funding round without appreciating that control provisions elsewhere in the documents have already weakened their command of the business. The numbers can look comforting while the underlying power migrates elsewhere.

That is why the earliest belief, the founder's belief, matters so much. It is not just a harmless misconception. It shapes behaviour. A founder who thinks ownership is naturally theirs may give away equity too casually because they assume their centrality can never really be displaced. Another founder, more defensive, may refuse to share ownership sensibly because they believe any dilution is a moral injury rather than a financing mechanism. Some founders will treat equity promises as tokens of gratitude, making verbal offers to friends, collaborators, or advisers without understanding that these promises may later collide with the formal capital structure.

Others will regard percentages as status markers rather than economic tools and become fixated on keeping a large number beside their name even when other terms in the deal matter more. In every case the initial misunderstanding about ownership creates later distortions.

The truth is both simpler and harsher. A founder does not own a company because they feel responsible for it. They own it to the extent that the legal structure says they do, and even that statement is only the beginning. The kind of shares they hold matters. The restrictions on those shares matter. The future claims against the company matter. The governance rights distributed elsewhere matter. The founder's stake may be large, small, economically weak, strategically powerful, vulnerable to dilution, or protected by circumstance. Ownership is not a mood. It is an architecture.

Yet it would be a mistake to swing too far in the opposite direction and speak as though the founder's initial belief is foolish. In a way, it contains a truth that later structures can obscure. The founder does often contribute the one element that cannot be bought at the outset, which is original commitment before there is evidence. Investors arrive when there is at least the possibility of an outcome. Employees join when there is at least the outline of a project. Advisers step in when there is something to advise upon. The founder comes before that. There is genuine value in being first to believe. One reason cap table conflicts become emotionally intense is that legal ownership and moral authorship are not the same thing, but both are real in different ways. The founder experiences the company as creation. The market experiences it as claims. A sophisticated understanding of startup ownership begins when the founder stops assuming those two things will automatically align.

This first section matters because everything that follows in the book will build on it. Before dilution can be understood, ownership must be stripped of fantasy without losing its emotional significance. Before investor rights can be examined, the founder's instinctive picture of the company must be made explicit. Before a cap table can be read, the reader must see why that table so often arrives as a shock. It is not merely a technical document. It is the first formal correction to the founder's private mythology.

And almost every founder has one.

They imagine that because the company began in their head, its future shape will continue to reflect that fact. Sometimes it does. More often, the world insists on translation. The idea becomes a company. The company becomes shares. The shares become percentages. The percentages become negotiations. The negotiations become a structure. From that moment onward, ownership is no longer simply what the founder feels. It is what can be counted, altered, priced, diluted, defended, and eventually realised.

That is the first shock of ownership, and every serious discussion of capitalization tables begins there.

Why Ownership Matters Before Revenue

One of the most persistent mistakes in early-stage company building is the belief that ownership only becomes important once a business begins to make money. Founders often assume that equity is a later concern, something to tidy up after product development, after traction, after the first real customer, after the first serious investor conversation, perhaps even after the first meaningful revenue. Until then, they tell themselves, the business is still too young, too uncertain, too fragile to justify detailed thought about who owns what. The company feels provisional, and because revenue has not yet arrived, ownership feels hypothetical.

That instinct is understandable, but it is wrong.

Ownership matters before revenue precisely because revenue has not yet arrived. In the absence of cash flow, ownership becomes one of the only meaningful currencies available to the company. It is what founders divide between themselves when deciding whether they are true partners or merely collaborators. It is what they promise to the technical builder who agrees to work below market rate because the upside may come later. It is what they hold out to a designer, an operator, an adviser, or an early employee when the company cannot yet pay what the work is truly worth. It is what an investor will study when deciding whether this business is disciplined enough to absorb outside money without descending into chaos. Revenue may be absent, but ownership is already doing work.

In fact, it is often doing the most sensitive work of all. It is carrying trust.

Before revenue, there is almost always a period in which multiple people are acting on faith. They believe in the founder, the product, the market, or the possibility that this could become something significant if enough intelligent effort is applied soon enough. During that phase, because the company cannot yet reward everyone in cash, ownership becomes the mechanism by which future reward is implied rather than delivered. That is why mistakes made in this stage are so potent. A badly structured ownership arrangement does not merely create future financial inefficiency. It corrupts the trust on which the company is trying to build itself.

If one founder feels under-recognised, ownership becomes resentment. If another has been given a large stake for modest contribution, ownership becomes a source of silent imbalance. If early promises are vague, casual, or undocumented, ownership becomes uncertainty. If a company has no clean record of who was granted what and why, ownership becomes a legal and strategic risk before there is even any revenue to fight over. The absence of money does not make ownership less important. It makes it more dangerous, because its meaning is being stretched across hope, gratitude, sacrifice, expectation, and fear.

This is the period in which many founders make decisions that feel minor because they cannot yet imagine scale. Five percent to a friend for some help with branding. Ten percent to someone who said they would be involved but has not really done much. A casual promise that someone is "basically a cofounder." A willingness to split things equally simply to avoid an uncomfortable conversation. The trouble is that these decisions are not small because the company is small. They are large because the company is small. When a company is at its beginning, every percentage point is attached to a structure that may later become extremely valuable. More importantly, the shape of that structure determines how future growth can occur.

A founder who dismisses ownership before revenue is usually imagining that the real substance of the business lies elsewhere. In the product. In the code. In the prototype. In the audience. In the hustle. In the pitch. In the sales effort still to come. And in one sense that is true. Ownership does not create demand. It does not fix engineering problems.

It does not win customers on its own. But ownership determines how the people doing those things are bound to each other. It influences whether commitment deepens or erodes, whether talent can be recruited intelligently, whether investors see a serious company or a founder's improvised mess, and whether future negotiations are built on clean foundations or plagued by old errors.

Revenue, when it comes, does not begin the ownership story. It exposes it.

The reason this matters so early is that revenue often arrives later than founders expect, but structural commitments are made much sooner. A company might spend months or years in the pre-revenue stage. During that time, real work is done, real relationships are formed, and real economic expectations begin to crystallise. The business may still look embryonic from the outside, but internally it is already becoming something with a capital structure, whether the founders acknowledge that or not. If they fail to shape that structure consciously, they do not avoid complexity. They merely postpone the reckoning until a more expensive and stressful moment.

This is especially important because the pre-revenue phase is where leverage is most distorted. Founders, desperate for help, often overpay in equity because they cannot yet see the full consequences. An early contributor who seems indispensable at the time may turn out to have been one useful person among many who could have filled that role. A cofounder split agreed in the first excitement of incorporation may look absurd eighteen months later when one person carried ninety percent of the burden. An adviser granted equity as a gesture of gratitude may disappear after two introductions. Because there is no revenue, and often little external validation, founders tend to make these decisions through emotion rather than structured judgment. Ownership is handed out to solve immediate discomforts rather than long-term problems.

That is one of the reasons investors care so much about early ownership even when the company is not yet producing meaningful income. A pre-revenue startup may be commercially immature, but its ownership structure can already reveal a great deal. It can reveal whether the founders understand discipline. Whether they can make difficult decisions early.

Whether they have confused generosity with strategy. Whether they appreciate future dilution. Whether they are capable of retaining enough unallocated space in the company for future hires, future rounds, and future corrections. A cap table with no revenue can still be either sensible or alarming. To a serious investor, the absence of revenue does not excuse a weak ownership structure. It often heightens concern, because if the company is already messy before outside money arrives, it will likely become worse afterward.

There is another, deeper reason ownership matters before revenue. Before the company has proven itself in the market, the core debate is not yet about profit. It is about belief, and belief is never distributed evenly. Some people believe more intensely, for longer, and at greater personal risk than others. Ownership is one of the only available mechanisms for recognising that unevenness in a way that can survive success if success comes. This is why early ownership decisions are so morally charged. They are not experienced merely as financial allocations. They are experienced as judgments about who mattered, who carried the idea, who gave up what, who took the risk, and who deserves what share of a future that does not yet exist.

That emotional charge often leads founders into one of two opposite mistakes. The first is overformalisation too early, where founders start behaving like miniature investment bankers before they have built anything real. They obsess over fractions and imagined outcomes rather than making progress on the product and market. The second, far more common, is underformalisation, where ownership is treated as a loose social understanding until circumstances force precision. Both are problems. The right approach is to treat ownership seriously without becoming paralysed by it. It must be structured early enough to prevent confusion, but not fetishised so much that it replaces company-building itself.

Seen properly, early ownership is less about exact perfection and more about preserving strategic integrity. The founder does not need omniscience. They need enough foresight to avoid irreversible stupidity. They need to understand that equity given away lightly cannot be reclaimed easily. That unclear promises create future disputes. That the absence of revenue does not make stakes imaginary.

That future investors will evaluate the company's ownership history as part of the company itself. That early employees may accept modest salaries only because ownership makes the sacrifice potentially rational. That each one of these realities exists before a single pound, dollar, or euro of true revenue has landed in the business account.

A company that misunderstands ownership before revenue often misunderstands it afterward as well, but now with more at stake. Revenue tends to make latent tensions visible. Once there is money, or the prospect of money, people revisit old assumptions. The quiet contributor wonders whether their early effort was properly recognised. The founder who gave away ten percent too easily now sees what that number might become. The cofounder who did little begins to act as though a paper entitlement should outweigh actual contribution. The investor reviewing the business notices unresolved promises. The employee option pool has not been thought through. The structure that looked harmless while the company had no market value suddenly feels decisive because revenue has turned possibility into evidence.

That is why mature founders learn to think of ownership as part of the company's infrastructure rather than as an afterthought. Before revenue, infrastructure matters even when it does not feel urgent. A business may operate for a while with weak systems, vague promises, and improvised structures, but each unresolved issue increases the cost of later correction. Ownership is no different. In fact, because it reaches into law, finance, incentives, and human relationships at the same time, correcting it is often harder than fixing a product decision or a process weakness. The product can be rewritten. A sales strategy can be changed. Ownership mistakes tend to leave longer shadows.

There is also a strategic asymmetry here that founders often miss. Before revenue, the company's future is uncertain to everyone, but not everyone bears uncertainty in the same way. The founder may experience the business as a mission, but other participants assess their involvement based on risk and reward. Ownership therefore becomes the bridge between present uncertainty and future justification. An early employee does not simply hear that the company has no money. They hear that the company has no money now but may later have value, and ownership is how that future value might be shared. An investor does not care that revenue is absent in itself.

They care whether the ownership structure has been prepared in a way that allows capital to enter without wrecking incentives. A cofounder does not simply want emotional recognition. They want to know that their effort translates into a durable stake.

For all of these people, ownership matters before revenue because it is the architecture of future reward before current reward is possible.

And this is where the intelligent founder gains an advantage. The founder who understands ownership early does not become obsessed with paper percentages for their own sake. They become capable of making clean agreements while the company is still flexible enough to absorb them. They can recognise the difference between a true co-founder and an early helper. They can resist overpaying in equity for short-term relief. They can plan an option pool before an investor forces the issue. They can understand why vesting is not an insult but a discipline. They can treat ownership as a serious instrument of alignment long before cash flow arrives to take over that role.

The phrase before revenue can sound like a period of suspension, as though the real business has not yet begun. In truth, much of the real business has already begun by then. The company is already deciding who it is, who it is for, who will carry it, and how its future will be shared if it survives. Ownership is part of that process from the first day the business becomes more than a private thought. It matters in silence, in draft agreements, in awkward conversations, in verbal promises, in emails sent too casually, in percentages assigned without reflection, and in all the structures that later participants will inherit whether they like them or not.

Revenue does not make ownership important.

Revenue merely removes the illusion that it was ever optional.

Why Investors Ask for the Cap Table So Early

To a first-time founder, it can feel almost insulting. They are still trying to explain the product, the market, the customer pain, the route to scale, the urgency of the problem, the quality of the team, perhaps even the technical elegance of the solution, and yet one of the first serious things an investor asks for is the cap table. Not always immediately, but early enough to unsettle. Sometimes before revenue. Sometimes before a term sheet. Sometimes before the founder feels the company has even become substantial enough to justify such scrutiny. The founder expects curiosity about growth. The investor asks about ownership.

That moment is often misread.

The founder may assume the investor is jumping ahead, becoming overly legalistic, or trying to reduce a living business to a spreadsheet before understanding what makes it exciting. But the investor is not asking for the cap table because they are bored by the product. They are asking because the cap table tells them whether the company is investable at all. A startup can have an interesting idea and still be structurally weak. It can have a promising market and still be burdened by a confused ownership history. It can even have early traction and still conceal patterns of future conflict. The cap table is one of the quickest ways an investor can test whether the business is merely ambitious or also coherent.

Investors ask early because ownership is upstream of many other issues. It affects incentives, control, dilution, governance, future fundraising, employee recruitment, exit outcomes, and the practical ability to complete a transaction without discovering hidden complications halfway through due diligence. A founder may think the business is not yet ready for ownership scrutiny because it is early. The investor often thinks the opposite. The earlier the company is, the more revealing the ownership structure can be, because small early decisions frequently become large later problems. If the founders have been sloppy when the cap table was simple, the investor has good reason to wonder how they will behave when the structure becomes complex.

What the investor wants, above all, is clarity.

They want to know who owns the company, what form that ownership takes, what rights attach to it, what promises have already been made, and what future claims may convert into equity later. They want to know whether the founders still hold enough of the company to remain meaningfully motivated. They want to know whether there is room for an employee option pool without making the structure unworkable. They want to know whether prior investors, if any, have unusual rights that could interfere with the current round. They want to know whether the company has a clean enough structure that new money can enter without triggering a tangle of renegotiations, legal corrections, or emotional disputes. The cap table does not answer every question, but it frames many of them quickly.

There is also a more practical reason investors look early. Early-stage investing is not just about choosing winners. It is also about avoiding preventable friction. An investor can tolerate uncertainty about market timing, customer behaviour, and future competition because those risks are inherent to startup investing. What they dislike are avoidable structural complications created by poor ownership discipline. Those complications do not make the startup bold. They make it expensive. Every unclear promise, undocumented grant, badly thought-out founder split, unresolved vesting issue, or informal equity arrangement increases the cost of the transaction. Not always the price, but the friction. More lawyer time. More negotiation. More delay. More explanation. More chances for someone to become offended, defensive, or opportunistic. Investors know that time lost in structural cleanup is time not spent building the business.

That is why the cap table is often read less as a portrait of current wealth and more as a diagnostic instrument. A clean, simple, well-reasoned cap table suggests a founder who understands that startups are built through structures as well as energy. A bloated or confusing one suggests the opposite. Investors are not looking only at the percentages. They are looking at the judgment that produced them.

For example, an investor who sees a company where four early "advisers" each own meaningful equity, with no obvious basis for the size of those grants, is not merely noticing generosity. They are seeing a founder who may have paid with equity instead of making hard decisions. An investor who sees a cofounder holding a large stake despite having left the company long ago sees not only a dead equity position but also a potential future resentment among active team members. A company in which ten or fifteen percent has been casually dispersed across minor contributors may still exist as a legal entity, but to an investor it begins to look structurally immature. The startup may not yet have much revenue, but it already has a history, and that history is visible in the cap table.

Investors also ask early because they are trying to assess whether the founder understands dilution before the investor has to explain it to them under pressure. This matters more than many founders realise. An investor wants to know whether the founder interprets ownership strategically or emotionally. A founder who treats every percentage point as sacred may become extremely difficult during negotiation because they experience even necessary dilution as personal theft.

On the other hand, a founder who has given away ownership carelessly may not appreciate how little room remains for future rounds. Neither extreme is attractive. Investors prefer founders who understand that ownership changes are inevitable, but who also appreciate the cost of those changes and protect the structure intelligently.

This is one reason the cap table has a predictive quality. It does not merely describe where the company is. It hints at how future conversations will go. A disciplined cap table suggests disciplined fundraising. A messy one suggests that the company may need saving from its own past before it can absorb new capital. For an investor deciding where to spend attention, that distinction matters immensely. Money is scarce, but attention is scarcer. No investor wants to begin serious work on a company only to discover halfway through that the founding team has spent eighteen months making undocumented promises and treating equity like an informal social currency.

There is also the question of control, which investors frequently assess before founders realise it is already on the table. An investor may not expect to own a majority of the company, especially at early stage, but they absolutely care whether the business can be governed coherently after they invest. The cap table helps them see whether voting power is likely to become fragmented, whether key stakeholders are aligned, and whether prior rights might obstruct future decisions. A founder may think the investor is merely asking who has what percentage. In reality the investor is often asking a deeper question: if I enter this company, will its structure support rational decision-making, or am I stepping into a future political struggle disguised as a startup?

That political element becomes visible surprisingly early. If there are multiple founders, the cap table can suggest whether their relationship was structured thoughtfully or simply equalised to avoid discomfort. If previous investors are present, the cap table may hint at whether the company has already accepted problematic terms. If there is an option pool, its size may show whether the founders have thought realistically about hiring. If convertible instruments sit off to the side, the investor will want to model how those claims will convert later and what that means for everyone's position. This is why experienced investors often ask for the cap table well before the founder expects them to. They are not being premature. They are reading the company at the structural level before they become emotionally attached to its narrative.

Narrative can be dangerous in investing.

A good founder can tell a compelling story. A good product can create excitement. A credible market can generate momentum. Investors know this, and many have learned, sometimes expensively, that story without structure is not enough. The cap table is one of the first documents that resists charisma. It forces exactness. Either the ownership is clear or it is not. Either the numbers reconcile or they do not. Either prior promises have been formalised or they have not. Either the structure leaves room for future growth or it does not. A brilliant founder may be able to carry a room on vision, but the cap table asks questions vision alone cannot answer.

There is a harder truth underneath all this. Investors ask for the cap table early because they know that many founders do not fully understand their own company until the cap table is laid out in front of them. That does not mean founders are unintelligent. It means startup ownership is easy to feel and surprisingly difficult to formalise. The founder may know who "basically" matters, who "sort of" has equity, who was "meant to" get something later, or who is "not really involved anymore but still on paper." These informal truths may have been adequate for survival in the pre-funding phase. They are not adequate for investment. The investor, by asking early, forces the company to become precise.

This can feel intrusive, but it is often one of the most clarifying moments in the life of a young company. When founders are required to show the cap table, they discover whether the company's ownership is real, current, and legible or whether it lives partly in assumption, memory, and unfinished paperwork. The document becomes a mirror. It reflects not the founder's aspiration, but the company's actual ownership condition. That is valuable not only for investors, but for founders themselves, even when the result is uncomfortable.

There is another reason sophisticated investors ask early: future rounds depend on present cleanliness. Venture finance is cumulative. Each round inherits the structure created by the previous one. If the company begins its financed life on an unstable ownership foundation, that instability does not disappear. It compounds. Later investors become more cautious. Negotiations become longer. Legal work becomes heavier. Employees become harder to incentivise cleanly. Exit calculations become more complicated. Investors know that the cheapest moment to understand the cap table is now, before new money enters and multiplies every existing imperfection.

Seen from the investor's side, then, the question is not why ask so early. It is why wait.
If the company is too early for the cap table to matter, it is probably too early for professional investment to matter as well. But once the founder is asking someone to put capital at risk, ownership becomes central. That capital is not entering a dream in the abstract. It is entering a company with a specific structure of claims. The investor needs to know where their money will sit, what it will dilute, what it will create, what it may be blocked by, and whether the people already inside the company still have enough incentive and enough discipline to justify the risk.

This is why the founder should learn to see the early cap table request not as a nuisance, but as a signal. It signals that the investor is serious enough to look beneath the surface. It signals that the company is crossing a threshold where narrative alone is no longer sufficient. And it signals that ownership, even before significant revenue, is one of the primary ways the business will be judged.

The founder may still feel that the real company lives in the product.
The investor is checking whether the company can survive contact with capital.
That is why the cap table comes early.

How a Simple Spreadsheet Becomes a Power Map

At first glance, a capitalization table looks almost disappointingly ordinary. It appears to be no more than a structured list of names, share classes, quantities, and percentages. The founder sees a spreadsheet. The investor sees an ownership model. The lawyer sees a formal record. The accountant sees a capital structure. All of them are correct, but none of those descriptions is complete. A cap table begins as an administrative instrument and quickly becomes something much more important. It becomes a map of power inside the company.

This transformation happens because ownership in a startup is never only about passive entitlement. A company is not a savings account where all parties simply wait for a return.

It is an evolving organisation in which decisions must be made, risks must be absorbed, resources must be allocated, and future claims must be balanced against present needs. The people on the cap table are not merely holders of percentages. They are participants in a structure that determines who can influence the company, who can block changes, who will be diluted, who will be rewarded, and who may discover that their apparently large percentage produces less real authority than they imagined.

The reason a cap table becomes a power map is that ownership affects behaviour long before any exit event occurs. A founder with a strong stake is likely to think differently about effort, sacrifice, and long-term reward than one whose stake has been whittled down without clear benefit. An early investor with meaningful ownership may expect access, information, and influence even if those rights are not fully apparent from the raw percentage alone. An employee option pool may not yet represent exercised shares, but it signals future economic participation and therefore shapes hiring, incentives, and future dilution. Every line in the spreadsheet points outward into some practical consequence. The table is static only on paper. In the life of the company, it is alive.

This is where inexperienced readers often focus on the wrong thing. They look at the cap table and think the main question is who owns the biggest percentage. That matters, of course, but it is not the whole story and often not even the most important part of the story. Two people can hold the same percentage of a company while standing in radically different positions with respect to control, liquidation outcomes, or future leverage. One may hold common shares with ordinary rights. Another may hold preferred shares carrying protections, influence, or superior economic treatment. A founder may own more than any individual investor and still find that the company cannot take certain actions without investor consent. An option holder may have no current voting power but still represent a meaningful future claim that affects how the whole structure must be understood. The cap table, in other words, records not just possession but position.

Power in startups is rarely distributed in a simple or perfectly transparent way. It exists at the intersection of equity, contracts, governance, and timing. The cap table is where these things begin to reveal themselves.

A founder who holds a large initial stake may look powerful, but if the company has promised substantial future equity elsewhere, or if later financing rights heavily favour incoming investors, that power may be more fragile than it appears. Conversely, a participant with a modest percentage may have strategic importance because of their board position, consent rights, information rights, or their role in enabling future rounds. The spreadsheet can therefore look numerical while actually describing a political system.

This is one reason sophisticated investors do not treat the cap table as a clerical attachment. They read it the way a strategist reads terrain. They want to understand where alliances are likely to form, where resentment may already be latent, whether founders are still properly incentivised, whether dead equity is clogging the structure, and whether future financing is likely to produce manageable dilution or structural stress. The cap table tells them whether the business is governable. A startup with a clean-looking product and an exciting market can still have an unhealthy internal structure if ownership has been distributed without discipline. In that case, the cap table begins to forecast not just economics but conflict.

Founders often resist this interpretation because it feels too political, almost cynical, as though the company were already being reduced to manoeuvre and leverage before it has even proved itself. Yet that resistance usually comes from confusing power with bad faith. Power is not the same as treachery. It is simply the capacity to affect outcomes. In a company, that capacity matters from the beginning. The founder who can appoint people, negotiate funding, decide hiring priorities, and maintain strategic direction has power. The investor who can refuse terms, delay a transaction, insist on protections, or influence board composition has power. The employee whose technical knowledge makes them difficult to replace has a different kind of power, even if their cap table stake is modest or deferred. The cap table does not capture every form of influence, but it captures one of the most durable and enforceable forms of it.

This is why early ownership decisions have effects far beyond simple fairness. When founders divide equity, they are not only deciding who gets what share of eventual upside. They are deciding how authority and alignment may work under pressure.

If one founder has a much larger stake, that may be entirely justified, but it will affect how future disagreements are experienced and resolved. If another founder holds a large percentage without vesting or ongoing contribution, that stake may later feel like a block of frozen power attached to someone no longer carrying the company. If advisers, friends, or casual early supporters have been granted equity in a loose or sentimental way, the result may not only be economic inefficiency but structural clutter. The cap table records all of this. It is not merely a statement of past decisions. It is an architecture for future negotiations.

The phrase power map is useful because it forces the reader to think spatially rather than sentimentally. A map shows position, relation, and movement. It tells you where different interests sit relative to one another. It reveals bottlenecks, concentrations, open space, and future pressure points. The cap table functions in much the same way. It shows whether ownership is concentrated or fragmented. It reveals whether room remains for future hires or future rounds. It shows whether an investor entering now will be joining a structure with clean lines or one already burdened by accumulated compromise. It also reveals the company's past behaviour. A disciplined table suggests disciplined decisions. A bloated one suggests a founder who has repeatedly solved immediate problems by handing out future claims.

This is particularly important once funding begins. The moment outside capital enters the company, ownership no longer serves only as an internal record. It becomes a bargaining field. Every new round changes not just the percentages but the relative positions of the participants. Founders may lose ownership yet gain runway, credibility, and growth capacity. Investors may gain protections that make their apparent ownership more powerful than the raw numbers suggest. Employees may gain options that do not yet vote but nonetheless alter how future dilution must be modelled. The spreadsheet that once looked simple is now the visible surface of a changing negotiation system.

There is a psychological lesson here as well. Many founders want the cap table to be neutral. They want it to function like a tidy account of who deserves what, as though it were a moral ledger. That hope is understandable, but the cap table cannot remain morally innocent once other parties arrive with different incentives. It becomes a contested space because the company itself is a contested future.

Everyone around the table may want the company to succeed, but they do not all define success in exactly the same way, nor do they all bear losses equally. Founders may care about mission, continuity, and control. Investors may care about return profile, downside protection, and timing of exit. Employees may care about whether their equity has realistic value. The cap table is where these interests begin to coexist in measurable form.

The intelligent reader therefore has to learn to see past the apparent simplicity of the document. A cap table is never just an output of arithmetic. It is the product of choices made under uncertainty by people with different expectations about value, effort, risk, and reward. That is why two superficially similar companies can have radically different internal realities. One may have a cap table that supports trust, disciplined fundraising, and future growth. Another may have a cap table that traps the founders in resentment, makes hiring harder, discourages new investors, and distorts the eventual distribution of exit proceeds. Both may look like spreadsheets. Only one is a healthy system.

This is also why the cap table matters to readers well beyond the founder. To the academic or technically minded reader, it is one of the clearest points at which corporate governance becomes visible in practical form. Abstract discussions of incentive alignment, control rights, residual claims, and strategic authority are important, but they become concrete in the cap table. It is where legal ownership meets financial logic. It is where valuation begins to interact with governance. It is where the company's internal constitution starts to emerge, often before the founders themselves realise that they are writing one.

Once this is understood, the cap table can no longer be treated as background administration. It becomes a primary object of attention. A founder preparing for a funding round must understand not only what percentages exist but what relationships those percentages create. An investor reviewing a business must understand not only who owns what today but how that structure will behave after the next round, the next option grant, or the next crisis. An employee evaluating an equity offer must understand not only the number presented to them but where that number sits in the broader ownership landscape. In each case, the spreadsheet becomes legible as a field of power.

That is why a simple cap table rarely stays simple for long. The company grows, people join, money arrives, rights accumulate, classes multiply, and what once looked like a short list of founders becomes an encoded description of the company's internal order. The earlier the founder grasps this, the better. If they continue to see the cap table as a piece of paperwork, they will be surprised by how much it determines. If they learn to see it as a power map, they begin to understand why ownership must be managed with the same seriousness as product, market, and capital itself.

The Hidden Danger of Casual Early Promises

One of the great weaknesses of the early startup phase is that it often feels too small, too personal, and too uncertain to justify formal seriousness. The company may still exist only as a prototype, a website, a deck, a few customer calls, a rough product, or a plan discussed at odd hours between people who know each other well enough to trust tone, gesture, and implication more than signed documents. That atmosphere can be energising. It can also be dangerous. In that stage, founders frequently make promises that feel temporary, informal, or harmless because everything still feels provisional. They tell someone they will "take care of them later." They say a contributor is "basically getting five percent." They hint that an early helper will "be part of the company." They reassure a friend that there will be equity once things settle down. Each statement may feel like a gesture of goodwill, gratitude, or motivation. Yet these casual promises can become some of the most corrosive forces in the future life of the company.

The danger lies partly in the mismatch between how the promise is made and how it is later remembered. The founder may experience the moment as conversational, encouraging, even diplomatic. They may believe they are expressing intent rather than creating an obligation. The recipient often hears something else. In a startup, where compensation is frequently uncertain and future upside is one of the few meaningful inducements available, an informal equity promise rarely lands as mere social warmth. It lands as economic significance. The person who hears it may begin mentally reorganising their place in the company around that expectation.

They may accept lower pay, work longer hours, or remain engaged through a difficult period because they believe they have been given or promised a real stake. The founder thinks they have bought time. In reality they may have created a claimant.

This is why early promises are so much more dangerous than they first appear. They do not simply create ambiguity. They create competing narratives of ownership. The founder remembers flexibility, context, and intention. The other party remembers the commitment. Neither may be acting in bad faith. That is what makes these situations so difficult. They are not usually battles between honesty and fraud. They are collisions between two sincere but incompatible memories of what was said, what was meant, and what was owed. Once the company begins to acquire value, those collisions become harder to smooth over because the numbers that once sounded abstract are no longer abstract at all. Five percent of nothing is a polite phrase. Five percent of something meaningful is an argument.

The startup world is unusually vulnerable to this because it is built on contribution before certainty. In a mature company, roles, compensation, and authority are usually defined with enough clarity that misunderstandings, while still possible, are somewhat constrained by systems. In a young company, by contrast, the business is often being assembled out of partial commitments. Someone helps with design. Someone writes code over weekends. Someone provides strategic introductions. Someone advises on product. Someone agrees to become more involved later if funding appears. At this point, because the company is not yet fully organised, founders are tempted to keep everything soft. Soft commitments preserve flexibility. Soft language avoids difficult negotiations. Soft promises maintain momentum. But softness in the present often hardens into dispute later because contribution and expectation have already begun to attach themselves to the company's future.

This is especially true when founders confuse appreciation with allocation. A contributor helps at a crucial moment and the founder feels genuine gratitude. They want to reward that help and also encourage more of it. The easiest available reward, especially when cash is scarce, is the suggestion of future ownership. Yet gratitude is an unstable basis for capital structure. It expands and contracts with circumstance.

In a stressful moment, one person can feel indispensable. Six months later, their actual role in the long-term company may look much smaller. If the founder made a casual promise in the heat of dependence, they may later feel trapped between fairness to the contributor and fairness to the company as a whole. Meanwhile the contributor, quite reasonably, may feel that the founder is retreating from a promise precisely because the company's prospects have improved. What began as emotional appreciation becomes structural tension.

There is also a hierarchy problem hidden inside informal promises. Founders are not always equally casual with everyone. They may make generous verbal commitments to people they know personally, or to people whose approval they seek, or to those who were present during the company's earliest and most chaotic stage. Later participants, who may contribute more in objective terms, may receive cleaner but smaller arrangements because by then the founders have become more disciplined. The result can be an ownership structure shaped less by strategic value than by emotional timing. Those who arrived during the romantic and disorganised phase may end up with better promises than those who arrived once the company began behaving like a company. This does not only create inefficiency. It creates moral confusion about legitimacy.

The phrase casual promise can sound too mild for what is really at stake. Often these are not just throwaway remarks but fragments of the company's unwritten constitution. They describe who is thought to matter, who is being invited to take risk, and who believes they are part of the future economic story. The problem is that unwritten constitutions do not stay unwritten. They emerge later through emails, text messages, recollections, half-finished documents, and emotionally charged conversations in which one party says, with complete sincerity, that they built their life around what was said. The founder, often equally sincere, says that nothing was final. From that moment onward, the company is no longer merely dealing with an administrative loose end. It is dealing with a conflict between expectation and formal structure, and those conflicts are hard to resolve cleanly because both sides can point to something real.

Investors understand this danger well, which is one reason they react badly to vague ownership histories. A founder who says that someone was "meant to get something later" is not describing a harmless loose end. They are describing a potential future claim. A company may have no signed grant, no board resolution, no issued shares, and still have a problem if a sufficiently important early participant believes a promise was made. Even if no legal liability arises, the existence of that expectation can distort hiring, fundraising, and governance because the issue hangs over the company until it is either resolved or denied. Investors do not like unresolved shadows in the ownership structure because shadows tend to become leverage at the worst possible time.

There is a particularly destructive version of this pattern that appears when founders use ambiguity strategically. They do not want to commit, but they do want help, loyalty, or continued effort. So they say enough to keep the other person engaged while preserving enough vagueness to retreat later if convenient. This may seem clever in the short term. It is usually disastrous in the long term. Even where the founder avoids a legal obligation, they often create reputational harm, internal distrust, and a company culture in which verbal commitments are treated as disposable. In a startup, where so much depends on people believing in a future not yet visible, that kind of cynicism is expensive. The founder may save equity. They may lose trust, and trust is often harder to rebuild than the cap table.

At the same time, it is important not to romanticise the other side. Not every recipient of an informal promise remains modest, reasonable, or proportionate in their expectations. Some people hear more than was offered. Some retroactively expand a vague suggestion into a firm entitlement. Some come to treat a period of early involvement as proof that they deserve permanent ownership regardless of actual contribution over time. This is why the problem cannot be solved by telling founders to simply be kinder or more generous. The solution is not emotional purity. It is clarity. If equity is being offered, it should be defined. If it is being considered but not granted, that should also be defined. If someone is helping informally with no expectation of ownership, that needs to be clear as well. What destroys companies is not merely selfishness. It is unresolved ambiguity around matters people care deeply about.

Founders sometimes defend ambiguity by appealing to uncertainty. They say the company is too early to know who deserves what. There is some truth in that. In the very beginning, many relationships are experimental. It may genuinely be too soon to decide whether someone is a cofounder, an employee, a consultant, or simply a helpful early ally.

But uncertainty is not a reason for vagueness. It is a reason for provisional structure. There are many ways to create staged clarity. Vesting. option grants that begin only after specific commitments are made. Written advisory arrangements with limited and explicit equity. Clear statements that no ownership has yet been granted and that any future allocation will depend on formal agreement. These mechanisms preserve flexibility without allowing fantasy to harden into grievance.

This is where casual promises become so expensive. They seem to preserve optionality, but often they destroy it. The founder thinks they are avoiding a decision. In reality they are making a weaker and more dangerous version of one. They are allowing expectation to form without giving themselves the protection of structure. Later, when they try to impose order, they discover that the company is not starting from zero. It is starting from a field of half-remembered commitments. At that point, almost every outcome is costly. If the founder honours every vague promise, they may cripple the ownership structure. If they refuse them, they may alienate important people or provoke disputes. If they try to compromise, everyone feels partially cheated. All of this was avoidable.

The deeper issue is that startup founders often underestimate the legal and emotional durability of spoken things. In everyday life, people say all sorts of hopeful, exaggerated, aspirational, and non-binding things to keep relationships moving. In a startup, where future upside can substitute for present payment, the same words carry a different weight. "We'll sort you out later" does not land like a vague courtesy. It lands like a placeholder for ownership. "You'll be part of this" does not sound symbolic when the company has no money. It sounds like a future economic position. Even where courts would dismiss such statements as too uncertain, the internal life of the company rarely dismisses them so easily. People remember. They compare what was said to what later happened. They form judgments not only about law, but about honour.

That is why disciplined founders learn early to separate enthusiasm from entitlement. They can still be warm, encouraging, and grateful, but they do not use equity language loosely. They do not promise percentages because a conversation is going well. They do not imply ownership to avoid conflict. They do not tell someone they are "basically a founder" unless they are prepared to formalise what that means. And if they are not prepared to formalise it, they say so.

This can feel uncomfortable in the moment, especially for founders who dislike confrontation or who want to keep everyone happy. Yet it is far kinder than allowing someone to continue under a false or inflated expectation.

The hidden danger, then, is not only that casual promises can produce legal complications. It is that they can deform the human structure of the company before the financial structure has even stabilised. They turn goodwill into contested memory. They replace strategy with drift. They create claimants where there should have been conversations. And because startups often reach their first real moment of external scrutiny only after months or years of this informal culture, the danger stays hidden until the company is finally asked to account for itself. At that point the spreadsheet must match reality, and reality often contains ghosts.

A mature ownership structure begins by refusing to create those ghosts in the first place.

Why This Book Exists

Most books on startup finance fail in one of two directions. They either simplify the subject so aggressively that the reader leaves with a few memorable phrases and almost no practical grasp of how ownership actually works, or they become so entangled in specialist terminology, jurisdictional detail, and technical abstraction that only a reader already comfortable with finance, law, or venture capital can move through them with confidence. In one version, the founder is reassured but not equipped. In the other, the serious reader is respected but the ordinary reader is effectively screened out. This book exists because capitalization tables deserve better treatment than either of those extremes.

A cap table is too important to be handled as a motivational sidebar, and too central to startup life to be left entirely to specialists. Founders encounter it early, often without preparation, and the consequences of misunderstanding it can echo through every later stage of the company. Employees may accept equity they do not understand. Advisers may be overpaid in ownership because no one paused to model the long-term effect. Investors may walk away from otherwise promising businesses because the ownership structure is weak, chaotic, or naïve.

Founders themselves may raise money without recognising what is being altered beneath them. By the time the company reaches a serious financing, an acquisition discussion, or a major internal dispute, the cap table may already contain the history of several avoidable mistakes. This book exists because too many people meet the ownership structure of their company only after that structure has begun to control them.

There is also a deeper reason. Capitalization tables are often presented as though they were merely technical records, tidy ledgers of equity distribution, as if their significance were administrative rather than strategic. That view is too thin. A cap table is not only a record of who owns what. It is one of the clearest descriptions of how a company has been built, how risk has been priced, how trust has been formalised, how future reward has been imagined, and how control may shift as the company grows. It sits at the meeting point of law, finance, governance, psychology, and ambition. That makes it much more than a spreadsheet, and that is why a proper treatment of the subject has to do more than define terms. It has to explain how the structure behaves.

This book therefore exists to do several jobs at once.

It exists to help the founder who has no finance background and has picked it up because someone, perhaps an investor or lawyer, has just asked for a cap table and they do not want to make a fool of themselves or, worse, make a permanent mistake. It exists to help the technically minded reader who wants a serious account of how startup ownership evolves through founder splits, vesting, option pools, priced rounds, notes, SAFEs, preferred stock, dilution, and exit. It exists to help the reader who understands some of the language already but has never quite seen how the pieces fit together into one continuous structure. It also exists, importantly, for the reader who may come from a more academic or analytical background and wants not only mechanics but concepts, not only outcomes but process, not only percentages but power.

That range matters. A book like this will only work if it can move between levels of understanding without becoming either patronising or opaque. The founder who is reading because they need urgent practical help should not be made to feel that the subject is reserved for insiders. The academic or highly literate reader should not be asked to endure a watered-down explanation that never rises above cliché.

The only honest way to serve both audiences is to build the discussion in layers, beginning with what the cap table is in practical life and then moving steadily into the deeper mechanics of ownership, governance, and venture finance. That is the method of this book. It will not assume expertise, but it will not avoid complexity simply because complexity is inconvenient.

This is also why the subject is being treated at length. A short guide can be useful for a narrow task, but capitalization tables do not live narrow lives. They begin with founding decisions, but they do not stay there. They shape how cofounders are bound to each other. They affect hiring. They determine how employee incentives are structured. They interact with notes, SAFEs, priced rounds, and investor protections. They influence control, not just economics. They determine how the company looks to future investors. They affect what happens during crisis, recapitalisation, acquisition, and IPO. In a well-built startup, the cap table is one of the few documents that touches nearly every important transition in the company's development. A short explanation can define it. It cannot adequately follow it.

Another reason this book exists is because the startup world often teaches ownership badly. Founders are exposed to fragments. They hear that dilution is normal, but not what kinds of dilution are harmless and what kinds are destructive. They hear that SAFEs are simple, but not how hidden claims accumulate before conversion. They hear that investors want preferred stock, but not how preferences alter the meaning of percentages. They hear that option pools are necessary, but not why their timing matters. They hear that ownership is about upside, while learning too late that it is also about governance, leverage, and constraint. In other words, they receive slogans instead of structures. The slogans are not always false, but they are usually incomplete. This book exists to replace fragments with continuity.

It also exists because of a problem of tone. Startup culture has an unfortunate tendency either to dramatise finance in breathless language about unicorns, rounds, and paper wealth, or to hide it behind a veil of professional detachment that implies real understanding belongs to lawyers, accountants, and venture capital firms. Both tendencies are unhelpful. The first distorts the subject into spectacle.

The second encourages founders to outsource thought. Neither is acceptable if the reader is trying to understand the ownership skeleton of their own company. The cap table deserves a tone that is serious, readable, and exact. It deserves to be explained as a practical instrument of company life rather than a sacred object of venture mythology.

There is a further reason, and it may be the most important of all. Ownership has moral consequences as well as financial ones. It is easy to talk about shares as though they were only economic units, but in a startup they are also expressions of contribution, trust, sacrifice, and expectation. A founder split is never purely mathematical. A vesting schedule is never only technical. An option grant carries meaning beyond its percentage. A liquidation preference changes not just a payout model but a hierarchy of protection. Casual early promises become disputes because people do not experience ownership merely as arithmetic. They experience it as recognition, legitimacy, and status within the story of the company. This book exists because good explanations of cap tables must acknowledge that human reality without surrendering to it. The reader needs to understand both the mechanics and the emotions that often distort them.

The research base behind this book also matters. Startup ownership is one of those subjects where practical life and serious scholarship overlap in fruitful ways. Venture finance literature helps explain why investors use particular instruments and how claims are structured. Governance scholarship helps show why ownership is never just about cash flow but also about control and strategic influence. Work on intellectual capital and valuation helps explain why equity structures matter even before tangible value is fully visible. The legal and contractual literature on term sheets, preferences, and investor rights helps reveal that the cap table is often the visible surface of a deeper structure. This book exists in part to bring those layers together in a way that remains usable. It does not exist to imitate an academic monograph, but neither does it exist to avoid the serious ideas that make the subject intelligible.

It also exists because the reader deserves to see the whole life cycle of ownership rather than isolated snapshots. A startup is often described through stages such as pre-seed, seed, Series A, and exit, as though each stage were a separate world. In reality the cap table ties them together.

The founder-only company is not a separate topic from the option pool. The option pool is not separate from the priced round. The priced round is not separate from dilution. Dilution is not separate from later control issues. Control is not separate from exit outcomes. The book exists to preserve that continuity. Each chapter will treat a particular part of the subject, but the reader should always feel that they are following one structure as it evolves, not jumping between disconnected lessons.

There is another sense in which this book is necessary. Founders are often told that they can always fix the cap table later. Sometimes they can. Often they can only fix it at a cost. The cost may be legal, financial, emotional, or reputational. A founder can try to reclaim equity from a departed cofounder, but the conversation may be ugly and the result incomplete. A company can clean up vague promises before a round, but only by spending time, money, and trust. An investor can accept a messy structure, but may demand terms that compensate for the risk. A bad early cap table does not always kill a company, but it often taxes it. This book exists because prevention is much cheaper than repair, and understanding is usually the first form of prevention.

For some readers, the most useful part of the book may be its practical clarity. For others, it may be the reframing of the cap table as a map of power rather than merely a spreadsheet. For still others, it may be the recognition that startup finance is not simply a chain of transactions but a sequence of structured reallocations in which every new layer of money changes the meaning of the old one. Whatever draws the reader here, the purpose is the same. The aim is not to make the reader sound knowledgeable. The aim is to make them genuinely less likely to blunder.

That is why this book exists.

It exists because the cap table is one of the hidden operating systems of the startup world, and too many people are expected to live inside it before they are ever shown how it works. It exists because ownership decisions made early can echo with surprising force. It exists because founders need more than slogans, and specialists are not the only people entitled to serious explanations. It exists because the company begins to take shape in ownership long before most people realise it. And it exists because once a founder understands the cap table properly, they begin to understand the company differently as well.

TWO

What a Share Actually Is

"Ownership means ownership."
- Peter Thiel

The Company as a Legal Shell

One of the most important transitions in the mind of a founder is the moment they stop thinking of the business as an idea they control and start understanding it as an entity that exists separately from them. That change sounds technical, but it is not merely technical. It is one of the deepest conceptual shifts in startup life. Before incorporation, the founder usually experiences the business as an extension of self. The product is their effort, the risk is their anxiety, the ambition is their ambition, and the future success, if it ever arrives, is imagined as something that will naturally belong to them because they originated it. Once a company is properly formed, that intuitive model begins to break down. The founder may still lead it, build it, and believe in it more fiercely than anyone else, but the company is no longer the founder in legal form. It is something separate.

That separateness is the foundation on which all later ownership rests.

A company is often described as a legal person, which can sound abstract or slightly theatrical if encountered for the first time. Yet the phrase exists for a good reason. The law needs a way to treat the enterprise as something capable of holding assets, entering contracts, taking on obligations, employing people, borrowing money, being sued, issuing equity, and continuing to exist even if the human beings who set it up change over time. If all of these things remained attached directly to the founder as a natural person, the business would be structurally fragile. Every contract would be personal. Every liability would flow more directly into the founder's own life. Every attempt to share ownership would be far messier because there would be no distinct object to divide. The company solves this by becoming the shell that contains the commercial activity.

The word shell is useful here, provided it is understood correctly. It does not mean emptiness in the dismissive sense. It means container. The company is the legal container into which the venture is placed. The name, the contracts, the intellectual property, the capital structure, the rights of investors, the obligations to employees, the record of shares, and the formal continuity of the business all sit inside that shell. Once that is understood, many other puzzles begin to make sense. A founder does not literally own the business in the way someone owns a chair or a car. They own shares in the company, and the company owns the business assets. That distinction is not academic nit-picking. It governs almost everything that follows.

This is also why people who are new to startup ownership often ask the wrong early questions. They ask whether they own the product, whether the business is still theirs, or whether bringing someone in means giving part of the company away as though the company were a physical possession cut into slices. The more precise way to think about it is this. The company exists as a separate legal structure, and different people can hold defined claims over that structure. Those claims are expressed through shares or similar rights. The company itself continues as the central vessel. It can therefore survive founder changes, funding rounds, employee hires, acquisitions, reorganisations, and even severe internal disagreements because the enterprise has been given legal form outside the private identity of any one participant.

For the founder, this can feel both empowering and unsettling. It is empowering because the company can now do things that a purely informal project cannot. It can contract properly. It can raise money. It can allocate ownership. It can create a board. It can hold intellectual property in a way investors and acquirers can recognise. It can outlast the mood, health, energy, or even continued involvement of its founder. At the same time, it is unsettling because it means the founder no longer occupies an absolute position. They may have created the company, but they are now relating to it through a formal structure. Their control, value, and future reward depend on how they sit inside that structure, not simply on the fact that they were first.

That is why the company as legal shell matters so much to capitalization tables. The cap table is not a list of who owns the product or who morally deserves the upside. It is a list of who holds what formal claim against the legal entity. Without the shell, the cap table is conceptually impossible.

There is nothing stable to capitalise. Once the shell exists, ownership can be divided, measured, transferred, diluted, protected, or converted because there is now a recognised structure through which those operations can occur. Put differently, the company makes shares possible because it creates something that shares can attach to.

This helps explain why early startup confusion about ownership is so persistent. Founders often make the emotional shift toward company-building before they make the conceptual shift toward entity-thinking. They begin acting as though the project is becoming real, but they still think about it as though it is personally fused to them. Then, when they incorporate and begin issuing shares, they are surprised by the implications. They thought they were creating administrative order around something already theirs. In fact, they were creating a structure in which their relationship to the business would now be mediated through ownership rights. The founder does not disappear from the picture, but they stop being identical with the company itself.

A serious reader should notice that this shift also changes how risk is understood. Before incorporation, the founder is often directly exposed. The project may still be small enough that all obligations, expenses, and informal promises flow through them personally. After incorporation, at least in principle and subject to the laws of the relevant jurisdiction, liability begins to be channelled through the entity. That is one of the reasons company formation exists in the first place. The shell is not merely about convenience or investment readiness. It is about structuring commercial life so that enterprise can be conducted through a legal form rather than through pure personal exposure. The fact that ownership later becomes share-based is therefore only one consequence of a deeper move. The venture has been given a body in law.

Once this is seen clearly, many practical realities stop looking arbitrary. Intellectual property should usually be assigned into the company because the company, not the founder personally, must be the thing investors are backing and acquirers are buying. Contracts should normally be entered into by the company because it is the operating entity. Shares are issued by the company because the ownership claim is against the legal shell. Even the idea of dilution becomes easier to understand, because what is being diluted is not the founder's private possession in a raw sense, but their proportional claim on the legal entity as more claims are created. The shell makes all of this coherent.

It also reveals something more subtle. Founders do not merely build businesses. They build structures capable of containing businesses. Some founders are strong on vision and weak on structure. Others over-focus on the shell and lose contact with the commercial reality it is supposed to serve. The wise approach is to understand that both are necessary. The shell without a viable venture is empty form. The venture without a proper shell becomes increasingly difficult to finance, govern, protect, and scale. The capitalization table sits precisely at this intersection. It is one of the clearest records of how the abstract shell has been populated with human claims.

This chapter therefore begins with the company itself because there is no sensible discussion of shares without first knowing what those shares are in relation to. A share is not a free-floating token of startup optimism. It is a defined unit of claim issued by a legal entity. The entity must exist before the claim can be coherent. That may sound obvious once stated plainly, but many founders behave for a long time as though the company were simply a label attached to their personal project. The whole architecture of ownership becomes clearer the moment they understand that the company is not merely their work wearing a formal name. It is the shell inside which the work, the capital, the rights, and the future structure of the business are all being organised.

Once that point is secure, the next question becomes unavoidable. If the company is the shell, then what exactly is a share inside it, and what kind of ownership does it really represent?

Shares as Slices of Ownership

Once the founder understands that the company exists as a separate legal shell, the next task is to understand what a share actually is. This is where the language of startup ownership begins to become clearer, because a share is the mechanism through which a person's claim on that shell is expressed. Founders often hear the word so early and so casually that it begins to feel almost decorative, as though shares were simply the official tokens used in company paperwork. In reality, a share is one of the most consequential units in the entire startup structure. It is small in form, but large in meaning.

At the simplest level, a share is a slice of ownership in the company. That sentence is accurate, but it needs to be handled carefully because it can mislead as easily as it can clarify. A slice is a useful image because it suggests division of a whole. If a company has been divided into shares, then each share represents a fraction of the total. But unlike slices of cake, shares are not merely passive portions. They are structured claims. Depending on the type of share, and the terms attached to it, that slice may carry economic rights, voting rights, information rights, liquidation rights, or some combination of these. Even where two parties each appear to hold slices of the same pie, the slices may not behave identically.

Still, the image is useful as a first principle. Ownership in a company is generally not held in one undifferentiated block. It is broken into units, and those units are allocated among participants. The founder may begin by holding all of them. Later, some may be transferred to a cofounder, issued to an employee option pool, sold to an investor, or reserved for future use. As that happens, the founder's relationship to the company changes. They do not cease to be central simply because other people now hold shares, but they are no longer the only formal claimant. The company's future is now being distributed through a structure of slices.

This matters because a share is not simply a symbolic badge that says someone is involved. It is a recognised form of entitlement. If the company becomes valuable, the share matters economically. If the company is sold, the share matters in the distribution of proceeds. If the company asks shareholders to vote, the share may matter in governance. If more shares are later issued, the relative meaning of existing shares can change. The share therefore connects the present structure of the company to its future possibilities. It is a small legal object with very long consequences.

Founders sometimes misunderstand this by thinking of shares as interchangeable with contribution in a loose moral sense. They assume that if someone helped a lot, that person should simply "get some shares," as though the company were handing out tokens of appreciation. That instinct is understandable but incomplete. Shares are not merely expressions of gratitude. They are claims against the company's future. To issue them is not just to thank someone. It is to bring them inside the ownership architecture. That means every decision to allocate shares has to be understood not only in terms of fairness today, but in terms of what the structure will look like tomorrow.

This is why experienced people become uneasy when they hear founders speak casually about handing out equity. A founder may think they are being kind, collaborative, or visionary. An investor or lawyer hears structural change. A share granted today is not just a present gesture. It is a future percentage, a future source of dilution for others, a future claim at exit, and sometimes a future source of influence. This does not mean shares should be hoarded or treated with fear. It means they should be issued with the seriousness appropriate to something that changes the ownership map of the company.

There is another subtle point here. A share is a unit of ownership, but its significance depends on context. One hundred shares can mean almost nothing or almost everything depending on how many total shares exist. This is one reason novice founders become confused by raw numbers. They focus on the count rather than the proportion. If a company has one hundred shares in total, then one share represents one percent. If the company has ten million shares, one share represents almost nothing. The number by itself tells you very little. What matters is the relationship between the number held by a person and the total number outstanding. That relationship is what turns shares into percentages, and percentages are what most people intuitively think of when they think about ownership.

Even then, one has to be careful. A percentage is not the whole truth either. It is a simplified expression of relative claim, and it can conceal differences in rights, class, timing, and future conversion. Two people might each hold ten percent and still stand in very different positions once the legal terms attached to their shares are taken into account. For now, though, the key point is simpler. Shares are the units from which those percentages are built. They are the basic grammar of company ownership. Without them, there is no clean way to express who owns what fraction of the legal shell.

This is why the language of slices can still be useful if kept under discipline. When a founder gives shares away, they are not giving away vague participation. They are dividing the company into more claimed pieces. When an investor buys shares, they are not merely supporting the company. They are purchasing part of the ownership structure. When an employee is granted options that may later convert into shares, the company is preparing to extend slices of the shell to that employee if certain conditions are met.

Every major step in startup finance can be translated back into this basic principle. The company is divided into structured slices, and those slices determine who stands where inside the enterprise.

It is also worth noticing that shares create the possibility of both alignment and tension. They align because they allow multiple people to care about the growth of the same entity. Founders, employees, and investors can all, in principle, benefit from the company becoming more valuable. That is one of the reasons shares are such a powerful organisational tool. They let future upside substitute, at least partly, for present compensation or present certainty. But they also create tension because the slices are finite in their relative meaning. To give one person more often means someone else has relatively less. To issue new shares may raise the value of the whole company while reducing the percentage of existing holders. Ownership through shares therefore always contains a political element. The slices permit collaboration, but they also structure competition over how the future will be divided.

For the founder, the practical lesson is that shares should never be thought of as mere abstractions. They are the way ownership becomes divisible, transferable, and investable. They are also the reason the startup can move from personal project to scalable company. A wholly informal venture cannot easily absorb new participants at the level of ownership. A share-based company can. That is one of the great strengths of the corporate form. It allows the enterprise to expand its circle of stakeholders without collapsing into pure personal bargaining every time a new contributor appears.

Seen properly, then, a share is both simple and profound. It is simple because it is just a unit of ownership in the company. It is profound because almost everything that matters later in startup finance is built from the arrangement, reallocation, and interpretation of those units. The cap table is simply the structured record of where those slices sit. The rest of the book will show how that record evolves, becomes more complicated, and interacts with law, finance, incentives, and power. But the foundation is here. The company is the shell, and shares are the slices through which that shell is owned.

Percentage Ownership Versus Number of Shares

One of the earliest and most persistent confusions in startup ownership comes from treating the number of shares as though it were more important than the percentage those shares represent. Founders often become attached to raw share counts because the numbers feel tangible. One founder has five million shares. Another has two million. An investor is being offered one million. An employee option grant might be twenty-five thousand. These figures sound concrete, and because they are expressed in whole numbers they appear to carry their own meaning. In reality, they do not carry much meaning at all unless they are understood in relation to the total number of shares in existence.

This is the point at which many readers discover that startup ownership is more relative than absolute. A share count in isolation tells you very little. Five hundred shares might represent half a company or almost nothing, depending entirely on the total number outstanding. The real question is never simply how many shares a person has. The real question is what fraction of the company those shares amount to. That fraction is what gives the number its significance.

This sounds simple, but the confusion persists because human beings are psychologically drawn to large and small numbers in ways that are not always rational. A founder may feel wealthier, more secure, or more important because they hold millions of shares rather than hundreds, even though the practical ownership meaning could be identical. Another may become distressed when a future financing reduces their percentage, even if the underlying value of their holding has increased. These reactions are understandable because the arithmetic of ownership is easy to read incorrectly when numbers are emotionally charged. The founder wants something they can hold onto, and a large share count often feels more substantial than a percentage that can later change. Yet the large share count is often little more than formatting.

Imagine two companies that are identical in all economically relevant respects. In the first, the founder owns 1,000 out of 1,000 total shares, which means they own 100 percent. In the second, the founder owns 10,000,000 out of 10,000,000 total shares, which also means they own 100 percent. The founder in the second company may feel as though they own something bigger because the number is larger, but in ownership terms nothing of substance has changed. The higher count does not create more company, more value, or more control. It merely changes the scale on which the ownership is recorded.

This is why experienced investors and lawyers often move quickly past the raw number and focus instead on the capitalisation as a proportion. They want to know who owns what percentage on a fully diluted basis, what claims exist beneath the current picture, and how that picture will change after a financing, an option pool expansion, or a conversion event. The count matters for calculation, but not for intuitive meaning. The percentage is what allows the ownership structure to be understood in human terms.

Even here, one has to retain some caution. Percentages can be clearer than raw numbers, but they can also create false comfort. A founder may say they own sixty percent of the company and take reassurance from that figure, while failing to notice that preferred rights held elsewhere in the structure may make that sixty percent economically weaker than it sounds. That deeper issue will come later. For the moment, the key lesson is more basic. A share count is the raw material. A percentage is the first real expression of ownership meaning.

This relative quality of ownership is one reason founders should be careful not to negotiate based on numbers that are psychologically flattering but economically empty. Consider a situation in which a cofounder is told they will receive one million shares. That can sound generous if no further context is given. If the company has ten million shares outstanding, it is a ten percent stake. If the company has one hundred million, it is one percent. The same number can describe very different economic realities. A founder who speaks in share counts without also speaking in percentages can therefore mislead others unintentionally, or occasionally intentionally, by allowing the number to do emotional work it does not deserve.

The same issue appears in employee compensation. Startups often offer option grants that sound large to people who are unfamiliar with capital structures. Fifty thousand options can sound extraordinary until one asks fifty thousand out of what. If the company's fully diluted share count is very high, the grant may represent only a modest fraction of the business. If the company is early and the total count is lower, the same grant may be more meaningful.

Employees who evaluate equity offers without understanding the denominator are effectively trying to judge size without knowing the scale of the map.

This relative logic also explains why companies can choose very different absolute share counts at formation without changing the underlying ownership relationships. Some companies begin with a small number of shares, perhaps a few hundred or a few thousand. Others begin with millions. The practical reasons for choosing one count rather than another may include administrative convenience, future flexibility, or customary practice in a given market or legal environment. What matters is not whether the count looks big or small. What matters is whether the structure is coherent, workable, and capable of supporting future allocations without creating unnecessary awkwardness. A company with ten million authorised shares is not automatically more sophisticated than one with ten thousand. The important question is whether the ownership proportions and future planning make sense.

There is, however, one practical reason large share counts often become common in startup environments. They make later grants and calculations feel more granular. It is psychologically and administratively easier to grant an employee 50,000 options than 0.5 shares, even if the economic meaning could be equivalent under a different share structure. Larger counts also allow founders and investors to model future issuances, pools, and conversions in units that feel less clumsy. But this is still a matter of formatting and convenience, not intrinsic economic superiority. The large number is a tool, not a signal of value.

It is also worth noticing how easily confusion between number and percentage can distort early founder conversations. One founder may suggest splitting the company by assigning specific share counts without any shared understanding of what those counts imply. Another may insist on a certain number of shares because it sounds large, even though the percentage on offer is unchanged under different total counts. Still another may believe dilution is measured by the reduction in share count rather than by the reduction in proportional ownership. These misunderstandings can create entirely unnecessary conflict because they focus attention on the wrong variable. The company does not care whether ownership is recorded in hundreds or millions. What changes the economic and governance reality is the proportion and the rights attached.

This distinction becomes especially important once new shares are issued. Suppose a founder owns 6,000,000 shares out of 10,000,000 total, giving them sixty percent. If the company later issues 2,000,000 new shares to an investor, the founder still holds 6,000,000 shares. Their raw count has not changed. Yet their percentage has fallen because the total has increased to 12,000,000. They now own fifty percent. This simple example captures a truth that underlies much of the tension in startup finance. You can keep the same number of shares and still own less of the company because ownership is measured proportionally. Many founders understand this intellectually once it is explained, but emotionally they continue to act as though static share counts should preserve static ownership. They do not.

The reverse can also be misunderstood. A founder may see their percentage decline and conclude they have become poorer or weaker in every relevant sense. Sometimes that is true. Sometimes it is not. If the company has raised capital at an attractive valuation, gained runway, improved its prospects, and increased the implied value of the founder's remaining stake, then lower percentage ownership may still correspond to greater underlying wealth. This is why percentage itself is not the whole story either. But it is a better starting point than raw counts because it at least reflects the founder's relative place inside the structure.

A disciplined reader should therefore begin to think of share counts as one layer of representation and percentages as another. The count is necessary because the company's ownership has to be divided into units. The percentage is what those units mean relative to the total. If the reader learns to ask out of how many every time they hear a share number, they will already be thinking more clearly than many people who spend years around startups. That question cuts through much of the noise. It forces scale, context, and proportion back into view.

This is also the moment to notice something subtle but important. Because ownership meaning depends on the denominator, the total share count becomes a strategic variable in its own right. Companies choose how many shares to authorise and issue, and those choices influence how future ownership conversations are framed. They do not alter the underlying economics by themselves, but they shape how legible the company is to founders, employees, and investors. A well-structured company uses share numbers in a way that supports clarity. A poorly structured one often uses them in ways that obscure it.

That is why this distinction is not just introductory arithmetic. It is part of the deeper discipline of startup ownership. Founders who learn early to separate raw counts from proportional meaning become harder to confuse, harder to flatter with large but empty numbers, and better able to understand what future rounds are actually doing to their position. They stop asking merely how many shares do I have and start asking what do those shares represent within the whole structure.

Authorised Shares, Issued Shares, and Outstanding Shares

If the difference between share count and percentage ownership is the first major conceptual hurdle in startup ownership, the next is understanding that not all shares sit in the same condition at the same time. Founders often assume that once shares exist, they simply exist in one uncomplicated category. In practice, company ownership is structured through several layers, and three of the most important are authorised shares, issued shares, and outstanding shares. These terms are close enough to be confused, but different enough that misunderstanding them can distort how the entire cap table is read.

Authorised shares are the maximum number of shares a company is permitted to issue under its constitutional documents or equivalent governing framework. They are the outer limit of what the company may create without first formally increasing that ceiling. Authorisation does not mean those shares have already been given to anyone. It means the company has legal room to create them. In that sense, authorised shares are best understood as capacity. They are the company's permitted inventory of ownership units, not the current distribution of those units.

This distinction matters because young companies often authorise far more shares than they initially issue. To a beginner, that can seem deceptive or inflated. Why authorise ten million shares if only a fraction of them are going to founders on day one. The answer is usually practical rather than theatrical. A company that expects to hire, grant options, raise funding, and perhaps restructure later needs room to issue new equity without having to revisit its constitutional framework every time the structure changes. The authorised figure provides flexibility. It is not, by itself, evidence that the company is worth more, or that anyone owns more, or that the founder has become richer by choosing a larger number.

It simply means the company has prepared legal capacity for future allocations.
Issued shares are different. These are shares the company has actually created and granted or sold to someone. Once issued, they stop being abstract capacity and become part of the real ownership structure. If the founders each receive a grant at incorporation, those are issued shares. If an investor later buys equity in a priced round, those are issued shares. If the company formally grants shares to an adviser, consultant, or employee rather than mere options, those too are issued shares. Issuance is the moment at which a share moves from possibility into actual allocation.

That makes issued shares much more central to the cap table than authorised shares. The cap table is concerned not with everything the company could theoretically issue, but with what it has already put into circulation and what claims now exist as a result. When founders talk loosely about "having ten million shares," they often mean the company has authorised ten million, not that ten million have been issued and allocated. Unless that distinction is made clearly, later conversations can become confused very quickly. A company may have a huge authorised number and only a modest issued count. In that case, most of the apparent ownership mass exists only as unissued capacity.

Outstanding shares narrow the focus further. These are generally the issued shares that are currently held by shareholders and remain active in the ownership structure. In ordinary conversation, many people treat issued and outstanding as though they were the same, and often, at least at early stage, they nearly are. But the distinction matters because issued shares can move into statuses that complicate the picture. Shares may be repurchased, redeemed, cancelled, or held in treasury depending on the jurisdiction and corporate actions involved. Once that happens, the total number issued at some point in history is not quite the same as the number currently outstanding as live claims in the company.

For most founders in the earliest phase, the practical lesson is this. Authorised shares tell you what the company is allowed to issue. Issued shares tell you what the company has actually granted or sold. Outstanding shares tell you what is currently in the hands of holders as part of the live ownership structure. If those layers blur together, the cap table becomes harder to read and easier to misstate. If they are kept distinct, the ownership architecture becomes much clearer.

This is not a matter of pedantry. Each category answers a different strategic question. Authorised shares answer how much room do we have. Issued shares answer what have we already allocated. Outstanding shares answer what is actually active in the ownership picture right now. A founder who does not know which category is being discussed can make serious mistakes. They may think the company has "lots of shares left" when in fact most of the authorised amount has already been issued or reserved. They may believe the dilution from a future round will be minor because they are looking only at current outstanding numbers without considering instruments that may later convert. They may even present ownership figures to investors in ways that are technically wrong, which is not a good advertisement for financial discipline.

This is also where the logic of future planning begins to show itself. Startups rarely stay frozen in their founding state. They hire, raise money, create option pools, and revise structures as they grow. Because of this, the company's authorised share count is often deliberately larger than what is initially needed. That can look odd to readers approaching the subject for the first time, because it seems to imply an inflation of ownership before value has even been created. In reality, it is more like drawing a large enough grid before the map is filled in. The company is preparing room for future issuances, not pretending those issuances have already happened.

The difference becomes especially important in conversations about employee options. An option pool may be carved out conceptually as part of the company's fully diluted structure, but the shares underlying that pool may not all be issued immediately to named individuals. They may exist partly as reserved future capacity within the company's broader capital framework. A beginner who looks only at currently issued founder shares may therefore underestimate how much of the company has already, in effect, been allocated for future use. This is why sophisticated readers of cap tables often care not only about what is issued and outstanding, but also about what is reserved, promised, or likely to convert. Ownership is shaped not only by present facts but by future claims already embedded in the structure.

Another common error appears when founders assume that authorised shares somehow belong to them by default until issued elsewhere. They do not.

The founder does not "own" all unissued shares simply because they incorporated the company. The company has the capacity to issue them, and future corporate actions may determine where they go. This can matter psychologically. A founder may feel that because only they currently hold issued shares, all remaining capacity somehow sits in waiting as their personal reserve. Once external finance enters the picture, that assumption breaks down. The company, acting through its governance mechanisms, may issue further shares to investors, employees, or others. The founder's relationship is to their existing allocation and whatever powers they have in governance, not to an invisible personal claim over all authorised but unissued capacity.

This is one reason investor conversations often become tense around option pools and future issuances. The founder may believe they are being asked to "give away more of their company," while the investor may see the matter as one of structuring future capacity sensibly inside the company's authorised framework. Both perspectives connect to something real, but the legal and capital structure logic lies with the latter. The company's share capacity is a resource to be structured, not an emotional extension of the founder's original idea of total possession.

At a more advanced level, these distinctions matter because cap tables are often modelled on different bases depending on the purpose of the conversation. A historical record may focus on issued and outstanding shares. A fundraising model may expand the frame to include options, warrants, SAFEs, notes, and other instruments on a fully diluted basis. A governance discussion may care especially about voting shares currently outstanding. A transaction document may define precisely which instruments count toward a particular threshold. The reader who understands only one undifferentiated idea of "shares" will struggle to navigate these shifts. The reader who understands authorised, issued, and outstanding as separate layers is already much better equipped.

This is also where startup ownership begins to resemble the careful management of space. The company does not merely divide what exists. It preserves room for what may need to exist later. Authorising a sensible number of shares is therefore partly an administrative act and partly a strategic one. Too little room can create repeated friction and procedural inconvenience.

Too much room is not inherently harmful, but it can confuse inexperienced founders if they begin to mistake authorised capacity for actual value. The intelligent approach is to treat authorisation as infrastructure, issuance as allocation, and outstanding shares as the current ownership reality.

If the reader keeps those three concepts distinct, much of the mystery around early cap tables begins to lift. A company may have a large legal capacity, a smaller actual distribution, and an even more focused active ownership picture. Each layer tells a different truth about the business. The art of reading a cap table lies in knowing which truth you are looking at and why.

Why Ten Million Shares Does Not Mean Ten Million Pounds

Few things flatter a new founder more quickly than a large share count. It produces an immediate and very human illusion of scale. If the company has been formed with ten million authorised shares, and the founder has been granted six million of them, the raw number can feel substantial in a way that six hundred or six thousand would not. The founder may not say it aloud, but the psychological effect is powerful. Millions suggest magnitude. They suggest value. They suggest that the company has already taken on a shape that resembles serious business rather than improvised ambition. This is one reason startup ownership is so easy to misread. The numbers look financial long before they become economically meaningful.

The problem is simple. Shares are units of division, not units of currency. A company can be divided into ten shares, ten thousand shares, or ten million shares without changing its underlying worth by that fact alone. The count is a matter of structure, convenience, and design. It is not a direct statement of value. Ten million shares do not mean ten million pounds any more than ten slices of pizza mean ten pounds of food. The number tells you how finely the whole has been divided, not what the whole is worth in money.

This distinction matters because founders, employees, and even some inexperienced investors can drift into a form of numerical superstition. They see the size of the count and begin to treat it as a proxy for value. A founder with several million shares may privately feel rich before the company has earned a single meaningful pound.

An employee may receive a grant of fifty thousand options and imagine a fortune because the number sounds large. Another founder may resist a restructuring because they are emotionally attached to their share count, even though the economic meaning of that count has changed or was never what they assumed. These reactions are natural, but they are not intellectually sound. A share count becomes financially meaningful only in relation to company value and the proportion of ownership represented.

To see why, imagine a company worth £100,000 in some hypothetical early-stage scenario. If that company has 100 shares in issue, each share is worth, in the most naive arithmetic sense, £1,000. If the same company has 10,000 shares, each share corresponds to £10. If the same company has 10,000,000 shares, each share corresponds to £0.01. Nothing about the company itself has changed in this example. Only the scale of division has changed. The founder with 6,000,000 shares in the third version is not richer than the founder with 60 shares in the first version if both own sixty percent of the same company. The absolute number is different. The economic reality is not.

This is one of the reasons serious discussions of startup ownership usually return so quickly to percentages and valuation. Those are the two things that begin to anchor the structure in actual economic meaning. The share count matters because it determines how the ownership is divided. The valuation matters because it determines what the whole may currently be considered worth in a transaction. Without both of these elements, the raw number is almost empty. A founder may own millions of shares in a company with negligible value. Another may own a modest share count in a company of significant worth. The count alone can mislead in both directions.

There is also a timing issue here. In very early-stage companies, the monetary value of shares can be not only low but profoundly uncertain. Founders often slip between two opposite illusions. In one, they treat their shareholding as if it already reflects future success and therefore behave as though the company's wealth has somehow arrived in advance. In the other, they treat the shares as nearly worthless because the company is early and therefore hand them out too casually. Both are mistakes. The shares may not have much current market value in a conventional sense, but they represent future claims whose value can change drastically if the company succeeds.

That is why founders must avoid both inflationary fantasy and dismissive carelessness. The shares are not cash, but they are not meaningless either.

The phrase ten million shares does not mean ten million pounds matters because it cuts through the vanity that large capital structures can create. Startup language often produces accidental theatre. A founder hears that their business has ten million authorised shares and begins to speak as though they are operating at a scale of wealth they have not yet earned. An employee hears that they have been offered one hundred thousand options and mistakes the generosity of the number for the generosity of the economics. Even outside observers can be fooled by the sound of it. Large numbers create a fog of seriousness. They make the company feel big before it is strong, and valuable before its value has actually been tested.

This is one reason professional investors rarely react emotionally to large share counts. They know the number can be changed, split, reorganised, or reverse-split if necessary. What they care about is what the share count means in the context of the company's total capital structure, the proposed valuation, the rights attached to the shares, and the future financing plan. A founder who boasts about having millions of shares is therefore revealing not sophistication but inexperience. The investor is not impressed by the count. They are asking what percentage does that represent, on what basis, with what rights, and how does it look after the next round.

This issue becomes especially important in compensation discussions. When startups use equity or options to attract talent, the count can be used, intentionally or not, to obscure the true economic significance of the offer. Telling someone they will receive 75,000 options sounds more impressive than telling them they will receive 0.75 percent, depending on the company's total count and maturity. Yet the latter is usually the more meaningful statement. The candidate needs to know what fraction of the company they are being offered, what the strike price is if applicable, how future dilution might affect the position, and what hurdles exist before the equity has any liquid value. A big raw number without that context is merely noise.

It is also important to understand that value itself is not the same thing as price. If a company completes a financing at a valuation of £5 million, that does not mean every share has some eternally fixed value derived from that round. It means that at that moment, in that transaction, investors were willing to invest on terms that implied a particular value for the company. Later developments may change that view. A company's implied share price in one round is therefore not a permanent truth. It is a pricing event. This makes the confusion between share count and pounds even more dangerous, because founders may take a financing valuation, multiply it mentally across their shareholding, and begin treating that notional figure as if it were accessible wealth. In most cases it is not. There may be illiquidity, vesting, preferences, future dilution, and a long list of other factors standing between nominal paper value and actual realised money.

That is why founders must learn early to distinguish between numerical size, proportional ownership, implied price, and realised value. These are related but not identical concepts. The company can have a huge number of shares and little present value. It can have a modest number of shares and significant value. A founder can hold a large share count and yet have no practical liquidity. A financing round can suggest a high paper valuation while leaving the founder years away from any personal financial outcome. Once these distinctions are seen clearly, much of the fantasy around startup ownership begins to recede. That is not depressing. It is clarifying.

There is a further strategic consequence. Because raw share counts do not themselves create value, founders should avoid negotiating as though preserving or increasing the number has intrinsic meaning. What matters is their actual proportion, their rights, and the economic context in which the company is developing. A founder who resists a sensible financing structure because they are emotionally attached to the number of shares they hold is confusing representation with substance. At the same time, a founder who hands out large option counts because they seem cheap in numerical terms may later discover that the apparently harmless grant represented a more meaningful portion of the company than they understood. In both cases, the mistake comes from treating the count as if it were inherently expressive of value.

It is often helpful to think of the share count as the ruler, not the thing being measured. One ruler may be marked in centimetres, another in millimetres, another in inches. The object being measured has not changed because the markings on the ruler differ. Likewise, a company can be divided into different numbers of shares without changing its economic reality by that fact alone. The share count is the measurement system chosen for expressing ownership. It matters because it structures how claims are recorded, but it is not itself the wealth.

This idea becomes more important as the company grows. Later rounds, option pool expansions, note conversions, and other capital structure events can all create new shares. The founder who has not yet detached emotionally from the raw count may find these changes confusing or threatening in the wrong way. The more mature founder understands that the count can expand while the company becomes healthier, stronger, and more valuable. They focus not on the seductive comfort of millions, but on what their stake really means inside an evolving structure.

That is the discipline this section is trying to establish. When you see a large share number, do not ask whether it sounds impressive. Ask what it represents. Ask what percentage it corresponds to. Ask what the company is worth, if a meaningful valuation exists at all. Ask what rights attach to the shares. Ask how future events will alter the structure. Once those questions are in place, the glamour drains out of the raw count and what remains is far more useful.

Ten million shares do not mean ten million pounds. They mean only that the company has been divided into ten million units. Everything that matters comes afterward.

Par Value and the Illusion of Precision

Once founders begin to feel more comfortable with share counts, percentages, authorised capital, and issued stock, another term usually appears and creates fresh confusion. That term is par value. It has the sound of something important and technical, which makes it easy to overestimate its significance. In practice, par value is one of those concepts that can distract inexperienced readers precisely because it looks more meaningful than it usually is in the life of a startup.

It is real, it has legal and formal relevance in some jurisdictions, and it should not be ignored, but it does not tell the founder what their company is worth and it does not convert a share count into genuine economic value.

Par value is best understood as a nominal or face value assigned to a share in the company's constitutional framework. Historically, the concept was tied to legal capital rules and creditor protection. The idea was that a company should not issue shares below a stated minimum, thereby preserving a floor under the capital formally contributed to the company. In modern startup life, however, par value usually functions less as a meaningful economic measure and more as a formal legal characteristic of the share. It is often set at a very low level for administrative convenience, and it frequently bears little or no relationship to the actual value at which investors later buy into the company.

This is where the illusion begins. A founder sees that shares have a nominal value attached to them and is tempted to assume that this figure says something important about what those shares are worth in a commercial sense. It usually does not. If a share has a par value of £0.001, that does not mean the share is worth a tenth of a penny in the market. It means only that the share carries that nominal legal designation in the company's structure. If the company later raises money at a far higher implied price per share, there is no contradiction. The par value has not been disproved, because it was never trying to describe market value in the first place.

This distinction is worth stressing because startup ownership is full of numbers that look precise while describing very different things. A share count tells you about division. A percentage tells you about proportion. A valuation tells you about what a transaction may imply the company is worth at a given moment. A price per share in a financing round tells you how the investor's money interacts with the current capital structure. Par value, by contrast, usually tells you something much narrower and more formal. It tells you the nominal base attached to the share in the company's legal design. That is why it can be simultaneously real and almost economically uninformative to the ordinary founder.

The danger lies in mistaking formal precision for financial truth. Founders often draw reassurance from numbers because numbers feel definite. They create the impression that the company has already been translated into something measurable and therefore more secure. Par value seems to offer that sort of certainty. It puts a figure next to the share and can therefore create the subconscious impression that the share's worth has somehow been established. Yet this is a false comfort. The presence of a nominal value does not solve the problem of what the company is actually worth, what a financing round may imply, or what the founder's holding might one day produce at exit. It merely adds another number to the structure.

This is why par value belongs in the category of formal precision rather than economic revelation. It is exact in the sense that it is stated clearly and has legal relevance. It is not exact in the sense that it tells you what the share means in wealth terms. A startup may have shares with an extremely low par value and still raise money at a high implied valuation. Another may have the same nominal structure and yet never become economically meaningful at all. The nominal figure remains what it was throughout. What changes is everything that actually matters commercially.

A useful way to understand the issue is to remember that the law and the market are not always trying to answer the same question. The law often wants categories, procedures, and minimum formal structure. The market wants price, risk, and expected return. Par value belongs more to the legal side of that divide than the economic side. It helps give the share a formal identity within the company's capital framework, but it does not tell the investor whether the company is attractive, whether the founder's stake is valuable, or whether the employee's options are meaningful. Those questions require a richer analysis of ownership, valuation, rights, and future prospects.

It is also important not to let the word value do too much work here. The startup world is already crowded with different meanings of value, and this is one reason founders get lost. There is nominal value, book value, market value, enterprise value, post-money value, pre-money value, and personal realised value, among others. A disciplined founder has to learn that these are not interchangeable labels for the same thing. They arise in different contexts and answer different questions.

Par value sits very close to the formal end of this spectrum. It is often one of the least interesting figures in the whole structure from the perspective of commercial interpretation, even though it may appear highly official on paper.

None of this means par value should be dismissed as irrelevant. In some jurisdictions, corporate law, accounting treatment, capital maintenance rules, or filing practices may make it important to understand. It can matter when shares are first issued, when constitutional documents are drafted, and when formal compliance is being checked. Founders should therefore know what it is and where it sits. They should simply resist the temptation to imagine that it reveals more than it does. Its importance is often procedural, not predictive.

This is a useful broader lesson in startup finance. Many of the most dangerous misunderstandings occur when a founder gives too much weight to a number because it looks official. Official-looking numbers can conceal as much as they reveal. A cap table may be technically tidy and still economically misleading if the rights attached to the shares are not understood. A company may have a perfectly clear nominal capital structure and still be badly designed for future fundraising. A founder may know the par value of every share and still have no serious understanding of dilution, preference stacks, or exit waterfalls. Precision without interpretation is one of the great traps of corporate finance.

Par value is therefore a good concept through which to learn humility about numbers. It reminds the reader that not every exact figure points to economic meaning. Some numbers exist because the law requires form. Others exist because transactions require measurement. Others again exist because internal administration needs categories. A founder who wants to understand capitalization tables properly must learn to ask not only what is the number, but what is this number for. Once that question is asked, par value settles into its proper place. It is part of the legal scaffolding of the share, but not a useful shorthand for what the company or the share is really worth.

That, in turn, helps protect the founder from a more general illusion. Startups often create the appearance of precision long before they possess stable reality. Shares have counts, classes, nominal values, issue dates, and percentages.

All of that can make the company look mathematically mature. Yet a startup can still be commercially uncertain, strategically fragile, and far from any meaningful external validation. Par value is one small example of how the formality of company structure can be mistaken for the substance of economic achievement. The wise founder learns early that paperwork may create order, but it does not by itself create value.

That is why par value belongs in this chapter. It helps draw the line between the administrative architecture of the share and the deeper economic questions that readers are often really trying to answer. A share can be formally exact and commercially uncertain at the same time. The founder must learn to live with that distinction, because much of startup ownership involves navigating structures that are precise in law long before they become clear in outcome.

* * *

THREE

Building the First Cap Table

"The first rule of any technology used in a business is that automation applied to an efficient operation will magnify the efficiency. The second is that automation applied to an inefficient operation will magnify the inefficiency."

- Bill Gates

The Founder-Only Cap Table

Every cap table begins in a state of deceptive simplicity. Before investors arrive, before employee options are carved out, before notes or SAFEs hang in the background waiting to convert, before lawyers begin layering preferences and protections into the structure, there is often just the founder and the company. That moment can feel almost too simple to deserve serious analysis. One person forms the company, receives the shares, and moves on to the "real" work. Yet this early stage matters more than it first appears, because the founder-only cap table is not merely the starting point of ownership. It is the template from which all later complexity will grow.

A founder-only cap table is the cleanest ownership structure a company will ever have. It may consist of a single line showing the founder's name, the class of shares held, the number of shares, and the percentage ownership. If no one else has yet been brought in and no options or convertible claims exist, the founder owns one hundred percent of the company. The clarity of that arrangement is powerful. It means the founder's legal, economic, and practical relationship to the company is still unified. There are no internal claims to negotiate, no competing interpretations of contribution, and no dilution to model. The shell exists, the shares exist, and all of them are held by one person.

That simplicity, however, should not be confused with unimportance. The founder-only cap table is where some of the most basic structural choices are made, often quietly and with far too little reflection.

The founder decides how many shares the company will authorise, how many will be issued at incorporation, whether there will be a single class of ordinary shares, whether vesting should apply even to founder holdings, how the company's records will be kept, and whether the intellectual property and founding assets have actually been placed inside the legal entity. These decisions may seem procedural because there is only one shareholder, but they are not trivial. They determine whether the earliest ownership record is clean enough to support everything that comes later.

There is a tendency among first-time founders to treat the founder-only phase as a period outside formal risk. Since there are no outside investors yet, no major employees, and often no meaningful revenue, they assume any structural imperfections can simply be corrected later. Sometimes they can. More often, what looks easy to repair in theory becomes harder once the company acquires momentum, acquires value, or begins speaking to sophisticated counterparties. A founder who has formed the company casually, issued shares without clear records, failed to assign core intellectual property, or muddled the share structure because it seemed easier at the time may later discover that the clean-up process is inconvenient, expensive, or strategically embarrassing. The founder-only cap table is therefore best seen not as a placeholder, but as the first real test of whether the company is being built with discipline.

This is especially important because the founder-only company often carries hidden assumptions about permanence. The founder sees the empty table and imagines that it describes a stable reality. In fact, it describes a moment of maximum concentration before the inevitable broadening of claims. The founder owns everything only because no one else has yet entered the structure. That does not make the one hundred percent meaningless, but it does make it temporary in most venture-backed scenarios. Future hires, cofounders, investors, option holders, and converting instruments will all, in different ways, challenge that original totality. A founder who understands this early tends to behave differently. They do not cling sentimentally to the opening figure as though it were an entitlement that must survive unchanged. Instead, they use the founder-only stage to establish the strongest possible base from which later changes can be made intelligently.

That base begins with clarity. The founder-only cap table should answer simple but crucial questions without hesitation. Who owns the issued shares. What class are they. How many have been issued. What percentage do they represent. Are any shares subject to vesting or other restrictions. Has the company reserved any shares for future use or is the capital structure still entirely founder-held. Has the company been documented in a way that an outside party can understand without oral explanation. If the founder cannot answer these questions clearly while they are still alone in the structure, it is not realistic to expect later negotiations involving multiple stakeholders to unfold smoothly.

There is also a psychological value in taking the founder-only cap table seriously. Many founders spend the early life of the company improvising around uncertainty, and that improvisation is often necessary in product, market, and commercial development. Ownership should not be left to the same improvisational habits. When the founder takes the time to build and understand a clean initial cap table, they begin treating the company as something more than a personal project with legal paperwork attached. They begin treating it as a structured enterprise capable of being read by others. That change in mindset is often as important as the table itself. It marks the shift from founding as private effort to founding as institution-building.

In practice, the founder-only cap table also reveals whether the founder understands that ownership is created through decisions, not discovered by instinct. A founder may feel they "obviously" own the company because they created it, but the table forces them to translate that instinct into formal structure. How many shares were issued to reflect that ownership. Under what authority. Recorded where. Held how. If another founder later joins, from where will that ownership come. If an option pool is later needed, how will it be created. If the company speaks to investors, what exactly will they be shown. The founder-only stage is therefore the first encounter with a truth that runs through the whole book. Ownership is not merely felt. It must be built.

There is another reason to linger over this stage. In the founder-only company, the relationship between simplicity and illusion is at its strongest. Because the cap table is clean, the founder may be tempted to think they understand cap tables in general.

They understand one hundred percent ownership held by one person, and that feels like understanding the topic. In reality, the founder-only cap table is only the easiest form the structure will ever take. It conceals all the later questions that make startup ownership difficult: fairness between founders, vesting discipline, employee incentives, outside investment, preferred rights, conversion mechanics, dilution, and exit distribution. That does not reduce the value of the founder-only stage, but it does mean the founder should approach it with humility. A simple cap table is not evidence that the ownership story is complete. It is evidence only that it has not yet become complicated.

Even so, this early simplicity offers one major advantage. It allows the founder to establish good habits before complexity arrives. If the company's records are clean now, they are easier to keep clean later. If the founder already understands the difference between authorised and issued shares, already knows why the raw share count is not the same as value, and already treats ownership as a formal structure rather than a loose narrative, then every later addition to the cap table can be handled with more confidence. The founder-only stage is the cheapest moment in the life of the company to become disciplined.

That is why this section begins here. Before cofounders, before employees, before investors, there is often a cap table with only one name on it. That table may look almost too bare to matter. In truth, it is the company's first statement of ownership reality. Everything that follows will either build on it cleanly or struggle against weaknesses introduced at the very beginning. The wise founder does not wait for complexity to begin caring about structure. They use the simplicity of the founder-only cap table to make sure the first line in the ownership story is written properly.

Single Founder Versus Multiple Founders

The difference between a single-founder company and a multiple-founder company is not merely a difference of headcount. It is the moment at which ownership stops being a simple record of initial authorship and becomes a negotiation about contribution, trust, future effort, and shared authority. A company with one founder begins from concentrated clarity. A company with two or more founders begins from relational structure. That shift matters immediately, because the cap table is no longer just a statement of what exists.

It becomes a judgment about how the company should be shared.
In a single-founder company, the ownership logic appears straightforward. One person formed the company, one person holds the issued founder shares, and the cap table reflects that concentration directly. The founder may still be wrong about many things, and later financing may still change the structure dramatically, but at least there is no internal dispute about who stood at the origin. The table records a unity between creator and owner, even if that unity will not last forever. There is power in that simplicity. Decisions can be made quickly. No one needs to negotiate a founder split. There is no immediate question of comparative contribution, no need to decide whether one person's idea was worth more than another person's labour, and no risk that resentment will arise because one founder thinks they carried more weight than the other. At least in its earliest phase, the single-founder cap table is structurally clean in a way that no multiple-founder table can ever fully be.

Yet that same simplicity can conceal its own risks. A single-founder company often depends on one person's judgment so completely that weaknesses in that judgment become structural weaknesses in the business. If the founder is poor at delegation, paranoid about control, or unclear about when genuine partners should be brought in, the clean cap table can become a trap rather than a strength. Future contributors may feel they are being invited into a company whose ownership story is already psychologically closed, even if the founder says otherwise. The single-founder structure is therefore powerful, but it can also become rigid if the founder begins to confuse current simplicity with permanent centrality.

Multiple-founder companies have the opposite problem. They often begin with flexibility, energy, and a broader spread of talent, but the ownership structure becomes more difficult immediately because the company has to decide not only who is involved but how that involvement should be translated into capital. This is one of the first genuinely adult decisions in the life of the startup. It cannot be solved by enthusiasm alone. The founders may all feel indispensable at the beginning. They may all have suffered through the same uncertain first months. They may all believe in the mission with equal sincerity. None of that tells them what the cap table should say.

The reason is simple. Multiple founders rarely contribute in identical ways, over identical timeframes, at identical risk, with identical replaceability. One founder may have had the original idea. Another may have built the product. Another may have brought technical depth, market knowledge, or the first serious credibility with customers or investors. One may be leaving a secure job. Another may be contributing part-time. One may have invested personal cash. Another may be essential operationally but impossible to evaluate cleanly at the beginning. When the company asks how this should be reflected in ownership, it is asking a much harder question than many founders first realise. It is not asking who feels committed. It is asking how the company should recognise unequal forms of value under uncertainty.

This is why founder splits are so emotionally charged. They are not merely financial decisions. They are the first attempt to convert belief into structure. To tell someone they own a certain percentage of the company is to tell them what their role means within the future economic life of the enterprise. Even if everyone agrees politely at the time, the number carries an interpretation. It suggests how central the person is, how much the business depends on them, and how much of the upside they are entitled to if success later arrives. A multiple-founder cap table is therefore never just a neutral allocation. It is a social and strategic statement.

Many early teams try to avoid this discomfort through equal splits. Equality feels clean, generous, and efficient. It avoids awkward arguments, preserves goodwill, and allows the founders to move forward without spending days or weeks dissecting their relative importance. In some cases, it is the right choice. If the founders are genuinely entering the business at the same time, with similar levels of commitment, similar exposure to risk, and similarly essential roles, then an equal split may be both fair and stabilising. But equal splits are often chosen not because they are clearly right, but because they postpone judgment. The team wants peace, and equality purchases a temporary form of it.

The problem is that the cap table is not temporary in the same way the mood of the founding team is temporary. What is comforting in the first month can become corrosive in the eighteenth. If one founder ends up carrying the company while another contributes far less, the original equal split may come to feel not generous but irrational.

Resentment often enters quietly. It appears first as a small discomfort, then as a pattern of interpretation. One founder begins to see every difficult week through the lens of ownership. They are doing more but not owning more. They are holding the company together while someone else retains the same percentage on paper. That is one of the fastest ways for the cap table to stop being a structure of alignment and become a structure of grievance.

This does not mean unequal splits are automatically superior. They bring their own complications. An unequal split forces the founders to make a more explicit judgment about comparative value at a moment when much of that value is still hypothetical. The founder with the larger stake may later be accused of having overreached or overvalued their own contribution. The founder with the smaller stake may accept the arrangement at first but become more sensitive to slights, exclusion, or changes in authority as the company develops. An unequal split can be strategically sensible and still emotionally unstable if the reasoning behind it is unclear, poorly explained, or no longer reflects how the company actually operates.

That is why the real issue is not equality versus inequality in the abstract. The real issue is whether the ownership structure has been built in a way that the founders themselves can continue to regard as legitimate once the romantic fog of formation clears. A multiple-founder cap table must be able to survive not only early enthusiasm but later asymmetry. People's effort changes. Circumstances change. The company discovers who it is and what kinds of labour matter most. A founder split that cannot survive those revelations is structurally weak even if it felt kind on the day it was agreed.

The single-founder versus multiple-founder distinction also matters because it changes how future investors interpret the company. A single-founder cap table may raise questions about concentration of risk. What happens if the founder leaves. Is there enough bench strength. Is this company too dependent on one person's energy or judgment. A multiple-founder cap table raises a different set of questions. Are the founders aligned. Is the split sane. Are all major contributors actually inside the structure. Are there dormant founders holding too much. Will future decisions require navigating hidden personal tensions.

Investors know that cofounder conflict is one of the most common ways young companies lose momentum, and the cap table is often the first clue to whether those conflicts are likely to emerge.

There is also a control dimension here. In a single-founder company, control and ownership initially sit in the same place. In a multiple-founder company, they are immediately distributed, whether evenly or unevenly. Even if the business is still small, authority is no longer naturally fused to one person. Decision-making, vision, and future economic reward now have to coexist within a structure of shared claims. That can be a strength if the founders have genuine complementarity and mutual discipline. It can also create paralysis if the ownership split gives everyone enough standing to contest decisions without enough clarity about who ultimately leads.

This is why multiple founders should never imagine that a split solves the leadership question. It only gives the leadership question a formal environment in which it will later be tested. Equal ownership does not guarantee equal judgment. Unequal ownership does not automatically justify unilateralism. The cap table records how the company has been shared, but the practical authority of the business still has to be lived. If the founders are unable to connect their ownership structure to a realistic way of working together, the numbers on the table will not rescue them.

In the end, the single-founder company and the multiple-founder company each begin with a different kind of strength and a different kind of vulnerability. The single-founder structure offers clarity but risks overconcentration. The multiple-founder structure offers breadth but introduces immediate complexity around fairness, legitimacy, and future control. Neither is inherently superior in all cases. What matters is whether the early cap table accurately reflects the reality the company is trying to build and whether it can continue to look sensible once the company stops being an idea and becomes an organisation under pressure.

That is why the move from one founder to several is not a small administrative change. It is the moment at which ownership stops being obvious and becomes contested, even if everyone is still smiling when the documents are signed.

How to Think About Founder Splits

The moment a startup has more than one founder, the cap table stops being a mere record and becomes an argument, even if that argument is quiet, polite, and disguised as practical discussion. A founder split is the first serious decision about how the company's future should be shared between human beings whose contributions are different in kind, uncertain in duration, and impossible to measure with complete confidence at the beginning. This is why so many teams get it wrong. They approach the split either as a problem to be solved emotionally or as a problem to be solved mathematically, when in reality it requires both judgment and structure.

To think properly about a founder split, one must begin by rejecting the idea that there is a universally fair formula. Founders often go looking for one because formulas are comforting. They promise objectivity. They seem to protect relationships by allowing the numbers to decide. If contribution could be reduced to a clean equation involving idea, labour, capital, network, and risk, then the founders could feed in their inputs and produce a justified answer. In practice, no such formula can capture the reality of early company formation without leaving out something important. Startups are too uncertain, human motives are too mixed, and future contribution is too difficult to predict. The split therefore has to be reasoned, not merely computed.

That does not mean reason disappears. It means the reasoning has to focus on the right questions. The first of those questions is not who had the idea. Ideas matter, but early-stage company building has taught the market over and over again that an idea alone is rarely the main source of enduring value. A founder who contributed the initial concept but cannot build, sell, organise, recruit, adapt, or endure may have been essential at the beginning and still not justify an overwhelming share of the company. Conversely, a founder who joined after the first spark but became indispensable in translating the concept into product, customers, or credibility may deserve far more than an amateur notion of originality would suggest. The split should therefore not begin from a romantic worship of inception. It should begin from the broader question of what each founder is genuinely bringing into the enterprise and what the company would look like without them.

This is a harder question than it sounds because founders contribute different things on different timescales. One may bring technical capacity. Another may bring commercial drive. Another may contribute capital. Another may have industry knowledge or relationships that make the venture more plausible. Another may provide operational structure or emotional stability of a sort that never appears on a deck but matters enormously when the company is under strain. A naive founder split treats only visible outputs as valuable. A more intelligent one also considers the less glamorous forms of contribution that change the company's chance of survival.

Even so, contribution at the point of formation is not enough. A founder split must also take account of expected future commitment. This is one of the most common failures in early ownership design. Teams negotiate based on what has been done so far rather than on who is really building the business from here onward. Yet companies do not become valuable because of what happened in the room where they were formed. They become valuable, if they do at all, because of future labour, discipline, and sustained execution. A founder who has been important in the set-up phase but is unlikely to remain fully committed should not automatically be treated as equivalent to a founder who is staking the next five or ten years of life on the company. Ownership that ignores this distinction often hardens into future resentment, because the cap table rewards past enthusiasm while the business depends on present endurance.

This is why time matters so much. It matters whether all founders are joining at the same moment or whether one is arriving later. It matters whether they are all leaving alternative employment or whether one is contributing around other commitments. It matters whether someone is all in or merely adjacent. It matters whether the role is existential to the company's core capability or genuinely replaceable in the medium term. To think clearly about founder splits, one has to move beyond symbolic language about partnership and ask what the company is actually being built out of and by whom.

There is also the question of risk. Founders often speak of risk in broad and dramatic terms, but it can be analysed more precisely. What is each founder giving up. Salary. time. reputation. career momentum. alternative opportunities. personal savings. stability. immigration status in some cases. relationships. emotional bandwidth. Different founders can believe equally in the company while bearing very unequal risk.

A split that ignores those asymmetries may feel morally thin later, especially if the founder taking the larger risk also ends up doing a disproportionate share of the work. At the same time, risk should not be fetishised as though sacrifice automatically entitles a person to ownership. Some founders take large personal risk not because the company needs it, but because of their own life configuration. The task is not to sentimentalise hardship. It is to judge how much of that hardship is integral to the venture and how much it should properly shape the ownership structure.

Another question worth asking is one founders rarely enjoy confronting. If we did not know each other, what would this contribution be worth in market terms. Friendship, history, and trust often shape the founding team, and rightly so, but they can also distort ownership decisions because they create pressure to recognise people for relational reasons rather than company reasons. A founder may be tempted to grant a generous stake because someone was present early, because they were supportive, because the relationship matters personally, or because refusing feels disloyal. Those motives are human, but they do not always produce a good cap table. Thinking in more detached terms can help. If this person were not my friend, sibling, former colleague, or emotionally important ally, would I still allocate this portion of the company for this contribution. That question is often clarifying in a way few others are.

At the same time, founder splits cannot be reduced to market pricing alone, because early company formation often involves forms of trust and commitment that would be difficult to buy directly. The technical cofounder who takes a leap on a fragile idea is not simply a contractor. The commercially gifted founder who opens doors before there is evidence is not just a consultant. Founders are not interchangeable service providers. They are people taking a structured gamble together under conditions of uncertainty. That means the split must recognise something larger than task equivalence. It must reflect the extent to which each person is entering the company as an owner in the full sense, sharing upside and downside through time rather than merely delivering a service.
This is why legitimacy matters. A founder split can be analytically defensible and still unstable if the founders themselves do not feel, over time, that the structure tells the truth about the company. The goal is not to produce a number that no one will ever question, because no such number exists.

The goal is to produce a split that can continue to feel principled once the company has passed through stress, asymmetry, fatigue, and the ordinary distortions of memory. If one founder later believes the structure never really reflected the business they were helping to carry, that feeling can infect every disagreement that follows. The founder split then stops being the background and becomes the emotional subtext of the company.

This is one reason vesting should be mentally paired with the founder split from the beginning. A team can accept a split more readily if everyone knows that ownership is connected to continuing contribution. Vesting does not eliminate the need for thoughtful allocation, but it softens one of the biggest dangers, which is that the company may lock in a permanent distribution before it has learned who will actually remain central. A founder split without vesting asks the early team to predict the future too precisely. A founder split with vesting recognises that commitment must prove itself over time.

It is also wise to think not only about fairness between founders, but about what the split leaves room for. A startup does not exist only for its founders. It may need to create an employee option pool, raise outside money, bring in key hires, and survive multiple rounds of dilution. A founder split that feels emotionally satisfying because it gives everyone a large and symmetrical share may leave too little structural flexibility for what the company actually needs. Conversely, a split that is too concentrated may make later contributors feel they are entering a business whose upside has already been hoarded. Thinking well about founder splits therefore means thinking one step beyond the founders themselves. The cap table has to support a company, not just validate a founding conversation.

There is no escaping the difficulty of this. The founder split forces the early team to do something most people are not naturally trained to do, which is to judge comparative value under uncertainty without pretending the judgment is neutral. That is why teams so often fall back on equal splits, on gut instinct, on deference to the loudest founder, or on whatever arrangement feels easiest to survive emotionally. Yet the wiser approach is neither to avoid the judgment nor to overclaim certainty. It is to make the best principled case one can at the beginning, document it clearly, connect it to vesting and future discipline, and accept that ownership in startups is always partly a forecast about what kind of company is being built and by whom. That is how to think about founder splits. Not as a calculation to be solved once and forgotten, and not as a sentimental statement of friendship, but as the first serious act of governance in the life of the company.

Equal Splits and Why They Go Wrong

The equal split has a peculiar status in startup culture. It is often treated as the decent default, the arrangement that proves goodwill, trust, and partnership. Two founders meet, decide they are building this together, and split the company fifty-fifty. Three founders come together in enthusiasm and divide it equally three ways. On the surface this looks admirable. It avoids ego. It avoids wrangling. It sends a signal that no one is trying to dominate the others. It allows the team to move forward quickly with the feeling that they are truly in it together. This is why equal splits are so common, especially in the earliest phase when everyone still wants the emotional experience of unity more than the discomfort of difficult judgment.

The problem is not that equal splits are always wrong. The problem is that they are often chosen for the wrong reason. They are frequently treated not as a considered outcome of real analysis, but as a mechanism for avoiding analysis altogether. The team senses, sometimes correctly, that asking who deserves more is awkward and potentially destabilising. So it reaches for equality as a moral shortcut. The split is no longer doing the work of reflecting contribution, commitment, risk, or expected future labour. It is doing the social work of preserving harmony in the room. For a time, that harmony can feel like wisdom. Later, when the company begins to reveal who is carrying what, equality can start to look less like fairness and more like a frozen evasion of reality.

The reason equal splits go wrong is simple. Founders are rarely equal in all the ways that matter, and the company rarely remains in the emotional condition in which equality first felt natural. One founder may have brought the original concept. Another may have been decisive in making it commercially real. One may work full time from the beginning while another remains partly committed elsewhere. One may carry the technical burden. Another may be more replaceable than everyone wanted to admit at the start. One may endure years of stress, fundraising, and execution while another drifts in importance or exits entirely. If the company has locked these people into equal economic positions without any mechanism for adjustment, the cap table begins to misdescribe the business almost as soon as the business becomes real.

This misdescription is not merely theoretical. It alters how effort is interpreted. A founder who begins to feel overburdened will not only resent the work itself. They will experience that burden through the lens of ownership. Every late night, every difficult hire, every investor conversation, every period of sustained pressure will be accompanied by the knowledge that someone else retains the same claim while bearing less of the actual load. Equality on paper can therefore become an amplifier of inequality in experience. That is one reason equal splits often feel most just at the beginning and most unjust later. They preserve peace while uncertainty is evenly distributed, but they become combustible once the company starts teaching the founders who is really indispensable.

This is particularly true in situations where equality was never genuinely deserved but was adopted out of politeness or fear. Many founders know, deep down, that one person is taking more risk, contributing more skill, or committing more fully. Yet they suppress that recognition because stating it aloud threatens the emotional tone of the partnership. They tell themselves that the business is too early to know, that things will balance out, or that true founders do not count in such a cold way. These thoughts can be humane, but they can also be evasive. If equality is chosen in full awareness that reality is already uneven, the later breakdown is not an accident. It is the delayed cost of refusing to make a harder decision when the company was still small enough to absorb it.

There is another reason equal splits fail so often. They create confusion about leadership. Ownership and authority are not the same thing, but people naturally tend to blur them. If two founders own the company equally, they often assume that major decisions should also carry some form of equal weight, even when one founder is much better positioned to lead a particular domain or the company as a whole. This can be manageable in a period of high trust and low pressure. Under real pressure, equal ownership can become a stage on which unresolved questions of direction and authority begin to play out. The founders may not be arguing about shares directly. They may be arguing about hiring, funding, pricing, product strategy, or pace. Yet beneath those disputes sits the cap table, quietly reinforcing the idea that equal ownership should correspond to equal standing in every consequential disagreement.

The equal split also becomes dangerous when it is given to people whose role is not truly that of founder in the full, demanding sense. Early-stage companies often include a circle of contributors who are close enough to the beginning to appear foundational, but whose actual future involvement is uncertain, partial, or less central than the term founder implies. If equality is used as a gesture of inclusion rather than as a disciplined ownership judgment, the company may find itself with multiple people holding major stakes when only one or two are actually carrying the business. This is one of the most common ways in which the word cofounder becomes expensive. Once someone has been treated as an equal founder, it becomes far harder, practically and emotionally, to correct the cap table later without seeming treacherous or revisionist.

What makes this particularly destructive is that equal splits often fail slowly rather than dramatically. There is not always a single moment when everyone realises the mistake. Instead, the team starts accumulating small asymmetries. One founder begins missing calls or delaying deliverables. Another becomes the face of the company by necessity. One grows in competence while another remains static. One keeps solving crises. Another retains status without weight. Because the ownership is equal, each new asymmetry feels harder to address. The founders may continue working together for months or years while privately building incompatible narratives of fairness. By the time the conflict becomes visible, it is rarely just about one issue. It is about everything that has happened under an ownership structure that no longer feels truthful.

It is important, however, not to overcorrect into a kind of reflexive contempt for equality. Equal splits can work. They work when the founders are in fact entering on highly similar terms, when their roles are genuinely complementary and equally essential, when commitment is matched, when risk is comparable, when the timing is aligned, and when vesting exists to protect the company if future divergence appears. In that situation equality may be not only reasonable but stabilising. It can remove unnecessary competition at the outset and allow the founders to focus on execution rather than internal comparison. The issue is not equality itself. The issue is false equality, symbolic equality, or fear-driven equality that is used to avoid facing real differences.

This is where vesting becomes indispensable. A truly equal split without vesting is one of the riskiest structures a young company can adopt, because it assumes a symmetry of future commitment that almost no one can guarantee. A truly equal split with vesting is a much more defensible arrangement, because it says in effect that the founders are beginning as equals but will earn that equality over time through continued participation. In practice, many of the horror stories associated with equal splits are not really stories about equality alone. They are stories about equality combined with permanence. It is the inability to correct for future divergence that makes the original decision so expensive.

Another subtle problem with equal splits is that they can distort the company's ability to communicate itself externally. Investors do not automatically dislike equal founder ownership, but they often look closely at it because they know it may conceal unresolved tensions or a lack of disciplined thinking. A perfectly justified equal split can still invite questions. Why was this divided equally. Did the founders truly join together at the same stage. Is there a clear operating leader. Are all founders still fully engaged. Was the split the result of thoughtful design or emotional convenience. If the founders cannot answer those questions convincingly, equality starts to look less like partnership and more like naivety. The problem is not the percentage itself. It is what the percentage suggests about the maturity of the team.

The deeper reason equal splits go wrong is that they often confuse moral equality with economic equality. Human beings may deserve equal dignity and respect inside the company without therefore deserving equal ownership. Friendship, trust, and mutual reliance do not automatically imply identical claims on future upside. In fact, treating these ideas as interchangeable can poison both the company and the relationship. The founder who begins to suspect that equality was granted in place of serious judgment may come to feel both commercially trapped and emotionally manipulated. The founder who receives an equal share but senses they have not matched the contribution of the other may become defensive, guilty, or quietly insecure. In that sense equal splits can damage not only cap table logic but also interpersonal stability.

The right way to assess an equal split, then, is not to ask whether it feels kind. It is to ask whether it is likely to remain intelligible once the company stops being an ideal and becomes an operating system under strain. Will this ownership structure still make sense when one founder has carried fundraising, another has built the product, and a third has contributed less than expected. Will it still make sense after twelve months of uneven sacrifice. Will it still make sense to an investor conducting diligence. Will it still make sense to the founders themselves when success or failure begins assigning sharper meaning to every percentage point. If the answer is uncertain, then equality may not be a foundation. It may be a delay tactic.

That is why equal splits deserve neither automatic praise nor automatic contempt. They deserve scrutiny. In the rare cases where equality reflects real parity of role, timing, risk, commitment, and ongoing contribution, it can work well, especially with vesting. In the more common cases where equality is a refuge from discomfort, it stores future instability inside the ownership structure. The startup may not feel that instability immediately, but the cap table remembers what the founders wanted to avoid, and sooner or later the company usually makes them confront it.

Unequal Splits and How to Justify Them

If equal splits often fail because they avoid judgment, unequal splits fail when judgment is made badly, explained badly, or defended through ego rather than principle. An unequal founder split is not automatically more mature than an equal one. It is simply more explicit. It acknowledges that the founders are not all entering the company on identical terms and that the ownership structure should reflect that reality. When done well, this can produce a cap table that is stronger, more honest, and more stable than a false equality ever could have been. When done badly, it can produce a structure that poisons trust from the start and leaves one or more founders feeling permanently diminished within a company they are still being asked to help build.

The challenge is that unequal splits force the founding team to do something very difficult. They must make a comparative judgment about value before the company has generated enough evidence to make that judgment feel comfortable.

They are deciding not only what each person has contributed, but what the company believes each person is likely to contribute over time. That makes the split partly retrospective and partly predictive. One founder may deserve a larger stake because they conceived the business, built the original prototype, supplied the first capital, or carried the venture alone before others joined. Another may deserve a smaller but still substantial stake because they are arriving later, bearing less risk, or playing a role the company needs but could replace more easily in the future. None of this is inherently unfair. It becomes unfair only when the reasoning is thin, self-serving, or disconnected from the real operating life of the business.

The first step in justifying an unequal split is to refuse the temptation to justify it through personality. Some founders slide into language that is revealingly weak. They say one person is "the visionary," another is "more junior," another is "supportive," another is "less founder-like," or that one person is "obviously" more important. These phrases are almost always signs that the thinking has not yet been done properly. A serious cap table cannot be built on aura. It has to be built on concrete questions. Who originated the venture and how much should that matter. Who is building the core product or technical capability. Who is committing full time. Who is taking greater financial or professional risk. Who is likely to be central to the company's execution over the next several years. Which roles are existential to the company's formation and which are valuable but not structurally equivalent. When those questions are answered soberly, inequality can become intelligible rather than arbitrary.

This intelligibility matters because unequal ownership has to survive scrutiny not only from the founders themselves but also from later investors, lawyers, employees, and, in many cases, from the founders' own future selves. The founder who receives the smaller stake may accept the arrangement at the beginning because they trust the others, because they want the company to get moving, or because they do not yet feel the weight of the difference. That acceptance is not enough. The structure must still make sense later when the company is tired, under pressure, and more valuable than it once was. If the smaller-holder founder looks back and can no longer see any principled basis for the original split, then the company has not solved the problem of fairness. It has merely postponed the complaint.

One of the clearest ways to justify inequality is through timing. If one founder built the company to a meaningful stage before the others arrived, that early labour and risk should often matter. A person who formed the company, developed the initial concept, perhaps built the first version of the product, and spent months or years turning vague possibility into something real has already contributed an extraordinary amount before any later founder appears. To ignore that would be naive. The late-arriving founder may still become indispensable and richly deserving of ownership, but they are entering a structure that has already absorbed effort and uncertainty. It is therefore entirely reasonable for the original founder to retain a larger stake, provided the difference is not exaggerated beyond what the continuing needs of the company can justify.

Timing alone, however, is not enough. A founder who arrived first but is no longer the key builder of the business cannot rely forever on chronological seniority. This is where many early founders become unreasonable. They assume that because they came first, their larger stake is morally untouchable even if someone else is now carrying equal or greater operational weight. In reality, the justification for a larger founder stake has to hold together across both the past and the future. If the company's future value will depend heavily on a later cofounder whose skill or labour is truly central, that person must be brought into the structure in a way that reflects the seriousness of their role. Otherwise the company may preserve historical justice while creating future instability.

The most defensible unequal splits therefore combine recognition of what has already been built with realism about what still remains to be built. That usually leads to a more balanced result than either extreme. The original founder may deserve a clearly larger share, but not such an overwhelming one that later indispensable founders feel like highly committed employees rather than genuine owners. The later founder may deserve a substantial stake, but not one that erases the disproportionate uncertainty and work absorbed before they joined. When both sides of this truth are held together, the resulting inequality is easier to explain, and what can be explained is far more likely to endure.

Another source of justifiable inequality is asymmetry of risk. If one founder is giving up far more, that can matter, especially where the risk is directly tied to the venture rather than merely to private circumstance.

Leaving a high-paying role, investing significant personal funds, relocating, foregoing immigration security, or staking professional reputation on the venture can all count toward a larger share, but only if those sacrifices are genuinely linked to the company's formation and growth. Risk should not be used as a melodramatic bargaining chip. Some people are simply in different life positions, and not every private sacrifice should automatically be capitalised into ownership. But where the asymmetry of risk is real and material to the business, an unequal split can reflect that without apology.

The same is true of irreplaceability. Some founding roles are much harder to substitute than others, especially in technical or highly specialised businesses. If the company's core product depends on one founder's deep scientific, technical, regulatory, or market-specific knowledge, it may make sense for that founder to hold more. This does not mean every technically skilled founder should automatically dominate the cap table, nor that non-technical founders are secondary by definition. It means that the company must be honest about what would happen if a given person disappeared. If one founder could be replaced with difficulty but plausibly, while another could not realistically be replaced without changing the nature of the venture itself, then treating them identically may be less fair than it appears.

Yet no unequal split can be justified by logic alone if it is communicated badly. Founders often underestimate this. They think that if the underlying reasoning is sound, the other party should simply accept it. That is not how human beings work, especially when ownership is involved. A smaller stake may be acceptable if the reasoning is openly discussed, tied to clear principles, and connected to vesting and future contribution. The same smaller stake can feel insulting if it is delivered as a fait accompli, justified through vague claims of superior vision, or framed in language that suggests hierarchy of person rather than hierarchy of contribution. An unequal split therefore has to be not only principled but narratively coherent. The founder receiving less must be able to understand why the company believes this structure is fair without feeling that they are being invited to build someone else's empire under the polite label of partnership.

This is where vesting again becomes crucial. Unequal splits are much easier to justify when everyone knows that ownership is earned over time through continued involvement. A later cofounder who receives a smaller stake may still accept the structure if they know the larger stake held by the original founder is also tied to vesting and ongoing engagement rather than treated as permanently sacrosanct. Vesting does not erase inequality, but it can transform the meaning of it. The message becomes not that one founder is simply more entitled, but that the company is trying to recognise different starting conditions while still insisting that future ownership must be lived into.

Investors often respond reasonably well to unequal splits when they are coherent. In fact, many investors prefer a thoughtful unequal split to a superficial equality, because it suggests that the founders have already been capable of making hard decisions. What investors dislike is not inequality but irrationality. If one founder holds a huge majority with no evident justification, that may look like ego or founder worship. If another holds a very small stake despite apparently functioning as a true cofounder, that may look like exploitation or naivety. But if the distribution reflects timing, risk, contribution, and continuing responsibility in a way that can be explained clearly, then inequality does not necessarily undermine the company's credibility. It may enhance it.

The danger, as always, is that founders often confuse justification with rationalisation. A founder may be able to produce a story about why they deserve more, but that story may simply be a polished version of self-interest. The test is whether the argument still looks strong when viewed from outside the founder's own ego. Would an investor find it credible. Would the smaller-holder founder still find it intelligible after a difficult year of work. Would the company still be able to recruit and retain top people without the structure looking lopsided or insecure. An unequal split that cannot withstand those questions is not truly justified. It is merely asserted.

Done well, however, unequal splits can prevent some of the deepest pathologies of startup ownership. They can acknowledge different realities at the outset rather than pretending away those differences for the sake of emotional convenience. They can help preserve legitimacy by making the cap table look more like the actual company and less like a fragile peace treaty.

They can also support the emergence of leadership without forcing everyone to inhabit the fiction that equality of ownership means equality of role. In that sense, a good unequal split is not a rejection of partnership. It is often a stronger version of partnership, because it is willing to base cooperation on a clearer understanding of what each person is really bringing to the business.

That is how unequal splits should be judged. Not by whether they make everyone equally comfortable at the beginning, but by whether they remain defensible when the company is no longer running on enthusiasm alone.

Founder Contributions, Money, Labour, Risk, and Timing

Once the founders accept that splits must be justified rather than guessed, the obvious next question is what exactly should count in that justification. This is where the conversation often becomes either too sentimental or too narrow. Some teams overvalue the original idea because it feels romantic and easy to point to. Others reduce the discussion to whoever is working the most hours in the first few weeks. Still others fixate on who put cash in earliest, as though financial contribution were the single clean measure of seriousness. In reality, founder contributions are multidimensional, and any serious attempt to structure the first cap table has to deal with that complexity directly.

The most obvious dimension is labour. Founders build companies through work before they build them through capital. Someone writes the first lines of code, drafts the first pitch, designs the first workflow, finds the first customers, tests the first assumptions, or takes the first calls no one else wants to make. In many early-stage companies, labour is the substance from which the venture is made. It is therefore entirely reasonable that labour should carry major weight in founder allocation. The problem is that not all labour is equally central, equally difficult to replace, or equally sustained through time. Ten hours of decisive technical work may matter more than fifty hours of loosely organised effort. One founder may work less in visible terms while doing the most important thinking. Another may appear industrious while contributing little that changes the company's actual trajectory. Labour matters, but it must be judged in relation to impact, not merely volume.

This is why founders should be wary of simplistic accounting exercises in which they compare their efforts like time sheets. Startups do not reward only sweat. They reward useful, difficult, and compounding sweat. The company has to ask not merely who worked hardest, but what kind of work was done and what would have happened without it. The founder who spends months trying to sell a non-existent product may be committed, but that commitment should not necessarily be valued in the same way as the founder who made the product possible in the first place. At the same time, the technical founder who built the first version but refuses to engage in the next hard phase of execution should not imagine that early intensity secures eternal superiority. Labour matters most when it is linked to the evolving needs of the company rather than frozen at one heroic early moment.

Money is another form of contribution, and it often creates disproportionate emotional weight because it feels measurable and costly in a direct way. A founder who puts in savings, pays company bills personally, finances incorporation, covers prototypes, or bridges the business through its earliest uncertainty has clearly contributed something real. Cash at the beginning is not trivial. It can create time, remove pressure, and allow the venture to move while others are still hesitating. Yet the role of founder cash is often misunderstood. Some founders treat personal financial contribution as though it should convert straight into large ownership increases. Others dismiss it too lightly, assuming that because the company will one day raise outside money, the founder who funded the early stage should not be specially recognised. Neither instinct is reliable.

The right question is how the money functioned inside the business. Was it seed capital without which the company could not have started at all. Was it a genuine risk-bearing contribution at a time when no one else would fund the venture. Did it merely cover routine early expenses that might more sensibly have been treated as a loan or reimbursable founder advance. Was the founder's cash contribution large relative to the scale of the business, or only symbolically large relative to their own private finances. Cash matters, but its role must be understood properly. Ownership is not always the correct tool for rewarding every financial contribution. Sometimes equity is appropriate. Sometimes a loan, reimbursement mechanism, or later adjustment is more rational. Confusing these categories is one of the ways founder splits become distorted by the emotional force of who paid for what.

Risk is harder to quantify and therefore easier to either exaggerate or ignore. Founders love to invoke risk because it flatters commitment. To say I risked everything sounds like proof of seriousness. Sometimes it is. Sometimes it is only rhetoric. The company has to distinguish between risk that is genuinely tied to the venture and risk that arises from a founder's wider life circumstances. Leaving a secure and well-paid role to build the company full time may justify greater ownership, especially if others remain comfortably employed elsewhere. Investing personal funds that may never be recovered may matter. Relocating, giving up visa security, staking professional reputation, or enduring material opportunity cost may all be relevant. Yet not all private sacrifice should automatically be translated into company ownership. Founders live under different personal conditions. One may have dependants, another may not. One may have savings, another may not. One may be naturally more risk-tolerant. These facts are real, but they are not all equally reasons to grant permanent claims on the future value of the company.

That is why risk should be evaluated not as drama, but as structural exposure. What has each founder put in motion that cannot easily be reclaimed if the company fails. What has each given up because of this venture rather than simply in the course of life. What asymmetries of commitment exist because one founder is fully dependent on the company's survival while another remains buffered by outside work or capital. Once risk is seen this way, it becomes a serious but disciplined consideration rather than a contest in autobiographical suffering.

Timing is often the quiet variable that shapes every other one. A founder who has been carrying the venture alone for a year before others arrive has already absorbed labour, uncertainty, and often emotional strain that later founders never had to bear. That should matter. The early solitary phase of company formation is not just a preface. It is part of the venture's real cost. The founder who survives it has already done work that no later equal split can erase without falsifying the company's history. At the same time, timing should not become a crude instrument of seniority. Arriving later does not necessarily mean contributing less in total significance. If a late-arriving founder becomes indispensable to product, fundraising, or execution, the company must not hide behind chronology to justify an ownership structure that now looks absurd.

Timing therefore matters in two directions. It matters because early work under greater uncertainty deserves recognition, and it matters because late-arriving but essential contribution may still merit substantial ownership. A good founder split reads both truths at once. It neither dismisses the weight of being first nor treats being first as a permanent shield against re-evaluation. This is one of the reasons early cap table design is so difficult. It forces the founders to honour the past without giving the past exclusive moral control over the future.

Another important category is the type of labour being contributed. Founders are often tempted to compare unlike things as though they were directly commensurable. The technical founder says the product would not exist without them. The commercial founder says the business would have no customers without them. The operational founder says the whole company would collapse into disorder without proper systems. All three may be right. The company's challenge is not to declare one category universally supreme, but to ask which forms of labour are actually existential at this stage of this company. In some ventures, the technical element is the venture. In others, distribution, sales, or domain access matter more. Founders get into trouble when they import generic assumptions about what should count rather than reading their own business honestly.

This also means that replaceability matters, even if founders dislike the coldness of the term. A contribution that is valuable but easy to hire for later may not justify the same ownership as one that is both valuable and highly difficult to replace. This is not a judgment on personal worth. It is a judgment on structural importance to the venture. A founder whose capability defines the company's uniqueness stands differently from one whose work, while useful and real, could realistically be purchased in the market without changing the character of the business. To ignore replaceability is to risk confusing effort with structural necessity.

Yet no founder contribution analysis should become so analytical that it loses sight of commitment as an enduring pattern. Some founders are not immediately dazzling in one narrow dimension, but they prove over time to be the people who stay, adapt, absorb burden, and keep the company moving. Others arrive with impressive credentials, high symbolic status, or strong early leverage but fade once the work becomes repetitive, ambiguous, or exhausting.

A good initial split cannot predict this perfectly, which is why vesting is essential, but teams should still try to judge not only current utility but likely staying power. Startups are built as much by persistence as by brilliance, and ownership that rewards only visible early glamour often ends up looking foolish once the company encounters its first real period of strain.

This is why founder contribution analysis cannot be a mere checklist. Money, labour, risk, and timing all matter, but they matter in relation to one another. A founder may bring less cash but more indispensable labour. Another may bring more early funding but be less central to long-term execution. One may join late but carry enormous future weight. Another may have built the original concept but no longer be the decisive operating force. The company has to think in terms of patterns rather than isolated factors. Which combination of contributions makes this person essential to the venture's creation and survival. Which founder is carrying what kind of burden, for how long, at what cost, and with what future centrality.

The hardest part is that this thinking must happen before the company has enough evidence to feel safe. That is why so many teams either default to equality or allow one loud founder to impose a structure. But if the cap table is going to be defensible later, the team has to at least try to reason through these dimensions honestly. A founder split that ignores money, labour, risk, and timing altogether is not generous. It is evasive. A split that treats one of them as everything is not disciplined. It is simplistic. The aim is not perfect justice at the beginning, because no startup can produce that. The aim is a principled first structure that reflects the company's best understanding of what is truly being put into the venture and by whom.

That is the real work of founder contribution analysis. It is not a ritual before the company starts. It is the first serious attempt to describe, in ownership form, what this company is actually being built out of.

Recording Ownership Properly from the Start

There is a peculiar moment in many young companies when the founders realise that they have already made ownership decisions without really recording them.

They know, in a loose and conversational way, who the founders are, who is meant to have what, who has been promised future equity, and how they have been talking about the company among themselves. Yet when someone asks for the actual structure in formal terms, the room becomes less confident. The founders may have an understanding, but they do not yet have a record. That gap between understanding and record is where many future cap table problems begin.

Recording ownership properly from the start is not glamorous work. It does not create product-market fit, it does not impress customers, and it does not generate the kind of momentum founders usually crave in the early stage. But it is one of the clearest examples of the difference between having a project and building a company. A company does not merely rely on what people intended. It relies on what has been formally structured, documented, and made legible to others. Ownership that exists only in memory, email fragments, or verbal consensus is not a stable capital structure. It is a dispute waiting for a trigger.

This matters because startups are built in environments where clarity is often sacrificed for speed. Founders are moving quickly. They are under pressure. They may believe that the understanding between them is strong enough that paperwork can follow later. Sometimes that belief is reinforced by trust, friendship, family ties, or a sense that formalising things too early feels awkward, cold, or somehow insulting. In that atmosphere, recording ownership properly can feel like a bureaucratic interruption to the exciting part of company building. Yet the opposite is closer to the truth. Good records are not a distraction from momentum. They are one of the conditions that make future momentum safer.

The reason proper recording matters so much is that ownership is cumulative. Every new person who enters the company, every funding discussion, every option grant, every future valuation conversation, and every later legal or tax question builds on what was done at the beginning. If the first layer is poorly recorded, every later layer becomes harder to trust. This is why a company with a brilliant product but a confused ownership history can suddenly look amateurish to sophisticated outsiders. Investors do not only care what the company says the structure is now. They care whether that structure has a clean and credible path backward through the company's actual history.

At minimum, recording ownership properly means that the company can answer certain basic questions without improvisation. Who was issued shares. On what date. In what quantity. Of what class. On what terms. Whether those shares are fully vested or subject to vesting. Whether any restrictions apply. Whether the company's constitutional documents support that issuance. Whether board or shareholder approvals, where required, were properly obtained. Whether the share register and related records actually match the story the founders tell about how the company was formed. If these questions cannot be answered cleanly, then the company's ownership is not yet properly recorded no matter how sincere the internal understanding may be.

This is not only a matter of legal defensiveness. It is also a matter of internal honesty. Founders often think they know their own cap table until they are required to set it down in precise form. That exercise frequently reveals ambiguities they had been carrying without noticing. One founder assumed someone was a full cofounder. Another assumed they were still deciding. One thought a promise of equity had already been finalised. Another thought it was still only provisional. One believed vesting had been agreed. Another assumed it was only a future discussion. A proper ownership record forces those assumptions into the open. In this sense, recording ownership is one of the first moments when the company becomes more exact than the conversation around it.

A disciplined company therefore begins to build its ownership record as soon as there is ownership to record, not when an investor later forces the issue. That means formal founder allocations should not remain trapped in draft emails or informal conversations. They should be reflected in the company's actual documents and records. The share count should match the decisions made. The percentages should reconcile properly. Any vesting arrangements should be written down rather than assumed. Any intellectual property transfer from the founders to the company should also be handled, because a founder holding one hundred percent of the shares in a company that does not actually own its own key assets is not standing on as solid a foundation as the cap table may suggest.

There is a practical mindset hidden in all this. Founders should learn early to treat the cap table as a living corporate record rather than as a one-off spreadsheet built only when needed for fundraising.

If the first version is created seriously, later updates become part of normal discipline rather than emergency clean-up. That means the company is less likely to lose track of old promises, less likely to discover inconsistencies under diligence, and less likely to find itself reconstructing its own ownership history from scattered messages and memory. The cap table should evolve as the company evolves, but its authority depends on the integrity of the starting point.

Another reason to record ownership properly is that memory deteriorates faster than founders think. In the earliest stage, everything feels vivid. Everyone remembers the formation conversations. Everyone remembers who said what and why. Everyone feels that the company is still close enough to its origin that nothing important could be misunderstood. This confidence rarely survives time. Months later, people remember selectively. Years later, they often remember structurally but not precisely. Meanwhile the company may have grown, relationships may have shifted, and the economic stakes may have become much larger. What once felt too obvious to document now becomes contested precisely because it was never given durable form. A proper ownership record protects against this erosion not by replacing trust, but by preserving what the trusted understanding actually was before later pressures began distorting it. The issue becomes even sharper when people leave. A founder departs. An early contributor fades out. A near-cofounder relationship never fully crystallises. A team member insists they were promised something more formal than what now appears in the records. In all such cases, the company is far stronger if it can point to a documented structure rather than a collection of recollections. This does not guarantee that conflict disappears, but it changes the company's position from uncertain improvisation to structured reference. Without that reference, every disagreement becomes a debate about the past. With it, the company can at least begin from something other than memory.

There is also a symbolic importance to good ownership records. A founder who records ownership properly is demonstrating to future participants that the company takes its own structure seriously. That matters to investors, yes, but it also matters to cofounders, employees, and advisers. It signals that the company does not intend to govern itself through loose implication. It suggests that future grants, promises, and negotiations will be handled with care rather than sentimentality. In a startup environment, where so much is uncertain, that kind of structural seriousness can itself become a form of trust-building.

Of course, recording ownership properly does not mean drowning a young company in unnecessary complexity. The goal is not to imitate the legal bureaucracy of a mature public firm. The goal is to ensure that the company's ownership structure is formal enough to be real, current enough to be useful, and clear enough to survive scrutiny. Founders often recoil from this because they fear the formal world will slow them down. In truth, what usually slows them down later is not too much discipline too early, but too little. A cleanly recorded founder cap table is one of the cheapest pieces of future-proofing a startup can purchase for itself.

This is also where the founder learns one of the deepest lessons of company-building. What the founders mean is not enough. What they can show matters. The startup world, for all its rhetoric of disruption and vision, still runs on documents whenever money, ownership, and control are involved. The cap table is one of those documents, and its authority depends on whether the underlying ownership has been recorded properly from the beginning. If it has, the company starts life with one of the rare advantages available to early ventures: structural clarity. If it has not, then even a simple beginning can cast a very long shadow.

* * *

FOUR

Vesting, Departures, and Early Discipline

"By failing to prepare, you are preparing to fail."

- Benjamin Franklin

Why Founder Shares Should Vest

One of the most common reactions a founder has when first encountering the idea of vesting is emotional rather than analytical. They hear that their shares should vest over time and immediately feel that something improper is being suggested. They started the company. They conceived it, named it, carried it through uncertainty, and often took the first real personal risk. To then be told that their ownership should not simply belong to them outright can sound like an insult. It can feel as though the company is refusing to recognise the fact that without them there would be nothing to vest in the first place.

That reaction is understandable, but it rests on a misunderstanding of what vesting is for. Vesting is not a denial of founding effort. It is a discipline imposed on ownership so that the cap table continues to reflect real commitment over time rather than freezing the assumptions of the first enthusiastic weeks into a permanent economic structure. A founder share grant without vesting assumes that the people who appear indispensable at the beginning will remain indispensable, committed, and present for long enough that the company never needs to revisit the question. In the real world, that assumption is often wrong.

This is why vesting exists. It is a recognition that companies are built over time, not in a single founding moment. The startup that exists in the founder's head, or in the first incorporation documents, is not yet the company that investors will one day fund, customers will one day use, or acquirers may one day buy. That future company will depend not only on initial belief but on sustained execution, endurance through uncertainty, and the continued contribution of the people listed on the cap table. Vesting ties ownership to that continuing reality. It asks a simple but necessary question. Is this person still building the company whose upside they claim.

Without vesting, founder ownership can become detached from founder contribution with remarkable speed. A person may be genuinely central during the first phase, then leave after six months, or drift into marginal involvement while retaining a stake that was granted as though lifelong commitment had been guaranteed. The company is then left in an awkward and often damaging position. A meaningful portion of its ownership is held by someone who is no longer helping to create value. That equity becomes what is often called dead equity. It still exists on the cap table. It still dilutes everyone else. It still claims part of the eventual upside. But it no longer corresponds to live effort inside the company.

Dead equity is one of the great silent distortions of early-stage companies. It may not kill a startup immediately, but it weakens almost everything. It demoralises active founders who know they are carrying the burden while someone absent retains a large economic claim. It discourages future key hires if the cap table already looks clogged. It complicates fundraising because investors do not like seeing meaningful ownership trapped with people who are no longer part of the operating business. It can also create ugly emotional asymmetries, because the departed founder may still feel morally entitled to the upside while those still doing the work increasingly experience that entitlement as irrational. Vesting does not eliminate all of these tensions, but it prevents many of them from becoming structurally permanent.

A founder who resists vesting often imagines the question in purely personal terms. They think, I know I am committed, so why should I be treated as though I might walk away. The difficulty is that the cap table cannot be built on private confidence alone. It must be built for a company that may eventually include cofounders, employees, investors, and advisers who all need to trust that the ownership structure has some internal logic beyond the current founder's self-belief. Vesting is one of the clearest signals that the company takes this seriously. It says that founder ownership is not just a reward for appearing at the beginning. It is a claim that becomes fully secure through continued participation in the company's development.

This does not mean the founder's initial effort is ignored. On the contrary, founder vesting arrangements often recognise that a meaningful amount of work has already been done before the formal structure is put in place.

In some cases, vesting schedules may be designed to acknowledge time already served or to grant an initial portion of the shares immediately. The precise mechanism can vary. What matters conceptually is that the company is refusing to assume that all value creation happened at the instant of formation. Founding matters, but building matters too, and the cap table should be capable of recognising both.

There is also a deeper organisational reason why founder shares should vest. Vesting changes behaviour not only at the point of departure, but throughout the life of the company. It creates a shared understanding that ownership is connected to continuing responsibility. This matters enormously in multiple-founder teams. Without vesting, even a mildly disengaged founder can become hard to confront because the ownership structure has already granted them permanent equality or near-equality. With vesting, the company has a framework that makes continued contribution part of the ownership story rather than a matter of personal pleading. The existence of that framework often improves discipline long before anyone actually leaves.

Vesting also brings founder ownership into line with a principle the company will almost certainly apply to others. Early employees, senior hires, and option holders are usually expected to earn their equity over time. If founders insist that everyone else should vest while they themselves should receive unconditional ownership from the first day, the company begins life with an internal inconsistency. That inconsistency may be emotionally satisfying to founders, but it is harder to justify once serious outsiders begin examining the structure. Investors in particular tend to view founder vesting as a sign that the team understands the basic logic of alignment. A company that refuses founder vesting entirely can look naive, overconfident, or insufficiently prepared for the realities of long-term company-building.

This is especially true because founders often overestimate how stable founding relationships will remain. In the early stage, optimism is not confined to the product or market. It also attaches itself to people. Cofounders believe they will remain equally committed. Friends assume loyalty will survive pressure. Family members imagine that trust eliminates the need for hard structure. Then the company begins to demand things the relationship has never had to bear before. One founder discovers they dislike operational grind. Another loses appetite for uncertainty.

Another wants a salary the company cannot support. Another becomes interested in a different venture or a different life altogether. None of this necessarily reflects bad character. It reflects the ordinary fact that early certainty about future human behaviour is often mistaken. Vesting is how the company protects itself against that ordinary mistake.

There is a legal and transactional dimension here as well. When investors conduct diligence, they are not merely checking whether shares have been issued correctly. They are trying to understand whether the ownership structure will remain viable as the company grows. Founder vesting is part of that viability. It reassures the investor that if a key founder departs, the company has a mechanism for preventing a large block of ownership from sitting permanently with someone no longer contributing. That reassurance matters because investors are buying into a future, not merely a past. They need to know that the cap table is capable of surviving personnel change without becoming structurally irrational.

At the same time, vesting should not be framed as a device for punishing founders. This is where some discussions go wrong. They treat vesting as though it were an expression of suspicion, a way of holding the founder under permanent threat. That is a crude view. Properly understood, vesting is not punitive but protective. It protects the company against premature allocation of permanent ownership. It protects cofounders from having to carry dead equity created by one another. It protects investors from entering a structure distorted by absent participants. It protects the founder as well, because if all founders vest, no one is being asked to shoulder the company while another keeps a full stake without earning it. Vesting is not a sign that the founder is distrusted. It is a sign that the company is being designed for the possibility that people, even sincere people, may change.

It is also worth noticing that the founder who truly intends to build the company over the long term loses less from vesting than they first imagine. If they remain, continue contributing, and help the company grow, the vesting schedule will run its course and their ownership will become fully theirs in the practical sense that matters. The pain of vesting is felt mainly when someone leaves early or disengages before the company has received the contribution that the original ownership grant implied. That is precisely when the company needs protection most. The founder who plans to stay is therefore often objecting to a mechanism whose primary effect is to constrain scenarios they say they do not intend to create.

In a broader sense, vesting is one of the first places where the startup learns to distinguish between sentiment and structure. Sentiment says this person was here at the beginning, therefore the ownership should simply be theirs. Structure says this person may indeed deserve substantial ownership, but the company should still protect itself against divergence between early appearance and later reality. Mature companies are built by repeatedly choosing structure where sentiment alone would leave too much exposed. Founder vesting is one of the earliest and most important examples of that principle in action.

That is why founder shares should vest. Not because the founder is unimportant, and not because the company wishes to humiliate the people who created it, but because the cap table must remain a truthful description of a living business rather than a monument to early optimism. The more seriously a founder intends to build something durable, the less threatening that idea should appear.

Standard Vesting Schedules

Once a founder accepts the logic of vesting in principle, the next question becomes practical. How does vesting actually work over time. This is where the concept stops being an abstract matter of discipline and turns into a schedule with real consequences for ownership. The details matter because a vesting schedule is not just a countdown clock attached to shares. It is the structure that determines when ownership becomes fully earned, how much remains vulnerable if a founder leaves, and how the company balances recognition of early effort against protection of future continuity.

In startup practice, the most common vesting schedule for founder shares is four years with a one-year cliff. That phrase is heard so often that it can begin to sound like ritual language rather than a real design choice, but it became common for a reason. It creates a period long enough to test commitment, long enough to cover the fragile early life of the business, and long enough to ensure that ownership reflects meaningful continued contribution rather than a short burst of enthusiasm. At the same time, it is not so long that the founder is kept in an indefinite state of insecurity. The one-year cliff means that no shares vest incrementally in the first year. Instead, the first portion vests only once that initial year has been completed, after which the remaining shares usually vest monthly or quarterly over the rest of the period.

This arrangement is worth examining carefully because it embodies several judgments about startup life. First, it assumes that the first year is a meaningful threshold. A founder who cannot remain engaged for a full year may have been important at formation, but the company is saying that such brief participation should not convert into lasting ownership at the same level as sustained commitment. Second, it assumes that after the cliff has passed, contribution should continue to earn ownership in a steady way. The founder is not rewarded once at the end as if the journey were indivisible. They earn the remaining stake through ongoing participation across the remaining three years. Third, it assumes that startup value is generally not created instantaneously. The schedule is a structural recognition of the fact that the company's real formation happens over time, not only on paper at incorporation.

The standard four-year schedule is not holy law. It is convention. That distinction matters because conventions can be wise without being universally correct. Some companies may have reasons to adjust the timeframe. A founder who has already worked for a substantial period before formal incorporation or before the vesting arrangement is implemented may argue for partial credit. A company in an unusually long development cycle may think carefully about whether its vesting logic should reflect that. In some situations, a shorter vesting period may be used, though this should not be done lightly. The more compressed the vesting schedule, the sooner ownership can detach from continuing contribution. In a high-risk early-stage company, that usually weakens the logic of vesting rather than strengthening it.

What makes the standard schedule useful is not that four years is a magical number, but that it tends to align reasonably well with the period in which startup fragility is highest. The first few years are usually when founder commitment matters most, when the company is least able to absorb dead equity, and when new capital is most likely to scrutinise the structure closely. A vesting schedule that reaches through this period forces the cap table to remain responsive to reality at the exact time when reality is most unstable. If a founder stays, the vesting will not feel punitive because it will simply pass. If a founder leaves early, the company retains a mechanism for preventing permanent structural distortion.

There is also a communication benefit to using a standard schedule. Founding teams often underestimate how helpful convention can be when a difficult conversation needs to be depersonalised. If one founder proposes a wildly unusual arrangement, the discussion can quickly become tangled in questions of motive. Why that period. Why that trigger. Why those percentages. A standard schedule gives the team a recognised baseline. It allows the company to say, in effect, this is how serious startups commonly protect themselves, and unless there is a compelling reason to do otherwise, we should start from a structure the market already understands. That does not eliminate negotiation, but it reduces the chance that the schedule itself becomes a proxy war over trust or status.

This is particularly useful when future investors enter the picture. Investors like structures they recognise because recognisable structures are easier to diligence, easier to model, and easier to trust. A founder cap table with a standard vesting schedule signals that the team is not improvising on fundamentals. It tells outsiders that at least one important piece of ownership discipline has been treated with maturity. Conversely, a company with no founder vesting, or with a highly unusual schedule unsupported by clear reasoning, may find itself needing to explain not just the structure but the judgment behind the structure. That explanation may be possible, but the burden of persuasion is higher.

One should also notice the internal behavioural effect of a standard vesting schedule. Because the schedule is gradual, it changes how the founders understand time inside the company. It makes clear that ownership is being earned through the ordinary, unglamorous sequence of months in which the startup either becomes real or does not. This has a healthy psychological effect. It resists the fantasy that all decisive effort happens at the beginning. Founders are reminded, month after month, that continued presence matters. The schedule becomes a quiet structural counterpart to the startup's lived reality, which is that value is usually built through endurance, adaptation, and repeated execution rather than through one dramatic founding gesture.

Of course, even standard schedules require care in implementation. A company can say founder shares vest over four years, but the actual effect depends on how the documents are written and how the company administers the arrangement.

Are the vesting terms clear. Is the cliff explicit. Is the vesting monthly after the first year or by another cadence. What happens if the founder leaves partway through a vesting period. Are unvested shares automatically repurchased or subject to some specific procedure. These questions matter because startup disputes often arise not from the absence of a general concept, but from the absence of precision in the actual terms. A "standard schedule" that exists only as a phrase in a conversation is not a proper vesting structure. It must be reflected in the company's records and legal documentation.

Another practical point is that standard schedules help with fairness between founders precisely because they create a common measurement of continuing commitment. In multiple-founder teams, differences in founder split may still exist, but if all founders are vesting against a similar temporal framework, then the company at least retains a shared principle. No one gets to treat their ownership as entirely exempt from future performance while others remain tied to it. This does not erase the importance of the original split, but it prevents the company from having to live with the worst version of that split if one founder disappears or disengages.

There is also a relationship between standard vesting schedules and future hiring. A startup that expects employees to accept four-year option vesting with a cliff should think carefully before exempting founders from similar discipline. The market may not demand perfect symmetry, but the logic should not become absurdly one-sided. If founders say to employees that long-term commitment should be tied to long-term equity earning, it becomes harder to defend the claim that founders alone should receive complete and unconditional ownership from day one. Standard founder vesting helps preserve consistency in the company's moral logic as well as its cap table logic.

The deeper point, however, is that standard vesting schedules are valuable not because they are standard, but because they reflect a realistic view of how startup companies are built. They assume uncertainty. They assume that people may change. They assume that effort has a duration, not just an origin. They assume that ownership should track some significant portion of that duration. These assumptions are not cynical. They are simply less naive than the assumption that a company can safely grant permanent founder ownership at the moment of formation and trust that future reality will always justify it.

For this reason, a founder should not ask first whether a standard schedule feels flattering. They should ask whether it helps the cap table remain truthful as the company passes through the period in which truth is most likely to diverge from early expectation. Four years with a one-year cliff is not the only possible answer, but it has become common because in many cases it does that job well enough to merit default status.

Cliffs and What They Actually Do

The word cliff sounds dramatic, and in startup ownership it should. A cliff is the part of the vesting schedule that says nothing is earned gradually during the initial period and then, if that period is completed, a defined block of equity vests at once. In the standard four-year vesting structure, that cliff is usually one year. The founder may work for eleven months and still have none of that scheduled equity vested. Work one more month, cross the first anniversary, and the first substantial portion, often twenty-five percent of the total vesting grant, becomes earned in one step. After that, the remaining shares usually vest incrementally.

Many founders hear this for the first time and think the cliff exists mainly to be harsh. They see it as an arbitrary punishment for anyone who leaves a little too early. That interpretation misses its real purpose. The cliff exists to distinguish between the founder or key participant who truly enters the company-building journey and the person who appears committed in the earliest burst of enthusiasm but does not stay long enough to justify a permanent claim on the company's future. It is a filtering mechanism, not merely a punishment mechanism. It asks whether the person remained long enough for the company to conclude that their participation moved beyond the experimental and into the foundational.

This matters because the earliest stage of a startup is full of ambiguity disguised as conviction. People say they are all in when what they often mean is that they are excited. People call themselves cofounders when what they often mean is that they are present during the formation period. People make sacrifices, but not always sacrifices that continue. The cliff gives the company a defined threshold before it has to treat early involvement as something deserving durable ownership. Without that threshold, even a relatively brief, intense, and emotionally important period of participation could produce a permanent equity stake. That is exactly the kind of cap table pollution vesting is designed to prevent.

The one-year cliff is especially significant because it marks the difference between real operating participation and initial possibility. In the life of a startup, a year is long enough for certain truths to emerge. It is long enough to discover whether the founders can actually work together, whether the company's direction survives first contact with reality, whether someone's commitment extends beyond the romance of starting, and whether each founder is still willing to bear the pressures that seemed abstract at the beginning. The cliff is therefore less about the calendar in itself than about what a year tends to reveal. A founder who leaves after three months may have been sincere, but the company is saying that sincerity without endurance should not be enough to secure founder-level ownership.

This is one reason cliffs are healthy even in teams with strong trust. Trust does not eliminate uncertainty about future behaviour. In fact, trust can sometimes make early structures weaker because founders assume they do not need protective mechanisms among friends or long-time collaborators. The cliff quietly corrects for that optimism. It does not declare distrust. It simply creates a formal point before which the company is not required to convert hope into permanent capital allocation. If everyone stays and contributes, the cliff will pass and the issue will fade. If someone leaves early, the company is protected from having to explain why a brief participant still holds a meaningful share of the future.

There is also a practical elegance to cliffs. Without one, vesting could begin immediately in tiny increments. That sounds fair in the abstract because it seems to reward every month of contribution proportionately. In practice, however, it often creates awkwardness. A founder who lasts only a very short time still accumulates a small but permanent stake. The amount may be modest, but modest dead equity is still dead equity. Enough small fragments of such equity can clutter a cap table, complicate later rounds, and create emotional or procedural headaches disproportionate to the actual economic value involved. The cliff avoids this by creating a probationary zone during which the relationship is being tested before ownership begins to vest in earnest.

This does not mean cliffs should be applied mechanically without reflection. Like all good startup structures, they have to be understood in context. If a founder has already spent substantial time building the company before the formal vesting arrangement is put in place, the team may discuss whether some credit for prior service should be recognised. If that happens, it should be handled explicitly, not vaguely. The company may decide that the cliff has effectively already been satisfied in part or in full because of earlier documented contribution. That can be reasonable. What matters is that the company knows what it is doing and records it properly. A cliff that exists on paper but is informally treated as negotiable through memory or sentiment ceases to be a useful structural tool.

It is also worth noticing that the cliff changes the emotional meaning of the first year. Without a cliff, the founders may treat the earliest months as though the ownership question has already been settled and merely awaits passage of time. With a cliff, the first year becomes the period in which the founding story is still, in one important sense, provisional. That is not a bad thing. It reflects the reality that the first year of a startup is often a test not just of the product but of the people. Can they endure uncertainty together. Can they make decisions under pressure. Can they disagree without collapse. Can they survive the ordinary humiliations and practical frustrations that attend young companies. The cliff recognises that until some part of this test has been passed, the cap table should remain guarded.

Founders sometimes worry that cliffs are too blunt because they create sharp differences between people who leave just before and just after the threshold. Someone who departs at eleven months may vest nothing, while someone who departs at thirteen months may keep a quarter of the grant. That can seem rough, and in individual cases it sometimes is. But every legal and economic structure contains threshold effects. The question is not whether a cliff creates a hard line. It obviously does. The question is whether that hard line serves an important function and whether the company is better off with it than without it. In most early-stage cases, the answer is yes. The bluntness is part of the usefulness. It avoids the slow leakage of ownership into very short-lived founder or near-founder participation.

There is another subtle advantage to cliffs, especially in founder teams. They force seriousness at the outset. A founder who knows there is a one-year cliff is less likely to treat the role as a prestigious experiment. The structure tells them that this is not a weekend identity or a short phase of interesting involvement. It is a commitment the company expects to see lived through a meaningful period before the corresponding ownership begins to vest. In this sense the cliff does not merely protect the company after the fact. It shapes behaviour before the fact by clarifying what the company is asking from those who call themselves founders.

This is why cliffs should not be confused with cynicism. They do not exist because everyone assumes failure, betrayal, or drift. They exist because startup life repeatedly proves that the early period is highly unstable and that ownership structures should reflect that instability rather than pretending it away. A well-designed cliff says to all participants that the company takes commitment seriously enough to wait before transforming it into durable equity. That message is not cold. It is mature.

The most important thing for the reader to understand is that a cliff is not just a timing trick inside a vesting schedule. It is the line between provisional participation and ownership that has started to earn permanence. Once that is understood, the cliff stops looking like an arbitrary obstacle and begins to look like one of the clearest safeguards a young company can give itself.

Good Leavers and Bad Leavers

Vesting answers one major question in startup ownership, which is how much equity a founder has earned over time. It does not answer every question that arises when someone leaves. Departure is rarely a neutral event. People leave for different reasons, under different conditions, at different moments in the life of the company. Some departures are understandable and dignified. Others are disruptive, damaging, or even openly disloyal. If the cap table treats all departures as morally and commercially identical, it may fail to protect the company where protection is needed most. This is where the concepts of good leavers and bad leavers enter the structure.

The language can sound melodramatic at first, but the underlying logic is straightforward. A company may decide that the treatment of a departing founder's shares should depend not only on how much has vested, but also on the circumstances of the departure. Someone who leaves because of illness, death, long-term incapacity, dismissal without wrongdoing, or some other condition that does not amount to voluntary abandonment or misconduct may be treated more favourably than someone who resigns abruptly, breaches obligations, joins a competitor in violation of agreed restrictions, or otherwise leaves in a way that harms the company.

The distinction exists because founders are not just shareholders in the abstract. They are also participants in an ongoing project, and the manner in which they cease participating may matter greatly to everyone left behind.

A good leaver is, in broad terms, someone whose departure does not carry the same moral or strategic stain as opportunistic or damaging exit. That does not mean a good leaver's departure is convenient. It may still be painful for the company. But the law and contract may recognise that the person should be allowed to keep vested shares, sell them on fairer terms, or otherwise leave with greater economic dignity than someone who has breached faith with the venture. The company is essentially saying that not all exits deserve the same treatment because not all exits are alike in cause or effect.

A bad leaver is the other side of that principle. The company is saying that certain kinds of departure justify more restrictive treatment. This can include forfeiture or repurchase of unvested shares, of course, but depending on the documents and jurisdiction it may also affect the treatment of vested shares, the price at which they can be repurchased, or the rights the departing founder continues to enjoy. The rationale is not mere vengeance. It is that a founder who leaves in a damaging, disloyal, or contract-breaking way should not necessarily walk away with the same economic outcome as someone who contributed seriously and then departed under circumstances that no reasonable person would view as misconduct.

This distinction matters because the startup is not a neutral machine. It is an organisation built on trust, contribution, and fragile alignment. A founder who leaves because life circumstances genuinely prevent continuation presents a very different case from a founder who has taken advantage of the startup's early uncertainty, extracted standing and ownership, and then exited in a way that leaves the active team carrying the cost. If the cap table and supporting agreements cannot tell the difference between those scenarios, then the company has failed to translate a real human distinction into a real structural distinction.

That said, good leaver and bad leaver provisions need careful thought because they can become abusive if drafted crudely or used as instruments of power rather than discipline.

A dominant founder may be tempted to define bad leaving too broadly, so that almost any disagreement, resignation, or underperformance can be used to strip another founder of equity. That is dangerous. It turns the departure framework into a weapon and undermines the legitimacy of the cap table itself. The purpose of these provisions is not to create a convenient way for stronger personalities to rewrite ownership after the fact. It is to protect the company against genuinely harmful forms of departure while preserving fairness where fairness is due.

This is why the definitions matter so much. A good leaver should not be defined sentimentally, nor a bad leaver vindictively. The company must ask what kinds of departure genuinely justify different treatment and why. Illness, death, incapacity, redundancy, removal without cause, or other non-culpable circumstances often support good leaver treatment because the person is not betraying the venture. Voluntary resignation in the early period may be more complex. It is not necessarily wicked, but if the founder is leaving by choice before the company has received what the ownership grant presumed, there may still be a logic for treating that departure less generously. Gross misconduct, fraud, serious breach of duty, refusal to perform agreed obligations, or direct competitive disloyalty are easier to classify as bad leaver circumstances because they attack the integrity of the venture itself.

One must also remember that good leaver and bad leaver provisions interact with vesting rather than replacing it. Vesting already determines what has and has not been earned over time. Departure provisions then layer additional treatment onto the question of what happens next. A founder who leaves after only a short period may simply forfeit most unvested equity regardless of whether they are a good or bad leaver. A founder who leaves after substantial vesting may then face different treatment of the vested portion depending on the character of the departure. The two systems work together. Vesting addresses time and contribution. Leaver provisions address the manner and context of exit.

The psychological importance of this should not be underestimated. Founders often agree to these provisions when relationships are good and imagine they will never matter. Later, if a departure occurs, the company is no longer deciding ownership in the middle of raw emotion. It is applying a structure that was agreed in advance while trust still existed. This is one of the great advantages of doing the hard work early.

A founder who leaves may still be unhappy, but the company is not improvising morality under pressure. It is relying on a framework designed precisely for moments when private trust can no longer carry the whole burden.

This also matters to investors. Investors are not only concerned with whether founders have vesting schedules. They are concerned with whether the company has sensible mechanisms for handling departure without descending into improvised bargaining or legal chaos. A founder who leaves badly but retains substantial influence or economic leverage can become a long-running problem. Good leaver and bad leaver provisions reassure outsiders that the company has at least considered these risks. They show that the startup understands one of the oldest truths in company-building, which is that conflict is easiest to regulate before it exists.

At the same time, there is a moral risk in overconfidence here. The distinction between good and bad leaving can look cleaner on paper than it does in life. Founders leave for mixed reasons. Someone may be burnt out, frightened, financially strained, and also underperforming. Someone may be pushed out after difficult conflict in which fault is shared. Someone may resign voluntarily but under conditions created by another founder's behaviour. Real departures rarely arrive in the pure categories the documents seem to anticipate. This is why drafting matters, but so does governance. The company must have a credible process for deciding how these terms apply. If the process itself is obviously partisan or manipulable, then even well-written categories may not produce legitimate outcomes.

There is a more strategic point beneath all this. Good leaver and bad leaver structures tell founders, from the beginning, that ownership is not just a trophy of having once shown up. It is connected to how one behaves within the company and how one exits it. That can have a healthy effect on culture. It makes clear that a founder role is not only about upside but also about responsibility. If you leave honourably, the structure may treat you with honour. If you leave destructively, the structure may reflect that too. The cap table is not becoming moralistic in a sentimental sense. It is simply refusing to be blind to conduct that materially affects the venture.

This should not be read as an invitation to obsess over worst-case scenarios or to assume that every founder relationship will end in bitterness. Most of the time, these provisions never become central because the founders remain, contribute, and build. Their value lies partly in the fact that they may never need to be used. Yet the company is stronger for having them because it is no longer relying solely on optimism to govern one of the hardest events in startup life. Departure is one of the moments when the difference between a romantic startup and a properly structured company becomes most visible. Good leaver and bad leaver provisions are part of that difference.

In the end, the logic is simple even if the drafting is not. A company should be able to distinguish between the founder who leaves under fair but unfortunate circumstances and the founder who leaves in a way that damages trust, continuity, or duty. If it cannot make that distinction structurally, the cap table is less intelligent than the life of the company itself.

What Happens if a Founder Walks Away

Few events reveal the true quality of a startup's ownership structure more quickly than the departure of a founder. While the company is young and everyone is still present, weaknesses in the cap table can remain hidden behind effort, urgency, and the natural optimism of people trying to build something from almost nothing. Once a founder walks away, however, the abstract questions become immediate. What shares have vested. What shares have not. What rights does the departing founder retain. Can the company repurchase anything. At what price. Does the founder remain a shareholder with information rights or voting influence. Does the departure trigger any restrictions. Is the company protected, or has it given away part of its future to someone no longer helping to create it.

These are not secondary questions. They go to the heart of whether the cap table still describes the real company or whether it has become a record of historical involvement detached from present value creation.

When a founder walks away, the first practical issue is usually vesting. If the company has sensible founder vesting in place, the starting point is at least clear. The founder keeps whatever has vested and loses or becomes subject to repurchase on whatever has not.

That does not make the situation emotionally easy, but it does make it structurally legible. The company is not forced into improvised bargaining over ownership that was never properly earned. The departing founder is not stripped of everything as though their contribution meant nothing, but neither do they walk away with a full long-term claim on a business they are no longer building. Vesting, in this context, does what it was designed to do. It limits the damage caused by a divergence between early promise and later participation.

If there is no vesting, matters become harder immediately. A founder who leaves may still retain the full stake originally granted, even if that stake was based on an assumption of years of future contribution. At that point the company has very few good options. It can try to persuade the departing founder to give some equity back, but persuasion under those circumstances is often expensive in every sense. The founder who is leaving may feel morally entitled to keep everything because the documents say it is theirs. The remaining founders may feel morally appalled because the structure now looks irrational. The company may attempt a negotiated buyback, but if the founder is no longer emotionally aligned, the price and tone of that negotiation can become ugly very quickly. What should have been handled quietly by structure now becomes a direct confrontation between law, resentment, and self-interest.

This is why a founder departure can have effects far beyond the simple percentage held by the person leaving. The immediate concern is usually dilution of the active team. A founder who remains on the cap table without remaining in the company still takes part of the upside if the company succeeds. But the deeper effects are often operational. Remaining founders may lose morale. Key hires may question joining a company where a large portion of ownership is frozen in dead hands. Investors may hesitate if they believe the company's cap table already contains a structural distortion that will complicate future rounds. Even decision-making can suffer if the departed founder retains rights, voting power, or a symbolic claim to status that the rest of the company no longer accepts.

The severity of the problem depends partly on when the departure occurs. If a founder leaves very early, before product, revenue, or real traction, the company can sometimes survive the event with limited damage provided the vesting and repurchase mechanisms are sound. If the founder leaves later, after substantial vesting, the legal outcome may be cleaner but the economic weight of the retained stake can be much heavier. In that case the company may be perfectly compliant and still feel strategically encumbered. A founder can walk away with a large vested holding that is fully legitimate in legal terms and still deeply frustrating to the people who remain, especially if the company's later value will be created largely without them.

This is where founders often confront a painful truth about ownership. Fairness at the moment of departure is not always the same thing as comfort for the people left behind. A founder who has genuinely given years of labour, accepted risk, and helped bring the company to a meaningful stage may deserve to keep a substantial vested stake even if they later depart. The remaining team may not like that outcome, particularly if they foresee years more work ahead, but the discomfort does not necessarily make the structure unjust. The cap table cannot be designed to eliminate all future resentment. It can only try to ensure that the ownership retained by the departed founder still bears a defensible relationship to what they actually contributed while present.

The way a founder walks away also matters. This is where good leaver and bad leaver concepts intersect with vesting. If the founder leaves because of illness, personal crisis, or circumstances not fairly characterised as betrayal or neglect, the company may treat their vested rights more generously and their departure with greater dignity. If they leave through misconduct, opportunism, or behaviour that harms the company, the company may have stronger grounds for repurchase, forfeiture of unvested equity, or other restrictive treatment. These distinctions matter not only because they affect outcomes, but because they tell the remaining team that the company is capable of recognising the moral difference between misfortune and disloyalty.

One must also consider intellectual property and know-how. A founder departure is not just about shares. It is also about whether the company actually owns what it needs to continue. If the founder held core code, patents, designs, trade secrets, or other vital assets informally rather than having them properly assigned into the company, then the departure can reveal that the cap table was only one part of the structural weakness. A founder may leave with no right to unvested shares and still retain dangerous leverage if the company never secured ownership of the key assets their work created. That is why proper early discipline has to extend beyond the share register. Ownership in the company is only part of the picture. Ownership by the company also matters.

There is another subtle problem that often arises after a founder leaves, especially in teams formed through friendship or mutual history. The remaining founders can become reluctant to confront the cap table consequences honestly because doing so feels like a personal betrayal. They may leave the departed founder's position unaddressed for months or years because the paperwork feels emotionally loaded. The company then drifts into a worse condition than the departure itself required. Instead of using its vesting and repurchase mechanisms cleanly and promptly, it allows ambiguity to persist. Later, when the issue finally has to be resolved during fundraising or acquisition, the emotional and structural costs are both higher. In this sense, founder departures do not just test the original documents. They test whether the active team has the courage to apply them.

What investors usually want to see is not that founder departures never happen, because everyone knows they do. What they want to see is that the company can survive them without becoming structurally absurd. A founder leaving should not automatically mean that twenty, thirty, or forty percent of the company is now trapped forever with a non-participant unless that outcome can genuinely be justified by what the founder already earned. Investors understand attrition. They are more concerned by cap tables that reveal no preparation for it. A startup that behaves as though founders never leave looks inexperienced. A startup that has a clear framework, clean records, and a plausible ownership story after departure looks much more investable, even if the departure itself was painful.

There is also a lesson here for founders still inside the company. Watching one founder walk away often forces the others to confront the reality of their own position. They see, sometimes for the first time, that founder equity is not simply a ceremonial confirmation of having been there at the start. It is part of a system designed to remain rational when circumstances change. This often deepens the team's understanding of vesting, discipline, and why ownership structures should be built for the company's life rather than the founders' initial emotional assumptions.

In the end, what happens if a founder walks away depends on what the company had the foresight to do before that day arrived. If vesting was in place, if departure categories were defined sensibly, if records were clean, and if company assets had been properly assigned, the situation may still be difficult but it is survivable. If none of that was done, then the departure often turns from a human problem into a structural one. The founder leaves, but the cap table keeps their shadow. The company then has to spend energy, money, and trust dealing with a problem that should have been handled quietly by design.

That is the real purpose of early discipline. It does not prevent people from leaving. It prevents their leaving from making the ownership structure less truthful than the company itself.

Why Early Discipline Protects Friendships as Much as Companies

One of the most damaging myths in early startup culture is the idea that formal structure threatens trust. Founders, especially those who know each other well, often feel that putting discipline around ownership is somehow a sign of coldness or suspicion. They worry that vesting schedules, repurchase rights, written founder agreements, and clearly defined cap table mechanics will make the company feel less exciting, less loyal, or less human. In reality, the opposite is usually true. Early discipline protects relationships because it removes from friendship the burden of carrying what structure should have carried all along.

This matters because many startups do not begin between strangers negotiating at arm's length. They begin between friends, siblings, spouses, former colleagues, university peers, or people bound by some prior loyalty that predates the company. That loyalty can be enormously valuable in the beginning. It allows founders to move faster, trust one another before evidence exists, and absorb uncertainty without demanding the kind of immediate safeguards outsiders might insist upon. Yet the very existence of that trust often tempts founders to postpone the formal decisions that matter most. They tell themselves they do not need paperwork because they know each other. They avoid hard conversations because the relationship feels more important than the structure. They assume that because everyone is aligned now, the alignment will somehow survive the strains of growth, scarcity, fatigue, and money.

That assumption is one of the fastest ways to injure both a company and a friendship.

The reason is simple. A friendship can survive many things, but it struggles to survive prolonged ambiguity about money, work, power, and recognition. Once the company starts making demands, the old relationship is forced to carry new weight. The friend is no longer only a friend. They are a cofounder, a shareholder, a person with claims on the future, a person whose contribution can be compared to yours, a person whose effort can feel unequal, a person who may leave while keeping ownership, or remain while demanding authority you no longer think justified. These are not normal pressures in ordinary friendship. If the company has not created a structure capable of handling them, the relationship becomes the structure by default, and that is usually too much to ask of it.

This is why early discipline is not anti-human. It is humane. It recognises that people change, memory changes, and circumstances change, and it refuses to demand that private affection absorb every commercial consequence of those changes. Vesting is humane because it prevents friends from having to beg one another to return ownership that should never have vested. Clear founder splits are humane because they prevent years of silent resentment from accumulating under a fake equality. Proper records are humane because they preserve what was actually agreed before later stress rewrites the story in each person's mind. Good leaver and bad leaver rules are humane because they stop moments of crisis from becoming entirely discretionary exercises in personal blame. In each case, discipline does not replace trust. It prevents trust from being used beyond its natural strength.

There is a pattern that recurs in failed founder relationships. At the beginning, everyone wants to prove they are different from the cynical world of lawyers, investors, and formal company-building. They pride themselves on being able to do things informally because they trust each other. Then the company becomes difficult. One founder works more. Another becomes distracted. One assumes a leadership role that was never fully acknowledged. Another still expects equal standing. A financing round forces the cap table into the open. An employee asks questions. A founder wants out. At that moment, every conversation becomes harder because the parties are no longer discussing only business logic. They are also defending their history as friends. The company has effectively made friendship the guarantor of its ownership system, and friendship is now failing under duties it was never designed to perform.

This is one reason so many founder disputes feel more painful than ordinary commercial disputes. They are not just arguments about equity. They are arguments about what the relationship meant. If one founder says an equal split no longer feels justified, the other hears not only a challenge to the cap table but often a challenge to their place in the story of the company and in the friendship itself. If a founder who leaves is asked to return unvested shares, they may hear not a structural necessity but a statement that their time never mattered. If one founder insists on documenting things more clearly, another may hear that as distrust. These interpretations are emotionally understandable, but they become much less likely when the discipline was present from the start. Early clarity depersonalises later necessity. It allows the company to say this is how we agreed the structure would work, rather than we now need to persuade you that our current interpretation is fair.

This is especially important because startups distort memory. In the beginning, everyone remembers the same late nights, the same excitement, the same mutual promises. Over time, however, each founder begins to narrate the company partly from their own burden. The founder who stayed longest remembers carrying. The founder who brought the original idea remembers conceiving. The founder who built the product remembers making the company real. The founder who raised the money remembers rescuing it from death. None of these memories is necessarily false, but they become selective. Without structure, each person's version of events slowly starts to compete with the others. A disciplined ownership framework cannot stop that psychological divergence, but it can prevent the company from having to decide major economic questions based on whichever memory shouts loudest.

Early discipline also protects friendships by making motives less suspect. If vesting, cliffs, repurchase rights, and clear founder allocation are all discussed at the beginning, they can be understood as part of the company's design rather than as tools invented later to target a specific person. This matters enormously. People are much more willing to accept a difficult structure when they know it was agreed in advance and applies generally.

They are much less willing to accept the same outcome when it appears only after tension has already emerged. In the latter case, even a fair proposal can feel manipulative. In the former, the same proposal feels like the company working as it was meant to work. Friendships survive structure more easily than they survive ad hoc reinterpretation.

It is also worth saying plainly that avoiding discipline is not the same thing as being kind. Founders sometimes imagine they are preserving harmony by leaving ownership matters loose. In reality, they are often only postponing the moment at which someone will feel hurt, and ensuring that the hurt will be larger when it arrives. A difficult conversation early, while the company is still small and the stakes are mostly conceptual, is usually far kinder than a much harder conversation later, when real money, real exhaustion, and real divergence have turned ambiguity into grievance. Founders who genuinely value their relationships should want less future improvisation, not more.

There is a further truth here that many founders do not see until too late. A well-disciplined company gives people something to retreat into when personal feeling becomes unreliable. That can save relationships that might otherwise collapse entirely. Two founders may no longer agree about one another's conduct. They may no longer trust each other fully. They may even no longer like each other very much. But if the cap table, vesting, and departure framework were built properly, they may still be able to separate as business participants without having to destroy the entire personal history between them. The structure acts as a buffer. It cannot remove disappointment, but it can stop disappointment from having to invent its own rules in real time.

This is why mature founders eventually stop seeing discipline as a concession to legalism and start seeing it as a form of respect. It respects the company by taking its future seriously. It respects future investors and hires by giving them a structure that makes sense. It respects the truth that people may change. And it respects the friendship itself by refusing to make personal loyalty carry more economic ambiguity than it reasonably can. Where there is no structure, friendship is often asked to do impossible work. Where there is structure, friendship has a better chance of remaining friendship rather than becoming a battlefield over a spreadsheet.

The paradox, then, is that startups formed among people who trust each other most strongly are often the ones that need discipline most urgently. Not because trust is weak, but because trust invites informality, and informality around ownership can become a slow-acting poison. Founders who understand this early give their relationships a much better chance of surviving whatever the company becomes. They do not assume affection is enough. They build a structure worthy of the affection.

That is why early discipline protects friendships as much as companies. It keeps the company from forcing private relationships to answer questions that should have been answered in the cap table from the very beginning.

Cleaning Up a Messy Early Structure

By the time many founders realise that their early ownership structure is weak, the company has already moved beyond the point where fixing it feels simple. The problem may reveal itself gradually. An investor asks for a current cap table and the founders discover that what they have is really a mixture of memory, assumptions, and half-finished paperwork. A former cofounder still appears to own a large block of shares despite having disappeared months ago. An early adviser was promised equity in vague terms that were never formalised cleanly but were also never withdrawn. Intellectual property sits partly with the company and partly with individuals. No one is quite sure what was issued, what was merely discussed, and what is now politically too awkward to revisit. At that moment the founders often feel both embarrassment and panic. They know the structure is messy, but they also know that touching it may trigger conflict.

This is why messy early structures are so dangerous. They do not just create technical untidiness. They create conditions in which every repair feels socially expensive. The company is no longer simply deciding how the cap table should look. It is deciding whether to challenge someone's sense of entitlement, whether to reopen an old conversation that was avoided for emotional reasons, whether to impose discipline late that should have existed early, and whether it still has the authority, trust, and legal basis to do so. Clean-up therefore always costs more than prevention, even when the legal work itself is modest. The real cost is often political and relational.

That said, messy structures can still be repaired, and founders should resist the fatalistic belief that early sloppiness automatically condemns the company. What matters is not perfection of origin but seriousness of response once the weakness is recognised. A startup that discovers a structural problem and addresses it honestly is in a far better position than one that continues to hide behind optimism while the cap table drifts further from reality. The aim of clean-up is not to rewrite history in a self-serving way. It is to restore enough alignment between the ownership record and the actual company that future growth, funding, hiring, or exit can proceed without old ambiguities poisoning every next step.

The first discipline in cleaning up a messy structure is to establish the facts before trying to negotiate solutions. This sounds obvious, but founders often move too quickly to the political conversation without first making a full map of the problem. They know there is confusion, so they begin trying to fix people. In reality they need first to fix knowledge. Who has actually been issued shares. What documents exist. What approvals were given. What promises were made verbally, in email, in draft agreements, or in investor conversations. What vesting terms, if any, were ever adopted. What former participants still hold legal rights. What intellectual property has and has not been assigned. What option-like expectations exist even if no formal option plan is in place. Until these questions are answered as clearly as possible, the company is trying to clean a room in the dark.

This fact-finding stage is often the first painful mirror the founders encounter. It forces them to see the difference between what they thought the company was and what the company is actually capable of proving. Many young businesses discover at this point that their ownership structure is less formal than they assumed, but also in some ways more dangerous. A promise no one took seriously may have been written down in language that now looks more concrete than anyone intended. A departed founder may still hold rights because no formal repurchase process was triggered. A helpful early contributor may have no legal claim at all, despite having built expectations around one. A founder may believe they own one hundred percent of what matters while failing to notice that the company itself does not yet own key work product. None of these problems can be solved by rhetoric. They have to be surfaced precisely before they can be handled intelligently.

Once the facts are known, the next task is to distinguish between what is legally binding, what is morally arguable, and what is merely awkward. Founders often blur these categories because they are under emotional strain. They feel that everything is simultaneously law, fairness, and politics. It is not. Some elements of the structure may be clearly documented and therefore hard to unwind except through consent or formal legal process. Other elements may be vague enough that they are not enforceable but still morally potent because someone relied on them in good faith. Others again may amount to nothing more than social discomfort, the residue of conversations everyone now wishes had been phrased differently. Clean-up becomes much easier once the company stops treating all unresolved matters as equal in force.

This distinction is especially important because not every messy element should be repaired in the same way. A former founder who clearly holds unvested shares may be subject to a fairly direct structural solution if the company's vesting documents and repurchase rights were properly drafted. An early adviser who was spoken to loosely about "some equity later" may require a very different approach, perhaps a candid clarification that no formal allocation exists, perhaps a negotiated token grant if the company judges that fair, perhaps nothing at all if the expectation was too vague to sustain. A founder who advanced money to the company may need reimbursement or loan treatment rather than extra equity. An unassigned piece of intellectual property requires transfer, not sentimental discussion. Clean-up fails when the company tries to use one tool for every kind of problem.

Another crucial principle is that clean-up should happen before the company is under maximum pressure if at all possible. Founders often wait until a financing, acquisition discussion, or legal diligence process forces them to act. That is understandable, because urgency finally overcomes avoidance. But it is also the worst possible moment to negotiate old ownership issues. People become more defensive when they know real money or a major opportunity is on the table. Former participants who might once have agreed to reasonable clean-up terms may become much harder to deal with if they suspect the company is on the verge of value inflection. Current founders may also become more desperate and therefore more prone to bad compromises. If the structure is messy and the company can see that clearly, it is almost always better to begin addressing it before the outside world turns the clean-up into a high-stakes event.

This is where honesty becomes strategically important. Founders cleaning up a bad structure are often tempted either toward excessive aggression or excessive appeasement. Excessive aggression means trying to deny or crush every inconvenient claim, treating all ambiguities as though they were obviously worthless, and assuming the company can simply impose its preferred narrative. Excessive appeasement means granting too much in order to avoid conflict, over-rewarding marginal contributors because the founders feel guilty, or preserving structurally irrational arrangements just to avoid difficult conversations. Neither approach is stable. The company needs something harder. It needs principled firmness. That means acknowledging real contribution where it exists, distinguishing it from imagined entitlement where it does not, and structuring outcomes in a way that future investors and future team members could still regard as sane.

There is also an emotional truth that founders need to face. Cleaning up a messy structure often feels like admitting failure at a level deeper than product or sales. It feels like admitting that the company was not built with the seriousness the founders now wish it had been. That embarrassment can create denial, and denial is one of the reasons messy cap tables survive long enough to become very expensive. The founders tell themselves the structure is "basically fine," that issues can be sorted later, that everyone is reasonable, or that the numbers are too small to matter. Then the company grows, the relationships cool, and the same small issue becomes far less small. The founders are no longer deciding whether to clean up an early mistake. They are deciding whether to do surgery on a living company in front of outsiders. This is why humility is useful. The founders do not need to defend the early mess as though it proves their authenticity. They need to fix it because the company deserves to become more coherent than its first chaotic months.

Professional help matters here as well. Founders can and should understand their cap table conceptually, but messy early structures often require legal, tax, and accounting advice to unwind safely. This is not because founders are helpless. It is because corporate clean-up touches areas where one seemingly simple correction can have implications the founders do not fully see. Share transfers, buybacks, cancellations, option treatment, tax exposure, IP assignment, board authority, and retrospective documentation can all carry consequences beyond the immediate interpersonal issue.

The wise founder does not outsource understanding, but also does not romanticise self-reliance to the point of making a delicate situation worse. A company that cleans up its structure well often emerges stronger than one that merely got lucky in the beginning. That may sound strange, but the process forces a seriousness many startups postpone for too long. The founders learn to separate memory from documentation, guilt from fairness, and convenience from structure. They also learn something invaluable about company-building itself. A startup is not only a machine for product and growth. It is a machine for making claims legible and governable. Cleaning up a messy structure is therefore not peripheral to the business. It is one of the moments when the business becomes more truly a company.

Of course, not every mess can be made elegant. Some startups carry structural compromises that can only be reduced, not eliminated. A departed founder may keep a larger stake than feels ideal because the company lacks grounds or leverage to do otherwise. An early promise may need to be honoured in some imperfect form because the alternative would be more damaging than the dilution itself. Clean-up is not a fantasy of perfect justice. It is an attempt to bring the structure back within the range of defensible rationality. If the company can do that, it has already moved a long way from the danger zone of improvisation.

This is the final lesson of the chapter. Early discipline is always cheaper than later repair, but later repair is still far better than pretending the company can grow on top of a cap table that no longer tells the truth. The purpose of cleaning up a messy early structure is not to erase the messy beginning. It is to make sure the future of the company is not permanently governed by the weakest decisions of its first days.

* * *

FIVE

The Cap Table as a Living Document

"The details are not the details. They make the design."
- Charles Eames

Why the Cap Table Is Never Finished

One of the easiest mistakes a founder can make is to think of the cap table as something that gets created once and then, for long stretches, can be mentally filed away as solved. This illusion is strongest just after the company has cleaned up its initial founder structure. The names are clear, the numbers reconcile, the early allocations make sense, and for the first time the business appears to have an ownership record that looks stable enough to trust. At that moment, the founder may feel a kind of relief, as though the cap table has finally been completed and the company can move on to more dynamic concerns like product, customers, hiring, and funding. In truth, the cap table is not a static achievement. It is a living document because the company itself is alive, and every meaningful change in the company's life has the potential to alter the ownership structure, the interpretation of that structure, or the claims already embedded within it.

This matters because startup founders often understand change commercially before they understand it structurally. They know that a new hire changes the team, that a funding round changes the balance sheet, that an option plan changes incentives, and that a departing founder changes operational reality. What they do not always realise quickly enough is that each of these events should also change, or at least be reflected in, the cap table. A startup is not merely a business that grows. It is a business whose internal claims evolve as growth, risk, and participation evolve. The cap table is where those changes become legible. If it does not change when the company changes, it stops describing the company accurately.

This is why the cap table should be thought of less as a certificate of ownership and more as an evolving record of ownership. A certificate suggests something final, sealed, and settled. A record suggests something current, maintained, and responsive to new facts. That distinction is critical. Founders who treat the cap table like a one-off historical document often discover later that the company has developed an active life around an inert spreadsheet. Promises were made. Options were discussed. SAFEs were signed. Shares were transferred. A founder left. A pool was created. An investor was issued stock. The company changed, but the cap table remained psychologically frozen in an earlier version of itself. Once that happens, the cap table ceases to be a tool of understanding and becomes a source of false reassurance.

A living cap table is necessary because ownership in a startup is rarely a closed system. Even when no new money is coming in, there may be movement. The founders may alter their understanding of what the company needs. An employee option pool may be created or expanded. Shares may vest month by month. Unvested shares may lapse back into company control when someone leaves. New service providers may receive equity grants. Convertible instruments may be signed that do not yet appear as issued shares but already represent future claims on the structure. In each of these cases, something real has happened to the ownership story whether or not the company has yet done the administrative work of bringing the cap table into line. A founder who understands the table as living knows that the failure to update it does not preserve reality. It only delays recognition of reality.

This becomes even more important as the company starts interacting with people who read cap tables professionally. Investors, lawyers, sophisticated hires, later-stage founders, acquirers, and in some cases tax or regulatory authorities are not only interested in what the founders believe the ownership structure to be. They want to know what it is now and how it got here. A cap table that has not been maintained loses authority in both directions. It fails as a current snapshot and it fails as a historical chain. The company may still be able to reconstruct what happened, but reconstruction is more fragile than continuity. A business that updates its cap table as events occur is building a reliable ownership history. A business that revisits it only when forced is building a memory test.

There is a deeper conceptual issue here as well. Founders often underestimate how much ownership is shaped by things that are not yet fully visible. A signed SAFE may not immediately alter the issued share count, but it changes the future structure and therefore belongs in the company's understanding of the cap table on a fully diluted basis. Vesting may occur gradually, which means the table should not be understood only in terms of gross grants but also in terms of what has and has not vested at a given moment. An option pool may exist partly as reserve rather than current issuance, but it still matters because it represents allocated future space in the company. In other words, the cap table is living not only because events happen, but because many ownership claims unfold through time rather than all at once.

This temporal dimension is one reason startup ownership can become confusing so quickly. Founders often want the cap table to be a present-tense document. They want it to say who owns what right now. But a useful cap table usually has to do more than that. It has to tell the truth about current ownership while also helping the company understand what the structure becomes after the next round, the next vesting event, the next option grant, or the next conversion. A static mindset is therefore dangerous because it assumes the table is only descriptive. In practice, the cap table is also predictive. It does not merely state the structure. It helps the company model where the structure is heading.

This predictive quality is why disciplined founders revisit the cap table even when no one is demanding it. They understand that ownership drift can happen quietly. A small promise here, an informal understanding there, a delayed paperwork update, a founder departure not fully processed, a note issued for convenience, an extra option grant made to retain someone important. None of these things looks like a dramatic event in isolation. Together they can significantly reshape the company. A founder who treats the cap table as alive notices that accumulation. A founder who treats it as finished does not notice it until someone external asks a direct question the company can no longer answer with confidence.

There is also a behavioural advantage in seeing the cap table as living. It encourages founders to integrate ownership discipline into ordinary company management rather than treating it as a separate legal ceremony.

When a new grant is contemplated, the founder asks how this affects the current structure and future dilution. When a founder departs, the founder asks not only what is emotionally fair but what the documents require and how the table must now change. When an investor discusses terms, the founder is already used to modelling the effect on the ownership map. In this way, the cap table becomes not an occasional burden but part of how the company thinks about itself. That habit is one of the clearest differences between founders who are merely surviving the cap table and founders who are learning to use it as an instrument of control.

The phrase never finished should also be understood with some restraint. It does not mean the company lives in permanent ownership instability, rewriting the structure constantly or treating equity as endlessly fluid. Quite the opposite. The point is that the cap table must remain accurate as the company moves through recognisable events. A living document is not a chaotic document. It is a maintained one. The discipline lies not in constant reinvention but in faithful update. The company should know what kinds of events change the table, what basis of ownership it is tracking, and how to keep the record aligned with the facts. That is a calmer and more rigorous idea than many founders first imagine when they hear that the cap table is "living."

What makes this especially significant in startup life is that so many other things are changing at the same time. The company is searching for product-market fit, finding customers, managing cash, making hires, and trying not to die. In that environment, it is very easy to let ownership maintenance slip because the consequences are not always immediate. The startup can continue operating for quite some time with a cap table that is partially outdated, conceptually thin, or administratively behind. This is precisely what makes neglect tempting. The penalty is delayed. But when it comes, it often arrives all at once, during due diligence, financing, exit preparation, or internal conflict. By then the company is not updating a living record. It is performing emergency archaeology on its own structure.

This chapter begins, therefore, with a change in posture. The founder must stop treating the cap table as something completed at birth and start treating it as something managed through life. That does not mean obsession. It means recognition. Every meaningful company event has an ownership dimension, and the cap table is where that dimension should be made visible.

If the company grows and the cap table does not, then the company's most basic ownership record is already falling behind the truth. That is why the cap table is never finished. The company is never simply what it was when the first shares were issued. It is what it has become through each addition, departure, promise, conversion, and financing event that followed. A serious cap table has to remain close enough to that becoming that it can still be trusted when the company most needs to know what it really is.

How Ownership Changes Over Time

A cap table begins by looking static because the company itself begins by looking small. At the very start, especially in the founder-only phase or in a young multi-founder structure, the ownership record can appear neat enough to suggest permanence. The names are few, the percentages are round, and the company has not yet gone through the events that force founders to confront how dynamic ownership really is. That early neatness is deceptive. Startup ownership is not a still photograph. It is closer to a sequence, because every significant stage in the life of the business has the potential to change who holds claims, what those claims mean, and how the balance of future upside is distributed.

The most obvious way ownership changes is through the creation of new shares. When the company issues shares to a new founder, an employee, or an investor, the structure is altered immediately. The total number of shares increases, and unless the new shares are somehow matched by proportionate issuance to existing holders, everyone else's percentage changes. This is the core arithmetic of dilution, but it is also something broader than arithmetic. The company is not merely adding new numbers to a spreadsheet. It is making a judgment about who else should now stand inside the ownership structure and what price the existing holders are willing, explicitly or implicitly, to pay for that addition. Ownership changes because the company changes who it needs.

Yet new issuance is only one form of movement. Ownership also changes through vesting. A founder or employee may have been granted a substantial stake on paper, but that stake is not fully earned at once. Month by month, quarter by quarter, the ownership reality matures. What looked like one clear allocation at the beginning is in fact unfolding across time.

This matters because a company that ignores vesting in its practical understanding of ownership can easily deceive itself. It may speak as though someone "has" a certain stake when in reality part of that stake remains contingent on continued involvement. The cap table must therefore reflect not only grants but earned position, because those are not always the same thing.

Departure changes ownership too, even when it does not always change it cleanly. If a founder leaves while substantial equity remains unvested, the company may repurchase or cancel what has not yet vested, thereby returning some portion of the structure to itself or to future reallocation. If the founder leaves after more vesting has occurred, the table may remain legally accurate while becoming strategically awkward. A meaningful percentage may now sit with someone whose role in value creation has ended. In both cases, the ownership story has changed. The cap table is no longer simply recording the people who built the company. It is recording the residue of people who once did, people who still do, and the tension between those categories.

Then there are the quieter changes, which are often the most dangerous because they arrive without the emotional drama of a founder departure or a formal financing round. A small advisory grant is made. An employee is promised options informally and the promise hangs in the background before documentation catches up. A founder advances money and expects some structural recognition later. An option pool is created or enlarged. A SAFE or convertible note is signed, not yet visible as issued equity, but already present as a future claim waiting to reshape the denominator when conversion occurs. None of these events may feel like the company has become different overnight. Yet each one shifts the ownership landscape. The cap table changes not only in moments of ceremony, but in the quieter accumulation of claims.

This is one reason startup ownership is so often misunderstood by people who think in snapshots. They ask what does the company look like now, but ignore the fact that the answer may already contain the seeds of several future structures. A founder might say they own sixty percent of the company, but that statement may only be true on a narrow present basis. Once the option pool is fully factored, once the note converts, once the SAFE triggers, once the promised employee grant is issued, once the next round lands, the founder may discover that their ownership was always more provisional than the static percentage suggested.

Ownership changes over time not merely because the company decides to rewrite itself, but because many of its commitments are temporal from the start.
Financing rounds make this dynamic unmistakable. Seed money, angel money, venture rounds, bridge financings, and later-stage capital all reshape the ownership structure. Sometimes the company receives cash in exchange for issuing new equity immediately. Sometimes it accepts a convertible instrument that defers the exact share impact until a later pricing event. Sometimes an investor insists that an option pool be increased before the round, which can change the economic burden even before the new investor's shares are issued. Each of these moves alters the relative position of founders, employees, and existing investors. The cap table therefore becomes a running record of the company's financing history as much as its original founding logic. To read it properly, one must see not only who is on it, but what sequence of decisions brought it to its current form.

This evolving quality is especially important because the meaning of ownership often shifts even when the raw percentage does not. Suppose a founder retains the same nominal shareholding through a period in which the company issues preferred stock with strong investor protections. The founder's numerical position may look stable enough to reassure them, but the economic and governance reality has changed. Their stake now sits inside a different hierarchy of rights. Similarly, a founder may watch their percentage fall in a financing round and panic, even though the company's increased valuation and survival prospects mean their smaller slice may now be worth far more in practical terms than the larger slice was before. Ownership changes over time, then, not only because the numbers move, but because the structure around the numbers becomes more complex.

There is also a deeper organisational truth here. Startups change what they are trying to solve as they mature, and ownership follows that maturation. In the earliest stage, ownership is often about binding founders to the uncertain labour of beginning. As the company grows, ownership becomes a tool for attracting talent, for aligning a broader team, for negotiating with capital providers, and eventually for shaping what happens at exit. The cap table therefore evolves because the company's needs evolve. A business trying to survive on founder effort alone requires one kind of ownership story.

A business preparing to recruit senior talent requires another. A business seeking outside capital requires another still. The percentages are not just moving arbitrarily. They are adjusting to changing organisational needs.

This is why founders must stop thinking of ownership as something lost whenever it changes. Sometimes ownership is lost in the narrow percentage sense, but gained in the broader company sense. Bringing in a critical technical leader, expanding the option pool to attract serious hires, or accepting capital that extends runway and accelerates growth can all reduce a founder's percentage while improving the quality, durability, and potential value of the company. The founder still needs to model these changes carefully and protect against giving away too much too early, but the mature mindset is not one of simple resistance. It is one of interpretation. What is this change doing to the structure, and does the company become stronger enough to justify it.

That said, not all change is healthy. Ownership can also worsen over time. A company that hands out equity loosely, expands pools without discipline, signs convertible instruments without understanding their cumulative effect, or repeatedly resolves pressure by giving away future claims may find that its cap table has evolved into something structurally weak. Founders may retain titles but lose meaningful incentive. Employees may discover that their options sit in a heavily diluted and preference-laden structure that offers less real upside than they assumed. Investors may see a cluttered and unstable table and decide the clean-up cost is too high. In these cases, change has occurred, but not in a direction the company should celebrate. A living cap table is not automatically a healthy one. It must be managed.

The practical lesson is that every event with ownership consequences should be viewed not in isolation but as part of a continuing narrative. A founder departure is not only a departure. It is an alteration to the future incentive landscape of the active team. An option pool is not only a hiring tool. It is a pre-allocation of future dilution. A SAFE is not only a convenient fundraising instrument. It is deferred structural change. A funding round is not only cash in. It is a rebalancing of claims, power, and expectations. The cap table is where all these meanings converge. To understand how ownership changes over time is to understand that the spreadsheet is not passively recording growth. It is recording the company's strategic choices about who gets to share in that growth and on what terms.

This is why good founders revisit the cap table not only when something has already happened, but when they are considering what should happen next. They understand that ownership is a moving system and that every decision enters that system with consequences. A static founder asks what do we own now. A dynamic founder asks what will this structure become if we take this hire, this round, this pool increase, this note, this concession, this exit path. The difference between those two ways of thinking is often the difference between being surprised by the cap table and actually governing it.

Ownership changes over time because startups are not founded once. They are, in a real sense, refounded repeatedly through each stage at which the company decides who must now be part of the future and how that future will be shared. The cap table is the written memory of those decisions. If it is treated like a living document, it remains useful. If it is treated like a relic of the founding moment, it quickly becomes less truthful than the business it claims to describe.

Why Every Promise Must Be Reflected Properly

One of the most dangerous habits in startup ownership is the habit of separating what the founders have said from what the company has actually recorded. This separation often begins innocently. Someone helps at a crucial early moment and is told they will be looked after. A prospective key hire is assured that equity will form part of the package once things settle down. A cofounder conversation produces broad agreement, but the founders move on before the documentation catches up. An adviser is told they will receive a small stake for introductions or strategic help. None of these moments necessarily feels dramatic. They occur in conversation, under pressure, in the spirit of momentum. Yet every one of them has the potential to become part of the company's ownership reality whether the company has formally acknowledged that reality or not.

This is why every promise must be reflected properly. A cap table can only be trusted to the extent that it corresponds not merely to paperwork already filed, but to the actual claims, commitments, and expectations the company has created. If the founders say one thing and record another, the business begins to split into two structures. One is the visible capital structure that can be shown to outsiders.

The other is the shadow structure of verbal commitments, unresolved expectations, informal bargains, and future obligations not yet admitted into the record. The longer those two structures are allowed to drift apart, the more dangerous the company becomes to itself.

The danger is not only legal, though legal trouble is possible. The deeper danger is structural incoherence. A company with unrecorded promises is living on borrowed clarity. It can still tell itself that the cap table is clean because the spreadsheet looks tidy, but the tidiness is false if meaningful expectations sit outside it. Someone believes they are owed equity. Someone assumes a promise will become formal. Someone has accepted lower pay or greater effort because of what was said. Someone has remained loyal during uncertainty because they believe they are economically inside the future of the business. If the cap table does not reflect these realities in some appropriate form, then it is no longer a serious map of ownership. It is merely a selective one.

Founders often resist this point because they worry that reflecting every promise properly will slow the company down or make the ownership structure more complicated before the business is ready. That fear is understandable, but it confuses recognition with overcommitment. Reflecting a promise properly does not always mean issuing shares immediately. Sometimes it means documenting that no grant exists yet and that any future allocation remains subject to specified conditions. Sometimes it means putting a formal option agreement in place rather than relying on goodwill. Sometimes it means clarifying that a discussion was exploratory and does not yet amount to an entitlement. What matters is not that every conversation instantly becomes permanent capital. What matters is that the company stops allowing economically relevant statements to float around without defined status.

This is especially important because startups create value not only through formal contracts but through reliance. People make decisions based on what they are told. An early employee may accept a reduced salary because the promise of future equity makes the sacrifice seem rational. An adviser may commit reputation and access because they believe they are being brought into the ownership story, even if only in a small way. A cofounder may continue through a difficult quarter because they believe the company has already recognised their stake, even if the paperwork remains unfinished.

If the founders later retreat into the claim that nothing counted because nothing was fully documented, they may be legally stronger than they are morally or strategically. That gap matters. A startup cannot build a trustworthy ownership culture on the belief that only what was written counts and everything else was merely atmosphere.

This does not mean every vague statement must be inflated into a formal equity position. Quite the opposite. One of the reasons founders get into trouble is that they speak too loosely in precisely those contexts where loose words generate hard expectations. The real discipline lies in making sure that promises stop being vague. If the company intends to grant equity, it should define the structure, the amount or range, the conditions, the vesting, the approvals needed, and the point at which the promise becomes binding. If the company is not yet ready to do that, then it should say so clearly and avoid language that implies more than it means. Proper reflection is therefore not just about administration after the promise. It is also about speaking in a way that can later be administered without betrayal.

This is one of the reasons so many cap tables become misleading long before a founder notices. The spreadsheet may show only issued shares and perhaps an option pool, but the lived ownership reality of the company has already become wider. There are side understandings. There are deferred commitments. There are people who feel included in the future economics of the company without being visibly represented. The founders may even prefer this arrangement because it preserves flexibility. Yet flexibility built on unreflected promises is fragile. It means the company is making economic use of expectation without taking structural responsibility for it. When the time comes to raise capital, hire more seriously, or settle a dispute, that fragility becomes visible all at once.

A serious cap table therefore has to be surrounded by a serious culture of reflection. If something has been promised, the founders should ask immediately what the proper formal expression of that promise is. Is it an issued grant, an option, a future conditional grant, a board-approved commitment not yet issued, a contractual advisory arrangement, or merely a discussion that should not yet be treated as a promise at all. Until the company answers that question, it has not really managed the ownership issue. It has only postponed it. And postponement in cap table matters has a way of turning into leverage for someone at exactly the moment the company can least afford the distraction.

There is also a governance reason why every promise must be reflected properly. Ownership is not only about eventual payout. It is also about internal legitimacy. If the company develops a reputation for saying one thing and recording another, the cap table begins to lose moral authority inside the organisation. People stop trusting that the structure tells the truth. They start reading ownership through rumour, private assurances, and perceived favour rather than through the formal record. At that point the cap table is no longer governing. It is being bypassed. That is one of the surest ways for the company to drift into cynicism. Once people suspect that equity talk is partly symbolic and partly political, every future grant becomes harder to interpret and every future negotiation harder to trust.

This is especially destructive because startups often use ownership language at moments of maximum emotional intensity. A founder says "you're part of this" during a crisis. A key early helper is told "we'll make sure you share in the upside." A future hire is encouraged with talk of joining "as a real stakeholder." In ordinary conversation, such statements might be motivational colour. In a startup, they are often heard as invitations into the ownership architecture. If the company does not intend that, it must speak differently. If it does intend that, it must record what it means. Anything in between is dangerous because it spends the currency of future equity while pretending no accounting is required.

This is where the cap table becomes not only a record but a discipline of truthfulness. It forces the company to align what it says, what it means, and what it is willing to document. That alignment is one of the clearest signs of maturity in a young business. Mature founders do not use equity language casually because they understand that ownership promises are among the most consequential things a company can say. They know that reflecting those promises properly is not legal theatre. It is a way of keeping the structure honest enough that future growth can happen without hidden claims continually breaking the surface.

There is an important subtlety here. Proper reflection does not always produce immediate simplicity. Sometimes it reveals that the company has already created obligations or expectations it would rather not have. In the short term, that can feel as though discipline is making the company messier rather than cleaner. But this is the right kind of messiness. It is the messiness of reality becoming visible rather than remaining concealed.

A company that sees its true ownership commitments can govern them. A company that hides them inside conversational ambiguity can only hope they never matter. Hope is not a cap table strategy.

The founders should therefore learn to ask, whenever they make or hear an ownership-related promise, where does this live in the actual structure. If the answer is nowhere, then either the promise should not have been made or the structure needs to be updated. There is no safe middle ground in which the company can indefinitely rely on equity rhetoric while keeping its formal ownership picture untouched. Eventually, someone will test whether the words meant anything. The company should know the answer before that moment arrives.

That is why every promise must be reflected properly. The cap table is only as honest as the distance between what the company has committed to and what it is willing to show.

The Dangers of Informal Side Agreements

If vague promises create one kind of cap table danger, informal side agreements create another, often more serious one. A side agreement is any ownership-related understanding that sits outside the clean, visible, and properly governed structure of the company. It may be written or unwritten. It may exist in an email chain, a private message, a hurried note after a meeting, or simply in a verbal understanding between two people who believed they could "sort the paperwork later." Sometimes it is born out of urgency. Sometimes out of friendship. Sometimes out of opportunism. Whatever its origin, the side agreement is dangerous because it creates a second ownership logic running alongside the official one.

This is why side agreements are so corrosive. They do not merely add complexity. They undermine the integrity of the cap table itself. A company can survive a complicated ownership structure if that structure is at least visible and internally coherent. What it struggles to survive is a split reality in which the formal record says one thing and various private deals imply something else. Once that happens, the cap table ceases to function as a common reference point. The company now has an official version of ownership and a hidden version of ownership, and no one can be entirely certain which one will assert itself at the most consequential moment.

Informal side agreements often emerge because founders are trying to solve a short-term discomfort without confronting the full meaning of what they are doing. A key contributor wants reassurance but the founders are not ready to issue shares formally. A cofounder relationship is evolving in a way the company does not yet want to announce. An adviser wants something in writing, but the company is not prepared to do the proper approvals. A founder wants to preserve flexibility while still making someone feel committed. So they create a private arrangement. They think this buys time. In reality, it often buys only ambiguity. The company has not really postponed the ownership issue. It has multiplied it.

This multiplication matters because side agreements rarely remain small. They tend to accumulate interpretive force over time. The person receiving the private assurance may begin to make decisions based on it. They may treat themselves as already inside the ownership story. They may accept lower compensation, invest more effort, or stay through difficulty because they believe the agreement means something durable. The founder who made the promise may tell themselves the understanding was conditional, limited, or still subject to formalisation. The gap between those two understandings widens silently. When the issue finally surfaces, it does not arrive as a minor paperwork correction. It arrives as a conflict between what one party thought had been secured and what the other thought had merely been discussed.

This is one reason side agreements are often more dangerous than openly documented arrangements that seem, at first glance, more onerous. A visible agreement can be evaluated, challenged, and integrated into the cap table. A side agreement exists in the dark, gathering expectation without receiving governance. The company is effectively allowing ownership implications to form without subjecting them to the discipline of the structure. That is not flexibility. It is ungoverned risk.

There is also a problem of legitimacy. A cap table only works as a governance tool if all relevant parties can believe that the visible structure is the real structure. Once informal side agreements become common, that belief deteriorates. Founders start wondering what other promises have been made privately. Employees begin to suspect that official equity policy may not be the whole story. Investors worry that the clean-looking table shown in diligence may hide off-record commitments.

The company's ownership culture begins to fray because transparency has been replaced by pockets of private arrangement. This is not just untidy. It is politically destabilising. People stop trusting the formal system and begin scanning for hidden deals.

That mistrust is particularly destructive in founder teams. If one founder makes a side agreement with a contributor or prospective partner without properly integrating it into the company's decision-making, the company is no longer dealing only with a promise to the outside person. It is dealing with an internal breach of governance. The other founders may reasonably feel that the structure has been altered without their consent, even if only in expectation. This can create two layers of resentment at once. The recipient may later feel cheated if the promise is not honoured. The cofounders may feel undermined because a potentially significant ownership matter was negotiated in private. Side agreements therefore do not only confuse the company's relationship with outsiders. They can also damage the alignment of the founding team itself.

A further danger lies in the temptation to use side agreements strategically. Some founders discover that private promises can function as cheap tools of influence. They can keep people warm, secure temporary loyalty, or avoid the hard work of formal decision-making by hinting at future ownership without having to commit the company openly. This is one of the most corrosive uses of side agreements because it turns ambiguity into method. The founder gets the motivational benefit of sounding generous while preserving the deniability of informality. In the short run this can feel clever. In the long run it is usually poisonous. The company becomes a place where ownership talk is no longer trusted and where promises are heard less as structured commitments than as instruments of convenience.

It is important to be clear that not every preliminary conversation is a side agreement. Startups need to explore possibilities. Founders need to talk to potential hires, advisers, and partners about what an equity relationship might eventually look like. The danger begins when these conversations move from exploration into private commitment without being brought into the proper formal process. A founder can say, we are considering an equity package subject to formal approval and documentation, without creating a side agreement. The problem begins when the company allows language to imply that a real economic arrangement already exists while the official structure remains untouched. The line is sometimes subtle, but it is crucial.

This is why the right response to side-agreement risk is not paranoia, but discipline of process. Ownership-related commitments should move through defined channels. If the company wants to grant equity, it should decide who has authority, what approvals are needed, how the grant will be documented, and how it will appear in the broader ownership structure. If the company is not yet ready to do that, then it should train itself not to speak as though the deal already exists. Startups often think process is the enemy of agility. In ownership matters, process is often the thing that prevents agility from becoming structural dishonesty.

There is also a legal and transactional consequence that founders frequently underestimate. Informal side agreements may not always be enforceable in the strongest sense, but they do not need to be fully enforceable to cause serious damage. They can create negotiation leverage, delay investment, prompt disputes, raise disclosure issues, or simply undermine the confidence of outside parties who now fear there may be more hidden arrangements. An investor who discovers one side agreement will immediately wonder how many others may exist. An acquirer doing diligence may view even informal ownership disputes as enough reason to slow down or alter terms. The company therefore pays for the side agreement not only if the claim succeeds, but whenever the mere existence of the hidden understanding makes the ownership story less trustworthy.

The practical rule should therefore be very simple. If a promise is significant enough that someone might reasonably change their behaviour because of it, it is too significant to leave as a side agreement. It either belongs in the formal structure or it should be clearly reframed as not yet agreed. Founders who live by this rule do not become less flexible. They become less dangerous to their own company.

In the end, informal side agreements are dangerous because they ask the company to live with two truths at once. The official truth is what the cap table says. The private truth is what certain people have been led to believe. Startups are already difficult enough without dividing reality in this way. A company that wants a cap table capable of surviving growth, scrutiny, and stress cannot afford to treat private ownership understandings as harmless background noise. They are not noise. They are hidden structure, and hidden structure is often the most unstable kind.

Spreadsheet Logic Versus Legal Reality

One of the easiest traps for founders to fall into is the belief that if the cap table works in a spreadsheet, then it works in the company. This is an understandable mistake because spreadsheets are seductive. They create order quickly. They reconcile numbers. They make dilution visible. They allow the founder to model different rounds, option pools, and ownership outcomes with apparent precision. Once the cells add up and the percentages balance, the structure can feel complete. The founder looks at the model and assumes the company now has a cap table. In reality, the spreadsheet may only be describing what the founder wishes the company's ownership structure to be. Whether that structure actually exists depends on something much less glamorous than arithmetic. It depends on legal reality.

This distinction matters because a spreadsheet is a representation, not an act. It can show a founder holding five million shares, an investor holding two million, an option pool taking ten percent, and a departing founder's unvested equity dropping away neatly on a date chosen by formula. The spreadsheet can do all of this in seconds. But the company does not become structured merely because a model of it exists. Shares have to be authorised, issued, approved, documented, and recorded in a way the company and, if challenged, the outside world can recognise. Vesting has to be more than a column heading. It has to be embedded in actual agreements. Transfers, repurchases, cancellations, option grants, and instruments waiting to convert have to be dealt with through the company's legal and governance machinery, not just through clean formulas.

This is one of the reasons founders can feel much more organised than they actually are. They may have built a cap table model that looks sophisticated, perhaps even beautiful in its clarity. Yet if the company's records, approvals, agreements, and constitutional framework do not match that model, the spreadsheet is not the cap table in the strongest sense. It is an aspiration. The founder has spreadsheet logic, but the company does not yet have legal reality. Problems begin when those two things diverge and the founder does not notice until someone else asks a question the spreadsheet cannot answer.

The distinction can be illustrated in many ways. A founder may assume an option pool exists because a tab in the spreadsheet reserves it, but unless the company has actually created the relevant plan or approved the necessary structure, the pool may not exist in any meaningful legal sense. A founder may model a cofounder's vesting and assume that if the person leaves, the unvested portion simply returns to the company because the formula says so. If the vesting terms were never properly documented, however, the legal position may be far murkier. A company may show a SAFE converting into equity in its projections, yet the actual terms of that SAFE, its trigger conditions, its cap, discount, or side provisions may produce a different outcome than the founder's model assumed. The spreadsheet may be elegant and still be wrong where it matters.

This is why good founders learn that spreadsheet logic is necessary but not sufficient. The spreadsheet is an analytical tool. It is how the company understands the implications of ownership decisions. It is how the founders compare scenarios, test dilution, model future rounds, and bring conceptual order to a changing structure. None of that should be underestimated. A company that cannot model its cap table clearly is already at a disadvantage. But modelling is only one part of ownership governance. Once a decision is made, the company has to move from logic into execution, from calculation into formal structure. Otherwise the spreadsheet remains a private interpretation rather than a reliable corporate record.

There is a psychological reason founders often ignore this. Numbers feel objective, and documents often feel procedural. The founder therefore grants more emotional authority to the spreadsheet than to the legal framework because the spreadsheet seems to tell the "real story" while the documents feel like the slower, less creative part that merely catches up later. In startup life, this intuition is dangerous. The spreadsheet tells one real story, but the documents tell another, and when money, control, or conflict are involved, the latter story usually has more force. The investor, the lawyer, the court, the acquirer, or the tax authority does not care very much that the spreadsheet always intended a certain outcome. They care whether the company actually created that outcome through the structures available to it.

This does not mean founders should become paralysed by legal formality. The lesson is not that the spreadsheet is unimportant. It is that the spreadsheet should be treated as a map that must eventually correspond to the territory. A good cap table process usually works in two stages. First the founder or the company models the structure, tests the consequences, and decides what should happen. Then the company ensures that the governance steps, approvals, documents, records, and instruments are actually put in place so that what should happen becomes what has happened. Startups get into trouble when they stop after the first stage and assume that understanding is the same as implementation.

This gap between logic and reality becomes particularly costly in situations of change. A funding round is agreed in principle. The spreadsheet is updated. Everyone knows how the ownership should look afterward. Yet if closing is delayed, if documents change, if the option pool is re-sized in negotiations, or if investor protections alter the effective structure, the final legal outcome may not match the original model. The same thing happens with founder departures, option grants, note conversions, and recapitalisations. The spreadsheet often moves first because it is easy to update. The danger is that the founder's mind then moves with it and starts treating the model as if the company has already crossed the same line. That is how businesses end up operating on structural assumptions that are not yet, or never become, legally true.

This also explains why diligence can feel so humiliating to an unprepared founder. Diligence is often the moment when the company is required to prove that the spreadsheet story and the legal story are the same story. If they are, the process may be tedious but manageable. If they are not, the company suddenly discovers that its confidence was built partly on private modelling rather than on completed structure. This is when phrases like "we still need to formalise that" or "that was agreed in principle" become dangerous. The outside party hears not flexibility but incompleteness. They hear a company that knows what it meant to do, but cannot yet show that it did it.

There is also a subtle governance problem when founders rely too heavily on spreadsheet logic. Spreadsheets are often built by one person or by a very small circle, and that can create a false sense that the ownership structure is whatever that person has currently modelled.

In reality, ownership is not simply what the most organised founder has entered into a file. It is what the company as an entity has properly created and maintained. This distinction becomes very important in teams, because it prevents one founder's private model from becoming the de facto constitution of the company without the relevant approvals, transparency, or challenge. A spreadsheet can be an excellent internal tool. It should not quietly become an ungoverned substitute for corporate process.

This is why startups need both forms of discipline. They need spreadsheet logic because without modelling they cannot think clearly about dilution, allocation, or future rounds. They need legal reality because without formal execution the model does not actually govern the company. Each discipline corrects the weaknesses of the other. The spreadsheet prevents founders from drifting into ownership decisions without understanding their arithmetic. The legal framework prevents founders from mistaking arithmetic for enacted structure. When both are present, the cap table becomes both understandable and real. When either is missing, the company is governing ownership on one leg.

A wise founder therefore learns to ask two questions of every cap table event. First, does the spreadsheet logic make sense. Second, has the company actually done what is necessary to make that logic true. These questions sound simple, but they are among the most powerful habits a startup can cultivate. They keep the company from confusing intention with accomplishment, and modelling with ownership reality. That distinction may seem technical in quiet times. Under pressure, it becomes decisive.

How Sloppiness Compounds Over Rounds

The danger of a sloppy cap table is rarely that it destroys a company in a single dramatic moment. More often, it behaves like a structural weakness that is tolerated because the company appears to keep moving. The founders tell themselves that the errors are small, that the unresolved promises are manageable, that the spreadsheet is close enough, that the missing approvals can be sorted later, that the departed founder's position is irritating but not fatal, that the adviser arrangement is vague but probably harmless. For a while, they may even be right. The company survives. Product work continues.

Customers arrive. A funding conversation begins. The reason sloppiness is so dangerous is not that it always causes immediate collapse. It is that each new round of growth, hiring, and financing multiplies the cost of whatever was left weak at the beginning.

This is what compounding means in ownership structure. A small defect does not remain small simply because its original size was modest. It becomes the base on which later complexity is built. If the first founder split was unclear, every later percentage discussion becomes harder because no one is entirely sure what kind of fairness the company believes in. If early equity promises were never reflected properly, future hires and investors are stepping into a structure with hidden expectations already coiled inside it. If vesting was absent or poorly documented, a founder departure can freeze dead equity in place, and every later round must then tolerate or work around a shareholder whose presence no longer corresponds to contribution. If option grants were discussed informally and documented late, the company's understanding of fully diluted ownership may already be unreliable before the first serious investment arrives. What began as one act of sloppiness turns into an inherited condition of the structure.

This effect becomes sharper with each round because new capital does not enter a blank company. It enters a capital history. Investors do not only care what the company looks like now. They care how it got here and whether the route it took suggests discipline or drift. A sloppy early structure therefore does more than create technical correction work. It sends a signal about the founders' relationship to governance itself. A company that repeatedly arrives at major financing moments with old ownership issues unresolved is effectively telling the market that momentum has been allowed to outrun structure. Some investors may tolerate that if the business is exceptional. Many will not. Those who do may demand protective terms, longer diligence, or more influence precisely because the company has shown it cannot be trusted to keep its own ownership record in order without outside pressure.

This is why each round magnifies sloppiness rather than simply layering over it. Consider a company with one departed founder still holding too much equity because no proper vesting and repurchase framework was enforced. In the early stage, the active founders may simply find this unfair.

By the time the company reaches a priced seed round, that same dormant stake begins to affect investor perception, option pool planning, and the founders' own dilution tolerance. By the time a Series A conversation appears, the problem is no longer just emotional. It affects whether the company looks clean enough for institutional money and whether later hires can be incentivised sensibly. The original failure was small enough to ignore. Its compounded effect becomes strategic.

The same pattern appears with informal side agreements. In the first months, an unwritten promise to an adviser or quasi-founder may feel too uncertain to worry about. After one round, it becomes awkward because a real valuation now exists and the implied value of the promised equity has risen. After two rounds, it becomes dangerous because the person holding that expectation may feel that the company grew on top of a promise that was never honoured, while the founders feel trapped by a claim they wish had never been made. The company is no longer deciding whether to clean up a vague conversation. It is negotiating under the shadow of real money and formalised capital structure. Sloppiness compounds because valuation compounds, and unresolved expectations become more combustible as the company becomes more worth arguing over.

Option pools provide another example. A founder who is casual about early grants or about the distinction between discussed grants and approved grants may think the problem is administrative. Then a financing round requires a clear fully diluted view of the company. Suddenly the difference between what was promised, what was modelled, and what was actually authorised begins to matter. If the company has to enlarge the pool as a condition of the round, all prior vagueness becomes more painful because the dilution burden must now be allocated on top of uncertainty. Later, if more hires are needed, the same sloppiness affects whether the pool is enough, whether earlier grants were sensible, and whether the company has room to continue using equity as a retention tool. A weak early discipline in one area becomes a repeated tax on every later financing decision.

Convertible instruments are especially good at exposing compounded sloppiness because they allow founders to defer ownership complexity while quietly increasing it. A SAFE or note may feel like a convenient way to avoid a priced round too early.

That can be true. But if several such instruments are signed without rigorous understanding of how they stack, interact, and convert, the company may later discover that the ownership picture it had in mind bears only partial resemblance to what the conversion mechanics actually produce. A company that is already sloppy in record-keeping, promise-making, or cap table maintenance is particularly exposed here, because deferred instruments demand clarity precisely where such a company is already weakest. Once again, nothing explodes at signing. The cost compounds until the conversion event, when the company is suddenly forced to discover what it really agreed to.

This cumulative effect also changes founder psychology. Early sloppiness tends to produce a habit of postponement. The founders tell themselves they will fix the issue at the next natural pause, but startups rarely provide natural pauses. There is always another hire, another customer problem, another funding milestone, another operational crisis. As the company grows, the founders become more practised at living with unresolved structure. That is one of the most dangerous forms of compounding because it is behavioural rather than numerical. The company becomes structurally tolerant of inaccuracy. It starts to rely on the belief that ownership mess can always be dealt with later, even as each new round makes later more expensive. What began as one instance of avoidance becomes a culture of avoidance.

There is also a dilution effect in the broadest sense. Sloppiness dilutes not only ownership but authority. Each unresolved issue reduces the founders' freedom to negotiate from a position of clarity. A founder with a perfectly maintained cap table can model a round, understand the consequences, and negotiate terms with a clean sense of what is at stake. A founder carrying structural mess negotiates under hidden uncertainty. They may not know exactly how much effective room remains. They may not know what dormant claim could surface. They may not know whether the company's own documents support the ownership picture they are presenting. Their strategic freedom is already impaired before the new investor even enters the room. That impairment compounds because each round adds new stakeholders, new rights, and new opportunities for inconsistency to become leverage in someone else's hands.

This is why founders should stop thinking of sloppiness as a local problem. It is not local. It is accumulative. It travels forward through the life of the company. A weak first layer does not stay at the bottom where no one can see it. It warps what is built on top. The spreadsheet becomes harder to trust. The company's story becomes harder to tell. The next round becomes harder to model. The fairness of dilution becomes harder to discuss internally. The credibility of the business becomes easier for outsiders to question. None of this may be visible when the company is tiny. That is exactly why founders underestimate it. They imagine that because the issue is survivable now, it will remain survivable later. In ownership structures, survivable now often means expensive later.

The opposite is also true, and it is worth saying because founders can become too fatalistic once they see their early mistakes clearly. Discipline compounds as well. A company that resolves sloppiness early, updates the cap table properly, reflects promises in real structures, handles departures through documented mechanisms, and models each new round against a reliable base becomes easier to finance, easier to govern, and easier to explain. Its later rounds are not burdened by silent archaeology. Its negotiations can focus on the new deal rather than on whether the old company was ever put together properly in the first place. That is one of the great strategic returns on early ownership discipline. It does not remove all future difficulty, but it stops difficulty from multiplying through preventable structural weakness.

This section matters because many founders intuitively understand dilution but not compounding. They know that new rounds change percentages, but they do not always understand that each round also increases the cost of any sloppiness already present. The cap table is therefore not just a record of ownership. It is a record of whether the company has been governed in a way that allows later complexity to remain intelligible. If it has not, each new layer makes the old confusion more expensive. That is why sloppiness over rounds is never really neutral. It is either being corrected, or it is being multiplied.

The Cap Table as Memory and Warning

By the time a founder has watched the ownership structure evolve through founder allocation, vesting, departures, promises, side agreements, and perhaps the first rounds of outside capital, the cap table begins to look less like a spreadsheet and more like a memory device. It carries the marks of what the company believed at different moments. It records who was trusted, who was rewarded, who was let in, who was protected, who left, and what kinds of discipline the business possessed when pressure arrived. In that sense the cap table is not only a map of current ownership. It is an archive of past decisions.

This is one reason experienced people can often read more from a cap table than inexperienced founders expect. A founder may look at the document and see percentages. A seasoned investor, operator, or lawyer often sees a history. A departed founder with substantial retained equity suggests one kind of past. A cleanly vesting founder structure suggests another. A bloated option pool, several small advisory positions, and stray legacy allocations suggest something else again. The table tells a story about how the company handled commitment, conflict, pressure, and growth. That story may be more flattering or less flattering than the founders would like, but it is there all the same. Ownership structures have a way of remembering what the company once chose not to confront directly.

This memory function matters because startups are full of narratives, and many of those narratives become polished over time. Founders explain their origin story. Investors speak about conviction. Early employees tell themselves they joined something coherent and promising. The cap table often cuts across these stories with a colder record of what actually happened. It remembers whether a cofounder was treated as equal because they truly were, or because the team wanted to avoid an awkward conversation. It remembers whether vesting was used as discipline or ignored out of sentiment. It remembers whether the company formalised what it promised or relied on optimism and memory to carry weight that should have been carried by structure. Even when no one says these things out loud, the cap table preserves them in form.

That preservation can be useful in a positive sense. A cleanly built cap table becomes institutional memory in the healthiest way. It allows the company to explain itself to new participants without relying entirely on the memory or charisma of the founding team. It tells future hires what kind of ownership culture they are entering. It tells investors that the company has not merely survived but has governed itself. It tells the founders themselves, if they are honest enough to look, whether the business they are now building rests on a structure that still reflects the values and realities they claim to believe in. Good records are not only evidence for outsiders. They are a way for the company to remain legible to itself as it grows.

But the cap table is also a warning. It warns the founder when the company's structure has started drifting away from the company's reality. It warns when legacy equity is becoming dead weight. It warns when promises have accumulated faster than formal grants. It warns when an apparently small concession, multiplied over time, is changing the ownership balance more than anyone feels in the moment. It warns when a pattern of delay, vagueness, or emotional avoidance has started hardening into the company's governance style. In this sense the cap table is not simply memory of what has been done. It is an early signal of what future problems are being prepared by today's habits.

This warning function is most valuable when the company is willing to read it before outsiders force the issue. Founders often discover the truth of their cap table only under examination, when an investor is asking hard questions, a departing founder becomes difficult, or a financing event exposes inconsistencies that everyone had privately learned to ignore. By then the cap table is still a warning, but it is a warning that has arrived late. The stronger company reads the warning sooner. It sees that the structure is beginning to tell an unhealthy story and corrects the story before it becomes more expensive to live with.

This requires a change in how founders look at the document. They cannot treat it as a passive administrative record, something that simply reflects whatever the company happens to do. They have to learn to interrogate it. What does this structure now say about us. Does it still reflect the people carrying the business. Does it show discipline or drift. Does it reveal a company that makes hard ownership choices clearly, or one that repeatedly hides from them. If someone who knew nothing else about the business saw this cap table, what would they infer about the way the founders govern. These are not abstract questions. They are ways of forcing the ownership record to speak more honestly than the company's internal mythology sometimes permits.

There is another reason the cap table acts as warning. Ownership has a way of turning silent tensions into future events. A founder may be carrying quiet resentment that their stake no longer feels justified relative to effort.

An early employee may believe an equity promise has still not been honoured. A departed contributor may remain economically present in a way that no longer makes strategic sense. None of this may cause immediate open conflict. Yet the cap table stores the conditions under which that conflict could later become explicit. A business with such tensions embedded in its structure is not stable simply because everyone is currently behaving. It is living beside delayed reactions. The cap table is where those delayed reactions can often be seen before they are felt.

That is why mature company-building involves not only maintaining the cap table but also learning from it. Every oddity in the structure asks a question. Why is this person here. Why is this grant shaped this way. Why was this option pool expanded. Why is this founder still carrying this percentage. Why does the fully diluted picture look more strained than the founders tend to admit in conversation. These questions do not all imply error, but they do imply that the structure is speaking and deserves to be listened to. If the founders are wise, they will hear not only the arithmetic but the diagnosis.

This chapter has argued that the cap table is a living document because the company itself changes through time. That truth leads naturally to a second one. A living document becomes a kind of institutional memory because it carries forward the traces of each stage through which the company has passed. And because it carries those traces forward, it also becomes one of the first places where future trouble can be seen. A cap table that is read only as a record is underused. A cap table that is read as memory and warning becomes a governance tool.

That is how the founders should learn to see it. Not just as the current answer to who owns what, but as the company's written memory of how it has handled the hardest questions of fairness, discipline, and growth so far, and as an early warning system for whether the way it is handling them now is preparing clarity or preparing trouble.

* * *

SIX

Dilution and the Mathematics of Growth

"Price is what you pay. Value is what you get."

- Warren Buffett

What Dilution Really Means

Dilution is one of the most misunderstood words in startup finance because it is one of the few words that founders often hear early, fear immediately, and only understand much later. The emotional reaction usually arrives first. A founder is told that raising money, creating an option pool, or issuing shares to new participants will dilute them, and the word lands with the force of warning. It sounds like loss, erosion, weakening, or surrender. In some cases it is all of those things. In other cases it is simply the normal arithmetic by which a growing company makes room for the people and capital required to keep growing. The difficulty is that founders often experience dilution as an injury before they understand it as a structure.

At its most basic, dilution means that a person's percentage ownership of the company decreases because the total number of shares or effective claims has increased and that person has not received enough of the new issuance to maintain the same proportion. Nothing mystical is happening. The company is being divided into a larger total set of claims, so the old slices become smaller as a fraction of the whole. A founder may still hold exactly the same number of shares and still be diluted, because dilution is about proportion, not simply count. That is the first discipline the reader must hold onto. Ownership can change without a founder giving up a single existing share. The denominator changes, and that changes the meaning of the founder's holding.

This arithmetic is simple enough in the abstract, but what gives dilution its power in startup life is that it is never only arithmetic. Each act of dilution reflects a decision about who else the company now needs and what the company is willing to exchange in order to secure that person, that capital, or that future flexibility. If the company issues shares to an investor, the founders are accepting that they will own a smaller percentage in exchange for cash, credibility, runway, and sometimes access to networks or governance support. If the company expands an option pool, the existing owners are accepting a smaller share of the future in exchange for the ability to recruit and retain talent. If a SAFE converts, earlier holders are discovering that past convenience was always going to produce present dilution once deferred claims became real. Dilution therefore means not only that the percentages change, but that the company has chosen to reallocate part of the future in order to make some next stage possible.

That is why dilution should not be understood as inherently good or inherently bad. It is a mechanism. Its meaning depends on the quality of what the company receives in return and on the wisdom with which the founders have modelled the consequences. A founder who is diluted because the company has brought in capital on sensible terms, extended its survival, improved its strategic position, and increased the likely future value of the business may be numerically weaker in percentage terms and economically stronger in every way that matters. A founder who is diluted because the company gave away equity carelessly, failed to understand the cumulative effect of instruments, or kept solving short-term discomfort through future claims may be weaker both numerically and strategically. The mistake is to treat all dilution as if it belonged to one moral category.

This is where early founder thinking often goes wrong. Founders tend to imagine their original ownership percentage as the natural shape of the company, and every later reduction as a departure from what properly belonged to them. That is psychologically understandable because the first cap table often feels intimate and total. The company begins with one founder or a small set of founders holding the entire structure. Those early percentages therefore feel like default reality. But for most startups that intend to hire, raise capital, and scale, the founder-only or founder-heavy cap table is not the natural endpoint of the business. It is merely the earliest form from which later forms will grow. To treat that first percentage as though it should remain untouched is to misunderstand what kind of organisation a startup is trying to become.

This does not mean founders should accept dilution passively. Quite the opposite. Understanding dilution properly is what allows founders to resist bad dilution while accepting useful dilution. A founder who sees all dilution as theft will either avoid necessary steps or negotiate from fear rather than strategy. A founder who sees dilution as automatically harmless because "everyone gets diluted" is just as exposed, because they may fail to notice when the company is exchanging too much of its future for too little in return. The mature posture is neither panic nor indifference. It is interpretation. What is causing the dilution. Who benefits. What does the company receive. What does the founder lose in percentage, and what may be gained in value, survivability, or capability. How does this round or grant affect the structure not only now, but after the next stage as well.

It is also essential to distinguish dilution from dispossession. Founders often use the language of dilution as though it meant that someone has taken part of what they already had in a direct physical sense. Usually that is not what is happening. The founder's existing shares have not been removed. Rather, the company has created additional claims, and this changes the founder's relative position within the whole. That distinction matters because it helps the founder see the process more clearly. New shares issued to others do not reach backward and erase the work the founder did. What they do is alter how much of the future upside and control remains concentrated with the original holders. This can still be painful or dangerous if done badly, but it is a different kind of event from simple confiscation.

There is another subtlety here that becomes more important as the company matures. Dilution is not only about equity percentages. It is also about incentives and governance. A founder who owns a smaller share than before may still be properly incentivised if the company is healthier and the likely value of the remaining stake is greater. But if dilution becomes severe enough that the active founders no longer feel that the upside justifies the burden they carry, then the cap table has begun to undermine the company's internal engine. Likewise, a founder who is numerically diluted may still retain practical control in some contexts, or may lose it faster than the percentage alone would suggest, depending on rights, board structure, and class differences. Dilution therefore has to be read not only in terms of wealth but also in terms of whether the company's internal alignment remains strong enough to support execution.

This is why modelling dilution is one of the central disciplines of startup ownership. Founders should never hear the word and merely recoil. They should ask immediately how much, from what, on what basis, into which structure, and with what expected return to the company. They should understand the present round but also the effect on the next round. They should distinguish between headline dilution and fully diluted reality. They should notice when apparently small concessions compound. They should resist the false comfort of looking only at current issued percentages if options, notes, or SAFEs are already waiting in the wings. A company that does not model dilution seriously is not governing its own ownership. It is allowing future arithmetic to surprise it.

The deeper truth is that dilution is the mathematics through which growth is often financed. A startup does not normally become a larger, more capable, better-resourced company while keeping the ownership structure frozen at its original founder shape. Growth usually requires new people and new capital, and those participants need to be brought into the future of the company somehow. Equity is one of the main ways that happens. The mathematics of that inclusion is dilution. Seen from this angle, dilution is not an external attack on the founder's position. It is the structural cost of building something bigger than a founder could usually build alone. That cost may be worth paying or not worth paying depending on the circumstances. But it is a cost that belongs to the logic of scale, not just to the malice of investors or the carelessness of founders.

This is where the Buffett quote at the head of the chapter becomes useful. Founders often focus on what they are paying in dilution, which is natural. But the more intelligent question is what value the company is receiving. A founder who gives up ten percent for nothing much has made a poor trade. A founder who gives up ten percent in exchange for the capital, talent, or infrastructure that meaningfully increases the future value of the remaining ninety has entered a more complex and potentially much better equation. Dilution becomes dangerous when the founder sees only the price and fails to judge the value, or sees the promise of value and fails to calculate the true price.

That is what dilution really means. It means the company is changing the proportion in which its future will be shared. Sometimes that is the right decision. Sometimes it is a foolish one. The arithmetic is simple. The judgment is not.

Why Dilution Is Not Always Bad

The first time founders truly feel dilution, they often experience it as a wound. The cap table changes, their percentage falls, and something that had once looked whole and self-evident now looks smaller. Even if they understood the arithmetic in advance, the emotional force of seeing a lower number beside their name can be surprisingly strong. Founders do not usually build companies so that they can own less of them, and so the instinctive reaction is to treat dilution as failure, weakness, or loss inflicted by outsiders. That reaction is powerful, but it is not always intelligent. Dilution is not always bad because percentages do not exist in isolation. They exist inside companies that are changing in value, capability, and survivability.

A founder who owns one hundred percent of a company with no meaningful market traction, no team, no capital, and no route to scale may be in an emotionally satisfying position but not necessarily a strong one. If that founder later owns sixty percent of a company with funded runway, a better product, stronger talent, clearer market credibility, and much higher implied value, the percentage has declined but the underlying position may have improved dramatically. This is the first hard lesson of startup finance that many founders resist because it offends intuitive ownership psychology. A smaller slice of something much stronger can be worth far more than a larger slice of something much weaker. The number that shrank may still sit inside a much more valuable whole.

This is why dilution cannot be judged by percentage change alone. It has to be judged by exchange. What did the company give up, and what did it gain. If a company dilutes its founders to bring in capital that allows it to survive, hire, build, and grow at a pace otherwise impossible, the founders may be paying part of their future upside in exchange for a much better chance of having meaningful upside at all. If the company dilutes to create an option pool that allows it to attract people whose labour is essential to making the venture real, the immediate percentage reduction may be the price of creating a team capable of increasing the value of everyone's remaining stake. In these situations, dilution is not the destruction of value. It is part of the mechanism through which value becomes more likely.

This does not mean the comforting slogan that dilution is fine because the pie gets bigger should be swallowed without scrutiny. Sometimes the pie does not get bigger enough. Sometimes the company gives away ownership for too little. Sometimes the capital is expensive, the investor unhelpful, the hires unimpressive, the round poorly timed, or the company's assumptions about future growth unrealistically optimistic. In those cases, dilution may indeed be bad. The important point is that dilution must be assessed in relation to what is purchased. It is a pricing event in the broadest sense. The company is paying in future claims. Whether the purchase is wise depends on the quality of what comes back.

There is a useful mental shift hidden inside this. Founders often think of dilution as something done to them. A more strategic founder thinks of it as something the company chooses to undertake under certain conditions. That shift matters because it moves the founder from victimhood to governance. If dilution is merely an injury inflicted by investors, then the founder's role is defensive. If dilution is a structural choice through which the company can buy time, talent, capability, and growth, then the founder's role is to judge when that trade is rational and when it is not. The second mindset is much stronger because it allows the founder to resist bad deals without becoming irrationally attached to avoiding all change in ownership.

This is where founder maturity begins to show. An immature founder says I do not want to be diluted. A mature founder asks what kind of dilution creates a company strong enough that my reduced stake is still worth far more than my original one. The difference between those two positions is not merely rhetorical. It determines whether the founder approaches financing, hiring, and incentive design as a series of threats or as a series of strategic allocation questions. A founder who cannot accept any dilution at all often ends up either underbuilding, underhiring, undercapitalising, or entering negotiations in a posture of fear. A founder who accepts every dilution on the grounds that growth requires sacrifice can lose discipline from the opposite side. The balance lies in understanding that dilution is sometimes the cost of turning possibility into a better-structured reality.

The reason this can feel so counterintuitive is that founders usually experience ownership in percentage terms long before they experience it in realised value.

The cap table shows sixty percent, forty-five percent, thirty percent. These are visible. The future commercial strength of the company is uncertain, modelled, hoped for, but not yet bankable. That creates an asymmetry in the founder's mind. The loss is present and clear. The gain is future and speculative. This is one reason dilution so often feels bad even when it may be strategically good. The founder is comparing a visible reduction against an invisible possibility. To assess dilution properly, the founder has to become comfortable reasoning across that asymmetry rather than simply obeying it emotionally.

Another reason dilution is not always bad is that it can improve not just economic value but organisational quality. Founders often underestimate how much stronger a company can become when ownership is spread in the right way. A startup with all its equity concentrated in one or two founders but lacking key technical, commercial, or operating talent may be structurally intact but commercially weak. A startup that uses ownership to attract serious long-term contributors can become more capable, more robust, and more likely to survive the ordinary shocks of growth. In that sense dilution can purchase not only value in a narrow financial sense but also institutional competence. The founder's remaining stake then sits inside a better company, one less dependent on founders doing everything themselves forever.

This logic is especially clear when looking at employee equity. Founders sometimes resent option pools because they understand, correctly, that pools dilute them even before specific hires are made. Yet if the option pool allows the company to attract the people without whom the business would stagnate or fail, then the dilution is part of what turns a founder-centric project into an investable, scalable organisation. The founder is not losing percentage to bureaucracy. They are making room for the people required to build the future value of the company. That room should be sized carefully, but its existence is often one of the conditions of serious growth.

The same principle applies to capital. A founder who refuses outside money in order to preserve a larger percentage may sometimes be making a wise choice, especially if the business can grow efficiently without heavy financing. But in many ventures, especially those requiring technology development, regulatory progress, rapid hiring, market capture, or long pre-revenue runways, capital is not decorative.

it is necessary. In those companies, preserving ownership at the expense of survival or strategic pace can be a very expensive form of purity. The founder ends up with a larger share of a weaker business, and sometimes of a dead one. It is not dilution itself that harms the founder. It is dilution without corresponding value, or the refusal of useful dilution out of fear.

There is another subtle reason why dilution is not always bad. In some cases it imposes healthy discipline on founders themselves. A founder who remains the near-total owner of a business for too long may become overly attached to control, underexposed to outside scrutiny, or insufficiently willing to build a structure that outgrows the founder's original habits. Bringing in investors, creating an employee ownership layer, or otherwise widening the ownership base can force the company to professionalise. This is not always pleasant, and it can certainly go too far if control is surrendered unwisely. But some dilution can be part of the transition from personal project to actual institution. The company becomes something larger than the founder's self-conception, and ownership changes to reflect that.

Of course, founders should never let the phrase not always bad become an excuse for lazy thinking. Every dilution event should still be modelled, challenged, and understood. The founder should ask what the new fully diluted picture looks like, what additional dilution future rounds are likely to impose, whether the round terms are sensible, whether the company is giving away room it may need later, and whether the likely increase in value or survivability is substantial enough to justify the trade. The point is not to celebrate dilution. It is to stop treating it as automatically equivalent to loss. In startups, some of the best ownership decisions look like loss in the short term because they are really exchanges between one form of claim and a stronger foundation for future value.

This is also why dilution should be discussed not only in numerical but in strategic language within founding teams. If the conversation is framed only as who is losing what percentage, the team may become defensive and narrow. If it is framed as what the company is buying with this change in ownership and what the likely effect is on the value and viability of the remaining stakes, then the conversation becomes more intelligent. It becomes possible to say yes to the right dilution and no to the wrong kind, rather than merely reacting to all dilution as a blow to founder pride.

In the end, dilution is not good because smaller percentages are somehow admirable, nor bad because founders naturally wanted to own more. Dilution is good or bad depending on whether it strengthens the company enough that the remaining ownership becomes more valuable, more durable, or more strategically meaningful than it would have been otherwise. The founders who understand this are not less protective of their position than other founders. They are simply more capable of judging when protecting the company requires them to accept a smaller share of something much stronger.

Percentage Loss Versus Value Creation

One of the central tensions in startup ownership is that founders can watch their percentage fall at exactly the same time their underlying position becomes stronger. This is the point at which dilution stops being a simple matter of arithmetic and becomes a matter of interpretation. The founder sees a smaller number and instinctively reads it as loss. The company may, however, have become better funded, better staffed, more credible, and more likely to survive. The challenge is that percentage loss is immediate and visible, while value creation is often delayed, probabilistic, and difficult to feel in the same clean numerical way. That is why many founders overreact to one and underappreciate the other.

To think clearly about this, the founder has to separate two related but distinct questions. The first question is what fraction of the company do I own after this event. The second is what is the likely economic and strategic quality of the company I now partly own. Those questions are obviously connected, but they are not the same question. A founder who moves from owning eighty percent of a very weak company to fifty-five percent of a far stronger one has clearly lost percentage. But whether they have become worse off depends on what happened to the company's real prospects in the process. If the company is now meaningfully more viable, better capitalised, and more capable of reaching a valuable outcome, then the founder may have lost relative share while gaining a much better position in every sense that matters beyond the spreadsheet's most immediate impression.

This is one of the reasons startup finance feels psychologically unfair to many founders. Human beings are much better at feeling subtraction than they are at pricing uncertain future improvement.

The founder knows what eighty percent meant. It meant control, pride, and a big number beside their name. The founder does not know with equal certainty what fifty-five percent of a newly funded, newly structured, still uncertain company will ultimately mean. So the mind compares a clear and tangible reduction against an improvement that may be larger in substance but softer in emotional texture. This asymmetry is why founders often speak as though percentage itself were the primary reality and everything else a speculative story investors tell to make dilution easier to swallow.

Yet that instinct can become very expensive if followed blindly. Startup value is not stored in the purity of the original percentage. It is created through the company's ability to become something more than it was when the founders first divided it up. This usually requires some combination of capital, talent, infrastructure, and credibility that the original founding team cannot produce entirely from within itself. When those things are acquired intelligently, percentage loss can be the price of moving the company into a new category of possibility. The key is not to deny the loss. The key is to measure whether the new possibility is substantial enough to justify it.

This requires founders to become more sophisticated about what value creation actually means. It does not mean simply attaching a higher notional valuation to the company and pretending that this solves everything. A financing round at a larger headline valuation can be real progress, but it can also be misleading if the terms are heavy, the company remains strategically weak, or the founder has not thought through how future rounds may continue to reshape the structure. Value creation should be understood more broadly. Has the company bought itself time. Has it improved the quality of its team. Has it gained strategic advantages that make later growth more likely. Has it reduced existential risk. Has it moved from being an idea with scattered execution into a credible business with better odds of surviving the next phase. These things may not all appear immediately as liquid founder wealth, but they are real components of value creation.

This is why founders should be cautious of speaking only in pre-money and post-money vocabulary without also asking what kind of company is being created through the transaction.

A founder may be dazzled by a round that seems to "increase value" while ignoring that the company has accepted terms or dilution patterns that weaken the practical meaning of the remaining stake. Another founder may recoil at dilution in a modestly priced round even though that round brings exactly the capital and structure needed to turn the business into something materially more valuable. Percentage loss versus value creation is therefore not a slogan. It is an evaluative discipline. Founders need to learn to think beyond the surface movement of numbers and ask what this ownership change is doing to the actual company.

There is also a strategic aspect to this distinction. Investors, senior hires, and acquirers do not usually evaluate the business by asking whether the founders preserved as much of the original cap table as possible. They ask whether the company became strong enough to matter. A founder who insists on maintaining very high ownership at the expense of company development may feel virtuous about avoiding dilution, but the market may see a company that remained underbuilt, undercapitalised, or unattractive to talent. In that scenario, the founder has protected percentage but failed to create enough value inside the protected structure. A smaller share of a company that becomes truly investable, operationally capable, and strategically credible is often superior to a larger share of a business that remained trapped by the founder's inability to exchange ownership for growth intelligently.

This does not mean founders should become casual about giving up ground. The distinction between percentage loss and value creation is not an excuse for soft thinking. It is possible for founders to talk themselves into almost any dilution if they rely too heavily on abstract future upside. That is why one must always return to what the company is concretely receiving. If the new capital is not enough to materially improve the company's prospects, if the hires are not genuinely transformative, if the investor brings little beyond money and the money itself is not sufficient, if the option grants are being used sloppily rather than strategically, then percentage loss may simply be loss dressed in the language of future possibility. The point is not that value creation always outweighs dilution. The point is that founders need to distinguish between deals that are truly buying stronger future value and deals that are merely diluting them without enough compensating gain.

This is especially important because value creation can be uneven across time. Some dilution events create immediate and obvious improvements. A financing round closes, key people are hired, product development accelerates, and the company quickly becomes stronger. Other dilution events are more ambiguous. The company may receive enough to survive, but not enough to thrive. It may buy time rather than transformation. In such cases the founder has to judge whether the percentage loss is a necessary defensive move, a bridge to something better, or simply the least bad option available. Startup life often contains dilution that is not glorious but still rational. The founder's task is not to demand that every reduction in percentage feel triumphant. It is to ask whether the structure after the change is more likely to lead somewhere worthwhile than the structure before it.

There is also a lesson here for internal team conversations. Founders often damage morale by speaking about dilution only in terms of what they are losing. That framing can make every ownership change sound like surrender and can teach the team to view necessary hiring or financing as zero-sum politics rather than company-building. A better framing is to acknowledge openly that percentage is being given up while asking what greater value or capability the company is trying to purchase. This does not magically eliminate tension, but it moves the discussion from injury to strategy. It reminds everyone that the cap table is not a museum piece. It is the structure through which the company decides who must be let into the future and on what basis.

One subtle but important consequence of this way of thinking is that founders become more resistant to vanity metrics in ownership. If the founder understands that value creation matters more than the superficial preservation of percentage, they are less likely to negotiate for symbolic victories that do not change the company's real strength. They stop chasing bigger-looking numbers for their own sake and begin asking whether the structure after the deal leaves them with a meaningful, motivated, and well-positioned stake in a stronger company. This is a much healthier way to think because it forces the founder to measure success not by the illusion of untouched ownership but by the actual condition of the business their ownership now represents.

The distinction between percentage loss and value creation is therefore one of the most important intellectual upgrades a founder can make. It does not ask the founder to become indifferent to dilution. It asks them to become serious about what dilution is buying. The founder who makes this shift is better equipped to evaluate rounds, pools, and grants without either sentimental panic or reckless optimism. They can say yes to the dilution that builds a materially better company and no to the dilution that merely transfers future upside without enough return. They begin to think less like the guardian of a shrinking fraction and more like the steward of a structure whose worth depends on what the company becomes.

That is the real test. The founder is not trying to die with the largest possible percentage of the original spreadsheet. The founder is trying to own a meaningful part of something that actually works, survives, and creates value worth sharing.

Simple Dilution Examples

Dilution becomes much easier to understand once the founder stops hearing it only in abstract language and starts seeing it in plain numerical examples. This is important because many founders think they understand dilution until the moment a real round or grant forces them to work through what actually happens to their stake. At that point, vague familiarity is no longer enough. The company has to know not just that dilution exists, but how it operates in the structure they are building. The examples in this section are deliberately simple because clarity matters more than sophistication at this stage. The goal is not to impress with complexity. It is to make the basic mechanics so intuitive that later, more complicated situations can still be read with confidence.

Imagine a company with a single founder who owns 1,000 shares out of 1,000 total shares outstanding. The founder therefore owns one hundred percent of the company. This is the cleanest possible starting point. Now imagine the company needs capital and issues 250 new shares to an investor. The founder still holds 1,000 shares. Nothing has been taken away. But the total number of shares is now 1,250. The founder's ownership is no longer one hundred percent. It is 1,000 divided by 1,250, which equals eighty percent. The investor owns 250 divided by 1,250, or twenty percent. That is dilution in its simplest form.

The founder's share count stays the same, but the founder's percentage falls because the whole has been expanded.
This simple example matters because it removes one of the most common confusions immediately. Dilution does not require the founder to transfer their own shares to someone else. The company can create new shares, and this alone changes everyone's relative position. Many founders understand this verbally, but not emotionally. They still feel as though their original ownership should somehow remain intact because they did not hand over anything. The arithmetic says otherwise. What matters is not whether the founder physically surrendered shares. What matters is that the company has created new claims and therefore changed the ratio between existing claims and the total.

Now consider a variation. Suppose the founder owns 800 shares out of 1,000 total, and an early employee owns 200. The founder therefore owns eighty percent and the employee twenty percent. The company then issues 250 new shares to an investor. The total rises to 1,250. The founder still has 800 shares, but now owns 800 divided by 1,250, or sixty-four percent. The employee still has 200 shares, but now owns sixteen percent. The investor owns twenty percent. Both existing holders have been diluted because the investor's shares increased the total while neither of them received any of the new issue. This is a useful example because it shows that dilution is not something that happens only to founders. It happens to whoever is already inside the structure when new claims are added without proportional participation.

The next step is to notice something that founders often miss in the emotional force of these changes. In the first example, the founder moved from one hundred percent to eighty percent. In the second, the founder moved from eighty percent to sixty-four percent. These can feel like painful reductions, and they are real reductions. But the founder should immediately ask what the company received. If the newly issued shares brought in capital that gives the company a much better chance of survival and growth, then the founder now owns a smaller percentage of a company that may be significantly stronger. If the company gave up twenty percent merely for symbolic interest or too little capital to matter, then the dilution may be poor. The arithmetic alone does not tell you whether the trade was wise, but it does tell you exactly what happened to ownership.

Another simple example helps show how dilution can continue over time. Begin again with a founder who owns 1,000 out of 1,000 shares. First, the company issues 250 shares to an investor, taking the founder to eighty percent. Later, the company creates an employee option pool of 250 shares. The founder still has 1,000 shares, but the total is now 1,500. The founder's percentage becomes 1,000 divided by 1,500, or about sixty-six point seven percent. The investor's original 250 shares now represent about sixteen point seven percent. The option pool represents the remaining sixteen point seven percent. This example matters because it shows how dilution compounds. The founder is not being diluted once and then done. Each structural change must be measured against the new total, not the original one. That is why founders who say "I only gave away twenty percent" can be misleading even to themselves if they later create pools, issue grants, or take additional rounds without re-running the whole picture.

Now consider what happens if the founder participates in the round. Suppose again that the founder owns 800 shares out of 1,000 total, and the company intends to issue 250 new shares. If the founder also buys some of those new shares, then their dilution can be reduced. Imagine the founder acquires 50 of the 250 new shares while the investor takes 200. The new total becomes 1,250. The founder now holds 850 shares, the employee still holds 200, and the investor holds 200. The founder's new percentage is 850 divided by 1,250, or sixty-eight percent. The employee has sixteen percent. The investor has sixteen percent. The founder has still been diluted from the original eighty percent, but less severely than if they had taken none of the new issue. This helps explain why pro rata rights and participation rights can matter so much later. They affect whether existing holders can preserve more of their relative position when new capital enters.

It is also useful to see how a small issue can still have a noticeable effect. Suppose a company has 10,000,000 shares outstanding and a founder owns 6,000,000, or sixty percent. If the company issues only 500,000 new shares, the founder's share count still remains 6,000,000, but the total becomes 10,500,000. The founder's new percentage becomes roughly fifty-seven point one percent. That is not a catastrophic change, but it is real. Even a seemingly modest issuance has altered the founder's position by nearly three percentage points. T his example matters because large share counts can sometimes disguise dilution psychologically. A founder sees millions of shares and assumes that a few hundred thousand more will not matter very much. But percentages do not care how impressive the raw counts sound. They care about the ratio.

Founders should also understand that dilution can happen before they fully feel it. If the company creates an option pool but does not immediately grant all the options, the founder may be tempted to think the dilution is not real yet because no named employee has received the shares. In structural terms, however, the company has often already allocated that ownership space. The founder's effective room has changed even if the grants are not yet fully dispersed. That is why sophisticated readers often look at the cap table on a fully diluted basis. They want to know not only who holds shares today, but what future claims are already embedded in the structure.

One more simple example helps clarify this. A company has 1,000 shares outstanding, all held by the founder. The company then reserves an option pool equivalent to 200 shares. Even if none of those options has yet been granted, the fully diluted picture may treat the company as effectively having 1,200 shares for modelling purposes. On that basis, the founder's stake is not viewed as one hundred percent but as 1,000 divided by 1,200, or about eighty-three point three percent. This can feel strange to new founders because the founder still literally holds all issued shares. But the market often cares about the structure the company is preparing to live with, not only the narrow legal count at this instant.

These simple examples are not the whole story, but they establish the habits of thought that matter. The founder should always ask four things. What is the current total. How many new shares or claims are being added. How many of those new claims, if any, are being allocated to me or other existing holders. What does the new total do to everyone's percentage. If the founder learns to run these questions automatically, dilution becomes much less mysterious and much easier to govern.

There is a final point worth stressing. Simplicity in examples does not mean simplicity in consequence. A movement from eighty percent to sixty-four percent can be perfectly rational or deeply damaging depending on what the company gained in return and what other future claims already exist. The arithmetic tells the founder what happened.

The strategic judgment tells the founder whether it was worth it. Both are essential. Founders who master only the arithmetic are still vulnerable to bad deals. Founders who ignore the arithmetic are vulnerable to surprise. The cap table requires both numerical clarity and commercial judgment. Simple dilution examples are where those two disciplines begin to meet.

Multi-Round Dilution Examples

A founder can grasp dilution perfectly well in a single round and still be unprepared for how dramatically ownership can change once several rounds are stacked on top of one another. This is where dilution stops feeling like a local event and begins to feel like the long mathematics of company-building. A startup does not usually raise capital once and then freeze. It hires, expands, revises plans, takes bridge money, creates or enlarges pools, and often raises again under different conditions. Each event is measured against the structure left by the previous one. That is why multi-round dilution matters so much. The founder is not being compared only with the original company anymore. The founder is being carried forward through a sequence of changing denominators.

The simplest way to understand this is to begin with a clean case and then watch the percentages evolve. Imagine a founder who initially owns 1,000 shares out of 1,000 total shares, or one hundred percent. In the first round, the company issues 250 new shares to an angel investor. The total becomes 1,250. The founder now owns eighty percent. The angel owns twenty percent. So far, the arithmetic is straightforward.

Now imagine the company grows and later raises another round. This time it issues 312.5 new shares to a seed investor. The total becomes 1,562.5. The founder still holds 1,000 shares, but now owns 64 percent. The angel still holds 250 shares, now worth 16 percent of the company. The new seed investor holds 20 percent. This is a useful moment to pause because it reveals a common misunderstanding. Founders sometimes think of each round as taking only a fresh percentage from them directly. In reality, each round is reshaping everyone who was already on the table. The angel who once owned twenty percent no longer does. The founder who was diluted in the first round is diluted again in the second. No one is insulated merely because they were already there.

Now add a third change that does not look like a financing round at all. Suppose the company creates an employee option pool equivalent to 208.33 shares so that the total rises to 1,770.83. The founder's 1,000 shares now represent roughly 56.5 percent. The angel's 250 shares represent about 14.1 percent. The seed investor's 312.5 shares represent about 17.6 percent. The option pool represents about 11.8 percent. This example matters because it shows how founders can undergo meaningful dilution from decisions that feel operational rather than financial. No investor wrote a cheque in this step. Yet the founder's position still moved materially because the company decided to make room for future hires. The cap table does not care whether the dilution came from capital or from talent strategy. It records both.

These round-by-round shifts are not merely interesting arithmetic. They are the reason founders must stop treating ownership as if it can be understood from a single snapshot. If the founder had looked only at the first angel round, they might have concluded that owning eighty percent still left them overwhelmingly strong. After the seed round and the pool expansion, the position has changed meaningfully. The founder still has a majority, but a much thinner one. The founder has not done anything obviously foolish in this example. The company may well be growing sensibly. Yet the multi-round effect is still real. Ownership changes more through accumulated events than through any single moment.

Another example shows this more starkly. Begin with three founders who together own 10,000,000 shares, allocated 5,000,000, 3,000,000, and 2,000,000. They therefore own fifty percent, thirty percent, and twenty percent. The company raises a seed round and issues 2,500,000 new shares to investors. The total becomes 12,500,000. The three founders now hold forty percent, twenty-four percent, and sixteen percent. Already their original percentages have changed significantly, even though they still collectively hold eighty percent.

Now the company expands the option pool by 1,500,000 shares before a Series A. The total becomes 14,000,000. The founders now sit at roughly 35.7 percent, 21.4 percent, and 14.3 percent. Then the Series A closes with 3,500,000 new shares issued. The total becomes 17,500,000. The founders now hold approximately 28.6 percent, 17.1 percent, and 11.4 percent. None of these steps is necessarily irrational. The company may be progressing well.

But the cumulative picture is very different from the original one. The lead founder who once held half the company now holds less than thirty percent. The founder who began at twenty percent now holds barely more than eleven percent. This is why early founders who say "we only need to think about the first round" are usually thinking too narrowly. The later rounds are not separate ownership stories. They are the continuation of the first one.

It is also important to notice that the pace of dilution is not always even. Some rounds may be relatively modest. Others may be highly dilutive because the company needs more capital than expected, the valuation has not risen enough, or earlier instruments convert in ways that suddenly widen the table. This is one reason founders need to model not only expected rounds but stressful ones. A founder who assumes every new round will occur at a substantially higher valuation may comfort themselves with the idea that later dilution will be mild. Sometimes that happens. Sometimes the company hits turbulence, growth is slower than hoped, or market conditions worsen, and the new money is far more expensive in ownership terms than the founder anticipated. Multi-round thinking must therefore include not only optimistic trajectories but realistic and adverse ones as well.

This is where the mathematics of compounding becomes emotionally important. In a single round, a founder may lose ten or fifteen percentage points and still feel that the position remains overwhelmingly theirs. After multiple rounds, option pool expansions, and instrument conversions, the founder may suddenly realise that the cumulative effect is far larger than any one step felt in isolation. That realisation often arrives late because each step was individually tolerable. This is exactly how dilution works in practice. Founders rarely lose control or incentive all at once. They lose it through a sequence of reasonable-looking events that were not viewed as one continuous process.

The same logic applies to early investors and employees. A small option grant that seems rich at the beginning may later represent a far smaller effective position after several rounds. An early angel who expected to retain significance may find that later institutional money has thinned the holding materially unless participation rights were exercised. This is why multi-round dilution is not only a founder issue. It is the broader mathematics of how the company's future is shared across time.

Every participant is being moved forward through a structure that becomes more crowded as the company grows.
There is, however, a strategic lesson that should temper panic. Multi-round dilution is not necessarily evidence of failure. In many successful companies, founders pass through several rounds and still build meaningful wealth and influence because the underlying company becomes so much stronger. The issue is not whether dilution occurs across rounds. It almost always does. The issue is whether the dilution is being exchanged for enough progress, enough value creation, and enough future possibility to leave the founders and other key holders in a strong enough position at the end. A founder who still owns twenty percent of a genuinely valuable company may be far better off than a founder who clung to sixty percent of a company that never became fundable or scalable.

This is why modelling multi-round dilution is one of the most important disciplines in cap table management. Founders should not simply ask what this round does to me. They should ask what this round plus the next likely round plus the likely pool expansion plus the likely instrument conversion does to me. That question is not pessimistic. It is realistic. It forces the founder to govern ownership as a process rather than react to each event in isolation. It also makes better negotiation possible, because the founder can see when a "reasonable" concession now may become a much more painful position later once other known or probable events are layered on top.

The wise founder therefore learns to look several moves ahead. They understand that every round is part of a chain, and that ownership is gradually rebalanced by each link in that chain. The cap table at any given moment is never merely the result of the last transaction. It is the cumulative result of everything that has been allowed into the structure so far. Multi-round dilution examples matter because they train the eye to see that continuity. Once the founder sees it, dilution stops being a series of isolated shocks and becomes what it really is: the rolling mathematics of company growth.

Psychological Mistakes Founders Make When Seeing Dilution

Dilution is mathematical, but founders rarely experience it mathematically at first. They experience it emotionally.

A percentage falls, a new investor appears on the cap table, an option pool expands, and the founder feels that something personal has been diminished. This is not surprising. Startups begin close to the founder's identity, and ownership is one of the first ways that identity becomes formalised. When the ownership share shrinks, the founder often reads that movement not just as a capital event, but as a judgment on importance, power, or status. That is where many of the most damaging mistakes begin.

The first mistake is to treat dilution as pure theft. Founders sometimes react as though every reduction in percentage ownership means that someone has taken something that properly belonged to them. In a narrow sense, this feeling can seem plausible, especially if the founder has spent months or years carrying the company through uncertainty before other people arrived. But the theft frame is usually too crude. In most cases, dilution occurs because the company has chosen to issue new claims in exchange for something: capital, talent, time, survival, or future capacity. That does not automatically make the exchange wise, but it does mean the founder is not dealing with simple dispossession. When founders see all dilution as theft, they often become incapable of distinguishing between the dilution that weakens them and the dilution that helps build a stronger company around their remaining stake.

The second mistake is the mirror image of the first. Some founders internalise the opposite slogan that dilution is normal, so they stop examining it seriously at all. They tell themselves that everyone gets diluted, that this is just how startups work, and that resisting it is amateurish. This can make them feel sophisticated, but it can also make them careless. Not all dilution is healthy. Some is simply expensive. Some is badly timed. Some is piled on top of earlier weak decisions. Some reflects investor leverage rather than company strength. A founder who normalises dilution too quickly may fail to notice when the company is giving away too much future upside for too little strategic return. In that sense, over-maturity can be as dangerous as immaturity. The founder becomes passive where judgment is needed.

A third psychological mistake is anchoring too hard to the original percentage. Founders often treat the first cap table as though it were the company's natural moral shape.

If they began with eighty percent, then eighty percent becomes the mental benchmark against which every future state is judged. Anything lower feels like damage. The problem is that the first cap table is usually not the natural final form of a startup that intends to hire, raise capital, and scale. It is simply the first form. A founder who anchors too strongly to that beginning will tend to experience each necessary change as a departure from rightful order rather than as part of the company's development. This makes later decisions much harder because the founder is comparing every new structure not with what the company needs, but with what the company looked like before it had to become anything more complex than a founding arrangement.

Another common mistake is confusing paper percentage with actual power. A founder may look at a dilution event and conclude that they have lost control because the number beside their name has dropped. Sometimes that is true, but often the reality is more nuanced. Control depends on more than headline ownership. It depends on voting rights, board composition, class structure, investor protections, and sometimes on the practical influence the founder retains over the business. Conversely, another founder may focus too much on keeping a numerically large stake and fail to notice that protective provisions elsewhere in the deal are changing the real balance of power more than the percentage itself. In both cases, the founder mistakes one visible metric for the whole structure. Dilution affects control, but it does not measure control all by itself.

The next mistake is a particularly human one. Founders often compare their diluted position not with realistic alternatives, but with a fantasy version of the company in which they somehow preserved the original ownership while still receiving all the benefits of capital, talent, and growth. This imaginary company is psychologically powerful because it makes every real deal look bad. In the founder's mind, there is always a version of events where the company raised less, hired differently, negotiated harder, or waited longer and somehow ended up just as strong with much less dilution. Sometimes a better deal was indeed possible. Often the fantasy ignores real trade-offs. The company may not have survived without the capital, may not have recruited the key people without the pool, or may not have had the leverage to force better terms. Founders who compare real ownership outcomes to impossible alternatives become needlessly bitter and strategically confused.

A related mistake is focusing only on the immediate round while ignoring cumulative effect. Founders may accept a dilution event because, taken alone, it seems tolerable. Ten percent here, a pool expansion there, a convertible instrument that does not feel real yet, another round later that can surely be handled when it comes. The founder reacts to each event locally and never fully processes what the whole sequence is doing. By the time the cumulative effect becomes emotionally obvious, the room for correction has narrowed. This is a psychological mistake because each individual event can feel small enough to avoid serious discomfort. Human beings are not naturally good at feeling compounding until it has already worked on them for some time. In ownership, that weakness can be extremely expensive.

There is also the mistake of treating dilution as humiliation rather than as structure. This appears most often when founders make dilution part of their identity story. They begin to see their ownership percentage as a measure of whether they are still truly the founder in the meaningful sense. A lower number therefore feels like demotion. This can become very destructive because it turns negotiations that should be commercial into negotiations about pride. The founder stops asking what ownership position will leave them well-motivated inside a stronger company and starts asking what number still feels worthy of their personal origin story. Once this happens, rational trade-offs become harder because the founder is no longer defending only economics. They are defending self-conception.

That self-conception can also distort how founders speak to one another. In multiple-founder teams, one founder may panic more than another about dilution because they are more attached to status than to economic interpretation. Another may act relaxed about dilution because they have not modelled the long-term consequences carefully enough. These different temperaments can create conflict that looks like disagreement over the deal but is really disagreement over what ownership means psychologically. One founder is protecting identity. Another is protecting future optionality. Another is trying to preserve harmony by pretending the details are smaller than they are. If the team does not name these psychological dynamics, they can end up arguing about numbers while actually disagreeing about emotion, trust, and fear.

Fear itself is perhaps the deepest psychological force here. Dilution can make founders feel that the company is slipping away from them even before any real loss of control has happened. That fear is not always irrational. Some founders do in fact lose meaningful influence through repeated financing. But fear becomes harmful when it prevents the founder from reading structure accurately. It can make them reject necessary capital, overreact to ordinary rounds, cling to inefficient ownership concentration, or treat everyone around the table as a threat. In that state, the founder is no longer governing the cap table. The cap table is governing the founder's emotional life.

The cure for these mistakes is not indifference. Founders should care about dilution. They should model it carefully, challenge it, and resist bad versions of it. What they need is not less seriousness, but a cleaner mind. They need to ask what is happening structurally, what the company is receiving, what future rounds are likely, what their post-dilution position means in terms of both incentive and control, and whether the value created is substantial enough to justify the percentage surrendered. That line of thought does not remove emotion, but it disciplines it. The founder stops reacting only to the shrinking number and starts evaluating the evolving company.

In the end, the great psychological trap of dilution is that it tempts founders to confuse visibility with importance. The percentage change is visible. The future value created by capital, hiring, runway, and strategic strength is less immediately visible. The wise founder learns to look past the first instinct and ask the more difficult question. Not how much smaller is my percentage, but what kind of company do I now own a smaller piece of, and is that company materially stronger than the one I had before.

The Difference Between Being Diluted and Being Destroyed

One of the most important distinctions a founder can learn is the distinction between being diluted and being destroyed. The two are often conflated because both involve a reduction in the founder's relative position, but they are not the same thing. A founder can be diluted and still remain highly motivated, economically significant, strategically relevant, and well placed to benefit from the company's future. A founder can also reach a point at which the ownership structure has become so distorted that the founder's stake, while still technically present, no longer functions as a meaningful engine of incentive or control. The first is a normal part of startup growth. The second is a structural failure. Founders who do not understand the difference often either panic too early or notice too late that the cap table has moved from healthy evolution into serious danger.

Dilution, in its ordinary form, means the founder owns a smaller percentage than before because new claims have been added to the company. That can be painful, but it does not by itself imply ruin. If the founder still owns a substantial stake in a company that is becoming stronger, if the rights attached to that stake remain meaningful, if the company's likely path to value creation remains attractive, and if the founder is still sufficiently aligned with the upside to justify carrying the burden of the work, then dilution may simply be part of the normal cost of scaling. The founder has lost proportion, but not their place in the business.

Destruction is something more severe. A founder is structurally destroyed when the cap table and associated rights leave them in a position so weak that the relationship between their labour and their likely reward has become irrational. This can happen in several ways. The founder may be diluted through repeated rounds until the remaining stake is too thin to carry the motivational weight that startup life demands. The founder may retain a non-trivial percentage on paper but sit beneath a stack of preferences, investor protections, or cumulative claims that dramatically reduce the practical value of that holding in likely exit scenarios. The founder may lose enough governance influence that they carry execution risk without retaining meaningful strategic authority. Or the founder may be squeezed between investor demands, legacy dead equity, and future dilution such that the company can continue, but their role inside it no longer feels economically coherent.

This distinction matters because founders often misread ordinary dilution as destruction simply because the percentage movement feels unpleasant. A founder who moves from sixty percent to forty-five percent in exchange for a sensible round, an expanded team, and real strategic progress may feel harmed, but in many cases that founder remains in a very strong position. The company may be better resourced, more credible, and more valuable, and the founder may still hold one of the largest and most meaningful stakes in the structure. If the founder treats that outcome as equivalent to being wiped out, they will often make terrible future decisions, either by resisting useful capital or by entering negotiations from an emotionally defensive posture that obscures what the company actually needs.

On the other hand, there are founders who comfort themselves with the word dilution when something much worse is happening. They tell themselves that this is just how startups work, that everyone gets diluted, that percentages are only numbers, and that what matters is building the company. Sometimes that attitude is mature. Sometimes it is a way of refusing to confront the fact that the company is ceasing to make sense for them. A founder who owns a small sliver beneath heavy investor preference, while also carrying the operational burden and having little real control, may not be merely diluted. They may be nearing the point where the economics of staying no longer match the sacrifices being demanded. To call that ordinary dilution would be a euphemism. It would conceal the structural damage behind a term that is too mild.

This is why founders need criteria for recognising the difference. The first criterion is incentive. After the dilution event, does the founder still hold enough of the company that the upside remains meaningful if the company succeeds. Meaningful is contextual. It depends on the type of company, the likely scale of exits, the stage of the business, the founder's life situation, and the expected future dilution still to come. But the question is indispensable. Startups demand years of uncertain labour, reputational exposure, opportunity cost, and emotional strain. If the founder's post-dilution position leaves only a remote or thin prospect of proportional reward relative to those burdens, the cap table may have crossed from dilution into something closer to structural dispossession.

The second criterion is governance. Can the founder still exercise enough influence over the strategic direction of the business that the role remains coherent. This does not mean the founder must control everything. In mature companies and heavily financed startups, full founder control is often neither possible nor desirable. But if the founder is left carrying enormous responsibility while having too little say in major decisions, then the ownership structure may be out of balance. Destruction is not only about losing money. It can also mean losing the practical relationship between leadership burden and authority.
The third criterion is exit reality. Founders often look only at their headline percentage without modelling how preferences, liquidation stacks, and future rounds may affect what they would actually receive in plausible outcomes.

A founder can appear to hold a respectable stake and still be in a deeply weakened position if the company would need to achieve a very high exit before the common equity beneath the preference stack begins to produce meaningful returns. In such a case, the founder's stake may have symbolic value but limited practical value in many real-world scenarios. This is one of the most common ways founders are "not destroyed" on paper while being far more exposed than they realise in practice.

The fourth criterion is room for future dilution. A founder may survive the present round comfortably but still be heading toward danger if the current structure leaves very little margin for later financing, later option expansion, or any correction of existing weaknesses. This is why destruction is often a process rather than a moment. A founder is not necessarily destroyed because of the current number alone, but because the current number, combined with what the company is likely to need next, implies a future in which the founder's position becomes too thin to remain sensible. Wise founders therefore judge not only the present round, but the likely path from here.

This distinction also helps founders think more clearly about negotiation. If a founder believes every dilution event is existential, they will negotiate as though any movement is catastrophic, which often leads to rigidity, fear, or refusal of beneficial deals. If a founder fails to recognise the possibility of actual structural destruction, they may negotiate too casually and notice the damage only when it is no longer easy to reverse. The useful middle ground is a sober understanding that many rounds will dilute the founder without destroying them, but some combinations of valuation, rights, timing, and accumulated prior mistakes can in fact begin to hollow out the founder's position in a way that should provoke much stronger resistance.

It is also worth noting that destruction is not always a function of the founder's raw percentage being low. In some highly successful companies, founders own relatively modest percentages and still become extraordinarily wealthy and influential because the company's scale is so large. Conversely, in smaller or more heavily preference-laden structures, a founder may retain what looks like a respectable percentage and still be in a weak practical position. This is why the distinction cannot be reduced to a fixed number. There is no universal line at which dilution becomes destruction. The question is always what the founder's remaining ownership means inside this actual company, with this actual capital structure, on this actual likely trajectory.

At a human level, the distinction is important because founders need language that is more precise than fear. If they feel every reduction in stake as annihilation, they will struggle to build rationally. If they lack language for recognising true structural harm, they may remain in arrangements that no longer make economic or strategic sense. The phrase being diluted should describe a founder whose share has decreased while a meaningful relationship to the company's future still remains. The phrase being destroyed should be reserved for situations in which that relationship has been weakened so badly that the founder's continuing role is no longer matched by the likely upside, authority, or strategic position left to them.

That is the real difference. Dilution is often a price paid to build something stronger. Destruction is what happens when the structure asks the founder to keep carrying the company after the cap table has ceased to reward, protect, or recognise that burden in any meaningful way. Wise founders must learn to tell those two situations apart, because one should often be accepted with discipline and the other resisted before it becomes irreversible.

* * *

SEVEN

Option Pools and Employee Equity

"If you want to build a great company, you have to give people a piece of the upside."

- Sam Altman

Why Startups Use Equity to Hire

A startup usually begins with too little of almost everything that established companies take for granted. It has too little cash, too little certainty, too little infrastructure, too little brand credibility, and often too little time. Yet it still needs serious people. It needs engineers, operators, designers, sales staff, researchers, marketers, product leaders, compliance specialists, or some other form of high-value labour without which the company cannot become more than a founder's ambitious outline. This is the central hiring problem of the startup. It must persuade capable people to join a venture that is riskier, poorer, less stable, and often more demanding than the alternatives available to them. Equity is one of the main tools by which startups try to solve that problem.

The logic is simple enough at first glance. If the company cannot pay top-market cash now, it offers a share in possible future upside later. In doing so, it tries to convert present weakness into future attraction. The employee is asked to accept some combination of lower salary, greater uncertainty, or higher workload in exchange for the chance that the company succeeds and their ownership becomes meaningfully valuable. This is why equity sits so naturally inside startup life. It allows the company to recruit not only with money already earned, but with a share of money that might one day exist if the company is built successfully.

That future-facing structure is one of the reasons equity is so powerful. Startups do not merely need labour. They need committed labour under uncertainty. They need people willing to endure ambiguity, partial systems, shifting priorities, funding stress, and the ordinary chaos of an immature business. Cash alone does not always buy that kind of commitment, especially when a better-funded employer can offer more cash with less risk. Equity changes the psychological and economic proposition. It says, in effect, that the employee is not merely being paid to do a job. They are being invited into a more owner-like relationship with the venture. Their reward, if the company succeeds, may rise far above what the cash salary alone would have suggested.

This matters because startups are not built only by the founders once the business becomes real. They are built by widening circles of contribution. The first key engineer who joins when the product is still fragile, the operator who creates internal order before the company has enough scale to deserve it, the commercial lead who turns scattered interest into repeatable revenue, the specialist who helps the startup cross a regulatory threshold or technical bottleneck, all of these people may contribute in ways that are disproportionate to their salary and even, at times, disproportionate to their formal title. Equity is one of the few tools the startup has for recognising that disproportion. It is a way of saying that some work matters to the future of the enterprise in a way that should not be treated as ordinary labour bought entirely with ordinary wages.

There is also a cash-management reason why startups use equity. In early-stage businesses, preserving cash is often as important as raising it. A company may have only limited runway, and every pound spent on payroll is a pound that cannot be spent on product development, infrastructure, customer acquisition, regulatory progress, or simply on buying time to reach the next milestone. Equity allows the startup to stretch its resources. By combining salary with ownership upside, the business can sometimes attract people it could never afford on a cash-only basis. This does not mean equity is free. It is not free at all. It is paid out of the company's future structure rather than out of current cash. But for a startup, that trade can be rational because present liquidity is often more constrained than future ownership capacity.

That trade, however, only works if the employee believes the equity means something real. This is where many founders get into trouble. They speak about equity as though it were automatically attractive simply because it exists. In reality, startup equity is only compelling when it is credible. The employee has to believe that the company has some plausible path to value creation, that the ownership grant has enough scale to matter if success occurs, and that the company understands the difference between symbolic participation and meaningful upside.

A grant that sounds impressive in raw numbers but represents a tiny and heavily diluted fraction of the business may not function as a serious hiring tool once the candidate understands the context. Equity therefore works not through magic but through legibility. The company must be able to explain what is being offered, under what conditions, and why it is worth taking seriously.

This is one reason employee equity sits directly inside cap table strategy rather than outside it. Founders sometimes talk as though hiring is one issue and ownership is another. In serious startups, the two quickly become inseparable. If the company expects to attract important people with equity, then it needs room on the cap table to do so. It needs to think about option pools, future dilution, and how much ownership should be reserved for the team that has not yet joined. This is not an afterthought. It is one of the central planning questions of startup building. A company that refuses to think about equity for employees often discovers later that it has preserved too much founder concentration at the cost of making serious recruitment harder. Conversely, a company that uses equity carelessly can weaken the founder position without actually building a stronger team. The challenge is not whether to use equity, but how intelligently to use it.

It is also important to see that equity changes the meaning of work inside the company. Someone paid only in salary is, in a narrow economic sense, compensated primarily for labour delivered in the present. Someone with meaningful equity is being linked to the long-term outcome of the business. That does not automatically make them a founder, and founders should be careful not to blur that line too casually. But it does change the relationship. The employee has a reason to care about future value creation, not merely current wages. This can strengthen alignment if handled well. It can make key hires think more like builders than like short-term contractors. It can also make the company feel more coherent because those helping to create the future are given some formal participation in it.

Yet there is a danger here too. Founders sometimes romanticise employee equity and assume it will solve all incentive problems by itself. It will not. Equity does not automatically produce loyalty, brilliance, or cultural cohesion. Poorly explained equity can breed cynicism rather than commitment.

Tiny grants sold as life-changing opportunities can make a company look unserious. Grants that are not properly documented or that sit inside a badly managed cap table may create confusion rather than alignment. The company must therefore resist the temptation to treat equity as motivational decoration. If it is going to be used, it has to be used as part of a real ownership strategy, not as a theatrical substitute for clear compensation thinking.

This is why employee equity is best understood as a bridge between two conditions. On one side is the startup's present inability to compete fully on salary, stability, and institutional polish. On the other is the possibility that the company becomes something valuable enough that those who joined early and contributed materially should share in that upside. Equity is the bridge between those two points. It asks employees to trust that the company may become stronger in the future, and it asks the company to make that trust concrete enough that it is not merely emotional manipulation. When done well, this is one of the most elegant mechanisms in startup finance. It allows the company to recruit with a mixture of realism and ambition, neither pretending it can pay like a mature business nor pretending that hope alone is adequate compensation.

There is also a broader economic truth beneath this. Modern startups often derive much of their value from intangible capital: code, product design, process knowledge, network effects, domain expertise, and the accumulated quality of the team itself. In such businesses, labour and value creation are tightly linked. The employee does not merely operate a machine whose value exists elsewhere. The employee is often actively creating the thing that later becomes valuable. Equity reflects that more accurately than salary alone can. It tells the truth that future company value may be built by a wider group than the founders, and that the ownership structure should, within limits, recognise this.

That is why startups use equity to hire. Not because equity is fashionable, and not because founders enjoy giving away part of the future, but because a young company often cannot become what it hopes to become through founder labour and cash salary alone. It needs a mechanism for sharing upside with the people whose contribution will help create that upside in the first place. Equity is that mechanism. Whether the company uses it well is another question, and the next sections will begin to answer it.

What Options Are and What They Are Not

One of the most persistent sources of confusion in startup ownership is the difference between owning shares and holding options over shares. Founders often speak loosely about "giving equity" to employees when what they really mean is granting stock options, and employees often hear the language of ownership before they understand the conditions attached to it. This looseness is dangerous because options are not the same thing as shares, and the difference affects value, timing, risk, tax, motivation, and the company's own cap table planning. A startup that does not understand this clearly is likely to miscommunicate with hires and mismanage its future ownership structure at the same time.

An option is, in essence, a right to acquire shares in the future, usually at a set exercise or strike price, subject to specified conditions. A share, by contrast, is an actual unit of ownership in the company. The distinction sounds simple, but its consequences are large. A person holding shares is already a shareholder. A person holding options may become a shareholder later if they satisfy the vesting conditions, remain in the company long enough, and in many cases choose to exercise the options in accordance with the plan rules. Until then, the option holder has a contingent position. They are economically connected to the future possibility of ownership, not yet sitting inside the ownership structure in the same way as someone who already holds issued stock.

This is why options are best understood as a bridge between contribution and ownership rather than ownership itself. The company is saying to the employee that if you remain, contribute, and satisfy the terms of this arrangement, you will have the right to buy into the company on terms set now, before the future is known. That can be highly valuable if the company succeeds, because the right to acquire shares at a low historic strike price may later become economically attractive. But the option is not the same thing as the share. It is the possibility of crossing into ownership later.

That difference matters immediately for how founders speak. When founders tell employees they are "getting equity," they often think they are simplifying. In reality, they may be blurring a crucial distinction. Equity granted as options is conditional. It usually vests over time. It may lapse if the employee leaves too early. It may require the employee to pay a strike price to exercise. It may have tax consequences depending on the jurisdiction and the timing of exercise. It may sit in a class of common stock beneath investor preferences. And it may derive most of its real value only in particular future scenarios. All of this can still make options a powerful and rational incentive tool, but only if the company is honest about what they are.

This is one reason employees often misunderstand startup compensation. A candidate hears that they are being offered 50,000 options and interprets that as immediate ownership. Another hears the raw number and imagines a life-changing payout without asking what fraction of the company the grant actually represents, what the fully diluted share count is, what the strike price will be, whether the options are tax-advantaged, or what happens if they leave before a liquidity event. The startup may even encourage that confusion unintentionally by speaking in emotionally generous language while remaining imprecise about mechanics. A serious company resists that temptation. It explains that options are a path into ownership, not ownership already in hand.

For founders, the option structure solves several problems at once. It allows the company to promise future upside without issuing all the shares immediately. It ties that upside to continued service through vesting. It keeps more structural flexibility in the early phase because unvested options can lapse if the employee leaves, rather than leaving the company with immediate dead equity. It also helps align incentives without requiring the founders to permanently allocate a large amount of current ownership before they know whether the hire will become central to the business. In this sense, options are one of the most practical instruments in startup design. They let the company link participation in future value to actual time and contribution rather than to hope alone.

Yet the fact that options are useful does not mean they are simple. Founders need to understand what they are not as much as what they are. They are not guaranteed wealth. They are not automatically equivalent to a salary sacrifice at a one-to-one emotional level. They are not immune to dilution. They are not always immediately exercisable. They are not senior to preferred rights just because the employee helped build the company. And they are not necessarily meaningful if the grant is tiny relative to the company's capital structure or if the likely exit outcomes would leave little for common holders after preferences are paid. An option can be real and still be of limited practical value.

That truth should not be hidden, because once employees discover it later, trust is harder to repair.

The option-versus-share distinction also matters for the company's own cap table discipline. A startup may have an option pool reserved for future grants, but until grants are made and then exercised, those options do not occupy the same position as already issued common shares. At the same time, they cannot simply be ignored. Sophisticated investors and founders often think in fully diluted terms precisely because options and other future claims already shape the structure the company is preparing to live with. The company therefore has to be able to hold two truths at once. Options are not the same thing as issued shares in current legal ownership. But they are part of the broader ownership story the company must understand when planning dilution, incentives, and future rounds.

There is also an important behavioural difference between shares and options. A founder or investor holding actual stock has already crossed the threshold into ownership and is experiencing the company from inside that position. An employee with options often experiences the company differently because their economic relationship is still partly anticipatory. They are earning toward something. This can be motivating if the company is healthy and the terms are clear. It can also become frustrating if the employee feels the grant is opaque, too small, or unlikely ever to produce meaningful value. In that sense, options create a psychological economy as well as a legal one. They ask the employee to believe in a future pathway to ownership, and that pathway has to look credible enough that the belief is not merely exploitative.

This is why the company's internal language around options matters so much. To say "you are an owner" to someone holding options is partly true in spirit and partly false in structure. The person has been invited into a route toward ownership. They may one day become a shareholder. They may be participating in the upside logic of the company. But if the startup uses the language of present ownership too casually, it sets up disappointment. A better discipline is to explain the instrument honestly and then explain why it still matters. Options are not second-rate shares. They are a structured way of aligning long-term contribution with future ownership. That is a respectable thing. It does not need to be oversold as something it is not.

Another reason this distinction is important is that option holders and shareholders may be treated differently in transactions. The terms of the option plan, the timing of vesting, acceleration provisions, exercise windows, and the structure of the exit can all affect what an option holder actually receives or can do. A share is already inside the cap table. An option is still partly governed by the route through which it becomes or fails to become a share. Founders who do not understand this can mislead employees without intending to, and employees who do not understand it can overestimate the certainty of what they have been granted.

In the end, what options are is a conditional right to step into ownership on terms set now for a future that is not yet known. What they are not is immediate, unconditional, fully realised equity in the same sense as already issued shares. That difference must remain clear if the company wants its hiring, compensation, and cap table strategy to remain credible. Once the distinction is secure, the next question becomes more practical. If options are the bridge, how should a startup build the pool from which those options are granted, and what does that do to the company's ownership structure overall.

The Difference Between Shares and Options

At a glance, shares and options can look like two routes to the same place, and in one limited sense that is true. Both relate to company ownership. Both can be used to align people with the future of the business. Both may ultimately lead to someone benefiting if the company becomes valuable. But they do not sit in the same legal, economic, or psychological position, and any startup that treats them as interchangeable will eventually confuse either its employees, its founders, or itself. The difference matters because the cap table is not governed by sentiment. It is governed by what people actually hold, when they hold it, and under what conditions that holding becomes real.

A share is an existing unit of ownership in the company. If you hold a share, you are already inside the ownership structure. The company has issued that share, and your rights arise from the fact that the share exists and belongs to you, subject to whatever restrictions or classes govern it. A share can carry voting rights, economic rights, information rights, and whatever other rights attach to that class of stock.

Even if some of those rights are limited or subordinated, the key fact remains that the shareholder is already a shareholder. The relationship to the company is present tense.
An option is different. An option is not itself a share. It is a contractual right, usually conditional and time-based, to acquire shares later, often at a pre-set exercise price. The relationship to the company is therefore not yet the same as that of a shareholder. The option holder has a future-oriented position. They may become a shareholder if the option vests, if they remain eligible, and if they exercise according to the rules of the plan and the law of the relevant jurisdiction. Until those conditions are satisfied, they are not in the same structural position as someone who already holds issued stock.

This difference matters immediately when thinking about control. A founder or investor who holds actual shares may have formal voting rights. An employee with options usually does not vote merely by holding the option. The employee may feel deeply invested in the company, and the company may treat them culturally as a long-term stakeholder, but that does not change the legal distinction. Options create a path toward ownership. They are not the same thing as current governance power. This is one reason options can be attractive to startups. They allow the company to promise future upside and alignment without immediately introducing new full shareholders in the same way direct share issuance would.

The economic distinction is equally important. A share has immediate economic existence, even if the market value of that share is uncertain or illiquid. An option has contingent economic potential. Its value depends on several things. It depends on whether it vests, whether the company becomes more valuable than the exercise price, whether the holder remains in a position to exercise, whether the company ever reaches a liquidity event, and whether the rights attached to the resulting shares produce meaningful returns in the actual exit structure. This does not make options weak or trivial. In a successful company they can be highly valuable. But that value is further away, more conditional, and more exposed to future structure than the value of already issued stock.
Founders need to understand this because the distinction shapes how they should communicate with hires. If the company says to an employee, you own this much of the company, when the employee in fact holds unvested options that may never convert into meaningful ownership, the

company is not being precise enough. It may feel encouraging in the moment, but it is laying the groundwork for future disappointment. A more serious approach is to say that the employee has been granted the opportunity to earn the right to acquire a certain amount of equity over time, and that the company will explain exactly what that means. That language may sound less glamorous, but it is more respectful because it tells the truth about the instrument being used.

The timing difference between shares and options also shapes incentives in different ways. Shares given directly to a founder or to someone else can create immediate alignment, but they can also create immediate dead equity if that person leaves and the shares are not subject to proper vesting or repurchase rights. Options are often preferred for employees precisely because they reduce this risk. The company does not have to issue full ownership at the beginning. Instead, the employee earns into that ownership. If they leave early, the unvested portion typically falls away, and the company can reuse that capacity for future hires. Options therefore give the startup a more controlled way to build a team without overcommitting the cap table too quickly.

This controlled quality becomes especially important in the first years of a startup, when no one yet knows with certainty which hires will become foundational. A direct share grant says, in effect, we are comfortable placing you inside the ownership structure now. An option grant says, we are prepared to create a structured path by which your continued contribution may bring you into that ownership structure over time. The second is often more appropriate because startups are experimental not only in product but in people. The company needs a mechanism that can recognise contribution without pretending too early that every hire will remain central forever.

At the same time, founders should not think of options as a painless substitute for shares. They still affect the cap table. They still consume ownership capacity. They still create dilution, especially on a fully diluted basis. And they still shape expectations about the company's future. A founder who behaves as though options are almost imaginary because they are not yet shares is making a serious error. The option may be contingent for the holder, but it is already part of the company's broader ownership planning. This is why serious cap table management tracks not only issued shares but also granted options, unallocated pool space, vesting schedules, and future conversion events. The distinction between shares and options is real, but it is not an excuse to ignore the latter until the last minute.

There is another subtle difference worth noticing. Shares usually sit closer to the founder and investor logic of the company. They are tied to people already recognised as part of the formal ownership base. Options sit closer to the company's long-term talent strategy. They are one of the instruments by which the startup translates future hope into present recruitment and retention. That means they often live at the intersection of finance and human motivation. A badly structured share grant can damage the cap table. A badly explained option grant can damage trust in the company's whole compensation philosophy. Founders therefore need to understand not only the legal difference, but the organisational role each instrument is playing.

The tax and practical implications can differ as well, though these vary heavily by jurisdiction and must not be oversimplified. Shares may trigger one set of consequences when issued. Options may create others depending on how the plan is designed, when they vest, when they are exercised, and what type of option regime is being used. This is one of the reasons startups should never rely entirely on intuitive language around equity. The word equity can cover instruments that behave differently enough to matter a great deal. A founder who does not respect that difference may think they are offering something elegant and end up offering something confusing or administratively harmful instead.

For employees, the distinction between shares and options should shape how they evaluate an offer. A share tells them they are already in the cap table. An option tells them they are being invited onto a path that may lead there. Neither is automatically better in all cases. In fact, options are often the more sensible instrument for employees precisely because they are tied to continued service and because they let the company manage its ownership structure more intelligently. But the employee should never be left to discover this difference accidentally. If the company wants equity to function as a serious hiring tool, it has to explain the instrument with enough clarity that the employee knows whether they are receiving present ownership, future conditional ownership, or merely the possibility of it.

The difference between shares and options is therefore not a technical footnote. It is one of the foundation stones of startup compensation and cap table design. Shares are current ownership. Options are a conditional right to move toward ownership later. Shares immediately place someone inside the company's formal capital structure. Options make them part of the company's future ownership planning. Shares are what the company has already issued. Options are part of what the company may later become if contribution continues and the relevant conditions are satisfied.

Once this distinction is secure, the next practical problem becomes unavoidable. If a company is going to use options seriously, it needs a pool from which to grant them, and the creation of that pool has consequences not only for hiring but for every existing holder on the cap table.

Creating an Employee Option Pool

An employee option pool is one of the first places where startup ownership becomes explicitly forward-looking. Up to this point, much of the cap table may have been concerned with claims already made, founder allocations already agreed, investor stakes already issued, and rights already sitting inside the company's structure. The option pool is different. It is ownership space reserved for people who may not even be in the company yet. In that sense it is both practical and philosophical. Practical because the business needs a mechanism to recruit and retain future talent. Philosophical because it forces the founders to admit that part of the company's future value will have to be shared with people who are not yet present but whose eventual contribution may prove decisive.

This is why the option pool matters so much. It is not simply a bucket of shares set aside for later administrative use. It is one of the clearest signals that the company is trying to become something larger than the current set of names on the cap table. The founders are saying, in effect, that they cannot build the whole company alone and that the ownership structure must leave room for the people who will help create the next phase of value. A startup that refuses to make that room may preserve founder concentration in the short term, but often at the cost of making serious hiring more difficult. A startup that creates the pool carelessly may dilute itself too early or too generously without actually strengthening the team. The challenge is to build enough room to recruit meaningfully without surrendering more future ownership than the company can justify.

At the structural level, creating an option pool usually means reserving a defined number of shares or a defined percentage of the company for employee equity grants.

This can happen early, even before many employees exist, because the company wants to plan ahead for the hires it expects to make. That planning is one of the pool's main virtues. It allows the startup to think in ownership terms before each individual hiring negotiation becomes urgent. Instead of improvising equity case by case under pressure, the company creates a framework in advance. That framework can then be allocated more strategically, with a clearer sense of what the company can offer and what that offering costs existing holders in dilution.

This is also why the pool sits so close to the heart of cap table management. The moment the pool is created, the ownership story changes. Even if no options have yet been granted, the company has effectively allocated future space inside the structure. On a fully diluted basis, that often means the founders and existing investors should already think of themselves as owning less than the current issued-share picture might suggest. This is one of the reasons founders so often dislike option pools emotionally. The pool feels like dilution without a named recipient. They see part of the company moving away before a single new person has yet arrived. That feeling is real, but it should be interpreted carefully. The company is not giving ownership away for nothing. It is reserving ownership capacity for the people it expects to need in order to grow.

The size of the pool is therefore one of the first genuinely strategic judgments in startup compensation. Too small, and the company risks repeated awkward expansions, weak offers to key hires, or a slow discovery that it has preserved founder ownership at the price of recruitment weakness. Too large, and the company may dilute itself in anticipation of hiring that never happens, or create a structurally inflated reserve that later investors push back against because it reflects poor planning rather than real talent needs. The right size depends on the stage of the company, the kinds of hires likely to be needed before the next financing event, the market norms for those roles, the current and projected capital structure, and the company's realistic growth plan. There is no single perfect number for all startups, but there is a very clear difference between a pool sized by strategy and one sized by guesswork.

This is where founders need to resist the temptation to think of the pool as a symbolic gesture. Creating an option pool is not merely about being able to say that the company offers equity. It is about having enough credible room to make offers that the right people may actually take seriously.

A startup that needs to hire a key engineering lead, a commercial builder, or a strong operator cannot assume that the candidate will be seduced simply by the word equity. The company must know what range of grants it can plausibly offer to different levels of hire and how many such hires it expects to need before the next major recapitalisation. Without that kind of thinking, the pool becomes either decorative or chaotic. It exists, but the company does not really know what it is for.

Another reason the option pool matters is that it disciplines founder psychology. Founders who build the cap table only around themselves and current investors often tell a story in which the company's future is already morally allocated. The pool interrupts that story. It says that a meaningful portion of the business must remain structurally available to future builders. This is often healthy. It pushes the founders to think less like sole proprietors and more like architects of an institution. At the same time, the pool can become a site of conflict because it makes the cost of future hiring visible. Founders may ask why they should be diluted now for employees not yet hired. Investors may prefer the pool to be created before their round so that the dilution burden falls more heavily on the founders than on the new capital. These tensions are not incidental. They are part of how the ownership structure negotiates the future.

That investor point deserves special attention because it is one of the most common moments at which founders discover what the option pool really means in practice. Investors often want the pool created or enlarged before a financing closes. The reason is simple. If the pool is created before the round, its dilutive effect falls principally on the existing holders, usually the founders and any earlier investors. If the pool is created after the round, the new investors are diluted along with everyone else. Investors therefore have an incentive to define the pre-money structure in a way that already contains enough option capacity for near-term hiring. Founders who do not understand this can end up thinking they negotiated one valuation while, in practical ownership terms, accepting something weaker once the pre-money pool expansion is factored in. This is one of the clearest examples of why the pool is not just an HR tool. It is a financing variable.

There is also an organisational question at the heart of pool creation. What kind of company is this business trying to become before the next major round or milestone.

A startup planning to remain lean and founder-driven for a longer period may not need the same pool as one that must rapidly recruit several high-calibre operators to hit product, revenue, or regulatory goals. The pool should therefore reflect the company's actual talent strategy rather than generic startup custom. Founders often look for a standard percentage because standards feel easier than bespoke thinking, but the wiser approach is to begin with expected hiring and work backwards. Which roles are essential. How many of them. At roughly what seniority. In what market context. Under what salary constraints. Only then does the pool begin to take on a rational shape.

One must also remember that a pool is not automatically a promise to every future employee. It is a reserve of capacity from which grants may be made. This distinction matters because founders sometimes behave as though creating the pool means the dilution is already emotionally justified by future hires who have not yet been evaluated. In reality, the pool should be treated as a resource to be deployed carefully. The company still needs discipline around who receives options, how much, on what vesting terms, and for what strategic reason. Creating the pool is not the end of equity discipline. It is the point at which that discipline becomes institutional rather than ad hoc.

This is why option pools should be revisited regularly but not casually. If the pool is being exhausted faster than expected, the company should ask whether that reflects good strategic hiring, overly generous grants, poor initial sizing, or changes in the business model. If the pool remains largely untouched for a long time, the company should ask whether it has reserved too much dilution for a hiring plan that never really materialised. A well-run startup does not create the pool and then forget it. It treats the pool as part of the living cap table, subject to the same need for maintenance, realism, and clear explanation as any other major ownership element.

At bottom, creating an employee option pool is an act of foresight. It is the company acknowledging that future value creation requires future participants and that those participants will need to be brought into the ownership structure in a way that is serious enough to matter. If the founders understand this, the pool stops looking like abstract dilution and starts looking like planned capacity. If they do not, it will feel like invisible loss and will often be handled badly, especially once investors begin pressing on it in real financing discussions. That is why the option pool deserves to be treated not as a technical side issue but as one of the central bridges between hiring strategy and ownership structure. It is where the company begins reserving part of its future for the people who have not yet arrived but without whom that future may never fully exist.

How Option Pools Dilute Founders

Option pools are one of the clearest examples of why founders need to understand dilution beyond investor rounds. Many founders begin their ownership education by thinking almost exclusively about capital. They imagine dilution as something that happens when an investor writes a cheque and receives newly issued shares. That is certainly one of the main ways dilution occurs, but it is not the only one, and in some startups the option pool becomes one of the earliest and most psychologically jarring sources of it. The founder is diluted not because outside capital has entered, but because the company has decided that future employees need room on the cap table before they even arrive.

This can feel especially strange because the dilution often appears before any obvious compensation has been received in return. In an investor round, the founder can at least point to the cash, the runway, the strategic partner, or the external validation. With an option pool, the founder sees percentage reduction while the company may still have no new hire, no new product capability, and no visible operational gain. The dilution is immediate in structural terms, but the value it is intended to purchase lies in the future. That temporal gap is one reason option pools often provoke anxiety. The founder feels the cost first and only later, if the hiring strategy is good, sees the benefit.To understand why this happens, the founder has to remember what the pool is doing. The company is reserving ownership space for people who are not yet on the team but whom the company expects to need. On a fully diluted basis, this means the founders and other existing holders should already think of those shares as part of the future ownership landscape. If the company creates a ten percent pool, the founders have in a very real sense accepted that ten percent of the company's future has been structurally earmarked for talent rather than retained entirely by current holders. That is dilution, even if the grants themselves come later and in stages.

A simple example shows the logic clearly. Suppose a founder owns 1,000 shares out of 1,000 total shares and therefore owns one hundred percent of the company. The company then creates an option pool of 200 shares for future employees. Even if those options have not yet been granted to named individuals, the fully diluted picture becomes 1,200 shares. The founder's effective ownership on that basis is no longer one hundred percent, but 1,000 divided by 1,200, or roughly eighty-three point three percent. Nothing has yet happened operationally. No new engineer has joined, no head of sales has accepted an offer, no product leader has arrived. Yet the company has already changed the founder's position because it has changed the structure the company is preparing to inhabit.

This is why founders often find option pool dilution more emotionally irritating than investor dilution. It feels anticipatory rather than earned. The company has given away room before it has actually secured the people who justify the room. That irritation is not foolish. It reflects a real tension in startup design. Founders are being asked to absorb present structural cost for future hiring that is still hypothetical. The answer is not to deny the irritation. The answer is to decide whether the planned hiring is genuinely necessary and whether the pool is sized in a way that makes sense relative to the company's stage and likely needs.

Another reason option pools dilute founders so visibly is that they are often created before financing rounds at the insistence of incoming investors. In such cases, the founder may initially believe they are negotiating one deal only to realise that the investor expects the company to enlarge the pool pre-money. This matters because if the pool is expanded before the new investment arrives, the dilution from the pool falls primarily on the existing holders, usually the founders and any earlier investors. The new investor then buys into a company that already contains the future hiring burden. Founders who are not paying close attention can therefore underestimate how much of the effective dilution in a round comes not from the investor's shares themselves, but from the pool expansion attached to the round.

This is where cap table sophistication becomes essential. A founder must ask not only what percentage is being sold to the investor, but what the company's ownership structure looks like before and after the pool is created, and who bears the economic cost of that creation. A founder who sees only the headline investor percentage may think the round is better than it is.

A founder who understands that the pool is also part of the transaction sees more clearly what the company is actually paying. This does not mean pool expansion is necessarily abusive. If the company truly needs that hiring capacity before the next round, creating the pool may be perfectly rational. But the founder must recognise that the dilution is real and should be priced into their understanding of the deal.

There is also a cumulative effect here. Option pool dilution rarely remains a one-off event. If the company hires aggressively, grants equity quickly, and then later needs to refresh or expand the pool, the founders can experience repeated rounds of pool-driven dilution over the life of the startup. This is especially important in talent-heavy businesses where the company must compete for scarce engineering, scientific, product, or regulatory talent. In those companies, the option pool is not merely a small side reserve. It becomes a continuing mechanism by which founder ownership gives way, bit by bit, to the workforce needed to build the company. Again, this may be the right trade, but it should never be invisible.

Founders also need to resist the temptation to think of option pool dilution as somehow less serious because it is going to employees rather than investors. It may feel nobler, and in some respects it is often easier to justify culturally. Employees are helping build the company. They may be taking salary risk and joining at an uncertain stage. But from the perspective of ownership mathematics, the company is still allocating part of the future away from current holders. Sentiment should not obscure that. If the grants are well chosen and the hires materially strengthen the business, the dilution may be excellent value. If the pool is oversized, the grants poorly disciplined, or the hires weak, then founder ownership may be thinning without enough corresponding increase in company capability.

This is one of the reasons option pool management is inseparable from hiring discipline. A startup that hires well and grants thoughtfully can use the pool to build a much more valuable business, leaving the founders with a smaller but stronger stake. A startup that hires loosely, over-grants to mediocre contributors, or uses equity as an easy substitute for clarity and cash discipline can erode founder ownership while failing to create the team quality that was supposed to justify the loss.

The option pool does not dilute founders in a morally clean way just because it is for employees. It dilutes them in a way that must still be judged by return on structural sacrifice.

Another subtle issue is that the founder often feels the dilution before the hires themselves feel fully real. A great new employee may take months to find, months to onboard, and longer still to prove transformative. During that period, the option pool already exists on the company's fully diluted picture. This can make the founder feel that the company is paying in advance for value it has not yet received. Sometimes that is exactly what is happening, and the trade is still sensible because that advance payment is the only way to compete for the people the business needs. But it does mean the founder must think probabilistically. The pool is a bet that future talent will be worth the structural cost. Like any bet, it can be well made or badly made.

This is why the right founder response is neither blanket resistance nor careless acceptance. Founders should ask how much pool is being created, what actual hires it is expected to support, what likely grant ranges those hires require, when the next financing event may occur, and whether the company is being asked to absorb more pre-money dilution than is truly necessary. Once those questions are asked, the founder can distinguish between a pool that is a rational piece of hiring infrastructure and a pool that has become an investor convenience or a founder blind spot. In both cases dilution occurs, but only one may deserve to occur.

In the end, option pools dilute founders because they reserve part of the company's future for people who are not yet on the cap table but whom the company expects to need. That dilution is real even before grants are made. It can be excellent strategy if it leads to hires who materially increase the company's value and strength. It can also become a quiet source of structural weakness if the pool is oversized, poorly negotiated, or badly used. The founder's task is not to deny the dilution, but to understand exactly what it is buying and to make sure the company receives enough in return for what it is giving up.

Why Investors Push Option Pools Before Funding

One of the first moments when many founders realise that the option pool is not merely an internal hiring tool but a central financing issue is when an investor insists that the pool be created or enlarged before the round closes. To the founder, this can feel like a strange and irritating demand. The company is trying to raise money, and yet the investor is focusing not only on the price, the amount raised, or the percentage being purchased, but also on how much ownership space will be reserved for future employees. At first glance this may look like unnecessary interference or even tactical opportunism. In truth, it is usually both a strategic concern and, very often, a pricing move.

The strategic concern is easy enough to understand. Serious investors know that the company they are funding will almost certainly need more people than it currently has. If the startup is going to use equity to recruit those people, then the structure has to contain enough room to do so. An investor who enters a company with no realistic pool, or with a pool that is too small for the next phase of hiring, knows that the ownership structure will have to be adjusted again soon. That future adjustment will dilute everyone, including the new investor. It is therefore rational for the investor to want the company's likely hiring needs addressed at the time of the financing rather than treated as a vague future problem.

That is the clean strategic explanation, and in many cases it is perfectly legitimate. Investors are not wrong to care whether the startup will have enough option capacity to recruit the next key engineer, product lead, commercial operator, or other essential hire before the next round. A company that raises money without enough room to build the next layer of the team may find itself constrained very quickly. From that perspective, the pool is part of making the financing actually fit the company's next phase of life.

But there is another, more transactional reality underneath this, and founders need to understand it clearly. The timing of when the pool is created matters because it affects who bears the dilution. If the option pool is created before the investment, then the pre-money holders, usually the founders and any existing shareholders, absorb most of that dilution. If the pool is created after the investment, then the new investor is also diluted by the pool expansion. Investors therefore have a clear economic incentive to prefer a pre-money pool. By insisting that the pool be created or topped up before they invest, they are protecting their percentage and shifting more of the hiring burden onto the existing owners.

This is one of the most important places where founders can

misunderstand the actual economics of a round. They may focus on the headline valuation and the stated percentage the investor is taking, while failing to notice that the option pool adjustment has changed the real deal. In effect, the founder may believe they are negotiating one price for the capital when, once the pre-money pool expansion is included, the ownership cost is higher than it first appeared. The round may still be reasonable. The investor may still be right that the company needs the pool. But the founder should never allow the mechanics to remain invisible. The pool is not a side detail. It is part of the price.

A simple example makes this clearer. Suppose a company has 1,000 shares outstanding, all owned by founders and earlier participants. An investor offers to buy 250 new shares, which would imply, in a simplified picture, that the investor owns twenty percent after the round and the existing holders own eighty percent. Now imagine the investor says the company also needs a pool of 200 shares in place before the financing closes. The structure changes before the investor's money even comes in. The existing holders are now being measured against a bigger pre-money denominator, and when the investor's shares are issued, the founder stake ends up thinner than the initial headline calculation suggested. The founder who understood only the twenty percent investor purchase has not really understood the transaction. The company has sold capital and reserved future hiring room at the same time, and both moves have been paid for out of the old owners' share of the future.

This is why sophisticated founders always ask a more exact question than what percentage is the investor taking. They ask what is the fully diluted cap table immediately before and immediately after the round, including any pool expansion required as part of the deal. They ask whether the pool size reflects actual near-term hiring needs or whether it has been padded beyond necessity for the convenience of the new capital. They ask whether the investor is pricing the company as though the pool already exists, while also asking the founders to absorb that pool before money arrives. These are not small technicalities. They are the mechanics through which the real economics of the round are expressed.

To be fair to investors, the desire for a pre-money pool is not necessarily predatory in itself. Investors know that early-stage companies often underestimate how much hiring they will need before the next round. They also know that founders, left to themselves, may resist creating enough pool because they feel the dilution too strongly in the present.

A company can therefore raise money at what looks like a healthy valuation and then almost immediately discover that it lacks enough equity capacity to recruit the team required to hit its next milestones. In that scenario, the investor's insistence on a sensible pool was not cynical. It was realistic. The founder's job is not to reject every investor request around the pool as inherently unfair. The founder's job is to understand when the request is justified by the company's actual needs and when it is being used to improve the investor's position beyond what those needs require.

This is where hiring strategy becomes inseparable from financing literacy. Founders who do not know what kinds of people they need, how many, at what rough equity levels, are very weak in these conversations because they cannot tell whether the proposed pool is sensible. They are negotiating blind. An investor says the company should have fifteen percent in the pool and the founder, having no grounded hiring model, either resists emotionally or accepts passively. Neither is strong. The stronger founder has a view. They know the roles they expect to fill, the likely grant ranges, the timeline before the next round, and therefore the approximate pool capacity the company actually needs. That knowledge allows them to distinguish between a realistic pre-money pool and an inflated one.

There is also a broader lesson here about how investors think. Investors do not only buy the current company. They buy a company as it must become in order for their investment thesis to work. That includes future hires. In that sense, investor pressure around the option pool is often a form of forward modelling. The investor is saying that the current team is not enough and that the cap table must already make provision for the next layer of talent. Founders should take that seriously, because it often contains real operational truth. At the same time, they should not let that truth obscure the financing consequence. The company may indeed need the pool, but it is still important to know who is paying for it.

This is also why the phrase investor is taking twenty percent can be a misleading simplification. The investor may be buying twenty percent on a post-money basis, but if the founders also have to enlarge the option pool pre-money, the effective cost to the founders may be meaningfully higher than the headline number suggests.

Startups that do not understand this often emerge from a round wondering why the founder stake fell further than expected. The arithmetic was always there. The founders simply did not treat the pool as part of the deal, when in fact it was central to it.

Another subtle issue is that investors often prefer the pool to be large enough that a further expansion will not be needed before the next financing. Again, this can be strategically sensible. Repeatedly revisiting the pool creates more complexity and more opportunities for conflict. But it can also produce over-sizing if no one challenges the assumptions behind it. A company can end up reserving more future dilution than its actual hiring plan justifies, effectively weakening the current holders for talent that may never be hired. This is one reason founders should not accept pool sizing as a generic norm. The correct size is not what everyone says is standard. It is what this company realistically needs in order to recruit its next layer of builders before the next major recapitalisation event.

In the end, investors push option pools before funding for two intertwined reasons. First, because they want the company to have enough ownership space to recruit the people needed for the next phase of growth. Second, because having that pool created pre-money protects the investor from bearing as much of the resulting dilution. Both reasons are real. Neither should be ignored. The founder who understands both can negotiate with much more intelligence than the founder who sees only one. The pool may be necessary. It may even be wise. But if it is part of the financing bargain, then it is part of the price, and the founder must learn to read it that way.

How Employees Misunderstand Equity Offers

If founders often misunderstand dilution, employees often misunderstand equity from the other side. The startup says it is offering upside, ownership, and the chance to share in something bigger than a salary. The employee hears hope, status, future wealth, and in many cases a kind of symbolic inclusion in the company's inner circle. Sometimes that hearing is justified. Sometimes it is based on partial truth, vague language, or a poor grasp of what the instrument being offered actually means. This is one of the most common points at which startup compensation becomes confused, because the employee is not only evaluating a financial proposition.

They are evaluating a story about belonging, reward, and future possibility.

The first misunderstanding is usually numerical. A startup offers an employee 50,000 options, 100,000 options, or some other large-sounding number, and the employee, especially if new to startup finance, interprets the count as evidence of major value. The number feels impressive because human beings react strongly to raw scale. Yet the number means almost nothing on its own. Fifty thousand options out of a company with five million fully diluted shares is a very different proposition from fifty thousand options out of a company with fifty million. Without the denominator, the employee is not really evaluating the offer. They are reacting to the emotional effect of the number. Many founders encourage this unintentionally by quoting the grant but not grounding it in the company's actual ownership structure.

The second misunderstanding is conceptual. Employees are often told they are "getting equity" when in reality they are being given options that vest over time and may require exercise to convert into actual shares. This can create a false sense of present ownership. The employee may begin thinking of themselves as already a shareholder in a fully realised sense, when in practice they hold a conditional right that may never fully turn into meaningful stock if they leave early, fail to vest, or never exercise. Again, this does not make the option offer worthless or deceptive by nature. It means only that the instrument must be understood for what it is. Employees who do not see the distinction may later feel misled when they discover that their apparent ownership was more contingent than they were led to believe.

A third misunderstanding concerns value itself. An employee may hear that the company is currently worth, for example, ten million pounds or fifty million dollars and mentally apply that valuation to the options being offered, as though this reveals what the grant is "worth." In practice, that kind of mental multiplication is often much too crude. The grant may vest only over time. The strike price may need to be paid to exercise. The company may raise more money and dilute the position further. Investor preferences may sit above the common equity. The company may never reach an exit. Or it may reach an exit at a level that sounds strong in a headline but leaves far less for common holders than the employee imagined. The employee is therefore not holding a small pile of certain wealth. They are holding a contingent claim on a future outcome filtered through many layers of uncertainty and structure.

This is one reason startup equity can produce either strong alignment or quiet cynicism depending on how it is explained. If the company treats options as though they are almost magical and allows the employee to believe that a large raw number or a current headline valuation tells the whole story, then disappointment is likely later. If the company explains the grant clearly, in percentage terms where possible, with reference to vesting, exercise, dilution, and the ordinary uncertainty of startup outcomes, then the employee may still accept the offer enthusiastically but with better judgment. The difference is not whether the company is optimistic. The difference is whether the optimism is anchored in a truthful understanding of the instrument.

Employees also misunderstand equity offers because they often fail to distinguish between upside and liquidity. A company may become more valuable on paper over several rounds, and the employee may see the implied value of their grant rising in theory, yet still have no practical way to turn that into money. There may be no market for the shares. The company may remain private for years. Exercise windows may create pressure or cost at awkward moments. Secondary sales may be unavailable. The employee therefore has to live with a peculiar form of value that can look substantial in conversation while remaining economically inaccessible in practice. Founders who talk about equity as if paper appreciation were the same as actual wealth are teaching employees the wrong lesson, even if they do not mean to.

Another common misunderstanding is to treat the option grant as a substitute for salary in a simple one-to-one way. Employees may sometimes accept lower cash compensation because the equity offer appears to make up the difference. In some cases this can be entirely rational, especially if the company has real promise and the grant is meaningful. In other cases, employees give up too much in present certainty for an option package that is small, heavily diluted, or unlikely to create enough eventual value to justify the trade. This is especially dangerous when the employee is early in their career, unfamiliar with startup finance, or emotionally influenced by the prestige of being in a startup with an exciting story. The company may not be acting maliciously, but if it relies on that misunderstanding rather than correcting it, the compensation culture becomes ethically weak.

There is also a social misunderstanding that often surrounds early employee equity. Employees may believe the grant means they are almost founder-like, that they are inside the deepest inner circle of the company, or that their relationship to the venture is now morally different from that of later hires. Sometimes that belief contains some truth. Early employees can be enormously important. But options do not automatically erase the structural distinction between founder risk and employee risk, nor do they guarantee equal strategic standing inside the business. If the company blurs those boundaries too loosely, it can create later resentment when employees discover that their formal rights, economic upside, or decision-making influence were never actually as expansive as the emotional language around the grant suggested.

This becomes particularly sensitive when dilution enters the picture. Employees often receive option grants when the company is smaller and then later watch financing rounds reduce the apparent fraction represented by those grants. If they were never properly taught how dilution works, they may feel that something has been taken from them unfairly. In reality, dilution is often part of the structure they entered from the beginning. But fairness in principle does not always feel fair in experience. A startup that wants equity to work as a retention and alignment tool has to prepare employees for the fact that percentages can change, that fully diluted ownership matters, and that the value of the remaining stake depends not just on the percentage but on what the company becomes through those rounds.

Another major misunderstanding is that employees often do not ask enough questions at the point of grant because they do not want to appear unsophisticated or ungrateful. The startup environment can make it feel awkward to ask hard questions about ownership. The employee worries that they will look cynical if they ask about percentage, strike price, exercise timing, tax treatment, dilution, or likely exit waterfall. So they accept broad language where clarity is needed. This is where responsible founders and leaders have a duty to explain more than the employee may know to ask. A company that truly wants equity to align people should not rely on silence and atmosphere. It should explain the instrument in a way that would still look fair if read years later by someone trying to understand whether they were treated honestly.

At the same time, employees can misread equity offers in the other direction by becoming too cynical too quickly. Some hear that options are not immediate cash and conclude that they are almost meaningless. That can also be wrong. In a genuinely strong company, a well-sized grant at the right stage can become very valuable. The point is not that employees should dismiss startup equity as fantasy. The point is that they should see it as structured uncertainty rather than guaranteed wealth. It is a contingent upside instrument whose significance depends on timing, scale, company quality, future dilution, and exit structure. That is a subtler and more mature view than either blind excitement or reflexive contempt.

Founders need to understand these misunderstandings because poorly understood equity is weak equity. It may still bring someone through the door, but it will not reliably create the trust, alignment, and long-term motivation that startups hope it will. If the employee later discovers that the offer meant much less than they believed, the company may have won short-term enthusiasm at the cost of long-term cynicism. A better approach is to speak plainly. Explain that options are not the same as shares. Explain the percentage, or the approximate fully diluted fraction. Explain vesting. Explain strike price and exercise in broad terms. Explain that future rounds will likely dilute everyone. Explain that value depends on what the company becomes and on where common equity sits in the eventual payout structure. A candidate who still wants to join after hearing all that is making a better decision, and is more likely to remain aligned when the company inevitably becomes more complex.

This is the real issue. Employees misunderstand equity offers because startup language often mixes motivation, hope, and ownership in a way that feels inspiring but leaves too much unsaid. The company has a choice. It can benefit from that fog for a while, or it can clear it and build a more serious ownership culture. The second path is harder in the moment but stronger over time, because people who understand what they have been offered are much less likely to feel betrayed by the very structure the company used to attract them.

Retention, Incentives, and False Generosity

The moral case for employee equity is often presented in simple, uplifting terms. The company is inviting people to share in the upside. The team is building something together. Those who help create the future should not be treated only as hired hands.

There is truth in all of this, and in many startups equity does function as a genuine bridge between risk, contribution, and reward. But there is another side to the story that founders need to understand if they want employee equity to work rather than merely sound noble. Equity is not only about generosity. It is about retention and incentive design, and when founders confuse those things they often create a compensation culture that feels humane in the beginning and exploitative later.

The reason is simple. A startup rarely gives equity away as a pure gift. It gives equity because it wants something in return. It wants the employee to join despite uncertainty. It wants them to stay through difficult years. It wants them to think beyond immediate salary. It wants them to care about the company's future, not only about their next pay cycle. It may also want to conserve cash while still appearing competitive in the labour market. None of this is shameful. In fact, it is often rational. But once these realities are recognised, the company can no longer pretend that all equity grants are simply acts of enlightened sharing. They are instruments. They are meant to shape behaviour.

This becomes especially clear when one looks at vesting. A company does not usually grant employee options in full and unconditionally on the first day because the purpose is not just to reward entry. It is to reward continued contribution over time. The startup wants to keep people. It wants the grant to make leaving more costly and staying more attractive. That is what retention means in this context. The employee does not simply receive upside. They are placed inside a structure designed to align their personal timeline with the company's timeline. If the company succeeds and the employee stays long enough, the grant may become meaningful. If they leave early, much of the option package may never vest. Equity therefore operates partly as deferred reward and partly as an anchor tying the employee to the company's future.

This can be healthy. Many businesses genuinely need mechanisms that encourage continuity, especially in the volatile early years when the loss of a key person can be severe. Startups often cannot offer the salary security, institutional prestige, or predictable career path available elsewhere. Equity helps compensate for that by saying that the employee is not merely selling time into uncertainty but participating in the possible upside generated by surviving that uncertainty. In this sense, equity can create a powerful bond between the employee and the company.

It can encourage long-term thinking, strengthen loyalty, and make it easier for the team to endure periods where the present compensation package alone might not feel sufficient.

The danger begins when founders use the language of generosity to disguise the fact that the grant is being asked to do several jobs at once, some of which are much more self-interested than the rhetoric suggests. An option package may be presented as though the company is sharing prosperity in a broad-minded and founder-like spirit, when in reality the grant may be small, heavily diluted, highly contingent, and calibrated partly to justify a lower salary than the market would otherwise demand. In that situation the company is not being generous in the full sense of the word. It is using future upside as an economic bargaining tool. Again, that may still be legitimate. The problem is not the economics. The problem is the false moral framing.

False generosity is dangerous because it creates the wrong expectations. If the employee believes the company is treating them almost like a co-owner in a strong substantive sense, but later discovers that the grant was structurally thin, heavily subordinated, or far less meaningful than the culture around it implied, then disappointment can become much sharper than if the company had been plain from the beginning. A grant that is honestly presented as a retention and incentive mechanism can still be attractive. A grant that is sold as an almost heroic sharing of destiny and later revealed to be modest in practical terms can feel manipulative even if the formal documents were accurate. The startup has then not only compensated badly. It has damaged trust.

This is why founders need to think carefully about what they are actually trying to achieve when they use equity in hiring. If the purpose is retention, the company should admit that to itself. If the purpose is to align someone with the long-term outcome of the business, that too should be clear. If the purpose is partly to offset lower present cash compensation, the founders should not hide from that reality either. Once these motives are seen clearly, the company can ask whether the grant is strong enough and honest enough to do the job it is supposed to do. Too many startups skip this step. They hand out equity under a haze of aspirational language and never quite decide whether the grant is meant to be a recruiting lure, a loyalty device, a long-term wealth creator, or merely a cultural signal. When one instrument is being asked to do all of these things at once without clarity, misunderstandings become almost inevitable.

Retention is often the least glamorous of these motives, but it may be the most important. A startup does not only need to attract people. It needs to keep the right people through the awkward, exhausting middle stages where the story is no longer new and the payoff is not yet visible. Equity can help because it gives the employee a reason to think in years rather than months. But that only works if the grant is large enough to matter and explained well enough that the employee can understand why staying changes their economic position. If the grant is too small, the company may tell itself that it has created alignment when in reality it has only created a talking point. If the vesting schedule and likely future dilution are not explained, the employee may overestimate what they are staying for. In both cases, the retention effect is weaker than the founders imagine.

Incentives are similarly easy to speak about and harder to design well. Founders often say that equity aligns incentives because everyone now wants the company to succeed. At a very general level that is true. But good incentive design requires more than broad desire for success. It requires that the person holding the equity can still see a believable connection between their effort and their eventual reward. If repeated dilution, tiny grants, confusing exercise rules, or weak communication obscure that connection, the incentive value of the equity begins to collapse. The employee may still say the right things, but inwardly the grant stops functioning as a serious source of motivation. The startup then continues talking about ownership culture long after the actual economics have ceased to support it.

There is also a subtle moral risk in giving equity too easily under the guise of generosity. Founders sometimes use broad grants or enthusiastic language because they want to appear expansive, team-oriented, and unlike the cold world of pure salary employment. But if the grants are not tied to a coherent philosophy of contribution and retention, the company may create future inequities between employees or between hires at different stages. Early grants may be oversized because the company was romantic and disorganised. Later grants may be smaller and more disciplined once investor scrutiny arrives. The result is a workforce in which people who contributed modestly early on may hold more attractive positions than later people carrying heavier actual burdens. That is not generosity. It is inconsistency, and inconsistent generosity becomes one of the most politically toxic features of startup compensation once the company matures enough for comparisons to become unavoidable.

This is why equity has to be governed, not merely distributed. A founder who wants to be generous should still ask hard questions. What role is this grant supposed to play. Is it large enough to retain this person meaningfully. Is it honest relative to the company's likely future dilution and exit structure. Is it proportionate to the person's role and stage of entry. Does it fit the broader grant philosophy of the company or is it an emotional one-off. A company that asks these questions can still be generous, but it becomes generous with discipline rather than with drift.

The strongest employee equity cultures are usually the ones that combine ambition with clarity. They do not apologise for the fact that options are meant to retain people and align them with the company's future. Nor do they pretend that every grant is an act of founder-level inclusion. Instead, they explain that the company is using ownership thoughtfully because it wants people to build for the long term and share in what they help create. That is a respectable position. It does not need to hide behind exaggerated rhetoric. In fact, the less it hides, the stronger the trust it tends to create.

The final lesson is that equity becomes false generosity when the startup uses the emotional aura of ownership to avoid being honest about the economics and behaviour it is trying to shape. It becomes real alignment when the company is clear that the grant is both an opportunity and a structure, both a reward and a retention tool, both a statement of trust and a disciplined mechanism for sharing future value. Founders who understand this are much less likely to promise more than the cap table can deliver, and much more likely to build an equity culture that people can still respect once the company has outgrown the romance of its earliest phase.

***

EIGHT

The Arrival of Outside Money

"Whenever you can, raise money when you don't need it."
- Marc Andreessen

The Difference Between Bootstrapping and Funded Growth

The arrival of outside money changes a startup in more ways than the bank balance reveals. Founders often talk about fundraising as though it were simply the moment when the company receives resources it did not previously have. In one narrow sense that is true. Capital enters, runway extends, salaries can be paid more confidently, product development can continue, and the business buys itself time. But this description is too thin. What really changes is the nature of the company's relationship to its own future. A bootstrapped company and a funded company may look similar from a distance, especially in the earliest stage, but they live under very different ownership, governance, and growth logics.

Bootstrapping is usually the condition in which the company is financed primarily by founder resources, founder labour, early customer revenue, or some combination of internal means rather than external equity capital. The bootstrapped startup is constrained, sometimes painfully so, but its ownership story is still relatively concentrated. The founders remain structurally close to the company. Their percentage ownership may still feel large, and their decisions, while difficult, are not yet being filtered through the rights and expectations of professional outside capital. The company moves more slowly, often with less margin for error, but it retains a certain purity of ownership and decision-making. The founders are carrying most of the risk, and in exchange they retain most of the future upside.

This arrangement has real strengths. A bootstrapped company often learns discipline early because it has no choice. It must think carefully about spending. It must hire more slowly. It must earn traction or revenue with fewer resources.

It cannot solve every strategic problem by reaching for the next round. In some businesses, especially those with relatively low capital requirements or faster routes to customer revenue, this can be an enormous advantage. The founders preserve ownership, avoid premature dilution, and retain a great deal of flexibility over the pace and shape of the company's development. The cap table remains cleaner for longer, and the company is less likely to absorb the preferences, controls, and structural obligations that arrive with outside capital.

Yet bootstrapping also imposes severe limits. The most obvious is time. A bootstrapped startup often has less of it than the founders admit to themselves. Even where cash burn is low, the company is usually consuming founder attention, founder stamina, and founder opportunity cost at a rate that can become unsustainable. If the business requires serious technical development, regulatory progress, significant hiring, market education, or rapid capture of a strategic opening, then internal financing may not be enough. In such cases the company is not merely choosing a more independent path. It may be choosing a structurally weaker one, in which speed, talent, or survivability are sacrificed in order to preserve founder ownership longer.

This is where funded growth begins to look different. A funded company has accepted that its ambitions, timeline, or competitive environment require more than internally generated resources. It brings in outside capital not merely to feel more comfortable, but because the founders believe the company can become significantly stronger, faster, or more defensible if additional money enters the structure. In doing so, however, the company gives something up. It gives up a portion of the future. That is the core fact that distinguishes funded growth from bootstrapping. The company is no longer trying to become more powerful while keeping the original ownership map largely intact. It is choosing to reallocate part of that map in exchange for the ability to attempt a larger or faster outcome.

This is why the arrival of outside money should never be reduced to a simple financing event. It is a structural transition. The cap table changes. The founder's percentage changes. The company's obligations change. The standard of documentation changes. The investor's expectations enter the room. The future hiring plan becomes more formal because the company now has money that needs to be deployed against milestones. The board may change. Reporting expectations may change.

Even the emotional logic of the company can change, because the founders are no longer carrying the entire burden privately. Their business is now partly financed by people who expect not only progress, but return.

That change can be healthy, and in many startups it is essential. Outside money can allow the business to move at a pace its market requires. It can give the founders room to hire people who materially improve the company's capabilities. It can allow product or technical work to continue long enough to reach an inflection point that bootstrapping alone might never have reached. It can also create legitimacy. The presence of respected investors can make later fundraising easier, signal confidence to employees and customers, and push the company into a more serious strategic category. A funded startup is therefore not merely richer than it was. It often becomes a different kind of entity, one that is being built not just from founder belief but from structured external conviction.

At the same time, funded growth creates its own dangers. Founders who romanticise fundraising sometimes forget that outside capital does not arrive as neutral fuel. It arrives with claims, rights, and expectations. It may make the company more powerful, but it also makes the ownership structure more crowded and the path more demanding. A founder who was once able to think of the company largely as their own project must now think of it as a shared financial instrument in which other people have invested on the basis of particular assumptions about growth and return. If the company takes money too early, too cheaply, or without a clear sense of what the capital is supposed to achieve, then the shift from bootstrapping to funded growth can weaken the company rather than strengthen it. The founders have diluted themselves without buying enough strategic improvement to justify the cost.

This is why the choice between bootstrapping and funded growth is not really a moral choice between independence and compromise. It is a structural choice about what kind of company is being built and what that company requires. Some founders are tempted to treat bootstrapping as inherently purer and therefore inherently better. Others treat funding as the obvious sign that the company is serious. Both instincts are too blunt. A bootstrapped company can become trapped by undercapitalisation just as a funded company can become distorted by premature dilution and investor pressure. The right question is not which identity sounds more admirable.

The right question is what the actual business needs in order to become viable, defensible, and worth the ownership structure being created around it.

This is also where cap table thinking becomes essential rather than optional. A founder who is considering outside money needs to understand that the company is about to move from one ownership regime into another. The company will no longer be governed only by founder allocation, employee incentives, and internal discipline. It will be governed as well by the terms on which outside capital enters. That means the founders need to know what they are protecting, what they are willing to trade, and what they are truly buying with the dilution. A bootstrapped company can often postpone some of these questions. A funded company cannot. The arrival of outside money is the moment when the company's ownership structure begins to matter not only to the founders, but to people whose capital is now tied to its future.

There is also a practical truth hidden inside this comparison. Bootstrapping and funded growth are not always mutually exclusive identities. Many strong startups move through both conditions. They begin bootstrapped, using founder labour and scarce resources to establish the company's earliest legitimacy, and then raise money once they can do so from a stronger position. Others raise early, then later try to behave with the discipline of a bootstrapped company rather than spending as though money itself were a strategy. The boundary between the two is therefore less ideological than temporal. What matters is that when the company crosses into funded growth, the founders recognise that they are not just improving liquidity. They are changing the ownership story of the business.

This chapter begins here because before founders can understand angels, venture capitalists, priced rounds, and investor negotiation, they have to understand what outside money actually means. It is not only relief. It is not only progress. It is the beginning of a different phase in which growth is financed by changing who shares in the company's future. The founders do not stop being central. But they are no longer alone in deciding what the company is worth, how fast it should move, and how much of its future can be spent in pursuit of something larger.

Who Angels Are

The word angel has always carried a slight risk of sentimental misunderstanding. In startup culture it can make early investors sound softer, kinder, or more benevolent than they necessarily are. The reality is more precise. An angel investor is usually an individual, or sometimes a small syndicate-like participant, who invests personal capital into young companies at an early stage in exchange for some form of ownership or a future right to ownership. Angels are often the first true outside money a startup encounters. That fact makes them enormously important, because they frequently stand at the boundary between the company as a founder-driven private project and the company as an investable financial structure.

What distinguishes angels from later institutional investors is not only size of cheque, though that often matters, but also position in the company's life cycle. Angels tend to enter when the business is earlier, less proven, more founder-dependent, and structurally less mature than the kinds of companies traditional venture funds often prefer. They are therefore investing under a high degree of uncertainty. In many cases, the startup may have a prototype rather than a finished product, early user or customer traction rather than repeatable scale, a compelling story rather than a stable business model, and a cap table that is still relatively simple compared with what it will later become. Angels enter before many of the company's larger proofs exist, and that willingness to tolerate uncertainty is part of what defines the role.

That does not mean angels are simply gamblers or romantics. Some are, but many are highly strategic. They may be former founders, operators, executives, domain experts, or individuals who have built enough capital and enough confidence to back companies they believe can become significant later. Their personal backgrounds often shape the kind of companies they support. A technically sophisticated angel may favour product-heavy or infrastructure startups. A former industry operator may back businesses they understand from the inside. A wealthy former founder may invest partly out of conviction, partly out of identity, and partly because they recognise in a very early company the kinds of signals they wish someone had recognised in theirs. In that sense, angels are often more heterogeneous than later professional funds. The category describes a structural position in startup finance, not one psychological type.

This heterogeneity matters because founders often make a mistake in thinking of angels as simply small venture capitalists. Sometimes angels behave very much like institutional investors in miniature. They negotiate carefully, push on terms, and think rigorously about ownership, governance, and future dilution. In other cases they behave more like high-trust early believers, investing partly on founder quality and partly on intuition about the market. Some bring useful networks, strategic introductions, sector insight, or credibility that matters beyond the cheque itself. Others bring capital and little else, which may still be valuable if the company needs runway more than advice. The founder should therefore not think of angels as one uniform species. The important question is not only whether the investor is an angel, but what kind of angel they are and how that fits the company's needs.

For the cap table, angels matter because they are often the first people to turn founder ownership into externally shared ownership. Before angels arrive, the company may still feel emotionally and structurally close to the founders. Once an angel invests, the startup has crossed a threshold. Someone outside the founding team now owns part of the future or holds a formal claim on future conversion into it. That changes the company in ways that are larger than the cheque size alone. The founder is no longer merely explaining the business. The founder is now structuring it for outside participation. This usually means the cap table must become more accurate, the documentation more serious, and the company's ownership story more legible to someone who did not live through its earliest improvisations.

This is one reason angels often have outsized influence relative to the size of their stake. They may not control the company, and in many cases they should not. But by being first, they help establish patterns. They influence how the founder thinks about financing, what level of discipline is expected in the cap table, whether the company begins using notes, SAFEs, or priced rounds, and what kind of outside scrutiny the founders must now get used to. The first angel can therefore act almost as a bridge figure between the intimate founding phase and the more formal world of venture-backed growth. If that bridge is crossed well, later rounds become easier to imagine and manage. If it is crossed badly, the company may lock in weak habits or awkward structures that later investors are much less willing to tolerate.

It is also important to understand that angels are usually investing personal money, and that changes the texture of the relationship. Institutional funds invest capital that belongs, at least structurally, to a fund vehicle with partners, mandates, time horizons, and portfolio logic. Angels are often investing out of their own balance sheet. This can make them more flexible, faster, or more intuitive. It can also make them more idiosyncratic. Their personal beliefs, temperament, and experience may shape the deal more directly than in an institutional process. Some angels are wonderfully founder-friendly because they know what fragile early companies are really like. Others can be intrusive or inconsistent because there is less institutional process constraining how they behave. The founder therefore has to evaluate not only the money but the person.

This is especially relevant because early capital is not neutral. The first outside investor can affect the company far beyond the immediate cash injection. Their name may influence who else is willing to invest later. Their behaviour may shape founder expectations about how investor relationships work. Their presence on the cap table may either reassure or concern future investors. A respected angel who is known to be constructive can strengthen the company's signalling power. A difficult or poorly chosen angel can become a lingering complication, especially if they negotiate unusual rights or if their style is misaligned with the company's next stage. In this way, angel money may be "small" in quantitative terms and still extremely consequential in structural terms.

Founders also need to resist the temptation to see angels as harmless simply because they are early and often less formal than funds. An angel cheque can look easier to accept than institutional money because the negotiation feels lighter, the person more approachable, and the amount smaller. Yet the cap table does not experience money sentimentally. If the company is issuing ownership or creating future claims in exchange for that money, the structural consequences still matter. A small cheque on bad terms can be more damaging than founders first realise, especially if it introduces awkward rights, valuation expectations, or cap table clutter that later rounds must inherit. Angel money may be more forgiving in process, but it is still real capital entering the ownership structure.

This is why the best founders think of angels in two frames at once. First, as early believers who can help the company cross the gap between fragile beginning and more credible next stage.

Second, as real participants in the cap table whose presence will influence future dilution, future fundraising, and the company's governance story. Neither frame is enough on its own. If founders see angels only as kind believers, they may under-negotiate or under-appreciate the structural consequences of the deal. If they see angels only as miniature institutions, they may fail to recognise the genuine strategic value that some angels bring through conviction, speed, and network.

The startup's need for angels often arises from a very specific mismatch. The company is too developed to remain only a founder-side project, but not yet developed enough to attract the capital it might later want from larger investors. It needs someone willing to bridge that gap. That is exactly where angels often matter most. They back possibility before the company has enough evidence to feel institutionally safe. In return, they receive ownership or the right to future ownership at a stage where risk is high and the cap table is still relatively uncluttered. This is one of the oldest and most important functions in startup finance, and understanding it clearly helps the founder read the next steps much better.
Angels are, then, neither saints nor simply small funds. They are early outside capital providers, often highly varied in character and value, who help transform a startup from something financed mainly by belief and internal sacrifice into something that has begun to formalise external confidence. The founder who understands who angels are is already beginning to understand what the first real dilution event means, and why the next question is not merely whether to take the money, but what that money is doing to the cap table and to the company's future shape.

Who Venture Capitalists Are

If angels are often the first outsiders to enter a startup's ownership structure, venture capitalists are usually the figures who make the company feel unmistakably transformed into a venture-backed business. This is not only because venture firms often invest larger amounts of money, though that matters. It is because venture capital arrives with a different institutional logic. The founder is no longer dealing primarily with an individual investing personal money under their own name and temperament. The founder is dealing with professional investors whose entire business model is built around placing capital into startups, managing portfolio risk, seeking outsized returns, and shaping the governance and growth trajectory of the companies they back. That difference changes both the cap table and the atmosphere around it.

A venture capitalist is typically investing through a fund or equivalent investment structure rather than simply from personal discretionary wealth. This matters because the money is governed by portfolio logic, return expectations, fund timelines, and formal decision-making processes. The venture capitalist is not only deciding whether they believe in this founder or this product. They are deciding whether this company fits a thesis, a stage, a risk profile, a likely return pattern, and a fund strategy capable of producing outcomes large enough to justify the model of venture investing itself. That institutional context shapes everything. It shapes how the investor evaluates the business, how they negotiate, what rights they want, how they think about future rounds, and what they expect the company to become.

This is one of the deepest differences between angels and venture capitalists. Angels can sometimes invest because they simply like the founder, understand the space, and are willing to take a relatively intuitive bet on a young business. Venture firms may still care deeply about founder quality, but they also have to care about portfolio construction. They are not trying merely to back good companies in the abstract. They are trying to back companies that, if successful, can return a meaningful amount relative to the size and expectations of the fund. This often means they are looking not just for businesses that can survive or become respectable, but for businesses that can become very large, strategically important, or extremely valuable. That requirement changes how they see the company. They are looking not only at whether the startup works, but whether it can scale into the kind of outcome venture capital is built to pursue.

For the cap table, this usually means greater seriousness. Venture capitalists do not simply want to know who currently owns what. They want to understand the whole structure in a way that supports later rounds, later investors, later hiring, and a plausible exit path. They tend to care more intensely about founder vesting, option pool sufficiency, prior investor rights, convertible instruments, dead equity, IP assignment, and the cleanliness of the corporate record. This is not because they are fussy for the sake of it. It is because venture money often enters at a point where the company is expected to become more legible, more scalable, and more capable of surviving multiple future financing events. A weak cap table that an angel might tolerate as early-stage mess is far more likely to concern a venture fund because the fund expects the company to grow on top of that structure.

This is why venture capitalists often feel less forgiving than angels to founders who are seeing institutional money for the first time. The founder may still be thinking of the business partly as an ambitious extension of the founding effort. The venture capitalist is already thinking several rounds ahead. They are asking what happens when later investors arrive, whether the option pool is large enough, whether the founder stake remains motivating after further dilution, whether the company's governance rights are robust enough to protect the new capital, and whether the current ownership structure leaves room for the business to keep evolving without becoming structurally irrational. In this sense, venture capitalists do not simply enter the current company. They enter the company's projected financing future, and they want the cap table to be able to survive that future.

This does not mean all venture firms are the same. Just as angels vary, venture funds vary by stage, style, sector, geography, risk appetite, and temperament. Some specialise in very early rounds and behave in ways not entirely unlike sophisticated angels, though with more process. Others focus on Series A and beyond, where the company is expected to have clearer product-market fit, stronger metrics, or a more developed operating base. Some are highly founder-friendly in tone and governance style. Others are much more formal or much more controlling. Some bring deep networks, sector expertise, and follow-on capacity. Others bring primarily money and signalling value. The founder therefore has to avoid the mistake of imagining "venture capital" as a single uniform type. It is an ecosystem of institutional actors whose common feature is not identical behaviour, but a professionalised relationship to startup investing.
Still, there are some common patterns. Venture capitalists typically care much more than angels about ownership structure as a system rather than as a moment. They often seek preferred shares, information rights, board representation or observer rights, protective provisions, pro rata rights, and other terms that allow them to protect downside and preserve upside. They are also more likely to think carefully about how the cap table will look after this round and the next one, not just after this cheque is written. That means they may push harder on pool sizing, on founder vesting, on cleaning up legacy issues, and on valuation relative to where the company must go from here. To a founder, this can feel intrusive or cold. From the venture capitalist's perspective, it is part of buying into a company that must now function as a serious financing vehicle, not merely as an exciting young business.

The role of the venture capitalist is therefore more political than many first-time founders realise. They are not just providers of cash. They become participants in the governance and strategic pressure structure of the company. Their presence on the cap table affects future investor confidence, future round pricing, employee perception, and sometimes the founder's own room to act. A strong venture partner can help the company professionalise, recruit, raise later money, and survive difficult strategic choices. A poor fit can create friction, pressure for premature scaling, misaligned incentives, or governance tension that drains management energy. The founder is not merely choosing money. The founder is choosing a participant in the future architecture of the business.

This is why venture money must never be evaluated purely on amount. Founders who are dazzled by cheque size without understanding the investor's logic, rights, expectations, and fit often end up with a stronger balance sheet and a weaker company culture or cap table. The most disciplined founders ask not only how much capital the investor brings, but how that capital arrives into the ownership structure. At what valuation. With what preferences. With what governance rights. With what expectations about pace, hiring, and future rounds. And perhaps most importantly, with what likely effect on the founder's continuing ability to build the company in a way that still feels coherent.

There is also a difference in how venture capitalists see risk. Angels may often be willing to place smaller bets in more personalised ways. Venture funds must think in return multiples and portfolio outcomes. That means they may prefer strategies that increase the chance of very large outcomes, even if those strategies also increase pressure, burn, or the need for later rounds. This can create real tension with founders who value control, durability, or moderate-but-solid growth. The cap table becomes part of this tension because each new round may push the company further into a path of funded acceleration, with dilution, governance, and expectation patterns that become harder to reverse. The founder should therefore understand that venture capital is not merely money that helps the same company do more. It can be money that changes the kind of company being built.

This is not necessarily negative. Many of the world's most important and valuable companies required that kind of capital and the institutional machinery surrounding it.

Some ventures simply cannot become what they aim to become through founder labour, revenue discipline, and angel support alone. They need deeper pools of capital and investors capable of supporting larger financing arcs. In those companies, venture capital is not a distortion but a necessary stage in the company's development. The point is not that venture capital is dangerous by definition. The point is that it is structurally transformative and should be understood as such.

That is who venture capitalists are. They are professional investors deploying institutional capital into startups with the expectation of outsized returns, the intention of participating in a company's growth and governance, and a strong interest in ownership structures that can survive and support later stages of financing. For the founder, their arrival is not just a bigger cheque. It is the point at which the cap table begins to matter in a more fully institutional way, and the next question becomes not merely who these investors are, but what they actually want from the company once they arrive.

What Each Investor Type Wants

Founders often make the mistake of thinking that all outside money wants the same thing and differs only in size, speed, or friendliness. That is too simple. Different investors may all speak the language of growth, upside, and partnership, but they approach the company from different structural positions, different risk tolerances, and different time horizons. If the founder does not understand what each investor type actually wants, then fundraising becomes a theatre of mixed assumptions. The company thinks it is taking money. The investor thinks it is buying into a particular future shape of the company. Those two interpretations can coexist for a while, but if they are never properly aligned, the cap table will later reveal the mismatch.

Angels usually want access to upside before the company becomes institutionally expensive. They are often entering when the business is still uncertain and the ownership structure is relatively uncluttered, so part of what they want is simple: a chance to participate early in something that could become much bigger later. But that is only the beginning. Some angels want proximity to interesting founders, sectors, or technologies. Some want to diversify personal wealth into startup risk. Some want to contribute experience or networks and thereby increase the value of their own early stake.

Others want to maintain the option of participating in later rounds if the company develops well. In cap table terms, angels usually want enough ownership or enough future conversion opportunity that the risk of investing this early still has a plausible return logic.

What they often do not want, at least in the same formal way as later venture funds, is heavy governance complexity from the start. Many angels are content with relatively simple structures so long as their position is clear, the founder appears disciplined, and the business has a believable route to future financing or value creation. That does not mean angels never care about rights, information, or protections. Many do. But early angel capital often tolerates a degree of structural youthfulness that larger funds will not. The founder should still remember that angels are not donating. They may be easier to satisfy procedurally than institutional investors, but they still want a position in the company that can become meaningful if the startup works.

Venture capitalists want something more exacting. They want companies that can plausibly generate venture-scale returns. This sounds obvious, but its implications are enormous. A venture fund is not usually looking for businesses that merely become respectable, modestly profitable, or stable enough for the founders to earn a living. It is looking for businesses that can grow large enough to matter to the economics of the fund. That means the venture capitalist often wants not only ownership, but enough ownership in a company that has enough upside that the stake can one day be worth a very great deal. This is why venture capitalists often focus so intensely on market size, scalability, speed of growth, defensibility, founder ambition, and the company's likely route through future rounds. They are not only evaluating the present. They are pricing the possibility of a very large outcome.

Because of that, venture capitalists often want more than economic participation. They want structure that protects the quality of their bet. This may include preferred shares, information rights, pro rata rights, board seats or observers, consent rights, liquidation preferences, anti-dilution provisions, and enough cap table discipline that future rounds remain manageable. The founder may interpret this as control-seeking, and sometimes it is. But it is also part of the venture fund's logic. The fund is not only trying to share in the upside. It is trying to shape the conditions under which that upside remains possible and not needlessly damaged by founder disorder, weak governance, or future structural chaos.

Then there are later-stage investors, growth funds, strategic investors, or other participants who may come after the company has already become more institutional. These investors often want something slightly different again. They may care less about the raw early-stage leap of faith and more about de-risked scaling. They may want exposure to a company that is already proving itself and now needs capital to accelerate expansion, internationalise, acquire, or otherwise move from strong business to very large business. Their ownership expectations, governance appetite, and valuation sensitivity may differ because they are entering at a stage where the company is more legible but also more expensive. These investors still care about cap table structure, perhaps even more in some respects, but their questions are often filtered through growth execution rather than just early-stage uncertainty.

It is also useful to distinguish between investors who want primarily financial return and those who want something broader or different. Some strategic investors may care about commercial alignment, access to technology, market positioning, supply chain relationships, or ecosystem influence alongside financial upside. That can make them useful, but it can also make them complicated. Their presence on the cap table may send strong signals to future investors or future acquirers. It may open doors. It may also narrow options or create perceived conflicts. The founder therefore has to ask not only how much money this investor offers, but what non-financial interest the investor has in being inside the company and how that interest will affect the business later.

Another category that founders sometimes overlook is the "tourist" investor, regardless of formal type. This may be an angel, a fund, or a strategic participant who wants the prestige, excitement, or signalling value of being in a hot company without bringing much sustained conviction or usefulness beyond the cheque. Tourist capital can look flattering because it often arrives wrapped in status. But it may become unhelpful if the investor lacks the patience, understanding, or follow-on commitment the company later needs. What this investor wants, at bottom, is exposure rather than true participation in the company's longer arc. That may still be tolerable in the right context, but the founder should know the difference between capital that is deeply aligned with the company's next stage and capital that is simply present.

This is why the question what each investor wants should always be answered on two levels. First, what do they want structurally. Ownership, rights, protection, follow-on ability, governance leverage, signalling, or strategic access. Second, what do they want psychologically or institutionally. Early upside, personal involvement, venture-scale returns, strategic optionality, prestige, portfolio diversification, or proximity to innovation. Both levels matter because they shape how the investor behaves once inside the cap table. Two investors may ask for similar percentages and yet behave very differently because what they are really seeking from the relationship is not the same.

For founders, this is not a purely academic distinction. It affects negotiation directly. A founder who knows what the investor actually wants is much better placed to trade intelligently. If the investor primarily wants enough ownership to make the bet economically meaningful, the founder may negotiate around size and structure. If the investor wants governance comfort because the cap table is messy, cleaning up the structure may create room to defend valuation or control more effectively. If the investor wants strategic access, the founder may need to think beyond the immediate round and ask what that access could later cost. If the investor wants a path to participating in later rounds, then pro rata rights and future signalling become part of the present negotiation. Understanding what the investor wants helps the founder see where the true pressure points are rather than reacting only to the headline terms.

This understanding also protects the founder from one of the more subtle startup dangers, which is confusing warmth with alignment. An angel may seem personally enthusiastic but still want a very strong economic position. A venture capitalist may seem highly founder-friendly and still be operating under institutional incentives that will matter later. A strategic investor may sound visionary while still wanting optionality that narrows the company's future. Conversely, a more formal or demanding investor may actually be well aligned if their capital, expectations, and rights match the company's real path. Founders who judge investors mainly by tone often miss what matters most. The cap table records alignment in structure, not in charm.

There is also an important internal consequence. Once founders begin to understand what each investor type wants, they start to see that fundraising is not simply about persuading someone to believe in the company. It is about choosing the kinds of participants the company can live with on its cap table and under its governance structure. This is a much stronger frame. It turns the founder from petitioner into selector, even when the company is still capital-constrained. The founder is not merely trying to get a yes. The founder is trying to decide which kind of yes improves the company's future and which kind of yes distorts it.

That is why this section matters. The arrival of outside money is not a generic event. It introduces different kinds of actors, each with different ambitions for what their capital should buy. The founder who understands those ambitions is much less likely to misread the round as a simple exchange of cash for shares. It is an exchange of cash for position inside the company's future, and different investors want different kinds of positions. Once that is clear, the next question follows naturally: how do investors actually read the cap table when deciding whether this company is worth entering at all.

How Investors Read a Cap Table

To a founder, the cap table often begins as a record of what has happened. To an investor, it is usually read first as a prediction of what will happen next. This difference matters enormously. Founders tend to look at the table and see the history of the company's formation, early promises, first hires, first money, and present ownership balance. Investors look at the same document and ask what kind of company this structure will allow, what kinds of problems it already contains, and how much pain is embedded in the future. In other words, investors do not read the cap table simply as an accounting of who owns what today. They read it as a diagnostic instrument for incentives, governance, scalability, and potential conflict.

The first thing many investors look for is basic cleanliness. Can they tell, quickly and without oral rescue from the founder, who owns the company, in what amounts, through what instruments, and under what broad conditions. A clean cap table does not have to be simple in the sense of tiny or early-stage. It has to be legible. If the table is full of ambiguous names, unexplained grants, unresolved founder exits, untracked options, or ownership positions that only make sense after twenty minutes of narrative explanation, the investor immediately learns something unhelpful. They learn that the company may not fully govern its own structure unless forced to. That is rarely a reassuring first impression.

Cleanliness, however, is only the surface layer. Once the investor can see the structure, the next question is whether it makes sense. Are the founders still meaningfully incentivised. Is there dead equity sitting with people who no longer contribute. Is the option pool large enough for likely hiring without being absurdly oversized. Are there convertibles, SAFEs, or other future claims that will significantly alter the picture later. Are earlier investors sitting on terms or rights that will complicate later financing. Does the current structure leave enough room for the next round without crushing the founder incentive base. A cap table can be tidy and still unhealthy if the distribution itself tells a story of poor judgment.

This is one reason investors often seem more interested in the cap table than founders expect. The product may be exciting, the market large, the technology interesting, but the cap table shows whether the business can realistically be financed and governed from here. A startup with a messy ownership history is not only administratively inconvenient. It is strategically expensive. An investor may worry that too much time, legal cost, or political energy will be consumed by cleaning up the past before the company can move cleanly into the future. Even when the business is promising, that friction matters. Investors are always comparing opportunities, and a structurally weak company has to compensate for its own ownership chaos with stronger traction, stronger founder quality, or stronger return potential than a cleaner company might need.

Founders often assume that investors are mainly looking for signs of whether the founders personally have "enough" left. That is certainly part of the analysis, but it is not the whole thing. Investors are not just asking whether the founder can still get rich. They are asking whether the founder has enough ownership left to remain properly motivated through years of future work and future dilution. That is a different question. A founder may still own a large-sounding percentage and yet, once future rounds, option expansion, and structural preferences are considered, be heading toward a position that will no longer align effort with reward strongly enough. An investor who sees that problem may hesitate, because misaligned founders are one of the most dangerous forms of cap table weakness.

Investors also read the cap table for evidence of founder judgment. A sensible founder split, founder vesting, a coherent option pool, and the absence of bizarre side allocations all suggest that the company has confronted difficult ownership questions directly rather than drifting through them. A table full of small advisory grants, dead cofounders, vague pools, odd percentages, or unexplained convertibles suggests the opposite. The investor is not only seeing numbers. The investor is seeing the residue of decisions. The cap table, in that sense, becomes a compressed record of whether the founders have been able to think structurally under pressure. For many investors, that is one of the deepest things the document reveals.

Another important thing investors read is future financing capacity. A startup is rarely judged only on whether this round can happen. It is judged on whether future rounds are likely to happen on a structure that still makes sense. If the current cap table already leaves the founders thin, leaves little room for employee incentives, or contains instruments that will heavily complicate the next step, then the investor has to ask whether the company is financing itself into a corner. That corner may not be visible to the founder yet because the current round still feels achievable. But the investor may already be imagining the next negotiation and seeing that the room is narrowing.

This is particularly important in early-stage venture deals because every current investor is, in effect, entering a future capital structure that does not yet fully exist. They want to know not only whether the company can absorb them now, but whether the table will still be governable after the next likely fundraise, after the next pool refresh, after the next conversion event, after the next founder departure if one occurs. A strong investor reads the current table with future states in mind. A founder who does not do the same is at a serious disadvantage in negotiation because the investor is pricing tomorrow while the founder may still be arguing from today's picture.

The cap table is also read for political risk. Investors know that percentages do not only determine payouts. They influence how people behave. A departed founder with a meaningful retained stake may not merely dilute returns. They may become a source of bitterness or obstruction. A cofounder split that no longer seems to match actual contribution may imply internal tension not yet visible in the pitch. An oversized early angel group with fragmented small holdings may create noise in future approvals or communications. A company where one founder dominates the structure overwhelmingly may raise questions about whether later hires and other founders can remain motivated or whether the governance environment is too concentrated.

The cap table therefore tells investors something about likely human conflict, not just about financial structure.

This is one reason some investors can look at a cap table and form a view about the culture of the company before they have spent much time with the team. A disciplined, legible, explainable structure suggests a company that respects hard decisions. A table built through sentiment, avoidance, or repeated informal compromise suggests a company that may struggle with clarity elsewhere as well. This is not always fair in a perfect sense, but it is often directionally correct. Ownership design and general company judgment tend to correlate more than founders like to admit.

Founders should also understand that investors read absences as well as presences. The absence of founder vesting is meaningful. The absence of a realistic option pool is meaningful. The absence of clarity around convertibles is meaningful. The absence of documentation behind an apparently settled ownership picture is meaningful. Silence in a cap table is not neutral if the company's stage implies that certain structures should already exist. In some cases the absence may be acceptable and explainable. In other cases it looks like inexperience or denial. A sophisticated investor is always comparing what is present on the table with what ought to be present given the company's claims about where it is heading.

This is why founders should prepare to read their own cap table through investor eyes before investors do it for them. If you were seeing this company cold, would the founder position still look motivating after the next round. Would the pool look credible. Would the old grants make sense. Would the instruments convert cleanly. Would the dead equity worry you. Would the structure suggest discipline or drift. These are not cynical questions. They are questions of realism. A founder who can answer them honestly is far better prepared both to fix what should be fixed and to defend what is already sound.

In the end, investors read a cap table as a compact theory of the company. It tells them how the business has handled scarcity, fairness, power, promises, and future planning so far. It tells them whether the current structure can support the next phase of hiring and financing.

And it tells them whether the company's ownership story is still coherent enough that new capital can enter without first having to untangle too much of the past. That is why the cap table is rarely a side document in serious fundraising. It is one of the clearest tests of whether the company that sounds promising is also built in a way that can survive real money.

What Makes a Cap Table Attractive or Unattractive

An attractive cap table is not one that flatters the founder. It is one that makes future company-building possible without requiring every new participant to first solve the mistakes of the past. This is an important distinction because founders often judge their ownership structure by how reassuring it feels to them in the moment. Investors, key hires, and later counterparties judge it by whether it looks governable, scalable, and credible from where the company stands now. A cap table can therefore feel emotionally comforting to the founders and still look unattractive to everyone else. It can also feel painful in the short term and yet look highly attractive because it has preserved the right conditions for growth.

The first thing that makes a cap table attractive is clarity. A serious outsider should be able to understand who owns the company, through what instruments, in what approximate proportions, and with what major caveats, without needing a rescue speech from the founder to explain away basic confusion. Clarity does not require the company to be simplistic. A company may have founders, investors, an option pool, some convertibles, and even a departed founder still holding a rational residual stake. All of that can still be attractive if it is intelligible. What makes a table unattractive is not complexity by itself, but murk. If the structure only makes sense after the founder starts saying things like "that person isn't really involved," "we sort of promised something there," or "this will all be cleaned up later," then the cap table is already becoming expensive.

Attractiveness also depends on founder incentive. Investors and sophisticated employees want to see that the people carrying the company still have enough ownership left to remain deeply motivated through the next stage and, ideally, through several stages after that. This does not mean the founders must still control an overwhelming majority. It means the structure must leave them with a stake that remains psychologically and economically meaningful after likely future dilution.

A founder who already looks over-diluted at an early stage makes the cap table unattractive because the outsider immediately starts asking what happens after the next round. If the founder position already feels thin, the future may look misaligned before it even arrives.

The opposite extreme can also be unattractive. A cap table in which founders have hoarded almost all ownership while failing to create realistic room for talent or future capital may look strong to a founder who fears dilution, but it can look naive or underprepared to an investor. A company that says it plans to hire strong people, scale quickly, and raise future money while leaving no sensible room on the cap table for any of that is not signalling strength. It is signalling that the founders have not yet fully accepted what kind of company they are trying to build. Attractive cap tables usually show some combination of founder commitment, future capacity, and structural realism. Unattractive ones often show emotional overattachment to the original ownership picture.

Another major factor is the treatment of dead equity. Investors and later hires do not like seeing large chunks of the company sitting with people who no longer matter to the business. A departed cofounder with an appropriately vested and explainable position may be tolerable or even entirely reasonable. A cap table clogged with absent participants, sentimental grants, obsolete advisers, or legacy allocations that no longer correspond to value creation is a different matter. This kind of structure is unattractive because it tells outsiders that current builders are carrying the business while historical passengers continue to drain the future. It also suggests that the company has either been unwilling or unable to confront hard ownership questions when they mattered most.

Option pool design plays a major role as well. A cap table is usually more attractive when it contains enough room to recruit meaningfully without looking bloated or careless. Too little room suggests the company will soon need awkward restructuring, which means today's round may not be cleanly future-ready. Too much room suggests the founders or investors have reserved dilution beyond what the company's actual near-term hiring plan justifies. The attractive middle ground is a pool that looks thought through. It signals that the company understands what kinds of hires it needs before the next financing event and has created enough but not absurdly more than enough space to support them.

The treatment of convertibles, SAFEs, and similar instruments also affects attractiveness. These tools are not inherently unattractive. Many good companies use them sensibly. What matters is whether their effect is understood and visible. A cap table becomes unattractive when there are multiple instruments hanging in the background whose future conversion is poorly modelled, poorly documented, or not clearly explained by the founders. That creates uncertainty around the true ownership picture, and uncertainty is almost always priced as risk. A startup that can show how these instruments sit within the broader structure, what their likely conversion effect is, and how the company remains healthy afterward looks much more attractive than one that treats them as vague future problems.

Attractive cap tables also tend to show discipline in the relationship between rights and percentages. This is not only about who owns how much, but about what those ownership positions mean. A company may have several stakeholders and still look attractive if the rights structure remains coherent and the founders can explain it clearly. A company becomes less attractive when headline percentages conceal deeper structural problems, such as severe preference stacking, badly designed rights, or odd arrangements that complicate later financing. An outsider wants confidence that the cap table is not a misleading front for a much more distorted economic reality underneath.

Another sign of attractiveness is that the table looks like it belongs to the company's actual stage. This is subtle but important. A very early company should not usually look like an over-engineered corporate labyrinth full of tiny fragmented positions, exotic instruments, and half a dozen categories of stakeholder whose presence only makes sense after years of mature financing. Conversely, a company that claims to be ready for institutional capital but still has the ownership looseness of a founder hobby project is also unattractive. A good cap table has stage-appropriate seriousness. It is neither more theatrical nor more casual than the company's real position justifies.

Investors also care about whether the cap table suggests future negotiation strength or future vulnerability. If the structure is already stretched, cluttered, or emotionally compromised, future rounds are likely to be harder, and future investors may use that weakness as leverage.

If the structure is clean, legible, and leaves room for rational expansion, then the current investor can feel more confident that the company is not financing itself into a trap. This is one reason a cap table can be attractive even if the founders have already given up a noticeable amount. The investor may prefer a founder owning a somewhat smaller but still strong stake in a clean and scalable structure over a founder owning a very large stake in a brittle and unrealistic one.

There is also an aesthetic of seriousness that should not be ignored. Attractive cap tables often look as though the company has been built by people willing to make difficult decisions before outsiders forced them to. Founder vesting is in place. Early grants make sense. Departures were handled. The pool is explainable. The instruments are visible. The structure tells the truth without requiring mythology to soften it. This creates confidence not only in the numbers, but in the people behind them.
An unattractive cap table, by contrast, often feels like a fossil record of avoidance. It shows that the founders postponed too much, promised too loosely, or governed too sentimentally.

This is why attractiveness in a cap table is not cosmetic. It is not about having pretty numbers or famous names. It is about whether the structure makes the company easier or harder to fund, easier or harder to hire for, easier or harder to govern, and easier or harder to believe in. A cap table is attractive when it says the company knows what it has done so far and still has room to do what comes next. It is unattractive when it says the future will have to spend its first energy cleaning up the past.

The First Real Funding Conversation

Every startup has a moment when talk about money stops being hypothetical. Before that point, founders may discuss fundraising in general terms, speculate about what kind of investors the business might one day attract, and loosely imagine how much capital would be useful. These conversations can still feel aspirational, almost strategic in the abstract. Then the first real funding conversation arrives. An angel, a syndicate, a family office, a seed investor, or some other outside participant asks direct questions. How much are you raising. On what terms. What does the cap table look like. How much has been promised already. What will the ownership structure be after this money enters. At that point, the founder is no longer talking about the idea of dilution.

The founder is beginning to price the future.

This moment matters because it is often the first time the founder is forced to translate private conviction into a structure another person might actually buy into. Until now, the business has largely been able to live inside its own story. The founders know what they believe the company could become. They know what effort has already gone in. They know what the next stage requires. The investor, however, is not buying belief alone. The investor is asking what part of the company is being offered in exchange for risk, and what kind of ownership structure they are stepping into if they say yes. The funding conversation therefore reveals whether the company has really moved from founder narrative into investable form.

This is where many founders discover that the cap table is no longer just a document they need for their own understanding. It becomes part of the company's argument. The founder is saying, explicitly or implicitly, that this is the current ownership structure, this is how new capital would fit into it, and this is why the resulting company is still attractive to everyone who must live inside it afterward. If the founder cannot make that argument clearly, then the weakness is not only in the presentation. It is in the company's understanding of itself. The funding conversation exposes that instantly because investors ask questions that a private company can postpone for a surprisingly long time but cannot avoid forever.

The founder's challenge is not simply to answer those questions, but to answer them without drifting into either fantasy or defensive panic. Fantasy appears when the founder speaks as though the company's current story already justifies a valuation or ownership position far stronger than the evidence supports. Panic appears when the founder hears the investor's questions and begins to treat every request as an existential threat to founder ownership rather than as part of a legitimate effort to understand the structure. The first real funding conversation requires a different kind of posture. The founder has to be realistic enough to know that outside capital is buying into uncertainty, but confident enough to understand what the company is actually worth, what it needs, and what ownership changes it can absorb without becoming structurally weaker.

This is one reason preparation matters so much. A founder going into a first funding conversation should know not only how much capital the company hopes to raise, but why that amount is the right amount for the next stage. They should know what milestones that capital is expected to buy, what hiring plans it supports, how much dilution the structure can realistically bear, what the option pool situation is, and what likely future financing needs still lie ahead. Without that grounding, the conversation becomes reactive. The investor asks how much room is left on the cap table, and the founder improvises. The investor asks what happens if the company needs another round sooner than hoped, and the founder discovers they have not modelled it. The investor asks how large the option pool should be before closing, and the founder realises they do not really know what the next layer of hiring requires. A founder unprepared in these ways is not only at a negotiation disadvantage. They are also at risk of learning too late that their company has been operating on assumptions rather than on a coherent capital strategy.

The first funding conversation is also where the founder begins to understand how investors actually think about the business. Founders often come into these conversations focused on the company's product, mission, or technical edge. Investors may well care about those things, but they are also immediately translating them into questions of ownership, risk, and future structure. How much of the company is this risk worth. Will the founders still be motivated after this round and the next one. Does the cap table leave room for future talent. Are there old promises or departing founders who could become problems. Is this a business that can take capital intelligently, or merely one that wants capital because capital feels like progress. These are not side questions. They are part of what the investor is buying.

That can feel jarring to a founder who still experiences the company in deeply personal terms. The business may still feel like an act of creation, endurance, and identity. The investor is already reading it as a structure of claims. This is not because the investor is blind to the human side of company-building. It is because capital enters through structure. The funding conversation is where the founder first has to fully inhabit that reality. The company is not only asking to be admired or believed in. It is asking to be entered. That means its ownership architecture can no longer remain private background. It has to hold up under external judgment.

There is also an emotional trap at this stage that founders must avoid. The first real funding conversation can produce a kind of identity shock. A founder who has lived for months or years with the feeling that the company is mostly theirs suddenly hears outside questions that imply it is a negotiable structure. That can trigger defensiveness, especially if the founder has not yet properly separated ownership arithmetic from self-worth. The investor asks about dilution, vesting, option pools, or governance rights, and the founder hears not merely structural questions but personal encroachment. This is one reason the earlier chapters of this book have focused so much on ownership as architecture rather than mood. By the time the funding conversation arrives, the founder has to be capable of hearing these questions as part of real company-building rather than as insults.

At the same time, the founder must not overcorrect by becoming too eager to please. Some first-time founders become so relieved that someone is seriously discussing funding that they allow the conversation itself to create pressure. They begin accepting the investor's framing as though any real interest must be taken on the investor's preferred terms. That is just as dangerous. The first funding conversation is not merely an evaluation of the company by the investor. It is also an evaluation of the investor and of the proposed relationship between new capital and the company's future structure. A founder who forgets this can easily agree to a deal that solves the immediate problem of cash while creating a much longer problem in ownership, governance, or future financing flexibility.

This is why the founder should think of the first funding conversation as the beginning of mutual legibility. The company is becoming legible to outside capital, and the investor's intentions are becoming legible to the company. The cap table sits at the centre of that exchange. It tells the investor what kind of business they are joining and tells the founder what kind of changes will be required if the money comes in. The conversation is therefore not only about valuation or cheque size. It is about what the company becomes once it accepts that this future will no longer be owned and governed exactly as it was before.

There is one final truth worth emphasising. The first real funding conversation is often remembered by founders as a moment when the company became more serious. That memory is usually correct, but not for the reason founders sometimes think.

The company does not become more serious merely because someone offered money. It becomes more serious because from that moment onward its ownership structure can no longer be treated as private, intuitive, or unfinished. Outside money forces the founders to see the company as an object others can price, question, and join. That is a major threshold. If crossed wisely, it can help transform the startup from a fragile project into a more credible business. If crossed carelessly, it can lock weakness into the cap table at precisely the moment the founders most need strength.

That is what the first real funding conversation really is. It is the moment when the company begins to discover whether the future it has been imagining can survive contact with capital.

* * *

NINE

Priced Rounds and the First Sale of Equity

"Everything is worth what its purchaser will pay for it."

- Publilius Syrus

What a Priced Round Is

There is a decisive shift in the life of a startup when outside money stops entering through loosely deferred structures and begins entering through a direct sale of equity at an agreed price. Up to that point, the company may have lived on founder capital, customer revenue, informal support, angel money, notes, SAFEs, or some combination of these. Those arrangements can still be highly consequential, but they often allow the company to postpone one of the hardest questions in startup finance: what is this business being valued at right now for the purpose of issuing actual ownership. A priced round is the moment that question is no longer postponed. The company and the investor agree, explicitly or implicitly through the transaction mechanics, on a value framework under which new shares are sold.

That is why a priced round matters so much. It is not just a fundraising event. It is the company's first full encounter with valuation as a live structural fact. The startup is no longer merely saying that it hopes to become valuable later. It is allowing outside capital to purchase a specific part of the company on the basis of a present pricing logic. This changes the cap table, the company's internal psychology, and the seriousness with which future investors will read the structure. Once a priced round has happened, the startup has crossed into a different level of financial legibility. It now has a concrete equity transaction that says something about how the market, or at least this investor, values the business at this stage.

A priced round usually means that new shares are issued to the investor in exchange for money, and the number of shares issued is determined by the agreed valuation framework and the amount invested. That sounds simple, but the simplicity can be misleading. Founders often hear the phrase priced round and think only of the company getting a number attached to it. In reality, a priced round is a package of decisions. It says how much the company is considered worth before the new money goes in, how much money is being added, how many new shares that money buys, what class of shares the investor receives, what rights attach to them, and what the resulting ownership structure looks like immediately afterward. The round is therefore a valuation event, a dilution event, and often a governance event all at once.

This distinguishes priced rounds from many convertible or deferred instruments. A SAFE or a note can bring money into the company without forcing everyone to agree immediately on the exact price of the equity being sold. That can be useful at very early stages when the business is hard to price cleanly and the company wants to move faster than a full equity round may allow. A priced round removes that deferral. The company has now decided, or been forced by circumstance, that the time has come to set terms on which actual ownership will be issued now rather than later. That change usually implies a higher level of maturity in the company, or at least a higher level of formal seriousness, because the founders and investors are no longer relying on future pricing events to settle the economics.

There is a psychological reason founders often find priced rounds both exciting and unsettling. On the one hand, the round can feel validating. Someone is not merely expressing enthusiasm for the company in the abstract. Someone is paying to own part of it now. That creates a sense of reality that earlier conversations may not have carried. On the other hand, the round forces the founders to confront the fact that the business is becoming divisible in a much more public and measurable way. The company is no longer a mostly founder-shaped enterprise with a few blurred edges. It is now a priced structure in which ownership is being sold and the future is being reallocated in hard numerical terms. That can feel like progress and loss at the same time, which is one reason founders often react so strongly to the first proper equity financing.

To understand a priced round properly, it helps to see that the price is not merely a flattering label attached to the company. It determines the exchange rate between capital and ownership. If the company is priced strongly, the investor gets fewer shares for a given amount of money, and the founders suffer less dilution. If the company is priced weakly, the investor receives more shares for the same money, and the founders give up more of the future to buy the same runway. This is why priced rounds are not only moments of prestige but of consequence. A high valuation can preserve founder ownership if justified. A weak valuation can materially reshape the cap table even if the absolute amount of money raised is unchanged. The company is not just receiving money. It is deciding how expensive its own future is in ownership terms.

This is also the point at which the class of shares begins to matter more sharply. In many priced rounds, especially institutional ones, the investor does not simply receive the same ordinary or common shares the founders hold. The investor may receive preferred shares with rights that alter the economic meaning of the cap table beyond the headline percentages. That is why founders should never think a priced round is fully understood once they know the valuation and the ownership percentage being sold. Those figures are essential, but they are not the whole structure. The round price tells you how much of the company the investor is buying. The terms tell you what kind of company they are buying into and what additional rights they are receiving along with that stake.

Another important feature of priced rounds is that they make the company easier to compare and easier to misunderstand. Once a startup has raised at a valuation, people inside and outside the company start using that number as a shorthand for worth. Employees may mentally multiply their option grants by the latest round price. Founders may begin speaking as though the company now "is" worth that amount in a broad and stable sense. Future investors may use the round as a reference point, whether to validate, challenge, or reset expectations. All of this gives the priced round a cultural power beyond its technical mechanics. Yet founders must remain disciplined. A priced round is evidence of what one investor or group of investors was willing to pay under a particular structure and at a particular moment. It is not a guarantee of liquidity, a permanent truth about the company's value, or proof that the cap table is now safe from future tension.

This is especially important because priced rounds often create a new baseline from which future dilution will be experienced. Before the round, the founders may have been diluted only through small early allocations, options, or convertibles. After the round, the cap table has a stronger numerical shape, a clearer market signal, and often a more formal set of expectations around later financing. The founders can now see more concretely what it means to sell part of the company. Future rounds will still change the structure, but the first priced round is often when dilution becomes emotionally and institutionally undeniable. The startup is no longer preparing to be financed. It has been financed through the sale of equity itself.

There is also a sequencing issue here that founders should understand. A priced round is often not just about current needs. It is a message to the future. The valuation, the investor type, the rights granted, the pool size, and the resulting founder position all influence how later investors will perceive the company. A round that is too aggressive in valuation may flatter the founders now but create pressure later if the company struggles to grow into that number. A round that is too weak may solve the immediate cash problem while leaving the founders with much less ownership than they should have had at this stage. A round with badly chosen terms may bring money in but complicate every future conversation. This is why priced rounds have such outsized significance. They do not only provide capital. They establish a structural reference point from which much else will follow.

For many startups, the first priced round is therefore the first true sale of the company's future in a formal market-like sense. The founders may still be the dominant force. The company may still be young. The investor may even be relatively friendly. But something fundamental has changed. The company now has a price at which actual equity was sold, and that price has altered the ownership map in a way that cannot be treated as symbolic. The cap table becomes more real, not because it was unreal before, but because it has now been tested through a direct exchange between capital and ownership.

That is what a priced round is. It is the moment when the startup stops deferring the price of equity and starts selling ownership on explicit terms. The amount raised matters. The valuation matters. The rights matter. The resulting dilution matters.

But above all, what matters is that the company has now crossed into a phase where its future is being structured through direct equity pricing rather than only through promise, projection, or deferred conversion. Once that happens, the founders have to think differently, because the cap table is no longer just their internal map of the company. It has become something the market has begun to write on with real money.

Pre-Money and Post-Money Valuation

Few phrases in startup finance create more confusion than pre-money and post-money valuation, not because the ideas are unusually difficult, but because the language sounds intuitive while hiding a structural distinction that matters enormously for ownership. Founders often hear the terms early, repeat them confidently, and still fail to understand exactly how they shape the cap table. That failure can be expensive. A founder who does not grasp the difference between pre-money and post-money is often not really reading the deal. They may think they are negotiating valuation while missing the fact that valuation only becomes meaningful once it is tied to timing, share issuance, and the resulting ownership structure.

Pre-money valuation is the agreed value of the company immediately before the new investment enters. Post-money valuation is the value of the company immediately after the investment enters. In the most straightforward arithmetic, post-money equals pre-money plus the amount of new money invested. That sounds simple enough, and at a basic level it is. If a company is valued pre-money at £4 million and an investor puts in £1 million, then the post-money valuation is £5 million. The investor has bought into a company that is now, for the purpose of this deal, valued at £5 million after their money has been added. Their £1 million therefore corresponds to twenty percent of the company on a post-money basis, while the pre-existing holders collectively own the remaining eighty percent.

This is the basic logic, but the reason founders get confused is that they often hear the bigger number and emotionally attach to it without tracking what it means for dilution. The founder may tell themselves that the company is now "worth" £5 million and take pride in that label, but the investor's money created part of that post-money number. The correct question is not simply what is the headline valuation.

It is what percentage of the company is being sold, on what pre-money base, and what does the structure look like after the new shares are issued. Without that second step, the valuation language can flatter the founder while obscuring the actual ownership movement.

This is why the distinction matters so much in a priced round. Pre-money valuation tells you how the existing company is being priced before the new capital is added. Post-money valuation tells you what the whole structure looks like once that capital is inside it. The founder's dilution is driven by how much of the post-money company the investor is acquiring. If the investor puts in £1 million at a £4 million pre-money, the investor gets twenty percent because £1 million is one-fifth of the £5 million post-money. If that same £1 million came in at a £9 million pre-money, the post-money would be £10 million and the investor would get only ten percent. The amount invested has not changed. The dilution has. That is why valuation is not decorative. It is the mechanism that prices ownership.

A simple numerical example makes this clearer. Imagine a company with 1,000,000 shares outstanding before the round. The founders and any existing holders together own all of them. The investor agrees to invest £1 million at a £4 million pre-money valuation. The company is therefore treated as worth £4 million before the money arrives. If 1,000,000 shares represent that £4 million pre-money value, then the implied price per share is £4. The investor's £1 million therefore buys 250,000 new shares at £4 each. After the round, the total number of shares becomes 1,250,000. The old holders still have 1,000,000 shares, which now represent eighty percent. The investor has 250,000 shares, or twenty percent. This is pre-money and post-money expressed not only in company-level valuation terms but in actual cap table form.

This example matters because it shows that valuation is not floating above the cap table. It is translated into the cap table through share price and new issuance. A founder who hears only that the round is being done at a £4 million pre-money and does not ask what that means for the number of new shares issued has not yet understood the deal fully. Similarly, a founder who hears only that the investor will own twenty percent after closing but does not ask whether an option pool is being created pre-money has not yet understood the real cost of that twenty percent. The valuation framework and the capital structure must always be read together. To separate them is to read only half the transaction.

This is where option pools re-enter the picture in a very important way. A founder may negotiate a pre-money valuation believing that the existing company consists of the current issued shares, only to discover that the investor expects a larger option pool to be included before the money comes in. That means the effective pre-money structure is broader than the founder first assumed, and the founder absorbs more dilution before the investor's ownership is even calculated. The headline pre-money valuation may remain the same, but the founder's effective economics are weaker because the pre-money denominator has been expanded. This is one of the common places where founders think they have defended valuation successfully while actually conceding more ownership than they realise. The problem is not that the words pre-money and post-money were false. The problem is that the founder did not ask carefully enough what counted inside each side of that distinction.

There is also a psychological trap in the way founders talk about these numbers after the round. Once a company has raised at a certain valuation, it becomes tempting to treat that number as a stable reflection of what the business is now "worth." Employees hear it. Friends hear it. The founders themselves begin to use it as a marker of progress. But the round valuation is not a simple truth about intrinsic worth. It is a deal-specific pricing event. It reflects what investors were willing to pay for a certain class of shares under certain terms at a certain moment, often with preferences and rights that matter to the economics. This does not make the number meaningless. It means only that it must not be confused with immediate founder liquidity or with a permanent and universally accepted value of the company. The founder who mentally converts the post-money number straight into personal wealth is usually reading the cap table far too loosely.

At the same time, founders should not become cynical and treat all valuation language as empty. Pre-money and post-money valuation are extremely useful concepts precisely because they force the company to express in structured terms how much ownership is being sold and what that implies about the current pricing of the business. The founder who understands them can compare deals more intelligently, model dilution more accurately, and avoid being distracted by flattering but unhelpful headlines. A good valuation at the wrong structure may be worse than a slightly lower one on better terms.

Conversely, a lower valuation may still be a rational choice if it brings in the right capital under conditions that materially strengthen the company. The key is that the founder must know how valuation is interacting with the cap table, not merely whether the number sounds impressive.

This interaction also reveals why founders need to think in sequence. Pre-money and post-money are not just present-tense labels. They help define the base from which future rounds will be judged. If the current round sets a high post-money valuation, that may help signalling in the short term, but it also means the next round must justify being priced above that level if the company wants to avoid the reputational and structural difficulty of a down round. If the current round is priced lower but sensibly, the company may preserve credibility and give itself more room to grow into the next stage. Pre-money and post-money are therefore not only measures of what is happening now. They are also reference points that future investors, employees, and founders will look back to when evaluating the company's trajectory.

There is an even more subtle lesson here. Pre-money and post-money teach the founder that valuation is always a relational concept. A company is not simply "worth" a number in the abstract. It is worth a number in relation to an amount of capital, a timing of entry, a class of shares, a specific cap table, and a specific deal structure. This is one reason two companies can both claim similar post-money valuations and yet leave their founders in very different positions. One may have achieved its number with a clean structure and sensible pool. Another may have reached the same headline through a combination of pre-money pool expansion, strong investor rights, and heavier-than-obvious dilution. Founders who focus only on the label and not the structure are often comparing the wrong things.

The safest habit a founder can cultivate is to ask, every time these terms appear, four linked questions. What is the pre-money valuation. How much new capital is being invested. What is the post-money valuation as a result. And what exact number of new shares, option pool changes, and structural rights does this create on the cap table. Once those questions are kept together, pre-money and post-money stop being mysterious or theatrical. They become what they should be: tools for understanding exactly how the company is being priced and how that pricing translates into ownership.

That is the real importance of the distinction. Pre-money tells the founder what the company is being treated as worth before new money arrives. Post-money tells the founder what the enlarged company is being treated as worth once that money is in. The space between those two numbers is not just accounting. It is the place where dilution is born.

How New Shares Are Created in a Round

For many founders, the most unsettling part of a priced round is not the idea of valuation but the moment they fully grasp how the investor's ownership actually appears. It does not usually appear because the founder hands over part of their own shareholding directly. It appears because the company creates new shares and issues them into the structure. That distinction is essential. A priced round is often not a transfer of existing founder stock, but an expansion of the company's capital base. The investor's position is created by enlarging the total number of claims, and that enlargement is what changes the founder's percentage.

This is the practical engine of dilution.

To understand it properly, the founder has to stop thinking of the company as a fixed pie and start thinking of it as a structure that can issue additional slices. The company begins the round with a certain number of shares already outstanding. Those shares represent the current ownership map. Once the company agrees a price per share for the round, it can calculate how many new shares must be created to match the amount of money the investor is putting in. If the investor is investing £1 million and the agreed round price is £4 per share, then 250,000 new shares are issued. The existing holders have not lost their own shares. What has changed is that the total has increased, and the investor now occupies part of that larger total.

This may sound mechanical, but the consequences are strategic. The company is not only taking in money. It is deciding how much new ownership must be manufactured in order to bring that money inside. That means every priced round is, in a literal sense, an act of capital creation. The company expands the number of claims because that is how it finances growth. Once the founder sees that clearly, the cap table becomes easier to read. The new investor's ownership is not mysterious.

It is the result of newly issued shares priced according to the round terms.

This is also why the starting share count matters less than inexperienced founders often think. A company with 1,000,000 existing shares and a company with 10,000,000 existing shares can both raise the same money at the same effective valuation, provided the implied price per share and number of new shares issued are adjusted accordingly. What matters is not whether the company's capital base is counted in thousands or millions. What matters is the relationship between the company's pre-round value, the amount invested, and the number of new shares that must be created to convert that investment into ownership. Founders who become too attached to raw counts often miss the more important point, which is that the round is creating a new proportional structure, not honouring the emotional comfort of the old one.

A simple example helps. Suppose a company has 2,000,000 shares outstanding before the round and is priced at a £6,000,000 pre-money valuation. That means the implied price per share is £3. If an investor puts in £1,500,000, then 500,000 new shares are issued at £3 each. After the round, the company has 2,500,000 shares outstanding. The investor owns 500,000 of them, or twenty percent. The existing shareholders collectively own the remaining eighty percent. This is not because anyone took twenty percent from the founders directly. It is because the company enlarged itself by exactly the number of shares required to translate £1,500,000 into the ownership proportion implied by the agreed pricing.

Once the founder understands that, a second truth becomes visible. Every new share created in the round sits equally inside the denominator when percentages are recalculated, but not every share may sit equally inside the economic structure once rights are considered. If the investor receives preferred shares and the founders hold common shares, then the round has not merely created more shares. It has created a new class of claim. The founder's percentage falls because the denominator expands, but the founder's practical relationship to the future may also change because the new shares may carry rights the old ones do not. That is why founders should never stop their thinking at the mere quantity of new shares. Quantity tells you how ownership is diluted. Rights tell you what kind of ownership has entered.

There is also a timing discipline hidden in this process. New shares are not properly "created" just because the spreadsheet has been updated. They are created when the company has actually taken the steps necessary to issue them under its governing documents and applicable law. This means approvals, resolutions, agreements, subscriptions, registers, and all the machinery that turns a model into corporate fact. Founders who update the cap table model before the round closes often begin psychologically living in the post-round structure before the legal structure exists. That can create confusion, especially if the round changes during negotiation or fails to close on the expected terms. The spreadsheet may predict the new shares. The company must still bring them into legal reality.

This is one reason good founders become very precise about the difference between proposed issuance and completed issuance. During a live round, there may be drafts, expected allocations, and modelled outcomes. Those are useful. But until closing happens properly, the company is still partly living in the old structure. Investors, lawyers, and serious finance people know this instinctively. Founders sometimes do not, especially when they are excited or relieved at the prospect of capital arriving. The emotional desire to treat the round as done can outrun the actual company mechanics. That is rarely wise. Ownership is too important to be governed by anticipation alone.

Another important point is that not all new shares in a round necessarily go only to the lead investor. If the company is simultaneously expanding an option pool, converting earlier instruments, or allowing existing investors to participate pro rata, then several streams of new issuance may occur around the same financing event. This is where founders often underestimate the true ownership impact of a round. They focus on the lead cheque and the lead investor, but the round is really a bundle of structural changes. New investor shares may be created. Pool shares may be reserved or issued. SAFEs or notes may convert into stock. Existing holders may take additional shares to preserve their position. The company's total share count after the round is therefore often the product of several creation events, not just one.

This is why founders should ask not simply how many shares is the new investor getting, but what total new shares are being created in connection with this round and for what reasons. That question produces a much more accurate reading of dilution. It also helps the founder spot when a round that looks acceptable at first glance has become significantly more expensive once all the associated issuances are counted. A company can believe it has sold, for example, twenty percent to a new investor when the effective structural cost is meaningfully higher once the new pool and all related issuances are included. If the founder does not trace how those shares are created, they are negotiating in a kind of numerical fog.

The language of creating shares also reminds the founder of something deeper. The company's capital structure is not a passive record of nature. It is an engineered structure. New shares are brought into existence by choice, and that choice should always be measured against what the company is buying in return. A strong company does not create claims lightly. It creates them to solve real problems, seize real opportunities, or secure real contributors. Every issuance is therefore both a financing step and a statement about what the company believes it needs badly enough to spend future ownership on. If the founder keeps that in mind, the mechanics of issuance become more than technical detail. They become visible expressions of strategic judgment.

This also explains why later rounds can feel so different from the first. Once the founder has watched the company create shares in one financing, the next financing is no longer conceptually abstract. The founder knows that the round is not only about valuation headlines and investor enthusiasm. It is about another enlargement of the ownership structure. Another reshaping of percentages. Another step in the movement from concentrated founding ownership toward a broader capital base. The more clearly the founder understands how shares are created in a round, the more capable they become of judging whether the next issuance is strengthening the company or merely thinning the old owners without enough return.

That is the central lesson. New shares in a priced round are the instrument through which cash becomes ownership. The company expands its capital structure to let the new investor in. Once the founder sees that process clearly, dilution becomes much easier to read, and the next question becomes sharper as well: once the new shares are created, how exactly is investor ownership calculated, and what does that mean for everyone else on the table.

How Investor Ownership Is Calculated

Once a founder understands that a priced round usually works by creating new shares, the next question becomes unavoidable. How does the company decide exactly how much of the post-round business the investor will own. This is where valuation stops sounding like a prestige label and starts operating as a conversion rule between money and control. Investor ownership is not guessed, and it is not simply the result of whatever percentage sounds tolerable to the founders. It is calculated from the relationship between the amount invested, the agreed valuation framework, and the resulting number of shares issued at the round price.

In the cleanest form, the logic is straightforward. The investor's post-money ownership percentage is usually the amount invested divided by the post-money valuation. If a company is valued at a £4 million pre-money and the investor puts in £1 million, then the post-money valuation is £5 million. The investor therefore owns £1 million out of £5 million, which is twenty percent. The pre-existing holders collectively own the remaining eighty percent. That is the percentage logic. The share-count logic then follows from it by calculating the price per share implied by the pre-money valuation and issuing enough new shares for the investor's cash to buy the appropriate stake.

This is one of the few places in startup finance where founders can help themselves enormously by holding the company-level view and the per-share view in their heads at the same time. At the company level, the question is what fraction of the enlarged company the investor is buying with the new money. At the share level, the question is how many new shares must be issued at the round price to produce that fraction. If either view is missing, the founder is likely to follow the deal only partially. With both views present, investor ownership becomes much easier to understand and much harder to misstate.

A simple example shows the two perspectives working together. Imagine a company with 1,000,000 shares outstanding and a pre-money valuation of £4 million. That means each existing share is being treated, for round purposes, as worth £4. If the investor puts in £1 million, then the investor receives 250,000 new shares at £4 each. After the round, the company has 1,250,000 shares in total. The investor's 250,000 shares represent twenty percent.

This is the same answer reached from the company-level logic, where the investor contributed one-fifth of the £5 million post-money value.

What this example really teaches is that investor ownership is not an independent number floating somewhere outside the round. It is produced by the deal structure. Change the pre-money valuation and the investor ownership changes. Keep the valuation the same but increase the amount invested and the investor ownership changes. Change the share count while keeping the economics consistent and the ownership percentage stays the same. Founders therefore need to stop thinking of investor ownership as a separate headline from valuation. It is the operational expression of valuation.

This is also why founders often become confused when they hear investors speak in both money and percentage terms. An investor may say they want to invest £2 million for twenty-five percent, or may say they are investing at a certain pre-money valuation and let the percentage follow from that. These are usually two ways of describing the same structural relationship. The founder should always be able to move comfortably between them. If the investor wants twenty-five percent and is putting in £2 million, then the implied post-money valuation is £8 million and the implied pre-money valuation is £6 million. If the investor says the pre-money is £6 million and they are putting in £2 million, then the post-money is £8 million and their ownership is twenty-five percent. The numbers are not separate claims. They are connected expressions of one deal.

At this point the founder also needs to remember that the apparently clean calculation can be affected by what is included in the effective pre-money structure. If the company is being asked to enlarge its option pool before the money comes in, then the investor's ownership may still be expressed as the same fraction of the post-money company while the founders bear more of the economic burden than they first expected. This is because the denominator from which the investor's shares are being calculated has been widened on the founder side before the new money lands. The investor's percentage may still be calculated cleanly from amount invested and post-money value, but the founder's retained ownership after all related changes may be less flattering than the headline round summary implied. This is one of the reasons founders must always ask not just what percentage the investor gets, but what exact pre-money structure is being used to calculate that result.

There is another subtlety here. Investor ownership is often discussed as though it is only a present-tense result, but in practice it is also a starting point for future rounds. An investor buying twenty percent today is not only acquiring a current stake. They are taking a position from which they may later try to preserve ownership through pro rata rights, support or resist future pool expansions, and influence the timing and structure of later financings. This means the founder should not think of the percentage as static in its significance. The percentage is the entry point. What matters next is what rights, follow-on behaviour, and future capital needs do to that position over time.

This is one reason sophisticated investors care about investor ownership in relation to eventual fund outcomes, not merely present control. A fund does not necessarily need majority control to achieve an excellent return. It needs a large enough stake in a company that could become very valuable, ideally one it can continue to support in future rounds if things go well. That is why founders often find venture investors more focused on ownership percentages than the emotional tone of the company-building story would seem to warrant. The investor is doing return math. A five percent stake in a modest outcome may not matter much to a venture fund. A fifteen or twenty percent stake in a company that can scale significantly may matter a great deal. The company's financing structure is therefore being designed partly around the investor's portfolio logic, not only around the founders' present comfort.

It is also worth noticing that the investor's ownership percentage tells outsiders something about how expensive the round was in founder terms. If an investor acquires a large share for a relatively modest cheque, that suggests either a lower valuation, a company at higher risk, or a negotiating position that did not favour the founders strongly. If an investor acquires a smaller share for a larger cheque, that may indicate stronger founder leverage, more traction, or a hotter market environment. This does not mean one should judge rounds simplistically by whether the investor received a "large" or "small" percentage. The terms, the company stage, the capital needs, and the strategic value of the investor all matter. But the investor's ownership is one of the clearest windows into how the company has priced itself and what it has had to give up to buy the next stage.

Founders should also learn to distinguish between the investor's ownership on an immediately issued basis and the broader fully diluted picture. If options, SAFEs, notes, warrants, or other instruments are already part of the structure, then the investor's percentage can look different depending on what basis of calculation is being used. Some conversations will refer to current issued ownership. Others will refer to fully diluted ownership. These are not interchangeable. A founder who does not ask which basis is being used can become confused very quickly and may think the investor's percentage is shifting mysteriously when in reality the underlying basis of measurement is changing. Precision in language matters a great deal here.

All of this means that investor ownership should never be treated as merely the investor's problem. It is one of the founder's most important tools for understanding the round itself. Once the founder knows the pre-money valuation, the amount being invested, the post-money valuation, and the exact structure into which the new shares are being issued, they can calculate investor ownership and therefore see much more clearly what the round is really doing to the company. Without that clarity, founders are often left reacting emotionally to dilution instead of understanding exactly how the new capital has been translated into a new position on the cap table.

That is the essential point. Investor ownership is not mysterious, and it is not arbitrary. It is the mathematical result of a pricing decision and a share issuance decision. When the founder understands that, the next step becomes easier to face as well: once the investor's ownership is fixed, what exactly happens to founder stakes, and how should the founders think about the shift from "our company" to "our company with outsiders inside it."

What the Round Does to Founder Stakes

The first priced round changes founder stakes in a way that is mathematically simple but psychologically much heavier than many founders expect. Before the round, the founders are usually still living, at least partly, inside the emotional afterglow of the original cap table. They know dilution is coming. They may even have modelled it. But the company is still experienced as something substantially theirs, and the first formal sale of equity makes that reality feel newly negotiable. Once the round closes, the founders can no longer think of outside ownership as a future possibility or an abstract idea. It is now written directly into the structure. The company has new participants inside its future, and the founders' own positions have been permanently recalculated around that fact.

At the most basic level, the round reduces founder percentages because the company has created new shares for the investor. If the founders previously owned one hundred percent, they now own less. If they previously held eighty percent collectively, they now hold less. This part is obvious. What matters more is how the founders interpret that change. A founder who reads only the falling percentage may conclude that the round has primarily taken something away. A founder who reads the structure more intelligently asks what the company received in exchange and whether the post-round founder position still leaves the people doing the work strongly aligned with the business's future.

This is the first serious test of whether the founders actually understand dilution or merely tolerate hearing about it. The round does not usually remove founder shares directly. It changes what those shares mean relative to the enlarged company. That is why the founder's share count may remain identical while the founder's stake becomes smaller in percentage terms. For many founders, this is the moment where theory becomes emotionally real. A founder who once owned 5,000,000 out of 10,000,000 shares may still hold all 5,000,000 after the round, but if the total expands to 12,500,000 then the founder no longer owns fifty percent. They own forty percent. The founder can say, truthfully, that nothing was taken from their certificate count. They can also no longer say they own half the company. The round has altered the founder's relationship to the whole.

This matters because founders do not only lose percentage. They gain context. Before the round, a large founder stake may sit inside a fragile company that lacks enough capital, credibility, or hiring capacity to become much more than promising. After the round, the founder may own less of a stronger enterprise. If the company has raised sensibly, the founders may now hold smaller stakes in a business with more runway, a more serious investor, a stronger signalling effect to future hires and capital, and a better chance of reaching the next milestone. That is the constructive version of what the round does to founder stakes. It trades some concentration for a stronger vehicle.

But there is a darker version too. If the round is poorly priced, badly timed, or structured around more rights and dilution than the company can comfortably bear, then founder stakes may become thinner without the company becoming strong enough to justify the cost.

This is why founders should never read their post-round position through percentage alone. Nor should they comfort themselves with vague narratives of progress if the post-round structure leaves them weak, demotivated, or badly exposed to future rounds. The important question is not merely whether the founder stake got smaller. It is whether the founder stake remains meaningful inside the company that now exists after the round.

That meaning has several dimensions. The first is motivation. Does each founder still hold enough that the upside remains worth years of uncertain work, later dilution, and the ordinary burdens of startup life. This is not a sentimental question. It is structural. If the founders are already thin after the first significant round, then future rounds, option pool expansions, or difficult financing conditions may leave them in a position where the cap table no longer supports founder-level commitment. Investors often understand this quite well, which is why they care about founder ownership not only as a present matter but as a trajectory. A round that feels acceptable now can still be dangerous if it leaves too little room for the founders to remain strongly aligned later.

The second dimension is internal balance. A round does not only change the founders versus the investor. It can also change the founders relative to one another. If one founder began with a much larger stake, that founder may still remain dominant after the round while another begins to look thin much sooner. If one founder is carrying more of the company's actual burden than the cap table already reflected, the dilution may intensify a pre-existing tension. The round therefore interacts with whatever the founder structure already was. It does not erase early choices. It carries them forward into a more formal ownership regime. That is one reason weak founder splits become even more painful once outside money arrives. The percentages no longer feel like internal matters alone. They now sit inside a capital structure that others are also relying on.

The third dimension is control. Founders often assume that losing percentage necessarily means losing control, but that is too simple. A founder may remain the largest holder after the round and retain practical leadership even if the percentage falls substantially. Another founder may still hold a numerically strong stake but lose meaningful freedom because the round also introduced preferred rights, consent thresholds, board representation, or other governance features that changed how decisions are made.

The round therefore changes founder stakes not only quantitatively but politically. It alters where founders stand in relation to future capital, future hires, and future strategic decisions. Sometimes that political shift is modest. Sometimes it matters far more than the raw percentage movement itself.

There is also an identity effect that founders should not ignore. After the first real round, many founders experience a subtle change in how they speak about the company. Before the round, they often say "my company" or "our company" in a way that still carries the intimacy of origin. After the round, even if those phrases remain socially natural, the founder now knows in a more formal way that the company has become a shared financial structure. This can be healthy. It can push the founder toward better governance, better reporting, and a more institutional mindset. But it can also create a quiet grief if the founder has not prepared emotionally for the fact that building something fundable usually means no longer owning it in the pure, concentrated way that the earliest stage allowed. The round does not only change the cap table. It changes the founder's mental relationship to the business.

This is one reason some founders become irrationally defensive after a first equity financing. They feel that something fundamental has been surrendered, and they react by overprotecting the remaining stake in ways that may later hurt the company. Others go the opposite way and become too relaxed, telling themselves that since dilution has already happened, future rounds are just more of the same. Both responses are unhelpful. The better response is to see the first round as a reset in ownership thinking. The founder stake after the round is the new reality. From that reality onward, the company has to be governed with a much more serious understanding of what each additional round, pool expansion, or rights package will do to the founders' continuing position.

What the round does to founder stakes, then, is not reducible to one line in the cap table. It changes percentages. It tests founder motivation. It carries forward old founder-split logic into a more formal environment. It may alter control. It may strengthen the company enough that the founders' smaller stake is actually much better than the old one was. Or it may reveal that the founders have paid too much for too little. All of that is inside the same event.

The smartest founders therefore look at the post-round cap table and ask more than how much do I own now. They ask, what kind of stake is this inside the company we have now built, what will this stake look like after the next likely round, and is it still large enough, clear enough, and properly situated enough that carrying this company forward makes economic and strategic sense. That is the real question a priced round asks of founder ownership.

Why the Round Price Matters More Than the Founder First Assumes

When founders first encounter priced rounds, they often focus on the most visible outcomes. How much money is coming in. What percentage is being sold. Whether the investor seems prestigious. Whether the round feels like progress. All of these things matter, but one variable often matters even more than founders initially appreciate, and that is the round price. The round price is not just a technical translation of valuation into per-share economics. It is one of the clearest mechanisms through which the company decides how expensive its own future will be in ownership terms. A founder who treats it as an accounting detail is usually underestimating one of the most consequential parts of the entire transaction.

The reason the round price matters so much is that it sits at the exact point where capital becomes dilution. Once the pre-money valuation has been agreed and the number of existing shares is known, the round price determines how many new shares the investor receives for the money being invested. The lower the round price, the more new shares must be created for the same amount of cash. The more new shares created, the greater the dilution to the existing holders. The higher the round price, the fewer new shares are needed, and the more ownership the founders preserve for the same capital. In other words, the round price is not simply descriptive. It is the exchange rate between runway and dilution.

This is one reason founders should resist the temptation to talk only in valuation headlines. A company may say it raised at a particular pre-money or post-money figure, but unless the founder understands the implied price per share and what that price did to the total share count, the real structure of the round may still feel vague. Investors usually understand this very clearly. They know that the same cheque can buy very different amounts of the company depending on the pricing. They know that a round with a lower price can create a much larger future claim. Founders, especially in a first serious round, sometimes remain too focused on the total amount raised and not focused enough on how much of the company the pricing quietly cost them.

A simple numerical comparison makes the point plain. Imagine a company with 1,000,000 shares outstanding. In one scenario, the pre-money valuation is £4 million, which implies a round price of £4 per share. A £1 million investor therefore receives 250,000 new shares and ends up with twenty percent of the company post-money. In another scenario, the same company raises the same £1 million, but the pre-money valuation is £9 million, implying a price of £9 per share. The investor now receives only about 111,111 new shares and ends up with about ten percent post-money. The money is identical. The difference lies in the round price, and the ownership consequence for the founders is enormous.

This is why founders should stop thinking of the round price as a technical by-product and start seeing it as a central strategic variable. It determines how much dilution the current amount of capital produces. It also influences how the company will be perceived later. A very low price may suggest weakness or urgency, which may be justified if the business is early or under pressure, but it still leaves the founders with less room for future rounds. A stronger price can preserve founder ownership and create a healthier base for the next financing, provided it is credible and not simply inflated beyond what the company can reasonably support. The founder's task is not to demand the highest imaginable price. It is to understand that price discipline is one of the few direct ways of defending ownership while still raising money.

The round price also matters because it affects how all later participants interpret the company. Employees who receive options after the round will often understand their grants, at least initially, in relation to the latest share price. Future investors will use the round as a reference point, whether they view it as a floor to beat, a benchmark to question, or a sign that the company may have been over- or underpriced. A poorly chosen round price therefore does not disappear once the money arrives. It becomes part of the company's financing history. If the price was too aggressive relative to the company's actual progress, later investors may resist or force a difficult reset. If it was too weak, the founders may spend years carrying the consequences of having sold more of the business than they needed to at an early stage.

This is one of the reasons founders should never celebrate a round price in isolation. A high price can feel like validation, but if it arrives with pool expansion, aggressive rights, or expectations the company cannot realistically meet before the next raise, then the apparent triumph may be more fragile than it looks. Likewise, a lower price may feel disappointing, but if it comes with clean terms, the right investor, and a realistic base from which the company can grow into a stronger next round, it may be strategically much healthier than a flattering but brittle valuation. The round price matters because it shapes the ownership cost of capital and the company's path into future financing, not because it flatters founder ego.

Founders also need to understand how the round price interacts with future dilution. A lower price today does not only cost the founder now. It changes the starting base from which later rounds will build. If the founder gives away more of the company than necessary in the first priced round, then later dilution events stack on top of a weaker existing position. That can produce compounding effects that become painful much sooner than expected. This is especially dangerous in companies that know they will need multiple rounds. A founder who thinks only about whether the present raise is survivable may miss the fact that the round price has already made the future cap table much tighter than it needed to be.

There is also a behavioural consequence. Founders often negotiate harder on headline valuation than on the underlying economics of round price because valuation language feels more strategic and impressive, whereas price per share can seem narrow or administrative. In reality, the latter often reveals the truth of the former. A round price that leaves the investor with more ownership than the founder expected, especially once pool changes are included, shows that the founder may have been comforted by the narrative of valuation without tracing how that narrative translated into share issuance. The investor is not ultimately buying "valuation." The investor is buying shares at a price. That is what enters the cap table, and that is what the founder must follow with precision.

This is particularly important when a company has issued convertibles or SAFEs earlier. Those instruments may convert based on discounts or caps that relate in some way to the round price. In such cases, the round price does not only determine the new investor's direct ownership. It may also trigger and price the conversion of earlier claims.

A lower price may therefore widen the dilutive effect far beyond the new investor alone. A founder who is not thinking carefully about round price in these contexts can be surprised twice: once by the investor's ownership and again by the conversion effects on the rest of the table. That is one of the clearest examples of why price is more than a current-round number. It can activate structural consequences across the whole financing history of the company.
The founder should also remember that price interacts with signalling. A stronger round price can create confidence around the company's trajectory, but only if the business genuinely has the momentum, metrics, or market position to support it. If the company raises at too high a price and then struggles, that price becomes a trap because the next investors must either validate it with an even higher one or force the company into a down round. A more moderate but realistic price can preserve strategic flexibility. The founder therefore needs to think not only what price feels best today, but what price the company can plausibly grow into by the next financing event. Round price matters because it is both a present economic fact and a future expectation-setting device.

At the human level, founders often underestimate round price because they still think emotionally in percentages and total raise size. The company is raising £2 million, which feels significant. The investor is taking a certain share, which feels manageable. But the founder may not instinctively feel how a slightly weaker price quietly changes the number of new shares created and therefore the shape of the cap table. This is why disciplined founders learn to convert all funding conversations into share-price consequences. They want to know what the price per share is, how many new shares are being issued, what the total becomes, how the pool is being treated, and what the founder position looks like on a fully diluted basis afterward. Once the founder can do that fluently, the round price stops being hidden inside the deal and becomes visible for what it is. That is why the round price matters more than the founder first assumes. It is the point where narrative becomes arithmetic and arithmetic becomes ownership. It determines how much of the company must be created anew to buy the capital coming in. It influences how the current round feels and how future rounds may unfold. It affects not only the investor's position but the founder's remaining room to build, hire, and survive future dilution. The company may remember the round by its headline valuation, but the cap table will remember it by the price at which the future was sold.

Walking Through a Full Early Funding Example

Abstract explanations of priced rounds are useful, but founders usually only feel that they understand them once they can watch an actual cap table move from one state to another and see how valuation, new shares, option pools, and founder percentages all interact in sequence. A full early funding example is therefore valuable because it turns separate ideas into one continuous event. The founder can see not only what each term means in isolation, but how the round reshapes the company as a whole.

Imagine a startup with two founders. Founder A owns 6,000,000 common shares and Founder B owns 4,000,000 common shares. The company therefore has 10,000,000 shares outstanding, and the founder ownership is split sixty-forty. There are no outside investors yet, no convertible instruments, and no option pool. The cap table is simple, and the founders together own one hundred percent.

Now suppose the company is preparing for its first real priced seed round. It has some early traction, a developing product, and clear evidence that it needs capital to hire more seriously and reach the next milestone. An investor is willing to invest £2 million, and the parties agree on a pre-money valuation of £8 million. On that basis, the post-money valuation will be £10 million. At the company level, this already tells us something important. The investor is buying twenty percent of the company after the round, because £2 million is one fifth of £10 million.

That is the valuation view. The share-issuance view takes us further. If the company is worth £8 million pre-money and has 10,000,000 shares outstanding, then the implied round price is £0.80 per share. The investor is putting in £2 million, so the company must issue 2,500,000 new shares at £0.80 each. After the round, the total share count becomes 12,500,000. Founder A still holds 6,000,000 shares, but now owns 48 percent rather than 60 percent. Founder B still holds 4,000,000 shares, but now owns 32 percent rather than 40 percent. The new investor holds 2,500,000 shares, or 20 percent. The founders have not transferred any of their old shares directly. The dilution has happened because the company expanded the denominator.

If the round stopped there, the mechanics would be fairly clean. But many real rounds do not stop there, and this is where the example becomes more useful. The investor says the company must also create an employee option pool of 15 percent on a post-round fully diluted basis because the startup will need to hire a lead engineer, a product manager, and a commercial operator before the next financing. The founders now face the issue many first-time companies underestimate: the pool is not separate from the round. It is part of the economics of the round.

To understand what this means, we have to ask when the pool is being created. Suppose the investor insists that the pool be created pre-money. That means the founders, not the new investor, will bear most of the economic burden of reserving that future hiring space. The company now has to determine how many pool shares are needed so that, after both the pool creation and the investment, the pool represents 15 percent of the company. This is where founders often realise that the round is more expensive than the headline valuation first suggested.

Let us walk through it carefully. Before the investor money comes in, the company has 10,000,000 founder shares. Let us call the number of new option-pool shares X. The pre-money fully diluted count becomes 10,000,000 plus X. The pre-money valuation remains £8 million, so the price per share for the round is now £8 million divided by 10,000,000 plus X. The investor is still putting in £2 million, so the number of investor shares issued becomes £2 million divided by that per-share price. After both the pool creation and the investment, the total shares become 10,000,000 plus X plus the investor shares. We want the pool to equal 15 percent of that total.

Solving it directly is less important here than seeing the consequence, but in this structure the required pool turns out to be materially larger than founders often guess. The pool has to be large enough not only to exist, but still to be 15 percent after the investor's new shares are also inside the table. Once the arithmetic is done, the founders discover that the company needs roughly 2,205,882 pool shares before the round, and the investor then receives roughly 3,051,471 new preferred shares. The total post-round fully diluted count becomes about 15,257,353 shares.

Now the cap table looks very different. Founder A still holds 6,000,000 shares, but now owns roughly 39.3 percent. Founder B still holds 4,000,000 shares, but now owns roughly 26.2 percent. The option pool represents about 14.5 percent if rounded from this simplified treatment, and the investor holds about 20 percent. In a more exact drafting structure the pool would be sized so it lands precisely at the negotiated percentage, but the lesson is already clear. The founders did not simply sell twenty percent to the investor. They also accepted substantial pre-money dilution to create the future hiring reserve.

This is the kind of moment that changes how founders think about fundraising. At first glance they thought they were raising £2 million at an £8 million pre-money and giving the investor twenty percent. In reality, once the required option pool is built in, Founder A has gone from 60 percent to roughly 39 percent, and Founder B from 40 percent to roughly 26 percent. The investor still gets twenty percent, but the founders' retained ownership is lower than a naive reading of the headline valuation would have implied. Nothing dishonest necessarily occurred. The founders simply had not yet understood that the pool was part of the real price.

Now imagine the company uses part of that pool over the next eighteen months. It grants 600,000 options to the lead engineer, 400,000 to the product hire, and 300,000 spread across several other early team members. The company grows, hits some milestones, and returns to market for a Series A. At this point, the cap table the next investors see is no longer just two founders and one seed investor. It is a founder pair, a seed investor, an option reserve partly granted and partly unallocated, and a company whose next round will be priced off the structure created by the seed financing.

Suppose the Series A investor offers £6 million at a £18 million pre-money. If the company has about 15.26 million fully diluted shares in its working structure, the implied Series A price is about £1.18 per share. The Series A investor therefore receives about 5.08 million new shares. The post-round total becomes about 20.34 million shares. Founder A's 6,000,000 shares now represent about 29.5 percent. Founder B's 4,000,000 shares now represent about 19.7 percent. The seed investor's 3.05 million shares fall to about 15 percent. The existing and remaining option pool position is also diluted proportionally, though specific granted options still retain their own economic significance within the now-larger company.

This second step is not included to frighten the founder. It is included to show what early financing decisions become once they are carried forward. Founder A has moved from 60 percent at incorporation to around 39 percent after the seed round and then to around 29.5 percent after the Series A. Founder B has moved from 40 percent to around 26 percent to around 19.7 percent. Neither founder has necessarily been treated badly. The company may now be much stronger, much better funded, and much more likely to produce a meaningful outcome. But the cap table has undergone a transformation that could not have been felt properly if the founders had looked only at the first round as an isolated event.

A second lesson emerges from this example. The option pool is not merely a staff perk layered gently on top of the "real" financing. It is part of the financing architecture. If the founders had ignored the pool in the seed round, they would have misunderstood both the investor's effective economics and their own post-round position. If they had oversized the pool beyond realistic hiring needs, they would have accepted unnecessary dilution. If they had undersized it, they might have faced another awkward and dilutive expansion before the Series A. In other words, the pool was not an HR detail. It was one of the main structural variables in the round.

A third lesson is that founder stake after a round must always be interpreted with the next likely round in mind. A founder looking only at the seed-stage post-round table might say that 39 percent or 26 percent still feels healthy. That may be true. But if the company obviously intends to raise again, then the real question is what those positions will look like after the next financing, after more grants, and after any future structural changes already implied by the company's growth plan. A founder who feels safe at seed because the percentage still looks large may discover later that the earlier comfort came partly from failing to think sequentially.

The value of a full example like this is not that it predicts what every company should do. Different businesses will have different valuations, different pool sizes, different numbers of founders, and different capital needs. The value is that it trains the founder to see the round as one continuous structural event. The founders begin with a simple cap table. They negotiate valuation. They set a price per share. They create new investor shares. They may expand the option pool. Their percentages change. The resulting structure becomes the base for the next stage.

Once a founder can watch that chain unfold clearly, priced rounds stop feeling like mysterious moments of dilution and start feeling like what they really are: deliberate re-engineerings of the company's ownership in exchange for resources that are supposed to make the company stronger than it was before.

That is the real purpose of walking through a full early funding example. It teaches the founder that fundraising is never only about the cheque. It is about the new company that exists after the cheque has been translated into ownership.

* * *

TEN

Convertible Notes and SAFE Agreements

"In theory there is no difference between theory and practice. In practice there is."

- Yogi Berra

Why Startups Use Deferred Pricing Instruments

One of the recurring tensions in early-stage finance is that startups often need money before anyone can price them with much confidence. The company may be too young, too uncertain, too pre-revenue, too experimentally structured, or too dependent on future technical and commercial proof for a full priced round to feel natural. Yet the need for capital is real all the same. The founders may need runway, early hires, product development time, or simply breathing room to reach the next milestone. This is the setting in which deferred pricing instruments become attractive. They allow money to enter the company now while postponing the hardest question of all, which is exactly how much the company is worth today for the purpose of issuing priced equity.

This is the core logic behind convertible notes and SAFE agreements. They are not primarily tools of legal elegance, and they are not just fashionable startup paperwork. They are mechanisms for solving a timing problem. The startup needs money before the company is mature enough, or before the parties are willing, to conduct a full priced round. Rather than forcing an awkward valuation too early, the company and the investor agree on a structure in which the money comes in now and the conversion into equity happens later, usually when a future financing round provides a more developed pricing context.

This can be very useful. A priced round requires more than cash need and enthusiasm. It usually requires a more defined cap table, more developed investor diligence, a clearer view of market progress, and enough confidence in current valuation that the company and investor are prepared to lock a price in.

Very young startups often do not meet that standard. Founders may have a strong vision and early evidence, but the range of plausible valuations can still be wide enough that trying to force precision too early may either overprice the company unrealistically or underprice it in a way the founders regret later. Deferred pricing instruments allow the parties to move forward without pretending that certainty already exists where it does not.

That does not mean these instruments avoid valuation entirely. This is one of the most common misunderstandings. Founders sometimes hear that a note or SAFE avoids a priced round and assume that it avoids valuation altogether. In reality, these instruments usually defer the final pricing event rather than eliminate it. The investor is not saying valuation does not matter. The investor is saying that valuation will be determined later through a specified mechanism, often with protections such as a discount, a valuation cap, or both. The company is therefore not escaping ownership consequences. It is shifting them into a future event where other terms and other capital will help define the final conversion.

This timing shift is what makes deferred instruments attractive to founders. In the short term, they can be faster, simpler, and psychologically easier than a full priced round. The founder does not have to endure an immediate negotiation over how many new preferred shares are being issued today. The company can often close small amounts of capital more quickly. Early investors who believe in the company can participate without forcing a fully institutional financing process too soon. The startup buys time, and sometimes that time is exactly what allows the business to reach a better later round on stronger terms.

But that same timing shift is what makes these instruments dangerous when misunderstood. Because the dilution is delayed, founders often fail to feel it properly. They know in theory that the money will convert into ownership later, but because no immediate share issuance is taking place in the obvious priced-round sense, the structural cost can feel softer, almost invisible. This is why founders sometimes sign several deferred instruments in succession, each of which seems individually manageable, only to discover later that the accumulated conversion meaningfully reshapes the cap table. Deferred pricing can therefore create a false emotional experience of cheap capital. The money feels easier because the dilution is not yet sitting in front of the founder in a new post-round percentage.

The dilution has merely been pushed forward in time.
This is one reason the phrase deferred pricing instrument is so useful. It reminds the founder that the issue is not whether ownership cost exists, but when and how that cost is going to be measured. The startup is not getting free runway. It is accepting a future ownership event whose exact form has not yet been fully calculated. If the company improves dramatically before that event, the founders may be glad not to have done a weak early priced round. If the company accumulates too many such instruments, or if the terms are badly understood, the later conversion can arrive as a structural shock. These instruments therefore demand more future thinking than they first appear to.

There is also an investor-side logic that founders need to understand. Early investors using notes or SAFEs are often willing to postpone the precise price of the company because they want to get into the company before it is fully priced by later capital. In return for taking that earlier risk, they typically want some protection so that when the later round does occur, they are not treated exactly the same as investors who waited for more proof. That is where discounts and valuation caps come in. The investor is effectively saying, I will allow the company to defer precise pricing now, but when the future round arrives, I want terms that recognise the fact that I came in earlier and under greater uncertainty. The deferred instrument therefore solves a timing problem for both sides, but not on neutral terms.

Founders should also notice that deferred pricing instruments often change the emotional dynamics of a financing discussion. A priced round forces everyone to confront dilution in the open. A SAFE or note can make the conversation feel more relational, faster, and more trust-based because the hardest ownership arithmetic is not yet fully on the table. This can be helpful in the right company at the right stage. It can also encourage founders to relax too much. When ownership is not being repriced today, founders may slide into thinking that the company is not really giving away much yet. That is the trap. The company is giving something away. It is just doing so through a future conversion framework rather than through immediate priced equity issuance.

This is especially important because startup companies often use these instruments at moments of weakness as well as moments of possibility. Sometimes a company uses a deferred instrument because it is too early for a priced round in a healthy sense.

Other times it uses one because the company is not yet strong enough to get a priced round on terms the founders could bear. Those are very different situations, but from the outside the documents can look similar. Founders therefore need to be honest with themselves about why they are choosing the instrument. Is it because the company is wisely postponing valuation until stronger proof exists, or because the company is avoiding a harsh current valuation it is not emotionally ready to face. The answer matters because it shapes how the founders should think about the eventual conversion and about the strategic urgency of reaching a stronger next stage before that conversion occurs.

There is another subtle reason startups use these instruments. They can make it easier to aggregate early believers without having to renegotiate the company's full capital structure every time a relatively small cheque appears. If several angels want to support the startup in an early phase, a deferred instrument structure may allow the company to take that money on broadly similar terms without constantly resetting the ownership picture through repeated tiny priced rounds. In the right context, this can preserve momentum and reduce procedural drag. But again, the founder must not confuse smoother procedure with lighter economics. The cap table is still being changed in substance, even if the exact percentage consequences are deferred until a later event.

What makes all this especially important is that many founders meet convertible notes and SAFEs before they are truly comfortable with dilution, option pools, valuation, or share issuance in priced rounds. The instruments therefore arrive in the founder's mind before the founder has built the conceptual equipment to read them properly. This is why they can feel deceptively simple. A few pages of documentation, a cap, maybe a discount, money in the bank, and no immediate dramatic change to the visible cap table. The company feels funded, and the founder feels relief. Later, the priced round arrives, the instruments convert, and the founder realises that the calm simplicity of the earlier moment was partly created by moving complexity out of sight rather than removing it.

That is why startups use deferred pricing instruments. They solve a real problem. They let money in before a full present-tense valuation is desirable or possible. They can be efficient, founder-friendly in the right circumstances, and strategically intelligent when used with discipline. But they are not escapes from pricing.

They are mechanisms for deciding that pricing will happen later under rules set now. The founder who understands that will be much better prepared for the next sections, because the question is no longer just why these instruments exist, but how each one actually works and what kind of future cap table they quietly prepare.

What a Convertible Note Is

A convertible note is, at its core, debt that is expected to become equity later rather than simply being repaid in cash. That sentence captures the essence, but it needs to be unpacked carefully because the instrument is easy to misunderstand if one sees only the word convertible and ignores the word note. A note is not originally stock. It is a loan-like instrument. Money comes into the company now, and the company accepts an obligation that, under specified conditions, will usually convert into shares at a later financing event instead of remaining a plain debt claim to maturity.

This hybrid character is what makes convertible notes both useful and potentially dangerous. They allow a startup to take in capital without doing a full priced round immediately, but they do so by using a legal form that begins life as debt. That means a note is not simply informal future equity. It is a structured claim with terms. Those terms often include a principal amount, sometimes an interest rate, a maturity date, conversion mechanics, and protections such as a discount and or a valuation cap. Founders who fail to respect the debt-like side of the note often treat it too casually. Founders who focus only on the debt label may become more frightened than necessary. The truth sits in the middle. A convertible note is usually designed with the expectation that it will convert, but until that conversion happens it is still a note, not already issued equity.

The reason startups use notes is closely tied to the problem described in the previous section. The company needs money before it is ready for a clean priced round. Rather than forcing everyone to agree today on the exact number of shares that should be sold, the note investor lends money into the company now and agrees that the note will turn into equity later when a future financing round creates a more mature pricing event. In that sense, the note defers the final ownership calculation. The company receives cash now. The investor receives a structured claim that is expected to translate into shares later.

This can be highly practical in an early company. A founder may be trying to extend runway by six or nine months, finish a product milestone, secure early traction, or get enough momentum that the next round can happen at a more credible and favourable valuation. A note can bridge that gap. It can also be quicker and procedurally lighter than a full priced round, especially when the amounts involved are relatively modest and the investor is comfortable with the broad trajectory of the company. The startup therefore buys time without immediately rewriting the visible cap table through a full equity issuance.

But this convenience comes with an important intellectual obligation. The founder must understand that the ownership cost has not disappeared. It has merely been delayed and partially hidden inside a future conversion event. The note is carrying a future share issuance inside it, and the exact terms of that issuance will usually depend on what happens in the next qualifying financing round. This is why founders who sign notes casually can later be surprised by the cap table impact. The note did not feel like a priced round when it was signed, but it was always a future equity event waiting for the right trigger.

The debt element of the note matters for another reason as well. Because the instrument begins as debt, it often includes a maturity date. That is the date at which, if no qualifying conversion event has occurred, the note does not simply become emotionally convenient to ignore. Something has to happen. Depending on the drafting, the note may be repayable, extendable, convertible under some fallback mechanism, or subject to negotiation between company and investor. This is one of the reasons notes can create pressure. A startup may imagine that it has bought itself time, but if the company does not reach a conversion event before maturity, the note may stop feeling like benign future equity and start feeling like a much more immediate capital structure problem.

Interest is another element founders often overlook. Because a note is debt, it may accrue interest over time. In many startup cases the note is not expected to be repaid in cash in the ordinary way, so the interest often converts alongside the principal into equity at the later financing event. This may not feel dramatic when the note is first signed, especially if the interest rate is modest, but it still matters. The investor is not only converting the principal money put in. The investor may also be converting accumulated interest. Once again, the theme is the same.

The economic effect is often greater than the founder feels in the moment of signing because some of the cost is deferred, layered, and waiting for later arithmetic to reveal it.

The key event in most convertible notes is the qualified financing, sometimes called a triggering financing or similar term depending on the documents. This is the future round at which the note stops sitting outside the share count and turns into stock. The company raises a priced round, and the noteholder does not usually receive cash repayment. Instead, the note converts into shares, often at a better price than the new investors are paying, because the noteholder took earlier risk. That better price is usually delivered through one or both of two mechanisms: a discount to the new round price, and a valuation cap that protects the noteholder if the company's valuation has increased significantly.

That is why founders should never think of a note as "just a loan from someone supportive." It is a loan-like instrument with an embedded future ownership consequence and usually with terms designed to reward early risk. If the company grows well, the noteholder may convert at terms more favourable than the next round investor. If the company grows poorly or fails to raise a qualifying round in time, the debt-like features of the note may become more visible and more uncomfortable. Either way, the note deserves to be read as a live cap table variable, not as a temporary side pocket of funding that can be understood later.

There is also a behavioural reason founders can get into trouble with notes. Because the early cap table does not always change visibly when the note is signed, the company may continue making other ownership decisions without fully factoring in the future conversion burden. Founders may speak as though they still own a certain percentage in a simple way, create option expectations too casually, or negotiate later rounds without having modelled how the note will actually land once it converts. This is why disciplined founders maintain a shadow or fully diluted view of the cap table even before the note has converted. The note may not yet be common or preferred stock, but it is already part of the company's ownership future.

Investors like convertible notes for their own reasons. They allow early participation in promising companies without forcing a full valuation debate too soon. They also let the investor capture some reward for coming in early, through discounts, caps, and the possibility of conversion into a stronger later round. In some cases, notes can also give investors a more familiar sense of downside structure because the instrument begins life as debt, though in practice startup notes are often underwritten with the expectation that equity conversion, not repayment, is the real path. Still, that debt framing can shape negotiation, especially in cases where the company struggles to reach the next financing event on time.

This means founders should not view notes as universally friendlier or harsher than priced rounds. They are different. A priced round forces present clarity and immediate dilution. A convertible note allows money to come in sooner and pricing to be deferred, but it creates a future conversion event with built-in investor protections and potential timing pressure. In the right company at the right stage, that can be very sensible. In the wrong company, or in the hands of founders who do not model the consequences carefully, it can create cap table surprises that feel far worse than the relative calm of the original signing suggested.

The safest way to think about a convertible note is this. It is not yet equity, but it is already ownership pressure. It is not ordinary commercial debt in the sense of a bank facility designed mainly for repayment, but it is also not costless founder-friendly money. It is a structured bridge between today's cash need and tomorrow's equity issuance. If the founder keeps that picture clear, the note becomes much easier to evaluate soberly. The next questions then follow naturally: what exactly is a SAFE, how is it different from a note, and why do so many startups and investors prefer one over the other in particular situations.

What a SAFE Is

A SAFE, which stands for Simple Agreement for Future Equity, was designed to solve much of the same early-stage financing problem that convertible notes try to solve, but with a different legal and conceptual shape. The startup still needs money before a full priced round is sensible or desirable. The investor still wants a structured way to come in early and convert into equity later, often with some reward for having taken that earlier risk.

The company still wants to avoid forcing a premature valuation event. But instead of using a debt instrument that is expected to convert, the SAFE begins from a different premise. It is not debt at all. It is an agreement that the investor's money will convert into equity in the future if specified trigger events occur.

That distinction matters immediately. A SAFE does not usually carry the same debt language as a convertible note. There is generally no principal-and-interest logic in the same sense, no ordinary maturity date in the same sense, and no initial framing of the capital as a loan awaiting repayment or later conversion. The investor gives the company money now and, in exchange, receives a contractual right to future equity under defined conditions. The SAFE is therefore simpler in one obvious way. It strips out much of the debt architecture that founders often find confusing or heavy in convertible notes and leaves behind a cleaner future-equity promise.

This is one reason SAFEs became so attractive to startups. They are often easier to explain, easier to document, and psychologically easier for founders to accept. There is no immediate sense that the company has taken on a conventional liability that may come due on a maturity date if things do not go well fast enough. The founders can tell themselves, with some justification, that they have raised money without taking on debt in the ordinary sense. That can feel much more aligned with how early-stage startup finance actually works, because many early backers of young companies are not really expecting bank-like repayment. They are expecting a future ownership event. The SAFE acknowledges that expectation directly rather than pretending the transaction is a loan first and an equity participation second.

Yet the simplicity of the SAFE can be deceptive if the founder interprets it as softness or as a kind of cap-table invisibility cloak. A SAFE is not debt, but it is still a real future claim on the company's ownership structure. The company has accepted money in exchange for an agreement that, under the right conditions, will convert into equity later. The fact that it is not debt does not make it harmless. It makes it different. The founder who hears simple and concludes light or consequence-free is making a serious mistake. A SAFE may feel less intimidating than a note at the moment of signing, but once multiple SAFEs accumulate or once the triggering round arrives, the cap table effect can be every bit as real and every bit as powerful.

This is why the phrase agreement for future equity should be taken literally. The SAFE is not present equity. It is not a share certificate in disguise. It is not immediate dilution in the same visible way as a priced round. But it is also not merely friendly support floating outside the structure. It is an agreement that future equity will be issued according to a conversion framework. The company is therefore writing future ownership into its financing present. It is deferring the visible cap table event, not escaping it.

The most common triggering event for a SAFE is a later priced financing. When that round happens, the SAFE converts into shares, usually at a price that reflects the terms of the SAFE, such as a discount to the new round price, a valuation cap, or both, depending on the specific form used. In this respect, the SAFE often behaves similarly to a convertible note at the point of conversion. The difference lies less in the conversion outcome than in the legal route taken to get there. The SAFE did not begin as debt. It began as a right to future equity. That is why founders often experience SAFEs as more founder-friendly, even though the eventual ownership effect can still be highly significant.

There is another reason SAFEs appeal to early-stage companies. Because they usually remove the maturity-date pressure associated with notes, they can feel more forgiving if the company takes longer than hoped to reach its next priced round. A startup using convertible notes may eventually have to confront the fact that the company is approaching maturity without a qualifying financing in place. That can create renegotiation pressure or at least strategic anxiety. A SAFE often avoids that particular kind of ticking-clock psychology. The company still needs to reach a financing event or another conversion trigger for the instrument to become equity, but the absence of the classic debt maturity structure can make the early capital feel less like a bridge with a drop at the far end.

That advantage, however, should not be romanticised. The lack of a maturity date can make it easier for founders to defer discipline too long. Because the SAFE does not always create the same immediate pressure to resolve itself as a note, founders may sign several of them, continue speaking as though the cap table is simpler than it really is, and then discover later that a priced round is about to convert a large amount of accumulated future ownership all at once. The company may feel calm while the SAFEs are sitting in the background, but that calm can be misleading. The cap table is not cleaner because the conversion has not happened yet. It is merely quieter.

This is one of the major psychological traps of SAFEs. They are called simple, and in some narrow drafting and conceptual respects they are. But simple is not the same as small. A simple path into future dilution is still future dilution. A founder who would have flinched at the same ownership cost if it had been presented in a current priced-round cap table may sign a SAFE more comfortably because the cost is still hidden inside later conversion mechanics. That is why SAFEs require the same seriousness of modelling as notes, even if they often feel friendlier at the point of entry. The founder still needs to maintain a fully diluted view of the company's future structure and still needs to ask what happens if several SAFEs convert at once into a later round.

It is also important to understand that SAFEs can vary. Some may use only a valuation cap. Some may use only a discount. Some may use both. Some may contain provisions tied to liquidity events, dissolution, or other outcomes. Founders should therefore resist the temptation to think of "a SAFE" as a single universal thing. It is a family of future-equity instruments built around a common concept. The company still has to read the actual terms. The instrument may be simpler than a note in one sense, but the practical effect depends on how the conversion logic is set up and how that logic interacts with later financing.

From the investor's point of view, a SAFE can be attractive because it preserves the essential bargain of early-stage investing without the complications of debt form. The investor still gets to come in before a full priced round, still has some protection through discount or cap mechanics, and still positions themselves for conversion into equity when the company reaches a more developed stage. In some cases the investor may also prefer the speed and standardisation of SAFEs, especially in ecosystems where they are common and well understood. The investor is therefore not choosing the SAFE because it is soft. The investor is choosing a cleaner legal path into a similar future-equity result.

For founders, the great temptation is to treat SAFEs as more benign than they are because they often arrive wrapped in speed, simplicity, and the absence of obvious current dilution. The wiser interpretation is more balanced. A SAFE is often an efficient and sensible way to bring in early capital before a priced round makes sense.

It can be more aligned with startup reality than a debt instrument pretending to be a loan first. It can save time, reduce friction, and remove some forms of short-term pressure. But none of that means the ownership consequence is minor. It means the company has agreed to deal with that consequence later under rules being set now.

That is what a SAFE is. It is not debt. It is not present equity. It is an agreement that turns today's money into tomorrow's stock if the triggering events occur. If the founder understands that clearly, then the next concepts become much easier to grasp, because the real power and danger of both notes and SAFEs often lies in the specific mechanics by which they reward early investors when the later round finally arrives.

Valuation Caps

A valuation cap is one of the most important and most misunderstood features in deferred pricing instruments because it appears, at first glance, to offer a strange kind of certainty inside a structure designed to postpone certainty. Founders often hear the term and assume it is simply a ceiling on what the company can be worth later for purposes of conversion. That is broadly true, but unless the founder understands exactly whose protection the cap is serving and how it reshapes the eventual cap table, the phrase can remain dangerously abstract. A valuation cap is not there primarily to help the founder. It is there to protect the early investor from being treated too much like a later investor if the company's valuation rises sharply before the conversion event occurs.

This is the central logic. Suppose an investor puts money into a company through a SAFE or convertible note when the startup is still very early, very uncertain, and difficult to price. The parties agree to defer the full priced round until later. If that later round happens after the company has improved dramatically, then a simple future conversion at the new round price could leave the early investor under-rewarded relative to the risk they took. They entered before many of the company's proofs existed. They did not wait for a cleaner, stronger, more validated business. A valuation cap solves this by saying, in effect, that even if the later round is priced much higher, the early investor's conversion will be treated as though the company's value were lower than that round price, up to the agreed cap. The investor therefore receives more shares than they would have received if they converted strictly at the later investor's price.

That is why the cap matters so much. It is not a statement of what the company is worth today in the same sense as a priced round valuation. It is a contractual protection on what valuation can be used to determine the early investor's conversion if the future round price becomes very high. Founders who miss this point often think of the cap as flattering. They say that the company has "raised on a £5 million cap" and speak as though this is equivalent to having been priced at £5 million in a current round. That is too loose. The cap does not necessarily mean the company was fully priced and sold at that valuation now. It means that, for this investor, the future conversion into equity will not be allowed to happen at a valuation above that ceiling.

A simple example makes the effect clearer. Imagine a startup takes £500,000 on a SAFE with a £4 million valuation cap. No priced round happens at that time. A year later the company raises a proper round at a £10 million pre-money valuation. If the SAFE had no cap and converted simply at the later round price, the early investor would receive equity as though they were investing into a £10 million company, which would often under-reward the fact that they invested when the company was far weaker. The valuation cap changes that. It says that for the purpose of calculating this investor's conversion, the company will be treated as if it were worth only £4 million, not £10 million. The early investor therefore receives significantly more shares than the new round investors receive for the same amount of money.

This is why caps can be so dilutive when founders do not model them properly. The founder may hear that the company has deferred pricing and feel relieved that no current equity round had to be done. But if the company improves and later raises at a much higher valuation, the cap effectively lets the early investor buy in at a much cheaper price than the new money. That is exactly what the cap was designed to do, but it can still shock founders who treated the early capital as though it had little present ownership consequence. The SAFE or note was always carrying future dilution inside it. The cap determines how generous that future dilution may become to the early investor if things go well.

There is another important psychological trap here. Founders often assume that a higher future valuation is unambiguously good because it means the company has grown more valuable. In broad terms that is often true.

But if the company has raised significant amounts of capped SAFEs or notes, a much higher priced round can produce a more dramatic conversion event than the founder expected. This is one of the strange ironies of deferred pricing instruments. The better the company does before the priced round, the more valuable the cap can become to the early investor, and therefore the more dilutive the eventual conversion can be to the founders and existing common holders. That does not make success bad. It means success interacts with prior financing terms in ways that founders must understand before they begin treating future growth as though it can only improve their ownership position.

This is also why valuation caps should never be negotiated emotionally. Founders sometimes reach for a high cap because it sounds prestigious, or accept a lower cap because they are eager to close the early money and have not yet learned to translate the number into future share issuance. Neither instinct is reliable. The cap should be judged by asking what likely future financing scenarios it creates and what the resulting conversion will do to the cap table. If the cap is very low relative to what the company may plausibly become before the next round, the early investor may end up receiving a very large equity position for a relatively modest cheque. If the cap is very high, the investor may feel insufficiently protected and may push back or rely more heavily on other terms such as discounts. The founder's job is not to treat the cap as a vanity number, but as a structural term that prices future dilution under success.

There is also a subtle distinction between a valuation cap and a direct valuation in a priced round. In a priced round, the whole company is being sold and repriced now. Everyone can see the price, the new shares, and the resulting ownership structure. With a cap, the company is not being fully repriced now in the same visible way. Instead, the early investor is being granted a private conversion ceiling that will matter later. This means the cap can create a second layer of valuation logic inside the company. New investors in the later round are buying at one price. The earlier capped investor is converting at another, cheaper effective price. This layered valuation reality is perfectly normal in startup finance, but it is one reason founders must not talk about caps as though they were the same thing as current priced-round valuations. They operate in a related but different way.

Caps also matter because they can accumulate. A company may raise several SAFEs or notes, each with its own cap, each signed at a different moment under different conditions. By the time the next priced round arrives, the company may discover that it is not dealing with one simple conversion event but with multiple early claims converting under a range of protective price ceilings. The founders who understood one cap in isolation may now find that the cumulative cap structure matters far more than they expected. This is one of the clearest examples of why deferred pricing instruments should always be modelled together rather than understood separately as small, convenient pieces of early capital.

Investors, naturally, like caps when they are sensible because caps protect early conviction. The investor who accepted early uncertainty wants assurance that if the company becomes much more attractive before the formal priced round, they will not be punished for entering first. The cap achieves that. It rewards early belief by allowing conversion on more favourable terms than later capital receives. From the company's side, that may be acceptable or even wise if the early investor truly provided capital at a stage where the startup badly needed it and where alternative funding was scarce. The founder simply must not forget that the favour shown to the early investor will be paid for later in ownership.

This is why the phrase valuation cap should trigger a specific line of thought in the founder's mind. Not just what number sounds tolerable, but what future round valuation could realistically occur, how much capital is being raised under this cap, how many shares would be issued on conversion in those scenarios, and what that would do to the founder's post-conversion position. If the founder is not asking those questions, they are not really negotiating the cap. They are only reacting to its name.

That is the real importance of valuation caps. They are one of the main ways by which deferred pricing instruments reward early investors for early risk. They postpone the visible dilution but pre-structure how generous that dilution will become if the company succeeds before the next round. A founder who understands caps properly does not panic at them, but neither do they treat them as harmless placeholders. They see them for what they are: private future pricing rules that can have very public consequences for the cap table when the conversion day finally arrives.

Discounts

If the valuation cap protects an early investor by setting a ceiling on the valuation used for future conversion, the discount protects the investor in a slightly different way. A discount says that when the later priced round eventually happens, the early investor will not convert at the exact same price per share paid by the new money. Instead, the early investor will convert at a lower price, usually expressed as a percentage reduction from the new round price. The logic is straightforward. The investor came in earlier, at a riskier stage, and should therefore receive a better deal on the equity than the investors who waited until more proof existed.

This makes the discount one of the clearest expressions of a simple startup finance principle. Early money should usually not be treated exactly the same as later money. The company that takes capital before it has fully proven itself is asking someone to bear uncertainty that later investors may not have to bear. A discount rewards that earlier risk by improving the investor's effective entry price when the true equity round finally occurs. In that sense, the discount is not a side feature. It is one of the main ways the deferred pricing instrument acknowledges that time and uncertainty should affect how ownership is ultimately priced.
A common example is a twenty percent discount. Suppose a startup signs a SAFE or convertible note with a twenty percent discount and later raises a priced round at £1 per share. The early investor does not convert at £1 per share. Instead, they convert at £0.80 per share. This means the same amount of money buys more shares for the early investor than it buys for the new round investor. The capital was put in earlier, so the conversion price is better. That is the whole function of the discount. It is a reward in share-price terms for having stepped into the company before the market had enough evidence to price it comfortably.

This is why founders must treat the discount as a real ownership cost, not as a piece of friendly legal formatting. The discount may not create visible dilution on the day the SAFE or note is signed, but when the priced round occurs it affects how many shares the early investor receives. More shares for them means less of the company left for everyone else than would have been the case without the discount. The founder who says, with relief, that the deferred instrument allows the company to avoid an immediate valuation fight must remember that the discount is one of the ways that fight has merely been moved into the future under predetermined rules.

At first glance, discounts can seem less dramatic than valuation caps because they are easier to understand intuitively. Twenty percent off the future round price feels more linear and more visibly tethered to the later financing event. A cap, by contrast, can create a very large ownership effect if the future valuation rises sharply. This often leads founders to underestimate discounts. They think of them as modest, almost gentle investor protections. In some scenarios they are indeed less severe than a low cap. But they are still meaningful. If the company raises several discounted instruments and then closes a significant priced round, the cumulative effect on the cap table can be far larger than the founders had emotionally registered at the moment of signing.

This matters especially because discounts tend to feel fair, and fairness can dull caution. A founder may tell themselves that a twenty percent discount is reasonable because the investor came in early. That may be entirely true. But fairness of concept does not eliminate the need for modelling. The startup still has to ask how much money is being raised under the discount, how likely the next priced round is to happen at a high or low share price, and what the resulting conversion would do to the founder's stake once all discounted instruments convert. A term can be fair and still be expensive. Mature founders learn to hold both thoughts at once.

The interaction between discounts and valuation caps is also important. Many deferred pricing instruments include both. In that case the investor usually converts under whichever mechanism produces the better outcome for them, meaning whichever one gives them the lower effective conversion price and therefore the larger number of shares. Founders often fail to appreciate this fully. They see cap and discount as though they are cumulative sweeteners stacked in the investor's favour all at once. In practice, the instruments usually operate so that one or the other determines the conversion economics, depending on the circumstances of the future round. But that does not necessarily make the structure less costly. It simply means the investor is protected across different future scenarios. If the round valuation rises very strongly, the cap may matter more. If the valuation is more modest, the discount may be the operative protection. Either way, the founder must model the actual likely outcomes rather than rely on impression.

There is also a behavioural consequence to discounts that founders should notice. Because a discount is tied directly to the future round price, it can make early capital feel more relational and less adversarial than a hard present-tense valuation discussion. The investor is not insisting on a fixed price today. They are saying, in effect, when the proper round happens later, I simply want a better price than the new money because I came in earlier. This can feel easier to accept than a current pricing debate. Yet the founder must not confuse ease of acceptance with lack of consequence. A discount does not avoid the ownership cost of early capital. It structures it in a way that often feels smoother today and becomes visible tomorrow.

This is one reason discounts are attractive to investors. They are simple, understandable, and directly linked to the future financing event. An investor does not need to predict exactly what the company should be worth right now if they are comfortable saying only that they deserve better pricing than later capital. For the company, this can also be useful when the valuation question is genuinely too unsettled for a cap to feel comfortable or when the parties want a cleaner, more intuitive mechanism. But again, usefulness does not mean softness. The better the company performs before the next round, the more valuable the discounted conversion becomes in share-count terms relative to the new money.

A founder should also notice that a discount changes not only the relationship between the early investor and the company, but also the relationship between the early investor and the later investor. The new priced-round investor is buying into the company at one price. The earlier deferred investor is converting at a lower price. This creates a multi-layered ownership event in which different capital enters or transforms under different economics. That is perfectly ordinary in startup finance, but it reinforces the point that the later cap table is not being built by one clean valuation event alone. It is being shaped by agreements made earlier, under uncertainty, that now decide who gets how many shares when the company finally reaches priced-round territory.

This can have signalling implications as well. If a founder has signed many discounted SAFEs or notes, the later priced round may convert a substantial amount of capital at better terms than the headline round price suggests. New investors understand this, which is why they usually ask to see the full conversion picture.

A founder who thinks only in terms of the round's new money may find the post-conversion cap table more crowded than expected. The discount was always there, quietly waiting for the new round to bring it into effect.

The right way to think about discounts is therefore not as harmless sweeteners, but as explicit share-price privileges for early capital. They are simpler than many founders fear and more consequential than many founders first assume. They say that when the real pricing moment arrives, the early investor gets to enter at a better rate than the later investor because of the risk they took. Whether that is a good trade for the company depends on how much money was needed, how much ownership room remains, and how intelligently the founders have modelled the conversion.

That is the key lesson. A discount is not a vague reward for early belief. It is a mechanism that turns early belief into more shares later. The founder who understands that will be much better placed to evaluate the next step, which is how the conversion itself actually happens when the triggering financing arrives and all these deferred promises stop being background structure and become live cap table reality.

Conversion Events

A deferred pricing instrument does not become important only because it exists. It becomes important when the event arrives that turns its quiet future promise into an actual cap table consequence. That moment is the conversion event. Until then, the note or SAFE sits in a peculiar position. It is neither ordinary current equity nor something the founder can safely ignore. It is a pending claim waiting for the company to reach the condition under which the claim stops being deferred and starts becoming shares. The conversion event is therefore the point at which hidden dilution becomes visible.

In most startup financing structures, the classic conversion event is a priced equity round, often defined in the documents as a qualified financing or equity financing above a certain threshold. The exact wording matters, but the broad logic is consistent. The company raises a formal round in which new investors buy shares at an agreed price, and that round becomes the trigger for the earlier note or SAFE holders to convert into equity as well.

This is the moment when the company stops carrying deferred pricing instruments as background obligations and starts translating them into actual ownership on the cap table.

This matters because conversion is not merely an administrative formality. It is one of the biggest structural transitions in the life of a young company. The founders are not only bringing in new money from the current round. They are also settling the ownership consequences of the earlier money that was allowed in before this pricing event existed. In practice, this means the round often creates more shares than the founders first think about when they focus only on the new investor's cheque. The current round investor buys newly issued shares. The SAFE and note holders convert into shares as well. Sometimes interest on notes converts too. The cap table that emerges after closing is therefore the product not only of the current raise, but of all the deferred promises now becoming real at once.

This is why conversion events can feel so jarring to founders who were comfortable with deferred instruments while they remained abstract. A SAFE or note may have seemed light, fast, and strategically convenient when signed. The company received cash. No immediate priced-round dilution had to be confronted. The founders could keep moving. Then the qualified financing arrives, and suddenly all the deferred economics come due in ownership terms. A round that looked, in the founder's imagination, like a simple exchange between current company and new investor turns out to be a multi-layered cap table reshaping involving discounts, caps, accrued interest, and the translation of earlier uncertainty into present shares.

The company should therefore never think of the conversion event as belonging only to the old instruments. It belongs to the round as a whole. The old and the new collide there. The later investor is buying into a company whose structure is not just being enlarged by their own shares, but also reordered by the conversion of prior capital. This is one reason new investors scrutinise deferred instruments so closely. They know that the conversion event is where the true cap table finally reveals itself. If the founder has not modelled that moment carefully, the company may walk into the round with an incomplete understanding of what the fully diluted structure will look like immediately after closing.

A simple example shows the mechanics. Suppose the company has 10,000,000 founder shares outstanding and one SAFE for £500,000 with a valuation cap that implies conversion at a favourable effective price. The company now raises a priced round of £2 million. The founders may initially think only about how many shares the new £2 million investor will receive. But before the cap table can be finalised, the SAFE must convert. If the SAFE converts at a lower price than the new investor is paying, the SAFE holder will receive more shares for their money than the new investor receives for the same amount. The result is that the total number of post-round shares is larger than the founders may have imagined if they modelled only the new raise and ignored the earlier instrument. The round has not merely brought in a new investor. It has also settled a prior claim on terms already embedded in the company's financing history.

This is why conversion events are structurally revealing. They force the founders to confront whether their earlier financing choices were disciplined or merely comfortable. A company that raised one modest SAFE or note on well-understood terms and tracked its fully diluted impact can usually move through conversion with relatively little surprise. A company that accumulated multiple instruments under varying caps and discounts, without fully appreciating how they would stack, may find the conversion event much more unsettling. What looked like a collection of small, manageable decisions can become a large ownership change once all those instruments convert together.

There is also an important sequencing point here. The conversion event usually happens before or as part of the financing close, not as a separate philosophical moment afterward. The company cannot properly describe the post-round cap table without including the converted holders. That means founders should model the structure in the order the deal will actually produce it. What existing shares are already outstanding. What convertibles will turn into shares at what effective prices. What new round shares will then be issued. Whether the option pool is also being resized in connection with the round. Which basis is being used for "fully diluted" in the documents. These are not mere details. They determine the real ownership picture the company will live with once the round is done.

Another reason conversion events matter is that they often settle uncertainty in a way that changes internal company psychology. Before conversion, founders may still speak about the notes or SAFEs as background financing. After conversion, the holders are now plainly visible on the cap table. Their stakes can be measured. Their presence becomes part of every future dilution discussion. The ownership story becomes harder, but also more honest. The company no longer has the comfort of vagueness. It has a real post-conversion structure, and from that point onward the founders must think from within it rather than from the simpler pre-conversion story they may have carried in their heads.

It is also worth noticing that not every conversion event is a happy growth moment. While the classic case is a strong priced round, some instruments may also contemplate conversion or alternative treatment in a liquidity event, dissolution, or other company-changing transaction. A sale of the business, for example, can create questions about whether the instrument converts, is repaid, or is treated under some formula tied to the sale price. The exact mechanics depend on the documents. What matters conceptually is that the instrument was never meant to float forever outside the ownership structure. Some future event was always expected to force resolution. The priced round is the most common version, but it is not the only one.

From the investor's point of view, the conversion event is the moment their early bet becomes real equity. Their earlier risk is translated into shares, often on terms better than those offered to the new round investor. From the founder's point of view, it is the moment the company discovers what those earlier financing decisions really cost in ownership terms. Both views are legitimate. That is why conversion events so often feel like moments of truth. They are where the company's financing past meets its priced-round present and becomes one capital structure.

The disciplined founder approaches this moment without surprise because the cap table has already been modelled as if the conversion were going to happen. The undisciplined founder experiences the conversion event as a sudden revelation that the round is more dilutive and more crowded than expected. The difference between those two founders is not luck. It is whether they understood that deferred pricing instruments are always waiting for a conversion event and that the day of conversion is not the day to begin asking what they really mean.

That is the lesson of conversion events. They are the point at which deferred instruments stop being quiet promises and start becoming active ownership. They reveal whether the company has been financing itself with foresight or with convenient vagueness. And because they often happen at the same time as a new priced round, they remind the founder of something essential about startup finance: the current cap table is never built only by the current round. It is built by everything the company chose to defer until now.

Why These Instruments Hide Future Dilution

The great seduction of convertible notes and SAFEs is that they allow the startup to feel funded before it feels diluted. Money arrives. Runway extends. The company can keep moving. No dramatic new post-round cap table has to be confronted immediately. No priced equity sale has forced the founders to look at a lower percentage beside their names in the present tense. This is precisely why these instruments are so useful in the right setting. It is also why they are so easy to misunderstand. They hide future dilution not because the dilution is unreal, but because the ownership consequence is structurally displaced in time.

That displacement matters enormously.

A founder who signs a priced round can usually see the ownership change immediately. The new investor receives shares, the total share count rises, and the founder's percentage falls. The cost is visible on the day the round closes. By contrast, a founder who signs a SAFE or note often experiences something much gentler. The company receives cash, but the visible common or preferred share counts may not move in the same dramatic way at that moment. The founder therefore feels the benefit of funding without yet feeling the ownership price in fully visible form. The dilution is real, but it is latent. It is waiting for the conversion event to bring it into the open.

This is what makes these instruments dangerous when handled casually. They create a gap between economic reality and emotional reality. Economically, the company has already accepted a future claim on its ownership. Emotionally, the founder may still feel that the cap table remains mostly as it was, especially if several months pass before any priced round forces conversion.

During that period, the company can make other decisions under the comforting illusion that ownership is simpler than it really is. Founders may continue talking as though they own certain percentages in a clean sense, discuss employee grants too loosely, or approach the next financing round without having fully modelled how much prior capital is already waiting to convert. The future dilution has been hidden not from the documents, but from the founder's intuition.

This is one reason deferred pricing instruments often feel much cheaper than they are. A £300,000 SAFE here and a £500,000 note there may not seem emotionally comparable to a full equity round in which a visible investor is taking ten or fifteen percent of the company. Yet once those deferred instruments convert, the founder may discover that the cumulative effect is substantial. The company did not avoid dilution. It accumulated it in a quieter form. This is why founders who say "we only raised small bridge amounts" can later be surprised to see how large a share count those amounts produce when converted on capped or discounted terms into the next round.

The hidden nature of the dilution also changes how founders negotiate. Because the cost is delayed, founders often become more relaxed at the point of signing than they would be in a present-tense priced round. They may accept caps or discounts they have not properly modelled because the immediate fundraising problem feels more urgent than the future cap table consequence. That is understandable. Early-stage survival often is urgent. But the company is still writing future ownership rules into its structure. If the founders do not translate those rules into likely dilution scenarios, then the apparent simplicity of the instrument becomes a trap. The company is financing the present by spending the future without clearly looking at the bill.

This hidden quality is especially powerful when the company is improving quickly. If a startup raises early deferred capital when it is still raw and then grows into a much stronger position before the priced round, the cap or discount may become highly valuable to the early investors. From the investor's point of view, that is exactly the point. They entered before the company became more expensive. From the founder's point of view, however, the later round can become an unpleasant revelation.

The company may be celebrating a stronger valuation while simultaneously discovering that the earlier deferred instruments now convert into more shares than the founders emotionally anticipated. The better the company performs, the more visible the hidden cost can become.

That is one of the strangest aspects of deferred dilution. Success can intensify the visibility of the earlier financing cost. In a priced round, a stronger valuation directly benefits the founders by reducing present dilution. In a capped SAFE or note, a stronger later valuation may still benefit the founders overall, but it also increases the advantage given to the early investor under the cap. The founder has to hold both truths at once. The company is better, and the early financing term is now more expensive because the company is better. That is not a contradiction. It is simply how deferred investor protection works.

Another reason these instruments hide future dilution is that they are often discussed one by one rather than as a set. A founder may sign each SAFE or note on its own day, under its own circumstances, with its own emotional justification. This one was needed to extend runway. That one was taken because a supportive investor was available. Another was signed to buy time before the next milestone. Each decision can seem reasonable in isolation. The founder rarely feels the whole stack at once. Then the priced round arrives, and all the instruments are now part of one conversion picture. What was once psychologically segmented becomes structurally unified. The hidden dilution was never only in each instrument individually. It was in the cumulative future share issuance those instruments were quietly building together.

This is why serious founders maintain a fully diluted shadow cap table even when no conversion has yet occurred. They do not wait for the priced round to discover what the company has promised. They model the company as if the notes and SAFEs were already part of the ownership future, because in substance they are. That does not mean pretending the exact final number is always known. Caps, discounts, and future round terms can still create scenario ranges. But it does mean refusing to let the founder's emotional model of the company remain cleaner than the company's actual financing obligations. A deferred instrument should never be allowed to become invisible simply because it has not yet become stock.

The hidden nature of the dilution also affects employees and later investors. Employees may be told that the company's cap table looks a certain way, not fully appreciating that a later priced round will bring earlier SAFEs or notes crashing visibly into the structure. Later investors may initially hear the headline story of the round and then realise, once they look more closely, that a significant portion of the post-round company will actually be going to earlier deferred holders at advantageous terms. This is why sophisticated investors ask about these instruments early and insist on seeing them modelled. They know the dilution is there even if the founders have not fully emotionally priced it yet.

It is important to be clear that hidden dilution is not the same as dishonest dilution. There is nothing inherently improper about SAFEs or notes. Many well-run companies use them responsibly. The issue is not that they conceal the truth from anyone reading the documents properly. The issue is that they conceal the future ownership effect from the founder's intuitive experience unless the founder forces that effect into view through modelling and discipline. The danger is therefore often psychological and organisational rather than legal. The company feels simpler than it really is, and that feeling can lead to weaker decisions.

The best defence against this is simple in principle and demanding in practice. Every deferred pricing instrument should be treated as a future cap table event from the moment it is signed. The founder should ask how much money is coming in, under what cap or discount, under what plausible next-round valuations, and how many shares that would likely produce on conversion. If several instruments exist, they should be modelled together, not separately. If the company is planning an option pool expansion or a major round, those assumptions should be included too. Once the founder sees the future dilution on paper, the instrument stops being deceptively light. It becomes what it really is: a delayed but very real ownership commitment.

That is why these instruments hide future dilution. They allow the company to separate the relief of funding from the pain of visible ownership change. That can be strategically useful. It can also be structurally dangerous. The founder's job is not to reject deferred instruments on principle, but to refuse the emotional convenience of acting as though deferred means negligible. In startup finance, deferred often means the same bill is coming later, with interest in the form of complexity, surprise, and accumulated cap table pressure if you did not look at it early enough.

How Founders Get Surprised Later

Very few founders are surprised by dilution because the math is impossible. They are surprised because the math was postponed, scattered across multiple instruments, softened by optimistic language, or never forced into one honest view of the future cap table until it was too late to remain emotionally comfortable. This distinction matters. Startup finance rarely tricks founders through complexity alone. More often, it surprises them because they let structure stay abstract until a later event turns abstraction into ownership reality all at once.

The first source of surprise is emotional sequencing. A founder signs a SAFE or note at a moment when the company needs money badly. The relief is immediate. Cash is in. Salaries can be paid. Product work can continue. The company survives another stretch of uncertainty. The ownership cost, however, is not immediate in the same visible way. The founder therefore stores the fundraising event in memory as a rescue rather than as a future cap table event. Months later, when the priced round comes and the instrument converts, the founder experiences the dilution as a fresh injury rather than as the delayed cost of the earlier rescue. Nothing dishonest necessarily happened. The founder simply did not live with the two parts of the event in one mental frame.

The second source of surprise is fragmented thinking. Founders often treat each deferred instrument separately. One note was for bridging a difficult quarter. One SAFE came from a supportive angel. Another was signed because a strategic introduction seemed useful. Each instrument feels manageable because it is considered alone. The founder tells themselves that none of them is large enough to be a real structural threat. Then the next priced round arrives and all the instruments convert together. What was once emotionally divided into three or four small decisions becomes one large share-issuance event. The founder is not surprised because the documents lied. The founder is surprised because the company was never being thought about as a whole.

A third source of surprise is the misuse of headline language. Founders hear that the round is being done at a certain valuation, or that the investor is only asking for a certain percentage, and they stop there. They do not push through to the next questions. What happens to the pre-money pool. What converts at close. What caps or discounts apply.

How many new shares are being created not only for the new investor but also for old deferred money. What does the fully diluted post-round picture actually look like. The founder therefore enters the closing process carrying a story of the round rather than a full model of the round. The surprise comes when the story and the model turn out not to be the same thing.

Another common cause is optimism about future valuation. Founders often assume that because the company is improving, the next round will be strong enough that everything will work out favourably. Sometimes that optimism is justified. Sometimes it becomes a substitute for modelling. A founder may sign a capped SAFE believing that the company will obviously be worth much more by the next round, without fully appreciating that this very success makes the cap more valuable to the investor and therefore more dilutive to the founder. In other words, the founder is surprised not by failure but by the fact that success itself has ownership consequences that earlier optimism never really traced through.

There is also the problem of spreadsheet avoidance. Many founders are willing to talk about dilution, caps, discounts, and future rounds conceptually, but they do not force those concepts into scenario models. They know, in a broad sense, that a cap means the investor converts more favourably later. They know that multiple SAFEs will dilute them. They know that an option pool matters. Yet until they actually model likely conversion outcomes under plausible future valuations, the knowledge remains too soft to shape behaviour. Later, when the company closes the round and the diluted founder position becomes visible in numbers rather than in vague principles, the result feels shocking. The shock is not caused by hidden math. It is caused by the founder having allowed the math to remain unmade.

A further source of surprise is that founders often underestimate how much the company changes between signing the deferred instrument and hitting the conversion event. During that time, the startup may hire, promise equity, expand plans, add pool capacity, or even accumulate more deferred instruments. The future conversion is therefore not arriving into the same company the founder imagined at the moment of the first SAFE or note. It is arriving into a structure that has become denser, more ambitious, and often more crowded.

The founder mentally compares the conversion with the simpler company they had in mind when they took the money, and the result looks harsher than expected because the structure around the instrument has evolved too.

Investors, of course, are rarely surprised in the same way. They understand that the deferred instrument is a claim designed to convert later under specified economics. They often model several scenarios and know how the cap or discount behaves if the next round is strong or weak. This asymmetry creates one of the classic founder pains in startup finance. The founder experiences the conversion as a revelation. The investor experiences it as the normal unfolding of a bargain already understood from the beginning. That does not make the investor predatory by default. It does mean the founder must learn to think with equal foresight or risk being emotionally outpaced by their own financing documents.

This is one of the deeper reasons why founders get surprised later. They confuse the absence of visible present dilution with the absence of future ownership consequence. In ordinary life, what is not in front of us is easier to discount emotionally. Startup finance takes advantage of that human weakness without necessarily intending to. Deferred instruments are rational tools, but they interact very powerfully with ordinary short-term psychology. The founder prioritises today's survival and allows tomorrow's ownership map to remain blurred. When tomorrow arrives and the blur sharpens, the company calls it conversion. The founder calls it surprise.

There is also a cultural problem in some startup environments. Deferred instruments are often spoken about as lightweight, founder-friendly, fast, and standard. Those descriptions can all be true in limited ways, but they can also produce complacency. If something is called simple often enough, the founder stops treating it with the seriousness that future equity deserves. This is how a company can accumulate a surprisingly heavy deferred structure while still telling itself that it has not really done much beyond taking some helpful early capital. Language matters. A SAFE may be simpler than a note. It is not simple in the sense of being economically trivial.

The cure for founder surprise is not suspicion of every instrument. It is disciplined anticipation. The founder should maintain a live, fully diluted view of the company that includes current shares, option pool effects, all SAFEs and notes, their likely conversion prices under plausible scenarios, and the founder position after likely future rounds. This does not mean predicting the future perfectly. It means refusing to let the future remain emotionally invisible. When the company raises the deferred money, the founder should already be able to say, under several likely next-round outcomes, this is approximately what happens to the cap table. A founder who can do that may still dislike the dilution when it becomes real, but they will not be ambushed by it.

That is the real lesson. Founders get surprised later because they allowed the ownership cost of early money to live in the future without forcing it into the present mind. Deferred pricing instruments are often useful, sometimes essential, but they are never free of consequence. The sooner the founder insists on seeing those consequences clearly, the less likely the future is to feel like a betrayal by mathematics that was there all along.

* * *

ELEVEN

Preferred Shares and Investor Rights

"Control your own destiny or someone else will."
- Jack Welch

Why All Shares Are Not Equal

One of the most dangerous assumptions a founder can carry into financing is the assumption that ownership percentage tells the whole story. In the earliest phase of a company, that assumption can seem close enough to true that it causes no obvious pain. The founders hold common shares. The cap table is simple. If one founder owns sixty percent and another forty percent, the meaning appears plain. Each person's share of the company seems to correspond directly to their place in the business and to their eventual share of the upside. Once outside investors begin to enter through priced rounds, however, this simplicity often breaks. The company is no longer just issuing more of the same ownership. It is often issuing a different kind of ownership.

This is the point at which founders need to understand a principle that becomes central to all later cap table analysis. Not all shares are equal. They may all occupy the same spreadsheet. They may all count toward percentages. But the rights attached to them may differ so much that two holdings with similar-looking percentages can produce very different economic and governance outcomes. The founder who does not understand this tends to make one of two mistakes. Either they take false comfort from a percentage that looks healthy while the rights underneath have shifted against them, or they panic at the visible size of an investor stake without realising that what matters most is not the headline number alone but the legal and economic structure attached to it.

The most common way this distinction appears is through the difference between common shares and preferred shares. Founders and employees often hold common stock. New investors in priced rounds often receive preferred stock. At a superficial level, both are forms of ownership in the company. At a deeper level, preferred shares are often designed to give investors special rights or protections that common shares do not carry. These rights may affect what happens if the company is sold, how future rounds work, what information investors receive, whether certain actions require investor consent, and how money is distributed in downside or middling outcomes. That is why a cap table can look ordinary in percentage terms while concealing a much more layered hierarchy underneath.

Founders sometimes resist this idea because it seems to violate the intuitive fairness of ownership. If someone owns twenty percent and another person owns twenty percent, should those positions not mean the same thing. In some moral sense one might think so. In the practical reality of venture finance, they often do not. The investor who buys preferred shares is usually not only seeking upside. They are also buying downside protection and governance influence. The founder, by contrast, is often carrying most of the company's execution risk through common stock. This asymmetry is not accidental. It is part of how venture-backed businesses are structured. The investor is bringing capital into a risky enterprise and wants not just exposure to success but also contractual advantages if the path becomes difficult, messy, or merely less extraordinary than hoped.

That is why founders must learn to stop equating percentage with position. Position is a function of percentage plus rights. A founder may own a large common stake and still find that an investor with a smaller preferred position is better protected in sale scenarios, better informed in governance terms, and more insulated from downside outcomes. None of this means the founder has been cheated by definition. It means the founder has entered a more sophisticated capital structure than the early company possessed. Once that happens, every serious reading of the cap table has to move beyond the visible percentages and ask what these shares actually do.

This question matters immediately in fundraising because many founders negotiate primarily on valuation and percentage sold while paying less attention to the architecture of the shares being issued. That is understandable in a first round. Valuation is easy to feel. Dilution is easy to fear. Rights are harder to visualise because they usually matter later and under specific conditions. But later is exactly when companies discover whether they understood what they sold. A founder can preserve more percentage than expected and still end up with a weaker practical position if the investor rights package is strong enough. Conversely, a founder may give up a meaningful stake on relatively clean terms and remain in a healthier long-term position than the percentages alone would suggest. The shares are not equal, so the stakes cannot be read only by size.

There is also a more subtle organisational consequence. When all shares are not equal, the company begins to operate with layered constituencies rather than a single undifferentiated ownership body. Founders, employees, angels, seed investors, and later funds may all sit in different positions relative to information, consent rights, economic preference, and influence over major decisions. The company is no longer merely a collective of owners with different percentages. It is a structured system of owners whose rights vary by class, timing, and contractual history. That can be entirely manageable in a well-governed startup, but it means the founder has to mature in how they think about ownership. The company is no longer simply divided. It is tiered.

This tiering is one reason preferred stock becomes so important to understand before the founder signs later-stage documents. It is not enough to know that the investor is taking fifteen percent or twenty percent. The founder has to know what kind of fifteen percent or twenty percent this is. Does it come with liquidation preferences. Does it come with anti-dilution protection. Does it come with board rights or consent rights. Does it carry participation rights in future rounds. Does it create a structure that is manageable if the company later sells for less than hoped. If the founder does not ask these questions, the cap table can become much more misleading than it looks.

It is important, though, not to become melodramatic about this. The fact that all shares are not equal does not mean preferred stock is inherently predatory or that venture finance is a trick. Preferred shares exist because capital providers and common holders are in different positions.

Founders typically gain their stake through creation, labour, and early risk. Investors enter later with money and want contractual protections tailored to their role. The company needs both. The issue is not whether different share classes should exist. The issue is whether the founder understands what the differences mean and whether the resulting structure still leaves the business governable, financeable, and worth carrying forward.

One should also notice that inequality among shares does not only affect exits and catastrophe. It shapes everyday power. An investor may have information rights that give them more formal access to company reporting than an ordinary common holder receives. Certain key company actions may require approval from preferred holders. Board composition may reflect investor rights associated with preferred stock rather than mere common percentages. Future financing decisions may be heavily influenced by who has pro rata rights or veto positions tied to a preferred class. In other words, the inequality of shares is not only about who gets paid first when something goes wrong. It is about how the company is governed while it is still alive and growing.

This is why the language of classes matters. Once the company begins issuing different classes of shares, the founder is no longer dealing with pure arithmetic. They are dealing with capital architecture. A percentage is still part of the picture, but it now sits inside a wider legal framework that determines how ownership behaves under pressure. The common founder share and the preferred investor share are not merely different labels on the same claim. They are often different instruments with different expectations built into them. The cap table remains one document, but it now contains multiple logics.

The founder who understands this early becomes much harder to surprise later. They stop asking only how much am I being diluted and start asking what kind of structure is being built around the diluted remainder. They stop taking comfort from headline percentages without reading the rights beneath them. They also stop assuming that apparent generosity in valuation automatically means generosity in the round as a whole. Once all shares are not equal, the real deal terms are distributed across valuation, dilution, rights, and future conversion effects together. That is a more demanding way to think, but it is also much closer to reality.

This chapter begins here because preferred shares and investor rights cannot be understood as isolated legal curiosities. They grow directly out of the fact that later-stage startup ownership is no longer flat. It has layers, preferences, and conditions. Once that is understood, the next question follows naturally. If common and preferred shares are different, what exactly is preferred stock designed to do, and why do investors insist on it so often in priced rounds.

What Preferred Stock Is

Preferred stock is best understood as equity with negotiated advantages attached to it. It is still ownership in the company, but it is not ownership on the same plain terms as common stock. If common shares represent the baseline ownership claim of founders, employees, and other ordinary holders, preferred shares represent a class of ownership designed to give investors additional protections, priorities, or controls in exchange for the capital they are putting at risk. That is why the word preferred matters. It signals that this stock sits in a more protected position than common stock in at least some important respects.

This is where many first-time founders get confused. They hear that an investor is buying shares and assume that the investor is simply joining the existing ownership structure as another holder on broadly similar terms. In reality, a priced round often does more than add another shareholder. It adds a new class of shareholder. The investor is not merely buying into the company. The investor is buying in through an instrument built to behave differently from the founders' stock if certain things happen later. Those differences may not matter much in ordinary day-to-day operations when the company is healthy and private, but they become very important in financing events, governance decisions, and sale outcomes. That is why preferred stock has to be understood not as a cosmetic label, but as a structural layer inside the cap table.

At the most basic level, preferred stock usually gives investors one or more of the following. It may give them priority in receiving money back in a sale or liquidation. It may give them the right to maintain ownership in future rounds. It may give them special voting or consent rights on important company actions. It may protect them in some way if later financing occurs on weaker terms. It may give them board influence or formal information access.

Not every preferred round includes all of these in the same way, and the exact package varies enormously. But the core idea is constant. The investor is not only sharing in upside. They are buying contractual position.

This position exists because startup investing is not symmetrical. Founders typically contribute idea, labour, time, and sustained operational risk. Investors contribute money and usually arrive later. Those two roles are not the same, and the law of venture finance reflects that difference. Preferred stock says that the investor is willing to enter the risk of the company, but not on the same bare terms as someone whose stake was earned through common founder ownership. The investor wants to participate in success while also shaping how the company treats capital if things become uncertain, disappointing, or merely less extraordinary than hoped.

One way to think about this is that preferred stock builds hierarchy into equity without turning the company into pure debt. The investor is still exposed. Preferred stock is not the same as a guaranteed bank repayment. If the company fails completely, preferred holders may still lose money. But preferred stock places the investor higher in certain queues and stronger in certain negotiations than common stock alone would allow. The result is a hybrid kind of ownership that still aims at upside, but with more carefully designed downside and control features than founders often imagine when they first hear the phrase investor equity.

This is why founders must not take too much comfort from the fact that preferred investors are technically still equity holders rather than lenders. Equity can still contain hierarchy. Preferred stock does not erase the essential startup risk of the investment, but it changes how that risk is distributed between investor and common holder. In many practical situations, it means the common founders are more exposed to middling outcomes than they first realise. If the company sells for an amount that sounds decent but is not large enough to clear the investor preferences comfortably, the founders may discover that their common stake participates in the outcome much later, and sometimes much less generously, than the headline ownership percentages suggested.

Preferred stock also changes how founders should think about later rounds. A company with only common stock can still be messy, but at least the ownership logic is relatively flat. Once preferred stock appears, the company begins creating layers of capital history. One round may have one preferred class, the next round another. One class may have certain rights, another additional ones. Earlier preferred investors may convert into common under some circumstances or retain preference under others. The business remains one company, but the cap table is now becoming a stacked structure rather than a single horizontal plane. This is one reason later-stage startup finance can feel so much more intricate than the founder-only or common-only phase. Preferred stock is one of the main devices by which that intricacy is built.

At the same time, founders should not imagine that preferred stock is inherently hostile. In many cases it is simply the normal and sensible way institutional capital enters a startup. An investor deploying meaningful money into a risky private company is usually not going to accept the exact same position as an employee option holder or a founder who came in at the beginning. The investor wants a defined package of rights that makes the investment worth making. That does not automatically mean the package is unfair. It means the package should be understood. Founders who approach preferred stock as though it were automatically toxic often fail to negotiate intelligently because they remain stuck in a mood of resistance rather than understanding. Founders who treat it too casually are vulnerable from the opposite side. The better stance is clarity without melodrama.

This clarity matters because preferred stock often hides its significance behind ordinary ownership language. The investor may say they are buying twenty percent. The founder hears twenty percent and imagines a dilution event. What the founder should also hear is that this twenty percent may have rights that make it stronger, safer, or more influential than twenty percent of common stock would be. If the founder does not ask how the preferred actually behaves, then they have only half-read the round. The cap table can appear mathematically comprehensible while being economically far more uneven underneath.

It is also worth noticing that preferred stock can influence company culture indirectly. Once a startup has outside investors holding preferred shares, the founders are no longer governing only with one eye on growth and one eye on dilution. They are also governing with an awareness that some company actions may now require investor approval, some sale outcomes may be distributed through investor preference layers, and some future financing decisions will be shaped by rights already issued.

The company becomes more formal, more legible, and sometimes more constrained. This is not always bad. In many businesses it is part of growing up. But it does mean preferred stock is not merely a technical financing choice. It alters the lived structure of the company.

There is another useful way to frame it. Common stock generally represents the residual claim on the company after stronger rights have been satisfied. Preferred stock often represents a negotiated improvement on that residual position. The investor still wants upside if the business becomes large, but also wants some assurance that if the business exits at a merely decent price, or if future rounds become difficult, they are not standing in exactly the same queue as everyone else. That is what preference means in practical capital terms. Not immunity, but improved position.

The founder who understands preferred stock properly becomes much more capable of reading term sheets and round structures. They stop asking only how much is being sold and start asking what class is being issued, what rights come with it, and how those rights affect real outcomes. That shift is vital, because once a company issues preferred stock, later financing cannot be understood simply by percentages anymore. The company now has differentiated ownership inside the same cap table, and the next task is to understand the baseline comparison that makes all of this intelligible: the difference between common and preferred as lived economic and governance positions inside the startup.

Common Stock Versus Preferred Stock

The cleanest way to understand preferred stock is to place it directly against common stock and ask not what they are called, but how they behave. In an early founder-only company, common stock often feels like the natural form of ownership. It is the baseline. It says who built the company, who owns the ordinary residual claim, and who stands inside the venture without special protections layered above them. Common stock is usually what founders hold. It is often what employees ultimately receive through options once exercised. It is the ordinary ownership from which later cap table complexity begins.

Preferred stock is different because it is designed not merely to participate in the company, but to participate from a more protected or more influential position. It is still equity, but it is equity that has been engineered. The investor holding preferred stock has not simply joined the founder on equal terms. The investor has entered through a class of shares that may carry special rights in liquidation, in future rounds, in information access, in board influence, or in company consent matters. Common stock says you are an owner. Preferred stock often says you are an owner with terms.

This distinction is easy to say and surprisingly hard for founders to feel until a real event forces the difference into view. As long as the company is simply operating, raising revenue, building product, and not yet distributing money or testing governance boundaries, the two classes may sit on the table without creating obvious day-to-day pain. Founders can look at the spreadsheet and still think largely in percentages. The trouble begins when the company hits one of the moments that reveal hierarchy. A sale, a down round, a recapitalisation, a major governance decision, or a conflict over approval rights can suddenly show that the investor's twenty percent and the founder's twenty percent were never the same thing at all.

This is why common stock is often described as the residual equity of the company. It gets what is left after stronger rights have been satisfied. That does not make common stock worthless or second-class in a moral sense. In a successful company, common stock can be extraordinarily valuable because once the company grows beyond the range where preferences dominate, the common holders may participate fully in large upside. Founders often make their real wealth through common stock because they own a lot of it and because the company succeeds at a scale large enough that the special investor protections matter less relative to the overall size of the outcome. But common stock is still residual in structure. It is what remains after the company has honoured the protections promised elsewhere.

Preferred stock, by contrast, is often designed to improve the investor's position before the company reaches that very large and unequivocally successful state. It says that if the outcome is merely moderate, or if the company encounters trouble, or if major structural decisions are being made, the investor should not be in exactly the same line as the common holders. This can mean the investor receives money back first in a sale.

It can mean the investor gets extra protection in down rounds. It can mean the investor's consent is needed for certain actions. It can mean the investor is entitled to more visibility into the company's operations. Common stock and preferred stock are therefore not simply different flavours of ownership. They represent different positions in the company's legal and economic hierarchy.

For founders, one of the most important consequences of this distinction is psychological. Common stock often carries the romance of authorship. It feels like the founder's natural stake because it was earned through creation, sacrifice, and prolonged risk. Preferred stock feels more transactional. It comes in later with rights attached and a term sheet behind it. This can make founders instinctively hostile to preferred rights because they experience them as a dilution not only of ownership but of purity. That instinct is understandable, but it can become unhelpful if it blinds the founder to the fact that these classes are designed for different roles. The investor did not found the company. The founder did not write the cheque in the financing round. The instruments reflect those different contributions.

At the same time, founders must not let this role difference lull them into underestimating how much preferred stock can reshape practical outcomes. Because common stock usually sits beneath preferred in important respects, founders can discover that a strong-looking common position on paper is weaker in middling real-world scenarios than they assumed. For example, if the company sells for an amount that is good but not spectacular, the preferred holders may receive their preference first, leaving less for common than the headline percentages would have led a naive observer to expect. In a large enough exit, the distinction may soften because everyone participates in a much bigger pool of value. In smaller or more complicated exits, the class difference can dominate the economics.

This means the comparison between common and preferred is not only a legal one. It is also a way of comparing how optimistic the company has to be before the founder's paper percentage starts behaving the way the founder imagines it behaves. A founder with common stock may do extremely well in a large success case and much less well in a merely decent one.

An investor with preferred stock may have given up some pure upside in exchange for stronger protection across a range of middling outcomes. That does not mean preferred stock always wins or common always loses. It means the two instruments are calibrated differently across different future states of the company.

There is also a governance comparison to make. Common stock in a founder-heavy early company often implies a relatively concentrated and intuitive control structure. The founders own the company and lead the company. Once preferred stock arrives, the company begins to separate those ideas. Founders may still run the business, but some decisions are now shaped by rights attached to investor capital. A preferred class may have protective provisions requiring consent for major actions such as issuing new shares, selling the company, changing the charter, or taking on certain forms of debt. Common holders may still matter greatly, but they are no longer the only constituency that the legal structure treats as decisive. This is one of the clearest ways preferred stock changes the lived reality of the startup.

Another key difference lies in future financing. Common stock usually does not come with the same built-in protections against later financing risk that preferred stock may carry. Preferred holders may have pro rata rights to maintain ownership, anti-dilution provisions to protect them in weak later rounds, or negotiation leverage that common holders simply do not possess. The founder therefore has to understand that common stock is often more exposed to the consequences of later financing than preferred stock is. Again, this is not an indictment of preferred stock by itself. It is a structural fact. The company is layering protections in favour of the capital entering now, and the common founders remain the more exposed residual claimants beneath that layer.

This comparison becomes particularly important when founders are looking at a term sheet and trying to decide whether the economics of the round are acceptable. A founder who asks only what percentage is being sold is not really comparing common and preferred. They are only reading the surface. A founder who asks what rights are attached, what happens in a sale, what future financing protections exist, and what governance approvals are being created is beginning to compare the actual instruments.

That is where real understanding begins. Once common and preferred are seen as structurally different forms of equity rather than just different names, term sheets become much easier to read with seriousness.

It is also worth saying that not every preferred structure is aggressive, and not every common position is weak. The details matter. Some rounds have relatively clean and founder-respectful preferred terms. Others create much more asymmetry. Some common positions remain highly attractive because the company still has enough founder ownership and enough likely scale that the residual stake is powerful. Others are already being squeezed too thin. The categories of common and preferred therefore establish the framework, but the actual consequences depend on how the rights are drafted and how the company performs. A founder must understand the class logic first in order to judge the actual deal second.

That is the real difference between common and preferred stock. Common is the baseline ownership of the company, usually residual and more exposed. Preferred is ownership with negotiated protection and often with stronger rights in specific scenarios. Both are equity. Both may participate in upside. But they are not equal in how they sit inside the company's structure. Once the founder sees that clearly, the next step is to look at the most famous and most consequential of those preferred rights, which is liquidation preference.

Liquidation Preference

If there is one preferred stock term that founders hear early, half-understand, and often underestimate until it matters, it is liquidation preference. The name itself can mislead. It sounds like something relevant only to catastrophe, bankruptcy, or the formal winding up of a failed business. In reality, liquidation preference usually matters in a much wider set of outcomes, including acquisitions and other sale events. It is one of the main reasons preferred stock is not just common stock with a nicer title. Liquidation preference determines who gets paid first, and sometimes how much they get, before the common holders fully participate in the distribution of proceeds.

At its simplest, a liquidation preference gives the preferred investor priority in recovering value from the company before common shareholders receive the remaining proceeds.

The classic form is a one-times non-participating preference. That means the investor has the right, in a sale or liquidation event, to receive an amount equal to the money they originally invested before the common shareholders receive the residual proceeds, unless converting into common would be more valuable to them. This sounds modest when first stated, and in many venture deals it is treated as ordinary. But even this "plain vanilla" version changes the economic meaning of the cap table substantially, especially in middling outcomes.

The easiest way to understand this is to compare what happens with and without the preference. Suppose an investor put £2 million into the company and received preferred stock. Later the company is sold for £5 million. If everyone simply participated on their ownership percentages with no preference, then the money would be split pro rata across the cap table according to share ownership. But if the investor has a one-times liquidation preference, the investor may first take back their £2 million before the rest is divided among the remaining claimants, unless converting to common produces a better result. The difference between those two distributions can be very significant, especially when the exit is not large enough for the preference to become economically irrelevant.

This is why liquidation preference matters most in outcomes that are respectable rather than spectacular. In a huge exit, common holders may still do very well because the total pool is so large that returning the investor's preference first does not meaningfully undermine the founders' remaining upside. In a poor or middling exit, however, the preference can dominate. The investor gets their money back first, and the common holders may discover that their paper percentages were never the whole story. This is one of the hardest lessons in startup finance for founders to internalise because they often imagine exits in terms of the total sale price and their visible stake, not in terms of what order different classes of shareholders get paid.

A simple example helps. Imagine founders hold common stock and together own eighty percent of the company. An investor holds twenty percent preferred and invested £2 million. The company is later sold for £3 million. A founder looking only at percentages might expect the investor to receive twenty percent of the proceeds, or £600,000, and the common holders to split the rest. But with a one-times liquidation preference, the investor may first receive £2 million off the top.

That leaves only £1 million for the common shareholders. The investor's percentage stake is no longer the most important fact. The preference is. In this case, the common founders are not sharing in the full sale price according to percentages from the first pound. They are receiving what remains after the preference has been satisfied.

This is why liquidation preference is not a technical footnote. It changes the payout sequence, and payout sequence changes real outcomes. A founder with a large common position can still do poorly in a modest exit if enough preferred money sits ahead of them. An investor with a smaller headline percentage can still recover much more strongly than that percentage alone would suggest because the preference allows them to step to the front of the line up to the agreed amount. The cap table therefore becomes layered not just in governance and future financing, but in the actual order of money distribution when the company has a liquidity event.

The common formulation of one-times non-participating preferred is often considered founder-friendlier than more aggressive variants because the investor usually must choose between taking the preference amount or converting into common if that would produce more. In other words, the investor does not get both in that basic structure. If the company sells for a very high price, the investor will often waive the preference and convert into common because their percentage share of the large exit is worth more than the return of their original investment. This is why founders should not treat all liquidation preferences as equally dangerous. The magnitude of the preference, whether it is participating or non-participating, and how many rounds of preferred stack on top of one another all matter immensely.

Still, even the "standard" form can be more consequential than founders first assume. A one-times preference sounds benign because it is "only" the original investment amount. But if the company has raised meaningful capital over several rounds, those amounts can stack. Multiple preferred rounds can create a substantial preference overhang, meaning that a significant portion of any sale proceeds must first go to investors before common holders see the residual. A founder who is casually comforted by a large common percentage without modelling the total preference stack is at serious risk of misunderstanding what a plausible sale outcome would actually deliver.

This is one reason later-stage cap table analysis often involves waterfalls rather than simple percentage tables. A waterfall shows how sale proceeds flow through the capital structure depending on the size of the exit. It makes clear that a company sold for £20 million may produce very different founder outcomes depending on how much preferred money sits ahead of the common and what rights those preferred holders have. Founders often avoid this thinking because it feels pessimistic or too legalistic. In reality, it is one of the clearest ways to understand what the cap table truly means under real exit scenarios.

Liquidation preference also influences behaviour before any exit happens. Investors know they have preference protection in downside or middling outcomes, and that may affect how they negotiate future rounds or how they view strategic decisions. Founders, if they understand the structure properly, know that not every sale at a decent number is actually decent for them. That can shape whether they are willing to accept acquisition offers, how they think about fundraising pressure, and how they evaluate the growing gap between company valuation headlines and common-stock economic reality. A company can look successful from the outside and still leave founders with much less than expected if the exit occurs below the level where common fully starts to matter.

It is also important to say plainly that liquidation preference is not inherently unfair. Investors are putting cash into highly risky private companies. They often want some assurance that if the outcome is merely acceptable rather than extraordinary, they are not treated identically to the common holders who did not contribute capital in that same form. The preference reflects that bargain. The issue for founders is not whether any preference should exist by default. The issue is whether the preference being granted remains proportionate, understandable, and survivable when combined with the rest of the cap table. A company with one clean preference round is a very different structure from a company with several rounds, cumulative protections, and little room left for common to matter in ordinary sale outcomes.

The founder should therefore learn to ask a small set of hard questions whenever preference appears. How large is the preference. Is it one-times or more. Is it participating or non-participating. How does it stack with earlier or later rounds. At what exit values do the founders begin to do well in real terms after the preference is satisfied.

These are not specialist questions to be handed off entirely to counsel. They are questions about what the company's ownership actually means. A founder who cannot answer them is not really reading the cap table under pressure.

That is why liquidation preference is one of the defining features of preferred stock. It is where the phrase preferred stops being theoretical and becomes plainly economic. It tells the founder that in some outcomes the investor is not simply a twenty percent partner alongside the founders. The investor is someone whose capital gets honoured first up to a defined level before the common holders receive what is left. Once that is understood, the founder is much better prepared for the next important distinction, which is what happens when the preference does not merely come first, but can also continue participating afterward.

Participating and Non-Participating Preferred

Once a founder understands basic liquidation preference, the next distinction becomes critical because it determines whether the investor's preference is simply a first claim or a first claim plus ongoing participation. This is the difference between non-participating preferred and participating preferred, and it is one of the places where founders can drastically misread how generous or aggressive a financing structure really is. Two investors may both appear to hold preferred stock with the same headline percentage and the same nominal preference multiple, yet the actual economic consequences for the common holders can be very different depending on whether the preferred participates after taking its preference.

Non-participating preferred is usually the cleaner and more founder-tolerable version. In this structure, the investor typically chooses between two alternatives in a liquidity event. They can either take their liquidation preference, usually the amount they invested multiplied by the agreed preference multiple, or they can convert into common and take their pro rata share of the total proceeds as a common holder. They do not generally get both. This matters because it places a ceiling on how much advantage the preference itself creates. In lower or middling exits, the investor may prefer to take the preference. In higher exits, the investor will often convert into common because their percentage share of the bigger outcome is worth more than merely getting their investment back first.

A simple example shows how this works. Imagine an investor put in £2 million for preferred stock and owns twenty percent of the company on an as-converted basis. The company is later sold for £6 million. Under a one-times non-participating preference, the investor asks which is better. If they take the preference, they receive £2 million first. If they convert to common, they receive twenty percent of £6 million, which is £1.2 million. In this case, the preference is better, so they take the £2 million. If instead the company were sold for £20 million, then twenty percent as common would be £4 million, which is better than merely taking the £2 million preference. So in that higher-exit case the investor would convert and take the common share instead. The investor is protected on the downside and middling range, but not entitled to double dip.

Participating preferred is different because it allows a form of double participation in the proceeds. In the classic participating structure, the investor first receives their liquidation preference and then also participates with the common holders in the remaining proceeds according to their ownership percentage, usually on an as-converted basis. That is why founders often describe it, not inaccurately, as the investor getting their money back first and then continuing to share in the company as though they had converted anyway. This can materially reduce what is left for common stock in outcomes that might otherwise have felt acceptable.

The same example shows the contrast clearly. Imagine again that the investor put in £2 million and owns twenty percent. The company is sold for £6 million. Under participating preferred, the investor first takes the £2 million preference. That leaves £4 million. The investor then also receives twenty percent of that remaining £4 million, which is £800,000. The investor's total proceeds are now £2.8 million, not merely £2 million or £1.2 million. The common holders receive the remaining £3.2 million. Compare that with non-participating preferred, where the investor would have had to choose only one path. The economic difference is substantial, and it comes directly out of what would otherwise have been common-holder proceeds.

This is why participation rights can be so significant in modest and middle-range exits. In an enormous exit, the common holders may still do very well despite participation because the overall pool is so large. In a small or mediocre exit, participating preferred can take a much larger bite out of the available proceeds than founders first realise. A company may sell for a number that sounds respectable in public, yet once the investor preference is paid and participation is layered on top, the founders discover that their personal economics are much thinner than the headline sale price implied. This is one of the most important reasons percentages alone are a poor guide to what founders will actually receive.

Founders often find participating preferred emotionally jarring because it violates their intuitive sense that preference should be about recovering capital first, not about staying privileged all the way through distribution. Non-participating preferred already gives the investor protection in weaker outcomes. Participating preferred goes further and says that the investor should keep that protection and still continue to share in the rest. From the investor's perspective, this can be justified as compensation for risk, especially in very early or high-risk deals. From the founder's perspective, it can feel like a much more aggressive extraction of value from the common. Both reactions have some logic. What matters is that the founder recognises the term for what it is and does not mistake it for ordinary "standard" preference if it is not.

There are also variations that soften participating preferred somewhat, the most common being participation with a cap. In this structure, the investor may first take the liquidation preference and then participate in the remaining proceeds, but only up to a specified total return. For example, the investor may be entitled to participate until they have received two or three times their original investment, after which they no longer continue to share. This does not remove the founder burden, but it can limit the severity of the double-dip effect in larger outcomes. A capped participation structure is still more investor-favourable than plain non-participating preferred, but less harsh than fully uncapped participation.

This is why founders should never ask only whether the preferred participates. They should ask whether it participates indefinitely or only up to a defined multiple. A participating preferred with a cap can still meaningfully distort moderate exits, but at least it does not allow the investor to continue enjoying preference-enhanced economics all the way into very large outcomes without limit. The cap matters because it determines whether participation is merely a stronger downside and mid-range protection or a much broader reallocation of exit economics across the full range of outcomes.

Another thing founders must notice is that participation becomes more dangerous when layered across multiple rounds. One investor with participating preferred may already be a serious issue in a modest exit. Several rounds of preferred, each with its own participation or preference rights, can create an outcome in which the common sits underneath a very thick stack of investor claims. At that point, the company may need a fairly large exit before the founders and other common holders experience the economics they had been informally imagining from their headline percentages. This is one reason later-stage cap table analysis increasingly depends on waterfall modelling rather than intuition. The structure can become too layered for back-of-the-envelope thinking to remain safe.

From a negotiation perspective, this means founders should be careful not to fixate only on valuation while treating participation terms as secondary. A strong headline valuation paired with aggressive participating preferred can be worse for common holders than a slightly lower valuation with clean non-participating preferred. The latter may leave the founders with a better real position in a wide range of realistic exits even if the former flatters the company more on paper in the moment. This is a recurring theme in cap table thinking. Headline numbers are not enough. Rights determine how those numbers behave.

It is also worth recognising that market norms vary by stage, geography, and financing climate. In some environments, one-times non-participating preferred is treated as the ordinary baseline and participation is viewed as more investor-friendly than founders should accept lightly. In tougher markets or weaker company situations, investors may push for stronger protections, including participation. The founder's job is not to moralise in the abstract, but to understand what each term does and whether the company is paying too much in structural economics for the capital it is receiving. Participation is not automatically unacceptable in every context, but it is never a trivial term.

The safest founder habit here is to run several exit scenarios. What happens at £10 million, £25 million, £50 million, £100 million, and beyond. How much does the investor receive under non-participating preferred. How much under participating preferred. When does conversion become more attractive than preference. If participation is capped, when does the cap cease to matter. These are not lawyer-only questions. They are the practical meaning of the cap table. A founder who cannot answer them is still thinking in headline percentages rather than in outcomes.

That is the real difference between participating and non-participating preferred. Non-participating preferred usually forces the investor to choose between protection and participation. Participating preferred often lets the investor have both. The words are short. The consequences are not.

Preference Stacks

A single liquidation preference is one thing. A preference stack is something much more consequential. The stack is what forms when multiple rounds of preferred stock sit on top of one another, each carrying its own claim to be paid before the common stock fully participates. Once that happens, the founder is no longer dealing with one investor preference that can be reasoned about in isolation. The company is now carrying a layered capital structure in which several investor classes may each have rights ahead of the founders and employees. This is where many founders stop thinking in percentages and start needing waterfall logic, because the order and size of those stacked claims can dominate real outcomes.

The reason preference stacks matter is simple. Every priced round that issues preferred stock can add another layer of money that expects priority treatment in a sale or liquidation event. One investor may have put in £2 million at seed. Another may later put in £8 million at Series A. Another may then put in £20 million at Series B. If each of those rounds carries a one-times liquidation preference, then the company may have £30 million of investor preference sitting ahead of the common stock before the founders receive the residual. In a large enough exit, that may not feel oppressive. In an exit below or around that level, it becomes everything.

This is one of the great hidden truths of venture-backed cap tables. A company can appear highly valuable on paper, can have raised substantial capital, and can still leave founders with much less than they imagined if the exit occurs in the range where the preference stack dominates. The headline valuation from the last round does not tell you who gets what in a sale. The stack does. This is why founders who talk excitedly about post-money valuations without also understanding the cumulative preference burden are often not really reading their own capital structure. They are reading the top line and ignoring the queue underneath it.

A basic example shows the shift clearly. Suppose a company has three preferred rounds. Seed investors put in £2 million. Series A investors put in £6 million. Series B investors put in £12 million. Let us assume, for simplicity, that each has a one-times non-participating liquidation preference and that there are no unusual multiples. The total stack is now £20 million. If the company sells for £15 million, the founders' common ownership percentages become much less relevant than they appear on the cap table, because the full stack cannot even be cleared. The preferred holders, depending on the exact seniority structure and rights, may absorb the entire exit value. Common may receive nothing. A founder can own a large common position and still be completely underwater in that scenario.

Now imagine the same company sells for £30 million. That sounds much better, and in public storytelling it may even sound like a meaningful success. But the stack still matters. If £20 million of preference must be satisfied first, only £10 million remains for the common, unless some or all preferred holders choose to convert because common participation would yield more. At that point the distribution depends on the exact ownership percentages and whether each class is better off taking preference or converting. The important lesson is that the founders are not automatically sharing the whole £30 million on their stated percentages. They are standing beneath a structure that decides first how much of that money must satisfy prior investor capital before common economics begin to look normal.

This is why the word stack is useful. It conveys height and order. Preferences do not sit beside one another in a morally flat way. They pile. Later money is often layered on top of earlier money. In some structures, later rounds may be senior to earlier rounds, meaning the most recent investor gets paid first even before earlier preferred holders receive their own preference. In other cases the preferred may sit pari passu, sharing preference payments together in proportion. Either way, the founders are dealing with accumulated investor priority, not a single simple right. The exact architecture of the stack therefore matters almost as much as its total size.

Founders often underestimate preference stacks because each round felt reasonable when it happened. The seed round preference seemed standard. The Series A preference also seemed standard. The Series B preference was maybe unavoidable in the market conditions at the time. No single layer looked outrageous. But together they create a very different company from the one the founders thought they were financing. This is one of the defining features of cap table complexity. Terms that are tolerable one at a time can become structurally dominant when accumulated. A founder who never steps back to look at the whole stack may continue telling themselves that each round was fine while failing to notice that the common stock is becoming less and less relevant across a wide range of plausible exits.

This is also where valuation can become a source of dangerous illusion. A company may have raised at a £100 million post-money valuation and yet still have a preference stack large enough that an exit at £60 million, while sounding substantial, is actually disappointing or even close to worthless for common holders. The founders may emotionally anchor to the idea that the company was once "worth" £100 million, but the real question in a sale is not what the last valuation said. It is how the current proceeds move through the stack. That is why founders should never rely on valuation headlines as a substitute for understanding exit economics. The stack is what makes those economics real.

Preference stacks also affect behaviour while the company is still operating. A founder who understands that common sits beneath a thick stack may make different choices about whether to raise another round, whether to consider acquisition offers, how to motivate employees with options, or whether the current strategy still makes economic sense for the common holders. A company can become what is sometimes called over-capitalised, meaning not simply that it raised a lot of money, but that it raised enough preference-bearing capital that the common's route to meaningful proceeds now requires a much larger outcome than before. At that point, founder incentives can start to warp. Some founders become highly risk-seeking because only a huge outcome now matters to them. Others become demoralised because moderate wins no longer feel like wins at all.

This is one reason investors should care about stacks too, even though they are often building them. A company with a very heavy preference stack can become strategically brittle. It may struggle to attract and retain talent if employees understand that their common or option upside sits beneath a mountain of investor priority. Founders may become less rationally aligned.

Acquisition conversations may become harder because sale prices that would once have been acceptable now leave key operators cold. In that sense, a preference stack is not only a downside protection device for investors. It is also a structure that can distort the company's operating psychology if it grows too high relative to realistic outcome paths.

The safest habit for founders is to stop thinking of preferences round by round and start thinking of them cumulatively. After each financing, the founder should ask how much total preference now exists, what the seniority structure is, and what sale outcomes would be needed before common begins to receive economically satisfying proceeds. These are not defeatist questions. They are reality questions. A founder who cannot answer them does not yet know what the company has actually become in economic terms.

This is also why preference stacks often lead naturally to waterfall analysis, because once several classes of preferred exist, ordinary percentage thinking becomes too crude. One has to ask not only who owns what, but in what order each class is paid, whether each class converts or takes preference, whether participation rights exist, and how much is left at each stage of the distribution. The more layers there are, the less useful intuitive cap table reading becomes. The company has to model outcomes, not just observe ownership.

That is the essential point. A preference stack is the accumulated hierarchy of investor priority built by multiple rounds of preferred financing. It can sit quietly in the company for years while the business operates, hires, and grows. Then a sale discussion or strategic reset arrives, and suddenly the stack reveals itself as one of the most important facts in the whole cap table. Founders who understand that early are far less likely to confuse headline success with real common-holder economics, and far more likely to see when another round is not just more dilution, but another layer in a structure that may eventually determine whether the common means very much at all.

Why Founders Must Read Rights, Not Just Percentages

One of the last habits founders lose, and one of the most important they ever lose, is the habit of reading the cap table as though percentages alone tell the truth. In the earliest life of a company that habit is understandable.

When everyone holds common stock and the structure is relatively flat, percentages do most of the explanatory work. Sixty percent means more than forty percent. One founder clearly owns more than another. The table feels intuitive. Once preferred shares, liquidation preferences, participation rights, board rights, protective provisions, pro rata rights, anti-dilution protections, and stacked financing rounds begin to enter the picture, that old intuition becomes dangerously incomplete. From that point forward, founders must read rights, not just percentages.

This is not a stylistic preference. It is a survival skill.

A founder who reads only percentages is reading the cap table as appearance. A founder who reads rights is reading it as behaviour. The difference is profound. Percentages tell you how ownership is divided in a broad numerical sense. Rights tell you what that ownership can actually do, what it gets paid in which order, what approvals it can demand, what protections it enjoys when the company struggles, and how strongly it can shape later rounds. A stakeholder with fifteen percent and strong preferred rights may occupy a more powerful economic or governance position than a stakeholder with a larger common percentage. If the founder does not understand that, then the founder is not really reading the company's ownership structure. They are reading only its surface.

This is why so many first-time founders feel blindsided later by outcomes they technically had enough information to foresee. The term sheet showed the rights. The charter reflected the classes. The round documents explained the preferences. But the founder's eye kept returning to the visible percentages because those were easier to grasp emotionally. When the company later faces an acquisition offer, a down round, a board conflict, or a middling exit, the founder discovers that the percentages they had been using as mental anchors are no longer enough. The rights are now doing the real work, and the founder is meeting them too late.

A simple way to see this is to remember that the cap table answers at least three different kinds of questions, and percentages only answer the first one well. First, who owns what fraction of the company in a broad arithmetic sense. Second, what rights attach to those ownership positions. Third, how do those rights and percentages interact under specific scenarios such as financing, sale, liquidation, or governance conflict.

A founder who reads only percentages is answering the first question and pretending the others do not exist. That may have been tolerable when the company was young and flat. It becomes reckless once institutional capital arrives.

The founder who has learned this lesson starts asking different questions automatically. Not just how much of the company is being sold, but what class is being issued. Not just what the investor owns, but what the investor can block, demand, or recover first. Not just what my percentage will be after the round, but what happens to my economics if the company sells for £20 million, £50 million, or £100 million. Not just whether this round feels "expensive," but whether the rights stack being created now will make future common ownership less meaningful than the percentages suggest. These are not lawyerly embellishments. They are the actual content of startup ownership once the company becomes financed in layers.

This also changes how founders should listen in negotiations. When an investor says the round is standard, the founder should not relax simply because the preference multiple sounds familiar or the headline valuation sounds acceptable. Standard is not a complete answer. Standard for whom, at what stage, in what market, with what cumulative effect when added to what is already in the cap table. A one-times non-participating preference may be ordinary in many venture contexts and still produce founder pain if the preference stack is already large. A pro rata right may sound harmless and still matter greatly later if it affects who can maintain influence over the company's financing path. A board seat may feel procedural and still reshape how the company governs itself under stress. Rights must be understood in context, not as isolated phrases that sound market-normal.

Another reason founders must read rights is that rights often become decisive exactly when percentages become least helpful. In a very large success, simple percentage thinking can come back into fashion because the company's overall value may be so high that preferences and protections matter less relative to the total proceeds. But in the real middle range of company outcomes, the range where many startups actually live or exit, rights are often far more important than founders expect. A company may sell for enough that everyone can say it was a real business, but not enough that all the preferred protections wash out harmlessly.

That is the zone where founders discover whether they understood the rights or merely memorised the percentages.

This is also why rights affect incentives. A founder who sees only their own percentage may believe they remain strongly aligned, only to find later that the common stock beneath the rights stack is worth much less than its headline size implied in plausible outcomes. Employees may receive option grants that sound meaningful until they realise how much investor preference sits ahead of them. Even investors read one another's rights carefully because their own future economics depend not only on what they own but on what later or earlier investors can demand. The cap table is therefore not a peaceful coexistence of percentages. It is an interaction of claims.

There is an ethical dimension here as well. Founders who do not read rights properly often end up misdescribing the company to employees, cofounders, or even to themselves. They speak about ownership in flat percentage language because it is simpler and more uplifting. "We still own most of the company." "This option grant is worth X percent." "The investor only took twenty percent." These statements may be technically incomplete in ways that matter a great deal. Once the company begins using that simplified language habitually, it starts building an ownership culture around a version of the truth that is too shallow. Later, when the real structure asserts itself, people feel misled even if the documents were available all along. This is another reason founders have to upgrade their own understanding first. The company usually speaks about ownership in the language the founders themselves are comfortable using.

Reading rights also makes founders better negotiators because it expands the set of tradeable variables. A founder who sees only valuation and percentage has only a few obvious places to fight. A founder who reads rights sees that some rounds are worse because of price, others because of preference, others because of participation, others because of board control, others because of future financing rights, and still others because of the cumulative interaction of all of these. That richer view allows a much more intelligent response. The founder can concede in one area and defend another. They can recognise when a slightly lower headline valuation with cleaner rights is actually better than a flattering number with harsher terms. They can distinguish between what sounds expensive and what really is expensive in the structure the company will live inside afterward.

The practical discipline that follows from this is very simple, even if living it is demanding. Every time the cap table changes, the founder should ask not only what new percentages result, but what new rights have entered the company, what old rights have been strengthened or subordinated, and how those rights behave in the next likely scenarios. Financing, sale, employee grants, down rounds, secondaries, and governance changes should all be read this way. A founder who does that consistently begins to see the cap table not as a static ownership report but as a live map of legal and economic power.

That is the point toward which this whole chapter has been moving. Once preferred stock enters the company, percentages stop being enough. They remain necessary, but they no longer tell the whole story. The founder who still reads only percentages after that point is driving with half the windscreen painted over. The company may continue for a while, but its most important structural realities will remain partly hidden until exactly the moment they become expensive.

That is why founders must read rights, not just percentages. Percentages tell you what the company looks like. Rights tell you how it works.

* * *

TWELVE

Pro Rata Rights, Anti-Dilution, and Investor Defences

"Risk comes from not knowing what you're doing."

- Warren Buffett

Why Investors Defend Their Ownership

One of the most revealing transitions in startup finance is the moment founders realise that investors are not only buying into the company as it exists today. They are also negotiating for how their position will behave when the company changes tomorrow. This is the deeper reason investor rights become so important after the first priced rounds. Investors are not passive owners waiting to see what happens. They are often trying to defend the economic and governance position they have just purchased against the predictable ways in which startups evolve: future rounds, future dilution, future re-pricing, future control shifts, and future restructuring. That is why investor protections exist. They are not random legal embellishments. They are tools for preserving value, influence, and optionality inside an unstable growth environment.

From the founder's point of view, this can feel slightly strange at first. The investor has already agreed to the round. They have priced the risk, signed the documents, and joined the cap table. Why are they still negotiating so much about what happens later. The answer is that startup investing is rarely a one-step event. The company is expected to change repeatedly after the investor enters. It may raise more capital, issue more shares, create or enlarge option pools, hit difficult markets, accept weaker later pricing, or take strategic turns that alter who holds influence. The investor knows this. So the investor wants to avoid being treated as though the first cheque alone is the whole relationship. They are buying a position inside a moving structure and often want rights that stop that position from eroding too easily.

This is why investors defend their ownership. Ownership in a startup is not static property. It is a stake in a system that keeps issuing new claims, changing valuation, and redistributing future upside as the company grows. An investor who buys ten or twenty percent today may see that position shrink meaningfully over several later rounds unless they have rights that let them maintain it or protect it. In some cases that shrinkage is completely acceptable, even expected. In other cases, especially where the company later raises on weak terms or where the investor wants to preserve a meaningful level of influence, the investor will push for mechanisms that keep their ownership from being diluted too easily or too unfairly. These mechanisms are not all the same. Some are about preserving percentage. Some are about protecting price. Some are about preventing value transfer in later financings. But they all arise from the same basic logic: investors do not want the stake they bought to lose its meaning faster than the risk of startup life already makes likely.

The most intuitive of these protections is the desire to keep participating in future rounds. If an investor believes in the company and wants to maintain roughly the same slice of the business as it grows, then it makes sense to seek a right to buy enough stock in later rounds to preserve their proportion. That is the logic behind pro rata rights, which will come shortly. Another line of defence is against weak future pricing. If a company later raises money at a lower valuation than the one at which an earlier investor entered, the earlier investor may argue that their old stake has been impaired not just by ordinary dilution but by a repricing that harms them more sharply than they had bargained for. That is where anti-dilution protection enters. Different rights respond to different threats, but the foundation is the same. The investor is trying to defend the economic meaning of the original deal.

This is also why founders should stop imagining investor rights as merely expressions of mistrust. Sometimes they are indeed signs of caution or imbalance in the relationship, but very often they are simply the natural language of capital entering a company that is expected to need more capital later. Investors know that the current round is not the end of the financing story. They are protecting themselves against the structure's future movement. A founder who understands that can negotiate more intelligently. Instead of hearing every defensive investor term as personal aggression, the founder can ask a better question: what future risk is the investor trying to guard against, and is the requested protection proportionate to that risk.

That question matters because not every investor defence is equally reasonable in every company or every market. Some are entirely ordinary and often healthy. Others can become excessive, especially when stacked across multiple rounds. A company that grants every investor a broad package of defensive rights without understanding their cumulative interaction can create a cap table that is not only protective for investors but brittle for the company itself. Founder incentives may weaken. Later financings may become harder. Decision-making may become cluttered with too many legacy entitlements. The problem is not that investors want to defend their ownership. The problem is that startup companies sometimes allow defensive rights to accumulate without asking what kind of company remains governable underneath them.

There is also a more subtle point. Investors do not all defend ownership for the same reason. Some want to preserve economic exposure because they think the company can become very valuable and they do not want their stake to thin too much before that happens. Some want to preserve influence because a certain threshold of ownership or board relationship matters to how they work with the company. Some want downside protection because they worry about weaker later rounds. Some simply want optionality: the right, but not the obligation, to continue investing if the company performs well. This means founders should not treat defensive rights as one generic bucket. The motivations matter because they shape how hard the investor pushes, which terms really matter to them, and where negotiation flexibility may exist.

The founder should also notice that investor defences are often strongest precisely in the scenarios founders least like to contemplate. Things go well but require more rounds than expected. The company raises on weaker terms. Option pools expand. Strategic pivots occur. A later round resets the pricing of the business. These are all moments when earlier capital may feel threatened. Investors know this. Founders often focus more on the ideal path than on the structurally plausible path. This difference in mindset is one reason investor protections can feel pessimistic from the founder side. In reality they are often designed around the ordinary instability of startup development. That does not mean every protection is justified. It means the founder should recognise that these terms are usually written for the stressful paths, not for the easy ones.

This is why the company's cap table becomes progressively more political as more investor classes enter. The founders are not only building a business. They are managing constituencies whose rights are designed to defend their own position as the company evolves. Those constituencies may align most of the time, especially in strong-growth scenarios. But alignment should never be assumed merely because everyone wants success in the abstract. The specific rights attached to investor stock are part of how those constituencies prepare for outcomes where success is slower, weaker, or more complicated than hoped. A founder who understands this early becomes much better at distinguishing between ordinary investor discipline and rights packages that go so far they begin to make the company itself harder to finance or motivate later.

There is another reason this chapter matters. Many founders become reasonably comfortable with dilution in the simple sense. They know future rounds reduce percentages. What they are often less prepared for is the idea that not all dilution is treated equally by all parties. Some investors can buy more in later rounds to preserve their share. Some are protected if later pricing falls. Founders and employees holding common stock often do not enjoy the same protections. This means that later financing events do not always land evenly across the cap table. The structure has been designed to distribute future financing pain asymmetrically. That is one of the deepest things investor defences do. They do not merely preserve investor economics in the abstract. They can shift how future pain is allocated across the company.

The founder should therefore read investor defences not as isolated legal tricks but as part of the company's future ownership politics. They affect who gets to stay strong in later rounds. They affect whether early investors can preserve or deepen their influence. They affect how much of the burden of weak future financing falls on founders and employees versus on earlier capital. Once the founder sees that clearly, terms like pro rata and anti-dilution stop sounding like technical clutter and start sounding like what they really are: structural answers to the question of who must absorb future uncertainty.

That is why investors defend their ownership. They know the startup is not a static object. It will raise again, reprice again, dilute again, and perhaps disappoint again before it ever reaches a final outcome. They want rights that keep their original deal from becoming economically fragile too quickly. Sometimes those rights are healthy. Sometimes they are too strong. The founder's task is not to resent the instinct behind them, but to understand it well enough to judge where sensible protection ends and harmful overreach begins.

Pro Rata Rights

Of all the investor protections founders encounter, pro rata rights are among the most common and, on the surface, among the easiest to accept. The basic idea seems reasonable enough. If an investor owns part of the company today and wants to keep owning roughly that same proportion tomorrow, then the investor should have the right to buy enough stock in a future round to maintain that position. In its simplest form, that is exactly what pro rata means. It is the right, but not usually the obligation, to participate in later financings in an amount sufficient to preserve the investor's percentage ownership.

This sounds straightforward, and in many cases it is. If an investor owns ten percent of the company and the company later raises another round, a pro rata right may allow that investor to buy enough of the new issuance to keep holding roughly ten percent afterward. Without such a right, the investor would simply be diluted along with everyone else if they did not join the round. With the right, they can preserve their stake if they choose to put in more money. That is why pro rata rights are often framed as ordinary fairness rather than as aggressive control. The investor is not asking to avoid future funding needs. The investor is asking to be allowed to keep backing the company on the same proportional basis if the company continues to develop well.

The reason investors care about this is not mysterious. Early investors often take more risk, enter at a stage when the company is much less proven, and may help the business reach the milestones that later make it attractive to larger capital. If the company starts performing strongly, those early investors do not want to be passively pushed into irrelevance by the very success they helped finance. Pro rata rights protect against that. They ensure that if the investor wants to keep supporting the company, the company cannot casually shut them out and force their stake to shrink purely because new capital is arriving from somewhere else. In that sense, pro rata is a defence not only of percentage but of continued relationship.

This is why pro rata rights can be healthy in the right company. They encourage early investors to stay engaged. They create continuity across financing rounds. They can reassure investors that supporting the company early will not automatically mean surrendering meaningful ownership later just because bigger money arrives. For founders, this can be beneficial too. An investor who knows they can maintain their position may be more willing to commit early, may be more patient through early uncertainty, and may become a useful source of follow-on capital when the next round comes. Pro rata rights can therefore strengthen the financing path rather than merely burden it.

Yet, like many seemingly ordinary investor protections, pro rata rights become more complicated once the company starts scaling and once multiple investors hold them at the same time. A right that feels modest when one angel or one seed investor has it can become much more consequential when several investors all expect to preserve their positions in a later round. The company is no longer just deciding how much of the round goes to the new lead investor. It is also deciding how much must be reserved or made available to insiders exercising pro rata rights. This can tighten the round, affect allocation politics, and reduce the founders' flexibility in choosing who comes into the company next.

This is one of the first places where founders discover that later financing is not simply about finding a new investor willing to write the cheque. It is also about managing the rights already sitting on the cap table. If a large portion of the round is taken up by existing investors exercising pro rata, then the company may have less room to bring in new names, less room to use a new strategic investor creatively, or less leverage in negotiations with a new lead who wants a certain minimum ownership stake. Pro rata rights do not just preserve earlier investors. They shape the available space in future rounds.

A simple example makes this clear. Imagine a seed investor owns fifteen percent of the company and has pro rata rights. The company later raises a Series A and plans to sell twenty percent of the post-round company to the new lead investor. If the seed investor exercises pro rata, they may also need to buy enough in the Series A to remain at roughly fifteen percent after the round. That means the total round may need to include not only the lead investor's target allocation but also additional shares for the seed investor's follow-on. If several investors do this, a round that looked clean in headline terms can become much more crowded.

The founders are not merely negotiating with one new cheque. They are allocating space among old and new capital simultaneously.

This is why pro rata rights can create subtle tension between different investor types. A new lead investor may want a large enough position to justify the work, reputation, and capital they are putting into the company. Earlier investors with pro rata rights may want to preserve their existing stakes. The founders may want enough room left over that the cap table remains healthy and future rounds remain possible. These interests can coexist, but they are not automatically harmonious. The more successful the company becomes, the more valuable those pro rata rights can be, because preserving a stake in a rising company is often exactly what early investors hoped to do.

For founders, one of the main mistakes is to think of pro rata as purely procedural. It is not merely a checkbox saying that an investor may write another cheque later. It is a structural claim on future financing capacity. Every strong pro rata holder is, in effect, reserving some right to remain inside the company's future capital raises. That can be very reasonable. It can also become restrictive if too many such rights accumulate or if the company does not understand how much of future rounds may already be spoken for. This is why founders should read pro rata not just as investor friendliness, but as future-round architecture.

There is also a psychological issue here. Founders often like pro rata rights when they are granted because the company is still small and every sign of investor loyalty feels positive. An early investor saying "we want the right to keep supporting you later" can sound encouraging, and often it is. The trouble comes when later rounds arrive and the company realises that those earlier rights are now part of the negotiation terrain. What once sounded like a flattering sign of commitment becomes a live allocation constraint. Nothing has gone wrong exactly. The founders are simply meeting the future meaning of a term that felt friendlier when it was still abstract.

This is another reason founders need to understand the scale of the right. Who has it. How much do they currently own. Is the right a standard pro rata right or something broader, such as super pro rata, where the investor may be allowed to buy more than their current percentage in future rounds.

What are the procedural conditions. Is the right automatic if the investor chooses to exercise, or can it be structured in ways that still leave the company room to manage the round sensibly. These details matter because pro rata can range from ordinary protective participation to a much more powerful tool for preserving or increasing investor influence over time.

It is also worth seeing pro rata rights from the investor's side with some sympathy. An early investor who helped finance the company before proof existed may reasonably feel that if the company becomes attractive later, they should not be frozen out while newcomers benefit from a cleaner, less risky entry point. Pro rata rights defend against that. They say that early risk should earn not just early entry but the opportunity to keep participating if the company grows into something better. That is a fair instinct. The founder's task is not to deny that instinct, but to make sure the resulting rights package does not make later rounds too inflexible or too weighted toward legacy capital.

In a healthy structure, pro rata rights can help hold the financing story together. They give early investors continuity, give founders follow-on support, and create a more stable bridge from round to round. In an overbuilt structure, they can contribute to cap table congestion and make later allocations harder than they need to be. The difference lies in scale, accumulation, and context. One or two meaningful pro rata holders in a growing company are often normal. A company where half the cap table expects to preserve its position every time new money enters may find that future financing has become a crowded room before the next lead investor has even arrived.

That is the essence of pro rata rights. They are not anti-dilution in the strict sense of changing the price of old shares. They are participation rights that let investors defend their percentage by putting in more money later. They sound modest because they preserve ownership through continued investment rather than through automatic repricing. But they are still powerful, because they reserve part of the company's future financing space for people who are already inside. The founder who understands that will be in a much better position to read the next line of investor defence, which is more technical, more feared, and often more misunderstood: anti-dilution protection.

Anti-Dilution Protection

If pro rata rights allow an investor to defend ownership by putting in more money later, anti-dilution protection addresses a different fear entirely. It is not mainly about preserving percentage through continued participation. It is about protecting the investor if the company later raises money at a lower price than the investor paid. In other words, anti-dilution is a response to the possibility of a down round. The investor is saying: if I bought into this company at one valuation and a future round effectively reprices the company downward, I do not want to absorb that loss in the same way as though nothing special had happened.

This is why anti-dilution protection is often one of the most sensitive terms in startup finance. It does not usually matter when everything is going well. In a strong company raising each new round at a higher valuation, anti-dilution may sit quietly in the documents and never become economically important. The term becomes decisive when the company struggles, or when market conditions worsen, or when the next financing can only be done at a price below the prior round. That is exactly why the term exists. It is written for the scenario founders least want to think about but most need to understand.

The basic logic is this. Suppose an investor bought preferred shares in a priced round at £2 per share. If the company later has to raise a round at £1 per share, the earlier investor has effectively paid twice the price of the new money for the same company. Without any protection, that earlier investor simply lives with the damage. Their stake has been diluted, and the new lower price has also made the earlier entry look expensive in hindsight. Anti-dilution protection softens that blow by adjusting the conversion price of the investor's preferred stock, often so that the investor ends up with more shares than they would otherwise have had. The investor is not usually being refunded in cash. They are being compensated through price adjustment inside the equity structure.

This is why anti-dilution is not ordinary dilution management. It is repricing protection. The investor is saying that if the company later sells equity more cheaply, the original bargain should be partially recalibrated in their favour. From the founder's point of view, this means that the pain of a down round does not fall evenly across the cap table. Common holders and less-protected stakeholders may bear more of the damage, because the protected preferred holders are cushioned by the adjustment mechanism. That is why anti-dilution can feel harsh. It does not merely record the pain of the company's weaker later financing. It redistributes that pain.

There are several forms of anti-dilution, but the most important distinction is between full ratchet and weighted average. Founders do not need to memorise these as legal jargon detached from reality. They need to understand what each one does to the company if the bad scenario arrives.

Full ratchet is the more severe version. Under full ratchet anti-dilution, if the company later issues shares at a lower price than the investor paid, the earlier investor's conversion price may be reset all the way down to that new lower price, regardless of how many shares were sold in the down round. This can be brutal for common holders and founders because it gives the earlier investor the full benefit of the new lower price even if the new issuance was relatively small. The company may have sold only a limited number of shares at the lower price, yet the anti-dilution effect on the earlier investor can be large because the investor's old preferred position is now treated as though it had originally been bought at the new cheaper price.

A quick example shows why founders fear full ratchet. Suppose an investor bought in at £2 per share. Later the company, under pressure, raises a relatively small rescue round at £1 per share. Under full ratchet, the earlier investor's conversion price may reset from £2 to £1. That means the investor's preferred stock now converts into twice as many common-equivalent shares as before. The down round did not just dilute everyone in the ordinary way. It also repriced the earlier investor's whole position as though they had come in at the cheaper price. The burden of that adjustment is borne largely by the common and other less-protected holders.

Weighted average anti-dilution is usually less aggressive and more common in more balanced venture structures. Here the adjustment depends not only on the fact that the new round price is lower, but also on how many shares were actually issued at that lower price. The company does not pretend the entire earlier round should be repriced fully down to the new level. Instead, it applies a formula that partially adjusts the earlier investor's conversion price based on the scale of the dilutive event.

A large down round at a much lower price produces a stronger adjustment. A small issuance at a somewhat lower price produces a milder one.

This makes weighted average anti-dilution feel more proportionate. It recognises that a down round is painful and that the earlier investor is being harmed by the lower pricing, but it does not transfer all of that pain onto the common in the same way full ratchet can. The exact formula matters and may use broad-based or narrow-based calculations depending on what counts in the denominator, but the conceptual difference is what founders most need to hold onto. Full ratchet reacts to the new lower price as though any lower price justifies a total reset. Weighted average reacts to the combination of lower price and actual scale of issuance.

That distinction matters enormously in negotiation. A founder who hears only "anti-dilution protection" and does not ask what kind may be agreeing to a much more dangerous structure than they realise. In a healthy market and a healthy company, full ratchet may never trigger. But the whole point of anti-dilution is that it is written for unhealthy scenarios. If the company later finds itself forced into a weak financing, the terms that looked remote and theoretical can suddenly dominate the cap table. This is why anti-dilution must be judged not by how it feels in good times, but by what it does when the company is vulnerable.

It is also important to see anti-dilution as part of the broader preference ecology of the cap table. It rarely operates in isolation. A company that has already issued preferred stock with liquidation preference, pro rata rights, and other protections is not dealing with anti-dilution as one more small term. It is adding another way in which later financing pain can be distributed unevenly. The investor with anti-dilution protection may also have the right to maintain ownership pro rata in the new round. The same investor may also sit ahead of common in liquidation. The founder should therefore not think of anti-dilution as a discrete technical clause. It is part of a cumulative architecture that determines who remains strongest when the company is weakest.

This is one reason anti-dilution protection can distort incentives if the cap table becomes too heavily layered. If founders and employees know that a down round will protect earlier investors substantially while leaving common more exposed, the common's relationship to future financing can become more anxious. A necessary rescue round may feel less like shared survival and more like an event that shifts value upward through the structure. Investors may consider that entirely fair given the capital risk they took earlier. Founders may experience it very differently. Both perspectives exist, which is exactly why these terms need to be understood before they are needed.

Founders should also remember that anti-dilution is not there because investors assume every company will fail to keep raising higher. It is there because startup outcomes are unstable. Markets change. Growth disappoints. Timelines slip. Products stall. Macro conditions tighten. Companies that once looked set for strong up rounds can find themselves needing defensive capital on weaker terms. Anti-dilution is a contractual recognition of that reality. It is not necessarily a sign of investor hostility. But it is also not a neutral term. When it activates, someone pays, and that someone is often the common stock.

The right founder response is neither outrage nor complacency. It is precision. What kind of anti-dilution is being requested. Under what trigger. How broad is the formula. What would happen in a small down round. What would happen in a large one. How much of the burden would shift onto the founders and the employee pool. If the company had to survive through a weaker later raise, would the cap table remain motivational and financeable afterward. These are real governance questions, not abstract legal curiosities.

That is what anti-dilution protection really is. It is a mechanism by which investors defend the price they paid if the company later sells stock more cheaply. It matters only in the scenarios founders most hope to avoid, which is exactly why founders must understand it before those scenarios arrive. Once they do, the next question becomes even more practical: what actually happens in a down round, and why can that event be so much more destabilising than founders expect from the phrase alone.

Full Ratchet Versus Weighted Average

Anti-dilution protection only becomes real when the company raises at a lower price than before, but once that happens, the type of anti-dilution provision matters enormously. Founders often hear the phrase anti-dilution as though it names one standard mechanism. It does not.

The difference between full ratchet and weighted average is one of the most important differences in the whole term-sheet landscape, because the two provisions redistribute the pain of a down round in very different ways. If a founder does not understand that distinction, they are not really reading the economic consequences of the deal.

Full ratchet is the harsher version. It says, in effect, that if the company later issues shares at a lower price than the investor originally paid, the investor's earlier conversion price will be reset all the way down to that new lower price, regardless of how many of those cheap shares were actually sold. That final phrase is what makes full ratchet so severe. It does not care very much whether the down round was large or small. It reacts primarily to the fact that a lower price now exists. Once that lower price exists, the earlier investor is treated as though they had effectively invested at that lower price too.

This can produce extremely aggressive outcomes for the common holders. Imagine an investor bought preferred shares at £2 per share. The company later has a difficult period and raises even a relatively small amount of capital at £1 per share. Under full ratchet, the earlier investor's conversion price may reset from £2 to £1. The practical effect is that the investor's preferred now converts into twice as many common-equivalent shares as before. The new, weaker round has therefore not only diluted everyone through ordinary issuance. It has also rewritten the economics of the earlier round in the investor's favour. The burden of that rewrite falls largely on the founders, employees, and other less-protected holders.

This is why founders should think of full ratchet as price shock with maximum force. It says that once a lower price appears anywhere in the structure, the protected investor should be moved all the way down to that price. There is no moderation based on the scale of the new issuance. A tiny down round can therefore trigger a surprisingly large cap table consequence. That is one of the reasons full ratchet is often viewed as particularly investor-friendly and particularly dangerous for common stock.

Weighted average works differently. It still protects the earlier investor from a later lower price, but it does so with more regard for proportion. Instead of resetting the investor fully down to the new lower price, it uses a formula that takes account of both the old price and the amount of new stock issued at the lower price.

The adjustment is therefore partial rather than absolute. A small number of low-priced shares causes some adjustment, but not the same dramatic reset as full ratchet. A very large and heavily discounted round causes a stronger adjustment, because the company really has changed its pricing meaningfully across a larger portion of the capital structure.

This makes weighted average feel more economically rational in many cases. It recognises that the investor has been harmed by the lower later price and deserves some protection, but it does not treat every lower-priced issuance as though the entire earlier round must be repriced from scratch. In that sense it spreads the pain more proportionately. The investor is cushioned, but the common is not hit with the same blunt-force reset that full ratchet can impose.

A useful way to think about the difference is this. Full ratchet asks only one big question: did the company later issue shares cheaper than my price. If yes, it resets hard. Weighted average asks two questions: did the company later issue shares cheaper, and how much of the company was actually issued that way. Because of that second question, weighted average is usually much less punitive in cases where the down round is relatively modest or where the lower-priced issuance is limited in size.

This distinction is not academic. It changes real company behaviour. Under full ratchet, founders may become terrified of even small lower-priced financings, because the anti-dilution effect can be disproportionate to the amount of rescue capital being raised. The company may need a relatively small bridge just to survive or to correct course, but the full ratchet mechanism can make that bridge much more expensive than its cheque size suggests. Under weighted average, the company still suffers in a down round, but the structural damage is often less extreme and more aligned with the actual size of the financing event.

This is one reason market participants often treat weighted average as more "standard" or more balanced in venture settings, while viewing full ratchet as a much more aggressive protection. That does not mean weighted average is harmless. It still shifts pain away from the protected investor and onto others. It still weakens common positions in a down round. It still matters a great deal. But it does so with more relation to the actual scope of the repricing event. Full ratchet, by contrast, can behave like a trapdoor under the common if the company later stumbles even in a relatively narrow financing context.

Founders also need to understand that weighted average itself has variants, most notably broad-based and narrow-based forms. The formulas differ in what counts in the denominator when the adjustment is calculated. Broad-based weighted average generally includes more of the company's existing capital structure in the calculation and therefore tends to be less harsh than narrow-based weighted average, which includes less and can produce a stronger adjustment in the investor's favour. For the founder, the key lesson is not to memorise formula jargon for its own sake, but to recognise that even within "weighted average" there are degrees of aggressiveness. A term that sounds acceptable at a high level may still need careful modelling before the company can understand what it will actually do.

This is where scenario work becomes essential. A founder should not accept anti-dilution language merely because counsel says it is there or because the investor describes it as market. The founder should ask what happens if we raise a small bridge at a lower price. What happens if we raise a substantial down round. What happens to the founder stake, the option pool, and the post-round common economics under full ratchet. What happens under weighted average. Once those scenarios are modelled, the difference stops sounding technical and starts looking like what it really is: an allocation rule for future pain.

It is also important to connect this distinction back to investor psychology. Investors ask for anti-dilution because they do not want to be left fully exposed if the company later reprices itself downward. Full ratchet expresses the strongest version of that fear. Weighted average expresses a more moderate one. Neither term exists because investors are confused about risk. They exist because investors understand risk and want contract language that decides who bears more of it if things go badly later. The founder's role is not to be surprised by that instinct. The founder's role is to see clearly how much of the downside reallocation the company is being asked to accept.

The practical negotiating insight is simple. A founder should almost never treat full ratchet and weighted average as roughly equivalent. They are not. One is a hard reset. The other is a proportional adjustment. One can turn even a relatively small weak financing into a major cap table distortion. The other still hurts, but usually in a way more tethered to the actual scale of the dilution event.

If the company is in a strong enough position to push for weighted average instead of full ratchet, that difference can preserve a very large amount of founder and employee value in later difficult scenarios.

That is the core distinction. Full ratchet says if the future price drops, my old price drops all the way with it. Weighted average says if the future price drops, adjust my old price partly, in proportion to how much lower-priced stock was actually issued. The words may look technical in the documents. In real company life, they can determine whether a bad round is survivable pain or a much more destructive rewriting of the ownership structure.

Down Rounds

A down round is one of the moments when startup mythology collides most violently with capital structure reality. Founders spend much of their early journey hearing that each round should move the company upward: more traction, more credibility, more valuation, more investor interest, more strategic momentum. That narrative is not always false, but it is not the only path companies travel. Sometimes the next round comes in below the price of the last one. Sometimes the market turns. Sometimes growth disappoints. Sometimes timelines slip, customer adoption stalls, or investor appetite cools. When that happens, the company may still need money, but the money now arrives at a lower valuation than before. That is a down round.

At one level, the definition is simple. The company sells new shares at a lower price than the price implied by the previous priced round. Yet the simplicity of the definition hides how destabilising the event can be. A down round does not merely mean the company is worth less in the eyes of current investors than it was before. It means the cap table, the founder psychology, the investor protections, the employee option story, and the company's internal sense of progress are all suddenly under stress at the same time. This is why down rounds are so feared. They are not just pricing events. They are structural stress tests.

The first reason they matter is obvious. A lower round price means more shares must be issued for the same amount of money. That means heavier dilution. If the company needs £5 million and the share price is now much lower than in the previous round, the founders and earlier holders will usually give up more of the company to get that same £5 million than they would have in a stronger round. This is dilution in the ordinary sense, and it is already painful enough. But the down round rarely stops there. Earlier investor protections may now activate, especially anti-dilution provisions. That means the company is not simply issuing new cheap shares. It may also be adjusting the economics of old shares in favour of protected investors. The pain is therefore not spread evenly. It can be concentrated on the common and on less-protected holders.

This is why a down round has a uniquely compounding quality. The company is already weak enough that it cannot raise at the old price. The founders are already dealing with the morale hit of that fact. Then the cap table mechanics intensify the damage. Anti-dilution may increase the effective share position of earlier investors. The preference stack may remain in place. New money may demand strong terms because the company's leverage is reduced. The option story may become harder to explain to employees whose grants were mentally priced against the old valuation. A founder who thought of the next round simply as "another financing" discovers instead that the company is being repriced downward while the old structural protections remain alive and, in some cases, become more powerful.

This is one reason down rounds are often more dangerous psychologically than founders anticipate. In an up round, dilution can be emotionally softened by the feeling that the company is progressing. The founders own less, but the business is supposedly worth more and has stronger external validation. In a down round, the founders own less and the company has also lost pricing ground. That double blow can be demoralising. Founders may begin to question not only the economics of staying, but the underlying story of the company itself. Employees may quietly infer that the business is weaker than previously claimed. Existing investors may split into camps over whether to support, defend, or control the company more tightly. The cap table becomes a site of tension rather than simply a record of financing.

A simple example shows how this works. Suppose a company raised its Series A at £2 per share. The founders, employees, and Series A investors have all organised their understanding of the company around that price. Time passes, and the business needs another round. But now the only available financing comes at £1 per share. That is the down round. New investors are buying in at half the previous price. Without any protections, this already means the company must issue twice as many shares for a given amount of capital as it would have if it were still financing at the Series A price. If the company also gave the Series A investors weighted average or full ratchet anti-dilution protection, then the earlier Series A shares may be recalibrated as well. The new round is therefore not just creating new cheap shares. It is also potentially reweighting old ones.

This is where founders begin to understand why down rounds are often discussed in whispers even though they are not especially rare in the real life of startups. They expose whether the company's earlier financing terms were merely tolerable in good conditions or actually survivable in bad ones. A company with clean one-times non-participating preferred, moderate pro rata rights, and balanced weighted-average anti-dilution may still suffer in a down round, but it may remain governable. A company with stacked aggressive preferences, strong investor controls, and harsh anti-dilution may find that the down round turns a difficult business moment into a cap table shock. The earlier terms now matter more than ever, because they decide how much of the damage gets pushed onto the common.

There is also a strong signalling effect. Outside observers often treat a down round as evidence that something has gone wrong, and often something has. But the meaning is not always identical across cases. Some down rounds happen because the company itself has underperformed. Others happen because the broader market has repriced a sector. Others still happen because the previous round was too aggressively priced in the first place and the new round is merely reality catching up. The founder therefore has to distinguish carefully between what the down round says externally and what it means internally. The market may read it as weakness. Internally, the real question is whether the new financing gives the company a viable path forward or merely prolongs decline under a more punishing structure.

This is why some down rounds are survivable and others are destructive. A survivable down round brings in enough capital, on terms the company can still live with, to reset the business onto a stronger path. It hurts, but it creates room to recover. A destructive down round leaves the company with heavier dilution, activated investor protections, damaged morale, and not enough strategic improvement to justify the pain. Founders often focus too much on whether the round is "up" or "down" and too little on whether the resulting company is still structurally coherent afterward.

The cap table, once again, matters more than the headline alone. Employees are often hit particularly hard by down rounds, even when they do not fully understand the mechanics. Their option grants may suddenly feel less valuable, either because the company's implied worth has dropped or because the future preference and dilution burden above the common has become more severe. This is one of the moments when founders discover whether they have built an honest ownership culture or merely an optimistic one. If employees were taught that valuation headlines equalled personal wealth, the down round can feel like betrayal. If they were taught that equity is a contingent upside instrument whose value depends on company trajectory and capital structure, the company still faces morale strain, but at least not moral confusion.

Another reason down rounds matter is that they can reset internal power. New investors entering in a weak round often demand stronger rights because the company has less leverage. Existing investors may exercise pro rata or anti-dilution protections. Founders may accept board changes or control concessions in exchange for survival. A company that felt founder-led before the down round may feel much more investor-shaped after it. This is not automatic, but it is common enough that founders should treat the down round as both a financing and a governance event. The question is not only how many shares are being sold. It is what kind of company will remain once this capital comes in.

Founders should therefore stop treating the phrase down round as if it were just a shameful label. It is a real structural category, and it deserves sober analysis. What is the new price. How much money is being raised. What anti-dilution triggers. What happens to founder ownership. What happens to the option pool. What rights are being added. What preference stack remains or grows. What exit values would now leave common with meaningful returns. And perhaps most importantly, does this round actually buy enough runway or strategic change that accepting the lower price is rational. If those questions are not asked, the founder is reacting to the stigma of the down round rather than governing the company through it.

That is the central truth. A down round is not just a lower price. It is the moment when all the defensive architecture of the cap table starts doing real work. The company is weaker. The new money is more expensive. Earlier protections may activate.

The founders and common holders often absorb a disproportionate share of the pain. But if the company understands the structure clearly, even a down round can sometimes become a painful reset rather than a death spiral. If it does not, the round may reveal that the company had far less room for error than the founders ever realised.

Why Later Investors Can Hurt Earlier Holders

One of the hardest truths in startup finance is that new investors do not enter a company neutrally. They enter through a round that changes the meaning of the positions already on the cap table. Founders often understand this in the narrow sense that later investors dilute earlier holders. What they do not always grasp quickly enough is that later investors can hurt earlier holders in ways far more specific than ordinary dilution alone. The new round can reprice the company, activate anti-dilution, alter governance, increase the preference stack, reshape future exit economics, and change which constituencies matter most in the company's next phase. A new investor is not merely joining the structure. They are helping rewrite it.

This matters because startup financing is cumulative. Every round sits on top of what came before. The earlier holders are still there, carrying their hopes, their rights, and their assumptions about what their ownership means. When later investors arrive, they do not arrive into empty space. They arrive into a pre-existing capital history and often negotiate terms that protect their own capital first. In doing so, they can damage earlier positions directly or indirectly. Sometimes this damage is simply the unavoidable cost of keeping the company alive. Sometimes it reflects hard but fair market repricing. Sometimes it reflects earlier founders having negotiated weakly in the past. But from the perspective of the earlier holder, the effect can still be painful. The company they thought they owned has changed underneath them.

The most obvious way later investors hurt earlier holders is through dilution. New shares are issued, and earlier percentages fall. That is basic. But in most serious financings the later investor's influence goes beyond the new shares they buy. If the later round is priced lower than an earlier one, then the later investor is not only diluting earlier holders through fresh issuance. They may also be triggering anti-dilution protections that partially rewrite the economic position of older preferred investors.

This means the founders, employees, and other unprotected holders can be hit twice. First by the new cheap shares. Second by the recapitalising effect of the old investors' protections. The later investor did not necessarily "cause" the earlier terms, but by arriving on weaker pricing they make those terms matter.

This is why later investors can harm earlier investors too, not just founders and employees. A seed investor with no strong anti-dilution may see a later round cut into the value and influence of that earlier position. A preferred holder from one round may be subordinated or diluted by a later, larger preferred holder. Pro rata rights can soften some of this if the earlier investor has the capital and desire to keep participating. But not every earlier investor can or will follow on. Those who cannot may discover that the company's financing path now belongs increasingly to newer money with larger cheques, stronger terms, and more strategic leverage. The startup world likes to speak warmly about early believers. The cap table often treats them much more coldly once bigger capital arrives.

Later investors can also hurt earlier holders through the preference stack. Every new preferred round can add another layer of money that must be paid ahead of common in a sale. This does not only threaten founders. It can also reduce the practical value of earlier preferred in middling exits, especially if the new round sits senior in the stack or if the cumulative preference burden becomes large enough that only very strong outcomes leave ample room beneath it. A company that once looked attractive to its seed investors can, after a few later rounds, become a business in which those early investors must now rely on a much bigger outcome than originally expected before their stake becomes truly exciting. New money may help the company survive and scale, but it can also push older capital into a more crowded and less cleanly rewarding structure.

Governance is another channel of harm. A later investor may negotiate board seats, consent rights, or other controls that alter the internal power balance of the company. Earlier holders can find themselves structurally weakened even if their raw percentage has not collapsed. Founders may discover that the company they once steered more intuitively is now operating under tighter investor oversight. Earlier investors may discover that their informal influence matters less once a larger or more institutional investor becomes the central outside capital partner.

New money often arrives with a stronger voice, not only because it is new, but because it is larger, later, and entering at a point where the company is more dependent on it. The older cap table is still present, but the practical centre of gravity may have shifted.
Employees can be particularly vulnerable in this process. Their options or common shares sit low in the structure, often beneath layers of preferred rights they did not fully understand when they joined. Later investors can therefore hurt employee economics even when employees are not directly part of the negotiation. A new round may increase the preference stack, create new dilution, or trigger terms that make the common less meaningful in likely exit ranges. Employees may still hold the same number of options. Yet the practical route from those options to real wealth may have become longer and harder because the company has admitted later capital on stronger terms. If the startup has not been honest about this possibility from the start, the damage can be not just financial but cultural.

There is also a more subtle problem. Later investors often force the company to become more realistic, and realism itself can hurt earlier holders who were living on a more flattering story. A company that raised an early round at an optimistic price may later need a weaker, more disciplined round that effectively tells the truth about where the business really stands. Earlier holders then feel harmed by the new investor, but part of what is happening is that the old ownership narrative is being corrected. This does not make the pain less real. It means founders should avoid blaming later investors too simplistically. Sometimes later capital is harsh because reality has become harsher. The company may still need that capital. But the repricing can reveal that earlier holders were carrying more paper comfort than durable economic strength.

This is why the phrase later investors can hurt earlier holders should not be understood as a moral accusation alone. It is a structural statement. New capital changes the environment in which old capital lives. It can reduce ownership percentages, reshape the preference stack, activate old protections, weaken common economics, alter governance, and shift who matters most in future rounds. Sometimes that harm is the price of survival. Sometimes it is the result of avoidable earlier mistakes. Sometimes it reflects investor opportunism in a weak company. Often it is some mixture of all three. The founder's job is not merely to resent the fact. The founder's job is to anticipate it.

That anticipation requires founders to stop thinking of each round as a self-contained deal. A later round must always be read from the perspective of the people already inside the company. What happens to their economics. What happens to their rights. What happens to their motivation. What happens to the preference stack. What happens in likely exit scenarios afterward. If the founder cannot answer those questions, then the company is financing itself without really understanding who is being protected and who is being sacrificed to make the financing possible.

There is also a strategic lesson here for the founders' own behaviour. A founder who understands how later investors can hurt earlier holders becomes more disciplined earlier. They resist weak founder splits, sloppy grants, overbuilt stacks, and aggressive terms that may feel survivable in isolation but become dangerous once later capital starts leaning on them. They also think more carefully about who is being let into the company now, because every new class of rights becomes part of the terrain future investors will build upon. In this sense, later-investor harm often begins as earlier-founder complacency.

None of this means later investors are villains by default. Many companies would die without later capital. Many later investors rescue or scale businesses in ways that benefit everyone overall, even if they still inflict structural pain on earlier holders in the process. But founders must not let that larger truth blur the local one. Later money is powerful precisely because it does not enter gently. It enters by changing the company. That change can be necessary. It can also be costly. Founders who understand both sides of that sentence are much better prepared for real financing life than founders who only celebrate the new cheque or only complain about the new dilution.

Why Founder Protection Matters Too

Once founders have spent enough time looking at investor rights, anti-dilution, pro rata, preferences, and down-round mechanics, a dangerous imbalance can begin to creep into their thinking. They may start to see the cap table as a structure in which only investors are allowed to defend themselves. The founders become the exposed class by default, carrying execution risk, dilution risk, governance pressure, and the residual uncertainty beneath every protective layer negotiated by outside capital.

That reading is understandable, because many startup financing structures do in fact place founders and employees in the most vulnerable position. But it is not the only possible reading, and it is not a healthy one if it leads founders to believe they should simply absorb whatever the financing process demands. Founder protection matters too.

This point needs to be made carefully. Founder protection is not the same thing as founder entitlement. It does not mean founders should be insulated from every future financing consequence or that the company should preserve founder comfort at the expense of raising the capital it genuinely needs. It means that if the company is going to remain worth building, the cap table must preserve enough founder ownership, enough founder motivation, and enough founder practical influence that the people carrying the company still have a real economic and strategic reason to keep carrying it. A cap table that protects investors beautifully while hollowing out the founder position is not, in any deep sense, well designed. It is just lopsided.

This is because the startup cannot be financed as though founder effort were infinitely available regardless of structure. Investors often act, rationally from their own perspective, as though capital can be protected layer by layer while management and founder drive will simply remain in place underneath whatever stack emerges. In reality, the founder's relationship to the company depends on what is left to them after all those layers are built. If repeated rounds, pools, rights, and preferences leave the founders with too little upside, too little room, or too little control, then the company may still be technically alive while becoming economically irrational for the people expected to build it. This is why founder protection is not sentimental. It is a condition of company viability.

The most basic form of founder protection is ownership that remains meaningful after realistic future dilution. This is not a precise universal number because stage, market, company ambition, and likely exit ranges all matter. But the principle is clear. A founder should not be left with a stake that only looks respectable today if it will become thin beyond motivation after the next likely round or two. This is why good investors often care about founder ownership as well. They know that a founder who is already over-diluted, or heading rapidly that way, may become less committed, less resilient, or less rational under pressure. Founder protection therefore serves not only the founder but the investor too, provided the investor is thinking beyond the current round and into the company's actual future.

Another important form of founder protection is vesting that is disciplined but fair. At first glance, vesting sounds like something that constrains founders rather than protects them. In reality, when applied across the founding team sensibly, it protects the active founders from being left carrying a company under a cap table clogged with departed cofounders who kept large stakes without staying to do the work. It also makes founder ownership more defensible to outsiders because it shows that the company has not treated founding as a one-day entitlement detached from continuing effort. Vesting is therefore not only investor comfort. It is also founder-to-founder protection and, in a broader sense, protection of the live company against dead equity.

Governance matters too. Founder protection does not necessarily mean founders must keep unilateral control forever, nor that every board seat should remain founder-dominated regardless of company maturity. But if the financing structure leaves founders with responsibility far in excess of authority, then the company is asking for trouble. Founders need enough practical influence that the role remains coherent. They should not be mere operators servicing a cap table that has already hollowed out their real stake in the venture. This is especially important in companies that are still highly founder-dependent for product, recruiting, customer belief, or strategic direction. A business can add outside oversight without turning the founder into a salaried hostage to investor architecture. That distinction matters enormously.

There is also founder protection in the way future rounds are negotiated. A founder who understands the cap table properly does not only ask what this round costs now. They ask what this round leaves me able to survive later. Is the valuation sane enough to support the next raise. Is the option pool being sized realistically rather than punitively. Are investor rights broad enough to reassure capital but not so broad that future financing becomes clogged. Is the preference stack still compatible with meaningful founder economics in plausible exits. These are all founder-protection questions. They are not selfish in a narrow sense. They are questions about whether the company is being financed in a way that still leaves the builders with a company worth building.

It is also worth recognising that founder protection has a cultural dimension. If the financing history of the company repeatedly teaches the team that every new round protects capital above all else while the founders and employees simply absorb the residual pain, then the company's internal ownership culture will often sour. Founders become more cynical. Employees begin to suspect that "upside" language is mainly for recruitment, not for reality. Even investors may discover that a company built on exhausted or disillusioned common holders is not as strong as the rights stack first made it seem. Founder protection therefore contributes to the broader credibility of the company's equity story. It signals that the business is not being financed as though only capital matters and labour can be structurally ignored.

This does not mean founder protection always wins when capital and founder interest conflict. Sometimes the company needs money badly enough that the founders must accept painful terms. Sometimes market conditions are poor. Sometimes the prior structure is already weak and there is no elegant path left. Founder protection is not magic. But even in those cases, the founder who has built the habit of asking protective questions is in a far stronger position than the founder who simply lets investor language define the whole frame. They may still have to compromise, but they will know what is being compromised and why. That knowledge alone often prevents the worst kinds of structural drift.

There is another subtle way founder protection matters. It preserves optionality. A founder with a still-meaningful stake, still-credible governance influence, and still-usable room for future rounds has choices. They can raise again, hire ambitiously, negotiate strategically, or consider acquisition offers from a position that still makes sense. A founder whose stake has been thinned too far beneath preferences and rights, or whose governance role has been overconstrained, loses those choices. The company may continue, but the founder is now moving inside a narrower corridor shaped mostly by other people's protections. That is often the real sign that founder protection has been neglected. The founder is still present, but no longer economically or strategically free in the way the company's health requires.

This is why smart founders do not apologise for protecting themselves in structural terms. They do not confuse self-erasure with maturity. They understand that investors are rightly defending their ownership because they know future rounds can change everything. Founders should think the same way. They should defend a structure in which their own continuing role remains worth the burden, in which later rounds do not automatically strip the common of meaning, and in which the company can still be led by people whose relationship to the upside has not been hollowed out by the cumulative force of every defensive right negotiated above them.

In practical terms, founder protection means asking hard questions earlier than most founders are comfortable asking them. What happens after the next round, not just this one. What exits still work for common after the current preference stack. Whether anti-dilution terms are survivable in a weak market. Whether pro rata rights are beginning to overreserve future financing space. Whether the board structure still matches the company's real founder dependence. Whether the option pool and investor rights together are leaving enough room for later hires and later capital without crushing the founders underneath. These are not special pleas. They are the mechanics of building a company that remains financeable and worth building at the same time.

That is why founder protection matters too. Investors are not wrong to protect capital. But capital is not the only thing a startup runs on. It also runs on people whose effort, imagination, and endurance must remain aligned with the outcomes the cap table still makes possible for them. A structure that forgets that can look sophisticated right up until the moment it discovers that well-defended money alone does not build companies.

* * *

THIRTEEN

Downside Scenarios, Waterfalls, and Exit Reality

"You only find out who is swimming naked when the tide goes out."

- Warren Buffett

Why Exit Math Matters Before Exit Day

One of the most common founder mistakes is to treat exit economics as something that can be understood later, once the company is large enough, funded enough, or close enough to a sale that the question feels concrete. Until then, many founders prefer to think in the more flattering language of headline valuation, ownership percentage, and general upside. That preference is understandable. Exit math often feels cold, defensive, or even pessimistic when the company is still trying to grow. Yet this instinct is precisely what makes so many founders vulnerable to shock when a real offer appears. By the time the exit is on the table, the cap table has already decided far more than the founder usually realises. Exit day does not create the economics. It reveals them.

This is why exit math matters long before any buyer appears.

A startup does not suddenly become economically legible at the point of sale. The sale merely activates rules that were written into the cap table over many rounds of financing, option grants, preferences, participation terms, anti-dilution protections, and structural compromises. Each of those decisions quietly shapes what different stakeholders will receive across different exit values. The founder who has not modelled that in advance is often still living inside a fantasy version of ownership, one where paper percentages and public valuation language are mistaken for actual payout logic. When a real offer comes in, the fantasy collapses quickly. The founder discovers that the company they thought they partially owned in one sense is distributed very differently in practice.

This is especially true because startups rarely exit only in the range founders like to imagine during optimistic periods. Some exits are spectacular. Some are respectable but not enormous. Some are acquihires dressed up as transactions. Some are distressed sales. Some are secondary-heavy recapitalisations that leave certain stakeholders better off than others. If the founder has only ever thought about the company in terms of the best-case path, then every middling offer feels confusing. The numbers may sound large in ordinary life and still produce much less for common holders than intuition suggested. Exit math matters because it allows the founder to see the difference between a company sale price and the founder's actual proceeds.

The most important reason this matters early is that financing decisions should be made with plausible outcomes in mind, not only with aspirational ones. A founder deciding whether to accept a new preference layer, a participating preferred structure, a large pool expansion, or an aggressive anti-dilution package is not merely deciding how the next round feels. The founder is deciding how future sale proceeds will move through the company if things go moderately well, very well, or less well than hoped. If those decisions are made without exit math, then the founder is effectively financing blind. The company may still raise the money it needs, but it will do so without understanding what kinds of eventual outcomes remain meaningful for the people building it.

This is one reason sophisticated investors almost always understand exit math better than inexperienced founders do. Investors are trained to think in return profiles, stack position, conversion choices, and scenario ranges. They know that a sale at £50 million can be excellent for one stakeholder and underwhelming for another depending on where each sits in the structure. Founders, by contrast, often think first in product, market, hiring, and survival terms. None of that is wrong. But if the founder never forces themselves to read the cap table through an exit lens, then they are letting other people understand the ultimate consequences of the structure better than they do.

There is also a motivational reason this chapter matters. Founders and early employees are carrying years of work under uncertainty. If the cap table has evolved to the point where only very large outcomes now meaningfully reward the common, that changes how the company should think about risk, fundraising, recruitment, and acquisition.

A founder who knows that a moderate exit barely touches the common after preferences and participation may reasonably behave differently from a founder whose common still matters strongly across a broader set of outcomes. Exit math is therefore not merely a liquidation exercise. It is a way of understanding what incentives the company is actually creating for the people inside it right now.

Another reason exit math matters early is that acquisition offers often arrive sooner and stranger than founders expect. Many founders imagine an exit as the final chapter of a long success story: a clean process, a very large number, enthusiastic buyers, and plenty for everyone. Real company sales are often messier. An offer may come while the company is tired, between rounds, under market pressure, or before the founders feel ready. An offer may sound high relative to where the company started and still be low relative to the structure now sitting on the cap table. If the founders have not already done the work of understanding what different sale prices mean, then they are trying to learn the company's true economics at the exact moment they also need to negotiate, decide, and lead.

This is where waterfalls become essential. A waterfall is simply a way of modelling how proceeds flow through the capital structure at different exit values. It shows who gets paid first, who converts, who takes preference, when participation matters, when the common begins to receive meaningful residual value, and how much each class actually gets in a range of scenarios. Founders sometimes avoid waterfall thinking because it sounds too financial, too late-stage, or too pessimistic. In reality it is one of the clearest tools for turning the cap table from an abstract ownership map into a real economic map. It does not ask whether the company will sell tomorrow. It asks what the current structure means if the company sells for £10 million, £25 million, £50 million, £100 million, or more.

This also helps founders avoid a very common form of self-deception. They may say, quite truthfully, that they still own a large percentage of the common. But if the preference stack is heavy enough and the investor rights strong enough, that common may only become powerful at high exit values. In smaller sales, the founder's large paper position may behave like a thin residual claim. The founder then discovers that "owning a lot" and "getting a lot" are not the same thing. Exit math matters because it closes the gap between those phrases.

It is important to say that thinking about downside or middling exits does not make a founder defeatist. It makes the founder literate. A founder who understands only the dream case is not more visionary. They are less prepared. Real ambition is perfectly compatible with structural realism. In fact, strong founders often make better growth decisions because they know exactly what outcomes remain meaningful and what financing terms would silently destroy those outcomes. Exit math is not about planning to lose. It is about refusing to let the cap table smuggle in consequences that the company only discovers when choices are already narrow.

This chapter begins here because before one can understand waterfalls, secondary sales, acquihires, management carve-outs, or the true meaning of "exit value," one has to accept a simpler truth. The economics of an exit are not written on the day the company is sold. They are written gradually in the ownership structure long before that day arrives. The founder who understands that early can still raise, hire, and build with ambition. But they will do so with open eyes, which is more than many founders can say by the time the first real offer lands.

What a Waterfall Analysis Shows

A waterfall analysis is the cap table forced to tell the truth about money. That is the simplest and most useful way to think about it. Before the waterfall, ownership can remain comfortably abstract. Percentages sit on a spreadsheet. Founders talk about dilution. Investors talk about preferences. Employees hear that their options may be valuable. Everyone has a rough sense of what they "own." But until those claims are run through an actual distribution scenario, much of the cap table remains conceptual. The waterfall changes that. It asks a blunt question: if the company is sold for a given amount, who gets paid what, in what order, and under what rights.

That is why waterfall analysis matters so much. It turns structure into outcome. It takes the company's financing history and converts it into a series of distribution maps. The founders stop talking about percentages in the abstract and start seeing what those percentages mean once liquidation preferences, participation rights, conversion choices, option holders, and stacked rounds all interact under a real sale price. In that sense, the waterfall is not a separate piece of finance from the cap table. It is the cap table under pressure.

A good waterfall analysis usually shows how sale proceeds flow at different exit values. For example, what happens if the company sells for £10 million, £25 million, £50 million, £100 million, and so on. At each level, the analysis asks who is entitled to get paid first. Do the preferred holders take their liquidation preferences. Do they convert into common instead because that gives them more. Are there participation rights that let investors receive both preference and a share of the remainder. How much of the proceeds are consumed by the preference stack before common holders begin to share meaningfully. Once those questions are answered, the company can see something much more real than a flat ownership table. It can see the economic behaviour of the cap table across a range of plausible outcomes.

This is especially important because startup exits are rarely all-or-nothing. Founders often mentally split the world into failure on one side and life-changing success on the other. Real transactions often live in the broad middle. A company may sell for a number that sounds large in ordinary life and still be a weak result for common holders once the waterfall is applied. Equally, a sale that sounds merely decent may turn out to be perfectly respectable for founders if the cap table is clean and the preference stack is light. The waterfall therefore helps founders stop relying on crude intuition about what an exit number "means" and start seeing what that number means inside this actual company.

A simple example shows the logic. Imagine a startup with founders holding common stock and one investor who put in £5 million on one-times non-participating preferred for twenty percent. If the company sells for £8 million, the investor will likely take the £5 million preference rather than convert to common, because twenty percent of £8 million would only be £1.6 million. That leaves £3 million for the common. The founders may still own eighty percent of the company on paper, but they are not receiving eighty percent of the full £8 million. They are receiving what remains after the preferred claim is satisfied. If the company instead sells for £40 million, the investor would likely convert to common because twenty percent of £40 million is £8 million, which is better than the £5 million preference. In that higher outcome, the economics look much more like the ownership table. The waterfall shows exactly where that shift happens.

That shift point is one of the most valuable things a waterfall reveals. It tells the company at what exit values preferred holders stop behaving like preference holders and start behaving like common-equivalent holders. That matters because below that point the company is living in a preference-dominated world. Above that point the common starts to behave more like founders intuitively expect. Without a waterfall, that boundary often remains invisible. Founders may think a certain sale price is safely in the upside zone when in fact preferences are still dominating much of the distribution.

Waterfall analysis also reveals the effect of participation rights. A non-participating preferred holder usually chooses between taking preference and converting. A participating preferred holder may take the preference first and then still join in the rest. The difference can be very large in middling exits. On a flat cap table, the investor's percentage may not look frightening. In the waterfall, the investor may suddenly absorb much more of the proceeds than the founder had emotionally budgeted for. This is why rights must be modelled, not merely read. The waterfall is where those rights stop being legal language and become cash outcomes.
Once multiple rounds exist, the waterfall becomes even more important. Seed investors, Series A investors, and Series B investors may each have their own preferred rights, their own investment amounts, and sometimes different seniority. The founders and employees sit beneath that stack. In a sale, the question is no longer just whether the investor takes preference or converts. It may be which investor class gets paid first, whether earlier rounds are pari passu or subordinated, whether later rounds stack above earlier ones, and how much of the sale price disappears before the common sees meaningful residual value. At that point, ordinary percentage reading is nearly useless on its own. The waterfall becomes the only honest way to see what the company's ownership actually means.

This is why serious boards and finance teams often revisit waterfall analysis after major financings, especially when the structure has become layered. They do not do this because they are eager to sell the company tomorrow. They do it because financing decisions today reshape outcome ranges later. The founders need to know what the new preference stack means. Employees need truthful communication about what their options sit beneath. Investors need to understand where future conversion and payout thresholds now lie. The waterfall is therefore not only an exit tool. It is a planning tool.

It also helps with acquisition discipline. When a buyer approaches the company, founders are often emotionally vulnerable to headline numbers. A £30 million offer may sound strong, especially if the business started with little and the founders have spent years struggling. But if the waterfall shows that the preference stack, participation rights, and existing obligations leave common with very little at that price, the company can evaluate the offer more soberly. Conversely, if a lower-sounding offer actually clears the stack well and leaves founders with meaningful proceeds, the company may avoid rejecting something rational simply because the gross number felt underwhelming. The waterfall gives decision-makers a cleaner view of the company's actual economics when the emotional pressure of a live offer is high.

Another reason waterfall analysis matters is that it exposes whether founder motivation still makes sense. If the cap table has evolved to the point where only very large exits deliver meaningful founder economics, then that fact should influence how the company thinks about risk, timing, and future financing. A founder who knows that £20 million and £30 million outcomes barely touch the common may behave very differently from a founder who knows those outcomes are still materially rewarding. The waterfall does not tell the founder what strategy to choose, but it does reveal what the current structure is rewarding and what it is effectively ignoring.

Some founders avoid waterfalls because they fear the analysis will be demoralising. Sometimes it is. But demoralising truth is still better than flattering ignorance. A founder who learns late that the cap table has made moderate exits almost meaningless for common has lost the chance to negotiate earlier rounds differently, manage expectations honestly, or make better strategic decisions while there was still room. The waterfall may not be pleasant, but it is clarifying. And clarity is worth more than mood when ownership structures are involved.

The best way to think about a waterfall analysis, then, is as a scenario machine for capital structure. It does not predict what the company will sell for. It does not decide what outcome is desirable. It simply shows what the current cap table does under different sale values. That is enough to make it indispensable. Once the company can see who gets paid what at each level, many abstract debates about dilution, preference, and fairness become much more concrete.

That is what a waterfall analysis shows. It shows not who says they own the company, but how the company's money would actually flow if the structure were forced to speak in cash rather than percentages.

Why Headline Sale Price Can Be Misleading

One of the most dangerous phrases in startup life is the phrase "the company sold for..." followed by a large number. It sounds definitive. It sounds like the answer to the whole story. It sounds like the moment at which all the years of risk, fundraising, dilution, and sacrifice are finally translated into a public measure of success. In ordinary conversation, that number often becomes the company's final reputation. People hear it and assume they know what happened. Yet in cap table reality, the headline sale price is often one of the least complete descriptions of what the transaction meant for the people inside the company. The company may have sold for a great deal of money and still left founders or employees with far less than outsiders would ever guess.

This is why headline sale price can be so misleading. It tells you what the buyer paid in gross terms. It does not tell you how that money moved through the structure. It does not tell you what portion went first to preferred holders under liquidation preferences. It does not tell you whether investors participated after taking preference. It does not tell you whether option holders were exercised, cashed out, or left with limited value. It does not tell you how much debt, transaction cost, or tax sat above or alongside the equity distribution. Most importantly, it does not tell you what the common stock actually received after the rights stack had done its work.

A founder who has not internalised this can make two opposite mistakes. They may hear a large offer and assume it is automatically life-changing for them because their paper percentage still looks substantial. Or they may reject a lower-seeming number because it sounds small relative to the last headline valuation, without realising that the actual distribution to common might still be meaningful at that level. In both cases, the founder is being misled by gross price language. The right question is never only what is the buyer paying. The right question is what does that price mean once it runs through this cap table.

A simple example shows why. Imagine a company sells for £40 million. On its face, that sounds impressive. Now imagine the company has £20 million of stacked preferred capital ahead of the common. Some of that preferred may convert rather than take preference depending on ownership and rights, but let us assume for simplicity that the stack remains materially relevant. Suddenly the founders are not sharing in forty million pounds from the first pound onward. A very large portion of that price may already be spoken for before the common receives the residual. If participating preferred is involved, or if there are transaction costs and debt obligations to clear as well, the founders' actual proceeds may be much thinner than the headline number would lead almost any outsider to imagine.

This is one reason founders can feel privately strange after an exit that the world calls successful. The public sees the sale price. The founder sees the distribution. The world says you sold your company for tens of millions. The founder knows what actually reached the common after years of dilution, preference stacking, and structural complexity. The gap between those two views can be emotionally disorienting. It is also one of the clearest reasons why founders must understand exit math early. Without that understanding, they may spend years orienting themselves around a type of success that no longer belongs to them in the simple form they imagine.

The reverse can also happen. A company may sell for a number that sounds modest compared with recent valuation headlines, and outsiders may treat it as disappointing. Yet if the cap table is relatively clean and the common sits in a strong position beneath a light preference stack, the founders may actually do very well in real terms. A £20 million sale can be far better for common than a £50 million sale in another company with a much heavier stack and more aggressive rights architecture. This is why comparing startup exits by gross price alone is often meaningless. The cap table determines whether the number is rich or thin for the people inside it.

It is also important to remember that sale price language often hides what kind of sale actually occurred. Was the transaction mostly cash, mostly stock, partly contingent earn-out, or heavily conditioned on retention packages. Were preferred holders paid cleanly in cash while management value was shifted into employment packages or bonuses rather than pure equity proceeds.

Did some founders or executives take secondary liquidity earlier, changing what the final sale means to them personally. Was part of the price really for the business, or partly for post-acquisition service commitments. These questions sit adjacent to the cap table and can further widen the gap between headline transaction value and what any one stakeholder truly received.

This matters a great deal for employees and option holders too. Employees are often particularly vulnerable to headline-sale misunderstanding because they may mentally value their options by taking the sale price and multiplying it by their paper percentage. That is almost never enough. Their options may still be unvested in part, may sit below the preference stack, may require exercise, or may be affected by the terms of the transaction itself. A company that has spoken loosely about equity for years can therefore find that an acquisition produces widespread confusion and bitterness, not because anyone lied in a legal sense, but because people were taught to think in gross price rather than in net structural outcome.

This is another reason boards and founders should not wait until a live offer appears before doing waterfall work. By then the emotional force of the buyer's headline number may already be shaping the room. Some participants may be dazzled. Others may be defensive. If the company has already modelled what different sale prices mean for each class and for the common in particular, then the conversation becomes much healthier. The board can say plainly what this offer means rather than allowing the number itself to do all the psychological work. A company that has not done this homework often ends up arguing not just about value, but about misunderstood value.

Headline sale price is also misleading because it can preserve the illusion that valuation and exit are part of one continuous upward line. Founders may think that if the company once raised at a £100 million valuation, then a £100 million sale must be good. In reality, the later financing terms may have made that sale much less attractive than the earlier paper number suggests. The valuation was never cash in founder hands. It was a financing reference point embedded inside a rights structure. When a real buyer arrives, the company is no longer living in valuation space. It is living in distribution space. Those are not the same thing, and founders who do not understand the difference are especially prone to being misled by headline exit numbers.

There is a broader social lesson here too. Startup culture often celebrates gross transaction values because they are easy to communicate. "Sold for £200 million" is a cleaner line than "sold for £200 million, of which the first £95 million effectively satisfied stacked preferences and transaction obligations before common began participating meaningfully." But what is communicable is not always what is useful. Founders who internalise the public language too deeply may begin building for optics rather than economics. They may chase valuation and headline sale scenarios that sound impressive while failing to notice that the structure beneath them is becoming less and less favourable to common holders. Exit math is the antidote to that vanity.

This does not mean headline sale price is irrelevant. It is obviously important. It shapes market perception, investor returns, founder reputation, and the broad scale of what is being distributed. But it is only the beginning of the analysis, not the end. A founder should hear the gross number and immediately ask what rights sit ahead of common, what conversion choices preferred holders will make, what the resulting waterfall looks like, and what portion of that price is truly distributable to the people carrying the common stock. Without those questions, the founder is reacting to publicity, not to economics.

That is why headline sale price can be misleading. It tells you what changed hands at the top of the transaction. It does not tell you what the cap table allowed to flow downward from there. Only the waterfall can do that. And once the founder sees the difference clearly, the next question becomes even more important: what happens to the distribution when preferences, participation, and multiple investor classes begin to interact in specific outcome ranges rather than in general theory.

How Preferences Change Real Outcomes

Preferences matter because they do not merely sit in the documents as legal ornaments. They change what an exit actually means. A founder can understand the definition of liquidation preference, can nod along to the distinction between participating and non-participating preferred, and can still fail to grasp the deeper point until a real or modelled sale forces the numbers into motion. The deeper point is simple. Preferences change outcomes not at the level of theory, but at the level of lived money. They decide whether a sale is rich, thin, or almost meaningless for the common.

They decide whether the founders are celebrating the same transaction as the investors or quietly living through a very different economic event beneath the same headline.

This is why preferences are so powerful. They alter the shape of the company's reward curve. Without strong preference rights, the founders and other shareholders participate more proportionately from the beginning of the distribution. With preference rights, the company's proceeds are routed through a structure that gives some holders a stronger first claim. That first claim is not just an accounting preference. It changes which outcome ranges feel good to different people. A sale that sounds attractive in gross terms may barely touch the common if the preference burden ahead of it is thick enough. A sale that would have felt life-changing in a flatter cap table can become something closer to partial capital recovery for investors and disappointment for founders.

A useful way to think about this is that preferences shift the point at which success begins for different classes of holders. The investor with preference protection may start getting meaningful proceeds at much lower sale values because their money comes back first, at least up to the amount protected. The founders and employees holding common may need the sale price to rise much higher before their economics become significant. In other words, the same company can contain multiple thresholds of "good outcome" depending on where each holder sits in the structure. This is one of the main reasons founders can become badly misaligned with their own cap table without noticing it immediately. They assume everyone wants the same sort of exit. The preference structure may already have made that false.

Consider a clean example. Suppose a company has £10 million of investor capital sitting in one-times non-participating preferred and the founders and employees hold the common beneath it. If the company sells for £12 million, the common is not sharing from pound one. The preference layer means that the first £10 million may effectively satisfy the investor's claim before the common fully begins to matter, unless conversion is better for the investor. In such a case, the investor may be relatively satisfied because the downside or middling outcome still returns most or all of their capital. The founders may feel the exact same sale very differently. They have carried years of execution risk and now discover that only a narrow slice of the total is really theirs. Preferences have not changed the gross sale price. They have changed the meaning of that sale price.

This is why it is so dangerous for founders to speak as though preferences are only relevant in failure. They are often most relevant in the broad middle where many real startup exits live. In a huge exit, preferences may matter less because the preferred holders often convert into common or because the total proceeds are large enough that the common still receives meaningful value after the preferences are dealt with. In a complete collapse, everyone may lose enough that the distinctions feel grimly obvious. It is in the middle where preferences do their most surprising work. The company may have built something real, attracted a buyer, and produced a transaction large enough to look impressive from the outside. Yet the preference structure can turn that respectable outcome into a relatively poor one for common holders.

This becomes even more pronounced when participation is involved. Under participating preferred, the investor does not merely recover the preference and step aside. The investor may recover the preference and then continue sharing in the remainder. That means the founder is not simply dealing with a first claim. The founder is dealing with a first claim plus an ongoing claim. In practical terms, this can make a moderate sale feel dramatically different from what the gross number suggests. The company has not just promised the investor protection on the way in. It has promised them a more powerful seat in the distribution itself.

The effect compounds further once multiple rounds exist. One preference may distort outcomes enough. A stack of them can remake the economic landscape entirely. Seed money, Series A, Series B, perhaps even later rounds, all sit ahead of common to varying degrees. Even where each individual preference once sounded reasonable, the combined structure can move the threshold of meaningful common returns far higher than the founders ever emotionally updated for. This is one of the quiet tragedies of poorly understood venture finance. A founder can spend years thinking they are building toward a very achievable definition of success while the cap table has already moved the real economic finish line far further away.

This is why preference-aware founders do not ask only "what is the company worth" or "what might we sell for." They ask "at what sale values does the common begin to do well under this actual structure." That is a different and much better question. It takes the founder out of vanity arithmetic and into actual economic planning. If the answer is that only very large exits now reward the common meaningfully, that fact should influence how the founders think about future rounds, employee options, strategic sales, and company risk. The cap table is already teaching the company what kinds of outcomes it now rewards. Preferences are one of the main instruments through which that teaching happens.

Another important consequence is cultural. Preferences can create hidden divergence between what the company says about success and what success actually means for different participants. If the founders continue recruiting employees using broad language about upside while knowing that the common sits under a thickening preference stack, then the company is drifting toward an ownership culture built on partial truth. Employees may still have meaningful upside in a strong enough outcome, but the range of outcomes in which that upside becomes real may be narrower than the rhetoric suggests. The same problem can affect founders themselves. A founder may keep speaking internally as though a certain sale range would be excellent without having fully processed that the preference structure has changed that calculus. Once a real offer appears, the mismatch between language and economics can become morally expensive.

It is also worth noticing that preferences do not only affect final sale value. They affect negotiating leverage in exit conversations. A founder who knows the common gets very little below a certain threshold may push harder against acquisition offers in that range, because such offers do not truly solve the founder's economic problem. Investors sitting on strong preferences may be more open to those same offers because their recovery position is better. This is one way preferences can change not just outcomes, but behaviour before the outcome is chosen. They can subtly reassign what counts as acceptable across the stakeholder group.

That is why later acquirers, boards, and serious investors often care a great deal about waterfall modelling. They know that preferences change what different constituencies want. A company is not one appetite. It is a structure of appetites shaped by rights. If founders do not understand how preferences have changed those appetites, they can misread both their own motivation and everyone else's. They may think a buyer's offer is being irrationally rejected or too quickly embraced when in fact the cap table has simply made the parties economically different in that range.

The founder's safest discipline is therefore to model outcomes repeatedly as the structure evolves. What does a £15 million sale mean now. What about £30 million, £50 million, £100 million. Who takes preference. Who converts. Who participates. At what point does common stop feeling residual and start feeling powerful again. These are not morbid exercises. They are the only reliable way to understand what the financing history of the company has already done to its future.

That is how preferences change real outcomes. They do not merely modify the edge cases. They redraw the economic map across much of the range where real exits occur. They determine whether the same gross sale feels like rescue, success, vindication, or disappointment depending on where each holder sits in the queue. And because they do that, they force the founder to stop asking only how much the company might sell for and start asking what that sale would actually mean after the structure has finished speaking.

Management Carve-Outs and Why They Exist

One of the more awkward signs that a cap table has drifted too far from founder and management reality is the appearance of the management carve-out. Founders often first encounter the idea with a mixture of confusion and suspicion. If the company is being sold, and if the cap table already tells everyone who owns what, then why would there need to be a separate pool of value carved out for management or key employees. Should the existing ownership structure not already answer that question. In a perfectly aligned company, perhaps it should. The very existence of a carve-out usually signals that something deeper has gone wrong or, at the very least, that the current capital structure does not distribute incentives in a way that supports the transaction the company is now trying to complete.

A management carve-out is, in essence, a negotiated allocation of sale proceeds or value specifically reserved for founders, executives, or key employees outside the ordinary waterfall logic of the cap table. It is often used in situations where the preference stack and other investor rights are so heavy that a proposed sale would leave little or nothing for the people still running the company, even though the board or the investor group believes those people are necessary to get the deal done, keep the business functioning through the transaction, or simply because the result would otherwise feel economically or morally absurd. The carve-out says, in effect, that the company cannot rely on the existing cap table alone to produce a workable outcome for management, so some separate economic accommodation has to be negotiated.

This is why carve-outs are so revealing. They are not usually signs of a beautifully designed capital structure. They are signs that the cap table, taken literally, is no longer doing enough to align the people the company still needs with the outcome on the table. A company may have a buyer. The investors may still recover something under their preferences. The board may believe the transaction is strategically or financially rational. Yet if the founders or management team are looking at the waterfall and seeing very little for themselves, the transaction can become unstable. The people who must help carry the sale through due diligence, transition, negotiation, and operational continuity may have too little reason to do so enthusiastically. A carve-out exists to solve that problem when the normal distribution mechanics no longer can.

This does not mean carve-outs are inherently illegitimate. In some cases they are quite rational. If a company is being sold in a difficult situation and the common is deeply underwater beneath a heavy preference stack, it may still make sense for investors to approve a specific carve-out for management rather than insist on the full purity of the existing waterfall. Investors may conclude that without some meaningful incentive for key people, the transaction may collapse, the company may deteriorate, or the operational handover may become much riskier. In that sense, a carve-out can be seen not only as a fairness adjustment but as a practical tool for preserving value in a constrained situation.

Yet the fact that carve-outs can be rational does not make them clean. They are often politically charged because they sit outside the normal economic expectations of the cap table. A founder who thought ownership percentages determined outcomes may suddenly discover that a separate negotiation is happening around who should receive value regardless of what the strict waterfall would produce. Investors may disagree among themselves about whether such a carve-out is warranted and, if so, how large it should be. Employees not included in the carve-out may feel excluded or misled. Earlier holders may wonder whether contractual rights are being bent in favour of management for reasons of expediency. The carve-out therefore solves one problem while often exposing several others. It is a practical device, not a sign that the structure is healthy.

This is one reason founders should not view carve-outs as comforting fallback mechanisms. They are sometimes necessary, but they are rarely ideal. A founder who tells themselves that a bad cap table can always be fixed later through some management accommodation is thinking too loosely. By the time carve-outs are needed, the company is usually already in a compromised position. It may be selling below the level at which common was expected to matter. It may be under investor pressure. The sale dynamics may be fragile. The management team may be tired, and the room for negotiation may be narrower than the founders would like. A carve-out can improve a bad situation. It is not a substitute for having built a structure that did not need rescue.

There is also a moral ambiguity to management carve-outs that founders should understand. On one hand, it can seem obviously right that the people who built and sustained the company should not walk away empty-handed while investor rights consume nearly all the proceeds. On the other hand, investors may argue, not unreasonably, that they negotiated their preferences precisely to protect capital in these weaker outcomes and that management already accepted the common position beneath that stack. The carve-out therefore lives in a tension between strict contractual logic and practical or equitable adjustment. That tension is one reason these negotiations can become so sensitive. They are not occurring on neutral ground. They are occurring at the point where the cap table's formal truth and the company's practical needs no longer line up neatly.

This makes carve-outs especially important for founders to understand in advance, even if they hope never to need one. A founder who sees a heavily stacked cap table, thin common economics in moderate exits, and a business still heavily dependent on management should at least understand that a future sale may require some special management arrangement if the company falls into the wrong valuation range. That does not mean the founder should count on it. It means the founder should recognise that the cap table may already be developing the conditions under which normal equity logic breaks down. The later appearance of a carve-out then becomes less surprising. It is seen for what it is: an attempt to patch an incentive gap created by prior financing structure.

Carve-outs can also teach a deeper lesson about how capital and labour interact inside a mature startup. Investors may have stronger formal rights. Founders and executives may have weaker formal claims. But when a transaction actually has to happen, formal rights do not always settle everything.

The company still needs human beings to cooperate, stay focused, and complete the process. If the formal structure leaves those human beings too exposed or too economically irrelevant, then the board or the investors may discover that capital structure alone is not enough to move the company through the transaction. The carve-out is one of the clearest acknowledgments of that reality. It says that the cap table, though legally authoritative, is not always operationally sufficient.

This can also happen in acquihire-like situations or distressed exits where the buyer is primarily interested in the team and perhaps only secondarily in the company's assets. In such cases, the company may not command enough value to satisfy all preferences and still reward common holders meaningfully. A buyer may still want key individuals to join post-acquisition. The board and investors may therefore support a carve-out or related arrangement because the value of the deal depends materially on those people staying motivated and saying yes. Again, none of this is pure principle. It is cap table reality colliding with transaction reality.

For employees and wider teams, carve-outs can be especially delicate. If only senior management is included, the rest of the team may feel that the company's repeated talk of shared upside has collapsed into a much narrower truth at the exit. In some cases that impression may be fair. In others, the carve-out may simply reflect the fact that a handful of people were essential to making the deal happen. Either way, the situation tends to expose whether the company has cultivated an honest ownership culture or merely a rhetorical one. The better the company has been at explaining real cap table economics over time, the less shocking the logic of a carve-out will feel when it appears. The worse the company has been at that, the more the carve-out will seem like an arbitrary and bitter political act.

This is why founders should read the possibility of a carve-out as both warning and lesson. It is a warning that the current structure may not reward common holders meaningfully in enough plausible sale scenarios. It is a lesson that formal ownership rights, however central, do not remove the need to keep the people who actually run the company economically connected to realistic outcomes. If the cap table fails to do that, the company may end up improvising at the point of sale in a way that reveals just how far the structure had drifted from lived company reality.

That is what management carve-outs are really about. They exist because sometimes the waterfall works too well for capital and too badly for the humans the company still needs. They are not elegant. They are not signs of perfect design. But they are often the clearest evidence that exit economics cannot be understood only in terms of the gross sale price or even in terms of the formal rights stack. One must also ask whether the resulting outcome still leaves the people carrying the business with enough reason to carry it through the final chapter.

Secondary Sales and Partial Liquidity

Most founders enter startup life thinking about liquidity in one of two dramatic forms. Either the company will eventually be sold, or it will eventually go public. Until then, ownership is imagined as paper wealth, meaningful perhaps, but unrealised. This binary view is understandable, but it is incomplete. In practice, many companies and many founders encounter partial liquidity before any final exit. That is where secondary sales enter the story. A secondary sale is not the company issuing new shares to raise fresh capital for itself. It is an existing shareholder selling some of their own shares to another buyer. In other words, money changes hands, but the company does not receive the proceeds. An owner does.

This distinction matters because it changes the meaning of liquidity entirely. In a primary financing round, the company sells equity and receives cash to fund growth. In a secondary transaction, an existing holder, sometimes a founder, early employee, or early investor, turns part of their paper ownership into actual money. The cap table still changes in the sense that one person now owns what another person used to own, but the company's balance sheet does not grow from the transaction in the same direct way. For founders, this can be psychologically significant. It introduces the possibility that not all economic reward must wait until the very end. Some liquidity can happen while the company is still private and still growing.

That possibility is both attractive and dangerous.

The attraction is obvious. Founders and early employees can spend years building a business while holding wealth that is real in theory but unusable in daily life. They may still be paying mortgages, supporting families, carrying personal financial stress, or simply wondering whether all their company risk will ever become actual money. A well-timed secondary can reduce that pressure. It can let a founder take some money off the table, de-risk their personal life, and continue building the company from a more stable position. That is why partial liquidity is not merely indulgence. In some cases it is one of the healthiest things a company can do for founder endurance and rationality.

The danger is that secondary sales can also change incentives. A founder who has taken meaningful liquidity may no longer be carrying the company with the same hunger or the same economic dependence on future upside. That is not inevitable, but it is a real concern, and investors often worry about it. Venture-backed companies frequently rely on the founders remaining highly motivated by the still-unrealised upside ahead. If a founder sells too much too early, later investors may fear that the founder has been derisked personally at the expense of keeping full alignment with the company's next stage. This is why secondary sales are often negotiated carefully and sometimes resisted. The issue is not simply whether a founder deserves some liquidity. The issue is how much, at what stage, and with what effect on the company's future.

This is one reason partial liquidity often becomes more acceptable at certain stages than others. Very early in a company's life, investors usually want founder capital to stay largely inside the business story rather than be extracted for personal relief. Later, once the company has grown, raised more substantial rounds, or achieved enough traction that the founder's long-term alignment is no longer in serious doubt, a modest secondary can feel much more reasonable. In such cases, investors may even welcome it if they believe the founder's personal finances are so strained that some partial liquidity will make the founder calmer, more durable, and less likely to make bad strategic decisions from private desperation.

Secondary sales also matter because they complicate how outsiders interpret the cap table. A founder may still appear to own a large stake, but if some of that stake has already been partially monetised, the founder's economic relationship to the future of the company is no longer quite the same as it once was. A new investor will often want to know not only the founder's current percentage, but whether the founder has already taken money out and how much. That affects the story of alignment. A founder who has sold a very small portion to solve life constraints may still look well aligned. A founder who has taken a large secondary early may prompt harder questions about appetite, ambition, and long-term commitment.

There is also an internal cultural dimension. Employees often understand, at least vaguely, that founders carry more risk and therefore may someday deserve more reward. But if the company allows substantial founder secondaries while employees are still being asked to accept thin salaries and illiquid options, the optics can become delicate. This is especially true if the company continues to talk in egalitarian language about shared upside while operating a very different reality beneath the surface. A secondary sale may be entirely rational for the founder and still need careful handling in how the company communicates about ownership, fairness, and timing. The issue is not merely economics. It is whether the company's story about who is carrying risk still matches the lived truth after some people have already begun cashing out.

Secondary transactions can also involve early investors rather than founders. An early angel may sell to a later fund. A seed investor may trim a position when a growth investor wants more room. These sales can be healthy if they refresh the cap table, bring in a more suitable long-term holder, or allow an early investor to realise gains while still leaving room for the next stage of company-building. But they can also alter the company's political structure. A new holder may be less patient, more institutional, or more demanding than the old one. Once again, the cap table is not only numbers. It is a set of relationships, and secondary sales can change those relationships even when no new money goes into the company itself.

This is why secondary liquidity should always be read through two lenses. First, what does it do for the person selling. Does it relieve unhealthy personal pressure, create founder stability, or reflect a sensible partial derisking after years of commitment. Second, what does it do to the company. Does it preserve alignment, improve cap table quality, or create future doubts about motivation and fairness. A secondary that helps the founder but weakens the company may still be a bad trade. A secondary that helps both may be one of the most rational and humane financing choices available.

There is another subtle truth here. Secondary sales can reveal whether the company and its investors understand that founder protection matters in practical life, not just in abstract upside. A founder who is expected to remain perfectly aligned for a decade with no chance of partial liquidity, while every investor enjoys preferences, pro rata rights, downside protection, and portfolio diversification, may begin to feel that the company's structure is fair only in one direction. Some carefully managed secondary liquidity can correct that imbalance without breaking the company's incentive logic. It can acknowledge that founders are not machines and that total illiquidity for too long can itself become destabilising.

That said, secondaries should rarely be treated casually. The quantity sold matters. The timing matters. The company's stage matters. The founder's remaining ownership matters. A small secondary that lets a founder buy a house or reduce personal financial stress while still leaving a very substantial stake in place is one thing. A large secondary that turns the founder into someone who has already largely won regardless of what happens next is another. Investors, boards, and founders all know the difference intuitively even when they disagree about exact thresholds. That is why secondary discussions are often as much about narrative and trust as about arithmetic.

From an exit-math perspective, secondary sales also remind founders of an important point. Liquidity does not always arrive in one dramatic block at the end. Ownership can convert into money in stages, under different conditions, through different counterparties. This makes the founder's economic story more complex than the simple percentage-times-exit-price formula many people carry in their heads. Some value may already have been realised. Some may still sit beneath a preference stack. Some may depend on future sale outcomes. Some may be tied to retention or employment conditions. The founder who understands secondary liquidity is better able to think about wealth, motivation, and cap table meaning in a more mature way.

That is what secondary sales and partial liquidity are really about. They sit between total illiquidity and final exit. They can reduce personal pressure, refresh the cap table, and create healthier founder endurance. They can also distort incentives, create optics problems, and weaken the company if handled badly. Like so much in startup finance, they are neither inherently good nor inherently corrupt. They are structurally powerful. The question is whether they are being used to make the company more buildable without quietly hollowing out the reasons its key people still need to build it.

Why Founders Must Know Their Own Exit Economics

A founder can spend years inside a company, raise multiple rounds, survive dilution, manage employees, negotiate with investors, and still reach the edge of a real transaction without knowing what they personally stand to receive in the most plausible outcome ranges. That is not rare. It is one of the most common forms of financial illiteracy in startup life. The founder knows the headline valuation history. The founder knows roughly what percentage of the common they still hold. The founder may even know the broad size of the preference stack. But when asked a direct question, what do you receive if the company sells for £20 million, £50 million, £100 million, many founders cannot answer with confidence. That is a serious weakness.

Founders must know their own exit economics because no one else in the company experiences the cap table in quite the same way they do. Investors know their protections. Lawyers know the documents. Finance people may know the models. But the founder is the one making strategic decisions under the emotional pressure of carrying the business. If the founder does not know what kinds of outcomes still matter for them personally, then they are navigating the company with a blurred understanding of their own incentives. That blur can distort everything from fundraising choices to acquisition decisions to how much risk the founder is willing to take late in the company's life.

This is not about greed. It is about coherence.

A founder who does not know their exit economics may overestimate what a moderate sale would do for them and therefore push the company toward apparently safe options that are not actually meaningful for the common. Another founder may underestimate what a reasonable sale would deliver and reject strong acquisition offers because they are still emotionally anchored to old valuation headlines rather than to the real waterfall. In both cases, the founder is not deciding from reality. They are deciding from a story. Cap table literacy exists precisely to replace story with structure where structure matters most.

This is especially important because founder sacrifice is not abstract. Years of work, stress, opportunity cost, reputation risk, and personal financial exposure eventually need to meet some answer.

That answer may be that the company is still worth carrying because the common meaningfully participates across a broad range of outcomes. It may be that only very large exits now matter because the stack above the common has become too heavy. It may even be that the founder has taken some secondary liquidity and therefore now relates to the future upside differently than before. All of these are real possibilities. But unless the founder has modelled them, they are living inside uncertainty not just about the company's future, but about the economic meaning of their own role.

This is one reason founders can become strangely irrational late in the game. Some become far too risk-seeking because only huge exits now make a difference to them, though they may not have consciously admitted that to themselves. Others become exhausted and overly willing to accept offers that sound large in gross terms because they assume their stake will translate more directly into money than it actually will. Both behaviours often reflect the same underlying problem. The founder has not forced the cap table to answer the question: what is my real economic position now across plausible company outcomes.

A simple discipline helps. Founders should know, at minimum, what their proceeds would look like at several sale values and financing states. What do I receive at £10 million, £25 million, £50 million, £100 million, and so on. What assumptions are being made about investor conversion. What preferences sit ahead of me. What participation rights matter. What transaction costs or debt may further reduce distributable proceeds. What happens if a later round occurs before sale. These do not have to be perfect predictions. They do have to be grounded enough that the founder is not shocked by their own economics at the moment they most need clarity.

Knowing your exit economics also changes how you negotiate while the company is still alive. A founder who understands that a particular preference layer or aggressive term would meaningfully destroy common economics across realistic outcomes can push back earlier and with far more confidence. A founder who knows that a moderate secondary sale would de-risk their personal life without undermining long-term alignment can discuss it more intelligently. A founder who sees that another round at a weak price would push the common too far beneath the stack can think more carefully about whether to raise, sell, or restructure. In each case, exit knowledge is not only about the end. It informs present strategy.

It also protects the founder from vanity. Startup culture encourages founders to think in public numbers: valuation, total raise, gross exit price, paper net worth. Those numbers are easy to repeat and easy to admire. They are also often poor guides to lived founder reality. The founder who knows their actual economics becomes much less vulnerable to being seduced by impressive-looking but economically thin outcomes. They can separate public prestige from private meaning. That is a powerful form of discipline, because it keeps the founder from building their emotional life around numbers the cap table may never let them actually experience.

There is an internal leadership benefit too. Founders who know their own economics are usually better at speaking honestly to senior employees and boards about what kinds of outcomes still make sense. They can explain why a certain offer is inadequate without sounding merely proud. They can explain why another round is dangerous without sounding generically dilution-averse. They can talk about motivation and alignment from a place of actual knowledge rather than vague discomfort. That tends to create more trust, not less, because the founder's position becomes legible instead of mysterious.

Of course, knowing your exit economics can be uncomfortable. Many founders avoid the exercise because they fear what they will learn. Perhaps the stack is heavier than they thought. Perhaps the common matters only at much higher prices than they had assumed. Perhaps the moderate acquisition they privately imagined as a win is barely meaningful after preferences. But discomfort is still an advantage if it arrives early enough to shape action. The founder who learns this late is trapped by it. The founder who learns it early can still negotiate, raise differently, sell differently, or at least understand what game they are now actually playing.

That is why founders must know their own exit economics. Not because the company is about to sell, and not because fixation on personal proceeds should dominate every decision, but because the cap table is already deciding what kinds of outcomes remain real for the founder. To lead the company without understanding that is to carry the business while partially blind to the economic meaning of carrying it. Once that blindness is removed, the founder is in a much stronger position to make hard decisions with seriousness rather than with hope alone.

FOURTEEN

Reading the Cap Table Like an Operator

"The map is not the territory."

- Alfred Korzybski

Why Founders Must Learn to Read Their Own Structure

A cap table is one of the few documents in a startup that can look deceptively simple while quietly controlling some of the most important truths in the company. At a glance, it appears to be a list of names, numbers, percentages, and share classes. Founders can therefore fall into the trap of treating it as an administrative object, something necessary for lawyers, accountants, and investors, but not something that needs to live at the centre of the founder's own operating mind. That is a mistake. A founder who cannot read the cap table properly is, in a very real sense, trying to run the company without understanding who the company economically belongs to, how that ownership behaves under pressure, and what future decisions the structure is already preparing.

This is why founders must learn to read their own structure.

The phrase read your own structure is important because it implies more than passive familiarity. Many founders can glance at the cap table and recognise the names on it. Some can even repeat the headline percentages from memory. That is not the same as reading it. To read the structure as an operator means understanding what the numbers do, what the rights attached to them do, what future scenarios they imply, and how the structure will behave when the company hires, raises, struggles, or sells. It means treating the cap table less like a static spreadsheet and more like a live operating system for power, dilution, and reward.

This matters because the cap table is not merely a record of the past. It is one of the most active forces shaping the future. Every founder split, every vesting schedule, every option pool, every SAFE, every note, every preferred round, every right granted to investors, every layer of preference and anti-dilution, all of it lives in the cap table or around it. When founders do not read that structure properly, they are effectively letting history accumulate into the business without fully understanding what that history is doing to the company they are trying to build. The company can continue moving for a while under that blindness, but eventually the structure will force itself into the foreground, usually at the moment when the founder most needs clear judgment.

That is the pattern. A financing is being negotiated. An investor asks what the fully diluted position looks like after conversion. A key hire wants to understand the real percentage behind a grant. A board discussion turns on who has consent rights. A buyer appears and the founders suddenly need to know what the common actually receives. In each case, the founder who never really learned to read the cap table finds themselves dependent on other people's interpretation of their own company. Lawyers explain. investors explain. Finance people explain. Sometimes they do it well. But none of them is carrying the company the way the founder is. The founder should not be learning the economic meaning of the business secondhand at the moment of decision.

This is one reason experienced operators are often far more serious about cap table literacy than first-time founders expect. They know that the cap table is not a side document. It is where sentiment stops and structure begins. It shows whether the founder can still be motivated after the next round. It shows whether the employee pool is real or theatrical. It shows whether the company is beginning to crowd itself with rights that will make later financing harder. It shows whether the founder's common stock still means what the founder thinks it means across plausible exits. These are operating questions. They are not only legal questions.

Founders sometimes resist this because they feel, often correctly, that too much focus on the cap table can make the company seem smaller, colder, or more financialised than the actual work of building product and serving customers. That resistance makes emotional sense. But it confuses priority with avoidance. No one is saying the founder should obsess over the cap table every hour instead of building the business. The point is simpler.

The founder should understand the economic machine they are inside well enough that when financing, hiring, or exit decisions arise, they are not reasoning from a fantasy version of ownership. You do not need to stare at the engine all day to drive a car. You do need to know whether the engine is working.

This becomes more important as the company matures because each new layer of capital makes the structure less intuitive. A founder-only company can often survive on rough understanding. A company with options, SAFEs, notes, preferred rounds, investor rights, and several possible future paths cannot. Once the ownership structure becomes layered, intuition starts lying. Headline percentage looks stronger than real economics. Valuation sounds more flattering than likely proceeds. "Standard" investor rights sound harmless until stacked together. The founder who does not actively learn to read these layers is likely to keep talking about the company using yesterday's simpler language while today's cap table is already saying something else.

There is also a discipline of honesty involved here. Founders often pride themselves on vision, endurance, and the ability to push through uncertainty. Those qualities matter enormously. But there is a weaker version of founder psychology that mistakes vagueness for optimism. It says the hard ownership details can be dealt with later, that percentages broadly make sense, that future rounds will probably be fine, that employees will understand the upside well enough, that exits can be analysed if and when they happen. This is not vision. It is avoidance wearing the costume of momentum. Learning to read the cap table properly is one of the clearest signs that a founder is becoming an operator rather than merely remaining an originator.

To read your own structure well, you have to ask a different class of questions. Not just who owns what now, but what happens next. If the company raises again, who gets diluted and who is protected. If the company sells modestly, who gets paid first and what remains for the common. If the option pool expands, what does that do to founder positions before and after the next round. If a SAFE converts, what does that really add to the share count. If a preferred investor has pro rata rights, how much future round space is already effectively reserved. These questions are practical, and more importantly, they are cumulative. The cap table is not a thing you understand once. It is a structure you keep re-reading as the company changes.

This is why a founder should think of cap table literacy as part of company stewardship. You are not merely raising money or issuing equity. You are changing the ownership architecture of the business. That architecture influences who is motivated, who is protected, who has leverage, and what kinds of outcomes remain meaningful. If the founder is serious about stewardship in product, hiring, and strategy, they should be serious about stewardship here too. Otherwise they are leaving one of the most consequential parts of company design largely to drift.

Another crucial point is that reading the cap table well does not require the founder to become a securities lawyer or to memorise every legal formula. It requires something more useful than that. It requires the founder to know enough that the structure cannot quietly move against them without their awareness. They should understand the major classes, the major rights, the major future triggers, and the major payout implications. They should know when they are looking at something ordinary, something aggressive, and something that needs modelling before it can be judged. They should know where they still need expert help. That is what practical literacy looks like. Not total technical mastery, but control over the meaning of the document.

This chapter begins here because the later-stage founder has to move beyond learning individual terms one by one and into a more operational discipline. It is no longer enough to know what liquidation preference is, or what anti-dilution is, or what a SAFE is. The founder now needs to be able to look at the whole structure and read it as a system. What kind of company does this cap table now create. What future pressures has it already written into the business. What choices does it leave open, and which ones has it quietly narrowed. Once a founder can do that, they are reading the cap table like an operator rather than like a spectator.

That is why founders must learn to read their own structure. Because eventually the company will ask them questions that only the cap table can answer, and by then it is too late to still be treating the answer sheet as background paperwork.

The Difference Between Looking and Reading

Most founders look at their cap table far more often than they read it. That distinction sounds rhetorical at first, but it is not. Looking means recognising the surface of the document.

The founder sees names, percentages, perhaps a class label or two, and feels a sense of familiarity. They know roughly who the major holders are. They know their own number. They may even know who came in during the last round and what the top-line dilution looked like. That is looking. It is not worthless, but it is shallow. Reading is something else. Reading means understanding what the structure is actually saying about power, incentives, and future consequences.

This matters because a cap table is one of the easiest documents in a company to mistake for something simpler than it is. A founder glances at it and sees order. The numbers add up. The percentages total one hundred. It feels complete. Yet the table is often like a map covered in symbols that only partly reveal what the terrain is really like. The founder who only looks at it sees the outlines. The founder who reads it sees the forces underneath. They see which percentages matter only in theory, which rights dominate in certain scenarios, which parts of the structure still leave room for growth, and which parts are already narrowing the company's future options.

This is why the difference between looking and reading becomes more consequential as the company matures. In the earliest stage, the gap may be small enough that it causes little damage. A founder-only table with a few common holders is still reasonably intuitive. A company with SAFEs, notes, an option pool, preferred rounds, pro rata rights, liquidation preferences, anti-dilution provisions, and stacked investor classes is not intuitive. At that stage, looking at the table may still create emotional reassurance because the founder recognises the broad shape, but reassurance is not understanding. The company can now be structurally complex while still appearing visually legible. That is a dangerous condition. It tempts the founder to mistake familiarity for comprehension.

A useful way to think about this is that looking answers the question what is here, while reading answers the question what does this do. Looking tells the founder that an investor owns fifteen percent preferred. Reading asks what kind of preferred, with what preference, what rights, what conversion logic, and what that fifteen percent means in a £20 million sale versus a £200 million one. Looking tells the founder there is a ten percent option pool. Reading asks whether that pool is already mostly allocated, whether it is enough for the next hiring phase, whether it was created pre-money, and what future expansion will do to the founder position. Looking tells the founder several SAFEs exist. Reading asks what caps and discounts they carry, how they stack, and what they convert into under plausible next-round prices. The table has the same cells in both cases. The founder's relationship to the meaning is completely different.

This difference is one reason founders can become blindsided by events they technically had enough information to foresee. The problem is not that the data was hidden. The problem is that the founder was using the table as confirmation rather than as inquiry. They were checking that the numbers were there, not interrogating what the numbers implied. A financing arrives, and the founder realises the round is more dilutive than expected once old instruments convert. A buyer appears, and the founder realises the preference stack eats more of the sale than the headline price suggested. A key hire wants to know what their grant really means, and the founder realises they have been speaking in raw option counts rather than in meaningful ownership context. In each case, the founder had been looking at the structure all along. They had not been reading it.

There is also a psychological comfort in looking that makes real reading harder. Looking allows the founder to stay close to the company's story as they want to tell it. We still own most of it. The round was good. The option pool is there. The note will convert later. The table remains something familiar and manageable. Reading is more demanding because it can force conclusions the founder does not particularly want. It may show that founder ownership is thinner than feels healthy once another likely round is added. It may show that the common only becomes powerful at exit prices far above what the team casually talks about. It may show that earlier "standard" investor rights have accumulated into something much less standard in combination. In that sense, reading requires the founder to exchange comfort for accuracy.

That exchange is exactly why it matters operationally. A company is not protected by the founder feeling reassured. It is protected by the founder knowing what the structure will do under pressure. The board does not need the founder to be vaguely familiar with the ownership map. It needs the founder to make decisions that take real ownership mechanics into account. A founder who only looks at the cap table may still negotiate, hire, and plan with confidence, but that confidence is fragile because it has not been tested against the actual logic of the structure. A founder who reads the table properly may sometimes feel less comfortable in the short term, but their decisions are usually more grounded.

This is why reading the cap table often begins with asking active questions rather than scanning passive numbers. What happens to these positions if we raise again. Which holders can preserve their ownership and which cannot. At what sale values do these preferences stop dominating. How much fully diluted ownership is already spoken for by promises not yet emotionally registered. Does the founder still have enough room after likely future rounds. Would a later investor find this structure attractive or crowded. A founder who approaches the table this way is not using it as a report card. They are using it as an operating instrument.

Another way to frame it is that looking treats the cap table as a photograph. Reading treats it as a machine. A photograph shows who is present in one captured moment. A machine tells you what happens when energy passes through it. Financing, hiring, dilution, exits, and governance stress are all forms of energy passing through the ownership structure. The founder who only has the photograph can still admire or worry about who is in the picture. The founder who understands the machine can predict how the parts move when pressure is applied. Startup life repeatedly applies pressure. That is why the machine view is the one that matters.

There is a practical consequence here for how founders should spend time with the document. Many review the cap table only when forced to do so by a round or a legal process. That reinforces the habit of looking rather than reading, because the interaction becomes reactive. A better discipline is to revisit the structure whenever the company changes in a way that could alter incentives or future economics. After a financing. After a pool expansion. After a major grant. After a SAFE or note issuance. After a founder departure. After the company begins discussing strategic alternatives. Each time, the founder should ask not only what the document now says, but what it now means. That habit gradually transforms the cap table from a periodic administrative burden into an ongoing instrument of strategic clarity.

The distinction also affects how the founder speaks to others. A founder who only looks at the structure tends to speak in broad and flattering simplifications because that is all they can safely see. We own X. The investor took Y. The pool is Z. A founder who reads the structure speaks more carefully. They understand the difference between issued and fully diluted. They explain that rights matter as much as percentages.

They know the likely exit ranges where common meaningfully participates. They can answer hard questions without hiding behind vagueness. This does not make them less inspiring. It makes them more credible.

In the end, the difference between looking and reading is the difference between comfort with the surface and command of the meaning. A founder can look at a cap table for years and still be surprised by it when the company is under stress. A founder who learns to read it starts seeing surprises earlier, when they are still merely implications rather than consequences. That is the shift that matters. Once it happens, the cap table stops being a thing the founder consults occasionally and becomes a thing the founder can actually use.

Which Questions to Ask Every Time the Cap Table Changes

A cap table change is never just a clerical event. That is the first principle the founder has to adopt if the structure is going to remain something they truly govern rather than something they periodically discover. New shares are issued, a SAFE is signed, an option pool is expanded, a founder leaves, a note converts, a secondary happens, a priced round closes. Each of these can be described administratively. But administration is only the surface. Underneath, every change is reassigning future upside, influence, and vulnerability. That is why the right response to a cap table change is not merely to update the spreadsheet. It is to interrogate what the update now means.

The easiest way to build that discipline is through a fixed set of questions. The founder should not rely on mood, memory, or optimism. They should know what they ask every single time the structure moves. This matters because the human mind is very good at treating each financing or ownership event as uniquely justified by current circumstances. This hire is essential. This investor is supportive. This bridge is only temporary. This pool increase is market standard. This founder departure is unfortunate but manageable. Each statement may be true. Yet if the founder never runs those events through the same core questions, the cap table drifts one reasonable-looking step at a time until the accumulated structure no longer reflects what the founder believed they were building.

The first question is the simplest and the most often skipped. What has actually changed. Not what story is attached to the event, not what motivation produced it, but what has changed in the structure itself.

Has the total share count increased. Has a new class entered. Has a future claim been added. Has a right been granted. Has dead equity been removed or left in place. Has the pool been resized. Has a conversion threshold moved. This sounds basic, but many founders rush straight from event to justification without forcing themselves to state, in plain structural terms, what is now different. If that is not clear, everything that follows is softer than it should be.

The second question is where dilution begins to become real. Who is being diluted or weakened by this change, and who is being protected or strengthened. Founders often talk about dilution as though it lands evenly across all pre-existing holders. In many startup structures it does not. A new round may dilute everyone in a broad sense, but pro rata rights let some investors preserve their position. Anti-dilution may protect earlier preferred while pushing more pain into the common. A pool expansion may fall primarily on founders if done pre-money. A secondary sale may not dilute at all but may still change influence and alignment. The founder should therefore not ask only whether dilution exists. They should ask where the pain and protection are being distributed.

The third question is temporal. What does this change mean now, and what does it probably mean after the next likely event. Many founders are willing to calculate the immediate effect of a round or grant. Fewer are disciplined enough to ask what that same change looks like after the next financing, the next conversion, or the next pool refresh. This is exactly where weak structures become dangerous, because something that still looks survivable in the present can become much less healthy once the next likely step is layered on top. A founder should get into the habit of asking not only what the table now says, but what this revised table will likely become if the company follows its next plausible path.

The fourth question is motivational. After this change, are the people who still need to build the company still meaningfully aligned with the outcome. This question matters for founders, key executives, and sometimes for critical early employees as well. A company can execute a structurally "clean" financing and still weaken itself if the common is thinned so far, or pushed so far beneath preferences and future likely dilution, that the people carrying the business no longer have a compelling economic relationship to the upside. Founders often assume alignment survives automatically. It does not.

It survives because the structure still makes the burden worth carrying. Every cap table change should therefore be tested against the question of whether the company's key builders still have enough left to remain rationally committed.

The fifth question is strategic. What future flexibility has this change preserved, and what flexibility has it quietly reduced. This is one of the most important operator questions because ownership changes are never only about current percentages. They affect room. Room for future hires. Room for later rounds. Room for attracting a lead investor. Room for making a moderate acquisition offer feel meaningful. Room for founder motivation after the next round rather than only before it. A founder who does not ask about room tends to think in snapshots. A founder who does ask starts to see whether each new event is making the company more financeable and buildable or simply more crowded.

Another necessary question is whether the structure is becoming more legible or less. Some cap table changes simplify reality. Cleaning up a departed founder, formalising a vague promise properly, converting old deferred instruments, or rationalising a messy early structure can all make the company easier to understand and govern. Other changes increase opacity. Small advisory grants made for convenience, loosely negotiated side promises, multiple tiny instruments on slightly different terms, poorly tracked option commitments, all of these can make the cap table more difficult to explain and less attractive to future investors. The founder should therefore always ask whether this event has made the ownership story cleaner or murkier. Legibility is not cosmetic. It is one of the clearest predictors of how painful future financing will become.

The founder should also ask a more uncomfortable question than most first-time teams like to ask. If I were seeing this company fresh from the outside, would this change make the cap table look stronger or weaker. This is the investor-eye question, and it is one of the best ways to escape founder self-soothing. Internally, every change usually has a reason that feels compelling. Externally, all those reasons collapse into structure. The outside investor or acquirer sees not why the company felt it had to do the thing, but what the company now looks like because it did. A good operator learns to make that outside reading before someone else does it for them.

A related question is whether the company is paying for certainty, speed, survival, or convenience, and whether the ownership cost matches what was purchased. This matters because cap table damage often enters through events that were justified in the moment by urgency. A bridge round buys time. A low-cap SAFE buys speed. An oversized pool buys negotiating convenience. A generous founder split buys emotional calm. A loosely documented advisory promise buys a quiet conversation. Some of those purchases are worth making. Some are not. The founder should ask, every time, what exactly are we buying with this structural concession, and is the price proportionate. Without that discipline, the company keeps spending future ownership for present relief without ever properly comparing the two.

There is also one question founders should ask that feels almost philosophical but is actually very practical. What kind of company does this change assume we are becoming. A large pool assumes significant hiring. A venture-style preferred round assumes a company that will likely need later rounds and must support institutional capital. A heavy preference stack assumes that much larger exits are still plausible and that common can wait beneath the structure. A founder secondary assumes the company can tolerate some personal derisking without breaking alignment. A SAFE stack assumes the company will later reach a priced financing that can absorb the conversion. In each case, the cap table change is not just moving numbers. It is making a bet about the company's future shape. The founder should know what that bet is.

These questions matter most when the event seems small. A major financing usually feels serious enough that people pay attention. The more dangerous moments are often the ones that appear too minor to deserve deep thought. One extra grant. One more small SAFE. One more special promise. One more rights package because the investor is helpful. The cap table is usually not ruined in one dramatic stroke. It is bent gradually by under-questioned decisions. That is why the founder's questioning discipline has to be habitual rather than situational.

In practice, what this means is simple. Every time the cap table changes, the founder should pause and ask: what changed, who was diluted or protected, what does this mean now, what will it likely mean after the next event, are the builders still aligned, what room is left, is the structure clearer or messier, how would an outsider read this, what exactly did we buy with the concession, and what future version of the company does this change assume. These questions are not overkill. They are the minimum needed to keep the cap table from becoming a machine that quietly outruns the founder's understanding.

That is the real difference between administrative maintenance and operational reading. One updates the sheet. The other protects the company.

Red Flags in Founder Ownership

A founder's ownership position is one of the clearest places where a cap table reveals whether the company has been built with seriousness or drift. This is because founder ownership sits at the centre of several competing truths at once. It has to reward creation. It has to preserve motivation. It has to leave room for future capital and talent. It has to remain credible to investors. It has to survive cofounder departures, later rounds, and years of company-building pressure. When founder ownership is healthy, the cap table usually feels demanding but coherent. When it is unhealthy, the red flags are often visible long before the company reaches a crisis. The problem is that many founders either do not know what those red flags are or prefer not to look at them too directly.

The first red flag is dead founder equity. This is one of the oldest and ugliest problems in startup structures. A person helped start the company, took a large stake, then left early or stopped contributing meaningfully, yet still remains on the cap table with a position large enough to burden everyone else. Founders often hesitate to confront this because it involves history, loyalty, or conflict. But from a structural perspective it is poison. Dead founder equity tells later investors, hires, and even the active founders themselves that the company is still paying the past for work the present must now carry alone. If a cap table contains large founder stakes held by people who are no longer building the company, it is already signalling a serious weakness in ownership discipline.

The second red flag is founder ownership that is already too thin too early. This is the opposite problem. Sometimes a founder has raised, granted, or compromised so much of the common position away by an early stage that the founder's remaining stake no longer looks capable of surviving realistic future dilution while still keeping the founder properly aligned.

This can happen through early weak pricing, oversized pools, sloppy cofounder allocation, overgenerous advisory grants, repeated small bridge financings, or simply a failure to think several rounds ahead. The founder may still feel reassured because the percentage is not yet tiny in absolute terms, but if the likely next round or two will drive it much lower, then the company is already moving toward a motivational problem. Investors often notice this before founders do.

A third red flag is equality without justification. Equal founder splits are not wrong by definition, but they are very often treated as emotionally convenient defaults rather than as conclusions earned through serious thinking. If the founders are not truly bringing comparable risk, skill, time, role commitment, and long-term burden, then a perfectly equal split may be less a sign of fairness than a sign that hard conversation was postponed at the moment it mattered most. This does not always blow up. But later, when one founder ends up carrying much more of the company than another, the cap table starts reflecting a past diplomacy that no longer matches present reality. Unearned equality is one of the most common early red flags because it often looks noble while quietly planting later resentment.

The fourth red flag is the absence of founder vesting or founder vesting that exists only weakly on paper. A company with several founders and no meaningful vesting discipline is effectively assuming that everyone who is present at the beginning will remain worthy of a permanent ownership grant regardless of what happens next. That is a dangerous assumption. Founder vesting is not only investor comfort. It is one of the main ways the active company protects itself from future drift, departure, and dead equity. If vesting is missing entirely, or if the company has emotionally decided it will never really be enforced, the structure is signalling softness at exactly the point where startup life most needs hardness.

Another red flag is founder ownership that can only be explained by story rather than by structure. This is when the founder split no longer makes sense on the face of the table and requires long narrative justification every time an outsider asks about it. "He had the original idea." "She was there at the start." "We meant to change it later." "He helped early on." A good cap table should not need a mythology layer to explain its basic founder economics. Some history will always matter, of course. But when the founder ownership only seems acceptable because everyone keeps retelling the same emotional backstory, that usually means the structure itself is weaker than the company wants to admit.

A particularly important red flag is founder overconcentration that leaves no serious room for talent or later capital. This is the founder-side mirror image of being over-diluted. Some teams protect founder ownership so intensely in the early stage that the cap table starts to imply a company that will somehow grow without enough room for key hires, option grants, or future financing. This can feel strong to the founders because they still "own nearly all of it." But if the actual business requires serious talent and outside money to become what the founders say it will become, then extreme ownership concentration can be a sign not of discipline but of denial. It says the founders are still attached to a founding-stage ownership fantasy while trying to build a company that will not fit inside it.

Then there is founder ownership that has become economically misleading because of the rights stack beneath it. This is a subtler red flag because the founder's percentage may still look healthy. On paper the founder may own a substantial share of the common. But if heavy preferences, multiple rounds, participation rights, and likely future dilution have already pushed the meaningful economic threshold far higher than the founder's intuition acknowledges, then the founder's ownership is partly theatrical. It exists, but it only behaves powerfully in very large outcomes. This is one of the most dangerous red flags because it flatters the founder while quietly hollowing out the common's practical meaning across a wide range of real scenarios.

A related warning sign is when the founder does not actually know what their own ownership means after the next likely round. If a founder can tell you their current percentage but cannot tell you what happens after the option pool expands, after the next priced round, after the SAFE conversion, or after a likely down-round scenario, then the founder is not truly governing their ownership. They are reciting a snapshot. That lack of forward visibility is itself a red flag, because founder ownership must be understood as a trajectory, not just a current number. A healthy founder position is one that still makes sense after the next likely stretch of company evolution, not only at this exact minute.

Another red flag appears when founder protection depends on informal trust rather than enforceable structure. The founders may say they would "never do that to each other," or that certain rights "wouldn't really be used," or that a departed founder "would give shares back if needed." Those statements may feel reassuring internally, but to a serious operator or investor they are warning lights.

A cap table built on informal promises rather than structural clarity is vulnerable precisely when stress arrives and trust is weakest. Founder ownership should not depend too heavily on everyone staying reasonable forever. The whole point of structure is to reduce how much has to rest on that hope.

There is also a broader pattern founders should notice. Red flags in founder ownership are rarely isolated. Dead equity, weak vesting, over-thin common, story-dependent splits, and poor forward modelling often cluster together. One weak decision at formation tends to invite others later because the company never really built the habit of taking founder ownership seriously as architecture. This is why looking for individual symptoms matters less than learning to see the overall condition. Does the founder position still look earned, disciplined, motivating, and survivable. Or does it look sentimental, overcompromised, opaque, or detached from the actual burden of building the company now.

The good news is that many founder-ownership red flags can still be addressed if seen early enough. Splits can be revisited before outside money hardens them further. Vesting can be put in place while the team is still intact enough to agree. Dead equity can sometimes be negotiated down or bought back before the company becomes much more valuable. Overconcentration can be softened with a rational pool strategy. Over-thin positions can shape how the next round is negotiated. The real danger is not that these red flags exist. It is that founders look at them so often they stop seeing them.

That is why founder ownership deserves especially hard reading. If the people carrying the company are structurally wrong on the cap table, then almost everything built on top of that structure will eventually feel some version of the same distortion. The founder who learns to see these red flags clearly is not becoming cynical. They are becoming capable of protecting the company from one of the oldest startup failures of all: a business whose ownership no longer tells the truth about who is actually building it.

Red Flags in Employee Equity

If founder ownership tells you whether the company still knows who is carrying it, employee equity tells you whether the company knows how to share the future honestly.

This is one of the clearest places where startups reveal whether they are serious operators or merely enthusiastic storytellers. Many companies speak beautifully about ownership culture, alignment, and giving people a piece of the upside. Far fewer build an employee equity structure that is coherent, credible, and durable once hiring pressure, later rounds, and investor rights begin to reshape the cap table. That gap is where the red flags appear.

The first red flag is vagueness disguised as generosity. An employee is told they are "getting equity," "becoming an owner," or "sharing in the upside," but no one explains what instrument they are actually receiving, what percentage it really represents, what the vesting terms are, how much fully diluted ownership exists, or where the common sits beneath the preference stack. This kind of language feels positive in the moment, and sometimes founders use it because they themselves do not fully understand the details. But structurally it is a warning sign. If the company cannot explain employee equity with precision, then it is very likely using ownership culture as an emotional recruiting tool while failing to govern the underlying economics properly.

A second red flag is grants that sound large in raw numbers but are tiny in real terms. A startup offers fifty thousand options, one hundred thousand options, perhaps more, and assumes the candidate will be impressed. The candidate often is, because large numbers feel important. Yet if the company never grounds that figure in the total share count or in the fully diluted percentage it represents, the offer is being framed in a way that can easily mislead. This is one of the oldest tricks of startup compensation, even when no deliberate bad faith is involved. The company speaks in counts because counts sound better than fractions. The founder who wants to read employee equity honestly should always ask whether the grant is being described in a way that makes its actual significance clearer or hazier.

Another red flag is the absence of a real equity philosophy. Some companies build option grants role by role, stage by stage, with at least a rough internal logic for how much ownership should go to which kinds of contributors and why. Others simply improvise. One employee gets a surprisingly large grant because they joined in a dramatic moment. Another gets very little because the company has become more cautious.

An early friend of the founders is overrewarded. A stronger later hire is underrewarded. The pattern becomes emotional rather than structural. Over time this creates one of the most politically corrosive forms of cap table disorder, because employees may have very different ownership positions that reflect founder mood, urgency, or sentiment more than actual role and contribution. A company does not need perfect uniformity, but it does need principles. If employee equity looks arbitrary, that is a serious warning sign.

A fourth red flag is a company that talks as though the option pool is an infinite moral resource rather than a finite economic one. Founders sometimes comfort themselves with the idea that because options are not immediate cash, they can be used liberally to solve recruiting or retention discomfort whenever it arises. In practice, every grant spends future ownership capacity. If the company keeps solving short-term people problems by handing out grants without modelling the cumulative effect, the pool becomes a quiet source of cap table decay. This is especially dangerous when the founders are simultaneously underestimating future hiring needs. The result is often the worst of both worlds: the company gives away meaningful slices to mediocre or panicked decisions and later discovers it still does not have enough room for the hires that truly matter.

There is also a red flag in grants that are too small to function as real incentives but are still spoken about as though they should inspire loyalty and sacrifice. This is one of the more ethically serious failures in startup equity culture. If an employee's option package is economically tiny relative to the company's structure, likely future dilution, and probable exit range, then the company should not pretend that the grant transforms the employee into a serious long-term stakeholder in any meaningful financial sense. It may still be worth something. It may still be part of a fair overall compensation package. But if the startup is using thin equity as if it were a substitute for stronger salary, deep alignment, or founder-level upside, then it is building morale on exaggeration. That usually ends badly.

Another clear warning sign is when the company itself does not know how the employee grants sit relative to the preference stack. Employees are given options, perhaps early and with genuine appreciation, but no one inside the leadership team has actually modelled what those options could mean at plausible sale values once preferences, participation, and later rounds are accounted for.

The company then ends up speaking about employee ownership as if it were equivalent to raw common percentage, when in reality the common may only become powerful at much higher exit values than anyone is saying aloud. A founder who cannot explain where employee common sits in likely outcomes is not really offering a serious equity culture. They are offering a partially understood hope.

A particularly dangerous red flag is overpromising around life-changing outcomes. Some startup cultures drift into language that makes every employee option grant sound like a potential fortune. In a tiny fraction of companies, that may turn out to be true. In most, the real economics are more conditional, more diluted, and more dependent on specific future structures than the rhetoric suggests. Founders do not have to become cold or pessimistic to avoid this mistake. They simply need to be honest. Options can be meaningful without being magical. They can be attractive without being sold as destiny. A company that cannot talk about equity without inflating it is usually compensating for a deeper insecurity about the offer.

There is also a warning sign in how the company reacts when employees ask hard questions. If a candidate or team member asks what percentage their grant represents, how dilution works, what the strike price is, how preferences affect common, or what the company's likely path to liquidity is, and the founders become defensive or evasive, that is not just a communications issue. It usually indicates that the company has not built an ownership culture capable of handling real scrutiny. Strong companies may not have perfect answers to every future scenario, but they can at least answer the current structural questions plainly. Weak companies often hide behind startup mystique because clear explanation would expose how little discipline has gone into the grant philosophy.

Another red flag is when the company keeps refreshing or enlarging the pool without also asking whether earlier grants still make sense. This creates a ratchet of dilution without much institutional memory. The company says yes to another pool expansion because it needs more hiring room, but no one revisits whether earlier option use was strategic or sloppy. Over time the founders may find themselves heavily diluted for a body of employee equity decisions that was never properly curated. At that point, the problem is no longer a single bad grant. It is the absence of governance over the pool as a whole.

Employee equity also becomes a red-flag zone when departures are handled inconsistently. One employee is allowed extended exercise rights. Another loses everything quickly. One senior person negotiates special treatment quietly. Another does not even understand what happens when they leave. If the company's approach to employee departures is opaque or selectively improvised, then the cap table is no longer functioning as a stable compensation system. It is becoming a political space where insiders with leverage get one outcome and everyone else another. Some variation may be justified by role or negotiation power, but if the company cannot explain the logic clearly, the structure is drifting from principled to opportunistic.

The deeper pattern in all these red flags is that employee equity stops being a governed instrument and becomes a rhetorical one. The company says ownership matters, but does not model it carefully. The company says everyone is aligned, but does not test whether the economics truly support that claim. The company says grants are meaningful, but often speaks in ways that exaggerate raw counts and understate structure. The result is not only cap table weakness. It is a credibility problem. Once employees discover that the company's ownership language outran the actual ownership economics, trust becomes much harder to rebuild.

The founder who reads employee equity properly therefore asks a few blunt questions. Are grants being explained clearly. Are they sized with any real philosophy. Do they remain meaningful after expected dilution. Is the option pool being used strategically or emotionally. Does the company understand what employee common is actually worth across plausible outcomes. Are departures handled by structure rather than by improvisation. If the answers are weak, the cap table is not just developing compensation issues. It is developing cultural fractures that will become more visible the longer the company lives.

That is why red flags in employee equity matter so much. Employees are often being asked to accept uncertainty, work hard, and believe in a future they cannot yet touch. If the company uses equity to make that bargain, then the structure has to deserve the language wrapped around it. Otherwise the cap table is not merely untidy. It is teaching people to trust a version of ownership reality that the company itself may not be able to honour.

Red Flags in Investor Terms

Investor terms rarely look dangerous at the moment they are first presented. They usually arrive wrapped in reasonableness. The investor wants to protect downside. The round should be market standard. The board needs some structure. The preference is ordinary. The anti-dilution is just there in case things go badly. The pro rata right simply lets supportive investors keep supporting. Each term can be explained plausibly on its own, and often the explanation is not even wrong. The problem is that founders who hear only the plausibility of each term and not the cumulative effect of all of them are often walking toward a cap table that becomes progressively less founder-legible, less common-friendly, and less strategically flexible. That is why red flags in investor terms matter. They are often the earliest signs that a financing is becoming more expensive in structure than it first appears in headline valuation.

The first red flag is any term that sounds standard but is never translated into scenarios. Standard is one of the most abused words in venture finance. A one-times preference may be standard. Weighted-average anti-dilution may be standard. Pro rata may be standard. Board consent rights may be standard. Yet "standard" tells the founder almost nothing unless the term is run through the company's actual structure and likely path. A term can be market-normal in isolation and still be damaging in combination with an already heavy stack, a thin founder position, or a company likely to need more capital than the founder wants to admit. The red flag is not the word standard itself. It is when standard is used to end thought rather than begin it.

Another warning sign is asymmetry that keeps growing round after round. One investor gets a preference. Another also gets a preference, perhaps stronger. One round includes pro rata. A later round adds stronger pro rata or super pro rata. Anti-dilution enters. Board rights deepen. Consent rights widen. None of these may look catastrophic when added one at a time, especially if the company is still chasing growth and each new cheque feels necessary. But if every round strengthens investor protections while weakening common economics and founder freedom, the company is not just financing growth. It is building an asymmetry machine. A healthy cap table can contain investor protection. A red-flag cap table becomes a structure in which almost every later financing deepens investor shelter while pushing more uncertainty downward into the common.

A third red flag is rights that feel modest because the investor's percentage is small. Founders often comfort themselves by saying the investor only owns ten percent or fifteen percent, so the attached rights cannot be that serious. This is exactly the wrong way to think. Rights and percentages are not the same thing. A relatively modest investor percentage can still carry meaningful board influence, information access, veto power over certain actions, preference protection, and future-round leverage. If the founder reads the percentage and emotionally discounts the rights because the stake looks "small," the founder is still reading the cap table as surface rather than as behaviour. Small-looking stakes can come with very real power if the terms are layered correctly.

Another major red flag is terms that are survivable only in success cases. This is one of the most common forms of hidden structural danger. In a strong up-round future, the preferences may convert and matter less. The anti-dilution may never trigger. The pro rata rights may feel manageable because demand for the round is high. The founder may therefore tell themselves that the term package is acceptable. But investor terms are not written mainly for the success case. They are written for the ambiguous, weaker, or more pressured paths. If the founder cannot look at the rights and ask what they do in a mediocre exit, a down round, a delayed financing, or a strategic sale that is good but not great, then the founder is not really evaluating the round. They are evaluating only the best version of the future and ignoring the one the rights were designed for.

A fifth warning sign is rights that reduce future financing flexibility in ways the founder has not modelled. Broad pro rata rights can crowd out later investors. Heavy preferences can make moderate exits unattractive to common and therefore distort company incentives. Aggressive anti-dilution can make rescue rounds or modest down rounds much more destructive than their cheque size suggests. Large consent packages can make strategic pivots or recapitalisations harder. Each of these is not just a present-round issue. It is a future-room issue. The red flag appears when the founder realises, or should realise, that the company is giving away not only economics but manoeuvrability. A well-built company can survive tough terms better than a company with no room left to move.

There is also a red flag in investor terms that seem to assume infinite founder endurance. This shows up when protections are stacked in a way that preserves investor economics very carefully while making little effort to preserve founder motivation through future dilution, moderate exits, or weaker financing conditions. A term package can be technically coherent and still economically absurd from the perspective of the people expected to keep building the business. If the rights structure seems to assume that founders will carry the company no matter how thin the common becomes or how distant meaningful liquidity is pushed, the company is entering dangerous territory. Investor protection is not the problem. Investor protection that quietly destroys founder meaning is.

Another sign to watch for is terms that no one inside the company can explain plainly. If the founder, the cofounders, and the senior team all rely entirely on counsel or the investor to interpret what the rights do, that is already a warning. This does not mean founders must become lawyers. It means the major economic and control consequences of the terms should be translatable into plain operating language. What happens in a sale. What happens in a down round. Who can block what. Who can keep buying later. What happens to the founders after another likely raise. If the terms cannot be explained in ordinary language, they are probably not understood deeply enough to be accepted with confidence. Complexity itself is not always avoidable. Unowned complexity is.

A further red flag appears when investor terms begin to solve investor anxiety by creating internal company fragility. For example, an investor may want very strong anti-dilution because they fear weaker later pricing. Rational from their side. But if that term would make any future weak round so painful that the company becomes harder to rescue, then the term is no longer merely protective. It may be destabilising. Similarly, a very strong liquidation preference may make the investor feel safe in middling outcomes, but if it pushes common economics so low that founders and key employees become increasingly indifferent to moderate exits or to continued effort beneath the stack, the company has traded investor comfort for organisational weakness. The founder should always ask whether a right protects capital in a way the company can still live with, or whether it begins solving one constituency's fear by creating another constituency's structural exhaustion.

Red flags also accumulate through precedent. Once one round grants a certain right, the next investor may treat that as a reference point, either insisting on parity or trying to improve on it. Founders who think only round by round often miss this. A term conceded today is not only a present concession. It may be the seed of tomorrow's baseline. That means a right that still seems tolerable now can become much worse once repeated, stacked, or enhanced later. This is one reason disciplined founders push back even on terms that they might barely survive in the current round. They know they are negotiating not just one contract but the tone of future contracts.

There is an emotional warning sign too. If the founder feels consistently relieved rather than clear after reading investor terms, that usually means they have accepted something because the money matters more urgently than the structure currently feels visible. Relief is not proof of a bad deal, but it is not proof of a good one either. A founder can feel relieved because the company got funded while still having accepted a rights package that will become painful later. The better emotional target is not relief alone. It is relief plus understanding. If the founder has the first without the second, caution is warranted.

The safest discipline is to test every investor term against a short list of future scenarios. What does this do in a moderate sale. What does it do in a down round. What does it do to future hiring room. What does it do after another likely raise. What does it do to founder motivation. What does it do to future lead-investor flexibility. The point is not to reject all investor protection. The point is to separate terms that support a serious company from terms that quietly convert the cap table into a structure that only works elegantly for capital.

That is what red flags in investor terms really are. They are not always dramatic. They are often reasonable-sounding protections whose cumulative effect is to make the company less fair, less flexible, less common-meaningful, or less survivable than the founder realises while the cheque is still fresh. The founder who learns to see those flags early is not becoming anti-investor. They are becoming capable of distinguishing between capital that strengthens the company and capital that enters with a rights package the company may later regret having normalised.

What a Healthy Cap Table Usually Looks Like

A healthy cap table is not one that flatters everyone, avoids all tension, or preserves some fantasy of perfect founder purity. It is one that remains coherent under growth. That is the best general test. The company can hire, raise, negotiate, and eventually consider exits without constantly discovering that old ownership decisions have made the next step harder than it should be. The structure does not need to be simple. It does need to be understandable, survivable, and aligned enough that the people carrying the business still have reason to carry it while the people funding it still have reason to keep funding it.

This is why health in a cap table is less about aesthetics than about function. A healthy structure usually tells the truth about contribution, leaves room for future development, and does not rely too heavily on hope to make the economics work. The founders are not overconcentrated to the point that talent and later capital have nowhere to go, but neither are they so diluted that the common has already become emotionally thin before the company has truly matured. The option pool is real enough to hire with, but not so bloated that it is an abstract tax on the founders for talent that may never arrive. The investor rights are serious enough to make outside capital comfortable, but not so layered that the common is crushed beneath a mountain of protections in every non-heroic outcome.

A healthy cap table is also legible. This is one of the most underrated features. An outsider with experience should be able to understand the basic story of the structure without needing a founder to rescue every awkward corner with narrative. The founders are identifiable. Their vesting or departure treatment makes sense. The options are trackable. The convertibles are modelled. The preferred classes and major rights can be explained plainly. The structure may still be complex, especially after several rounds, but it is complexity with order rather than complexity with drift. That distinction matters because legibility is a proxy for governance quality. Companies that cannot explain their cap table cleanly usually do not fully control it.

Founder motivation is one of the clearest markers of health. A strong cap table leaves founders with enough meaning in the common that the next stage is still worth building. Not because founders must always hold huge percentages, but because the relationship between effort and plausible reward remains rational. If the common only becomes meaningful at unrealistically high outcomes, then the structure may look fine on a spreadsheet while quietly damaging the company's internal engine. A healthy cap table keeps the common alive across a meaningful range of outcomes, not only at the most extravagant edge of possibility.

The same principle applies to key employees. Healthy employee equity is neither symbolic theatre nor founder-like excess. It is explainable, proportionate, and still meaningful after likely dilution. Employees may not all receive life-changing grants, but the company should not be relying on grants too thin to function while speaking as though everyone is deeply aligned. A healthy cap table usually supports an honest equity culture. The company can tell people what they have in terms that match the structure the company is actually building, rather than relying on inflated rhetoric to make small grants feel large.

Investor rights in a healthy cap table usually look balanced rather than maximal. Preferences exist, often because they are normal and reasonable, but they do not stack so aggressively that moderate exits become nearly irrelevant to common. Pro rata rights may exist, but not in a way that turns every future round into a crowded inheritance fight. Anti-dilution, if present, is usually the kind that protects against genuine repricing harm without making later rescue or recalibration impossible. Board and consent rights create discipline without turning the founders into functionaries in their own still-founder-dependent company. None of this requires softness. It requires proportion.

Another sign of health is that the cap table leaves room. Room is one of the most important and least visible features of a good structure. Room for the next round. Room for a key hire. Room for the company to survive a weaker market. Room for the founders to still matter after the next likely dilution event. Room for a moderate strategic acquisition to still be economically interesting to the common. Unhealthy cap tables often feel tight. Every future move seems to require a structural apology. Healthy ones feel as though the company can still become more than it is without first having to undo half its prior financing history.

A healthy cap table also tends to show evidence of earlier discipline. Founder vesting was not ignored. Dead equity was not allowed to fester without challenge. Early adviser and friend allocations were not handed out sentimentally in ways that still distort the present. SAFEs and notes were not allowed to pile up without modelling. Option pools were not treated as decorative. These are not glamorous achievements, but they matter because they show that the founders were willing to make hard choices before outside pressure forced them to. A healthy structure usually reflects those earlier moments of seriousness.

It is also worth noting that a healthy cap table is not necessarily one with the highest valuation history or the most famous investors. Those things can coexist with health, but they are not the same. Some of the least healthy tables are found in companies that raised impressively on paper while quietly giving away too much room, too much priority, or too much future flexibility. Likewise, some companies with more modest valuation histories have very healthy cap tables because they financed in ways that preserved founder meaning, employee credibility, and future strategic room. Health is not glamour. It is whether the ownership structure still supports the company the founders say they want to build.

A final sign of health is that the cap table can be discussed without embarrassment. Founders who know their structure and are not trying to hide from it tend to speak about it with clarity. They know the founder position, the pool, the convertibles, the major investor rights, and the broad exit economics. They do not need to pretend everything is perfect, but they are not afraid of the document either. That is often the simplest practical test. An unhealthy cap table tends to produce avoidance, euphemism, and emotional flinching. A healthy one still contains trade-offs, but the people leading the company can face those trade-offs directly.

This chapter has been about reading the cap table like an operator rather than like a spectator. A healthy cap table is what that operator is trying to preserve. Not some idealised ownership purity, but a structure that remains honest enough, flexible enough, and aligned enough that the company can keep moving without the economic machine quietly turning against its own builders.

* * *

FIFTEEN

Common Cap Table Mistakes and How to Avoid Them

"An ounce of prevention is worth a pound of cure."

- Benjamin Franklin

The Most Common Early Mistakes

Most cap table disasters do not begin as disasters. They begin as conveniences, evasions, optimistic shortcuts, or decisions made under social pressure at moments when the company still feels too small for structure to matter very much. This is why the earliest mistakes are often the most dangerous. They are made before the founders fully understand dilution, before investors arrive with harder questions, before the company has enough value for the consequences to feel heavy, and before anyone involved wants to believe that a few messy choices can later shape millions in value, years of conflict, or the difference between a clean financing and a painful one. Yet that is exactly what happens.

The first common mistake is treating the founding moment as if clarity can be postponed. Two or three people start the company, everyone is enthusiastic, nobody wants to poison the mood by talking too hard about roles, vesting, departures, future effort, or what happens if someone stops contributing. The founders split the ownership quickly, often equally, because equality feels polite and uncertainty makes all future contribution seem unknowable anyway. Sometimes that works out. Very often it plants the first structural weakness. The company begins life with a cap table designed to preserve emotional peace in the moment rather than to reflect how a startup actually evolves under strain.

The second mistake is confusing goodwill with governance. Founders assume that because they currently trust one another, the structure does not need to be rigorous. Vesting is delayed or ignored. Intellectual property assignment is treated casually. Equity promises are made in broad language rather than through disciplined documentation.

A departed contributor is left on the table because "we'll sort it later." This is one of the deepest errors in early-stage company building. Structure is not there because people distrust one another. Structure is there because trust alone is a poor operating system once time, fatigue, money, and misalignment begin to do their work.

A third very common mistake is giving away equity before the company has learned how expensive equity really is. In the earliest stage, percentages feel abstract. One percent here, two percent there, a few points to a helpful adviser, a meaningful chunk to a prospective cofounder, perhaps an informal promise to someone who made introductions or did a brief but memorable burst of work. These allocations can feel generous without feeling costly because the company is still small, uncertain, and unpriced. The founders are spending from a future they cannot yet emotionally value. That is why early-stage equity sloppiness is so common. The company is writing cheques on a value structure that only later becomes legible.

Another mistake is speaking about equity far more loosely than the company is willing to document it. Founders say things like "we'll make you whole," "you'll have a piece of this," "you're in from the ground floor," or "there'll definitely be upside for you" without deciding what those statements mean structurally. The result is a company with two cap tables. One is the visible one on the spreadsheet. The other is the shadow one made of expectations, half-promises, remembered conversations, and emotionally live but formally unresolved claims. That shadow table is one of the most reliable predictors of later conflict. The company believes it has kept flexibility. In reality it has accumulated ambiguity.

The next major mistake is not distinguishing between current ownership and future ownership pressure. Founders sometimes think the cap table is only about issued shares. They may ignore the effect of deferred instruments, option pools not yet fully granted, or promised grants not yet documented. This produces a form of blindness that can persist for months or years. The founder sees the clean present picture and does not emotionally register the claims already waiting in the wings. Then a financing or a sale forces those hidden elements into the open and the founders feel shocked by how much of the future was already spoken for. The problem was never that the information did not exist. The problem was that the founders treated the current issued picture as the whole truth.

Another early mistake is failing to think sequentially. A founder may calculate that a current round, grant, or pool expansion is survivable and stop there. What they do not ask is what that position becomes after the next likely financing event. This is one of the most dangerous forms of cap table naïveté because a founder can be right in the narrow present tense and still be heading rapidly toward an over-thin or over-layered structure. Startups rarely stop after one round, one pool, or one conversion event. Every decision lives inside a chain. Founders who think in isolated moments often make choices that seem tolerable now and become destructive later.

There is also the mistake of treating legal documents as though they are for later translation rather than immediate comprehension. Some founders are comfortable not fully understanding the details of notes, SAFEs, preferences, or anti-dilution because they assume counsel or investors will explain them if and when the terms matter. That attitude is expensive. It means the founder is participating in the creation of the company's ownership architecture without really knowing what kind of company is being architected. Professional advice is essential, but it is not a substitute for founder understanding. A founder who signs what they do not truly understand is not merely outsourcing detail. They are outsourcing part of their own future bargaining position and economic literacy.

A further common mistake is assuming early-stage mess can always be cleaned up cheaply later. Sometimes it can. Often it can be reduced rather than eliminated. But later clean-up nearly always costs more than early discipline, because by then the stakes are higher, the relationships are colder, and the value at issue is more real. An adviser who might once have accepted a token grant or a clarification may become far less flexible once the company looks valuable. A departed cofounder who could once have been bought out cleanly may now hold leverage. A vague promise that felt socially soft at the beginning may harden into a live dispute once real money is on the table. The company that keeps postponing ownership discipline is usually not avoiding pain. It is compounding it.

Another mistake is failing to align the cap table with the kind of company being built. Some companies are capital-light, revenue-driven, and can preserve founder ownership longer without great harm. Others are talent-heavy, capital-hungry, and likely to need multiple rounds plus serious employee equity.

Founders often borrow structural instincts from startup culture generically instead of from the real demands of their own business. One company hoards founder ownership as though it will never need serious external capital. Another gives away equity too liberally as though dilution is always harmless because "that's what startups do." Both are reading a myth rather than their company. The cap table should follow business reality, not startup folklore.

There is also the very human mistake of letting embarrassment delay correction. Once founders realise the table is weaker than they want to admit, many stop looking closely because looking would force them to acknowledge that the company is living on borrowed clarity. This avoidance is understandable. It is also destructive. A messy structure does not improve because the founders stop staring at it. It simply remains quiet until an investor, acquirer, employee dispute, or financing event makes silence impossible. Some of the worst cap table outcomes happen not because the founders never understood anything, but because they understood enough to be embarrassed and then chose not to act while there was still room.

What ties all these early mistakes together is not stupidity. It is a repeated refusal to let structure become real while the company still feels young, personal, and emotionally fluid. Founders want momentum, hope, harmony, and speed. The cap table asks for definition, discipline, and consequences. When the founders keep choosing the former without enough of the latter, the company gets an ownership history that feels friendly at the beginning and expensive later.

That is why the most common early mistakes deserve such serious attention. They are not minor blemishes on an otherwise strong business. They are often the first cracks in the foundation of the ownership system itself. A company can survive many of them. But the earlier they are seen for what they are, the better the chances that the cap table becomes a structure the company can still grow inside rather than a record of all the moments when people chose comfort over clarity.

Splitting Founder Equity Badly

Few cap table mistakes do more long-term damage than a bad founder split made early and then left to harden. This is because founder equity is not just one allocation among many. It is the base layer on which almost everything else gets built. Future hiring, investor confidence, founder motivation, governance trust, and even the emotional tone of the company often rest on whether the founding ownership structure still makes sense once the romantic blur of the beginning has passed. If that base layer is wrong, later rounds and later rights do not replace the problem. They build on top of it.

The most obvious bad split is the one that is plainly unfair in hindsight, but that is not the only kind. Some bad splits are lopsided from the start. One founder takes almost everything while others are expected to contribute at a level the ownership clearly does not honour. Those cases are easy to identify. The more common and more subtle bad split is the one that feels superficially fair because it avoided conflict at the beginning. Equal thirds. Equal halves. Equal quarters. Everyone was excited, everyone mattered, everyone wanted to move quickly, and nobody wanted to poison the energy by asking who would still be here in three years, who was taking the real career risk, who was working full time, who brought a replaceable skill, and who was actually carrying the business idea into the market. So the split was made for peace rather than for truth.

This is why bad founder splits often look noble before they look weak. They are presented as trust, solidarity, friendship, or team spirit. Sometimes they are all of those things. But a startup is not a symbolic gesture. It is an evolving burden. The real test of the split comes later, when one founder is working twelve-hour days, another is still "advising" around a day job, another leaves, another underperforms, and another turns out to be central in a way no one fully saw at formation. At that point the early split stops being a moral gesture and becomes a piece of infrastructure. If it was not designed to survive unequal reality, it begins to feel unjust.

The reason this becomes so damaging is that founder equity has a way of turning private disappointment into structural drag. If one founder feels underrewarded relative to what they now carry, that feeling does not remain purely emotional. It affects decisions, negotiation stance, willingness to stay through hard periods, and sometimes how aggressively the founder pushes to correct the structure later. If another founder feels overprotected by the early split, they may unconsciously rely on a position no longer earned by their current contribution. The company then starts operating inside a false ownership story. Everyone may continue behaving politely for a while, but the cap table is already out of sync with the work.

This is one reason investors care so much about founder splits. They are not only asking whether the founders like each other. They are asking whether the ownership structure still reflects a plausible operating reality. A cap table in which one founder appears clearly overcompensated for current contribution, or one in which a critical founder is already thin relative to burden, signals risk. The company may still succeed, but it is carrying a built-in incentive distortion. Later financing cannot solve that neatly. In fact, later dilution often makes it worse, because once everyone's percentages fall, a founder who was already misallocated begins to feel the mismatch even more sharply.
A particularly dangerous form of bad founder splitting happens when one founder is brought in late but treated as if they were there from the very beginning, or when someone with an important but narrower function is treated as a full economic equal to the person carrying the company's whole strategic and operational weight. Again, this can feel generous or harmonious at the time. But if the roles are not truly equal in risk and burden, then the ownership equality becomes unstable. The company eventually discovers that equality of sentiment is not the same as equality of contribution. By then, changing the split may be emotionally and legally much harder than getting it roughly right would have been earlier.

Another common error is failing to separate idea value from company-building value. Founders sometimes give large equity weight to the person who first articulated the concept, even when that person is not the one turning the concept into an actual enterprise. Ideas matter. But in most startups, the overwhelming share of value is created after the idea stage, through execution, hiring, iteration, sales, fundraising, and endurance. A founder split that overpays for conception and underpays for sustained execution is often a split that will age badly. The company becomes trapped inside an origin myth while the real work happens elsewhere.

This is where vesting becomes indispensable. A founder split can begin imperfectly and still remain survivable if vesting exists and is taken seriously. Without vesting, a weak split hardens immediately. With vesting, the company at least retains a mechanism by which continued participation determines how much of the initial allocation becomes permanent. That is not a magic cure. A badly chosen split can still cause pain even under vesting. But vesting turns founder ownership from pure declaration into something more conditional and more aligned with actual staying power.

When founder splits are made badly and vesting is absent or ignored, the company has almost no structural defence against future resentment or dead equity.

A founder who wants to assess whether the split is bad should ask a short set of uncomfortable questions. If we started this company today, knowing what we now know about actual roles and actual burden, would we allocate it the same way. If one founder left tomorrow, would the remaining structure still feel rational. After likely future dilution, who will still be meaningfully motivated and who may already feel thin. Does this split reflect friendship, conflict avoidance, or narrative sentiment more than it reflects present and future contribution. Those questions do not produce perfect answers, but if the honest answer to several of them is no, the split is probably weaker than the team wants to admit.

This is also one of the areas where delay becomes costly very quickly.

A weak founder split is easiest to address when the company is still early enough that everyone can acknowledge uncertainty and adjust with relatively modest pain. Once outside money arrives, once valuation rises, or once one founder has emotionally attached their identity to the percentage they hold, correction becomes harder. The company moves from "we should fix this" to "how do we unwind this without blowing up trust or losing someone." That is why bad splits so often persist long past the point where everyone privately knows they are wrong. They become too expensive socially to revisit, and then even more expensive economically to live with.

It is important not to become simplistic here. There is no universal correct founder split formula. Some equal splits are entirely justified. Some unequal splits are excellent. The point is not that one pattern is always right. The point is that a good split must survive contact with actual startup life. It must be able to carry unequal burden, uncertain future roles, possible departures, and later dilution without turning the founder layer of the company into a source of permanent low-grade instability. A split that cannot do that is bad even if it felt virtuous when signed.

That is why splitting founder equity badly is not merely one common mistake among many. It is one of the foundational mistakes from which later cap table distortion often grows. If the people meant to carry the company do not have a structure that still makes sense once the work becomes real, every later financing event enters a weakened human system.

And once that happens, the cap table is no longer just recording ownership. It is preserving an early misunderstanding of what the company would require.

Delaying Vesting Too Long

Few ownership decisions are regretted as consistently as delaying founder vesting because everything feels harmonious at the beginning. The startup is still small. Everyone is energised. The company may not even feel fully real yet. At that stage, vesting can seem unnecessarily formal, almost insulting. Why talk about what happens if someone leaves when everyone is still speaking the language of mission, belief, and shared sacrifice. This is exactly why vesting gets delayed, and exactly why delaying it is so often a mistake. By the time vesting feels emotionally easy to introduce, it is usually much harder economically and politically to impose.

The problem is not that founders fail to understand vesting in theory. Many know perfectly well that vesting exists to prevent someone from walking away early with a large permanent stake. The problem is that the early atmosphere of trust makes the risk feel hypothetical. The team thinks in present loyalty rather than future divergence. But startups are machines for creating divergence. Roles change. Energy changes. Skill differences become visible. One founder goes full time while another hesitates. One becomes central. Another becomes peripheral. Personal lives intervene. Health changes. The market proves harsher than hoped. By the time these differences become obvious, the ownership already exists if vesting was delayed or ignored. The company is then left trying to retrofit discipline into a structure built on early optimism.

This is why delayed vesting is so dangerous. It takes what should have been a routine founding safeguard and turns it into a later political event. If vesting is in place from the start, it feels normal. It is simply part of how the company works. If it is introduced later, it feels accusatory. Suddenly the founders are no longer talking abstractly about good governance. They are talking, however politely, about the possibility that someone in this very room may not deserve to keep everything they currently appear to own. That is much harder. The same term that would have felt ordinary at formation now feels personal because reality has already begun to separate the team.

A common pattern looks like this. Two or three founders split the company, perhaps equally, perhaps just quickly. No vesting is put in place because everyone assumes they will sort out the paperwork later. The company starts moving. After six months or a year, one founder has done far more than the others. Another has become intermittent. Another is clearly less committed than their ownership suggests. Now the active founder realises that if someone leaves, the cap table will be stuck with a large block of dead equity. Vesting is suddenly urgent. But urgency has arrived after the moral innocence of the founding moment has gone. The conversation is no longer about principle. It is about whether people who have already mentally accepted their ownership will agree to place conditions on it.

This is one reason some of the worst founder disputes begin not with money itself, but with timing. Everyone might have accepted vesting at the start. Later, one founder sees it as essential protection and another sees it as a retroactive threat. The company is then arguing not only about fairness but about history. "If you wanted vesting, you should have said so earlier." "We all assumed this was earned at formation." "I have already given up a year for this." "You have barely been here for half of it." The longer vesting is delayed, the more these arguments shift from abstract governance to personal grievance.

Delaying vesting also distorts investor conversations. Sophisticated investors expect founder vesting or at least founder ownership that has been structured with similar discipline. If the company reaches an external financing without vesting in place, investors often push for it then. Founders sometimes misread this as intrusive or distrustful. In reality, the company is now being forced to confront a basic structural weakness it should have addressed itself earlier. Worse still, if vesting is imposed only at the point of financing, the founders may feel that discipline was introduced for the investor's benefit rather than for the health of the company. That can create resentment even when the investor is right. Early self-discipline avoids that.

Another problem is that delayed vesting makes founder departures much more expensive. If a founder leaves early and there was no vesting, the company may have little leverage to reclaim or repurchase the unearned portion on sensible terms. What should have returned automatically to the company is now a negotiation, and negotiations in these situations are rarely clean. The departing founder may feel morally entitled to keep a large stake because they were there at the beginning.

The remaining founders may feel betrayed by the idea that an early but short contribution should permanently burden the business. Without vesting, both sides have room to feel justified. The cap table is left carrying the cost.

There is also a subtler cost. Even if no founder leaves, the absence of vesting changes how contribution is felt internally. If ownership is fully locked in too early, then later differences in effort do not naturally feed back into the structure. That can create a low-grade sense of unfairness even inside a team that remains outwardly intact. One founder knows they are carrying more than another and also knows the cap table no longer has any built-in mechanism for recognising that fact. Over time, that knowledge hardens. The company continues, but the founder layer becomes more brittle because the structure no longer feels responsive to actual burden.

It is important to say that vesting is not only a punishment device. Founders sometimes speak about it as though it exists to threaten people who might leave. In a better reading, vesting is a way of matching long-term ownership to long-term building. It protects the active team. It protects future hires from being asked to work under dead equity. It protects later investors from inheriting unexamined founder drift. It even protects the founder who remains, because it prevents them from discovering too late that the company's first layer of ownership was built on trust alone when trust could no longer do the work.

The practical lesson is blunt. Vesting is easiest and healthiest when agreed before anyone has much leverage to personalise it. If the company has already delayed too long, then the founders should still confront the issue rather than hide from it, but they should do so knowing the conversation is now harder because they waited. The longer the delay, the less vesting feels like governance and the more it feels like accusation. That is the real cost of postponement.

A founder reading the cap table properly should therefore treat absent or weak founder vesting as a red flag even if the team currently feels stable. Stability now is not proof the structure is sound. It may simply mean the company has not yet reached the moment that tests whether ownership was tied to staying power or handed out as though the future were already known. Startups have a brutal habit of revealing exactly how little of the future was known at formation.

That is why delaying vesting too long is such a common and expensive mistake. It takes one of the clearest early tools for keeping founder ownership honest and waits until honesty has become socially difficult. By then the company is not preventing dead equity. It is negotiating with it in advance.

Giving Away Advisory Equity Too Easily

Few equity mistakes feel smaller in the moment and larger in hindsight than giving away advisory equity too easily. This is because advisers often arrive at exactly the stage when founders are most vulnerable to flattery, most uncertain about what kind of help they truly need, and least emotionally calibrated to the future cost of ownership. A well-connected person shows interest. Someone experienced offers guidance. A former operator, investor, executive, or industry figure says they would like to help. The founders are grateful, excited, and often a little intimidated. Equity then becomes the easy language of seriousness. Instead of asking what work is actually being done, over what period, with what accountability, and for what measurable value, the company often jumps straight to the symbolism of giving someone "a piece" of the business.

That is how advisory equity becomes expensive.

The first problem is that advisory relationships are usually much looser than founders imagine at the start. A cofounder is expected to build. An employee is expected to work. An investor is expected to fund. An adviser, by contrast, often occupies a much more ambiguous space. They may genuinely want to help, but the help may be irregular, soft, hard to measure, and highly dependent on circumstance. A few calls. Some comments on strategy. One or two introductions. Occasional encouragement. Sometimes that can be valuable. But the startup often grants equity as though the adviser is entering a much more durable and accountable relationship than reality will later support.

This is why advisory equity is so often over-granted. Founders price the relationship according to what they hope it will become rather than what it actually proves to be. The adviser is imagined as someone who may open big doors, transform fundraising, shape major decisions, or lend enormous credibility to the company. Sometimes that happens. More often the relationship settles into something much thinner.

A founder who looked at the future glow of the adviser's reputation and gave away a meaningful piece of the company may later realise that the actual return on that equity was a handful of calls and some goodwill. The problem was not always bad faith. It was that hope was mistaken for contribution.

Another reason this mistake is common is that advisers often arrive before founders have developed any discipline around valuing ownership. In the very early stage, a quarter of a percent, half a percent, even one percent can sound small. The company is not yet priced. The founders are not yet thinking in waterfalls. The cap table still feels mostly like a conceptual map of possibility rather than a machine that will later allocate real value. This makes advisory equity feel cheap. It is only later, when multiple such grants exist or when the company becomes more valuable, that the founders begin to see they were not giving away something symbolic. They were allocating future ownership capacity to people whose long-term claim on the company may never have deserved that scale.

A further problem is that advisory work is easy to confuse with investor friendliness, networking, or founder reassurance. Someone knowledgeable may speak to the founders for an hour, make them feel seen, and offer a few useful suggestions. That interaction can feel significant because the founders are under pressure and hungry for guidance. But significance of feeling is not the same as significance of long-term company value. Equity should usually reward durable contribution or durable alignment, not merely moments of useful attention. When founders start paying in ownership for emotional uplift or aspirational access rather than for structured help, the cap table begins to absorb sentiment in a form it will later struggle to justify.

This is why a bad advisory grant often has a particular smell to it. The company cannot clearly explain what the adviser was meant to do, what they actually did, what the grant size was based on, how long the relationship was meant to last, or why the contribution could not have been handled through a much smaller grant, a vesting schedule, a cash fee, or simply informal goodwill. The ownership is there. The story is hazy. That mismatch is a red flag. A healthy cap table should be able to explain why each meaningful line item exists. If an adviser's equity only makes sense when told through a glow of founder gratitude, then the grant was probably too loose from the start.

One of the clearest mistakes is granting advisory equity without vesting. This is almost always structurally weak. If the adviser disappears after two meetings, loses interest, or never produces the hoped-for value, the company is then left with dead equity in one of the least defensible forms. The whole point of vesting in these contexts is to match actual continuing service with continuing earning of the grant. Without it, the company is effectively paying upfront for a future relationship that may never really exist. That is the sort of bargain founders only make when they are still thinking of equity as cheap.

Even with vesting, founders often still make the error of granting too much because they never defined the role tightly enough. An adviser should usually be understood as a specific, bounded contribution relationship. Not a mystical elder hovering above the company, but someone expected to help in identifiable ways over a defined period. If the role is broad, vague, and reputation-based, the company is much more likely to pay for imagined strategic gravity rather than actual delivered value. This is why disciplined companies often ask simple questions before any advisory grant is made. What exactly do we need from this person. What would good performance look like. How often will they engage. What access are they truly giving. What comparable help could we buy with cash later if needed. If those questions do not produce concrete answers, equity is usually the wrong instrument or at least the wrong scale.

There is also a compounding danger. One advisory grant may be survivable even if it is a little generous. Several such grants, made over time to different impressive or supportive figures, begin to create a fog of legacy ownership with very weak operational justification. Later investors notice this. Future employees notice this if they understand the table. Active founders feel it when they realise meaningful pieces of the company are sitting with people who are not carrying current burden. The harm is not only arithmetic. It is symbolic. The cap table starts saying that the company paid liberally for peripheral contribution while expecting deep sacrifice from the people still doing the real work.

This becomes especially toxic if the advisers are retained mostly for signalling. Some founders give away equity to have names associated with the company, hoping it will impress later investors or customers. That can sometimes have strategic value, but it is often overestimated.

If the person's involvement is shallow, the market eventually sees that shallowness. The founder then discovers they spent real ownership for a layer of reflected prestige that did not translate into durable leverage. Again, the mistake is not that signalling never matters. It is that signalling is often too soft a reason to support a lasting equity grant unless the strategic value is unusually concrete.

A disciplined founder should therefore be sceptical of any advisory equity decision that is being made quickly, emotionally, or out of vague ambition. The right questions are not glamorous. Is the grant small enough to reflect the role honestly. Is there vesting. Is the advisory relationship specific enough to evaluate. Is the company buying something it could not reasonably secure through cash or gratitude or informal contact. Would we still think this grant made sense a year from now if the adviser contributed only modestly. If the answer to that last question is no, the company is probably granting from excitement rather than judgment.

None of this means advisers are useless or should never receive equity. Some advisers are genuinely pivotal. They may open critical commercial doors, provide sustained technical guidance, help recruit major talent, or shape the company's path in ways well worth rewarding. But those cases are the exception, not the default. The founders who understand this are much less likely to confuse prestigious association with real company-building. They reserve meaningful ownership for people whose contribution will still look meaningful when the romance of the early relationship has faded.

That is why giving away advisory equity too easily is such a classic early mistake. It feels sophisticated, relational, and low-cost when the company is young. Later it often looks like one of the purest forms of undisciplined spending the cap table ever recorded.

Ignoring Small Grants That Add Up

One of the easiest ways a cap table gets quietly worse is not through one dramatic mistake, but through a series of small grants that each seem too minor to worry about. A quarter of a percent here. A few options there. A small advisory promise. A token allocation to someone helpful. A special case made for an early supporter. None of these looks fatal on its own. That is exactly the problem.

Because each grant feels small, the founder often treats it as beneath serious structural scrutiny. The company is not giving away "real" ownership, only a tiny sliver. Yet the cap table does not care whether the founders felt relaxed when they made the decision. Small grants accumulate. Over time they become real.

This is one of the most common forms of cap table drift. The founders are usually not behaving recklessly in a dramatic sense. They are simply failing to apply the same seriousness to small allocations that they would apply to a major financing event. The logic feels harmless. It is only a little bit. This person helped. The amount is tiny. It avoids an awkward conversation. It keeps someone warm. It shows goodwill. The company keeps spending future ownership to solve present social discomfort, and because no single act looks large enough to trigger alarm, the cumulative effect remains psychologically invisible until much later.

That invisibility is what makes this mistake so dangerous.

A founder who would resist giving away five percent in one clean motion may end up giving away more than that across a year of tiny, emotionally justified exceptions. The harm is not just numerical, although the numbers matter. The harm is that each micro-allocation lowers the discipline threshold for the next one. Once the company has established that equity can be used casually to smooth relationships, reward informal help, or purchase goodwill without much internal challenge, it becomes much easier to keep doing it. The cap table then develops not as a strategic architecture, but as a sediment of small compromises.

This matters especially because small grants often go to people whose contribution is difficult to revisit later. The company may not even keep close track of why each grant was made. A founder may remember the general mood but not the specific bargain. Years later, a meaningful slice of the business may be sitting across several names that no longer feel central, and no one can cleanly explain why those people are there in the size they are there. This is one of the reasons later investors dislike cluttered cap tables. The problem is not only that the grants exist. It is that they reflect a company that spent ownership in increments too small to feel serious while still being large enough to matter in aggregate.

There is also a measurement problem. Founders often think small in percentage terms without converting those percentages into share-count reality or later economic reality. Half a percent sounds tiny. In a company that later becomes valuable, it may be worth a great deal. Even before that, it may represent significant hiring room, founder room, or future flexibility. This is why strong operators do not ask only whether a grant is small. They ask whether it is small relative to what the company still needs to reserve for later and whether the contribution being rewarded truly justifies permanent space in the structure. A grant can be small and still be a bad use of ownership.

Another version of this problem appears inside option pools. A founder may tell themselves that a particular grant is not worth serious thought because it comes "out of the pool" rather than directly from founder shares. But the pool is not free. It is already diluted space. Each small grant still spends part of a finite resource the company will later need for stronger hires or retention decisions. A company that treats the pool as a soft cushion for every minor people issue often discovers later that the pool was eaten by a thousand tolerable-seeming decisions instead of being concentrated on the people who truly mattered most.

This is also where fairness becomes slippery. Small grants often feel easier to approve because denying them can make the founder feel petty. The amount is modest. The recipient was helpful. Refusing can feel meaner than giving. Yet this is precisely how cap tables become emotionally governed rather than structurally governed. The company starts using ownership not as a long-term strategic instrument, but as a politeness tool. Strong founders learn to separate generosity from ownership. They can be grateful without writing permanent cap table entries every time gratitude is deserved.

One of the best tests here is simple. If this grant were multiplied by ten similar grants over the next year, would the company still feel comfortable. If the answer is no, then the founder is not evaluating the grant properly as part of a pattern. Another good test is whether the company could explain the grant to a future investor without embarrassment. "This person did a little bit and we wanted to be nice" is not usually a strong structural reason for ownership. If the founder would not want to defend the grant in a serious financing conversation, that is a warning sign even if the percentage looks tiny today.

The discipline required is not complicated. Small grants should still be forced through the same core questions as large ones. What exactly is being rewarded. Why is equity the right instrument. Is the amount proportionate. Is there vesting. What future room is being spent. Would this still look sensible if repeated several times. If those questions are not worth asking because the grant feels "too small," that usually means the founder is thinking in emotional units rather than capital structure units.

That is why ignoring small grants that add up is such a classic mistake. It is cap table entropy in slow motion. No single decision looks serious enough to trigger fear, but together they create a structure full of weakly justified ownership that the active company must later live beneath. The best way to avoid it is not to become miserly. It is to remember that ownership is most often damaged not by one reckless moment, but by many easy ones.

Letting the Cap Table Drift Without Review

One of the most damaging habits in startup ownership is not a single bad decision but the absence of a recurring discipline. The company makes a founder split. It adds an adviser. It grants a few options. It signs a SAFE. It raises a round. It enlarges the pool. It hires someone senior. Another note appears. A founder leaves. A secondary happens. None of these events is ignored in the moment. Papers are signed. Numbers are updated. The spreadsheet changes. Yet the cap table as a whole is never really reviewed. It is maintained, but not governed. It moves, but no one stands back and asks what it has now become. That is drift.

Drift is dangerous because cap tables do not usually announce when they have crossed from healthy complexity into structural weakness. They simply become a little harder to explain, a little more crowded, a little less founder-aligned, a little more preference-heavy, a little more dependent on hopeful assumptions about future rounds or future exits. Each change has a justification. The company keeps moving. Because there is no obvious moment of collapse, the founders tell themselves that the structure must still be broadly fine. In reality, they may simply have stopped examining it at the level required to notice that the company is gradually financing itself into a narrower and narrower future.

This is why review matters so much. A cap table is not a one-time design problem solved at formation and then occasionally touched when external events force it. It is a living structure that needs periodic interpretation. Not because founders should become obsessed with the spreadsheet, but because without review the business loses one of the few chances it has to detect structural weakness before that weakness becomes expensive. The company reviews product. It reviews finances. It reviews hiring plans. It reviews strategy. If ownership is never reviewed with the same seriousness, then one of the most consequential systems in the company is being left largely to inertia.

The easiest way to spot drift is to ask whether the founders can still answer basic structural questions without hesitation. Who owns what on a fully diluted basis. What meaningful rights sit above the common. What happens if the SAFEs convert in the next priced round. How much room remains in the pool. What does the founder position look like after the next likely financing. What sale values still matter for common. Which small grants are still justified. Which legacy lines on the table would be awkward to defend to a serious new investor. If the answers to these questions have become fuzzy, stale, or dependent on opening multiple old files and reconstructing history from memory, drift has already begun.

A particularly common form of drift occurs when the company keeps updating the table mechanically but never re-reads it strategically. The share counts are current. The percentages sum properly. The latest round is entered. The model is technically "right." Yet no one has asked whether the new state still makes sense. This is one of the clearest examples of the difference between bookkeeping and governance. Bookkeeping records what happened. Governance asks whether what happened has created a company that is still worth building inside. A startup can be very tidy administratively and still be drifting strategically.

This becomes especially serious after financing events. A round closes and everyone feels relief. The company now has cash. The legal work is done. Attention returns to execution. That is understandable. But the post-round moment is exactly when the founders should revisit the cap table in its new form. What is the real founder position now. What future rights have entered. What preferences are stacked. What pool room remains. What has become easier, and what has quietly become harder.

If that review never happens, the company may continue talking internally as though it still occupies the simpler pre-round structure that existed emotionally before the financing, even though the actual company has changed materially.

Another form of drift comes from treating old assumptions as if they remain valid after the company evolves. The founders may still be quoting option percentages or valuation narratives that made sense two rounds ago. They may still think of a certain adviser grant as negligible even though the company is now much more valuable. They may still assume a particular exit range is attractive without having re-run the waterfall after new preferred layers were added. The cap table has changed, but the mental model has not. This is one of the most dangerous kinds of drift because the company begins making present decisions through an outdated ownership imagination.

Review is also where founders catch the buildup of small errors that no single event seemed important enough to challenge. A few under-analysed grants. A slightly too-generous early concession. A stale option pool assumption. A conversion effect no one has re-modelled since the market changed. None of these may matter much alone. Together they can produce a company whose ownership logic no longer matches its operating reality. Without recurring review, the founders only discover the accumulation when an investor, acquirer, or conflict forces the entire structure into the open at once.

There is also a human reason drift happens. Reviewing the cap table properly can be unpleasant. It may reveal that the founders have less room than they thought, that common economics are thinner than hoped, that some earlier generosity was structurally foolish, or that future financing will be more painful than current optimism likes to admit. Founders therefore postpone review not because they do not know it matters, but because they sense that real review may remove comforting illusions. This is understandable. It is also exactly why the discipline matters. Structures do not become kinder because they are left unexamined.

A good review process does not need to be elaborate. It needs to be regular and serious. After every major financing. After every meaningful pool expansion. After any significant founder departure. After signing deferred instruments.

Before major hiring phases. Before acquisition discussions. And periodically even without any crisis, simply because the company has changed enough that the ownership structure deserves to be re-read. In those reviews, the founders should ask not only what the cap table now says, but whether it still looks healthy, financeable, legible, and motivational.

The best companies also understand that review is not only for investor benefit. It is one of the few forms of founder self-protection available in a structure that tends naturally to become more complex over time. A founder who reviews the cap table regularly is much less likely to be ambushed by later dilution, preference consequences, or option-pool shortfalls. They may still have to accept painful realities. But they accept them earlier, while there is still room to adapt, rather than later, when the company is already cornered.

That is why letting the cap table drift without review is such a serious mistake. It turns ownership from something the company is actively designing into something the company passively inherits from its own prior decisions. By the time that inheritance becomes visible, it is often heavier than the founders realised. Review is how you stop the cap table from quietly becoming a stranger to the company that depends on it.

Fixing Problems Before Investors Force You To

There is a large difference between a company that cleans its cap table because it understands the need for discipline and a company that cleans it because an investor has finally made avoidance impossible. The difference is not only pride. It is cost, leverage, and timing. When founders fix ownership problems early, they usually still have some control over the process. When investors force the clean-up, the same issues are often resolved under pressure, under scrutiny, and with much less room for nuance. That is why one of the best habits a founder can build is simple: fix the problem before someone outside the company turns it into a condition.

This matters because investors are very good at spotting structural weakness once they care enough to look. Dead equity. Missing vesting. Option pools that make no strategic sense. SAFEs or notes piled up without clear modelling.

Founder splits that no longer match reality. Shadow promises never properly resolved. Old grants the company seems embarrassed to explain. These things may sit quietly for months or years while the startup is small. Once a real financing is in view, they stop being background noise. They become friction. The investor is not only asking whether the company is exciting. The investor is asking whether the structure is clean enough that new money can enter without first inheriting a mess.

That is where founder timing becomes decisive. If the company addresses those issues first, it can often do so from inside its own logic. The founders can explain the problem to one another honestly. The team can negotiate with a departed cofounder before outside valuation makes their stake feel heavier. Vesting can be added or tightened while the conversation is still about prudence rather than suspicion. Small grants can be revisited while they are still small enough that adjustment feels possible. The company can frame the clean-up as part of becoming more serious. Once investors are pushing, the same clean-up may feel accusatory, defensive, or reactive. The company is no longer fixing itself because it wants to. It is doing so because capital has made that repair a gate.

This is one reason self-directed clean-up is almost always cheaper. Not only in legal fees, though that matters, but in emotional and structural cost. A founder who goes back to an old adviser or early contributor before the company looks obviously financeable may still have room to renegotiate, clarify, or reduce a questionable grant. The same conversation later, when the business has investor attention and a live financing process, is much harder. The person on the other side knows there is now something real at stake. What could have been solved by straightforward discussion may now require leverage, formal concessions, or awkward side arrangements. Delay makes nearly every ownership problem more expensive.

Another reason early fixing matters is that investors interpret reactive clean-up differently from proactive clean-up. A company that says, before being asked, we reviewed our structure, identified weak spots, corrected them, and can explain why, sounds disciplined. A company that says, after an investor points to the issue, yes, we know that is a problem and we are trying to sort it, sounds like a company that needed to be told. The underlying structural flaw may be the same in both cases. The signal about founder judgment is very different.

Since so much of fundraising rests on trust in the founder's ability to govern complexity, that signal matters more than many first-time founders realise.
This is especially important because investors are not always wrong about what needs fixing, but they are not always aligned with the company's softest or most humane path to fixing it either. When an investor spots a cap table issue, their instinct is usually to remove uncertainty before they commit money. That is rational from their side. But it can make the company's repair work harsher than necessary. They may push for clean outcomes quickly, with little patience for emotional history or founder nuance. If the company has already done the work itself, it can often preserve more control over how the solution is reached and avoid being pushed into a repair process shaped mainly by the investor's risk tolerance rather than by the company's broader health.

A good example is dead founder equity. If the active team recognises early that an old split or unvested position no longer reflects contribution, there may still be time to negotiate a sensible repurchase, reduction, or reset while the issue is morally clear and before the company's rising value intensifies everyone's sense of entitlement. If the matter is left untouched until a lead investor says this must be fixed before we invest, the conversation often becomes much sharper. The departed founder may feel they are being squeezed out because money is on the line. The active founders may feel humiliated that their old avoidance is now visible to outsiders. The investor may have little interest in the emotional delicacy of the history. The same problem, left too long, becomes structurally and socially harder.

The same principle applies to convertible instruments, pool sizing, informal promises, and muddled advisory grants. Problems that can still be described internally as things we should clean up tend later to become things that now threaten the round. Once that happens, urgency enters. Urgency is bad for ownership conversations. It makes everyone more defensive, more positional, and more aware that the outcome now affects immediate financing leverage. Founders who fix earlier are not only being tidier. They are preserving the chance to solve ownership questions before urgency distorts them.

It is also worth noticing that some problems are easier to fix gradually than suddenly. A company can develop a habit of reviewing tiny advisory allocations, rationalising stale commitments, tightening grant language, and modelling deferred instruments properly over time. These are small acts of maintenance. If ignored, they later present as a single big clean-up project under investor glare. The founders then tell themselves they are dealing with one painful episode, when in truth they are paying the accumulated price of not having maintained the structure continuously. That accumulated price is almost always heavier than the cost of gradual correction would have been.

Another reason to fix early is founder morale. Cap table problems left untouched have a way of draining confidence even before outsiders comment on them. Founders may not talk openly about it, but many know when the structure contains weak spots. They know the old split is soft. They know the adviser grant looks silly. They know the SAFE stack has not been modelled tightly enough. That knowledge sits in the background and subtly erodes the founder's sense of control. When the company finally addresses those issues, especially before a financing crisis forces the matter, it often feels not merely like administrative improvement but like regaining authorship over the company's own structure.

This is why one of the strongest operator habits is to ask, regularly, what would a serious investor make us fix if they looked at this today. Then fix as much of it as the company reasonably can before anyone asks. That question is not about becoming subservient to investor taste. It is about using outside scrutiny as a mirror before the stakes of that scrutiny become immediate. A founder who can answer it honestly is usually already halfway to the correct clean-up list.

Of course, not every problem can be fully fixed. Some old grants cannot be unwound easily. Some departed founders will not cooperate. Some weak earlier rounds cannot be erased. A company may have to live with some scar tissue. The point is not perfection. The point is ownership of the repair process. Founders should never wait for an investor to be the first person in the room taking the cap table seriously. By then the company is already negotiating from weakness.

That is why fixing problems before investors force you to is one of the clearest signs that a founder has moved from reacting to structure to governing it. You are not just trying to make the table look nicer for due diligence. You are trying to make sure the company is not carrying avoidable weaknesses into the moment when capital becomes expensive, scrutiny becomes real, and every old compromise starts asking to be paid for.

* * *

SIXTEEN

Repairing, Reframing, and Living With an Imperfect Cap Table

"Do what you can, with what you have, where you are."
- Theodore Roosevelt

Not Every Bad Cap Table Can Be Made Perfect

One of the most important emotional shifts a founder has to make is the shift from wanting a perfect cap table to wanting a workable one. This matters because once a company has been alive for any length of time, especially if it has already raised, hired, promised, drifted, or improvised, the structure usually contains some scar tissue. There may be an early split that no longer feels ideal. There may be an adviser grant that was too generous. A departed founder may still hold more than the active team wishes they did. A SAFE stack may be untidier than the founders would design from scratch. The option pool may have been used unevenly. None of this is unusual. The mistake is to assume that because the cap table is imperfect, it must either be completely repaired or else it is hopeless. Real companies usually live somewhere in between.

That is why this chapter begins with a difficult but useful truth. Not every bad cap table can be made perfect.
This is not defeatism. It is the beginning of operational maturity. A founder who understands this stops wasting energy on fantasies of total structural purity after the company has already accumulated history. Instead, they start asking better questions. What can still be improved. What cannot be fully undone but can be contained. Which weaknesses are actually fatal to future financing or motivation, and which are merely unattractive but survivable. Which line items are ugly but economically tolerable, and which ones are actively distorting the company's future. This is a much stronger posture than either denial or perfectionism. Denial says the table is fine when it clearly is not. Perfectionism says the table is ruined because it no longer matches an imaginary clean version that only exists in hindsight.

The reason perfection is often impossible is simple. Ownership hardens. Once equity has been granted, once rights have been issued, once founders have mentally and legally attached themselves to certain percentages, the company cannot always rewind to the point before those decisions were made. Time gives cap table decisions social weight as well as economic weight. People build identities around their stake. They make life choices around their expected position. They interpret later correction attempts through the lens of what they believe was already earned. Even when a founder can see clearly that an old allocation was wrong, that does not mean it can be painlessly reversed. By the time the truth is obvious, the company may have to bargain with reality rather than overwrite it.

This is especially true if the company has become more valuable. A weak grant made when the company was little more than an idea may have been easy to revisit six weeks later. Two years later, with traction, investors, or a live financing in sight, the same grant may feel much more expensive to the recipient and much more politically dangerous to challenge. The company is then no longer asking whether the original decision was wise. It is asking what can still be done now that the wrong decision has had time to become real in other people's minds. That is a fundamentally different problem.

There is also a practical limit. Some structural damage can be reduced only by creating other forms of friction. You can renegotiate with a departed founder, but you may reopen old conflict. You can compress an option pool or reprice some grants, but you may unsettle the team. You can try to buy back dead equity, but that may require cash or concessions the company would rather use elsewhere. You can force clarity around old promises, but you may lose goodwill you still need. The founder therefore has to stop thinking in the abstract language of "fixing" and start thinking in the more grounded language of trade-offs. Every repair has its own cost. The right repair is not always the most total one. It is often the one that improves the company materially without causing more damage than it removes.

This is why some imperfections are best understood as tolerances rather than emergencies. A slightly generous old grant that no longer feels ideal may still be acceptable if it does not meaningfully distort hiring, financing, or founder motivation. A small awkward line item on the table may be unattractive but not worth major political effort to remove.

A nonfatal scar is still a scar, but it is not necessarily the place to spend the company's most precious attention if there are deeper structural priorities elsewhere. Mature founders learn to distinguish between clean-up that matters and clean-up that only satisfies a fantasy of elegance.

At the same time, accepting imperfection should never become an excuse for cowardice. The fact that perfection is unavailable does not mean the company should simply live with every weakness. Some problems really do need intervention even if the intervention is incomplete. Dead founder equity that meaningfully burdens the active common is not merely ugly. It affects incentives. A stack of unmodelled SAFEs is not just messy. It threatens future financing clarity. A founder position that becomes too thin after the next likely round is not just unfortunate. It can hollow out the company's internal engine. These are not scars to admire stoically. They are live problems. The fact that the ideal fix may be impossible only means the company should pursue the best available fix, not abandon the field.

This is where the founder's judgment becomes more important than their desire for neatness. The question is no longer "can we make this perfect." The question is "what condition does this cap table need to reach in order for the company to remain financeable, buildable, and aligned." That target is much more realistic and much more useful. Financeable means the next investor can enter without inheriting nonsense the company refuses to acknowledge. Buildable means the active founders and key team still have enough room and motivation that building the company makes sense. Aligned means the rights stack has not drifted so far from the human reality of the company that moderate outcomes or future rounds become structurally demoralising. A cap table that reaches that state may still be imperfect. It may also be completely good enough.

It is important to say this plainly because many founders secretly torture themselves with hindsight after they become more literate about ownership. Once they understand founder splits, vesting, preference stacks, or advisory mistakes more clearly, they begin mentally rebuilding the company from day one and comparing the live structure to the ideal one they would create now. That comparison can be instructive for learning, but it can also become paralysing if taken too far. The real company is not competing against the perfect hypothetical company. It is competing against its own actual future. The only question that matters now is whether the current structure can still support a viable next phase if repaired and governed intelligently from here.

Another reason imperfection must be accepted is that startups themselves are not perfect institutions. They are built under uncertainty, fatigue, and partial knowledge. Some structural roughness is not evidence of failure. It is evidence of being a real company rather than a case study designed from hindsight. The founder's job is not to erase every sign that the company was built by humans under pressure. It is to prevent the roughness from becoming so great that the ownership structure stops serving the business. That is a more realistic standard and a better one.

This also changes how founders should talk to boards, investors, and teams about cap table issues. The wrong tone is either false reassurance or theatrical despair. The better tone is sober control. Yes, the structure has weaknesses. Here is what they are. Here is what we can still improve. Here is what we probably have to live with. Here is why the resulting company is still workable. That kind of framing builds trust because it treats the cap table as a governable system rather than as either an embarrassment to hide or a ruined object beyond repair.

That is why not every bad cap table can be made perfect, and why that fact should not frighten a founder into passivity. The cap table does not need to become pure. It needs to become truthful, legible, and livable enough that the company can keep moving without being quietly undermined by its own structure. Once the founder accepts that, repair becomes much more practical. The question is no longer how to erase history. It is how to stop history from having more power over the future than it deserves.

Which Problems Are Worth Fighting to Fix

Once a founder accepts that not every cap table weakness can be erased, the next question becomes more important than purity. Which problems are worth the cost of trying to fix. This is where many teams go wrong in the opposite direction. Some become fatalistic and leave too much untouched because repair feels awkward. Others become obsessed with tidying everything and spend political, legal, and emotional capital on issues that are unattractive but not actually decisive. Good cap table repair depends on triage. Not every flaw deserves the same level of attention. The founder has to learn which weaknesses are merely inelegant and which ones are actively threatening the company's future.

The first category worth fighting over is anything that materially damages founder motivation. If the active founders are carrying the business while the structure leaves them too thin, too subordinated, or too exposed beneath rights they did not fully appreciate, that is not a cosmetic issue. It goes to the heart of whether the company remains worth building. A founder who knows that the next likely round will push the common into a range that no longer feels meaningful should not treat that as just another unfortunate detail. That is a core structural problem. If it can be softened through negotiation, timing, pool discipline, or other repair, it is worth serious effort.

The second category is dead equity with real weight. Not every legacy line item needs war. But a departed founder or stale holder with enough ownership to distort incentives, future hiring, or investor perception is very often worth confronting. This is especially true when the gap between contribution and retained stake is obvious to everyone still doing the work. Dead equity is one of the few cap table problems that poisons both morale and financeability at the same time. If a repair is realistically available, even if imperfect, it is usually worth pursuing earlier rather than later.

A third category is anything that threatens the next financing directly. Some cap table problems are ugly but tolerable until the company needs more capital. Others are exactly the kind of weakness that will cause investors to hesitate, reprice, or force harsher terms. Unmodelled convertibles, unclear founder vesting, strange side grants, badly sized pools, or rights clutter that makes the next round hard to allocate all fall into this category. If the founders can already see that an issue will become a term-sheet problem later, they should treat it as a present operating problem now. The investor does not create the weakness. The investor merely reveals its cost.

Another class of problems worth fixing is anything that makes employee equity unbelievable. If the company is still recruiting and retaining people on the basis of ownership, then the structure under that promise matters. A pool that is too small, too misused, or too disconnected from a real grant philosophy is not just messy compensation design. It weakens the company's ability to hire honestly. Likewise, if the rights stack has become so heavy that moderate outcomes leave common with almost nothing, then the company needs to at least understand and, where possible, repair what can still be repaired before continuing to sell the upside story in lazy terms. This does not mean every employee equity imperfection demands emergency surgery. It means that if the company's actual ownership logic is no longer compatible with how it recruits, that gap is worth fighting to close.

There are also problems worth fixing because they distort strategic decisions. A cap table can become so preference-heavy, so round-dependent, or so rights-constrained that the company no longer behaves rationally in real-world exit or financing ranges. Moderate acquisition offers become nonstarters for the common. Rescue capital becomes far more expensive than it appears because anti-dilution or other protections will activate harshly. Later investors are hard to bring in because too much round space is already spoken for. These are not minor irritants. They shape what options the company can realistically take. If a repair increases real strategic flexibility, that repair usually deserves more weight than a purely cosmetic improvement.

By contrast, some issues are not worth major conflict. A small early grant that feels slightly generous but does not meaningfully affect financing, hiring, founder morale, or exit economics may simply be a scar. It may irritate the founders every time they look at the table, but irritation is not enough. Likewise, minor asymmetries in grants or small imperfections in advisory allocations may not justify the time and political damage of reopening them if they are economically trivial in the company's real future. This is where founders need emotional discipline. Not every line item that offends retrospective taste is worth active repair. Some are tuition fees from the company's earlier ignorance.

A useful way to think about it is to ask four questions. Does this problem change whether the company can raise. Does it change whether the people building the company are still meaningfully aligned. Does it change whether the company can hire and retain credibly. Does it change whether plausible exits or strategic moves still work for the common. If the answer is yes to one or more of those, the issue is probably worth serious attention. If the answer is no across the board, the company may be looking at something annoying rather than something dangerous.

Another good test is whether the issue compounds if left alone. Some problems are static. An ugly old grant remains ugly, but it does not necessarily become much worse over time. Other problems get more expensive every month they are left untouched.

Unvested founder issues harden. Deferred instruments pile up. Thin founder positions become thinner after the next round. Weak pool discipline keeps allocating future room to weak uses. Problems that compound are often worth fighting earlier because delay itself is part of the damage.

It also matters how fixable the problem is. Some issues are important but practically immovable. A departed founder may have too much leverage. A round term may be baked in. A historical rights package may be difficult to reopen without a live financing or a major transaction. In those cases, the company should still understand the problem clearly, but may need to focus on containment rather than full repair. That is still a valid outcome. Knowing what cannot realistically be fixed now allows the founders to spend their effort on issues where intervention still has a real chance of improving the structure.

There is also a social dimension. The company should ask not only whether a repair is economically justified, but whether it is worth the relationship cost. Some fights destroy more trust than the improvement they produce. Others clarify the structure in a way that strengthens trust because everyone knows the company is finally telling the truth. This is a judgment call, but it should be made consciously. Founders often either avoid conflict entirely or rush into it under the banner of fairness. Better operators weigh the likely economic gain against the probable human damage and act with both in mind.

The strongest repair priorities usually have one thing in common. They make the company more liveable going forward rather than merely more elegant in hindsight. That is the real test. A good repair is one that improves the future operating reality of the business. It helps the next raise, restores founder meaning, improves the honesty of employee equity, reduces dead weight, or reopens strategic room. If a "fix" does none of those and mainly satisfies the founders' desire to make the table look as though they had known more earlier, it is probably lower priority than it feels.

That is why some cap table problems are worth fighting to fix and others are better treated as scars, constraints, or lessons. The mature founder is not the one who tries to win every historical argument against the table. It is the one who can tell which weaknesses threaten the company's future and which ones merely offend the company's memory of how it wishes the past had gone.

Buying Back Shares, Renegotiating, and Other Repairs

Once a founder has decided that a cap table problem is worth fixing, the next challenge is practical rather than philosophical. What can actually be done. This is where many teams get stuck, because they know the structure is weak but treat repair as if it comes in only two forms: either the company somehow rewinds the mistake completely or else nothing can change. Real repair is usually more varied than that. Shares can sometimes be bought back. Grants can sometimes be reduced or restructured. Vesting can be introduced or reset. Rights can sometimes be renegotiated in connection with a new round. Dead equity can sometimes be compressed, exchanged, or neutralised in other ways. None of these routes is easy by default, but together they form the practical toolkit by which an imperfect cap table can often be improved.

The most obvious repair is a buyback or repurchase. This usually arises when someone holds stock that the active company no longer believes they should continue to hold in full. Perhaps a founder left early. Perhaps an adviser received too much. Perhaps the company retained a repurchase right that can still be exercised over unvested or partially vested shares. In the cleanest case, this is straightforward. The governing documents already gave the company a mechanism to repurchase unvested stock, and the company simply uses it. In more difficult cases, especially where the equity has already vested or where the legal position is looser, the company may need to negotiate. That negotiation can still produce a good outcome, but the founders should be honest with themselves: if the company is asking someone to give up stock they currently believe belongs to them, this is not administration. It is bargaining.

That is why price matters so much in buyback conversations. Founders often want to think morally. The person did not do enough. The grant was too generous. The company now needs the equity back. All of that may be true. But once the equity is real, the person on the other side is likely to think economically as well as morally. A repurchase may therefore require cash, installment payments, some alternative form of compensation, or another compromise. The founders must decide whether the economic cost of getting the stock back is lower than the long-term structural cost of leaving it where it is. That is not always a pleasant calculation, but it is the real one.

Another repair route is renegotiation without full repurchase. A founder who left may not be willing to surrender everything, but may accept a reduction. An adviser with an oversized grant may agree to convert part of it into a smaller continuing relationship and release the rest. A cofounder whose stake no longer reflects reality may agree to a revised vesting arrangement if the conversation happens early enough and honestly enough. These partial repairs are often much more realistic than total reset fantasies. Founders should not dismiss them simply because they do not produce a perfectly clean table. Reducing a bad problem is often far more valuable than insisting on a perfect solution that never arrives.

There is also the possibility of changing future structure rather than undoing past structure. This is especially important when some old rights or allocations cannot be cleanly reversed. For example, a founder may not be able to remove an old grant, but can decide to be much stricter with all future grants so that the bad old line becomes a contained scar rather than the first of many similar mistakes. A company may not be able to eliminate an awkward SAFE stack immediately, but can model it properly and structure the next round to absorb it with maximum clarity. A founder split that is politically hard to reopen may still be made more tolerable if founder vesting, board structure, or future role-based grants are handled more intelligently from this point onward. Not all repair is subtraction. Some repair is building a healthier future around an imperfect past.

Renegotiation often becomes easiest when tied to a real company event. This is an important operational truth. People are much more willing to revisit ownership when some larger transition is already happening. A financing round, a founder departure, a major hire, a strategic review, or a clean-up before investor diligence can all create moments when the company's need for structural clarity is more visible and more legitimate. That does not mean the founders should manipulate events cynically. It means they should recognise that ownership renegotiation is often easier when connected to a broader turning point than when raised out of nowhere as a pure retrospective complaint.

This is especially true with investor rights. Earlier investor terms are often hard to reopen in a vacuum. But if the company is doing a new round, refinancing old instruments, or trying to attract a new lead investor, there may be room to rationalise or simplify some older rights as part of the process.

A company might not be able to erase prior preferences or protections entirely, but it may be able to harmonise terms, compress complexity, or exchange one kind of right for another in a way that makes the cap table more workable. These opportunities are highly context-dependent, but they are real. Founders who assume old investor terms are untouchable forever often underestimate how much can be renegotiated when new money or new strategic need enters the room.

There is also a repair path through clarity itself. Some ownership problems are worsened because no one has actually stated the issue plainly. The company knows there are loose expectations, poorly explained grants, or confusion about what certain instruments mean, but avoids naming them because naming them may force discomfort. In such cases, one of the most powerful forms of repair is simply to get the structure onto the table honestly. Model the SAFE conversions. Show the likely exit ranges. Explain the preference stack. Clarify what certain grants actually represent. This may not change the legal structure immediately, but it changes the company's relationship to it. That is not trivial. A team making decisions from clear truth is already in a better state than a team operating on half-myths.

Another route is to separate economic recognition from cap table permanence. Sometimes founders use equity because they feel they need to reward someone, but by the time they revisit the issue they realise permanent ownership was the wrong tool. In some cases, especially before matters harden too far, the company may be able to restructure the arrangement: a smaller equity position plus a consulting fee, a retention bonus, a transition payment, or some other non-equity recognition. This does not always work. But it is worth remembering that the company is not limited to all-or-nothing cap table thinking. Some problems exist because equity was used for a purpose better served by another instrument. Repair may therefore involve moving some value recognition out of the ownership structure rather than fighting only over percentages inside it.

Founders should also be realistic about sequencing. The company does not need to solve every issue at once. In fact, trying to do so can make repair harder because it creates a sense of wholesale structural panic. A better approach is often to rank the repairs. Deal first with what affects financing, founder motivation, and major dead equity.

Then address grants, clarity problems, and future process discipline. Not because the smaller issues do not matter, but because cap table repair works best when it improves the company's ability to operate rather than overwhelming the team with an attempt at total historical purification.

There is a final point worth making. Some repairs will fail. A former founder may refuse to negotiate. An adviser may cling to a weak grant. An investor may not reopen rights outside a new round. A team may be too late to change a split without creating more damage than it removes. That does not mean the repair effort was pointless. Attempting repair often clarifies what is truly fixed, what is merely contained, and what future strategies must now account for. A company that knows exactly where it remains structurally wounded is still in a far better position than a company that keeps telling itself everything is broadly fine because the alternative felt socially difficult.

That is why buying back shares, renegotiating, and other repairs matter so much. They are the practical means by which founders move from regret to governance. The company may never become the perfectly clean structure hindsight imagines. But it can often become something much more important: a structure whose flaws are smaller, better understood, and less powerful over the company's future than they would have been if left untouched.

When to Accept Imperfection and Move On

One of the most valuable skills a founder can develop is knowing when a cap table problem has moved from being something that should be fixed to something that should be understood, contained, and then carried. This sounds like compromise, and it is. But compromise is not always weakness. In ownership matters, as in operations more broadly, there comes a point where the pursuit of a cleaner past starts costing more than it returns to the future. The founder who cannot recognise that point can end up turning cap table repair into a second business, one that consumes time, trust, and momentum while producing less improvement than the company hoped.

This is why accepting imperfection is not laziness. It is triage with discipline.

The key is that acceptance should follow analysis, not replace it. A founder should never move on from a problem simply because it is awkward, embarrassing, or politically sensitive. That is avoidance. Acceptance becomes legitimate only after the company has asked the hard questions. How much does this issue really distort financing, hiring, founder motivation, or exit economics. What are the realistic repair options. What would those repairs cost in cash, trust, legal effort, or internal distraction. What improvement would they actually buy. Once those questions are answered honestly, the founder can decide whether this is a live structural threat or an old wound that no longer deserves to dominate the company's attention.

A good test is whether the issue materially changes the company's next important decision. If an imperfect grant, a stale allocation, or an old awkward line on the table is unattractive but does not meaningfully alter the next financing, the next key hire, the founder's motivation, or the economics of plausible outcomes, then it may not deserve major intervention. The founders do not have to love that fact. They simply have to recognise it. Some cap table ugliness is mostly historical. It is not beautiful, but it is also not steering the car. The company should not let irritation masquerade as urgency.

Another test is whether the issue compounds if left alone. If the answer is no, acceptance becomes more reasonable. A static imperfection is often easier to live with than a dynamic one. An old grant that is larger than ideal but no longer growing may be tolerable. An under-modelled SAFE stack that keeps expanding is not. A legacy founder holding an awkward but manageable amount may be a scar. A founder split that is still actively corroding motivation is not. Acceptance makes sense when the structure has stopped worsening and the remaining harm is bounded. It is much less sensible when the problem continues to deepen with time.

There is also the question of leverage. Founders sometimes know a fix would be good in theory but have almost no practical leverage to get it. The other party is entitled enough, distant enough, or legally protected enough that reopening the issue would require a fight the company is unlikely to win cleanly.

In those situations, insisting on repair can become a form of self-harm disguised as principle. It may be better to acknowledge the weakness, incorporate it into future planning, and protect the company elsewhere than to drain leadership energy into a battle whose likely result is limited. This is especially true if the repair would consume emotional oxygen the company badly needs for product, hiring, fundraising, or survival.

A subtle sign that it may be time to accept imperfection is when the company's best path forward lies not through undoing the old issue but through building enough future strength that the issue matters less. For example, a founder may not be able to claw back an overly generous early allocation. But if the company becomes disciplined about all future grants, keeps the founder common meaningful, avoids overstacking preferences, and preserves employee credibility, then the old mistake becomes a smaller percentage of a much healthier overall system. This is not denial. It is scaling around scar tissue rather than trying to remove it surgically after removal has become disproportionate.

Founders also need to watch their own emotions here. Cap table repair can become attractive not because it is the highest-value work, but because it offers the psychological pleasure of fighting a past mistake. There is something seductive about the idea of finally correcting what should have been done properly from the start. Sometimes that instinct is exactly right. At other times it becomes a way of spending present attention on old injustice because the company's current strategic problems are harder, less morally clear, and less emotionally satisfying to tackle. Strong operators learn to notice this in themselves. Not every structurally imperfect line item deserves the intensity of unresolved regret.

Accepting imperfection can also be a form of respect for reality. A startup is not built in a laboratory. It is built under uncertainty, pressure, partial information, and human mess. Some wrong turns will become permanent features of the landscape. If every such feature is treated as intolerable, the company will never finish repairing yesterday long enough to build tomorrow. The founder has to be able to say, with clear eyes, this is not how I would design it now, but it is not large enough, live enough, or repairable enough to justify more energy than we have already spent. That sentence is not surrender. It is a mature allocation of scarce leadership time.

This is especially important for the people still carrying the business. Founders and key employees can become demoralised if the company keeps reopening old ownership pain without producing meaningful change. A repair process that drags on without resolution may do more to weaken morale than the original structural flaw now would. In such cases, decisive acceptance can be healthier than indefinite attempted correction. The company says: this is the scar, here is what it means, here is how we account for it, and here is why we are no longer spending disproportionate energy trying to erase it. That kind of clarity often restores more operational confidence than a permanent half-repair campaign.

Of course, acceptance should never become rhetorical camouflage for cowardice. That is why the discipline matters. The founder should be able to explain why this issue is now being carried rather than fought. Because it does not affect the next financing. Because it is bounded in outcome. Because the repair cost would exceed the gain. Because leverage is gone. Because future structure can be made stronger around it. If the founder cannot explain the acceptance clearly, the company is probably still rationalising avoidance rather than making a real decision.

A healthy company often contains both repair and acceptance at the same time. Some lines are worth fixing. Others are worth monitoring. Others are simply worth understanding. This mixed condition is normal. The goal is not to emerge with a perfect cap table. The goal is to emerge with a cap table whose remaining flaws no longer quietly dominate the company's most important future choices. Once that threshold is reached, more cleaning may still be possible, but it is no longer urgent in the same way.

That is when to accept imperfection and move on. Not when the issue is uncomfortable, but when it is no longer one of the company's highest-leverage structural battles and when the work of erasing it would take more from the future than the scar still takes from the present.

How to Explain a Messy Cap Table Honestly

A messy cap table becomes much more dangerous when the company tries to speak about it as though it were cleaner than it is. This is one of the most important founder disciplines in later-stage ownership management. A weak structure is one problem.

A weak structure wrapped in evasive language is a much bigger one. Once that happens, the company is not only carrying economic and governance friction. It is also creating a credibility problem with investors, employees, boards, and sometimes with the founders themselves. That is why honest explanation matters so much. You do not need a perfect cap table to be trusted. You do need a truthful account of the one you actually have.

This is harder than it sounds because founders often confuse honesty with self-harm. They fear that if they explain the messy bits too plainly, they will make the company look amateurish, fragile, or poorly governed. So they soften. They speak in broad terms. They emphasise the current headline structure and hope the rough edges will either seem smaller than they are or disappear into the background. Sometimes that works for a few minutes. It almost never works for long. Serious people who matter to the company eventually ask the next questions. When they do, they are not only judging the structure itself. They are judging whether the founders understand it and whether they can be trusted to speak about it without fiction.

This is why the right goal is not to make the cap table sound pretty. It is to make it sound understood.

A founder explaining an imperfect structure honestly should start with the basic rule that clarity beats defensiveness. If there is dead equity, say there is dead equity and explain its size, origin, and current practical impact. If there is a SAFE stack, explain the instruments, the likely conversion effects, and whether they have been modelled. If the founder split is not ideal, explain why it ended up that way and what, if anything, has been done or can still be done about it. If the pool is tighter than it should be, say so and explain what that means for the next hiring phase. This does not mean narrating every historical embarrassment in dramatic detail. It means naming the issue plainly enough that the listener can trust they are not being led through fog.

One of the strongest ways to explain a messy cap table honestly is to separate the problem into three parts. What the issue is. What it actually affects. What the company has done or plans to do about it. That structure matters because many founders either understate the issue or overstate it. Understatement sounds evasive.

Overstatement sounds panicked. A better explanation sounds like this: there is a legacy founder allocation that is larger than ideal, it does not currently block financing but it does slightly weaken the common layer, and we have already explored repurchase options while adjusting future grants and pool strategy to contain the impact. That kind of explanation does not pretend the issue is trivial, and it does not make the company sound structurally helpless either. It shows control.

Another important principle is to quantify wherever possible. Words like messy, crowded, heavy, or awkward may be emotionally accurate, but they are not enough on their own. If the company says the SAFE stack is meaningful, say how much capital is in it and what that likely means in share terms under a plausible next round. If the preference stack is large, say how much capital sits ahead of the common and at roughly what exit ranges it becomes dominant. If founder ownership feels thin, show what the founder position looks like after the next likely financing rather than relying on vague discomfort. Numbers do not solve the problem, but they do make the explanation more trustworthy because they show the founder is reading structure, not just describing mood.

This is especially important with investors. Serious investors are often more forgiving of structural imperfections than founders expect, provided the imperfections are understood, bounded, and not disguised. What they do not like is drift combined with vagueness. If the founders know the weak spots, have modelled them, and can explain why the resulting company is still workable, the conversation becomes much healthier. The investor may still care. They may still want fixes. But the founder is now negotiating from literacy rather than from embarrassment. That changes the tone completely. A messy cap table handled honestly can still support confidence. A messy cap table hidden behind soft language often amplifies concern because it suggests the founders themselves are still partly strangers to the structure.

Employees require a slightly different kind of honesty. The company does not need to dump every financing complexity onto the whole team in exhaustive legal form. But if the startup is using equity as part of its culture and compensation logic, then key people especially deserve explanations that are more truthful than aspirational.

The company should be able to say what the option pool is for, how the common fits beneath investor rights in broad terms, and what kinds of outcomes still matter for employee upside without pretending all equity automatically behaves like raw percentage. The goal is not to drain inspiration from the culture. It is to make sure the inspiration sits on a foundation that will not later collapse into resentment when reality finally asserts itself.

There is also an internal founder benefit to speaking honestly about the structure. A cap table the founders can explain plainly is often a cap table the founders can govern more calmly. One of the hidden costs of mess is that it creates a low-grade shame or avoidance response. The founders know there are weak spots, so they avoid looking too directly or talking too clearly. That avoidance then weakens decision quality. Honest explanation, even of something imperfect, often restores a sense of authorship. The company is no longer pretending. It is saying this is the structure, here are the scars, here is the real meaning, and here is why we still believe the next phase makes sense. That is a much stronger operating posture than anxious prettification.

A common mistake founders make in these conversations is overusing story to defend weak structure. Story matters. History matters. But it should not be used to smother analysis. "He was there at the beginning" or "we all trusted each other" may explain how something happened. They do not explain what it now means. Strong explanation uses history only as context, not as a substitute for structural clarity. The listener still needs to know current impact and forward plan. If the explanation remains trapped in sentiment, it usually signals that the company is still emotionally governed by the origin story of the mistake rather than by the present consequences of it.

Another key point is that honest explanation should include limits. Founders do not build trust by pretending every cap table issue is already solved. Sometimes the strongest statement is simply that a problem exists, the company has assessed repair options, and complete correction is not currently realistic. That kind of sentence can sound exposed, but it often increases credibility because it makes clear the founders are not promising structural miracles. They are distinguishing between what is repairable, what is containable, and what must simply be carried knowingly. Investors, boards, and senior employees usually trust that kind of realism more than sweeping language about everything being "fine."

The tone matters too. Honest explanation is not self-flagellation. The founder does not need to speak as though every early mistake proves the company is naïve or broken. The better tone is sober and precise. Yes, this is a weak spot. Here is why it exists. Here is the actual magnitude. Here is how it affects the next stage. Here is what has already been done. Here is what still remains imperfect. Here is why the business is still workable anyway. That tone tells the listener that the founders are capable of diagnosing their own structure without either panic or denial. That is the tone of an operator.

That is how to explain a messy cap table honestly. Not by making it sound elegant. Not by pretending the scars are virtues. But by proving that the company knows what the scars are, what they cost, and why they no longer control the whole future of the business.

How to Rebuild Credibility After Cap Table Mistakes

A cap table mistake does not only damage structure. It can also damage trust. Founders often focus first on the numeric or legal problem because that is the visible part. The split is wrong. The grant was too large. The pool is too tight. The SAFE stack was not modelled properly. The preference burden is heavier than expected. Those are all real issues. But once other people have seen that the founders let the structure drift, a second problem appears. The company is now carrying a credibility gap. Investors may wonder whether the founders really understand dilution and rights. Employees may wonder whether ownership language in the company means what they thought it meant. Cofounders may wonder whether hard topics will always be delayed until someone external forces them. That is why rebuilding credibility matters almost as much as repairing the table itself.

The first step in rebuilding credibility is to stop pretending the mistake was smaller than it was. Founders often try to preserve authority by minimising the issue. It is only a small grant. It is only one ex-founder. It is only a few SAFEs. It is only a temporary mismatch. That instinct is natural and usually harmful. The people who matter most can often tell when the company is softening the truth to reduce embarrassment. Once they sense that, the founders lose not only on the original issue but also on the interpretation of it. A much stronger approach is to say plainly what the problem is, what its real scope is, and what it does to the structure.

Authority is rebuilt faster through clarity than through defensive understatement.
The second step is to show that the founders now understand the mechanics, not just the optics. A company does not rebuild trust merely by admitting error. It rebuilds trust by proving it can now explain the consequences accurately. If the issue is a badly sized early grant, the founders should be able to say what percentage it represents, why it is too large relative to contribution, and how it affects future hiring room. If the issue is a stack of unmodelled notes or SAFEs, the founders should be able to show likely conversion outcomes and post-financing effects. If the issue is founder dead equity, they should be able to explain what it does to motivation and future financing. The goal is not to become performative about the mistake. The goal is to demonstrate that the company is no longer confused about its own structure.

This is why specific modelling is so powerful in credibility repair. People trust correction more when they can see that the founders have moved from vague discomfort to precise understanding. "We realised the table was messy" is weak. "We reviewed the structure, modelled the next likely financing, identified that the option pool and two legacy grants were distorting our post-round founder position, and have already taken steps A and B while evaluating C" is much stronger. The second kind of statement does not sound more polished merely because it is more detailed. It sounds more trustworthy because it shows operational command rather than emotional reaction.

Another crucial part of rebuilding credibility is visible process. A cap table mistake often signals not just a bad past decision but the absence of a decision-making system. The company did not have a standard for grants, did not review the table regularly, did not model deferred instruments, did not revisit founder alignment, did not ask how the next round would reshape the common. If the company wants people to believe the same class of mistake will not simply recur, it has to show that the process has changed. That may mean scheduled cap table reviews, tighter approval rules for grants, better modelling around SAFEs and notes, explicit scenario analysis before financings, or more disciplined founder governance. The exact form matters less than the principle. Credibility is not rebuilt by apology alone. It is rebuilt by making recurrence less likely.

This is especially important with investors. Investors do not need founders to have been perfect. They do need some reason to believe the company will not keep manufacturing structural surprises. If the founders can show that the weakness has been diagnosed, partly repaired where possible, and now sits inside a stronger internal process, many investors will treat the issue as part of the company's maturity curve rather than as proof of permanent unreliability. If the founders simply say they understand now but cannot point to any changed discipline, the investor is likely to assume the company's understanding remains too mood-dependent to trust.

Employees require a slightly different kind of credibility repair. In many startups, ownership language has a moral charge. People were told they were getting equity, becoming owners, or sharing in the future. If the cap table later reveals that some of that language was looser or more flattering than the structure justified, then the company cannot repair the breach by legal correctness alone. It has to become more honest in how it speaks going forward. That means fewer inflated claims, clearer explanation of what grants really are, more discipline about percentages and fully diluted context, and less reliance on startup mystique. Employees do not need every detail of venture law. They do need to feel that the company is now telling the truth as clearly as it can.

There is also a personal founder dimension here. Founders often lose credibility with themselves after cap table mistakes. They realise they did not understand something they should have understood, or they allowed discomfort to delay structure for too long, or they used equity too casually because it still felt abstract. That self-doubt can quietly weaken later judgment if it turns into shame rather than learning. One of the strongest ways to repair that internal credibility is to become more exacting, not more apologetic. Learn the mechanics. Rebuild the process. Ask the harder questions earlier. Once the founder can see themselves governing the structure more clearly than before, confidence starts returning on a more durable basis than mere optimism ever gave.

Another important piece is sequencing communication correctly. The company should not wait until every repair is complete before speaking honestly, because some repairs take time and some may never become perfect. But it also should not announce broad structural self-criticism before it has even worked out what the problem actually is and what it intends to do.

The most credible sequence is usually this: assess, model, define, begin repair, then explain. That way the company is not speaking from either panic or ignorance. It is speaking from diagnosis. If a founder talks too early, they may sound overwhelmed. If they talk too late, they may sound as though they were hiding the issue. Timing matters.

One of the clearest markers that credibility is rebuilding is when the company can discuss the cap table without emotional flinching. That does not mean enjoying the imperfections. It means being able to answer direct questions plainly, explain trade-offs, admit what remains weak, and still sound in control of the future. This is true in fundraising, in board conversations, and inside the founding team. A founder who has rebuilt credibility around the cap table sounds different. Less vague. Less defensive. Less reliant on flattering shorthand. More grounded in scenario, structure, and consequence. That change is often more powerful than the structural clean-up itself because it affects every later decision.

It is also worth saying that credibility is sometimes rebuilt not by eliminating the problem but by surviving it well. A company may never fully remove a legacy grant or perfect an old founder split. But if it becomes highly disciplined from that point onward, models the issue clearly, makes later financings intelligently, and keeps the common meaningful enough for the active team, then the old mistake stops defining the company. It becomes part of its history, not its operating identity. That is often the realistic goal. Not innocence restored, but reliability established.

The final point is that rebuilding credibility takes repetition. One clean explanation helps. One stronger process helps. One well-handled financing helps. But trust around structure usually returns through a pattern of competence. The company keeps reviewing the table. Keeps explaining it clearly. Keeps avoiding the old shortcuts. Keeps making choices that show the lesson actually stuck. Over time, that pattern becomes more persuasive than any single mea culpa ever could.

That is how credibility is rebuilt after cap table mistakes. Not by pretending the mistake did not matter, and not by drowning in retrospective guilt, but by proving that the company now understands its structure better than the weakness ever did.

The Difference Between a Broken Table and a Scarred One

One of the most important judgments a founder can make is the difference between a cap table that is broken and one that is merely scarred. These are not the same thing, and confusing them leads to two opposite errors. Some founders minimise serious structural damage by calling it normal startup mess when in fact the ownership system is now actively undermining financing, motivation, or exit logic. Others look at a table with visible imperfections and conclude that the whole structure is ruined, when in fact the company can still function, raise, hire, and eventually exit with perfectly acceptable outcomes if those scars are understood and managed properly. The distinction matters because repair strategy depends on it.

A scarred table is one that bears the marks of real company history without being fundamentally unable to support the next stage. It may contain an overgenerous early adviser grant, a founder split that is not how the team would do it now, a few awkward but bounded legacy lines, a slightly inefficient pool history, or some deferred instruments that are untidy but modelled and absorbable. None of this is ideal. But the company remains structurally live. Founders are still meaningfully aligned. Financing is still possible without existential surgery. Employee equity can still be explained honestly. Exit economics may be less clean than a textbook case, but not absurd. The table is not pretty. It is usable.

A broken table is different. It does not merely contain mistakes. It changes what the company can realistically do. Financing becomes hard because the structure is too cluttered, too thin on the founder side, too opaque, or too burdened by unresolved legacy claims. The active founders are no longer properly motivated because the common has become too weak beneath preferences or future likely dilution. Employees are being sold an upside story that the structure no longer supports in any honest way. A moderate exit that should have been strategically viable is meaningless to the common because the stack has become too heavy. Dead equity is large enough to distort everything. The table is no longer just wounded by history. It is being governed by it.

This is why the distinction cannot be made by visual untidiness alone. Some tables look a bit messy and still work. Some look clean at a glance and are structurally broken underneath because the rights stack has hollowed out the common or the next likely financing will crush what remains. A founder should not ask only whether the table feels elegant. They should ask whether the structure still supports a credible next phase of company life. Can we raise. Can we hire. Can the active people still care rationally. Can plausible exits still mean something. If the answer is yes, the table may be scarred rather than broken. If the answer is increasingly no, the problem is deeper.

A useful test is to imagine the next serious outside conversation. If a real investor looked at this table, would the likely outcome be discomfort followed by a manageable clean-up plan, or would it be a fundamental repricing of confidence in the company. If a buyer looked at the waterfall, would the distribution still support a coherent internal decision, or would the company become politically impossible to sell in most realistic ranges. If a strong hire asked what their equity really means, could the company answer honestly without hollow language. A scarred table can still survive those conversations. A broken one usually cannot without major structural intervention.

Another way to tell the difference is by asking whether the flaws are bounded. A scar is bounded. It has edges. The founders can say this grant is larger than ideal, this line is awkward, this founder departure left some inefficient residue, but here is the real impact and here is why it does not control the company's future. Brokenness is harder to bound. The issues bleed into one another. The founder split is weak, which makes later dilution more dangerous, which makes the common thinner, which makes hiring harder, which makes the next round less attractive, which increases dependence on harsher investor terms. When the weaknesses start reinforcing one another rather than sitting as isolated imperfections, the table is moving from scarred toward broken.

This is why founder morale is such an important indicator. In a scarred table, the founders may dislike some of the history but can still see a rational path forward. The company still feels worth carrying. In a broken table, the founders often begin to feel trapped inside economics that no longer match the burden they are being asked to bear. That feeling may initially present as vague exhaustion or unusual sensitivity around financing terms. But structurally it usually means the ownership system is no longer supporting the builders well enough. A founder who cannot distinguish normal frustration from structurally rational demoralisation is at risk of missing one of the clearest warnings the table can give.

A scarred table is also often explainable. Not beautifully, but honestly. The founders can tell the story of what happened, what the weak points are, what has already been fixed, what remains, and why the structure still works. Broken tables are much harder to explain without either evasion or collapse into defensive narrative. The company cannot get through the explanation without sounding as though too many crucial things depend on hope, future clean-up, or people being unusually accommodating later. Explanation is not the only test, but it is a good one. If the founders cannot explain the structure without sounding structurally dependent on luck, the table is probably in more trouble than they want to admit.

This distinction also matters emotionally because founders often attach shame to imperfection. Once they become more literate about cap tables, they look back at earlier decisions and feel that any visible weakness proves amateurism. That feeling can make them over-diagnose brokenness. But real startups are built by people under uncertainty. Scars are normal. The mature question is not whether the table is flawless. It is whether the imperfections have crossed the line into controlling the future. That is the threshold that matters.

At the same time, the idea of a scar should never be used as a comforting euphemism for structural harm. Founders sometimes call something "just a scar" because admitting brokenness would force hard action. That is why the distinction has to be made against actual company function. Does this issue materially impair our next raise, our key team incentives, our exit logic, or our governance coherence. If yes, the company is not merely carrying a scar with grace. It is absorbing live structural damage.

The right response follows naturally from the diagnosis. Scarred tables need clarity, containment, and disciplined future choices. Broken tables need real intervention, even if imperfectly executed. The mistake is to apply the wrong response. If you treat a broken table as though it merely needs better storytelling, the company drifts deeper into structural weakness. If you treat a scarred table as though it requires total reconstruction, you may waste precious energy trying to eliminate history rather than govern it.

That is the difference between a broken table and a scarred one. A scar remembers the past. A broken structure dictates too much of the future. The founder's job is to know which one they are living with. Once that judgment is correct, the company can stop oscillating between denial and despair and start acting with proportion.

SEVENTEEN

Building a Cap Table Culture Inside the Company

"Culture is what you tolerate."

- Bill Walsh

Why Ownership Culture Matters

A cap table is not only a legal structure. It is also a cultural one. This is one of the last things many founders learn, and one of the most important. The company may have lawyers, term sheets, option grants, board approvals, and a spreadsheet that balances neatly. All of that can exist while the people inside the business still do not really understand what ownership means there, how it is talked about, what it is used for, and whether the language around equity matches the actual economics beneath it. That gap between structure and culture matters more than founders often realise, because once the company starts hiring, granting options, raising multiple rounds, and speaking publicly or internally about upside, ownership stops being a private founder concern. It becomes part of how the company teaches people what this business is and what belonging to it means.

This is why ownership culture matters.

A startup with a weak ownership culture usually falls into one of two patterns. Either it romanticises equity, speaking as though everyone is becoming a meaningful owner without really explaining dilution, rights, or where the common sits in the structure. Or it becomes so technical and guarded that only investors and lawyers are allowed to understand what the cap table means, while everyone else works under slogans. Neither pattern is healthy. The first creates disappointment later. The second creates mistrust and distance. A strong ownership culture sits in the middle. It does not pretend the cap table is simple or universally generous, but it does make the company's logic around ownership clear enough that people are not building their relationship to the company on fantasy.

This matters especially because startups ask a lot from people before certainty exists. Founders ask employees to join with less salary than they might get elsewhere, under more ambiguity, with more risk, and often with more emotional commitment than a standard job would demand. Investors ask founders to keep building under dilution and governance pressure. Cofounders ask one another to trust that early splits, vesting, and role evolution still mean something fair. In all these cases, ownership is one of the main ways the company explains why this burden is worth carrying. If the ownership culture is sloppy, inflated, or evasive, then one of the company's core moral languages is weak.

This is one reason cap table mistakes often become cultural wounds. The numerical issue may be real, but the deeper damage comes when people realise that the company's language around ownership was not as grounded as they assumed. An employee hears for years that they have a meaningful piece of the upside, then learns at exit that the structure above the common is heavier than they understood. A founder believes a moderate acquisition would be life-changing, then discovers the stack says otherwise. A cofounder accepts an equal split in the name of trust, then later realises the company never built a culture capable of revisiting hard truths once contribution diverged. In each case, the problem is not only cap table mechanics. It is that the company taught people to relate to ownership in a way that reality could not sustain.

A strong ownership culture therefore starts with honesty about what equity is and is not. Equity is not a magical substitute for salary. It is not a guarantee of wealth. It is not the same thing for founders, employees, and investors. It is not fully understandable from raw share counts alone. But neither is it meaningless. It is a structured claim on future value that can become very significant in the right company and under the right conditions. The company has to be able to hold both sides of that sentence without sliding into either hype or cynicism. That is harder than it sounds, and many startups never manage it.

Another reason ownership culture matters is that the cap table influences behaviour long before any exit occurs. If people inside the company believe their upside is real and legible, they often behave differently than if they suspect the ownership language is mostly decorative. If founders know their common still means something across plausible outcomes, they tend to carry the business differently than if they quietly suspect the structure has pushed meaningful reward too far away. If employees know how their grants actually work, they are more likely to ask intelligent questions, make mature comparisons, and trust the company's compensation philosophy. In that sense, ownership culture affects not just morale but decision quality.

This is also why founder language matters so much. Founders set the tone for how ownership is understood. If they constantly speak in flattering simplifications because the truth feels more awkward or less inspiring, the company learns to treat equity as a piece of brand language rather than a serious instrument. If they are too cold or overly legalistic, the company may treat ownership as something abstract and remote, relevant only to investors and senior leadership. The best founders speak with precision and proportion. They can explain why equity matters without overselling it. They can explain dilution without sounding apologetic about every round. They can explain that rights matter, that exits are not just gross sale prices, and that common stock behaves differently from preferred, without turning every team conversation into a finance lecture.

Ownership culture also matters because it affects how a company handles hard moments. When a down round comes, when an option pool must expand, when a founder leaves, when a secondary is discussed, when a buyer appears, the company's prior culture around ownership determines whether those conversations feel like clarifications or betrayals. In a weak ownership culture, every structural truth arrives as a shock because people were trained on simplified hope. In a strong one, the same events may still be painful, but they are less likely to feel morally deceptive because the company has already taught people that equity is real, conditional, layered, and shaped by capital structure.

This is not only about internal communication. It also affects how the company is read from outside. Investors often notice whether founders can speak coherently about equity culture or whether they rely on vague startup mythology. A company that understands its own ownership culture tends to recruit better, negotiate better, and survive financing stress better because it is not constantly discovering that its public language and private economics have drifted apart. That kind of coherence is rare enough that it becomes a signal of maturity in itself.

There is another subtle point here. Ownership culture is not formed only by what the company says. It is formed by what the company does repeatedly. How grants are explained. How departures are handled. Whether the founders model dilution before speaking about upside. Whether small equity decisions are governed or handed out emotionally. Whether employees are encouraged to ask questions or quietly discouraged from looking too closely. Whether secondaries are framed as rational alignment tools or handled in a way that makes the rest of the team feel ownership is one story for some people and another for everyone else. Culture is not a memo. It is a pattern.

This is why the company cannot leave ownership culture to chance. If it does, the default culture will usually be a mixture of startup cliché, partial truth, and emotional convenience. That may be enough in the earliest months. It will not be enough once the cap table becomes layered and the company starts asking people to trust the meaning of equity over longer periods. By then, the absence of culture is itself a culture, and usually a weak one.

That is why ownership culture matters. Because the cap table is not merely a list of who owns what. It is part of how the company teaches people what kind of future they are working toward, who gets protected, who carries risk, and whether the language of ownership in the business deserves to be believed

How Founders Should Talk About Equity Internally

The way founders talk about equity inside the company is often more influential than the documents themselves, because most people do not live emotionally inside legal wording. They live inside repeated explanation. They absorb tone, examples, shorthand, promises, and omissions. That is why founders need to think carefully about how they speak about ownership. A company can have technically accurate documents and still build a misleading equity culture if the internal language around those documents is inflated, vague, or selectively simplified. In the same way, a company with a complicated structure can still build trust if the founders speak plainly enough that people understand the broad truth of what they hold and what they do not.

This is why founder language matters so much. Equity is not just granted. It is interpreted.
The first rule is that founders should speak about equity as something meaningful but conditional. Those two words belong together. If the founder speaks as though equity is automatically life-changing, they are setting people up for later disillusionment. If they speak as though equity is merely symbolic and not worth understanding, they are weakening one of the company's core incentive tools. A much stronger tone is this: equity can matter a great deal, but its value depends on company success, future dilution, where the grant sits in the structure, and what kind of outcome the company eventually reaches. That framing is neither cold nor dishonest. It teaches people to respect ownership without mistaking it for guaranteed wealth.

The second rule is that founders should speak in percentages or percentage equivalents whenever possible, not just in raw share counts. Raw counts are too easy to misuse, even unintentionally. Fifty thousand options can sound enormous or trivial depending on the denominator, and most people do not have the denominator in their head unless the company gives it to them. Founders do not need to turn every grant conversation into a securities seminar, but they do need to avoid the lazy habit of letting big-looking numbers create false impressions. If the grant represents a certain fully diluted percentage or approximate range, that is usually far more honest and informative than the raw count alone.

Another important rule is that founders should explain the difference between owning equity and being granted a path toward equity. Many startups talk as though every option grant makes someone a full present-tense owner in the same sense as a founder or current shareholder. That is too loose. Options matter. They can become highly valuable. They can align people deeply with the company's future. But they are not the same as already-issued stock. Founders should be able to say this without draining the offer of energy. In fact, doing so usually builds trust because the company sounds like it understands its own instruments rather than just using "ownership" as inspirational fog.

Founders should also talk about dilution early rather than only when it becomes painful. This is one of the strongest cultural habits a company can build. If employees hear about equity only in optimistic language during recruiting and then meet dilution only after the company raises more money, they will often experience the later truth as a disappointment or a bait-and-switch. A healthier pattern is to explain from the beginning that if the company succeeds and keeps growing, there will likely be more rounds, more hires, and therefore more dilution. The point is not to make equity sound fragile. It is to show that dilution is part of the company's growth path, not a secret reversal of the original promise.

This is especially important because many founders talk about fundraising as if it only adds strength and never redistributes meaning. Internally, they celebrate the round, quote the valuation, and speak about momentum. All of that can be true. But if they never also explain that new capital changes the ownership structure and often brings in holders with different rights from the common, then the company is training people to hear only the flattering half of financing. Strong founders do not need to narrate every term of every round to the whole team. They do need to avoid letting fundraising language become pure theatre detached from the cap table consequences it actually creates.

Another good habit is to distinguish clearly between company valuation and personal or employee payout. This is one of the biggest areas where internal ownership language goes wrong. A company raises at a certain valuation and people begin casually speaking as though that number can be mentally multiplied by their stake to tell them what they "have." Founders should interrupt that instinct early. A private valuation is not the same as cash in hand. It is a financing event under specific terms. Liquidity, preferences, and future rounds all matter. Employees do not need a cynical lecture every time valuation is mentioned, but they should not be left with the impression that each valuation step is simply a transparent increase in their realised wealth.

Tone matters here. Founders should not sound frightened of their own cap table, nor should they sound like marketing copywriters for it. The strongest tone is calm, specific, and repeatable. Equity matters. It is part of how we share future upside. It takes time to vest. The company will likely raise more. Different classes of holders can have different rights. Not every headline number translates directly into common-holder proceeds. We will explain your grant clearly and answer questions honestly. That kind of language creates a company in which people learn to take ownership seriously without needing fantasy to stay motivated.

Founders should also make it safe for people to ask basic equity questions. A weak ownership culture often treats such questions as slightly awkward, slightly cynical, or slightly too technical for normal conversation. That is a mistake. When employees feel they cannot ask what their grant actually means, the company teaches them that equity is something to feel about, not something to understand. A much healthier culture says the opposite. Ask what percentage it represents. Ask how vesting works. Ask how future rounds may affect it. Ask where common sits relative to investor rights in broad terms. The founders do not need to promise that every answer will be simple. They do need to make clear that the questions are legitimate.

There is also a difference between talking to the whole company and talking to senior hires or key operators. Founders should recognise that not every audience needs the same level of detail. A broad team explanation may need to stay high level while still being truthful. A senior hire taking meaningful equity, however, should usually be given a more grounded discussion. The more the company is relying on someone's grant to attract and retain them, the more honest and specific the company should be about what that grant means inside the real structure. High-leverage people deserve something stronger than slogans.

Another essential discipline is consistency. Founders damage trust when their equity language changes depending on the situation. If they talk about everyone being owners during recruiting, but speak like only investors matter during financing, or like only founders matter during secondary discussions, people notice. A healthy culture does not require identical treatment of different stakeholders, because founders, employees, and investors genuinely occupy different positions. It does require that the company's explanation of those differences remain coherent across contexts. Otherwise equity starts to feel like a rhetorical tool rather than a serious internal logic.

One subtle but powerful habit is to speak about ownership as part of company design, not only as compensation. Equity is often discussed only when someone is being granted something. But the better founders also explain, at the right times, how the company thinks about structure. Why vesting exists. Why option pools matter. Why future rounds change the cap table. Why the company cannot just grant endlessly without consequence. This teaches people that ownership is not just a perk machine. It is part of how the company is built.

That shift in mindset creates much better long-term conversations later when the company has to make harder structural decisions.
That is how founders should talk about equity internally. Not as myth, not as trivia, and not as an occasional legal footnote. They should talk about it as real, conditional, valuable, structured, and worth understanding. If they do that consistently, the company's ownership culture becomes far harder to break when financing, dilution, or exit reality eventually demands that the words line up with the cap table beneath them.

Explaining Equity Without Overselling It

One of the hardest communication disciplines in a startup is explaining equity in a way that remains attractive without becoming dishonest. This is difficult because founders are usually trying to do two things at once. They are trying to recruit, motivate, and retain people in an uncertain environment, and they are trying to describe an instrument whose value depends on future events no one can guarantee. The temptation is obvious. Soften the uncertainty, brighten the upside, and let the emotional power of ownership do the recruiting work. That temptation is understandable. It is also one of the fastest ways to create later distrust if the company's words run too far ahead of the cap table's real meaning.

This is why founders need to learn how to explain equity without overselling it.

Overselling usually begins with one of two habits. The first is inflation. The founder speaks as though the grant is likely to become life-changing simply because the company is ambitious and the grant exists. The second is simplification. The founder strips away too much of the structure and ends up describing the grant as if it were a direct slice of future sale proceeds with no dilution, no preferences, no vesting, and no uncertainty. Both habits can be persuasive in the short term. Both are dangerous because they teach the recipient to build expectations on a version of the company's ownership reality that does not actually exist.

The better approach is not to become cold or deflating. A founder can still say that equity matters, that early participation can be meaningful, and that joining now creates upside exposure that later hires may not get in the same way. Those things can all be true.

The difference is that the founder also makes clear what kind of claim is being offered and what conditions shape its value. It vests over time. The company will likely raise more capital. Different classes of stock can have different rights. The value depends on how well the company performs and what sort of exit or liquidity event eventually occurs. This does not make the offer less real. It makes it more trustworthy.

One of the strongest ways to avoid overselling is to shift from promise language to scenario language. Promise language sounds like this: this could be worth a fortune, you are getting in at the ground floor, this will make a huge difference later. Scenario language sounds more like this: if the company grows well and reaches a strong outcome, early equity can become very meaningful, but it is still subject to dilution, structure, and the timing of any eventual liquidity. The first style tries to create excitement by blurring conditions. The second creates seriousness by naming them. Seriousness tends to age much better than hype.

Another useful discipline is to avoid treating current paper valuation as if it were direct evidence of future grant value. This is one of the most common ways founders oversell unintentionally. The company just raised at a strong valuation, and someone is receiving a grant. The founder is tempted to mentally multiply the grant's percentage by the latest round value and let that number hover in conversation, even if only implicitly. That is usually misleading. A private financing valuation is not cash. It is a priced event under specific rights and terms. If founders want credibility, they should avoid turning those paper numbers into casual pseudo-wealth calculations for employees or hires.

This matters especially because many recipients are not financially naive, only structurally inexperienced. They know uncertainty exists. What they often lack is a working model of how startup equity actually behaves. Founders do not need to solve that lack of knowledge with complexity, but they should not exploit it with simplification either. A better explanation says, in effect, this is real upside, not guaranteed upside. It reflects your place in the company, but it will be shaped by future financing, future growth, and the company's eventual path. That kind of statement often makes strong candidates trust the company more, not less, because it signals that the founders are not trying to win commitment through ambiguity.

Another good rule is never to use equity to disguise a compensation weakness the company is unwilling to admit. If the salary is lower because the company is early, say so. If the company is offering meaningful upside partly because it cannot yet compete on cash, say so. That honesty is not a liability. It is usually a sign of maturity. What damages trust is when the company tries to make thin or uncertain equity sound like a direct replacement for the cash security and institutional clarity it cannot yet provide. Equity can offset some of that gap. It does not erase the gap altogether. Founders who admit that usually sound more credible than founders who behave as though ownership makes every trade-off disappear.

It is also important to explain the instrument in the right order. Many companies begin with the dream and add the conditions later, if at all. A better sequence is to explain what the person is receiving, how it vests, what it represents approximately, and then why it can still be valuable if the company succeeds. That order grounds the excitement in structure rather than letting structure arrive later as a correction. It changes the emotional experience from "I thought this was bigger and simpler than it is" to "I understand what this is, and it still sounds worthwhile." The latter is far better for long-term trust.

Founders should also watch for a very common internal rationalisation. They tell themselves they are overspeaking now because everyone in startups does it, because the person needs to be inspired, or because they can clear up the details later once the company has more time. That is almost always a mistake. Later clarification rarely feels like clarification. It usually feels like reduction. People remember the emotional meaning of the first explanation and compare the later detail against that memory. If the first explanation was inflated, the later truth feels like retreat. It is much better to start from a grounded explanation and let later company progress make the grant feel better, rather than start from exaggerated potential and let later structure make it feel worse.

A healthy company also avoids overselling by being consistent across contexts. If founders speak cautiously and accurately in board meetings but dramatically and simplistically in recruiting, the inconsistency will eventually show. The same is true if internal descriptions of employee grants sound ownership-rich while founder conversations privately admit that the common beneath the stack is much thinner than public language suggests. Consistency does not mean identical detail for every audience. It means the broad truth should not change depending on whether the company is trying to persuade or trying to analyse.

There is a strategic benefit here too. A founder who can explain equity well without overselling it is usually much better at judging the people they are hiring. Candidates who still find the grant attractive after hearing the real structure are often making a more mature choice than candidates who only respond to inflated visions of windfall. That may slightly narrow the pool. It usually improves alignment inside the pool that remains. The company ends up with people who are choosing the actual startup, not the simplified myth of one.

The point is not to drain all emotional energy from ownership conversation. Equity should feel meaningful. Joining early should feel different from joining late. The company should be able to say that if it succeeds, early grants can matter a great deal. But excitement should be built on real architecture, not on omission. The founder's job is not only to make the offer sound good. It is to make the offer sound true in a way that will still feel true when the company is larger, more layered, and under more financial scrutiny than it is today.

That is how to explain equity without overselling it. Say enough that people understand why it matters, but never so much that the future has to come back later and take the shine off by force.

Why Employees Should Understand Dilution Too

One of the quiet weaknesses in many startup cultures is that dilution is treated as something employees do not really need to understand until much later, if ever. Founders and investors discuss it. Lawyers model it. Finance people track it. Employees, meanwhile, are often left with a much simpler story: you have equity, the company is growing, and growth is good for everyone. That story is emotionally convenient. It is also incomplete in a way that can become corrosive. If employees are going to be asked to care about ownership, then they should understand not only upside but how that upside changes as the company raises more capital, enlarges option pools, and layers investor rights above the common. Otherwise the company is asking them to believe in an instrument it is not willing to explain honestly.

This is why employees should understand dilution too.

That does not mean every employee needs a masterclass in venture law.

It means the company should not behave as though dilution is some secret technical weather system that only senior people are allowed to comprehend. Dilution is one of the main things that shapes what an employee grant will actually mean over time. If the company is serious about using equity as part of compensation, then understanding dilution is part of understanding compensation. To hide or avoid that topic is not protecting employees from complexity. It is protecting the company from having to explain the real terms of its own bargain.

The reason this matters so much is that employee grants often feel largest at the moment they are made. The company is smaller. The team is thinner. The future is wide open. The founder may speak with excitement about upside and early participation. Then the company begins to grow. It raises capital. It hires more people. It may refresh the option pool. It may sign notes or SAFEs that later convert. Each of these events can change the fully diluted ownership picture. The employee is still holding the same grant count or roughly the same vested path, but its share of the overall structure may now be smaller than it felt at the beginning. If that possibility was never explained, the employee experiences ordinary startup development as a kind of hidden shrinkage rather than as the predictable structural trade-off it really is.

This is one reason dilution often feels more unfair than it actually is. Not because the company necessarily did anything improper, but because the employee was not prepared to see it as part of the growth story. A strong company says early, clearly, and repeatedly that if the business succeeds it will probably need more people and more money, and that this means ownership percentages usually do not stay frozen. The grant can still become more valuable in absolute terms if the company becomes stronger, even while the percentage becomes smaller. That is a subtle idea, but employees can understand it perfectly well if the company respects them enough to explain it.

There is also a practical reason employees should understand dilution. It changes how they interpret company milestones. A new financing round can be both good news and a dilution event. A larger pool can make it easier to hire the people needed for growth and still mean the ownership base is becoming broader. A high valuation can be exciting while still not translating directly into employee wealth.

If employees have never been taught how dilution works, they are left to process these events through headlines and mood. That usually produces one of two reactions. Either they assume every round automatically makes their grant more valuable in a simple linear way, or they later become disillusioned when they realise that the path from company growth to personal upside is more structured than they were led to believe.

Teaching employees about dilution also strengthens the company's credibility during hard moments. If the business ever has to do a weaker round, reprice grants, or revisit option strategy, a team that already understands dilution will not love the pain, but it is far less likely to feel deceived by the existence of the mechanism itself. A team that was taught only to associate equity with upward emotional language is much more likely to interpret any structural complication as betrayal. The same cap table event therefore lands very differently depending on the ownership culture built beforehand.

Another important point is that employees do not all need the same depth of explanation. A very broad team explanation can stay simple. Equity represents a claim on future upside. The company will likely raise more money and hire more people. That means ownership is diluted over time, though the company may also become more valuable if things go well. Rights and preferences can affect what common ultimately receives. That is already far better than saying nothing. Senior hires, early employees, and anyone receiving meaningfully large grants usually deserve more detail than that. The more heavily the company is relying on a person's equity package to recruit and align them, the stronger the company's duty to explain dilution clearly.

There is also a moral advantage in being more open about dilution. Many startups want employees to think like owners. But real owners do not only hear about upside. They also understand the ways their position can change. If the company wants maturity from its people, it should model maturity in how it talks about equity. An employee who understands dilution is often a better long-term participant in the company than one who has been kept on a simpler emotional script. They ask sharper questions. They evaluate grants more intelligently. They are less likely to swing from exaggerated hope to exaggerated bitterness later. In other words, teaching dilution is not just educational. It is cultural stabilisation.

A founder might worry that this will make equity sound less attractive. In some cases it may remove a little of the mystical glow. That is usually a good trade. A grant that remains compelling after honest explanation is much stronger than one that required haze to feel meaningful. The goal is not to make employees cynical. It is to make them informed enough that trust can survive the normal structural changes of startup life. If the company has to hide dilution to make equity sound worthwhile, that usually means something deeper is already weak, either in the grant itself or in the way the company is framing it.

One subtle benefit of teaching dilution is that it helps employees understand why the company cannot hand out equity endlessly to solve every people problem. If the team sees the option pool as a real, finite ownership resource rather than as a magical compensation cushion, it becomes easier to have adult conversations about grant size, role importance, and hiring priorities. The company can then speak about equity as design rather than as pure reward. That tends to create a healthier culture around both grants and fairness.

This is particularly important in companies that want to scale. A growing startup will almost certainly change its ownership shape several times before any exit. Employees who join early and stay through that growth should not have to piece together what dilution means from rumours, internet threads, or moments of personal disappointment. The company should teach them enough that the mechanics never arrive as a surprise. Surprise is what destroys trust. Difficulty does not have to.

That is why employees should understand dilution too. Because ownership culture is not honest if it explains only the pleasant half of ownership reality. If the company wants people to care about equity, it should also help them understand how equity changes as the business becomes more real.

Why Silence About Ownership Breeds Distrust

Most companies do not create ownership distrust by openly lying. They create it by staying too quiet for too long. Silence leaves space, and in that space people build their own assumptions. Employees assume their grants mean more than the structure supports.

Cofounders assume old allocations still feel fair because no one has challenged them. Senior hires assume a strong headline valuation means their common stock is sitting closer to cash than it really is. Investors assume the founders understand more than they do because the founders never admit uncertainty. Silence does not preserve simplicity. It produces private mythology.

This is why silence about ownership breeds distrust.
A founder may believe they are protecting the company by avoiding detailed equity conversations. They may think the structure is too technical, too sensitive, or too easy to misunderstand. Sometimes they simply do not feel confident enough in their own understanding to invite questions. All of that is human. But once the company begins using ownership as part of compensation, motivation, or identity, silence becomes costly. People do not stop thinking about equity because the company avoids the subject. They just think about it without guidance. That almost always produces a worse outcome than imperfect but honest explanation would have done.
Silence is especially dangerous because ownership has emotional weight. People hear the word equity and attach meaning to it quickly. It sounds like stake, belonging, and future reward. If the company does not explain what kind of stake, under what conditions, and beneath what rights structure, then the emotional meaning rushes far ahead of the structural meaning. The gap may remain invisible for months or years. Then a round happens, a sale appears, a grant is questioned, or someone leaves, and suddenly that gap becomes visible. What the company experiences as clarification, the employee or cofounder may experience as reduction. Not because the truth changed, but because silence allowed the first version of the truth in their mind to grow unchecked.

This is one reason ownership distrust often feels more moral than technical when it surfaces. The cap table mechanics may be perfectly legal. The documents may have been available. But if the company relied on silence while letting more flattering assumptions flourish, the people affected often do not experience the later explanation as neutral information. They experience it as the company having benefited from their earlier misunderstanding. Even when no deliberate manipulation occurred, the emotional result can be similar. Silence made the company look safer, more generous, or more aligned than the actual structure justified.

Founders sometimes imagine that silence is neutral because they are "not saying anything inaccurate." In practice, silence in a startup is rarely neutral. It usually advantages the more informed party. Investors often understand dilution. Founders may understand it partly. Employees and junior hires often understand it least. If the company chooses not to explain, the people at the bottom of that information hierarchy pay the highest cost later. This is why silence is not just an omission. It is a distribution choice. It decides who gets to live inside understanding and who gets to live inside hopeful inference.

Another problem is that silence weakens the company's response when hard moments come. If the company has never built a language for talking about dilution, preferences, option pools, or exit economics, then the first real conversation often happens under stress. A down round. A disappointing offer. A pool expansion. A confusing secondary. A founder dispute. Those are the worst moments to begin teaching ownership reality from scratch. People are already emotional, and the company has no prior trust reserve on the subject. What could have been a painful but understandable structural explanation becomes a credibility crisis because the silence before it made the truth feel sudden.

Silence also creates internal inconsistency. Different people start receiving different partial stories. One founder explains equity enthusiastically in hiring conversations. Another speaks much more cautiously in board settings. Finance or legal people know one version. Employees hear another. Because there is no shared ownership language inside the company, each context produces its own convenient translation. Over time, these differences collide. The company then does not only have a cap table problem. It has an interpretive problem. Different groups think the same ownership system means different things because the founders never made one coherent internal explanation the norm.

This matters with cofounders too, not just employees. Some of the worst founder disputes are not caused by the percentages alone, but by the fact that ownership subjects were left unspoken because everyone preferred peace. Vesting is delayed. Expected roles are never tied back to economics. Departure scenarios are not discussed. Everyone lets the table sit in a kind of respectful quiet. That quiet feels harmonious until reality diverges. Then all the conversations that should have happened incrementally arrive at once, and each one now carries the weight of accumulated avoidance. Silence turned manageable structural maintenance into emotionally loaded renegotiation.

A healthy company does not solve this by making ownership omnipresent or by turning every team conversation into a finance seminar. It solves it by making silence unnecessary. The company has a clear way to explain grants. A clear way to explain dilution. A clear way to explain what financing means for common holders. A clear way to answer questions without embarrassment. Once that exists, people no longer have to infer the company's ownership reality from tone, gossip, or occasional overheard fragments. They can ask. The company can answer. That alone removes a huge amount of avoidable distrust.

There is also a reputational reason to avoid silence. Companies develop internal memories. People remember whether equity questions were welcomed or brushed off. Whether founders answered directly or retreated into vague reassurance. Whether hard truths appeared early in understandable form or late in defensive form. These memories shape how future explanations are received. If the company has been silent or slippery, even a truthful explanation later will be heard through suspicion. If the company has been consistent and open, even painful news lands in a context where people know the founders are not inventing clarity only because they have been cornered.

Silence can also tempt founders into their own self-deception. If no one is asking ownership questions and no one is forcing scenario analysis into the room, the founders themselves may keep operating on simplified assumptions longer than they should. In that way, silence is not just something leaders impose downward. It can become a shared company habit of not looking too closely. That may feel easier. It also makes the eventual reckoning harsher because the founders now have to confront not only what the structure means, but how long they allowed themselves to avoid knowing it fully.

The cure is not overexposure. It is repeated, proportionate candour. Explain enough early that people do not build fantasy where the company should have built understanding. Explain enough consistently that later structural events feel like developments inside an already known system rather than sudden revelations. Explain enough precisely that the company does not have one ownership culture in recruiting, another in board meetings, and a third in moments of crisis. Once that pattern exists, ownership stops being a quiet source of future distrust and becomes part of the company's shared operating reality.

That is why silence about ownership breeds distrust. Not because every person needs every detail at all times, but because people will always form a relationship to the equity story whether the company guides that relationship or not. If the company refuses to speak, assumption fills the gap. And assumption is almost always kinder, simpler, and less structurally accurate than the cap table that was there all along.

Teaching New Hires What Their Grant Really Means

One of the clearest tests of a company's ownership culture is what happens when a new hire receives equity for the first time. This moment matters because it is where abstract philosophy becomes a concrete offer. The company is no longer merely saying that ownership matters in principle. It is placing a specific instrument in front of a real person and, through the way it explains that instrument, teaching them what kind of relationship this company expects them to have with risk, reward, and the future. If that teaching is weak, confused, or inflated, the damage begins immediately. The hire may still accept the offer, but they will accept it on terms of understanding the company did not really earn.

This is why new hires should never be left to decode their grant alone.

A founder may assume that because the documents exist, the meaning has been adequately conveyed. That is rarely true. Most people, even smart and capable people, do not have an intuitive grasp of how startup equity actually behaves. They may understand salary. They may understand bonuses. They may understand a pension or a stock grant in a public company. A private-company option grant, sitting inside a cap table that may later be diluted, repriced, or layered beneath investor preferences, is something else. If the company simply hands over the documents and expects the candidate to infer the practical meaning, it is not communicating. It is outsourcing understanding to guesswork.

The first thing a new hire should understand is what they are actually receiving. Not just "equity," but what kind. Is it an option grant. Restricted stock. Some other instrument. Does it vest over time. Is there a strike price. Is it already-issued ownership or a right to acquire ownership later. These basics matter because they determine what the person even has in hand. A company that skips this and jumps straight to enthusiasm is already inviting misunderstanding.

Excitement without instrument clarity is one of the oldest startup bad habits.
The second thing the company should explain is scale in a way that is honest. Raw share counts are not enough. If a person is receiving 25,000 or 100,000 options, that number should be placed in context. Roughly what fraction of the company does that represent on a fully diluted basis. Is it a meaningful early-stage grant for this level of role, or a smaller participation grant that should be understood as such. The company does not need to perform a full capital markets lecture in every hiring conversation, but it does need to avoid the lazy use of big numbers to create emotional impact. Scale without denominator is theatre.

The third thing a new hire should be told is that the grant will almost certainly change in relative meaning over time because the company is likely to raise more money, hire more people, and expand the structure. This is the point at which many companies become vague because they fear that dilution will make the grant sound weaker. In practice, careful explanation usually does the opposite. It makes the company sound more serious. The right message is not "your grant will be diluted and therefore disappoint you." It is "your grant may represent a smaller percentage later because the company will probably grow and finance itself further, but if that growth is strong enough the absolute value can still rise significantly." That is a mature explanation. It respects both structure and possibility.

A strong hiring conversation also explains the difference between valuation and liquidity. New hires often hear that the company raised at a certain valuation and instinctively connect that to their own grant. Founders should break that connection gently but clearly. A private valuation is a financing marker, not cash in hand. It may say something about company momentum, but it does not tell the hire what their grant is presently worth in an actionable sense. Nor does it tell them what they would personally receive in an exit without reference to the rights stack, future dilution, and eventual sale structure. This does not need to be framed ominously. It just needs to be framed truthfully.

Another important part of teaching is setting the right emotional frame. The company should not present the grant as either a lottery ticket or a formality. It should present it as a meaningful long-term upside instrument tied to the company's future performance and the person's continued participation.

That framing matters because it invites the hire to take the equity seriously without making them feel manipulated by extravagant promise. A candidate who joins after hearing that kind of explanation is usually entering the company with stronger psychological footing than one who joined mainly because the grant was allowed to shimmer in vagueness.

The company should also explain vesting with more seriousness than many do. Vesting is often treated like a minor technicality when in fact it shapes the person's whole relationship to the grant. How long before the first tranche vests. Whether there is a cliff. What happens if they leave before or after certain milestones. These are not small questions. They determine whether the grant is a long-term incentive with real staying logic or simply a flattering figure in an offer letter. New hires do not need to be frightened by vesting. They do need to understand it.

For more senior hires, the explanation should go further. If the company is relying heavily on equity to recruit someone into a key operating, technical, or commercial role, then a surface-level explanation is not enough. Senior people should usually be told where the common sits broadly relative to investor rights, what the company's likely financing path still looks like, whether the option pool is likely to need expanding again, and how the founders think about plausible outcome ranges. This is not because senior hires need exhaustive legal detail. It is because the more important the role and the larger the grant, the less acceptable it is to let misunderstanding carry the motivational burden.

There is also a retention benefit here. People stay better when they understand what they are staying for. If the company teaches new hires only the glamour of equity, their motivation may be strongest at the beginning and weaken later when the structure becomes more complex. If the company teaches them the real logic of the grant from the start, they are more likely to remain aligned through financing rounds, changing percentages, and the long middle years in which the company is neither obviously failing nor obviously winning. Clear explanation turns equity from a recruiting story into a durable incentive.

A further advantage is that this kind of teaching improves the company's internal standards. Once founders know they will have to explain each grant clearly, they tend to grant more carefully. It becomes harder to hand out weak, arbitrary, or emotionally motivated grants when someone will soon ask what this actually means. In that sense, teaching new hires is not only good for them. It is good for the founders because it forces discipline upstream. Companies that cannot explain their grants often grant badly. Companies that explain well usually get sharper about what they are issuing and why.

This does not mean overwhelming every candidate with complexity. The company should adapt to role, seniority, and context. But the principle remains fixed. Every new hire who receives equity should come away understanding what instrument they received, roughly what it represents, how vesting works, why dilution matters, and why the grant is still potentially meaningful if the company performs strongly. That is not too much to ask. It is the minimum needed to make ownership culture something more than marketing.

That is how a company teaches new hires what their grant really means. Not by draining all excitement from the offer, but by making sure the excitement is attached to a structure the company can still stand behind later.

Building a Company That Can Speak Honestly About Ownership

A company can only speak honestly about ownership if it has first decided that honesty is more important than convenience. That sounds obvious, but in practice it is one of the hardest cultural commitments a startup can make. Convenience is tempting at every stage. It is convenient to keep early founder conversations warm rather than exact. It is convenient to describe grants in raw numbers rather than in real context. It is convenient to let employees feel broadly optimistic rather than teach them dilution too early. It is convenient to celebrate valuations and stay quiet about preferences. It is convenient to postpone hard explanations until someone asks. Honest ownership culture begins the moment a company chooses not to take that easier route.

This matters because ownership truth is cumulative. A company that speaks loosely in the beginning rarely becomes sharply honest later without friction. The early habits harden. Founders get used to flattering shorthand. Employees learn to hear equity as a story of future abundance rather than a structured claim with conditions. Investors may receive one language while the team receives another.

By the time the company becomes complex enough that honesty is unavoidable, the earlier convenience has created a translation gap. The company is then no longer simply trying to explain structure. It is trying to reconcile old emotional promises with present structural reality. That is much harder than building the habit of truth earlier.

A company that can speak honestly about ownership usually has a few visible characteristics. First, the founders themselves understand the structure well enough that they do not need vagueness to sound confident. They know the difference between common and preferred. They know how dilution works. They know what the option pool is for. They know what a round did to founder stakes and what likely future rounds may do next. They know the broad exit economics well enough that they are not frightened by their own cap table. Without that internal literacy, honest external communication is almost impossible. People speak vaguely most often when they do not fully trust their own grip on the facts.

Second, the company has a repeatable internal language. Not a script, but a coherent way of explaining grants, vesting, dilution, and financing events that does not change opportunistically depending on the audience. Employees may hear a simpler version than investors. A senior hire may get more detail than a junior one. But the broad truth remains the same. Equity is real but conditional. Dilution is normal in growth. Valuation is not the same as liquidity. Rights matter. Early grants can be meaningful, but not all grants are founder-level. This consistency is one of the strongest markers that ownership culture is being governed rather than improvised.

Third, the company does not punish curiosity. People can ask what their grant means. They can ask about dilution. They can ask what a financing round changes. They can ask how preferences affect common in broad terms. They do not need to become experts, but they are not made to feel rude or disloyal for wanting to understand the instrument the company uses to align them with its future. When that kind of questioning is normal, ownership becomes part of the company's real operating language. When it is subtly discouraged, ownership becomes mystique. Mystique is always weaker than literacy.

Another sign of honesty is that the company does not rely on crisis to begin explaining reality. A weak ownership culture waits until something painful happens and then starts telling the truth because it has run out of alternatives. A stronger one teaches enough along the way that painful events still hurt, but they do not feel like revelations. A new round may dilute the common. An option pool may expand. A buyer may appear at a price that sounds large but distributes unevenly. In an honest ownership culture, these are developments within a known system, not moments where the company suddenly admits that the system was always more complex than it let on.

This kind of culture also changes how founders think about their own incentives. If the company can speak honestly about ownership, it usually means the founders are not hiding from their own economics either. They know whether the common still matters for them across plausible outcomes. They know whether the stack has become too heavy. They know when another financing would change the meaning of founder ownership materially. That self-knowledge matters because companies often become dishonest outwardly only after the founders have already become vague inwardly. Internal clarity tends to support external clarity. Internal avoidance almost always produces external simplification.

An honest ownership culture is also less likely to use equity as emotional glue for unrelated problems. If a company needs to hire, it does not automatically reach for inflated equity language to compensate for a weak cash package. If it needs to retain someone, it does not pretend a small top-up grant is transformational when it is not. If it needs to thank an adviser, it does not casually convert gratitude into permanent ownership without asking whether ownership is really the right instrument. This discipline comes from seeing equity as a serious structural resource rather than as a soft social token.

There is an investor benefit here too. Companies that can speak honestly about ownership are usually easier to finance because they are less likely to produce unpleasant surprises in diligence or in internal alignment later. An investor may not love every line on the table, but they will usually trust a founder more if the founder can explain the weak spots plainly, quantify them, and show how the company thinks about them. The same principle applies to hires, boards, and acquirers. Honesty does not erase structural weakness. It makes the weakness governable because it is no longer hidden behind rhetoric.

This does not mean the company should make ownership the centre of every conversation. Culture can become distorted in the opposite direction too, where equity is discussed so constantly and so technically that people stop hearing it as part of a shared mission and start hearing it only as a financial instrument. That is not the goal. The goal is proportion. Ownership should be explained enough that no one has to build their own fantasy version of it, but not so obsessively that the company sounds like a spreadsheet with a product attached. A healthy company knows when to teach, when to answer, and when to keep building.

The deepest reason all of this matters is that ownership culture determines whether the company's internal story can survive contact with reality. Startups ask people to trade certainty for possibility. That is a legitimate bargain only if the possibility is described with enough honesty that people can choose it knowingly. The company does not owe everyone a guarantee. It does owe them a version of the truth that will not later need to be revised downward by force. When that standard is met, even hard structural realities become easier to carry because people feel they were not tricked into believing something simpler than the company itself believed.

That is what it means to build a company that can speak honestly about ownership. It means the cap table is no longer treated as a private technical object with a public myth layered over it. It means the company's words and its structure are close enough that future rounds, future dilution, and eventual exits do not constantly expose the gap between what was said and what was real. And that, in the end, is one of the strongest forms of trust a startup can build.

* * *

EIGHTEEN

The Cap Table as Strategy, Not Administration

"Plans are only good intentions unless they immediately degenerate into hard work."

- Peter Drucker

Why Ownership Structure Is Part of Company Strategy

One of the last illusions founders give up is the illusion that the cap table belongs mainly to lawyers, finance people, and fundraising moments. At first that illusion feels practical. The founders are busy building product, finding customers, hiring people, surviving uncertainty, and trying to keep the company alive. Ownership structure seems like background machinery. Important, yes, but not central. Something to maintain rather than to think through continuously. That view is understandable early on. It becomes dangerous later. Because once a company begins to hire with equity, raise across multiple rounds, layer investor rights, and shape its future around possible exits or long private growth, ownership structure stops being mere administration. It becomes strategy.

This is why the cap table should be understood not only as a record of what the company has done, but as a set of decisions about what kind of company it will still be able to become.

Every meaningful ownership decision carries strategic implications.

A founder split is not only a fairness question. It decides whether the founding team will remain aligned when contribution diverges. An option pool is not only a compensation bucket. It decides how much room the company has left to attract future talent without destabilising the common. A priced round is not only a cash event. It decides how much of the future must be sold to buy the next stage and what rights will now sit above the founders and employees. A SAFE or note is not only a bridge. It decides how much future dilution is already quietly waiting for the next round. A secondary is not only liquidity. It changes how the founder now relates to future upside and how others read that relationship. These are strategic consequences, whether the founders choose to think of them that way or not.

That is why treating the cap table as administration is so risky. Administration records the consequence after the decision. Strategy examines the consequence before the decision is locked in. A founder who stays in administrative mode updates the spreadsheet after the round, the grant, the note, or the departure. A founder thinking strategically asks beforehand what this move will do to founder motivation, hiring room, financing flexibility, and exit economics. The table will record either kind of choice. Only one kind is actively governing the future.

This becomes even clearer when you ask a simple question. What things most determine whether this company can survive its next major transition. The answer is rarely only product or revenue. It is often also whether the founders still have enough ownership to care, whether the employee grants still mean enough to retain key people, whether the next investor can be brought in without inheriting structural nonsense, whether the preference stack still leaves moderate outcomes meaningful, and whether the current rights package has preserved room for another round without turning the company into a hostage to its own past financing. Those are all cap table questions. They are also plainly strategic questions.

A cap table is strategic because it allocates not only value, but future options.

This is one of the most underappreciated points in startup building. A good structure leaves room. Room to hire. Room to raise again. Room to take a good strategic acquisition if one appears. Room for a founder to stay rational after another round. Room for investors to support the company without making later allocations impossible. Room for employees to believe the ownership story without needing fantasy. When founders protect only the immediate moment and ignore room, they often discover too late that the company can still operate but can no longer move easily. That is not merely an ownership issue. It is a strategic narrowing of the company's future.

This is also why ownership structure shapes behaviour long before any exit or crisis appears. A founder whose common only becomes meaningful at very high outcomes will often behave differently from one whose economics still work in moderate but respectable outcomes. A company with a light preference burden can consider a wider range of strategic offers than one whose common is nearly irrelevant below heroic numbers.

A startup with a well-sized pool can recruit differently from one that has already spent most of its future room on emotional or poorly governed grants. The structure is therefore not passive. It influences what kinds of actions the company is likely to take because it changes which outcomes are still economically real for the people involved.
Investors understand this better than many first-time founders do. That is one reason they negotiate for rights so carefully. They are not only trying to own part of the company. They are trying to shape how their ownership behaves across future strategic states. Will they be protected in a weak round. Can they maintain position in a strong one. Are they senior in middling exits. Do they have enough information and control rights to steer or block certain moves. These are strategic questions from the investor side. Founders need to become equally comfortable seeing the cap table through that same lens rather than assuming that strategy lives only in product, market, and hiring while ownership lives in the back office.

There is another way to see this. Most founders would agree that choosing the wrong market can damage a company, that hiring the wrong senior team can damage a company, and that taking the wrong kind of customer or partner can damage a company. Yet many of the same founders still speak about ownership as if it were mainly a matter of recording percentages accurately after the "real" decisions have been made. That is far too narrow. Ownership structure determines who remains motivated, who has leverage, who has vetoes, who can keep investing, who gets paid first, and what kinds of outcomes count as success for different stakeholders. A system that does all of that is not administrative in any serious sense. It is part of the company's core design.

This is particularly important in companies that expect multiple rounds, significant hiring, or a long path to liquidity. In such companies the cap table becomes a running theory of the business. It expresses how the company thinks value will be created, who will need to be brought in to create it, how much capital it will take, how much of the future must be sold to buy that capital, and what sort of exit or continuation would still make sense for those carrying the load. If that theory is weak, the business may still grow for a while, but its internal incentives and financing logic will become increasingly strained. That strain usually appears first as discomfort, then later as conflict or poor strategic choices. Again, that is not separate from company strategy. It is company strategy showing up through the ownership architecture.

A strong founder eventually starts asking strategic questions in cap table language almost automatically. If we raise this round, what kind of company are we becoming. If we grant this pool, what kind of hiring future are we assuming. If we accept this preference stack, what kind of exits are we still really building for. If we let this dead equity stay, what does that say about who is paying for the past versus who is building the future. If we speak about ownership this way internally, what kind of culture are we creating around incentives and trust. Those are strategic questions expressed through structure rather than through product roadmaps. That is exactly the shift mature operators make.

This is why the founder who still thinks of the cap table as administration is often already behind. They are not necessarily careless. They may even be diligent in updating the numbers. But they are letting the ownership machine shape the company without fully engaging its strategic meaning. Eventually the machine forces itself into the foreground anyway, often at the worst possible moment. A financing gets harder than expected. A founder no longer feels motivated by the common. A buyer appears and the common economics are thinner than the headline suggests. A key employee asks what their grant really means and the founders realise the answer is weaker than the culture implied. All of these are moments when administration proves insufficient and strategy, neglected earlier, arrives late.

That is why ownership structure is part of company strategy. Because it decides not only who has what, but what the company can still credibly do next, what kinds of outcomes still matter, and whether the people expected to carry the business are still connected strongly enough to the future they are being asked to build. Once a founder sees that clearly, the cap table stops being a spreadsheet that happens to matter and becomes what it always was: one of the core strategic maps of the company itself.

How Financing Choices Shape the Kind of Company You Build

Founders often talk about financing as though it were mainly a question of how much money the company can obtain and on what timeline. That is only the surface of it. Every financing choice also shapes what kind of company the business is still capable of becoming. This is one of the deepest strategic truths in startup life, and one of the least appreciated early on. Capital does not enter a neutral machine.

It enters by changing the machine. The amount raised matters. The valuation matters. The rights matter. The preferences matter. The future expectations matter. Put together, those things decide not only how well funded the company is, but what strategic paths are still open, what incentives remain live, and what sorts of outcomes the business is now effectively building toward.

This is why financing choices are never only financial choices. They are design choices.

A bootstrapped or lightly funded company behaves differently from a heavily venture-backed one not simply because one has more cash. It behaves differently because the ownership structure, the expected pace, the tolerance for moderate outcomes, and the relationship between founders and future rounds are different. A company that raises a great deal of capital early often buys speed, talent, and runway. It may also buy a higher threshold for what counts as success. A company that preserves ownership longer may move more slowly, but it may also remain economically meaningful to the common across a wider range of exit values. Neither path is automatically superior. The point is that the financing path becomes part of the company's strategic identity whether the founder articulates it that way or not.

This can be seen most clearly in how later rounds shape ambition. A company with a light preference stack and a meaningful common layer may be able to consider a respectable acquisition, a strategic merger, or a period of durable independent growth without those paths becoming economically absurd for the founders and team. A company that has raised aggressively at high prices with multiple preferred layers may find that only very large outcomes now make sense for the common. That does not just change economics at exit. It changes present behaviour. The company may become more risk-seeking, more dependent on further capital, and less able to choose moderate but rational paths because the financing history has silently redefined what "winning" now means.

This is one of the main ways financing shapes company type. It changes the minimum viable success case.

A founder who understands that will read every round differently. The question stops being only can we raise this money. It becomes what kind of company will we have to become in order for this round to make sense later.

If the answer is that the company must now grow much faster, hire much more aggressively, and ultimately reach much larger outcomes before the common economics are attractive, then the founder should be honest that they are no longer just financing growth. They are accepting a strategic ratchet. The company now has to live up to a larger narrative because the ownership structure beneath it has been priced around that expectation.

This is why the same amount of capital can be healthy in one company and distorting in another. A business with long development cycles, high technical risk, or genuine network-scale potential may rationally need deep financing early. A capital-light business that raises in the same style may simply be building unnecessary pressure into the cap table. Founders sometimes borrow financing habits from the ecosystem around them instead of from the actual demands of their own business. The result is not just overfunding or underfunding. It is a mismatch between structure and strategy. The company ends up financed for one kind of future while trying to live inside another.

There is also the issue of who the company becomes answerable to. A financing choice does not only decide how much runway exists. It decides what kind of constituency the company is now carrying. A round led by patient angels is different from one led by a fund that needs venture-scale outcomes. A round that introduces heavy preference and control rights is different from one that leaves more flexibility in founder hands. A round that expects frequent follow-on financing is different from one that genuinely extends runway toward self-sustaining optionality. These are strategic differences because they shape how much freedom the company retains to choose among futures rather than being pulled toward one by the logic of its capital.

Hiring strategy is affected too. Once a company raises on certain terms, it often creates not only financial capacity but structural obligation to use that capacity in specific ways. A large option pool implies a company that expects to hire significantly. A heavily funded round often implies a burn pattern that must justify itself through growth. A tighter structure may force more discipline and slower team building. In each case, the financing choice has already expressed a view about how the company should scale. The founders may still imagine they are deciding that later. Often the cap table has already made much of the decision for them.

This is one reason founder self-awareness matters so much. Some founders genuinely want to build companies that can only make sense at large scale with multiple rounds and strong investor involvement. Others want more strategic flexibility, more room for moderate but meaningful outcomes, or more founder control over timing. Neither instinct is childish. The mistake is when the founder's financing choices quietly commit the company to one path while the founder still speaks emotionally as though they are pursuing the other. That is how companies drift into internal contradiction. The founder says they want optionality, but the structure only really rewards aggressive scale. Or the founder says they want venture-scale ambition, but they refuse financing terms that would actually support building that sort of company seriously.

This is also where valuation vanity becomes dangerous. A founder may choose a financing structure because the headline valuation sounds strong, not because the resulting company remains strategically healthy. A higher price can preserve more common in the immediate round, but if it also sets unrealistic expectations for the next raise or pushes the company into a path where only further high-priced growth rounds make the story cohere, then the strategic cost may be higher than it first appears. Once again, financing choice is not just about current dilution. It is about what future shape of company the business is now being forced to justify.

Another strategic effect lies in exit timing. Some financing paths leave the company able to say yes to offers that are good, though not spectacular. Others make such offers almost meaningless to the common. That difference feeds back into strategy years before any buyer appears. A company whose structure has preserved moderate-outcome relevance can remain more pragmatic. A company whose common only becomes powerful in very large exits often has to behave as though anything short of that is failure. That may be rational for some businesses. It may be ruinous for others. The financing path is what often decides which mindset the company is structurally pushed toward.

A founder thinking strategically therefore asks financing questions in future-tense terms. If we take this round, what sort of growth path must follow. What exits still matter afterward. What future rounds are we implicitly signing up for. What happens to founder and employee meaning if those rounds occur. How much room remains if the market cools or timelines slip.

These are not defensive questions. They are the real content of capital strategy. Without them, financing becomes a series of present-tense wins that may gradually produce a future the company is much less free to choose.
That is why financing choices shape the kind of company you build. They determine not only what resources the company has, but what ownership burden, incentive structure, and strategic threshold now sit underneath those resources. The founders can still execute brilliantly or poorly inside that structure. But the structure itself is already deciding what counts as enough, what paths remain attractive, and what sorts of futures are still economically coherent for the people involved.

Why Too Much Capital Can Be as Dangerous as Too Little

Founders are often warned about undercapitalisation, and rightly so. Too little money can suffocate a company before it reaches product maturity, before it hires the right people, before it survives the normal delays and mistakes that real businesses almost always encounter. But there is a second danger that startup culture sometimes treats too lightly because it arrives wearing the costume of success. Too much capital can be as dangerous as too little. Not because money itself is bad, but because capital always comes attached to structure, pace, expectations, and rights. When a company takes in more than it can use intelligently, or more than its actual business model justifies, the damage is not only financial. It becomes strategic and cultural.

This is one of the hardest lessons for founders to accept because raising money usually feels like winning. An investor says yes. A round closes. The company looks validated. The team relaxes. Ambition expands. But capital is not neutral fuel. It has to be converted into company-building through hiring, product development, go-to-market execution, and time. If the company takes in more capital than it can turn into real progress at a healthy rate, then the cap table has been spent on a future the business may not actually be able to justify. The company is now more diluted, more preference-burdened, and often under pressure to behave like a larger business before it has earned the right to do so.

This is why excess capital can be dangerous. It can distort both pace and perception.
The pace distortion is often the first problem. A heavily funded company may feel it has to hire faster, expand faster, launch faster, and signal scale faster because the amount of money raised itself becomes a kind of strategic promise. Even if no investor says it directly, the round creates an implied question. What is all this capital for if not aggressive movement. A founder who might otherwise have been disciplined is now running inside a structure that rewards visible momentum, because a large raise with little visible acceleration starts to look like underperformance. The company may then hire before it has clarity, spend before it has efficiency, and broaden before it has real fit. None of this is caused by bad intentions. It is caused by the financing structure making patience more difficult.

The perception distortion is subtler but just as serious. Once a company raises a substantial round, people inside and outside the business start treating it differently. Employees may assume the business is safer than it really is. Founders may assume product-market fit is closer than it is because sophisticated investors backed the company. The market may start seeing the company through valuation and total-raised headlines rather than through operating fundamentals. This can create a dangerous internal drift where the startup begins performing maturity instead of earning it. The company looks bigger on paper than it is in fact, and the cap table has already been sold as though that paper status meant something durable.

This matters because too much capital almost always changes the minimum acceptable outcome. If a lightly funded company sells for a respectable figure, that can still be meaningful to founders and employees. If a heavily funded company with stacked preferences sells for the same figure, the common may receive very little. The extra capital did not only buy more runway. It also raised the threshold at which the common economics begin to feel rewarding. This is one of the clearest strategic costs of overcapitalisation. The company does not merely have more money. It now needs a larger success to make the ownership structure feel worthwhile for the builders underneath it.

That in turn affects behaviour. Founders who know, consciously or not, that only very large outcomes still matter to the common often become more risk-seeking.

Moderate outcomes lose emotional force. Strategic acquisition offers that would once have been sensible now feel like surrender because the structure above the common absorbs too much of the proceeds. The company starts behaving as though only one kind of future is acceptable, not necessarily because the founders are visionary in a disciplined way, but because the cap table has made other futures less meaningful to them. This is one of the hidden ways excessive capital reshapes company strategy. It narrows what still counts as success.

There is also an employee effect. A company that raises too much too early often ends up distributing options in a context where the common already sits beneath a larger preference burden than the team fully appreciates. The hires may look strong, the grants may sound impressive, and the brand of the company may rise. Yet the actual path from employee common to meaningful value may be thinner than it appears. If later financings continue, the situation can worsen. The company has then used capital to buy growth optics while simultaneously weakening the range of outcomes in which its ownership culture remains convincing.

This is why founders should ask not only can we raise this money, but can we use this money without becoming structurally more fragile. The answer depends on the business. Some companies truly do need deep capital early because the problem is technically hard, regulation is heavy, hardware is expensive, or the market opportunity justifies aggressive scaling. In those cases, large financing may be rational. But even then, the founder should still be honest about what kind of company that financing path creates. It creates one that must justify more capital, more rights, and often a higher threshold for what counts as success. If the founder wants that, good. If the founder merely likes the feeling of being heavily funded, the company is drifting into a very costly illusion.

One of the most reliable warning signs is when capital arrives faster than the company's operating discipline matures. The round may be strong. The company may be in fashion. The market may be hot. But if the founders have not yet built the habits needed to allocate ownership carefully, hire carefully, and measure progress honestly, then large amounts of money can amplify immaturity rather than solve it. The company does not become stronger simply because it can spend more. It becomes louder. If the underlying judgments are weak, more capital means more room to make bigger mistakes while also selling more of the future to finance them.

This is why some of the healthiest companies are not the ones that raised the most, but the ones that raised in proportion to what they could actually convert into durable advantage. They used capital to solve real constraints, not to purchase status. They preserved enough common meaning that later strategic options still felt broad. They did not force the business into scale theatre before the product, team, and customer logic had caught up. Their cap table remained a support for strategy rather than a pressure system demanding performance the business had not yet structurally earned.

The founder's best defence here is to think in terms of fit. Not whether capital is available, but whether this amount of capital, on these terms, at this stage, fits the company's real needs and real capacity. Can we spend it intelligently. Can we preserve enough room beneath it that future rounds or moderate outcomes do not become economically hollow. Will it help us find reality faster, or encourage us to postpone reality beneath a bigger burn rate and a more flattering paper story. Those are strategic cap table questions, even though they begin with fundraising.

That is why too much capital can be as dangerous as too little. Too little can starve the company. Too much can pressure it into becoming the wrong version of itself while weakening the common beneath a heavier structure. The ideal is not poverty. It is proportionality. Enough capital to solve the real next stage, not so much that the ownership system now requires a future the business may not be built to deliver.

Using Equity to Buy Time, Talent, or Trust

Equity is one of the most flexible instruments a startup has, which is exactly why it is so often misused. Founders reach for it in moments of pressure because ownership can seem to solve multiple problems at once. It can bring in capital when cash is scarce. It can attract talent when salaries are weak. It can calm a cofounder dispute. It can thank an adviser, retain an executive, or persuade someone important to keep believing in the company a little longer. In all these cases, equity is being used to buy something. That is the right way to think about it. The problem is that founders often buy without asking clearly enough what they are buying, how much it is actually worth, and whether ownership is the right currency for that purchase.

This is why equity should never be treated as a sentimental reward alone. It is a strategic spending instrument.

The first thing founders often buy with equity is time. Convertible notes, SAFEs, bridge rounds, and even hurried grants can all be ways of purchasing more time before the company has to face a harder truth. Sometimes that is exactly the right move. A company may need six more months to finish a product, hit a milestone, or reach a financing event under better conditions. Equity can buy that runway when cash from operations cannot. But time purchased with ownership is never free. The founder has to ask whether the time being bought is likely to create enough additional value that the ownership spent on it was justified. If the company is merely delaying a truth it is not usingfully approaching, then equity has been spent not on time but on denial.

The second common purchase is talent. This can be highly rational. Startups often cannot get the right people on salary alone, especially in the early stage. Equity can bridge the gap by saying, in effect, join us now at lower certainty and share in what we build. That is a legitimate bargain. But the company has to be disciplined about what kind of talent is worth permanent ownership and at what scale. Founders often overpay in equity when they are emotionally impressed by a candidate, under pressure to fill a role, or using ownership to compensate for their own uncertainty about what the person will really contribute. The right question is not simply whether the hire is good. It is whether the long-term ownership cost is proportionate to the actual strategic value the person is likely to create.

The third thing equity often buys is trust. Founders use it to keep people close, to make others feel included, to show seriousness, to smooth relationships that might otherwise become strained. A small grant to a helpful early supporter. A founder-level allocation given to preserve harmony. An adviser stake offered more out of gratitude or social pressure than out of clear structural need. This is where equity becomes especially dangerous, because trust bought through ownership often feels successful in the moment. The relationship warms. The awkwardness reduces. The person feels recognised. But unless the contribution being rewarded is durable and significant enough to justify a real claim on the future, the company has paid for emotional peace with structural cost. That trade is often much more expensive than it first appears.

This is why founders should always ask a brutally simple question when using equity: what exactly are we buying. Not in vague startup language, but in concrete terms. Are we buying twelve months of runway to reach a real milestone. Are we buying a critical technical leader who will carry a major part of the product. Are we buying a chance to preserve founder commitment through a painful phase. Or are we buying reassurance, politeness, status, and the feeling of momentum. These are not the same purchases. Some are good uses of ownership. Others are often signs that the company is spending future value to avoid discomfort in the present.

A good way to see this is to notice that equity is most often misused when cash is emotionally difficult but structurally more appropriate. Founders may avoid paying cash for a real consulting project, a temporary adviser, or a bounded piece of work because cash feels scarce and equity feels abstract. So they pay in ownership instead. That may help today's budget. It can also leave the company with permanent cap table residue from contributions that were temporary or replaceable. In many cases the better question is not "can we afford to use cash." It is "can we afford not to," given what permanent ownership actually costs if the company works.

The same logic applies to investor capital. When a company raises money, it is buying time and possibility with dilution and future rights. That may be entirely right. But if the founders are not precise about what the capital is meant to buy, then equity has been spent without a disciplined purchase thesis. The round then becomes expensive in a deeper way. The company is not only diluted. It is diluted without clear strategic gain. That is usually how too much capital becomes dangerous: ownership was sold to buy optionality, prestige, or relief rather than a sharply defined next phase of real value creation.

Using equity well therefore depends on fit between instrument and purpose. Equity is strongest when the thing being bought is itself long-term, uncertain, and deeply tied to the company's future. A cofounder who will build for years. A key early hire whose contribution is central and enduring. Capital that extends the company toward a materially stronger future state. In these cases, ownership is being exchanged for something that lives on roughly the same timescale as the ownership itself. Equity is weakest when it is used to pay for short-term, ambiguous, or emotionally motivated needs. Then the company is using a permanent future claim to buy something temporary, fuzzy, or avoidable.

Another way to frame it is that equity should usually buy leverage, not just survival. Survival alone may justify it in true emergency, but if that becomes a pattern, the company is repeatedly spending future value to stay alive without strengthening the engine enough to make the spend worthwhile. By contrast, when equity buys a stronger team, clearer product progress, more credible future fundraising, or a more defensible strategic position, the ownership cost can be rational because the company has become genuinely better rather than merely less immediately threatened. The founder's task is to know the difference.

This also explains why equity discipline is inseparable from strategy. If the company knows clearly what next milestone matters most, what hires are genuinely pivotal, and what financing amount truly extends it into a stronger strategic position, then equity can be used precisely. If the company is vague about all of that, then ownership tends to be spent vaguely too. The cap table becomes a record of all the times the founders purchased hope in different forms without pinning down the actual object of the purchase. That is not strategy. It is drift financed by dilution.

One practical habit helps enormously here. Before any meaningful equity decision, ask not only what we are giving, but what specific thing the company will have afterward that it would not otherwise have had. More time to do what. More talent for which mission-critical function. More trust with what continuing contribution attached. More capital leading to what measurable next state. If those answers are thin, then the company is probably using equity too loosely. If the answers are strong, ownership may well be the right tool.

That is why equity should be seen as a strategic currency. It can buy time, talent, or trust, but only some purchases justify permanent claims on the company's future. Founders who understand this stop using ownership to soothe the present and start using it to build the future more deliberately.

Why Every Ownership Decision Has a Strategic Cost

The easiest way to become careless with a cap table is to treat ownership decisions as though they only have arithmetic cost. A founder gives away one percent, sells ten percent, expands a pool by five percent, signs a SAFE for a certain amount, and thinks mainly in terms of visible dilution. The numbers go down.

The spreadsheet updates. Something has been spent. That is true, but it is only the shallowest version of the truth. Every ownership decision also has a strategic cost. It changes not just how much of the company belongs to whom, but what kinds of moves the company can still make later, what kinds of outcomes still feel meaningful, and how much room remains for the next necessary stage.

This is why ownership should never be priced only in percentages. A founder who gives away one percent to an adviser may think they have paid a small price. But what if that one percent comes from room the company later needs for a genuinely critical early engineer. What if it sits on the table as one more weakly justified line that future investors read as evidence of sloppy governance. What if it is one of ten such "small" decisions that together make the pool tighter and the founder thinner. The strategic cost of that one percent may therefore be much larger than the arithmetic alone suggests. It has not only reduced ownership. It has reduced optionality.

This is the recurring theme. Ownership decisions spend future room. A founder may decide to raise more money now because the cheque is available and the valuation sounds strong. The arithmetic cost is visible: new shares, lower founder percentages, more preferred stock. But the strategic cost may be even more important. The company may now need a larger next round to maintain the narrative. The preference stack may become thick enough that moderate exits lose meaning for the common. The founder may become structurally committed to a much larger outcome than the actual business model once required. The company has not simply sold part of itself. It has narrowed the set of futures that still make economic sense.

That is what many first-time founders miss. Ownership does not only distribute value. It shapes the threshold at which value still matters. This is why a seemingly generous hiring grant can be strategically expensive, even if it looks affordable in isolation. Suppose the company gives a meaningful option package to a hire who is good but not truly pivotal, partly because the founders are under pressure and want to close quickly. The arithmetic cost is the grant itself. The strategic cost is that later, when a truly indispensable hire appears, the pool may be too tight, forcing the company into either a weak offer, a new pool expansion, or a financing structure that shifts more pain onto the common.

What seemed like one manageable concession has altered the company's later hiring posture.

The same is true with investor rights. A liquidation preference, anti-dilution clause, or broad pro rata right is often understood first as a term in a deal. But each right also changes the company's strategic behaviour later. A heavy preference stack can make the founders less interested in moderate acquisition offers. Strong anti-dilution can make rescue capital much harder to accept. Broad pro rata rights can crowd future round allocation. These are not abstract side effects. They are part of the price the company pays for current capital. If the founder looks only at the current cheque and the current percentage sold, they are underpricing the real transaction.

That is why strong founders begin asking a different kind of question before ownership decisions. Not just how much of the company does this cost now, but what future flexibility does this consume. Can we still raise cleanly after this. Can we still hire. Can we still make a sensible sale decision in a moderate range. Can the founders still care enough after another likely round. Can employees still believe in the common honestly. These are strategic cost questions, and they are often more important than the immediate dilution percentage.

Another way to understand this is to think of ownership as carrying both financial weight and directional weight. Financial weight is the visible reduction in percentage or increase in obligations. Directional weight is what the decision now nudges the company toward. A big round may push toward scale and further rounds. A thin founder position may push toward risk-seeking because only huge exits still matter. A weak pool may push toward underhiring or overpromising. A messy SAFE stack may push toward financing complexity later. Once founders start seeing directional weight, they stop treating the cap table as passive background and start seeing it as a steering mechanism.

This is one reason hindsight around cap tables can be so painful. Founders often look back and realise that what hurt was not one dramatic dilution event, but a chain of ownership decisions that each quietly altered the company's future logic. A soft early founder split made later motivation harder. A few casual grants made the pool weaker. A bridge round delayed a harder truth without buying enough real progress. A large round raised the outcome threshold beyond what the business naturally wanted to become. None of these was only a number. Each was a strategy choice wearing financial clothes.

It is also why not all expensive-looking ownership decisions are actually bad. Sometimes a company spends real ownership and buys something strategically decisive in return. A key technical founder joins. A crucial early executive takes a meaningful grant and changes the company's trajectory. A financing round gives enough runway to reach a genuinely stronger state rather than merely extending ambiguity. In these cases the arithmetic cost may still be painful, but the strategic cost is justified because the company is now stronger in a way that preserves or increases future optionality rather than shrinking it. The key is not to avoid ownership spending. It is to know what you are buying and whether the future you are giving up is smaller than the future you are making possible.

Founders also need to understand that strategic cost accumulates asymmetrically. Some ownership decisions mainly reduce present percentage. Others specifically damage later manoeuvrability. Those are usually the most dangerous. A founder may emotionally focus on the dilution they can see while missing the deeper strategic loss they cannot. For example, a round that only modestly dilutes but introduces heavy rights may be more strategically expensive than a slightly more dilutive round with cleaner terms. This is why percentage alone is such a weak measure of deal quality. Strategic cost often lives in the rights stack, not just in the share count.

A healthy habit is therefore to ask of every ownership decision: what future problem are we solving, what future problem are we creating, and which of those two is likely to matter more. If the company cannot answer that, the decision is probably being made too reactively. Equity should not be used simply because it is available to spend. It should be used because the thing it buys is worth the future strategic narrowing it causes.

That is why every ownership decision has a strategic cost. The cap table is not a ledger sitting beside the company. It is one of the systems that decides what kind of company can still emerge from the one you have today.

Designing for the Next Round Before It Arrives

One of the strongest habits a founder can build is the habit of designing the cap table for the next round before the next round is real. Most founders do the opposite. They design for the current problem.

They need money now, a hire now, a bridge now, a compromise now, a pool expansion now. The structure is shaped to solve immediate pressure, and only later, when another financing appears, does the company discover what that pressure relief quietly cost. By then the company is no longer designing freely. It is negotiating from inside the consequences of its earlier choices.

This is why the next round should be considered before the current decision closes.

A startup almost never experiences ownership in isolated events. A round is followed by another round, or by a pool increase, or by conversion, or by a strategic reset, or by a sale discussion shaped by what the earlier financing already did. That means the true cost of any ownership decision cannot be read only in present tense. A founder who says "this round is survivable" but has not asked what the company looks like after the next likely round has only done half the work. And in cap table terms, half the work is often where the danger hides.

Designing for the next round means asking a set of forward-facing questions now, before the company is under time pressure again. If we raise this capital on these terms, what does founder ownership likely look like after the next financing. If we expand the pool now, will it still be enough for the next stage or are we just delaying another awkward expansion. If we allow these SAFEs or notes to accumulate, what happens when they convert into a priced round later. If we grant these investor rights, what room remains for a future lead investor to enter cleanly. If we take this valuation, can the company plausibly grow into a stronger next round or have we set a benchmark that later becomes a trap. These are not pessimistic questions. They are strategic questions asked at the only time when they can still shape the answer.

This matters because the next round is often where hidden weakness becomes visible. A founder may feel comfortable after a current financing because the company has cash and the percentages still look acceptable. Then the next round appears and several things happen at once. Deferred instruments convert. The pool must grow again. The earlier investor exercises pro rata. The founder position, which looked acceptable in isolation, now becomes thin. The company realises it cannot offer a new lead enough room without displacing someone else or expanding the round more than intended. None of these things arrives as a surprise in the legal sense. They arrive as surprises only because the company did not design forward when it still had the chance.

This is one reason sophisticated investors often seem to think one round ahead while inexperienced founders think one cheque ahead. The investor is not only asking whether this deal works now. They are asking whether the company that emerges from this deal is still a financeable company later. Founders need that same reflex. A company that raises money in a way that makes the next round structurally awkward has not simply bought time. It has bought time while reducing future negotiating freedom. That is often a much worse bargain than it first appears.

Another reason to design forward is that future investors do not evaluate the company from a blank slate. They inherit the structure. Every right, every preference, every pool assumption, every founder percentage, every convertable instrument, every legacy line. They are not only assessing product and traction. They are assessing what kind of ownership system they are being asked to enter. A founder who understands this stops seeing the current round as self-contained and starts seeing it as the draft that the next investor will mark up. That mindset changes decisions. It encourages cleaner terms, clearer modelling, and more restraint with seemingly small concessions that may later create disproportionate friction.

This also applies to employee equity. A company that grants aggressively without modelling the next stage often discovers later that its pool is too weak for the hires that truly matter. Or the opposite: it expands the pool too broadly out of current caution and creates needless founder dilution before the company even knows whether that space will be used intelligently. Designing for the next round means sizing and using the pool with an actual future hiring sequence in mind, not just as a soft buffer for the present moment's staffing anxiety. Again, the issue is not whether the current decision is explainable. It is whether the current decision leaves the next decision easier or harder.

A useful way to think about this is that every round creates a draft of the next term sheet. Not literally, but structurally. A round with a heavy preference stack drafts a later exit conversation. A round with broad pro rata rights drafts a later allocation fight. A round with aggressive anti-dilution drafts a later down-round pain pattern. A round with an undersized pool drafts a later hiring constraint. A round with a founder position already near its motivational limit drafts a later morale problem. Founders who see that clearly become much more exacting, because they realise they are not just signing for today's capital. They are writing part of tomorrow's negotiation terrain.

This does not mean founders must become paralysed by future modelling. The goal is not to predict everything. It is to rule out preventable structural fragility. A founder cannot know exactly when the next round will happen, at what price, or under what market conditions. But they can know whether the current structure leaves enough room, enough clarity, and enough founder meaning that a future round is still likely to be workable across a sensible range of scenarios. That is already enough to improve decision quality materially.

One practical habit helps here. After any major cap table change, model at least one plausible next financing before treating the current structure as settled. Not because that future financing is certain, but because doing so reveals whether the current setup still supports one. If the next likely round would crush the founders, exhaust the pool, create intolerable conversion pain, or leave too little room for a lead investor, that information matters now. It may not kill the current transaction, but it should shape how the founders negotiate valuation, rights, pool sizing, or grant discipline while there is still some leverage.

This forward design mindset is also a form of founder protection. It prevents the company from celebrating current survival while quietly financing itself into a position where only harsher future terms remain available. Founders who think one round ahead are often calmer, not more anxious, because they are less likely to be blindsided by consequences that were always implicit in the current deal. They can still make painful choices. They simply make them knowingly, which is the difference between strategy and drift.

That is why the next round should be designed for before it arrives. The cap table is not just a record of this financing. It is the terrain from which the next financing will begin. A founder who forgets that keeps solving present problems by borrowing against future room. A founder who remembers it starts building a company that can keep taking the next step without each step making the one after it needlessly harder.

The Founder Who Understands the Table Has More Strategic Freedom

There is a practical difference between a founder who merely lives inside the cap table and a founder who truly understands it. The first founder reacts.

The second founder chooses. That is the clearest way to put it. Both may have the same structure on paper, the same investors, the same pool, the same SAFEs, the same rights, and the same burdens. But the founder who understands the table sees consequences earlier, negotiates from clearer ground, explains the company more honestly, and retains more freedom because they are not constantly surprised by the ownership machine they themselves are operating inside.
This is why cap table literacy is not just defensive. It is a source of strategic freedom.

Founders often think of ownership knowledge as something grim, restrictive, or mainly useful for avoiding mistakes. That is too narrow. Yes, it helps prevent errors. But more importantly, it expands the founder's ability to move deliberately. A founder who understands the table can see when a financing is genuinely useful versus when it is buying present comfort at too high a future cost. They can distinguish between a hire worth stretching the pool for and one who is merely being overpaid in equity because the company is under pressure. They can tell when an acquisition offer is truly weak versus when it only sounds weak against vanity valuation memories. They can push back on investor terms not from instinctive defensiveness but from specific knowledge of what those terms will do in later scenarios. All of that is freedom. Not the freedom to escape structure, but the freedom to act inside it intelligently.

The founder who does not understand the table often feels less constrained in the short term because they have not yet forced the structure to tell them the truth. That feeling is misleading. It is not real freedom. It is deferred limitation. The company can still sign the round, make the grant, tell the story, and move on. Later, however, the founder discovers that certain options are no longer truly available. Moderate exits no longer work for the common. The next round requires more cleanup than expected. The founder position is thinner than it felt. The pool is weaker. The rights stack is heavier. The founder did not have more freedom earlier. They had less awareness of what they were already giving away.

This is why understanding the cap table changes negotiation psychology so profoundly. A founder who has not modelled the structure tends to negotiate around headlines and feelings. Valuation sounds good. Percentage sounds survivable. The investor seems supportive.

The company needs the money. By contrast, a founder who knows the table can ask much sharper questions. What does this do after the next likely round. How does this preference sit on top of the existing stack. If we accept this pool size now, what room is left for the hires that matter most. If this SAFE converts at the cap, what does it do to the founder position in the Series A. Those questions do not make the founder difficult for the sake of it. They make the founder harder to manipulate with partial truth.

Strategic freedom also appears in timing. A founder who understands the table is usually better at knowing when to raise, when to delay, when to push for cleaner terms, and when to accept a hard but necessary structure because the company's alternatives are genuinely weaker. That timing judgment is incredibly valuable. Many founders raise too early, too late, too much, or too little because they are interpreting need only through runway or sentiment. A founder who sees the ownership consequences as well can evaluate timing with much more depth. The question becomes not only do we need capital, but what kind of company will still exist for us after we take it now versus later.

The same is true in hiring. Equity is one of the most strategic tools in a startup, but only for founders who understand what it costs. A founder who reads the table well can use ownership precisely. They know when a meaningful grant is justified, when a smaller grant is more honest, when cash should do the job instead, and when the pool needs defending for future hires who will matter even more. This is real operating freedom. The founder is not just reacting to each candidate emotionally. They are allocating a scarce strategic resource with awareness of what later room still matters.

Another form of freedom is communicative. Founders who understand the table can speak about it without hiding, overselling, or sounding brittle. That gives them more room with employees, boards, and investors because trust rises when the company sounds like it understands its own structure. A founder who cannot explain their own economics usually compensates with vagueness. Vagueness narrows freedom because it creates future distrust. Clear explanation widens it because it allows the company to have harder conversations earlier without moral collapse. The founder is not constantly trapped between silence and oversimplification. They can tell the truth proportionately, and that makes later decisions easier to carry.

This matters especially in difficult periods. Down rounds, strategic sales, founder departures, pool expansions, investor clean-up conversations, and secondary discussions all become much more manageable when the founder already understands how the structure behaves. The event may still be painful. But pain is different from confusion. Confusion makes the company reactive and politically fragile. Understanding makes it capable of choosing among hard options. That is why literacy is freedom. It does not remove constraint. It reduces avoidable helplessness.

There is also a deeper kind of freedom here, which is freedom from ownership mythology. Many founders are partly governed by stories they inherited from startup culture rather than by the actual economics of their company. Raise more if you can. Equity is always motivating. Valuation means progress. Everyone should want the same kind of exit. Early grants are small enough not to matter. The next round will sort things out. These myths are convenient, and they reduce strategic freedom because they make the founder think in borrowed narratives instead of in the logic of the table they actually have. Once the founder understands the cap table properly, they can stop inheriting strategy from clichés and start building it from structure.

This is one reason the founder who understands the table often feels calmer, not more anxious. At first, learning the structure can feel sobering because it removes some comforting simplifications. But after that initial discomfort, it usually produces steadier judgment. The founder knows where the pressure points are. They know what outcomes still work. They know what kinds of concessions are genuinely dangerous and which are merely unattractive. They know what needs repairing and what can be carried as a scar. That kind of clarity is psychologically stabilising. It replaces ambient worry with defined reality.

And defined reality is almost always more usable than vague optimism.

This is the strategic culmination of everything in this book. The cap table is not a back-office artefact to be updated after the real decisions are made. It is one of the main places where the real decisions are made, because it determines who remains aligned, what capital costs, which futures still make sense, and how much room the company still has to keep becoming itself. A founder who understands that does not become less ambitious. They become more exact in what ambition now requires.

That is why the founder who understands the table has more strategic freedom. Not because the structure disappears, but because they are no longer being quietly governed by something they have not yet fully read.

* * *

NINETEEN

The Founder's Long View of Ownership

"The essence of strategy is choosing what not to do."

- Michael Porter

Why Ownership Should Be Managed Across the Whole Journey

One of the most common founder errors is to experience ownership in fragments. Formation is one fragment. The first hire is another. The first SAFE is another. The seed round, the option pool expansion, the Series A, the founder departure, the secondary, the acquisition conversation. Each event feels immediate, local, and explainable on its own terms. The founder solves the problem in front of them, updates the table, and moves on. This way of living inside the cap table is understandable because startup life is pressurised and sequential. But it is also one of the reasons ownership structures drift so badly. The company is being built across a whole journey, while the founder is governing ownership one emotional scene at a time.

This is why ownership should be managed across the whole journey rather than through isolated episodes.

The cap table is not a set of separate transactions that happen to touch the same spreadsheet. It is a continuous narrative of how the company allocates power, risk, patience, and reward over time. The founder split is still present when the first investor arrives. The first investor's rights are still present when the second one arrives. The early option decisions are still present when later hiring becomes expensive. The deferred instruments are still present when the priced round finally happens. The preference stack is still present when the buyer appears. Nothing truly disappears. Each decision becomes part of the terrain on which the next one stands. The founder who understands this stops asking only "does this make sense now" and starts asking "what kind of ownership story are we writing if we keep making decisions like this."

That shift matters because the startup journey almost always lasts longer and becomes stranger than the founders imagine at the start. In the beginning, ownership feels like a founding matter. Then it becomes a fundraising matter. Then it becomes a hiring matter. Then it becomes an incentive matter. Then it becomes an exit matter. In reality it is all of those at once, just with different parts of the structure becoming louder at different times. A founder who keeps seeing ownership as something that belongs mainly to whichever phase is currently most visible will usually be outmanoeuvred by the structure's continuity. The spreadsheet remembers what the founder has emotionally moved on from.

This is why the long view is so powerful. It forces the founder to hold multiple truths at once. A grant can help close a candidate today and still weaken future hiring room. A round can save the company this year and still make moderate exits less meaningful three years later. A founder split can feel fair in the first month and still corrode motivation in the fourth year. A secondary can reduce founder pressure now and still affect how investors read alignment later. None of those statements cancels the others. The long view simply refuses to let the present consume the future without being priced for what it is doing.

There is also a psychological benefit in taking the long view. Many founders oscillate between overprotectiveness and overgenerosity because they are reacting to the immediate emotional atmosphere around each ownership decision. In one moment they are terrified of dilution. In another they are generous because the company badly needs help. In another they are flattered by investor interest. In another they are tired and use equity to smooth disagreement. A founder with the long view is not emotionless, but they are less easily pushed around by the local drama of each ownership event because they can see where it fits in the longer sequence. The question is not only "how do I feel about this decision today." It is "what does this decision become once the next three predictable things have happened."

This is one reason the long view improves fairness as well as strategy. Fairness in ownership is often misjudged when founders look only at the immediate scene. The person who feels helpful now may not still look central later. The equal split that feels diplomatic now may not survive contact with unequal burden. The investor term that feels tolerable now may later redirect too much pain downward. The long view does not make fairness obvious, but it makes shallow fairness much easier to detect.

It exposes the difference between a decision that feels kind in the moment and one that remains coherent across the life of the company.

Another crucial point is that ownership is one of the few parts of the startup that compounds morally as well as financially. Every decision teaches the company something about what ownership is for. Is it for enduring contribution or for early emotional settlement. Is it for serious long-term alignment or for short-term persuasion. Is it a strategic currency or a politeness tool. Is it explained truthfully or wrapped in motivational haze. Once those habits form, they repeat. The long view therefore is not only about the future arithmetic of the table. It is about the culture of ownership the founders are building through repeated choices. Those choices eventually become the company's reflex.

The founder who manages ownership across the whole journey tends to ask different questions very early. If we make this founder split now, can it survive departures, divergence, and dilution later. If we use the option pool this way now, what does that leave for the people we have not met yet but will later need badly. If we take this round now, what sort of exits or future raises are we structurally making more important. If we explain grants this way now, what kind of expectations are we planting for years. Those questions are not signs of pessimism. They are signs that the founder has stopped confusing motion with strategy.

This long view also changes how one experiences repair. A founder who thinks only in episodes tends to see cap table repair as an embarrassing interruption. Something went wrong. We now have to fix it. A founder who thinks across the whole journey sees repair more naturally as part of ongoing governance. The table evolved. Some parts became weak. We now strengthen them where we can. This is a much healthier posture because it removes some of the shame that causes founders to delay repair until outsiders force it. A company can have history and still be well governed. The long view makes that easier to accept.

It is also worth noticing that the long view does not require certainty. The founder cannot know exactly what rounds will happen, who will leave, what the market will do, or how the company will exit. That is not the point. The point is to stop behaving as though the absence of certainty means the absence of pattern.

There are predictable categories of future pressure: later financings, more hiring, possible dilution, founder evolution, investor rights becoming louder, exit logic eventually mattering. The founder who manages ownership well does not predict the details of those moments perfectly. They simply refuse to design as if those moments will not come.

This is what separates the founder who merely survives the cap table from the founder who governs it. Survival is episodic. Governance is longitudinal. Survival says we got through this round, this hire, this problem. Governance says we are still building a company whose ownership structure can carry the next phase without constant surprise. That is a much stronger ambition, and it is the right one.

That is why ownership should be managed across the whole journey. Because the company experiences itself as a sequence of urgent presents, but the cap table experiences the company as one long accumulation of choices. The founder who learns to think the same way gains one of the rarest forms of startup advantage: the ability to make present decisions without letting the future arrive later as a stranger.

Thinking in Decades, Not Rounds

Most founders are taught to think in rounds because rounds are the visible milestones. Pre-seed. Seed. Series A. Series B. Each one feels like a chapter marker, and the company's ownership story gets narrated accordingly. The founder raises, survives, updates the table, and then starts preparing emotionally for the next round. That rhythm is understandable, but it can quietly shrink the founder's imagination. A company is not built in rounds. It is built across years of compounding decisions, relationships, expectations, and structural consequences. That is why the founder who wants real command over ownership has to learn to think in decades, not rounds.

This does not mean literally predicting ten or twenty years of exact cap table events. It means taking a longer structural view than the next financing calendar. A founder thinking only in rounds often asks, can we get this round done, can we survive the dilution, can we keep enough room for the next raise. A founder thinking in decades asks a different question.

What kind of ownership life are we creating for this company. Are we building something that remains meaningful to the people carrying it over a long arc, or are we repeatedly solving short-term financing problems in ways that make the company harder and harder to live inside later.

This matters because ownership decisions age. Some age well. Others harden into burdens. A founder split may feel reasonable in year one and absurd by year five. A generous adviser grant may feel harmless early and look embarrassing a decade later. A preference stack may seem manageable across two financings and become strategically distorting across six. Employee grants given under one ownership culture may later sit inside a very different company from the one they were emotionally sold into. The round-by-round mindset tends to underweight this aging process. The long view sees that every line on the cap table is not only a present allocation but a future memory.

Thinking in decades also changes how a founder relates to dilution. In the short term, dilution is often experienced emotionally and defensively. The founder sees the percentage fall and feels loss. In the longer view, dilution becomes less about the pain of this one event and more about whether the remaining stake still makes sense across the whole life of the business. That is a much more useful standard. The question is not whether any one round hurts. It usually will. The question is whether the cumulative structure still leaves founders, key employees, and even investors in a company whose likely future remains coherent. A founder thinking in decades cares less about winning the optics of one round and more about preserving enough meaning across many phases of company life.

This is one of the reasons overcapitalisation can be so dangerous. A founder thinking only in the current market may see available capital and take it because the round looks attractive now. A founder thinking in decades asks what kind of company this capital path creates if we carry it through. What preference burden does it build. What exit thresholds does it imply. What founder motivation does it preserve or destroy later. What kinds of future rounds does it quietly assume. The long view often makes today's flattering choice look much more expensive than it first appeared.

The same principle applies to employee equity. A round-based mindset often treats grants as local hiring tools. We need this person now, what gets them over the line. A decade-scale mindset asks what kind of ownership culture this pattern creates. Are we using equity in a way that can still be defended later. Are we creating a company where long-serving employees can look back and feel the ownership language matched reality closely enough. Are we spending pool room on roles that will still seem strategically important in hindsight. The founder cannot know every answer in advance, but asking the longer question changes the quality of the grant decisions immediately.

Another benefit of the long view is that it weakens vanity. Round-based thinking is highly susceptible to vanity because rounds are public, legible, and easy to compare. Valuations, cheque sizes, famous funds, all of it flatters the present. Decade-scale thinking is much less interested in whether the current event looks impressive. It asks whether this ownership structure will still look intelligent after years of later financing, departures, option use, and strategic stress. That is a far harder standard to satisfy, but it is also a much more useful one. Plenty of cap tables look glamorous in year two and disappointing in year eight.

Thinking in decades also makes founder repair decisions better. A founder focused only on the next round may be tempted to patch the table just enough to satisfy immediate investor scrutiny. A founder with the longer view asks which fixes will still matter three, five, or ten years from now. Is this dead equity only cosmetically awkward, or will it still corrode the common later. Is this rights package merely tolerable now, or will it become a recurring source of distortion in future financings and exits. The longer frame helps separate repair that is merely tactical from repair that actually improves the life of the company.

This does not mean every company will last a decade or should plan as though it certainly will. The point is not duration in itself. The point is structural continuity. Even a company that exits in five years is still being shaped by long-running ownership effects, not by isolated round logic alone. And a company that lasts much longer than expected will be especially punished if the founders built the cap table as though only the next eighteen months mattered. The longer frame is therefore a form of resilience. It protects the company from being repeatedly surprised by the cumulative meaning of its own history.

There is also a human difference. Founders thinking in rounds often become emotionally hostage to financing cadence. Confidence rises and falls with the last raise, the next pitch, the latest headline valuation. Founders thinking in decades are usually steadier. They still care deeply about financing, but they are less likely to confuse capital events with the whole meaning of the business. Ownership becomes part of a longer architecture of stewardship rather than a recurring drama of dilution and validation. That emotional steadiness often leads to better decisions because the founder is less likely to spend the future for the sake of looking stronger in the present.

In practical terms, thinking in decades means asking broader questions more often. If we keep making ownership decisions in this style, what kind of company exists five years from now. What kinds of exits still work. What sort of financing dependence are we creating. What does the common mean after repeated ordinary growth, not only after one heroic success. What kind of ownership story will long-serving employees and investors be able to tell about this company later. These questions are not abstract philosophy. They are strategic design in long form.

That is why the founder's ownership horizon has to become longer than the next round. Rounds matter, but they are only the punctuation marks. The real sentence is the long life of the company, and ownership is one of the main ways that sentence either remains coherent or gradually stops making sense.

What You Owe Future Versions of the Company

One of the most useful ways to think about cap table discipline is to stop treating the company as though it only exists in its present form. Every ownership decision is being made by one version of the company and handed to another version that does not yet exist. The founders of today choose the split, the grant, the SAFE, the round, the pool, the rights package. The company of tomorrow inherits all of it. That later company may be stronger, more complex, more employable, more financeable, or more fragile because of what was chosen earlier. This is why ownership is a stewardship problem as much as a financing problem. Founders are not only making choices for themselves. They are placing burdens or creating room for future versions of the business.

That is why a founder should ask, more often than most do, what do we owe the company we are trying to become.

The answer is not perfection. The future company does not need flawless paperwork and a fantasy cap table designed with omniscience. What it needs is not to be made weaker for the sake of present emotional convenience. It needs room. It needs legibility. It needs enough founder meaning left that the people still carrying the business are not asked to do so under structurally irrational economics. It needs enough hiring capacity left that future talent can still be brought in without tearing open the structure every time. It needs a rights stack that future financing and future exits can still live with. In other words, the present company owes the future company decisions that do not quietly make its life harder than necessary.

This is one reason so many early ownership choices age badly. They are made as though the company of the moment is the only one that matters. Founders want to preserve harmony now, so they use equal splits without enough thought. They want to reward someone now, so they hand out equity without asking whether that grant will still make sense later. They want to close the round now, so they accept terms without modelling what those terms will do after the next likely financing. In each case, the present wins relief and the future inherits friction. That is not always avoidable. But it should at least be recognised for what it is: a transfer of burden forward.

A strong operator becomes uncomfortable with making the future company pay for present convenience unless the trade is genuinely worth it.

This applies to almost every part of the cap table. A founder split should be something the later company can still defend. An option pool should be sized for the people the future company will actually need, not only for the emotional fear of missing hires today. A convertible instrument should be understood in terms of what it will do to the next financing, not merely in terms of how much relief it gives this month. A financing round should be judged partly by whether the company it creates is still capable of another rational round later. A secondary should be judged partly by whether the founder who remains after it is still aligned enough for the future company to trust.

This long-duty perspective is especially important because future versions of the company usually have less room to fix old mistakes than the present one had to avoid them. That is one of the cruellest asymmetries in ownership. The early company can often choose discipline cheaply. The later company usually has to buy back indiscipline at a higher price, if it can buy it back at all. The present founder therefore has leverage the future founder will not always possess. To waste that leverage is not only a tactical error. It is a form of negligence toward the company that comes later.

There is also a cultural obligation here. Future versions of the company inherit not only the numbers on the table but the meaning attached to them. If today's founders teach that equity is a vague symbol, then tomorrow's company must somehow explain real dilution and real hierarchy to people raised on softer language. If today's founders use ownership to avoid awkward conversations, tomorrow's company will be forced into harder conversations under worse conditions. If today's founders hand out grants casually, tomorrow's company will discover that its option story is weaker than its recruiting narrative assumed. The future company is always paying for the habits the present company normalised.

This is why ownership culture itself should be thought of as an obligation to the future. A company that learns to speak honestly about grants, dilution, rights, and exit logic is giving later versions of itself a far better chance of surviving hard moments without trust collapse. A company that relies on romance, vagueness, and silence is leaving the future to explain why the emotional story and the structural reality were never quite the same. That is an avoidable debt.

Another useful test is this. If the company five years from now could speak back to you, what would it thank you for and what would it resent you for. It would probably thank you for founder vesting handled early, for dead equity challenged before it hardened, for careful use of the option pool, for not overselling grants, for rights packages that preserved future manoeuvrability, for not chasing flattering valuations that turned the next round into a trap. It would likely resent you for lazy splits, emotional grants, unmodelled SAFEs, casual dilution of the common, or using ownership as a substitute for hard present-tense judgment. This is not a sentimental exercise. It is often a very sharp way of identifying whether the current decision is stewardship or drift.

The founders also owe the future company honesty about scale. Some financing paths create a business that must become much bigger for the common to matter. That may be right. But the future company deserves founders who understand that they have made that choice. If the present company raises and spends as though scale is obviously the only route, while the founders still emotionally imagine a wider range of acceptable outcomes, then the future company inherits contradiction. It now needs a giant result to make the cap table cohere, while the leadership may still be making decisions as if smaller but respectable outcomes remain equally meaningful. That is unfair to the future because it hands down confusion rather than strategy.

This way of thinking also changes the emotional tone of discipline. Cap table rigor can feel narrow or joyless if it is framed only as constraint. It becomes easier to accept when framed as duty to the company that will later depend on what you decide now. You are not being stern merely to satisfy legal neatness. You are trying not to leave the future company with dead weight, broken incentives, and avoidable complexity. That is a creative act, not merely a restrictive one. It is part of building the business, not separate from it.

Of course, no founder can fully protect the future company from everything. Markets move. people leave. products fail. capital dries up. Not every later structural pain is proof of an earlier moral failure. But many are proof of earlier choices that were softer, lazier, or more present-bound than they needed to be. The founder cannot guarantee a clean inheritance. They can decide whether to make the inheritance heavier than it has to be.

That is what you owe future versions of the company: not perfection, not prophecy, but a structure that does not needlessly reduce their room to act, hire, raise, explain, and remain worth building. Once a founder starts thinking that way, the cap table stops being merely about today's negotiation and becomes part of a larger obligation to the business across time.

The Company You Build Is the Company the Table Allows

Founders often like to believe that the business is shaped mainly by vision, effort, talent, and market reality, while the cap table sits beside those things as a record of who benefits if the company succeeds.

That is only partly true. The table does not determine product quality, customer demand, or founder intelligence. But it does determine what kinds of company remain buildable once all those human and market forces begin pushing against structure. This is the harder truth. The company you build is, in part, the company the table allows.

This is not because ownership is mystical. It is because ownership creates incentives, rights, thresholds, and constraints. A company with a thin founder common layer behaves differently from one with a thick one. A company with a light preference burden can accept kinds of outcomes that a heavily stacked company no longer can. A company with enough pool room can hire opportunistically when the right people appear. A company whose future round space is already crowded by rights and expectations cannot move as freely. In each case, the table is not replacing strategy. It is setting the conditions under which strategy can still function.

This is why two companies with similar products, similar markets, and even similar headline valuations can still become very different businesses over time. One may remain flexible, founder-driven, and able to take moderate but sensible wins seriously. The other may become structurally committed to chasing only very large outcomes because the common beneath the stack no longer has much to gain from anything less. One may be able to recruit intelligently because the pool was preserved and used well. The other may discover that earlier casual grants and poorly planned expansions have left little room for the people it now most needs. The difference is not only operational. It is architectural.

A cap table allows some futures and makes others less realistic.

This is why founders need to stop thinking of ownership as something that mainly matters at exit. Exit simply reveals the end-state consequences most sharply. Long before then, the structure is already shaping what the company can plausibly say yes to. Can it raise again without founder economics becoming absurd. Can it accept a strategic acquisition at a non-heroic price and still keep the common meaningfully involved. Can it retain key people under the actual grant logic it has built. Can it survive a weak round without triggering so much structural pain that the company's core actors become demoralised. These are all questions about what the table allows.

The phrase allows is important because it suggests a range rather than a single outcome. A cap table rarely makes only one future possible. What it does is change the range of futures that remain rational for the people inside the company. A healthy table leaves a wider range. Moderate exits may still matter. Later financing may still be workable. The founders can still care after another round. The company can hire without constantly reopening structural pain. A weaker table narrows the range. Suddenly only a giant exit feels worthwhile. Only high-priced future rounds keep the narrative coherent. Only increasingly elaborate investor accommodation keeps capital flowing. The company is still alive, but the set of strategically tolerable paths has shrunk.

That shrinking can happen quietly. This is one of the reasons founders miss it. The company still operates day to day. Customers are still being served. Product is still shipping. Meetings are still happening. The narrowing lives in the structure until an event activates it. An offer appears. A key hire asks for more equity. A new investor wants room. A founder privately models their own proceeds. Only then does the company realise that what it thought was one business is actually two. The business it wanted to build, and the business the table will still reward.
This is also why founder morale can become such an important signal. If founders begin reacting strangely to moderate acquisition talk, to financing proposals, or to the cumulative effect of dilution, that reaction is often read as emotional volatility. Sometimes it is. But often it is the table speaking through them. The structure may now reward a narrower set of outcomes than the founder's earlier intuition still assumes. The founder feels that mismatch before they can always articulate it. A company whose table still allows broad strategic freedom tends to produce calmer decision-making. A company whose table has become outcome-rigid often produces either desperation or avoidance.

The same pattern applies to employees. A company may say it wants a culture of ownership, patience, and long-term commitment. But if the actual common economics beneath the structure only become meaningful in a very small range of huge outcomes, then the table is not really allowing the culture the company claims to want. It is allowing something thinner. Perhaps loyalty powered partly by hope, or perhaps a two-speed company where investors and founders understand the real economics while the broader team works inside a softer narrative. That may function for a while. It is not the same as a company whose ownership structure genuinely supports the long-term alignment language it uses.

This is one reason founders should read the table not only by looking at percentages and rights, but by asking what behaviours it now makes rational. Does it make it rational to keep building through another likely financing. Does it make it rational for a key early hire to stay. Does it make a moderate but credible acquisition worth considering. Does it make another pool refresh survivable. Does it make the next round attractive to new money without leaving the old company hollowed out. If the answers are increasingly conditional, the table is already narrowing strategy.

There is another way to say this. A cap table is a machine for converting events into meaning. The same financing round means one thing in a company with strong founder common and modest preferences, and something else in a company already pressed thin. The same sale price means one thing in a clean structure and something else in a stacked one. The same option grant means one thing in a company that preserved room and another in one that spent it emotionally. The company is not only what happens to it. It is what its structure makes those events mean. That is why the table does not merely track the business. It helps define the business.

This should not make founders fatalistic. The table does not erase leadership. A strong founder can still repair, renegotiate, simplify, or strategically adapt around structural weakness. But such repairs are themselves proof of the same principle. They matter because the structure matters. If the table were only administration, none of those efforts would change the kind of company being built. The fact that they do shows why ownership architecture belongs in the core of strategy rather than on its edge.

That is why the company you build is, in part, the company the table allows. Vision decides what you want. Effort decides how far you can push. Market decides what is possible. The cap table decides which of those possibilities still make economic and political sense once the company has to live inside its own ownership history.

Why Ownership Discipline Is a Form of Leadership

Leadership in a startup is often described through visible acts. Setting vision. Making hires. Raising capital. Taking hard calls under uncertainty. Holding morale together when the business is under strain.

All of that matters. But there is another form of leadership that is quieter and, in many companies, far less developed. It is the willingness to govern ownership with seriousness before ownership chaos forces seriousness upon the company. This is why ownership discipline should be understood not as legal tidiness or founder paranoia, but as a form of leadership.

A founder who treats the cap table carelessly is not merely making spreadsheet mistakes. They are teaching the company that difficult structural truths can be postponed, softened, or traded away for immediate relief. A founder who treats the cap table seriously is teaching something different. They are teaching that incentives matter, that fairness must survive contact with reality, that future builders deserve room, that capital should be taken with open eyes, and that present convenience is not always worth future distortion. Those lessons do not live only in the spreadsheet. They live in the culture and in the quality of later decisions.

This is why ownership discipline is leadership. It is one of the ways a founder proves they can govern a system rather than merely drive momentum through it.

The first leadership quality embedded in ownership discipline is clarity. Strong leaders reduce ambiguity where ambiguity will later become expensive. They do not leave founder splits vague because the conversation is awkward. They do not hand out equity loosely because gratitude is easier than precision. They do not let vesting drift because everyone currently likes one another. They do not treat dilution as something to be explained only after people have already built expectations around a softer story. In each case, the leader is choosing clarity over temporary emotional ease. That is a deeply general leadership trait, not a cap table quirk.

The second quality is courage. Many ownership problems persist not because founders do not know better, but because they do not want to have the hard conversation. A cofounder split needs revisiting. A dead grant needs confronting. An investor term needs pushing back on. An employee deserves a more honest explanation of what their grant means. A secondary should be discussed in alignment terms rather than hidden behind celebratory language. None of these conversations is pleasant. But leadership is often the art of being willing to create short-term discomfort in order to avoid long-term damage. Ownership discipline is one of the clearest places where that art is tested.

The third quality is stewardship. A founder with ownership discipline behaves as though the company will one day be inherited by later versions of itself. They think about future hires, future rounds, future exits, future motivation, future credibility. They do not use equity only to solve the problem in the room. They ask what this decision leaves behind. That is stewardship in the pure sense. It is leadership expressed not through charisma or urgency, but through responsibility to people and choices that do not yet exist.

This is one reason weak cap tables so often correlate with weak founder leadership in broader ways. The same habits that create ownership drift tend to appear elsewhere. Hard issues are postponed. Structure is avoided until an outsider forces it. Emotional harmony is purchased with future complication. Public optimism outruns private understanding. None of this means a founder with a messy table is bad or unserious by definition. But it does mean that ownership discipline often reveals whether the founder can lead beyond the immediate atmosphere of the moment.

There is also a fairness dimension here that matters greatly. Leadership is not only about making tough calls. It is also about ensuring that the company's reward structure continues to tell the truth about who is carrying the burden. That is why dead equity matters. That is why founder over-thinning matters. That is why employee option language matters. A founder who lets ownership drift into a place where the present builders are paying too much for the past, or where the company speaks more generously than the structure justifies, is not merely tolerating an accounting oddity. They are tolerating a fairness failure. Strong leaders notice that and act on it before the company's internal trust erodes.

Ownership discipline is leadership for another reason too. It improves decision quality under pressure. A founder who understands the table can make better calls in financing, hiring, acquisition, and retention because they know what each move really costs and what room still remains. That is practical leadership. It makes the founder less reactive, less likely to be dazzled by headline terms, and less likely to oversell or undersell the company's options. Teams feel that difference, even if they do not always name it. A founder who knows the structure usually sounds more grounded because they are not making strategic decisions from partial information.

It is also worth saying that leadership through ownership discipline is often invisible until its absence causes pain. No one throws a party because the founders handled vesting early, resisted a weak advisory grant, sized the pool intelligently, or modelled the next round before taking the current one. Those acts do not have the glamour of a big customer or a successful raise. Yet later, when the company can hire well, raise cleanly, survive a hard financing, or explain its structure without embarrassment, much of that strength often comes from those earlier unglamorous acts of discipline. That is the nature of some of the best leadership. It looks quiet on the day it is exercised and decisive years later.

This does not mean leaders must become rigid. Ownership discipline is not the same as joyless severity. Companies still need generosity, flexibility, and the ability to make exceptions when the situation truly calls for them. The point is that exceptions should be conscious, priced, and rare enough that they do not become the company's default governance style. Leadership here means knowing when to bend and when bending is simply drift with a nicer emotional story attached.

Another sign that ownership discipline is leadership is that it protects the company from becoming dependent on investor-imposed adulthood. A founder who governs the table well does not wait for the next lead to point out the obvious clean-up list. They know what the weak spots are before diligence does. They have already thought about room, rights, founder alignment, and the next likely financing path. This makes the company stronger not only structurally but politically. It is much easier to negotiate with outsiders when the founders have already shown they can govern themselves.

At the deepest level, ownership discipline is leadership because it answers a basic question: can this founder be trusted with systems of consequence, not just with moments of momentum. Many people can sell a vision, push through fatigue, or persuade others to believe. Fewer can preserve coherence in the slow-moving, cumulative structures that shape a company's real future. The cap table is one of those structures. A founder who takes it seriously is demonstrating a kind of leadership that is more durable than inspiration alone.

That is why ownership discipline should be seen as part of leadership, not adjacent to it. It is one of the clearest ways a founder shows whether they are merely carrying the company forward or actually governing the conditions under which it can keep becoming itself.

Leaving a Better Ownership System Than the One You Inherited

Very few founders begin with a truly clean ownership understanding. Most inherit something, even if what they inherit is only the startup folklore of the world around them. They inherit ideas about equal splits, about how much dilution is normal, about what investors are allowed to demand, about how employees should be motivated, about what counts as a successful raise, about when liquidity should happen, about whether equity is mainly a reward, a weapon, a bargaining chip, or a language of belief. Some founders also inherit a literal structure from earlier decisions they did not fully make themselves: an old cofounder agreement, a grant policy that predates them, a pile of notes and promises, a board habit, a financing style, a rights stack, a culture of silence. Whether cultural or literal, inheritance shapes the starting point.

The real test of leadership is not whether the founder started from a perfect system. It is whether they leave a better one than they found.

This matters because ownership systems have a way of outliving the people who first normalised them. A founder may inherit a company where grants are explained loosely, where dilution is only mentioned after the fact, where adviser equity was treated casually, where investor rights accumulated without much modelling, where the common's real meaning is quietly thinner than the internal language suggests. If that founder simply continues the pattern, then they are no longer inheriting weakness. They are transmitting it. The company becomes a vehicle for carrying old ownership confusion forward into new generations of hires, new rounds, and new expectations.

Leaving a better ownership system begins with refusing to romanticise what came before. This can be difficult because founders often feel loyalty to the company's story, to earlier people, or to the way things have "always been done." But ownership systems should be judged by what they now do, not by the emotional history that first produced them. If the inherited structure is thin on founder meaning, soft on discipline, vague with employees, or overprotective of capital at the expense of the people still building, then the right response is not reverence. It is repair, clarification, and better habits from this point forward.

A better system is not necessarily a simpler one. This is important. As companies grow, they often become more structurally complex. More rounds, more classes, more grants, more hires, more scenarios. Complexity itself is not failure. A better ownership system is one where complexity is governed rather than denied. The founders understand it. The key people can have it explained to them honestly. The weak points are known. The rights are legible. The common still means enough for the active team. The company no longer relies on fog to make the structure sound attractive. In that sense, better does not mean cleaner in appearance. It means truer in operation.

This is also why founders should think in institutional rather than merely personal terms. It is not enough for one founder to privately understand the table if the rest of the company still lives inside weak ownership language and loose grant discipline. A better system changes the organisation's reflexes. Grants are explained more honestly. Small allocations face stronger scrutiny. Vesting is not treated as optional sentiment. Deferred instruments are modelled, not merely signed. Financing conversations include what the current choice does to the next one. Employees are not taught that valuation is the same as wealth. Founders do not use equity as a politeness tool when cash, clarity, or boundaries would be more honest. These habits become part of the company's way of operating, which means they can survive individual personalities better than private understanding alone.

There is a long-term justice dimension here as well. Startups often ask future people to live inside structures built by past people. That is inevitable. The question is what sort of inheritance those future people receive. Do they inherit dead equity, vague promises, and motivationally hollow common. Or do they inherit a company that, while not perfect, at least tries to match ownership to contribution, explain equity seriously, preserve room for builders, and prevent capital structure from quietly swallowing the company's strategic options. When a founder improves the ownership system, they are not only protecting themselves. They are reducing the amount of hidden unfairness later people will have to absorb.

This is especially important with employees. Many companies speak as though equity is one of the most meaningful parts of belonging to the business, yet leave employees to navigate an ownership culture built on half-truths and selective simplification.

A founder who leaves a better system changes that. They may not make every grant huge. They may not erase dilution or the reality of investor rights. But they can make the company one in which employees are not invited into ownership through mythology. That alone is a profound improvement, because it replaces a culture of private disappointment with one of informed participation.

The same is true with future investors. A founder who improves the ownership system leaves behind a company that can be financed from a position of greater dignity. Later rounds no longer have to begin by discovering what was never governed properly. Investors may still negotiate hard, as they should. But the company meets them with literacy rather than with embarrassment. That matters. It changes the company's leverage, its tone, and the quality of the capital relationships it can sustain.

There is also a personal legacy question hidden here. Founders often imagine their legacy in product terms, market terms, or headline terms. What they built, how much they raised, what customers they served, whether they sold, how large the company became. Those things matter. But one of the quietest and most enduring parts of a founder's legacy is the ownership system they leave behind. Did they normalise discipline or drift. Did they teach people to understand the table or only to feel inspired by it. Did they spend equity like a strategic resource or like emotional currency. Did they leave a structure that later people could still inhabit without constantly paying for old softness. Those are legacy questions too, whether founders name them that way or not.

A better ownership system is also one that tolerates less self-deception. This may be its most important feature. Many weak ownership cultures survive because everyone learns to say the flattering thing and avoid the structuring question beneath it. We still own plenty. The pool is fine. The round was great. The grant is meaningful. The table is a little messy but basically healthy. A founder who leaves a better system leaves behind a company where those sentences are harder to say unless they are actually true. That is not only an improvement in honesty. It is an improvement in strategic capacity, because the business can now make decisions from the real structure instead of from its own preferred mythology.

Of course, no founder finishes the work completely. Ownership systems remain alive. Later rounds will still change them. Later leaders may still weaken or strengthen them. Markets will still test them. That is not a reason to aim low. It is a reason to think in transmission rather than completion. You may not leave perfection. You can leave stronger habits, clearer language, better defaults, cleaner incentives, and a company less dependent on future people having to untangle what you could have governed more carefully.

That is what it means to leave a better ownership system than the one you inherited. It means the next person inside the company starts from more truth, more room, and less accumulated confusion than you did. In the long life of a business, that is not a small contribution. It is one of the most serious forms of stewardship a founder can offer.

Owning the Consequences Without Being Ruled by Them

There comes a point in every founder's relationship with the cap table when the most important task is no longer learning the terms, spotting the mistakes, or even repairing what can still be repaired. The most important task becomes psychological and strategic at the same time. Can the founder own the consequences of the structure without becoming ruled by them. This is a harder question than it first appears, because once a founder really understands the cap table, they often feel two opposite temptations. One is regret. The other is fatalism. Regret says we should have done all of this differently. Fatalism says it is too late now, so the structure rules us. Both are understandable. Neither is a good operating posture.

To own the consequences means something more disciplined.
It means accepting that the cap table is now part of the company's reality, not a draft of it. The founder split happened. The rounds happened. The grants happened. The rights were issued. The preferences exist. The SAFEs were signed. The pool was used this way rather than that way. The company now lives in the structure those choices created. Pretending otherwise is childish. But being ruled by the structure means something different. It means allowing the table to become a kind of psychological tyrant, a document so powerful in the founder's mind that it narrows judgment, poisons morale, and causes the company to behave as though no meaningful agency remains. That is just as dangerous.

This distinction matters because real founders often pass through a phase of overcorrection. Once they finally understand what the cap table truly means, the earlier simplifications fall away. Moderate exits may not matter as much as they thought. The founder position may be thinner than it once felt. The preference stack may be heavier. The future rounds may be harder. This can produce a sharp clarity, which is good, but also a dark exaggeration, which is not. The founder begins to see every structural limitation as destiny. They stop asking what can still be chosen, negotiated, or built from here. The cap table becomes not a map of constraints, but a story of defeat.

That is what must be resisted.

A founder who owns the consequences properly starts by naming them accurately. This round reduced our room. This old grant remains a scar. This preference stack means certain exits are weaker for the common than outsiders would assume. This founder split is not how we would design it now. This next round, if it comes, needs to be negotiated carefully because the common cannot absorb the same pattern again without real damage. All of that is ownership of consequence. There is no denial in it. But then comes the crucial second step. Given those truths, what freedom remains. What can still be strengthened. What paths still work. What repairs are still worth making. What outcomes still matter. That second step is what prevents consequence from turning into rule.

This is one reason the founder's emotional relationship to the cap table matters so much. A founder who has not yet accepted the real structure will usually oscillate between fantasy and panic. A founder who accepts it too passively may become timid or numb. The stronger posture is harder. It says this is the actual machine we are inside, and I will neither idealise it nor submit to it as though it now thinks for me. That is a mature way of handling constraint. It is the same posture good leaders bring to markets, regulation, competition, and technical limits. The cap table deserves the same level of seriousness, no more and no less.

There is also a practical advantage in this stance. Once the founder is no longer trying to escape the truth of the structure or collapse under it, they become much better at communicating. They can speak to investors without embarrassment. They can speak to employees without myth-making.

They can speak to cofounders without dressing structural questions up as purely emotional ones. They can say this is where we are, this is what it means, this is what we can still do. That tone creates confidence because it sounds like governance rather than like either apology or delusion.

Owning the consequences also means resisting the temptation to turn every future decision into a referendum on the past. This is a common failure mode. A founder finally sees that the table contains earlier mistakes, and from then on every financing, grant, or strategic discussion gets emotionally tied back to those old errors. That is understandable, but it can make the company clumsy. The better approach is to let the past instruct the present without letting it dominate it. The company does not need to forget what went wrong. It needs to stop using every present-tense decision as a vehicle for relitigating prior weakness. Otherwise the cap table becomes not only a structural burden but a narrative trap.

This is especially important because some consequences are genuinely permanent. A dead line may never fully disappear. An old rights package may never become elegant. A founder may never recover the exact position they might have had in a cleaner history. These things can be true without meaning the company is doomed or the founder is merely a victim of old choices. The structure is not obliged to become beautiful before the business can still be worth building. But the founder has to stop making beauty the condition of motion. That is another way of saying the same thing. Own the consequences, but do not let them become a veto on future action.

A useful test is this: when looking at the cap table, does the founder mainly ask what was lost, or what is still possible. Both questions matter, but only one leads. If the founder is only counting loss, they are already being ruled. If they can count loss and still ask what strategic range remains open, they are leading again. This is not motivational fluff. It is operationally essential. Companies are almost always built under imperfect conditions. The question is whether the imperfection has become information or identity.

There is another layer to this as well. Founders are often role models for how the rest of the company interprets ownership reality. If the founder behaves as though the cap table has become a prison, others will often absorb that mood even if they do not fully understand the mechanics.

If the founder behaves as though the table means nothing, others will absorb a different but equally dangerous unreality. The founder who owns the consequences calmly helps create a company that can live inside structure without melodrama. That is a cultural achievement as much as a strategic one.

This does not mean the founder should accept every consequence quietly. Sometimes the correct response is to fight, renegotiate, simplify, or restructure. Owning the consequences includes that. The difference is that the action comes from clear diagnosis rather than from denial or rage. The founder is not trying to erase the fact that the structure has power. They are deciding where that power can still be challenged usefully. Again, that is governance.

That is what it means to own the consequences without being ruled by them. The cap table is real. Its history is real. Its burdens are real. But the founder is still a strategic actor inside that reality, not merely its passive product. Once that becomes true, the company can stop treating ownership understanding as the end of innocence and start treating it as the beginning of steadier leadership.

* * *

TWENTY

Closing Principles for Founders, Builders, and Future Stewards

"The future depends on what you do today."

- Mahatma Gandhi

The Cap Table Is Never Just a Spreadsheet

If there is one final lesson founders need to carry from everything that has come before, it is this: the cap table is never just a spreadsheet. It may appear in spreadsheet form. It may be updated in percentages, classes, strike prices, option counts, conversion assumptions, and ownership columns. Lawyers may send it as a schedule. Investors may review it as part of diligence. Finance people may model it in scenarios. But none of those formats captures its full nature. The cap table is not merely a document that stores information. It is a living record of what the company has believed about value, trust, contribution, control, sacrifice, and the future.

That is why cap table literacy is not a specialist hobby or an administrative side skill. It is part of understanding the company itself.

Every line on the table is an answer to a past question. Who mattered enough to be made a founder. Who was trusted enough to receive equity. What kind of capital the company accepted and what rights it was willing to grant in return. How much room it preserved for future talent. Whether it governed dead equity or allowed history to remain expensive. Whether it used ownership as a strategic currency or as a way to avoid hard present-tense conversations. Those answers accumulate. When a founder looks at the cap table properly, they are not only looking at percentages. They are looking at the company's memory of its own judgment.

This is one reason the cap table so often feels heavier than its cells should. Founders sense, even before they can articulate it fully, that the document contains more than numbers. It contains old optimism, early diplomacy, rushed decisions, disciplined choices, strategic foresight, weak compromises, later repair, investor pressure, and the simple passage of time. It contains, in compressed form, the story of how this company kept deciding who would bear risk and who would own the reward. No serious founder should treat that lightly, because that story does not only belong to the past. It continues shaping the future every time the company hires, raises, explains equity, or considers a strategic outcome.

That is why a founder should never ask only whether the cap table is accurate. Accuracy is necessary, but it is only the floor. The deeper question is whether the table still tells the truth about the company in a way the company can live inside. Does it still reflect contribution closely enough that the active builders remain motivated. Does it still preserve enough room for future talent. Does it still allow the company to raise intelligently rather than reactively. Does it still make a believable ownership promise to employees. Does it still leave the common meaningful across enough plausible outcomes that the business is worth carrying. If the answer to those questions is no, the problem is not that the spreadsheet is badly formatted. The problem is that the company's ownership system and the company's lived reality are drifting apart.

This is also why so many founder mistakes around ownership begin with underestimating what the table really is. If the cap table is imagined as just a spreadsheet, then small grants feel small, future dilution feels abstract, vague promises feel manageable, and investor rights feel like legal decoration. The founder assumes the "real" work is happening elsewhere and that ownership will simply track it afterward. In reality the ownership system is one of the places where the real work of company design is happening all along. It is deciding how much future is being spent, who is being protected, who is being asked to remain patient, and what kinds of success the structure will later reward.

That is why the spreadsheet metaphor can actually be dangerous if it is used too casually. Spreadsheets feel controllable. They give the illusion that if the formulas balance and the percentages sum properly, the underlying system must be healthy enough. But the cap table is not a neutral calculation sheet.

It is a strategic and moral architecture rendered numerically. Two companies can have cap tables that are equally neat in arithmetic terms while being completely different in fairness, future room, and exit logic. The cells can be tidy while the incentives are broken. They can be visually simple while the rights stack is already making moderate success irrelevant to the common. The founder who confuses neatness with health is still reading surface rather than structure.

There is another reason the cap table is never just a spreadsheet. People live inside it. Founders build under it. Employees trust it, even when they do not understand it fully. Investors negotiate through it. Buyers eventually discover its true meaning through it. A spreadsheet can be cold. A cap table is never purely cold because human endurance, reputation, and expectation are attached to its outcomes. It can decide whether a founder still feels rationally connected to the upside after years of dilution. It can decide whether an early employee later feels proud of the risk they took or quietly misled by the language that surrounded it. It can decide whether a company can accept a respectable acquisition or must reject it because the stack above the common has made the economics too thin. No document that does all of that deserves to be spoken of as if it were only back-office plumbing.

This is why the best founders eventually become bilingual. They learn to speak both the emotional language of building and the structural language of ownership. They do not surrender one to gain the other. They understand that ambition without structure becomes drift, and structure without ambition becomes dead administration. The cap table sits exactly at that junction. It translates dreams into claims, growth into dilution, financing into rights, trust into vesting, and exit into distribution. To ignore it is not to stay focused on the real company. It is to leave part of the real company unread.

A founder who truly understands this begins to treat ownership differently in every phase. Formation becomes not only an origin story but a lasting allocation of burden and belief. Hiring becomes not only a staffing exercise but a careful use of future room. Financing becomes not only a cash event but a decision about what sort of company the common will still inhabit afterward. Culture becomes not only motivation but also the truthfulness with which the company teaches people what ownership means. Exit becomes not only a sale but a final reading of every structural choice that came before. Once all of that is visible, the cap table cannot honestly be called just a spreadsheet anymore.

The deeper truth is even simpler. The cap table is one of the places where the company decides what kind of future it deserves to have. A business that spends ownership carelessly is not only giving away percentages. It is narrowing its later room, weakening its future explanations, and altering what kinds of outcomes will still make sense to its builders. A business that treats ownership with discipline is not merely being cautious. It is protecting future coherence. That is why this subject matters so much. Not because founders should become fixated on percentages, but because they should understand that the structure beneath those percentages is one of the strongest long-term forces acting on the company they are trying to build.

That is the closing principle this chapter begins from. The cap table is never just a spreadsheet. It is the company's ownership memory, its incentive architecture, its financing history, its future room, and, in many ways, its quietest form of strategy.

What Good Founders Learn Earlier Than They Wanted To

There is a particular kind of maturity that arrives in startup life when a founder realises that ownership is not a reward system floating above the company, but one of the core structures through which the company either stays coherent or slowly turns against its own builders. Most founders do eventually learn this. The difference is when. The stronger founders usually learn it earlier than they wanted to. Not because they enjoyed the lesson, but because they were willing to stop treating ownership as something that could remain soft, symbolic, or postponed until the company was "more real." The company was already real enough for ownership to matter.

This is one of the defining differences between founders who merely endure cap table complexity and founders who eventually govern it well. The latter tend to accept some uncomfortable truths sooner.

They learn earlier than they wanted to that equal is not always fair. A clean emotional split at the beginning may age badly if roles, risk, or burden diverge. They learn earlier than they wanted to that trust and structure are not rivals. In fact, trust without structure often becomes the thing that later fractures trust most painfully.

They learn earlier than they wanted to that equity is expensive even when the company still feels small, and that tiny-looking grants can become very real parts of the future. They learn earlier than they wanted to that dilution is not a later technicality but a present strategic force. They learn earlier than they wanted to that investor rights are not decorative, that preferences change real outcomes, and that headline valuation is often much less important than the structure beneath it.

These lessons rarely arrive in a neat academic sequence. They usually arrive through discomfort. A founder leaves. An investor asks a harder question than expected. A pool proves too small. A grant looks foolish in hindsight. A financing term that sounded standard starts to reveal its future cost. A moderate exit scenario looks much thinner for the common than the founders had once imagined. The founders then have a choice. They can treat the discomfort as a temporary nuisance and keep reaching for softer narratives, or they can let the discomfort teach them the thing they were trying not to see. Good founders learn earlier because they do the latter more often.

This matters because timing changes cost. A lesson learned before the round changes the round. A lesson learned before the grant changes the grant. A lesson learned before a cofounder leaves changes the departure. The same lesson learned later may still be valuable, but now it arrives in the form of repair rather than design. That is why early pain is often cheaper than late regret. Founders rarely enjoy being forced into ownership clarity ahead of schedule. But the companies that survive structurally are often the ones whose leaders accepted the cost of earlier clarity while it was still affordable.

Another thing good founders learn earlier than they wanted to is that not all growth is healthy if the cap table underneath it is weakening the people doing the growing. This is a hard lesson because startup culture rewards visible momentum. More money, more hires, more rounds, more valuation, more public proof. It takes some maturity to say that a round can be successful in one sense and still make the company worse in another if it leaves the common too thin, the stack too heavy, or the future too narrow. Founders who learn that early become much harder to impress with vanity. They begin to care more about what the structure lets the company remain than about what the headline lets the company claim.

They also learn earlier than they wanted to that employees deserve more honesty than many startups instinctively give them. That does not mean dumping every technical detail onto every new hire. It means recognising that if the company is using ownership as part of the bargain, then ownership must be explained like a real instrument rather than sold like a mood. This lesson often arrives when founders realise that silence does not preserve simplicity. It breeds assumption. Good founders learn that before the company's first real ownership disappointment becomes a trust problem.

A further lesson comes in the form of humility. Founders often begin with the unconscious belief that product brilliance, effort, or mission intensity will somehow compensate for structural sloppiness. Later they discover that ownership systems are not overawed by vision. A bad split is still a bad split even if the product is exciting. A heavy preference stack is still heavy even if the company is culturally strong. A weak pool is still weak even if the team is loyal. Good founders learn earlier than they wanted to that the cap table is not impressed by charisma. It responds only to what was actually signed, granted, modelled, and governed.

This does not make strong founders more cynical. It usually makes them more proportionate. They stop using equity as a politeness tool. They stop postponing vesting because everyone currently gets along. They stop assuming the next round will somehow solve what the current one is quietly making worse. They stop speaking about ownership in one language to investors and another to employees. They stop treating discomfort as proof that the topic should be avoided. Instead, they begin using discomfort as a signal that the company has reached the edge of something it now needs to understand properly.

One of the deepest lessons they learn is that a founder's job is not to keep the ownership story emotionally easy. It is to keep it structurally true enough that the company can survive real events without discovering that its own internal language has become a liability. That is a much harder standard. It requires more discipline, more conversation, and more willingness to look at unpleasant numbers before those numbers are attached to live negotiations or disappointed people. But it is also one of the clearest marks of serious stewardship.

The reason these lessons matter is not that they make founders perfect. No founder learns everything early enough. Every real company contains hindsight. The difference is that good founders let ownership understanding arrive in time to influence design rather than only to explain damage afterward. They do not need to enjoy that education. They only need to stop resisting it once the company has become large enough that resistance itself is expensive.

That is what good founders learn earlier than they wanted to. They learn that ownership is not background, that structure is not hostility, that dilution is not a later inconvenience, that rights are not mere legal texture, and that future trust depends heavily on whether the company tells the truth about equity while there is still time for truth to shape the table rather than merely describe it.

Why a Cap Table Is a Record of Past Courage or Past Avoidance

A cap table is often described as a record of ownership. That is true, but incomplete. It is also a record of how the founders handled difficulty. Every meaningful line on the table reflects some earlier moment when a hard question had to be answered. Who deserves what. Who is staying. What happens if someone leaves. How much future should be sold for present capital. How much room should be preserved for people not yet hired. Whether a weak grant should be challenged. Whether a preferred term should be resisted. Whether a founder conversation should happen now or be postponed until later. The cap table stores the answers. That is why, if you know how to read it, it often reveals not only financial history but moral and managerial history as well.

This is why a cap table can be read as a record of past courage or past avoidance.

Courage in this context is rarely dramatic. It does not usually look like a heroic refusal in a boardroom. More often it looks like early vesting that everyone agreed to before anyone wanted to imagine leaving. It looks like a founder split that was discussed seriously instead of settled diplomatically. It looks like a weak advisory grant not being made just because someone seemed impressive. It looks like a round being negotiated not only for valuation optics but for long-term structural sanity.

It looks like dead equity being dealt with before the company became more valuable and the conversation more painful. These choices often feel awkward in the moment. Later they read as discipline.

Avoidance looks different. It often arrives disguised as kindness, speed, trust, gratitude, or momentum. The founders do not revisit the split because everyone currently gets along. They delay vesting because it feels too cold. They grant a little equity because saying no would be uncomfortable. They do not model the convertibles because the next round still feels far away. They accept the rights package because the money is needed and the future can be sorted out later. Each decision can be explained sympathetically. That is exactly why avoidance is so common. It rarely announces itself honestly as cowardice. It sounds reasonable, humane, and temporary. The cap table is where those temporary avoidances become permanent features.

This is one reason strong operators learn to read the table historically. They ask not only what percentages exist, but what conversations must have happened, or failed to happen, to create them. An overgenerous founder split often means early emotional diplomacy won over structural truth. Missing vesting often means the founders preferred harmony over discipline. A clutter of tiny grants usually means ownership was used to smooth the present rather than to design the future. A crowded stack of deferred instruments may mean the company repeatedly bought time without confronting what the time needed to produce. A common layer that has become too thin may reveal a history of capital acceptance without enough strategic defence of founder meaning. The table is not only telling you where the company is. It is telling you how the company behaved when earlier choices still felt reversible.

This way of reading matters because founders often flatter themselves by remembering only the intention behind their decisions. We trusted each other. We were grateful. We needed speed. We had no choice. Sometimes all of that is true. But the table does not preserve intention. It preserves outcome. Later versions of the company have to live with the structure, not with the emotional atmosphere in which it was first created. That is why reading the cap table as a record of courage or avoidance can be such a sobering exercise. It removes some of the comfort of origin stories and replaces it with a more useful question. When things were still pliable, did we face the truth or soften it.

This is not a moral judgment in the simple sense. No real founder handles every ownership decision bravely. Every company contains some mixture of discipline and avoidance. That is normal. The important thing is whether the pattern is being recognised. A cap table with a few scars may reflect a company that was mostly disciplined and occasionally too soft. A cap table with repeated weak grants, absent vesting, dead founder equity, vague employee ownership language, and repeatedly unmodelled financing choices is showing a more consistent pattern. The company did not merely make a few errors. It developed a habit of paying future cost to avoid present discomfort.

That pattern often reaches beyond ownership. This is why the cap table can be such an honest mirror of leadership. Founders who avoid hard structural truths in equity often avoid them elsewhere too. Hiring becomes soft. Performance conversations drift. Product decisions are delayed because they may upset someone's emotional investment. Strategy becomes a series of present-tense relief moves rather than a designed path. None of this means the cap table explains everything. It does mean the same founder tendencies often appear there in unusually concentrated form because ownership decisions are so good at exposing whether a leader can tolerate clarity before clarity becomes unavoidable.

There is also something hopeful in this way of reading. A cap table that records past avoidance can still become the place where future courage starts to show. A founder may look at the structure and finally recognise the pattern. Here is where we were too soft. Here is where we delayed. Here is where we let gratitude, fear, or optimism spend future room too easily. Once that becomes visible, the next decisions can be made differently. The company cannot erase its history, but it can stop repeating it. In that sense, the table is not only a record of failure or success. It is also a teaching device, one of the clearest records of which truths the company was willing to face at the time and which truths it kept pushing forward into a more expensive future.

This is why some of the most important cap table work a founder ever does is interpretive rather than mechanical. The spreadsheet may already be up to date. The percentages may already sum. But until the founder can say what kinds of past behaviour the table now reflects, they have not fully learned from it.

They may still be operating as though the numbers appeared through neutral process rather than through human choices under pressure. That illusion is dangerous because it prevents the founder from seeing the behavioural roots of structural weakness. If they do not see those roots, they are likely to regrow them.

A company that understands this becomes much less likely to romanticise mess. It can still be compassionate about why the mistakes happened. It can still recognise that uncertainty, pressure, and inexperience are part of real startup life. But it no longer treats those conditions as excuses for letting the same pattern continue. Instead, it starts asking a harder and more useful question. When the next ownership decision comes, what will this look like later. Will it read as one more moment where we chose temporary emotional ease, or as one where we accepted short-term discomfort to leave the future company stronger.

That is why a cap table is a record of past courage or past avoidance. It remembers whether the founders faced reality when it was still cheap to face, or whether they kept sending the bill forward. The numbers may look neutral. The story they tell is not.

The Table Punishes Vagueness and Rewards Clarity

One of the hardest facts about ownership is that the cap table eventually forces precision on every area where the founders previously allowed themselves to stay vague. This is why weak ownership decisions so often feel tolerable at the beginning. Vagueness is comfortable in early company life. It preserves relationships. It keeps momentum high. It allows the founders to defer awkward conversation while the business still feels fragile and full of possibility. But the table is patient. It does not need to punish vagueness immediately. It simply waits until money, time, hiring, dilution, or exit pressure make the cost visible. When that happens, what once felt like harmless softness begins to harden into expensive reality. That is why the table punishes vagueness and rewards clarity.

A vague founder split becomes a concrete imbalance when roles diverge. A vague promise to "take care" of someone becomes a live claim when the company starts to matter. A vague understanding of how SAFEs or notes will convert becomes very specific dilution when the priced round arrives.

A vague assumption that the option pool will somehow be enough becomes a hard hiring constraint once the next key candidate appears. A vague internal story about employee equity becomes distrust when people discover that what they thought they had and what they actually had are not the same. In each case, the cap table is not being cruel. It is simply doing what structure always does. It turns ambiguity into consequence.

This matters because many founders still treat vagueness as a form of flexibility. They tell themselves that by not defining something too tightly, they are keeping options open. Sometimes that is true in the very short term. More often, they are not preserving flexibility. They are preserving uncertainty until a later moment when the company has less leverage, less emotional room, and higher stakes. At that point the ambiguity has not remained soft. It has become contested. The company then discovers that what felt like optionality was often just deferred conflict.

Clarity works differently. It can be uncomfortable earlier, but it is usually cheaper. A clear founder agreement may feel heavy in the first week and save years of resentment later. A clearly modelled SAFE stack may feel sobering today and prevent financing shock later. A clearly explained option grant may sound less intoxicating now and create much stronger trust over time. A clearly bounded adviser relationship may feel less flattering in the moment and save real ownership room for future hires. The reward of clarity is not emotional ease. It is that the company does not keep having to pay for truths it already could have known.

This is one reason disciplined founders become more direct over time. Not because they become harsher people, but because they learn that ownership systems do not respect hopeful blur. The table will eventually ask specific questions no matter what. How much does this person really own. What rights do these shares have. What happens if this founder leaves. What does this convert into. What happens in the next round. What does this sale mean for common. The only real choice the company has is whether to answer these questions while there is still room to shape the answers, or whether to let them arrive later as expensive revelations.
The table also punishes vagueness in culture. If the company uses loose language about being owners, sharing in the upside, or building together without teaching what that actually means inside the real structure, the later correction almost always feels worse than the earlier honesty would have.

Employees do not usually resent complexity as much as founders fear. What they resent is discovering that complexity was always there while the company chose the softer story because it was easier to recruit, reassure, or avoid awkwardness. The table rewards clarity because clarity builds a culture that can survive real financing, real dilution, and real exit logic without moral collapse.

This applies to investor conversations too. Founders often fear that if they speak too plainly about cap table weakness, they will damage the company's image. In reality, serious investors are often far more concerned by founders who remain vague about issues they clearly should understand. An imperfect structure described with clarity is usually easier to trust than a weaker structure wrapped in uncertainty, overconfidence, or soft language. The reward of clarity here is not that the problem disappears. It is that the founder sounds like someone who governs the table rather than someone being quietly governed by it.

There is also a strategic reward to clarity. A founder who sees the structure clearly can make sharper trade-offs. They can distinguish between a weak term that is survivable and one that is not. They can tell when a grant is worth the room it consumes and when it is not. They can tell whether another financing strengthens the business or merely postpones a truth under a heavier stack. Vagueness removes this precision. It forces the company to act from mood and impression. Clarity restores design. That is one of the greatest rewards the table gives to those who are willing to read it honestly.

A useful way to think about this is that vagueness usually feels generous at the beginning and expensive later, while clarity often feels strict at the beginning and generous later. Vague splits feel kind until they become unfair. Vague grant language feels exciting until it becomes misleading. Vague financing assumptions feel flexible until they become dilution shock. Clarity reverses that pattern. It asks more of the company now so that the future company has to suffer less later. Founders who understand this stop confusing immediate softness with long-term health.
This is not an argument for endless technicality. Clarity does not mean drowning every ownership conversation in legal detail. It means making sure the company has real answers where it needs them, and truthful language where others depend on it.

It means not allowing ambiguity to live in places where the cap table will later force painful precision anyway. It means naming what is being granted, what is being promised, what is being sold, what rights are entering, and what future effects are already quietly implied. That is enough. It is also much more than many companies manage.

That is why the table punishes vagueness and rewards clarity. It turns blurred choices into hard outcomes and truthful choices into durable structure. The founder who learns this early stops treating ownership clarity as a burden and starts seeing it for what it really is: one of the cheapest forms of future protection the company will ever have.

Future Value Is Usually Spent Long Before It Is Felt

One of the most sobering truths about ownership is that founders rarely feel the cost of a cap table decision at the same moment they make it. They feel something else. Relief. Gratitude. Speed. Validation. Harmony. Momentum. The company closes the round, makes the hire, grants the options, signs the SAFE, calms the disagreement, or gets through another difficult month. In the present tense, the decision usually feels productive because it solved a live problem. The cost is real, but it is deferred. It sits in the future, waiting for a financing, a sale, a dilution event, a hiring constraint, or a founder morale problem to make it felt in concrete terms. That is why future value is usually spent long before it is felt.

This delay is what makes ownership discipline so hard.

If every weak equity decision caused immediate pain, founders would become careful much faster. If an overgenerous grant instantly blocked a critical later hire, the lesson would arrive on the same day. If a poorly negotiated preference stack immediately cut founder motivation in half, the round would be understood differently in the room. If every vague promise instantly turned into a dispute, people would stop making vague promises. But the table usually works on a lag. The present gets the benefit first. The future receives the bill. That lag is the perfect breeding ground for bad ownership habits because it lets founders confuse successful problem-solving with good structural judgment.

This is why so many cap table mistakes look harmless while they are being made. A small grant feels small because the company is still young. A SAFE feels efficient because the dilution is not yet visible. A founder split feels fair because real contribution has not yet diverged. A pool expansion feels prudent because the future hires are still abstractions. A rights package feels tolerable because the painful scenario it was written for has not yet happened. In every case, the future value is already being spent. It just has not been converted yet into something painful enough to interrupt the present story.

This dynamic matters because it changes how a founder should interpret comfort. Comfort at the moment of an ownership decision is not evidence that the decision is cheap. It is often evidence that the cost has not ripened yet. A founder who understands this becomes much more suspicious of easy emotional wins in cap table matters. Not because ease is always wrong, but because ownership decisions that feel too easy are often the ones most likely to have exported their real cost into a later chapter of the company's life.

A simple way to see this is to compare ownership spending with ordinary cash spending. If the company pays cash today, the account balance changes today. Everyone sees the reduction. Equity is different. When ownership is spent, the company often experiences the purchased benefit immediately while the balance-sheet feeling of the spend remains emotionally hidden. The founders still "feel" like they own the company. The option pool still "feels" available. The future exit still "feels" broad. It is only later, once the structure is activated by real events, that the company notices how much of its future was already allocated.

This is one reason later rounds are so often shocking to first-time founders. They think they are negotiating only with the present cap table, when in reality they are also negotiating with all the future value previously spent in quieter ways. The old SAFEs now convert. The early grants now matter. The founder split now bites. The pool now proves thin or wasteful. The investor rights now crowd the room. The company has not suddenly become more expensive. It is simply feeling today what it already spent yesterday.

The same pattern applies to exits. A founder may look at a respectable acquisition offer and feel bewildered by how little the common receives. That bewilderment often comes from the same timing illusion. The future value was spent years earlier in rounds, preferences, rights, and dilution decisions that felt useful or even necessary at the time. The exit is not where the value was lost. It is where the loss becomes visible. Understanding that distinction is crucial, because it changes how founders think about every earlier ownership choice. They stop asking only whether the present problem got solved and start asking what future value is being quietly consumed to solve it.

This is also why employee equity can become a trust issue so easily. If the company grants options with enthusiastic language while saying little about dilution, financing layers, or how common behaves under pressure, employees often build their understanding from the present emotional meaning of the grant. Years later, when the company is more valuable but also more structurally layered, they discover that some of the future they thought they were holding was already partly spent by decisions made long before they understood enough to notice them. The problem again is not only economic. It is temporal. The company let the value feel larger before teaching how and when that value could be reduced.

A disciplined founder therefore learns to read ownership decisions through time rather than only through immediate effect. This grant helps now, but what does it consume later. This round extends runway now, but what threshold of success does it impose later. This rights package gets the deal done now, but what strategic room does it close later. This vague promise avoids discomfort now, but what conflict does it create later. These are not gloomy questions. They are the only way to stop using future value as if it were an invisible resource.

There is also a moral point here. Future value is often spent by one set of people and felt by another. Early founders make choices that later employees must live under. One version of the founder team buys relief that a later version of the team pays for. Today's investor protections may leave tomorrow's common thinner. This makes ownership discipline a stewardship issue, not merely a self-protection issue. The lag in consequence means the people making the decision are not always the ones who suffer most from it. That is exactly why seriousness is needed at the moment of spend.

Of course, not every future-costly decision is wrong. Sometimes spending future value is completely rational. A financing round may be expensive and still save or transform the company. A strong hire may consume meaningful ownership and still be worth every basis point. A bridge may buy the specific time the business genuinely needs. The lesson is not never spend future value. The lesson is to know that you are spending it, and to know what you are buying in return. Once that awareness is present, the founder is no longer being seduced by the time lag between benefit and cost.

That is why future value is usually spent long before it is felt. The cap table gives the present the reward quickly and sends the bill forward. Founders who understand this stop treating ownership as an easy way to solve current problems and start treating it as a serious strategic resource whose cost is measured not on the day it is granted or sold, but on the day the future finally arrives to collect it.

The Best Time to Protect the Future Is While the Present Still Feels Easy

Most ownership damage is done at moments when the company does not yet feel endangered enough for discipline to seem urgent. That is what makes the problem so persistent. Founders become serious about the cap table when the next round is hard, when an exit is on the table, when a founder leaves, when the pool is tight, when a major hire wants clarity, when an investor starts pointing at weak spots. By then the structure is already loud. The company is reacting. But the best time to protect the future is earlier, when the present still feels easy enough that people are tempted to believe structure can wait.

This is one of the deepest strategic truths in ownership management.

When the company is small, the founders still trust one another, the grants still look tiny, the rights still feel theoretical, and the next round still seems far away, that is exactly when the future is cheapest to defend. Vesting can be put in place without sounding accusatory. A founder spllt can be debated before percentages harden into identity. Advisory equity can be restrained before gratitude turns into permanent cap table clutter. Option pool logic can be established before emotional grants begin draining it.

Deferred instruments can be modelled before conversion becomes a shock. Investor terms can be questioned before desperation narrows leverage. None of these actions feels dramatic when the present still feels manageable. That is precisely why they are so often postponed.
The irony is brutal. Founders wait until the present feels difficult, and by then the future is much more expensive to protect.

This is why easy moments deserve more suspicion than founders usually give them. Ease creates the illusion that there is still plenty of time to get serious later. The company is young. The stakes are low. Everyone means well. The document can be cleaned up next month. The grant is too small to matter. The round is just to get moving. All of this sounds harmless because the consequences are still latent. But the table is already learning from these choices. It is already becoming the structure that later versions of the company must inhabit. The present may feel easy because the future has not yet arrived to complain.
A strong founder therefore treats early ease as a window, not as permission.

This applies to communication as much as to structure. It is easier to explain equity honestly when nobody has yet built grand assumptions around it. It is easier to teach dilution before dilution becomes painful. It is easier to say that valuation is not liquidity before the company has several rounds of paper milestones behind it. It is easier to create a culture where people ask ownership questions before silence has trained everyone to treat the subject as slightly taboo. Once again, the company is always making future trust cheaper or more expensive. The easiest time to do it well is before the company most emotionally needs the trust.

There is also a leadership lesson here. Founders often want proof that a hard ownership conversation is necessary before having it. But that proof usually arrives as damage. The cofounder has already drifted. The grant already looks wrong. The investor already wants cleanup. The next round already exposes the weakness. Great ownership discipline does not wait for proof in that form. It acts when the structural logic is already visible, even if the pain has not yet become undeniable. That is a rarer kind of leadership because it requires founders to tolerate short-term awkwardness without the social comfort of being able to say "well, now we obviously had no choice."

This is also why prevention is so much more valuable than repair in cap table life. Repair matters, and many later companies need it. But prevention has one enormous advantage: it happens before the people involved have had years to build entitlement, memory, and emotional attachment around the weaker structure. A fair vesting agreement is much easier before a founder has mentally spent their fully vested stake. A smaller grant is easier before someone has told their family what their oversized one might someday be worth. A cleaner rights package is easier before the market turns and the investor's protections become emotionally non-negotiable. Easy presents are the last moments when good structure is sometimes still cheap.

Of course, founders cannot protect every future risk while things are calm. That would be paralysis. The point is not to become neurotic. It is to identify the decisions that are cheap to get right early and expensive to revisit later. Founder splits. Vesting. Small grants. Advisory equity. Pool logic. Deferred instrument modelling. Financing terms that set precedent. Ownership language that shapes employee belief. These are exactly the areas where present ease is least trustworthy as a signal. They are easy now because the future has not yet made them hard. That is why they deserve attention now.

Another way to frame it is this: if a decision feels too minor to deserve structure, it may be exactly the kind of decision that later becomes expensive because it never received structure when it was still small enough to govern cheaply. The tiny grant, the informal promise, the delayed vesting, the "we'll sort it later" founder issue, the little bridge, the modest SAFE. The table rarely becomes distorted through one huge moral failure. It is more often shaped by many moments when the present felt too easy to justify doing the harder but better thing.

This is what disciplined founders learn to reverse. They stop asking whether the current pressure level makes a structural choice feel urgent. They ask whether the future cost of not acting is likely to be much higher once the present stops feeling easy. That is the better test. It is forward-facing, not mood-based.

That is why the best time to protect the future is while the present still feels easy. Because that is when the company still has the most room, the most softness for honest conversation, and the lowest price for getting the structure right enough before history begins charging interest on every lazy choice.

Why the Table Eventually Reveals What the Founder Really Believed

A founder can say many things about the company. They can say they valued fairness. They can say they cared about long-term alignment. They can say they believed in the team, respected employees, negotiated hard for the future, and thought seriously about what the company was becoming. Some of that may be true. Some may be partly true. But eventually the cap table becomes a harsher witness than the founder's own description. Because over time the table reveals what the founder really believed strongly enough to structure, and what they only believed loosely enough to say.

This is one of the final truths of ownership.

The table eventually exposes whether the founder truly believed contribution should match ownership, or whether they only believed that until the first awkward founder conversation. It reveals whether they really believed future hires mattered, or whether the option pool was treated as an afterthought until talent became hard to close. It reveals whether they genuinely believed employees deserved honest equity language, or whether optimism was allowed to do too much of the recruiting work. It reveals whether they truly believed in preserving founder meaning through later rounds, or whether they kept spending the common to solve present pressure while telling themselves the next milestone would somehow justify it. It reveals whether they thought investor rights were strategic forces to be weighed carefully, or merely paperwork to be gotten through so the money could arrive.

This is why the cap table is so unforgiving as a historical record. It does not preserve what the founder intended to value. It preserves what the founder actually priced.

A founder may sincerely value fairness and still leave behind a structure that repeatedly chose emotional convenience over fair durability. They may sincerely care about the team and still operate an ownership culture built on more inspiration than truth. They may sincerely believe in founder resilience and still accept rounds that gradually made the common too thin for that resilience to remain economically rational. The table is not mocking them. It is simply showing the final result of repeated choices. Belief, in startup ownership, is measured less by speeches than by what made it into the structure.

This is why real cap table literacy is so morally clarifying. It removes the founder's ability to hide fully behind narrative. A messy table may still be understandable. A weak choice may still have been necessary. A painful round may still have saved the company. But the founder has to see what happened without the protective blur of intention. The adviser grant stayed. The founder vesting was delayed. The rights stack grew. The common thinned. The employee story outran the economics. Those things are what the company believed strongly enough, in practice, to tolerate. Whether the founder would phrase those beliefs that way is almost beside the point. The table already has.

There is something useful, even hopeful, in this harshness. Because once a founder understands that the table will eventually reveal what they really believed, they start making different choices now. They stop treating structure as secondary to values and start seeing structure as the place where values become credible. If they really believe future builders deserve room, they preserve it. If they really believe founder burden should still matter after likely dilution, they negotiate with that in mind. If they really believe employees deserve honesty, they explain grants and dilution clearly enough that the company's later reality does not feel like a betrayal. If they really believe the future company deserves a better inheritance, they stop spending ownership as though the future were somebody else's problem.

This is one reason the cap table can become a better guide than the founder's mood. Mood changes. Pressure changes. Markets change. The temptation to soften, delay, flatter, or defer is always present. But if the founder keeps asking what this decision will later say about what I really believed, the quality of the decision often improves immediately. That question cuts through a great deal of startup self-romance. It forces the founder to ask not whether the current explanation sounds good, but whether the resulting structure will later prove that explanation was real.

It also changes how founders should think about legacy. Most people imagine legacy in public terms: the size of the company, the product built, the customers served, the valuation achieved, the exit secured. The cap table suggests another standard. What did the founder normalise. What did they repeatedly protect. What did they keep telling themselves would be sorted later. What kind of ownership system did they leave for the next people to inhabit. In this sense, the table is not only a financial record.

It is a record of the founder's operational ethics. Not ethics in the grand abstract, but ethics expressed through who was protected, who was diluted, who was told the truth, and whose future room was defended.

Of course, no table reveals perfect purity. Every company contains compromise. Every founder sometimes chooses the less elegant path because the company needs cash, needs speed, needs survival. The point is not that every hard trade-off proves bad faith. The point is that repeated patterns prove something. If over time the structure consistently shows that short-term convenience beat long-term coherence, or that present fundraising beat future common meaning, or that ownership language stayed softer than ownership reality, then the founder should not hide from what that pattern says. The table has already done the harder work of saying it.

This is the right place to end the argument. Because once a founder really understands that the cap table eventually reveals what they believed, they no longer need to be told that ownership discipline matters. They know. They know that every split, grant, round, pool, promise, note, and right is becoming part of a record that future investors, future employees, future founders, and perhaps even the founder's older self will one day read. And when that day comes, the question will not be what did you mean to build. It will be what did you actually build into the structure when it still felt easier not to decide too clearly.

That is why the table eventually reveals what the founder really believed. It strips away the flattering commentary and leaves behind the only thing the company can truly live inside: the architecture of choices that was real enough to sign.

* * *

TWENTY-ONE

Final Working Principles for the Founder at the Table

"First say to yourself what you would be; and then do what you have to do."
- Epictetus

Read the Structure Before the Structure Reads You

There is a stage in startup life when the founder stops merely living through ownership events and starts recognising that the cap table is always reading the company back. It reads whether the founders really believed in vesting strongly enough to impose it. It reads whether equity was used carefully or casually. It reads whether the founders protected future room or spent it to ease present discomfort. It reads whether investor rights were negotiated with foresight or accepted in a haze of relief. In that sense, the table is always interpreting the company, whether the company interprets the table well or not. The founder who waits too long to understand the structure usually discovers that the structure already understands them perfectly.

This is why the final working principle is simple. Read the structure before the structure reads you.

To do that means more than looking at percentages. It means asking what the company has already committed itself to, what kinds of outcomes still work, which future decisions have already been made easier or harder, and what present choices are quietly being written into later pain or later freedom. A founder who reads the structure early is rarely free of trade-offs, but they are much less likely to be ambushed by them. A founder who delays that reading often enjoys a period of comforting blur and then pays for it when a round, a hire, a departure, or a sale forces the cap table to speak in harder terms.

This is one of the reasons startup ownership feels so unlike ordinary compensation or ordinary business accounting. The table is not passive. It keeps converting vague choices into precise consequences. It keeps asking whether this company really wants the future its current structure is buying. It keeps narrowing or preserving room depending on how the founders behave. And because of that, every founder eventually reaches a moment where ownership can no longer be treated as background. Either the founder becomes capable of reading the table strategically, or the table becomes one of the main things dictating the founder's strategic life without having been properly examined first.

That is why the strongest founders treat cap table understanding as part of their craft, not as a side subject. They do not become obsessed with it for vanity. They become literate in it because they understand that ownership is one of the last places where wishful thinking can survive for years and then collapse all at once. Reading the structure early is how they reduce the collapse.

The founder who does this learns to ask a different class of questions almost by reflex. What does this round do after the next one. What does this grant consume later. What kind of exit does this stack now require. What does this employee promise actually mean under dilution. Is this a scar or a structural threat. Are we spending future value knowingly or merely using ownership to buy present calm. Once those questions become habitual, the founder stops treating the table as a static document and starts using it as one of the main instruments of company design.

And that is where all of this was always headed. The cap table is not something you finish understanding once. It is something you keep re-reading as the company changes, because the company and the table are always translating one another. If the founder leads that translation, the structure becomes a tool. If not, it becomes a delayed form of judgment.

That is the final principle. Read the structure before the structure reads you.

Every Percentage Hides a Story About Power

Founders are often first taught to read ownership through percentage because percentage is the simplest visible language on the table.

Twenty percent. Ten percent. Two founders splitting sixty-forty. A pool at twelve percent. An investor taking fifteen percent in the round. Those numbers are useful, but they are also dangerously incomplete if taken at face value. A percentage is never just a number. It is a compressed statement about rights, timing, hierarchy, bargaining strength, and future consequence. That is why one of the most important habits a founder can develop is to stop asking only how much and start asking what kind.

Every percentage hides a story about power.

A founder's thirty percent common stake may sound substantial, but if it sits beneath a heavy preference stack and another likely dilutive round, its real strategic meaning may be much narrower than the number suggests. An investor's twelve percent may look modest, but if it comes with preferred rights, board influence, information rights, pro rata, and strong downside protection, that twelve percent can matter far more in practice than a larger-looking common position elsewhere on the table. An employee grant may look tiny as a percentage and still be deeply meaningful if it was given early in a company with preserved room and honest economics. Another grant may look larger and yet sit inside a structure where the common has already become thin in most realistic outcomes. The percentage itself does not tell the full story. It is the doorway, not the room.

This is why founders who rely on percentage alone often misread both fairness and risk. They assume a large percentage means strong position. Sometimes it does. Sometimes it means a large residual claim with weak practical power in the outcomes that are actually likely. They assume a small investor percentage means limited influence. Sometimes it does. Sometimes it means a carefully protected minority position that can shape rounds, exits, or governance much more than its headline size suggests. They assume a modest grant means modest consequence. Sometimes it does. Sometimes ten or fifteen "small" grants have together consumed future room that the company will later desperately need. In each case, the hidden story under the percentage is what matters.

That hidden story usually begins with timing. Early ownership and later ownership are not the same thing, even when the percentages look comparable. Early founders take risk before anything is proven.

Early employees often take lower cash and higher uncertainty. Early investors come in before later validation. Later investors may take different risk but often enter with more protections, more information, and a clearer company. This means percentage alone does not tell you who is carrying what kind of burden. It tells you only what fraction is visible at the moment. The story underneath it includes when the claim was made, what the company looked like then, and what rights were layered in to reflect that timing.

The next hidden story is class. Common and preferred are not interchangeable. Two holders can each have ten percent and still occupy very different positions in sale scenarios, later financings, and governance events. This is why percentage thinking becomes especially dangerous once the company has raised priced rounds. The founder may keep speaking the old flat language of who owns what, while the real structure has already become tiered. In that setting, a percentage that looks equal in arithmetic may be profoundly unequal in consequence.

Another story hidden inside percentage is future room. A grant or round is never only about what exists now. It also says something about what has been spent from the company's later flexibility. A founder looking at a five percent pool increase should not only see dilution. They should see a strategic choice about the kind of hiring future the company thinks it needs. A founder looking at a pro rata position should not only see a current investor stake. They should see a future claim on round allocation space. A founder looking at their own percentage should not only see current ownership. They should see what that percentage likely becomes after the next plausible events. In other words, percentage is not static. It is a current expression of a moving strategic path.

This is also why founders need to become suspicious of the emotional effect of clean-looking numbers. Round percentages, founder splits, option grants, and ownership charts can produce a false sense of comprehension simply because percentages feel precise. Precision of display is not the same as precision of meaning. A cap table can be numerically exact and strategically misunderstood at the same time. The founder who really understands the table keeps translating every number into a series of harder questions. What rights sit under this. What happens to this under dilution. What does this mean at exit. What did this cost us in future room. What kind of company does this percentage now imply we must become for it to make sense.

There is also a cultural implication here. When founders speak in percentages without explaining the stories beneath them, they often teach the company to misunderstand ownership. Employees hear that they have some percentage and attach simple wealth logic to it. Founders hear that they still own some threshold and assume motivation is structurally safe. Outsiders hear the round percentage and assume they understand the deal. Over time, this habit creates a company that uses the appearance of clarity as a substitute for actual clarity. That is one of the ways weak ownership cultures persist for years before harder events expose the missing story underneath.

A better founder habit is to narrate percentages more responsibly. Not by turning every conversation into a lecture, but by remembering that every percentage answers several questions at once. What share of the company is visible. What rights are attached. What future dilution is likely. What strategic room has already been consumed. What likely outcomes still make this meaningful. A founder who thinks this way becomes much harder to impress with flattering surface numbers and much harder to frighten with raw dilution rhetoric alone. They start seeing ownership as structure rather than as display.

This is one of the final stages of cap table maturity. The founder stops reading the table as a picture and starts reading it as a set of compressed histories and future obligations. A percentage is no longer just a percentage. It is a sentence about power written in numbers. The better the founder can read those sentences, the less likely they are to confuse appearance with position.
That is why every percentage hides a story about power. The founder's job is to learn to read the story before the number is allowed to do too much of the thinking on its own.

Protect Room Before You Need It

One of the most repeated cap table mistakes is waiting until room is already scarce before starting to value it. Founders do this with option pools, with founder ownership, with future financing space, with strategic flexibility, even with the emotional room the company needs to have hard ownership conversations without panic. The pattern is always similar. While room exists, it feels abundant and therefore easy to spend. Only once it tightens does its real value become obvious.

By then, protecting it is much more expensive than it would have been earlier.
That is why one of the strongest working principles is simple: protect room before you need it.
Room matters because startups are not built only from what is already known. They are built from what must still be added later. Future hires are not here yet. Future investors are not here yet. The next hard negotiation has not happened yet. The next market downturn has not arrived yet. The founder does not yet know which executive will become indispensable, which financing will be harder than expected, which strategic partner will require space, or which exit range will later matter emotionally to the common. Room is what allows the company to meet those unknowns without every new demand becoming a structural emergency.

This is why room is not waste. It is strategic capacity.

A founder who keeps too little room in the option pool may feel efficient today and trapped tomorrow. A founder who gives away common too casually in the early phase may feel generous today and over-thin later when the real dilution begins. A company that fills future rounds with too many rights claims, too much pro rata crowding, or too many legacy expectations may feel comfortably funded today and awkwardly unfinanceable later. In each case, the immediate choice looked manageable because the missing future counterparty had not yet walked into the room to reveal the scarcity.

Protecting room begins with resisting the instinct to allocate every visible gap just because it exists. Empty pool space is not a waste simply because no one holds it yet. Unused founder ownership is not greed simply because someone could be granted a little more. A round that leaves some strategic flexibility on the table is not automatically a failure simply because more capital was technically available. These are hard ideas for founders because startup culture often praises maximum immediate motion. But maximum immediate motion and maximum long-term flexibility are not the same thing. Very often they are in tension.

This is especially true in hiring. A company that protects room is able to say yes later to the hire who really changes the business. A company that spends room emotionally on every decent candidate often discovers that when the exceptional candidate appears, the ownership structure has already been softened by earlier convenience. Then the company must either under-offer, dilute again, or scramble for some awkward exception. None of those is as good as having defended the room in the first place.

The same principle applies to financing. Founders often evaluate rounds by asking how much cash can be secured now. A better question is how much future room survives after the round closes. Room for the next round to be attractive. Room for the common to remain meaningful. Room for a moderate strategic outcome not to become worthless beneath the stack. Room for the company to survive if the market turns and the next raise is not as flattering as hoped. The round that looks slightly less triumphant in the present can often be the one that leaves the company much stronger in its next phase because it preserved room instead of consuming it.

There is also a cultural form of room. A company that has been honest about ownership, disciplined about grants, and clear about dilution usually has more room to handle hard future conversations without trust collapse. A company that has oversold, avoided, and smoothed everything with vague optimism has much less room. When the harder moment comes, it arrives into a company that already used up its credibility buffer. This too is room, and it too should be protected before the company needs it.

A founder protecting room is therefore not behaving timidly. They are recognising that future strength depends heavily on what has not yet been spent. This is one of the deepest shifts in ownership maturity. The founder stops seeing every unallocated percentage, every ungranted option, every unclaimed future slot, as something waiting to be used immediately. They start seeing it as part of the company's reserve of strategic freedom.

That is why protecting room before you need it is such a central principle. Once the company needs room visibly, it is already negotiating from scarcity. The best time to defend it is earlier, while abundance still makes restraint feel unnecessary.

Model the Pain Before the Pain Arrives

One of the most reliable signs that a founder is still treating the cap table too passively is that they only model outcomes once those outcomes have become immediate threats. A down round becomes real, and only then do they ask what anti-dilution does. A buyer appears, and only then do they ask what the common actually receives. A key hire pushes for more equity, and only then do they realise how little room is left in the pool. This reactive pattern is common because modelling pain early feels unnatural.

It can seem pessimistic, distracting, even disloyal to the company's own ambition. But it is one of the strongest forms of ownership discipline a founder can build. Model the pain before the pain arrives.
This does not mean becoming obsessed with worst-case thinking. It means refusing to let the structure remain flattering only because it has not yet been tested. The cap table can feel healthy in calm weather for exactly the same reason a weak bridge can look sturdy before real weight crosses it. The point of modelling pain is not to assume disaster. It is to find out whether the company's ownership architecture still behaves coherently when ordinary startup stress is applied.

There are several kinds of pain worth modelling. The first is financing pain. What happens if the next round is smaller, slower, or lower-priced than hoped. What happens if deferred instruments convert at less comfortable terms. What happens if the pool needs to be expanded before the next raise rather than after it. What happens to founder ownership if a likely investor exercises pro rata and the company still needs to make room for a new lead. These are not edge cases. They are normal venture-life possibilities. A founder who has never run them is still partly relying on optimism as a substitute for structure.
The second kind is exit pain. Not the fantasy exit, but the uncomfortable middle. What happens at £15 million, £30 million, £50 million, not only at the giant outcome everyone prefers to discuss. What do preferences do. When do investors convert. How much of the proceeds are consumed before the common begins to matter in a real way. Which sale ranges still produce rational founder alignment, and which ones reveal that the structure now only really works for capital above the common. If the company has not looked at those ranges before a buyer appears, then it is not prepared to negotiate from knowledge. It is waiting to be emotionally surprised by its own waterfall.

The third kind of pain is personnel pain. What happens if a founder leaves. What happens if a critical hire must be brought in tomorrow. What happens if the company has to retain a key operator after a hard year and the only tool left is ownership. What happens if employees begin asking sharper questions about dilution and the company has to explain a thinner common story than its culture has implied. These are all ownership events even when they first appear as people events. The company that models them early is less likely to be cornered into weak grants, confused promises, or rushed structural concessions later.

The value of modelling pain is not only numerical. It is educational. It forces the founder to discover what the cap table is really saying before the company is too emotional to hear it properly. A founder may learn that the structure is stronger than feared. Good. They may learn it is thinner than hoped. Better to know. They may learn that one more weak round would materially break founder meaning, or that one more pool expansion would require much stricter grant discipline elsewhere, or that a moderate sale no longer works for the common without some form of carve-out or deeper strategic rethink. None of this knowledge is pleasant for its own sake. All of it is useful.

This is also why modelling pain is an antidote to vanity. Headline numbers flatter. Scenario modelling humbles. A founder can feel proud of a valuation, a round size, or a paper percentage until the table is forced through real-world strain. The strain then asks the only question that really matters: how does this structure behave when the company does not get the easiest possible future. Founders who ask that question voluntarily become much harder to fool, including by their own momentum.

Another reason this principle matters is that pain rarely arrives alone. A weaker round may coincide with a hiring need. A founder departure may coincide with a financing. An acquisition offer may arrive when morale is already uneven. The company is therefore rarely experiencing one clean structural pressure at a time. Modelling pain early helps the founder see where those pressures might stack. A table that can survive one difficulty in isolation may still become unstable when two or three ordinary startup complications happen together. The time to discover that is not when they are already in the room.

A disciplined founder therefore treats scenario analysis as a normal part of ownership stewardship. Not because they distrust the future, but because they respect how expensive surprise can be. The cap table should be asked hard questions while there is still time to do something intelligent with the answers.

That is why you model the pain before the pain arrives. Because once it has arrived, the company is no longer learning. It is paying.

Use the Table to Tell the Truth, Not to Hide It

A cap table can be used in two opposite ways. It can be used as a tool for making reality clearer, or it can be used as a shield behind which the

company hides reality until reality becomes too loud to ignore. This is one of the final disciplines founders need to learn. The numbers themselves do not guarantee honesty. A founder can have a perfectly updated spreadsheet and still use it deceptively by speaking around it, simplifying only in flattering directions, or letting other people infer things the structure does not really support. In that sense, the table is morally neutral. It can support clarity, or it can support avoidance, depending on how the founder uses it.
That is why the table should be used to tell the truth, not to hide it.

The most common way founders use the table to hide reality is not through outright falsehood. It is through selective visibility. They talk about current percentage but not future dilution. They talk about valuation but not preference. They talk about grants but not vesting or where common sits beneath the stack. They talk about ownership culture but not how little of the company still remains uncommitted for future builders. They let the spreadsheet stay technically correct while the company's actual ownership language becomes strategically incomplete. The table is present, but it is not being allowed to do its clarifying job.

This matters because the cap table is one of the few places where a startup can force itself out of comforting narrative and into measurable structure. If the founder refuses that use, the company loses one of its best internal truth mechanisms. A financing round sounds strong until the table shows what it did to the common. A grant sounds small until the table shows how many similar "small" grants now exist. A founder still feels aligned until the table shows what another likely round would do. A moderate sale sounds attractive until the table shows the waterfall. In each case, the table is not inventing bad news. It is making hidden meaning visible. That is exactly what founders should want from it, even when the answer is inconvenient.

The opposite approach is to use the table as a defensive object. The founder knows the structure is complicated and assumes that complexity itself will discourage scrutiny. People will not ask too much. The documents are technically there. The numbers exist if anyone really wants to dig in. Meanwhile the company keeps speaking in easier summaries because those are more useful for recruiting, morale, fundraising optics, or avoiding embarrassment. This is a weak use of ownership knowledge. It turns structure into a private instrument of control rather than a shared instrument of truth.

Strong founders do the opposite. They use the table to sharpen their own explanations. They do not hide behind it. They refer back to it to make sure the language around ownership stays tethered to what the structure will actually do under pressure. If the company says a grant is meaningful, the founders should know in what sense. If they say dilution is normal, they should know how much and where it lands. If they say a round was good, they should know what strategic cost it carried and why it was still worth it. If they say a sale offer is weak or attractive, they should have already run the table far enough to know that judgment is not just emotional theatre.

This is why the table is one of the best anti-myth tools in the company. Startups naturally generate myth because people need stories to act under uncertainty. That is normal. But if myth is never disciplined by structure, the company slowly becomes easier to motivate and harder to trust. The table is where myth meets arithmetic, rights, and consequence. Used properly, it helps the founders keep the story honest enough that later reality does not feel like betrayal. Used badly, it becomes a private back room where the real company sits while the public company runs on more flattering language.

There is also a leadership advantage here. Teams tend to trust founders more when it is clear that the founders are willing to let structure constrain narrative rather than the other way around. That does not mean sharing every technical detail with everyone all the time. It means the company's broad language about ownership remains compatible with what the table would show if examined. Once that compatibility exists, people can survive complexity much better. Once it does not, every future clarification starts to feel like reduction.

Another practical benefit is that a founder who uses the table to tell the truth is less likely to fool themselves. This may be the most important benefit of all. Founders are often the first audience for the company's oversimplifications. They repeat them externally and gradually start believing them internally. We still own enough. The pool is fine. The next round will be manageable. The common will still matter. The table, if actually used, can interrupt that drift. It can say no, here is the real position. That interruption is often uncomfortable. It is also one of the strongest forms of strategic protection available.

The discipline, then, is simple to say and hard to maintain. Whenever the company is about to use ownership language, ask whether the table supports it in substance or whether the language is leaning on omission. Whenever the company takes a structural step, ask what truth that step now creates, not only what comfort it gives in the present. Whenever a hard scenario appears, let the table answer before the room's emotions do.

That is how the cap table becomes a truth instrument instead of a hiding place. And that is one of the final habits that separates founders who are merely accompanied by their structure from founders who are actually governing it.

Build for the Outcome You Can Actually Live With

One of the most dangerous habits in startup ownership is building a cap table around an outcome the company may admire but cannot realistically count on. Founders often do this indirectly. They do not say aloud that only a giant exit matters now. They do not always admit that the common has become thin enough that moderate success no longer feels meaningful. They simply keep taking financing, granting equity, and layering rights in ways that quietly move the company toward a narrower acceptable future. The result is a business whose structure only really works if a very particular kind of success arrives. That is a fragile way to build.

This is why one of the final working principles is to build for the outcome you can actually live with.

That does not mean aiming low. It means being structurally honest. A founder should know what kinds of outcomes still make sense for the common, for key employees, and for the company as a whole. If only very large exits now produce meaningful economics beneath the stack, the founder should recognise that and understand what sort of strategic behaviour that structure will encourage. If moderate exits still work well enough, that matters too. The key is that the company's ownership decisions should not keep drifting toward a future that the founder is unwilling to name while simultaneously making other futures less and less real.

This principle matters because the cap table does not only record ambition. It prices it.

A lightly financed company with a clean common layer may be able to live with a broader range of outcomes. It can pursue large success if possible while still finding smaller but real wins meaningful. A heavily layered company with repeated rounds, strong preferences, and thin common often cannot. It must keep climbing because too much of the future has already been sold. Neither structure is morally superior in the abstract. But they are not building for the same livable outcome. A founder who does not see that difference is likely to make strategic decisions in one emotional register while the table is quietly forcing another.

This is also why valuation vanity is so dangerous. A founder may celebrate a strong round because it looks like progress, even while the terms underneath it push the company into a future where only bigger and bigger rounds or much larger exits remain satisfying. The business is not just growing. It is committing itself. If the founder would not actually be content to live inside that narrower future, then the financing path is not merely aggressive. It is misaligned. The company is building toward an outcome the table demands more than the founders have truly chosen.

A good founder therefore keeps asking a blunt question: after this decision, what kind of success must now happen for the structure to feel worth carrying. If the answer keeps moving upward with every round and every right granted, that is not automatically wrong. It is, however, something the founder must confront directly. Because if the company will only feel coherent at one extreme of possible outcomes, the founders are no longer simply pursuing upside. They are increasingly dependent on it.

This affects culture too. Employees cannot be told one ownership story while the table is quietly making only far narrower outcomes meaningful. Investors cannot be brought in on one understanding while the founders privately hope for another. A company that builds for an outcome it cannot actually live with usually ends up needing more hope in its internal language than the structure can support. That is a dangerous place to operate from.

The better posture is to make ownership choices that leave the company able to live with a realistic range of futures, not just the most flattering one. That may still include high ambition, repeated rounds, and venture-scale goals. But if that is the path, it should be the real path, not a drift into structural extremity because each local decision sounded fine in isolation.

The founder should know what the company is now financially requiring from the future and decide whether that requirement is a future they actually want to build under.

That is why you build for the outcome you can actually live with. Because the table will eventually force the company to discover whether the futures it still rewards are ones the founders consciously chose or ones they wandered into while calling each step progress.

Leave the Company More Legible Than You Found It

The final working principle may be the simplest to say and the hardest to live consistently: leave the company more legible than you found it.

Legibility matters because a startup is always being handed from one version of itself to the next. Early founders hand it to later founders. One financing environment hands it to another. Early employees hand it to later employees. One board era hands it to the next. If the ownership system becomes more confusing, more euphemistic, more dependent on private memory, more loaded with poorly explained exceptions, then every future version of the company starts from weaker ground. It has to waste energy reconstructing what should have been known, explaining what should already have been explainable, and carrying the emotional cost of structural ambiguity that earlier people could have reduced.

A legible company is not necessarily a simple company. It may still have multiple rounds, preferences, SAFEs, options, scars, and compromises. But it is readable. The founders understand it. The next investor can make sense of it. A key hire can have their grant explained honestly. The employee ownership story is compatible with the real structure. The weak spots are known as weak spots, not hidden behind vague language. The company may not be elegant, but it is not obscure.

This is why legibility is such a strong form of stewardship. When you make the company more legible, you are not just tidying documents. You are reducing the amount of future confusion that others will have to pay for. You are turning hidden complexity into manageable complexity. You are making it less likely that a later financing, a later sale, or a later internal dispute will feel like a revelation rather than a development inside a system that was already understood.

Founders often underestimate how much damage obscurity does. A company can survive a scar better than it can survive a mystery. A slightly ugly grant that everyone understands is easier to live with than a "small" line item nobody can explain. A known founder imbalance can be managed more intelligently than a founder story everyone politely avoids naming. A modelled SAFE stack is easier to finance around than one that remains emotionally invisible until conversion day. Legibility does not erase pain. It lowers surprise, and surprise is one of the most expensive things a cap table can produce.

Leaving the company more legible also means improving its language, not only its structure. Founders should want the next people inside the business to inherit fewer myths and clearer explanations. Fewer inflated ownership claims. Fewer fuzzy promises. Fewer casual uses of share count without denominator, valuation without structure, upside without dilution, common without stack. A better company is one where people can ask ownership questions and receive answers grounded in the real architecture rather than in whatever tone is most convenient for the moment.

This is one of the deepest forms of maturity in company building. You stop asking only whether the cap table is technically current and start asking whether the company can now explain itself with more truth than it could before. If the answer is yes, then even an imperfect structure is becoming a better governed one.

That is the right place to end.

The cap table is not just where ownership sits. It is where the company stores its seriousness. It remembers whether the founders faced difficult truths early or delayed them. It reflects whether capital was taken with foresight or with haze. It shows whether employees were invited into ownership through honesty or through simplification. It reveals whether the future was protected when it was still cheap to protect, or billed later at a much higher cost.

And because of that, the founder's task is not only to get the numbers right. It is to keep the company readable enough that the next hard decision can be made from truth rather than from reconstruction.

That is the final principle.

Leave the company more legible than you found it.

***

References

Feld, B. and Mendelson, J. (2019) Venture Deals: Be Smarter Than Your Lawyer and Venture Capitalist. 4th edn. Hoboken, NJ: Wiley.

Holloway (2023) The Holloway Guide to Raising Venture Capital. Available at Holloway.

Holloway (2022) The Holloway Guide to Equity Compensation. Available at Holloway.

National Venture Capital Association (NVCA) (2025) Model Legal Documents. Available at NVCA.

National Venture Capital Association (NVCA) (2025) Model Term Sheet. Available at NVCA.

National Venture Capital Association (NVCA) (2025) Stock Purchase Agreement. Available at NVCA.

Y Combinator (2013) 'Announcing the Safe, a Replacement for Convertible Notes.' Available at Y Combinator.

Y Combinator (n.d.) Safe Financing Documents. Available at Y Combinator.

Y Combinator (n.d.) Primer for Post Money Safe v1.1. Available at Y Combinator.

Y Combinator (n.d.) 'Understanding SAFEs and Priced Equity Rounds.' Available at Y Combinator.

Y Combinator (n.d.) 'A Guide to Seed Fundraising.' Available at Y Combinator.

Y Combinator (n.d.) The Y Combinator Deal. Available at Y Combinator.

Disclaimer

This book is intended for general educational and informational purposes only. It is not legal advice, investment advice, tax advice, accounting advice, or regulated financial advice. The material in this book is designed to help founders, operators, employees, and readers think more clearly about capitalization tables, ownership structure, dilution, investor rights, and related startup finance concepts, but it should not be relied upon as a substitute for professional advice tailored to your specific circumstances.

Capitalization tables and venture financing structures can have major legal, financial, tax, and personal consequences. Small differences in wording, jurisdiction, timing, company structure, shareholder agreements, employment status, securities law treatment, and investor rights can produce very different outcomes. Because of this, readers should consult appropriately qualified professionals before making decisions about founder equity, share classes, option plans, SAFEs, convertible notes, investment rounds, vesting, employee grants, secondaries, acquisitions, or any related matter.

The author and publisher make no guarantees regarding accuracy, completeness, commercial outcome, fundraising success, company valuation, legal enforceability, tax treatment, or financial result. Laws, regulations, market norms, and investment practices change over time and may differ by country, state, or industry. Readers remain solely responsible for their own decisions, agreements, negotiations, and business conduct.

Any examples, scenarios, models, or illustrations in this book are simplified for clarity and education. They do not reflect every legal, commercial, accounting, or tax variable that may apply in real transactions. References to companies, investors, founders, financing tools, or market practices are provided for discussion and explanatory purposes only and should not be interpreted as endorsements, recommendations, or predictions of future performance.
By reading this book, you acknowledge that you are using the information at your own risk and that neither the author nor the publisher shall be liable for any loss, claim, liability, damage, or expense arising from reliance on its contents.

Also by TechEyeSpy
The Rough Start Guide Series

The Rough Start Guide to Starting an Enforcement Agency
The Rough Start Guide to Starting a Private Detective Agency
The Rough Start Guide to Starting a Security Firm
The Rough Start Guide to Raising from Angels and Family
The Rough Start Guide to Building a Cap Table
The Rough Start Guide to Term Sheets and Negotiation
The Rough Start Guide to Launching an Enforcement Agency
The Rough Start Guide Cinema Manual

www.ingramcontent.com/pod-product-compliance
Lightning Source LLC
LaVergne TN
LVHW082016200926
848481LV00010B/2872